V&R

Schriften des Hannah-Arendt-Instituts
für Totalitarismusforschung

Edited by Günther Heydemann

Volume 46

Vandenhoeck & Ruprecht

The Extreme Right in Europe

Current Trends and Perspectives

Edited by
Uwe Backes and Patrick Moreau

Vandenhoeck & Ruprecht

Bibliographic information published by the Deutsche Nationalbibliothek

The Deutsche Nationalbibliothek lists this publication in the
Deutsche Nationalbibliografie; detailed bibliographic data
available online: http://dnb.d-nb.de.

ISBN 978-3-525-36922-7
ISBN 978-3-647-36922-8 (E-Book)

Cover:
Demonstration of "autonomous Nationalists" in Paris, May 8, 2011
Photo: Capucine Granier-Deferre

Typesetting by: Hannah-Arendt-Institut, Dresden
Printed and bound in Germany by ⊕ Hubert & Co, Göttingen

Printed on non-aging paper.

Contents

Introduction

Uwe Backes/Patrick Moreau

The extreme right in Europe is no longer a terra incognita of research. On the contrary: scientific literature has become almost unmanageable. There are historic reasons for this. But this boom is also connected to the periodic new updates of the phenomenon: Election successes of respective parties, the vitality of militant scenes and subcultures, or the aftermath of frequently scandalizing forms of articulation arouse the interest of a broader public in the intellectual-cultural realm at times. As the imposing number of new publications shows, the strong interest in the topic continues to persist and does not subside.[1]

This applies especially to the numerous studies within the national framework. But there is no lack of transnational research of a comparative character any longer. Special emphasis is placed on research on the extreme right parties, their electoral basis, and the conditions for their success. Nevertheless, the state of the research shows a strong east-west gradient. For easily comprehensible reasons, the countries of Eastern Europe are generally less well researched than the Western ones. Concerning the non-partisan organized part of the spectrum, the yield is equally modest for the West as well as the East. Few authors have investigated militant scenes and subcultural phenomena transnationally. The number of those, who have, in recent years, studied cultural phenomena (ideologies, theory circles, artistic forms of expression etc.) in a comparative and transnational way, is even smaller. In spite of the numerous publications available within the national framework, the topic is, thus, by no means "exhausted".

The plan for the present edition emerged in the run-up of the elections to the European Parliament that were held in all the EU-member states from June 4 to June 7, 2009. The 7th direct elections offered an opportunity for measuring

1 In view of the large number of publications, only the following editions of the years 2010/2011 will be named as pars pro toto: Botsch/Kopke/Rensmann/Schoeps (Eds.), Politik des Hasses; Eatwell/Goodwin (Eds.), The New Extremism in 21st Century Britain; Lebourg, Le Monde vu de la plus extrême droite; Mayer/Odehnal, Aufmarsch; Minkenberg (Eds.), Historical Legacies; Moroska, Prawicowy populizm a eurosceptycyzm; Pankowski, The Populist Radical Right in Poland; Rodrigues/Donselaar (Eds.), Monitor Racisme & Extremisme; Spöhr/Kolls (Eds.), Rechtsextremismus in Deutschland und Europa; Stöss, Rechtsextremismus im Wandel; Zick/Küpper/Hövermann, Die Abwertung der Anderen.

the conditions of power at the right wing of the national party systems and to comparatively classify the total potential. Most authors contributing to this volume met in Strasbourg in November 2009 to present the first results of their research, to hold discussions, and to prepare the proposed publication. This also comprised the coordination of topics and the central leading issues that were to result in an edition of the greatest possible evidential value and unity.

The presented volume aims at setting new accents in various ways and at expanding the state of knowledge on the European level. *Firstly,* all contributions use a comparative approach exceeding the national framework. The authors fall back on previous research on the countries in order to bring out differences and common denominators in selected European states. *Secondly,* partially due to the inclusion of states such as Turkey and Serbia, which are not EU-members yet, Eastern Europe is represented in an approximately balanced fashion although the state of research is much less favorable than for Western Europe. In spite of the existing gaps, hope seems justified that from this volume, impulses for further research efforts will arise. *Thirdly,* the research presented here does not only deal with partisan organized right-wing extremism and the election activities connected with it. It equally includes two additional broad realms: on the one hand, militant scenes and subcultures including some paramilitary phenomena in Eastern Europe, on the other hand, the broad realm of political ideas and cultural trends and their influence on European political culture. Here, again, these topics are treated in a comparative and transnational manner.

All the contributors to this book deal with their research subjects with the tools of the historian, the political scientist, and the social scientist as discriminatingly as possible and sine ira et studio. The selection of the topics in the realm of the "extreme right", however, cannot do without a normative framework determining the direction and allowing for the setting of limits. The scale is based on the fundamental values last set down in the Treaty of Lisbon which all the member states are obligated to. They stand in a long tradition of constitutional history which in the examination of lack of freedom, intolerance, tyranny, and heteronomy led to an "agreement of fundamentals" as recorded in Par. 2: "The Union is founded on the values of respect for human dignity, freedom, democracy, equality, the rule of law and respect for human rights, including the rights of persons belonging to minorities. These values are common to the Member States in a society in which pluralism, non-discrimination, tolerance, justice, solidarity and equality between women and men prevail".

The contributions in this volume deal with the impairment of these values which, for the most part, stem from an anti-egalitarian (and often at the same time anti-liberal) attitude that negates the ethos of fundamental human equality implicitly and explicitly. Aside of the sober analysis of the represented phenomena it is the intention of the publication to point out threats to the peaceful and liberal co-existence of mankind and to allow the judging of the extent of the endangerment. For this, it is necessary to go partially beyond the edge of the – in a narrower sense – "extreme right", to examine transitional zones and to grasp discriminations also where they are not accompanied by an unambiguous and in every respect disloyal attitude toward the basic values and rules of conduct of European constitutional states. In contrast, the issue of how the dangers pointed out in such a way can be confronted appropriately is being omitted.[2]

This publication has many fathers. It is foremost the product of a German-French cooperation, particularly between the Hannah-Arendt-Institut für Totalitarismusforschung an der Technischen Universität Dresden and the Laboratoire Cultures et Sociétés en Europe (University of Strasbourg/CNRS), whose director, Pascal Hintermeyer, has accompanied its creation with support and advice from the very first planning stages to going to print. The Laboratoire was the host of the Strasbourg Conference in November 2009 and also made possible the workshops and coordination meetings that followed, without which the project would hardly have gotten off the ground. The Cercle Gutenberg, which awarded the German publisher of the edition a "Chaire Gutenberg" in the research year 2010/2011, thus laying the foundation for research that went far beyond the framework of this edition, offered important support. Additional valuable assistance was offered by the Région Alsace and the partner cities Strasbourg and Dresden. The creation of this book was for the most part entrusted to the Hannah-Arendt-Institute. The editors are grateful to its editorial department and experienced publishing team led by Walter Heidenreich. Many expert translators transmitted French, German, and Czech texts into English like Rachel Ives, Elisabeth Orrison, Rita Schorpp, and Mirko Wittwar to name only a few. Special thanks also go to Isabel Eisfeld who maintained the contacts with the authors and edited the papers. Any possible flaws are the sole responsibility of the publishers.

2 The following publication contains important insights to this: Bertelsmann Stiftung (Ed.), Strategies for Combating Right-Wing Extremism in Europe.

I.
Parties and Elections

The Populist Radical Right in European Elections 1979-2009

Gilles Ivaldi

I. Introduction

The resurgence of populist radical right parties in European democracies has been one of the most scrutinized and thoroughly documented political phenomena in the past four decades. Few nations across the continent have proved totally immune to the development of this new breed of partisan actors located on the right end of the political spectrum.[1] The electoral consolidation of this party family in a number of Western European countries throughout the 1980s and the 1990s has been echoed with similar parties gaining substantial political ground in the younger post-transitional regimes of Central and Eastern Europe in the more recent period.

The overall significance of the populist radical right and the challenge it poses to liberal democracy can be judged from the vast amount of literature devoted to the phenomenon. Beginning in the late-1980s, scholars have striven to identify propitious conditions for the success of the populist radical right in the deep structural socio-economic, political and/or cultural changes that have taken place in post-industrial societies.[2]

For their part, comparative empirical studies have focused on factors that account for the observed variance in the electoral performances of those parties across time and space. Not surprisingly, immigration features prominently here.[3] In most cases, it is brought into explanation for the electoral fortunes of the populist radical right.[4] On the supply-side of electoral politics, these parties have successfully managed to frame multifaceted public concerns about immi-

1 This was demonstrated recently by the outbreak of populist radical right parties in some countries traditionally regarded as the most "tolerant" such as the Netherlands, Sweden or Finland.
2 See for instance Betz, Right-Wing Populism; Kitschelt, Radical Right in Western Europe; Ignazi, The Silent Counter-Revolution.
3 See Van der Brug/Fennema, Protest or Mainstream?
4 See Jackman/Volpert, Conditions Favouring Parties; Lubbers et al., Extreme Right-Wing Voting; Golder, Explaining Variation; Swank/Betz, Globalization; Jesuit et al., Electoral Support for Extreme Right-Wing Parties.

gration into a broader set of salient issues in the competitive space.[5] Their voters tend to be significantly more xenophobic and wary of ethnic or religious pluralism.[6] Simultaneously, a great deal of attention has been given to the "populist" dimension in the electoral appeal of those parties. Betz or Taggart, for instance, have emphasized the populist radical right's ability to mobilize public resentment towards the political elite.[7] The examination of the broader political context has led to further consideration of historical, political opportunity structure and organizational factors behind the variation in levels of electoral support for those parties across European nations.[8]

So far, the bulk of the existing comparative research on populist radical right parties has been mainly concerned with first-order elections in Western Europe, although there has been growing interest in a broader pan-European perspective.[9] If only because of the quasi absence of non-European immigration, the analysis of party systems in CEE countries provides a most fertile ground for a theoretical (re-)assessment, refining and possible expansion of some of the core concepts that are customarily employed in the literature on Western Europe.[10] These efforts are in line with the general assumption that populist radical right parties in former communist countries share some core ideological similarities with their Western counterparts notwithstanding the regional peculiarities in the historical transformation of post-communist political systems.[11] This is true, for instance, of the issues of territoriality, fierce anti-Communism or widespread political corruption in the East. There are also interesting prospects for future research in the functional analogy whereby hostility towards neighboring countries and negative attitudes towards inner minorities in Central and Eastern Europe are satisfactorily employable as substitutes for anti-immigrant feelings in the West.[12]

Implications of populist radical right success are far reaching and evidently go beyond the sole academic sphere. At the political level, there are well-founded concerns with the policy impact by those parties, either because of their joining national coalition governments such as in Italy, Austria, Slovakia, Poland or the Netherlands, or simply due to their ability to exert influence on mainstream pol-

5 See Rydgren, Is Extreme Right-Wing Populism Contagious?; Givens, Voting Radical Right.
6 See Arzheimer/Carter, Political Opportunity Structures; and his chapter in this volume.
7 Cf. Betz, Right-Wing Populism; Taggart, New Populist Parties in Western Europe.
8 See for instance Arzheimer/Carter, Political Opportunity Structures; Art, The Organizational Origins.
9 See Norris, Radical Right; see also Mammone et al., The Extreme Right in Contemporary Europe.
10 See Bustikova, The Extreme Right in Eastern Europe; Stefanova, Ethnic Nationalism.
11 See also Mudde, Populist Radical Right Parties in Europe, p. 4.
12 See Kopeček, The Far Right in Europe.

icy making while remaining in opposition.[13] Such concerns have also become central to international bodies, above all the European Union.[14]

The European dimension is of further importance because of the contribution by post-Maastricht Euroscepticism and rejection of supra-nationality to the electoral dynamics of the populist radical right on both the supply and demand sides. Most parties of the populist radical right take a negative stance towards the European Union, although the intensity of their opposition varies across time and space.[15] As will be discussed, the European Parliament is also an arena that allows if not encourages cross-national co-operation by parties of the populist radical right.

The objective of this chapter is to examine the fluctuation in the electoral performances of populist radical parties in European elections across all Western and Eastern member states. The simultaneity in the 2004 and 2009 waves of elections permits to examine cross-national factors of variation in the electoral support for those parties. It also allows to look more specifically at how European elections are linked to the national election cycle and the degree of constancy they exhibit with the political developments in the domestic arena. Because of the predominance of "second-order" dynamics, it is of particular interest to assess the "bellwether" status of European ballots and the extent to which the latter provide specific political opportunity structures for parties of the populist radical right.

Based upon one commonly used academic definition of the populist radical right idiosyncrasy, this chapter suggests a brief account of the presence of this party family in European parliament since the first set of Euro elections in 1979, together with a political mapping of its location in the collaborative space within the European arena. The second section of this chapter then looks more specifically at the status and role of EP elections within the national election cycle, and addresses the issue of regularity and change in the existing inter-relations between European and national first-order elections across EU-member states.

13 Cf. Albertazzi/McDonnell, Twenty-First Century Populism; Centre-Right Parties and Immigration and Integration Policy in Europe, Special Issue of the Journal of European Public Policy, 15 (2008) 3.

14 See for instance Fieschi, European Institutions. Let us recall that in 2000 the controversial forming of the ÖVP-FPÖ coalition in Austria had led to the EU taking unprecedented action and issuing temporary diplomatic sanctions against Schüssel's "Schwarz-Blau" government. In June 2006, the European Parliament voted a text on the "Increase in racist and homophobic violence in Europe" whereby it expressed anxiety about how "some political parties, including those in power in a number of countries or well represented at local level, have deliberately placed issues of racial, ethnic, national, religious and gay intolerance at the heart of their agenda, allowing political leaders to use language that incites racial and other forms of hatred and stokes extremism in society". European Parliament, Document no. P6_TA(2006)0273, http://www.europarl.europa.eu/meetdocs/2009_2014/documents/ta/23/04/2009%20-%200273/p6_ta-prov(2009)0273_de.pdf.

15 See Mudde, Populist Radical Right Parties in Europe, pp. 158–183.

II. Political mapping of the populist radical right in European parliament

Any attempt to examine parties of the populist radical right empirically and comparatively is inevitably confronted with the issue of concept formation, the lack of inter-subjective agreement on case categorization and more generally the absence of a commonly accepted perimeter for the phenomenon.[16] The plethoric literature on the subject has long identified major shortcomings in delineating clear boundaries around the different manifestations in this heterogeneous party family. The diversity in the anthropology and trajectories of its members within their respective party system is another factor that has hindered the many efforts to achieve a single definition for this party family.

A general debate about the merits and limitations of existing definitions would clearly fall beyond the scope of this chapter. The analysis presented here adopts the theoretical framework proposed by Mudde in his conceptualization of the populist radical right's core ideological features combining nativism, authoritarianism and populism.[17] This definition allows for a categorization of a number of parties that can be identified as members of the populist radical right family as well as some "borderline" cases. For example, it provides the criteria that are needed to assess the location of newly formed right-wing populist or anti-establishment actors with strong anti-immigrant appeal such as the Dutch LPF and PVV or the *True Finns* in the Finnish context.

Figure 1 below shows the populist radical right parties and their position in the various networks of cross-national collaboration that have developed in-and-outside the European Parliament since the late 1970s. Historically, the French FN has been at the centre of gravity of this constellation of parties, together with the Austrian FPÖ and the *Flemish Bloc* (VB). The centrality of the FN's position is consistent with both the identification of the party as perhaps one of the most typical - or least debated - instances of the populist radical right, and its leading role in a number of attempts at unifying nationalist parties across Europe.

Yet as can be seen, there are only partial overlaps between academic classification and those parties' actual location on the EU political map. Their actual spread shows a greater deal of heterogeneity. To date some well-established representatives of the populist radical right family such as the Greek *Popular Orthodox Rally* (La. O. S.), the *Danish People's Party* (DF), the *League of Polish Families* (LPR) or the Italian *Lega Nord* (LN) have not entered formal co-operation with other core members such as the French FN, the Austrian FPÖ or, more recently, the *British National Party* (BNP). Whilst Euroscepticism and anti-federalism are clear common denominators to the bulk of populist radical right parties represented in European institutions, movements cluster into distinct

16 See Kitschelt, Radical Right in Western Europe; Zaslove, The Populist Radical Right.
17 See Mudde, Populist Radical Right Parties in Europe.

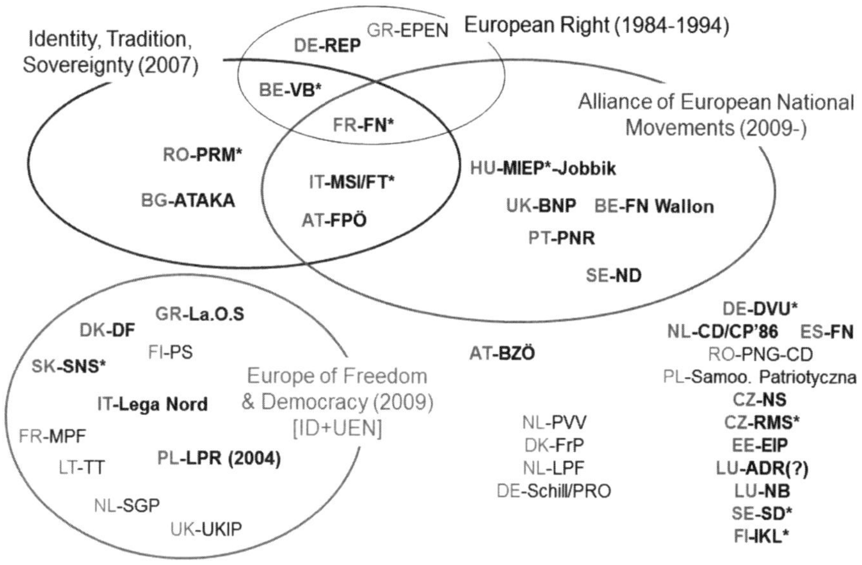

Figure 1: A political map of the European populist radical right

In bold: "Populist radical right parties" as identified by Mudde, Populist Radical Right Parties in Europe, pp. 305–308.
*Current or past member of EURONAT

political groups, mostly the short-lived Identity, Tradition, Sovereignty (ITS) and Europe of Freedom and Democracy (EFD).[18] In the latter group, populist radical right movements coalesce with another heterogeneous collection of right-wing anti-federalist Eurosceptics such as Lithuania's *Order and Justice* (TT), the French *Mouvement pour la France* (MPF), the *Dutch Reformed Political Party* (SGP) or the UK *Independence Party*. Some parties with a strong anti-immigration agenda such as the now defunct Danish *Progress Party* (FrP) or Dutch *List Pim Fortuyn* (LPF), as well as the Dutch *Party for Freedom* (PVV), distance themselves from either group of actors.

Outside the European parliament, the evolution for instance of the EURONAT network initiated by French FN leader Jean-Marie Le Pen in 1997 shows similar trends of instability and lack of unity over time although the make-up of the organization would appear to be more homogeneous with regard to its constitutive parties' political pedigree.[19] In October 2005, EURONAT

18 Formed in July 2009, the EFD group brought together former Eurosceptic "Independence/Democracy" (ID) and "Union for a Europe of Nations" (UEN) outgoing parliamentary parties in 2009. Following the break up of the ITS group in November 2007, most populist radical right parties will seat as non-attached members (non-inscrits) in the 2009–2014 European parliament.

19 With the exception of "Social National Party of Ukraine" (SNPU) and the "Italian New Force" (FN), all current or past members of EURONAT are listed as populist radical right parties by Mudde, Populist Radical Right Parties in Europe.

comprised six member parties in Western Europe (French FN, the *British National Party*, the Dutch *New Right*, the Italian *Fiamma Tricolore*, the Swedish *National Democrats* and the *National Democracy* in Spain). In the late 1990s, the pan-European network had managed to bring together a larger number of organizations (n=10), including Central and Eastern European participants such as the Hungarian MIÉP, the *Greater Romania Party* or the *Slovak National Party*, which subsequently left over political disagreement.

The most recent attempt at federating nationalist parties within the Alliance of European National Movements (AENM) represents another significant reshuffling of the formal agreement that had underpinned the creation of the ITS group in 2007 or the reactivation of EURONAT two years earlier. The Alliance was formed in October 2009 under joint leadership of French MEP Gollnisch and *British National Party*'s chairman Griffin. Membership was expanded from seven to nine national parties at the organization's first general assembly in Strasbourg in June 2010 with the addition of the Portuguese PNR and Swedish *National Democrats* (ND) (see Figure 1).[20] In line with the general Eurosceptic orientation of all previous nationalist networks, the common declaration issued by the Alliance insisted on the "creation of a Europe of free, independent and equal nations in the framework of a confederation of sovereign nation states, refraining from taking decisions on matters properly taken by states themselves", while calling simultaneously for the "rejection of any attempt to create a centralist European super state".

Reasons for this heterogeneity in political positioning by the populist radical right are diverse and essentially practical rather than ideological. First, the accumulation of unsuccessful attempts at unifying the pan-European nationalist camp results from the prevalence of strong and often diverging national interests. Antagonistic views were revealed for instance in the dispute that sparked the collapse of the ITS group after Italian MEP Alessandra Mussolini played the anti-Romanian card in alleging a relationship between immigration and criminality in domestic politics. Despite clear ideological convergence on some key socio-cultural issues, there have also been strategic image-seeking concerns that have prevented party leaders from collaborating with some of their potentially more "fiendish" counterparts in Europe. A controversial figure in the Netherlands, PVV chairman Geert Wilders does for instance take great care in distancing himself from other populist radical right leaders in Europe.

Lastly and perhaps most importantly, the reminiscence of old historical irredentist or ethnic disputes has precluded forming more stable and broader cross-national federations of parties.[21] This had already been the case within the group of the European Right between 1989 and 1994 where longstanding disagree-

20 The Alliance also comprises the All-Ukrainian Union "Svoboda" which is classified as a populist radical right party by Mudde, Populist Radical Right Parties in Europe, p. 308.

21 Mareš, The Extreme Right in Eastern Europe.

ments between the German *Republikaner* and Italian MSI over the South Tyrol region had complicated efforts of pragmatic co-operation in the European parliament. At the time of building the Alliance of European national movements in October 2009, leaders of the Hungarian MIÉP-*Jobbik* coalition fiercely rejected any attempt at bringing in the Romanian PRM or Bulgarian *Ataka* because of their strong nationalist anti-ethnic Hungarian agenda. Similarly, the increased salience of the linguistic cleavage in Belgium made very difficult formal collaboration between the Walloon FN and its Flemish VB counterpart.

III. The electoral weight of the pan-European populist radical right: 1979–2009

Is the populist radical right on the rise on the European stage? To some extent, the answer to this question again depends on which individual parties are counted as members of the populist radical right family. Performances in Euro elections by those parties over the 1979–2009 period are summarized in Figure 2. As can be seen, the populist radical right remains a relatively stable yet marginal transnational political force averaging less than 6 % of the vote across all seven waves of EP elections since the late 1970s (slightly more in 2009 if we include the Dutch PVV as shown on the chart). The unweighted conditional means displayed in Figure 2 show no clear discernible trend over time and at the very least dispel the myth of an ineluctable electoral growth of extreme forces on the right of the European political spectrum.[22]

Looking at seat ratios as a more proportional measure of electoral impact relative to population size across member states leads to similar conclusions. In the last set of elections in June 2009, populist radical right parties stricto sensu won 31 seats (4.2 %), a proportion very similar to that achieved by those parties in the late 1980s and throughout the 1990s prior to Eastern enlargement of the EU. Using a broader definition that would encompass borderline cases such as the Dutch PVV or, even more extensively perhaps, the *True Finns* (PS), a total of thirteen parties received 38 seats in the last European elections, that is 5.2 % of all MEPs compared with 4.8 % in the previous wave of 2004/07. This can be contrasted for instance with the outcome of the 2009 elections for the *European Green Party* or the *European United Left-Nordic Green Left* (EUL/NGL) whose member organizations totalled 46 seats (6.3 %, up to 55 seats if we include the *European Free Alliance*) and 35 seats (4.7 %) respectively.

However, this relatively modest electoral impact should not conceal a substantial amount of inter-country variance and the changing balance of forces

22 Nor do we find significant differences if we consider the regional divide between Western and Eastern Europe across the 2004–2009 waves of European elections. In 2004–07, the populist radical right achieved 4.5 and 5.5 % of the EP vote in Western and Eastern member states respectively; in June 2009, comparable figures were 6.4 and 6.0 %.

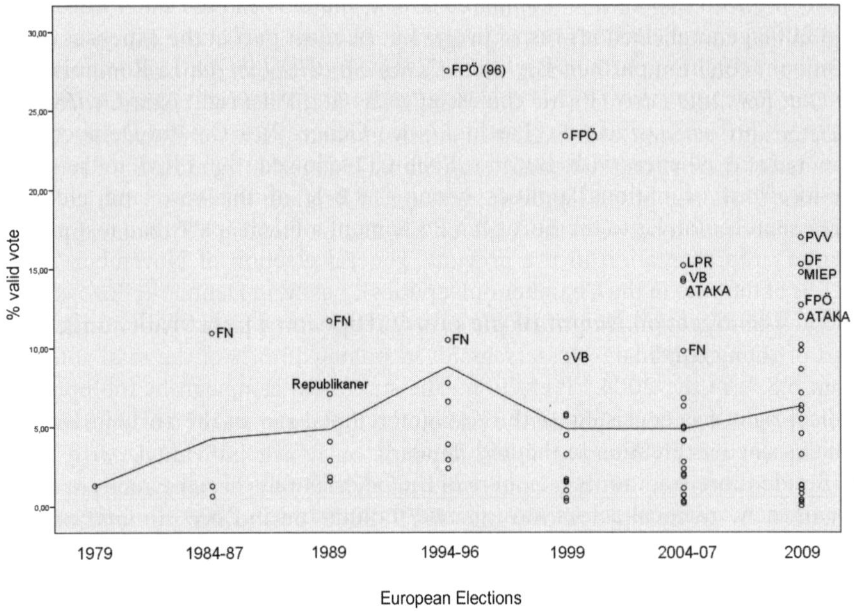

Figure 2: Vote cast for populist radical right parties in European elections, 1979–2009

within the populist radical right family. Table 1 below has a brief summary of election results for this group of parties in the 2009 and 2004 EU parliamentary contests. In recent years, some of the well-established members of the populist radical right have experienced electoral setbacks or decline. This is the case for instance in Austria where the FPÖ-BZÖ duopoly has only recovered part of the former strengths of the unitary FPÖ in the 1990s. Similarly the populist radical right has lost ground in Flanders (VB), France (FN), Bulgaria (Ataka) and most dramatically in Poland where the *League of Polish Families* (LPR) joined the Libertas coalition and polled a mere 1.1 % of the vote in 2009 as opposed to 15.2 % in the 2004 ballot. A flash phenomenon in the 1989 Euro election, the *Republikaner* (REP) have become largely irrelevant to German politics since the mid-1990s.

This contrasts with the strengths of other parties such as the Italian *Lega Nord* (LN), the *Greater Romania Party* (PRM) or the *Danish People's Party* (DF), which have all made substantial electoral gains in the 2009 EP elections. In Italy, the *Lega Nord* benefited from the polarization of its proprietary immigration and law-and-order issues in the domestic arena.[23] Bossi's party increased its

23 The 2009 European election took place concurrently to the parliamentary debate over the most contentious centre-right government's bill criminalising irregular immigration

share of the vote to 10.2 % (compared with 5 and 8.3 % in the 2004 European and 2008 general elections respectively) for the most part at the expenses of its dominant coalition partner, Berlusconi's *Popolo della Libertà*. In Romania, the *Greater Romania Party* (PRM) coalesced with nationalist right *New Generation Party - Christian Democrat* ("Partidul Noua Generație - Creştin Democrat"). The tactical alliance with Becali's PNG-CD allowed the PRM to re-stage the forefront of national politics winning 8.6 % of the vote and electing three representatives to the European Parliament after the party had lost parliamentary representation in the previous general election of November 2008 (3.1 % of the vote in the Chamber of Deputies). Lastly, in Denmark, Eurosceptic and anti-immigration *Danish People's Party* (DF) won a large victory under the lead of young candidate Messerschmidt by polling 15.3 % of the total vote, up from 6.8 % in the 2004 EP election. The successful campaign by the populist radical right was consistent with the uninterrupted rise of the party in Danish politics since its creation in the mid-1990s.[24]

Beside those traditional members of the populist radical right family, a number of 'new' political actors have gained momentum in 2009. In Greece, the *Popular Orthodox Rally* (La.O.S.) has received 7.1 % of the vote cast. In Hungary, the *Justice and Life Party* (MIÉP) has joined forces with the *Jobbik* movement to receive 14.8 % of the vote coming third in the polls. The populist radical right vote was boosted by the deep economic crisis and the anti-incumbent vote that was expressed against the ruling *Socialist Party* in office since 2002. In the UK, Nick Griffin's *British National Party* (BNP) has made entry into European parliament for the first time with 6 % of the vote and two seats, as have the *National Party* (SNS) in Slovakia or the *True Finns* (PS) in Finland. In the Finnish case, the high performance achieved by Soini's party in the most recent EP election (9.8 %) follows the acceleration in the upward trend observed since the 1999 general election at both national and local level, as revealed by the party's score in the 2008 local council elections (5.4 % as opposed to only 0.9 % four years earlier). In the Netherlands, Geert Wilders' *Party for Freedom* (PVV) has come second in the polls behind the *Christian-Democrats* and won an impressive 17 % and four EU parliamentary seats.

and the right for citizens to organise anti-crime vigilante patrols. The bill was approved by the Lower Chamber on 13 May 2009 with a majority vote of confidence of 316 to 238. The law was passed by the Senate in July 2009.

24 It was boosted by controversies over the possibility of holding a Euro referendum and the July 2008 ruling by the European Court of Justice against the tightening of Denmark's immigration laws that had resulted from the DF offering parliamentary support to the minority centre-right government.

Table 1: The populist radical right in the 2009 European elections

Country	Party	Full name and acronym	% 2009	Seats 2009	% 2004
AT-Austria	Freedom Party Alliance for the Future of Austria	Freiheitliche Partei Österreichs, FPÖ Bündnis Zukunft Österreich, BZÖ	12.71 4.58	2 -	6.31 -
BE-Belgium	Flemish Interest National Front	Vlaams Belang, VB Front national, FN	9.85 1.33	2 -	14.34 2.79
BG-Bulgaria	National Union Attack	Ataka	11.96	2	14.20[d]
CZ-Czech Republic	National Party Workers' Party	Národní strana, NS Dělnická strana, DS	0.26 1.07	- -	0.67 -
DE-Germany	National Democratic Party; German People's Union Republicans	Nationaldemokratische Partei Deutschlands, NPD (Die Nationalen); Deutsche Volksunion, DVU Republikaner, REP	0.40 1.30	- -	0.90 1.90
DK-Denmark	Danish People's Party[c]	Dansk Folkeparti, DF	15.28	2	6.80
FI-Finland	True Finns[a] The Finnish People's Blue-whites	Perussuomalaiset, PS Suomen Kansan Sinivalkoiset, SKS	9.79 -	3 -	0.54 0.20
FR-France	National Front	Front national, FN	6.34	3	9.81
GR-Greece	Popular Orthodox Rally	Laïkós Orthódoxos Synagermós, La.O.S.	7.14	2	4.12
HU-Hungary	Hungarian Justice and Life Party	Magyar Igazság és Élet Pártja, MIÉP-Jobbik	14.77	3	2.35
IT-Italy	Northern League[b] The Right-Tricolor Flame	Lega Nord La Destra-Fiamma Tricolore	10.20 0.79	9 -	5.00 0.70
LV-Latvia	All for Latvia!	Partija Visu Latvijai!	2.81	-	-
MT-Malta	National Action	Azzjoni Nazzjonali, AN	0.64	-	-
NL-Netherlands	Party for Freedom[a]	Partij voor de Vrijheid, PVV	16.97	4	-
PL-Poland	League of Polish Families	Liga Polskich Rodzin, LPR	1.14	-	15.20

Country	Party	Full name and acronym	% 2009	Seats 2009	% 2004
PT-Portugal	National Renewal Party	Partido Nacional Renovador, PNR	0.40	-	0.30
RO-Romania	Greater Romania Party	Partidul Romania Mare, PRM	8.65	3	4.15[d]
SE-Sweden	Swedish Democrats	Sverigedemokraterna, SD	3.27	-	1.13
SI-Slovenia	Slovene National Party	Slovenska nacionalna stranka, SNS	2.86	-	5.00
SK-Slovakia	Slovak National Party[b]	Slovenská národná strana, SNS	5.50	1	2.01
UK-United Kingdom	British National Party	British National Party, BNP	6.04	2	4.90

(a) Parties not considered by Mudde, Populist Radical Right Parties in Europe, Appendix A: pp. 305–308;
(b) incumbent at time of EU election;
(c) parliamentary support to the ruling coalition;
(d) 2007 European election.

IV. European elections and the national election cycle

Cross-national variability in the electoral performances of the pan-European populist radical right needs of course to be considered within each particular national election cycle. The "second-order" model formulated by Reif/Schmitt in the early 1980s emphasizes some key features of EP elections in relation to the political situation of the first-order arena. One central claim by the authors is that European elections are in fact largely dominated by the domestic agenda.[25] Another original proposition of particular relevance to the present analysis is that voters are more prone to cast "expressive" votes for peripheral and fringe parties in European contests. As suggested by Reif in his follow-up study of the 1979 and 1984 sets of Euro elections, the tendency by voters to "follow their heart" in second-order elections benefits smaller, new and more radical movements whose prospects in European elections are often brighter than those of established parties.[26]

Because of their strong anti-establishment appeal, populist radical right parties are propositionally in a favorable position to mobilize dissatisfied voters, even more so in second-order ballots where citizens have a greater propensity to "vote with their boots" against mainstream parties. Populist radical right parties could therefore be expected to perform somehow better in European elections than in contiguous national contest. In countries with majoritarian electoral systems in principal elections such as the UK or France, the change to proportional representation in EP elections is another factor that might further boost votes for those parties in the second-order arena. Lastly, the Eurosceptic focus of the populist radical right political platform might appeal to those voters who in varying proportions across member states tend to disagree with the European integration process generally supported by larger parties of government.

One way to test the populist radical right party short-term gain hypothesis is to compare aggregate national election results for domestic and European elections at the level of individual parties. A simple calculation can be performed by looking at differences in party size from the general election immediately preceding each European contest. On average, performances in EP elections represent a modest 0.7 % improvement on the parties' showings in the preceding first-order contest (sd=3.9, n=69 over the 1979–2009 period). Alternatively, in order to examine more closely the extent to which European elections are independent from the first-order electoral cycle, one can choose to look at the previous but also the subsequent first-order ballot. Where data are available, a hypothetical "mid-term" performance can be computed by averaging the populist radical right's electoral returns in general elections immediately preceding and following each European contest. Actual scores in European ballots are then

25 See Reif/Schmitt, Nine National Second-Order Elections.

26 See Reif, National Electoral Cycles and European Elections 1979 and 1984, pp. 244–255.

contrasted with this measure of expected electoral performances between adjoining general elections. Populist radical right parties win on average 0.4 % more than their mean score in the two concomitant first-order elections, within substantial range and with a significant amount of variance across time and space (sd=3.1, min=-7.45, max=7.28, n=60 over the 1979–2010 period of time).

Put in comparative and longitudinal perspective, the observed variance in party performances between first and second-order elections gives only partial evidence of any such political opportunity structure that would foster the populist radical right vote in European ballots. The data fail to reveal systematic sweeps in favor of those parties. At country level, cases of recurring European electoral bounties are relatively few. They include the *National Union Attack* (ATAKA) in Bulgaria, the Greek *Popular Orthodox Rally* (La.O.S.) and to a much lesser extent irrelevant fringe parties such as the *Workers' Party* (DS) in the Czech Republic or the *National Renewal Party* (PNR) in Portugal or the Italian MSI-*Fiamma Tricolore* following the 1995 breakaway from Fini's *Alleanza Nazionale* (AN).

Demarcation is perhaps clearer in Britain and Germany where performances by the populist radical right are more compatible with the second-order hypothesis of short-term deviations in electoral choices away from traditional party allegiances. In Germany, the *Republikaner* (REP) have enjoyed higher levels of popular support in European elections compared with concomitant domestic contests. In Britain, the change in the electoral system from FPTP to party list prior to the 1999 election has certainly created a favorable structure of opportunity for minor parties, which has benefited the BNP and eventually led to the party's first notable success in returning two MEPs in 2009.

In contrast, there are cases where populist radical right parties tend to underperform in European elections if not simply fail to enter the competition. For example, the small *Estonian Independence Party* (EIP) did not run in the 2004 and 2009 EP elections despite being present in the 2003 and 2007 general elections. In Italy, the electoral showings of the *Lega Nord* and predecessor party *Lega Lombarda* were poorer in European elections throughout the 1990s, at a time when the party had not yet completed its process of ideological radicalization on immigration. Similarly, the *Sweden Democrats* (SD), the *Slovak National Party* (SNS) or the *Danish People's Party* (DF) have often underperformed in EP contests although, as discussed above, the most recent 2009 election in Denmark showed a sharp increase in Euro votes for Kjærsgaard's party.

There are of course limitations to such a rudimentary approach. The second-order model draws attention to the temporal location of European elections in the domestic electoral sequence. Using a simple difference assumes a "smoothed" linear trend between elections whereas there have long been suggestions of the existence of more complex popularity cycles for governments and opposition parties.[27] The propensity for disillusioned voters to defect to third

27 See Tufte, Determinants of the Outcomes of Midterm Congressional Elections; Schmitt, The European Parliament Elections.

parties in rebellion against incumbent and/or mainstream opposition parties may be expected to vary according to whether the European election takes place during the so-called "honeymoon period" just after the general election or, on the contrary, at mid-term when government popularity usually reaches a nadir.

Figure 3 below shows the distribution of changes in populist radical right parties' scores compared with the preceding first-order election based on the location of the European contest within the national electoral cycle. The traditional first-order popularity cycle hypothesis of different effects at different points in time is materialized by the third-order polynomial curve in Figure 3. As can be seen, however, there is only limited support for the hypothesis of consistently higher gains for the populist radical right in cases of European elections taking place around mid-term, as opposed to smaller changes either earlier or later in the domestic cycle closer to general elections. Such variability across the cycle is exemplified in a number of cases. In Austria, both the 1996 and 2009 elections were contested early in the national cycle and yet gave very contrasted outcomes for the FPÖ when compared with the party's score in the 1995 and 2008 general elections (+5.6 and -4.8 respectively). In Hungary, the *Justice and Life Party* (MIÉP) significantly increased its share of the European vote (+12.6) in June 2009 only a few months ahead of the 2010 general election, whereas the party had lost 2 % in the mid-term 2004 EP contest. In the 2007 Euro elections, the *Greater Romania Party* had suffered heavy electoral losses on its preceding performance in the 2004 general election (-9.5 %) in the final quarter of the national cycle. In 2009, on the other hand, Tudor's movement increased its score by more than 5 % during the honeymoon period for the coalition government that had emerged from the 2008 legislative election a few months earlier.

As briefly alluded to in the opening section of this chapter, a whole host of interrelated structural socio-economic and political opportunity factors help account for the variation in support for the populist radical right across elections. If only because of the existing links between first and second-order electoral arenas in most countries, none of those factors can be considered peculiar to European elections alone – with the exception perhaps of changes that might take place in the electoral system for EP contests. The connection between the parties' ups and downs in EP elections and the next general elections will be examined below. Attention should be briefly given here to shorter-term variables that might also affect the populist radical right vote in European elections.

First, the differentiation process that occurs in the European election party system should not be overlooked. Across several EU member states, the shape of the competitive space is temporarily altered by single-issue parties entering the European electoral arena. In some cases, these actors compete directly for the electoral constituency of the populist radical right on issues of national sovereignty and the rejection of EU "bureaucracy". The breed of anti-EU movements in Scandinavia such as the *Danish June Movement* ("JuniBevægelsen") or *Swedish June List* ("Junilistan") is one instance of single-issue parties with a broad appeal to cross-sections of the electorate in European elections, which

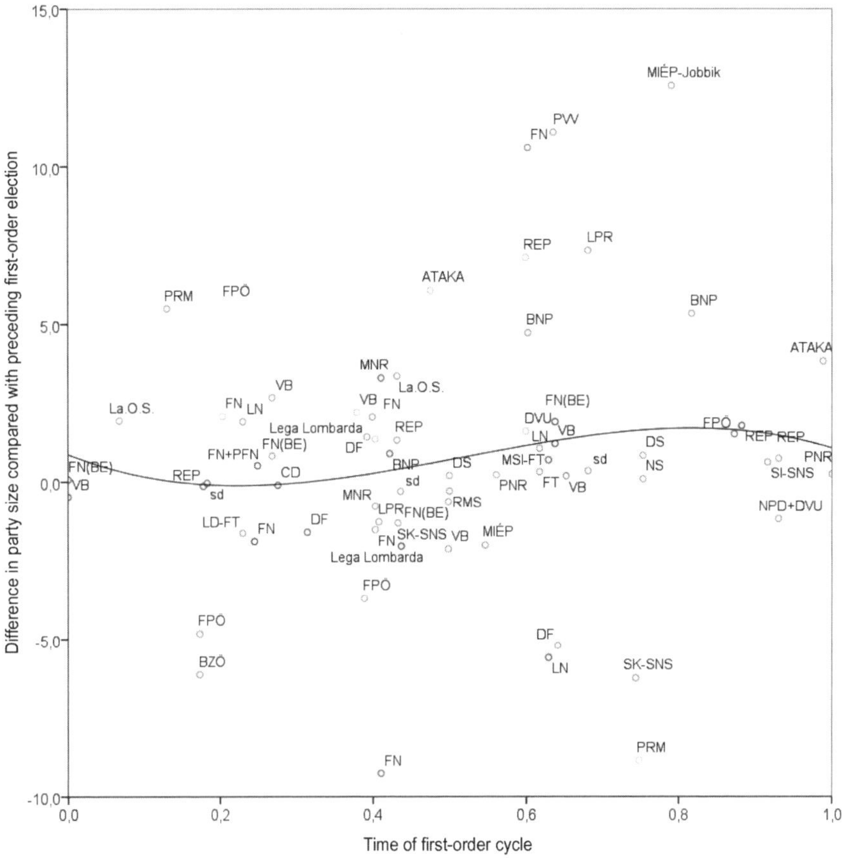

Figure 3: Change in populist radical right votes from first-order to European election according to the position in the national election cycle

X = Time of first-order cycle expressed as the proportion of time elapsed.
Y = Score in European election - Score in preceding national election (legislative in semi-presidential systems).

subsequently exit the first-order arena.[28] In France, the emergence of Villiers' conservative anti-Maastricht movement as early as 1994 altered the balance of forces on the right of the French political spectrum. In Austria, the rise of Hans-Peter Martin's List with 14 % of the vote in the 2004 EP election participated in the electoral debacle of the FPÖ albeit not its primary cause.

28 This is also true of other Eurosceptic actors such as the "UK Independence Party", the "People's Union of Estonia" ("Eestimaa Rahvaliit", ER), the "Lithuanian Order and Justice" ("Tvarka ir teisingumas", TT), the "Independent Democrats" ("Nezávislí demokraté", NEZDEM) in the Czech Republic, or, more recently, the broader federation of Eurosceptics gathered under the Libertas banner in the 2009 European election.

More prominently perhaps it is important to consider the impact of individual party change across elections. Some of the variation observed in the electoral fortunes of the populist radical right in EP contests cannot be accounted for without looking at tactical alliances, temporary amalgamations of competing parties, nor the splits into rival factions often found in this party family. To cite one instance of significant change in the organizational structure of parties with substantial impact on electoral performances, we should recall the 1999 schism that took place within the French *Front national*, which led eventually to the forming of the *National Republican Movement* (MNR) and its first competing against the FN in the 1999 European election. Conversely, the process of ad hoc co-operation by parties of the Romanian populist radical right (PRM+PNG) in the 2009 EP contest provides an example of a pragmatic strategy successfully rewarded in electoral terms.[29]

Lastly, we cannot ignore the systemic trajectory of the populist radical right. Across some EU member states, the electoral consolidation of those parties has paved the way to their entering national coalition governments. The ongoing research on patterns of populist incumbency reflects on the variety of experiences where those parties have effectively managed to get their way into office either nationally or locally.[30] Accounts of recent developments in Italian or Swiss politics show for instance that some populist radical right parties have successfully managed the transition from opposition to government. Sustainable electoral success is often achieved through complex strategies of "keeping one foot in and one foot out".[31] In other cases, however, populist radical right incumbency has led to electoral failure and the demise of parties at national level. This model has been well documented in Austria (2002), the Netherlands (2003), Poland (2007) or Slovakia (2010), where parties of the populist radical right have suffered heavy electoral losses following participation in national government.

The negative incumbency effect is by no mean restricted to national elections and can be found to replicate in second-order contests that are close to the "re-instating" general election within the domestic cycle. The 2004 European elections in Austria or the Netherlands provide examples of such lagged negative incumbency effects. In the former case, the FPÖ continued to lose votes after the already severe setback faced by the party in the 2002 general election. In the 2004 Dutch election to the European Parliament, the LPF political epiphe-

29 In coalition with Becali's PNG, the PRM list won 8.7 % of the vote in the 2009 European parliamentary election. This represented a significant gain from the party's previous showings in the 2008 legislative and local elections (3.2 and 3.7 % of the vote). The reshuffling of the balance of forces within the populist radical right camp was evident however in the subsequent presidential election of November 2009 where the PRM and PNG ran independently and received 5.6 and 1.9 % respectively.

30 Cf. Heinisch, Success in Opposition; Albertazzi/McDonnell, Twenty-First Century Populism.

31 See Albertazzi/McDonnell, The Lega Nord in the Second Berlusconi Government.

nomenon was well on its way down to political irrelevance after the party's score had dropped from 17 % of the vote in the 2002 general election to only 5.7 % in 2003 and would further collapse in the 2006 legislatives with less than 0.5 %. In a similar vein, the Polish EP election of June 2009 seems to have been an extension of the decay phase that was inaugurated by the LPR in the 2007 general election where the party lost 6.7 % on its previous performance of 2005 (8 %) following two years in government with conservative *Law and Justice* (PiS) and populist *Samoobrona* (SRP). More recently, the 2009 European election in Slovakia announced the forthcoming reverse of the *Slovak National Party* (SNS) in the June 2010 general election (5.1 % down from 11.7 % four years earlier) after the party had joined in controversial coalition with Fico's populist left-wing SMER in June 2006.

V. European elections as "bellwethers" of populist radical right success?

In most countries, European elections are regarded as "real life" polls of public opinion with palpable repercussions on the balance of forces in the next general election. What do European elections tell us about party system change and more specifically about the subsequent fate of the populist radical right in national politics? If we simply take a glance at the most recent wave of EP elections of June 2009, there is some evidence of a link between the performances by those parties in European elections and their showings in the subsequent general election.

In Hungary, the rise of the MIÉP-*Jobbik* alliance in the 2009 EP election heralded the return of the populist radical right in Parliament after its joint platform had failed to win any seat in the 2006 general election. In the first round of the April 2010 legislative election, Vona's *Jobbik* alone gathered 16.7 % of the vote and 26 seats coming in third place behind the mainstream conservatives of *Fidesz* and the *Hungarian Socialist Party* (MSZP). Similarly, in the general election of June 2010, the *Dutch Party for Freedom* confirmed its showing in the 2009 Euro contest by winning 15.5 % of the vote and 24 seats in the House of Representatives. In Greece, the success of the *Popular Orthodox Rally* was replicated in the general election of October 2009 where Karatzaferis' La. O. S. won 5.6 % of the vote and 15 seats in the Hellenic Parliament prior to the outbreak of the debt crisis. In September 2010, the *Swedish Democrats* (SD) confirmed their previous performance of the 2009 European election and won 20 out of the 349 seats in national parliament (5.7 % of the vote). A similar conclusion applies to cases where populist radical right movements showed an electoral fall in June 2009, as suggested earlier in the Slovak case. In Belgium, the underperformance by the *Vlaams Belang* with 7.8 % of the vote in the June 2010 legislative elections was detectable in the party's showing in the EP ballot one year before (9.8 % as opposed to 12 % in the 2007 general election).

The relationship between European elections and the next general election can be explored in a more systematic way. According to Marsh, European election results have a significant domestic impact and provide a guide to the next general election results.[32] The author suggests to model gains or losses by parties between adjacent national elections as a linear function of the changes observed in the intervening European contest. A similar approach can be considered to assess the strengths and weaknesses of the populist radical right in EP elections since 1979.[33]

European election results are indeed pointers to populist radical right performances in the national space. Shifts manifested at European level have significant consequences on the subsequent political development of those parties in the first-order arena. The simple linear model employed here gives an adjusted R^2 of 0.48 (SEE=2.8). The coefficient for change in European elections is 0.66 and statistically significant. Consistent with previous considerations is that electoral swings occurring in European elections are slightly larger in magnitude than those that take place in the next general election.[34]

VI. Conclusion

With the specter of interwar fascist mass parties haunting public debates, the rise of new waves of populist radical right parties since the early 1980s has become a crucial matter of concern. The wealth of studies devoted to examining the dynamics behind the elector success of those political actors bears testimony to the critical importance of the phenomenon both domestically and internationally.

The main objective of this chapter was to assess the development of the populist radical right in the European arena by using the accumulated experience of the seven waves of EP elections since 1979. Looking first at the map of populist radical right parties in European parliament has pointed to the heterogeneity in this collection of political actors. Despite many attempts at unifying all "nationalists" across the continent, a number of historical and practical factors have hindered efforts of building networks of cross-national co-operation between parties that share core ideological features otherwise – most notably a strong Eurosceptic stance and a fierce rejection of European federalism.

Cross-national examination of the performances by populist radical right parties in Euro elections over the 1979–2009 period has underlined both the rela-

32 Cf. Marsh, Testing the Second-Order Election Model, p. 606.

33 A total of 60 cases are included in the analysis where all data for previous general election, European election and next general elections are available.

34 The data show no clear regional divide when contrasting Western member states and former communist countries (adj. R^2 of 0.43 and 0.59 respectively), bearing in mind the limitations inherent in the smaller number of cases available from the 2004–09 series of EP elections in Central and Eastern European nations, n=12).

tive marginality and the stability in the electoral weight of the populist radical right at about 6 % of the total European vote. Such European average of electoral scores conceals of course the substantial amount of variance that is found across EU member states, and the ever-changing balance of forces within the populist radical right family. As illustrated in the most recent wave of EP election of June 2009, "new" political actors have emerged on the European scene and their success has compensated for the decline of more established members of the populist radical right elsewhere.

In line with the traditional "second-order" model for European elections, this variability in the electoral performances of the populist radical right has been considered in the context of each particular national election cycle. Put in comparative and longitudinal perspective, there was limited evidence of any such political opportunity structure that would boost the populist radical right vote in European ballots. Despite a strong populist appeal to dissatisfied voters, EP election scores were found to represent only a slight improvement on the parties' showings in concomitant first-order contests. Controlling for the location of the European contest within the national election cycle showed no further evidence of a greater propensity by those parties to capitalize electorally on public discontent at any particular point in time in between first-order elections.

A systemic relationship was found between the first and second-order arenas with respect to the fluctuation in the electoral results of the populist radical right at European elections. A glance at all available data since the late 1970s revealed a significant link between the performances by those parties in European elections and their showings in the subsequent general election. Consistent with other studies of EP elections was that European election results had indeed a significant domestic impact and provided a 'bellwether' pointer to the next general election results.

One more general implication emerging from all this is that the electoral performances of the populist radical right in European elections cannot be dissociated from the broad national political environment in which they take place. Whilst there are no discernible trends at the pan-European level, close links exist between the first and second-order arenas in individual EU member states. Such consistency in populist radical right voting across distinct sets of elections with clearly dissimilar political statuses lends lesser support to a theory of short-term insincere voting for those parties in EP elections. Citizens might be keener to express discontent in low-profile elections by voting for the populist radical right, yet in the end, they do not necessarily return to the mainstream when the time comes to make effective decisions that will weigh on domestic government formation.

Electoral Sociology – Who Votes for the Extreme Right and Why – and When?

Kai Arzheimer

This chapter profiles the social base of electoral support for the parties of the Extreme Right[1] in Western Europe, i. e. the question of whether some groups in society are more susceptible to the appeal of these parties than others. This issue is relevant for a number of reasons: First, by looking at the social composition of European societies we might be able to better understand why parties of the Extreme Right are more successful in some countries than in others. Second, a careful analysis of the link between the social and the political might help us to gauge the potential for future right-wing mobilization in countries which currently have no electorally successful parties of the Extreme Right. Third, knowing who votes for a party might help us to get a clearer understanding of the underlying motives to cast a vote for the Extreme Right.

Over the last fifteen years or so, analyses of the Extreme Right's electorate(s) have become a minor industry within the larger context of (comparative) Political Sociology. By necessity, this chapter aims at summarizing the main findings from this research program, but cannot strive for a comprehensive presentation of all that has been achieved during these years. More specifically, findings from national and small-n studies are (almost) completely ignored. Much by the same token, I will not delve into the fascinating literature on the social bases of the Interwar Extreme Right in Germany and in other countries.[2]

Recent events in Central and Eastern Europe provide an intriguing complement to this Western perspective.[3] However, much like Central and Eastern European parties and electorates themselves, our (comparative) knowledge of the social base of the Extreme Right in CEE is still very much in flux. Therefore,

1 A staggering number of labels and definitions have been applied to the parties whose electorates are analyzed in this chapter (see section 1.1). For simplicity's sake, I use the term "Extreme Right", arguably the most prominent in the international literature. This does not imply that all or indeed a majority of the relevant parties are "extremist", i. e. opposed to the values of Liberal Democracy.

2 See Childers, The Nazi Voter; Falter, Hitlers Wähler; King/Tanner/Wagner, Ordinary Economic Voting Behavior; Küchler, The NSDAP Vote in the Weimar Republic; O'Loughlin, The Electoral Geography of Weimar Germany.

3 See Mudde, Racist Extremism in Central and Eastern Europe.

the chapter aims to provide a comparative perspective on developments in Western European electoral politics since the 1980s.

I. Theory

1. Definitions

Much of the early literature on the Extreme Right is devoted to the twin debates on the correct label and on the proper criteria for membership in this party family. Initially, the newly successful parties of the "Third Wave" that began in the late 1970s were seen as closely linked to the Extreme Right of the Interwar years.[4] While such connections do exist in many cases, scholars soon began to pinpoint the differences between a) the current and the Interwar right and b) between different members of the emerging new party family. As a result, scholars came up with a plethora of definitions, typologies and labels, including (but not limited to) the "New Right", "Radical Right", "Populist Right" and "Extreme Right", to mention only the most popular ones. As recently as 2007, Cas Mudde, one of the most prolific scholars in this area, made an attempt to bring a semblance of order to the field by suggesting that "nativism", the belief that states should be inhabited exclusively by members of the "native" group, is the largest common denominator for the parties of the Third Wave including those in Central and Eastern Europe.[5] Like a Russian doll, this family contains two subgroups which are nested into each other: Parties of the "Radical Right" combine nativism and authoritarianism, whereas the "Populist Radical Right" add populism as an additional ingredient to this mixture. In a departure from his earlier work, the label "Extreme Right" is reserved for anti-democratic (extremist) parties within the all-embracing nativist cluster.[6]

While Mudde's proposal is remarkably clear and was very well received in the field,[7] it matters most to students of parties. Scholars of voting behavior, on the other hand, tend to go with a rather pragmatic approach that was concisely summarized by Mudde a decade earlier: "We know *who* they are, even though we do not know exactly *what* they are".[8] As this quote suggests, there is (definitional questions not withstanding) actually a very broad consensus as to which parties are normally included in analyses of the Right's electoral base. These include the *Progress Party* in Norway, the *Danish People's Party* and the *Progress Party* in Denmark, *New Democracy* and the *Sweden Democrats* in Sweden, the *National Front*, *National Democrats* and *British National Party* in Britain, the *National Front* and the *National Republican Movement* in France, the *German*

4 Prowe, 'Classic' Fascism.
5 Mudde, Populist Radical Right Parties in Europe, pp. 18–24.
6 Ibid., p. 24.
7 Cf. the symposium in Political Studies Review 2009.
8 Mudde, The Paradox of the Anti-Party Party, p. 233.

People's Union, *Republicans* and *National Democrats* in Germany, the Centre Parties, *Lijst Pim Fortuyn* and the *Freedom Party* in the Netherlands, the *Vlaams Blok/Belang* and the *National Front* in Belgium, the *Freedom Party* and the *Alliance for the Future* in Austria, the Italian *Social Movement/National Alliance*, the *Northern League* and the *Tricolour Flame* in Italy, the *Falange Parties* in Spain, *Political Spring*, the *Popular Orthodox Rally* and various smaller and short-lived parties in Greece, and the *Christian Democrats* (PDC) in Portugal. There is even a remarkable agreement on which parties should best be seen as borderline cases: the Scandinavian Progress Parties before they transformed themselves into anti-immigration parties during the early 1980s, the *National Alliance* after Fini began to develop its "post-fascist" profile in the mid-1990s, the *Swiss People's Party* in Switzerland before it became dominated by its 'Zurich Wing' led by Blocher and the *True Finns* in Finland and the *Social Democratic Centre/Popular Party* in Portugal.

Amongst scholars of voting behavior, there is little doubt that these parties attract similar voters and should be grouped together in a single, albeit very heterogeneous, party family. "Extreme Right" is currently the most popular label for this group. Its use does not (necessarily) signify the respective parties' opposition to the principles of liberal democracy but rather adherence to a convention in the field.

This is not to imply that differences between these parties do not exist, do not matter for voting behavior or should be analyzed by different typologies. The German NPD, for instance, is unapologetically neo-fascist, whereas the Norwegian *Progress Party* is, at least on the surface, remarkably moderate and libertarian. Rather, it is next to impossible to incorporate the existing differences between parties into studies of voting behavior because it is very rare to concurrently observe two or more electorally viable parties of the Third Wave competing for votes. Therefore, party sub-type effects are inseparable from other constant and time-varying country effects.

2. Explanations

Over the last eight decades or so, historians, sociologists and political scientists have developed a multitude of theoretical accounts that aim to explain the electoral support for the Interwar and modern Extreme Right. While many of these accounts are highly complex, they can usefully be grouped into four broad categories.[9]

A first group of scholars focuses on largely stable and very general attributes of the Extreme Right's supporters, that is, personality traits and value orientations. The most prominent example of this line of research is without doubt the original study on the so-called "Authoritarian Personality's" support for the Nazi

9 See Winkler, Bausteine einer allgemeinen Theorie des Rechtsextremismus.

party by Adorno and his collaborators.[10] More recent contributions include work by Altemeyer and Lederer, who both aim at developing "modern" scales for measuring authoritarianism.[11] In a related fashion, authors like Ignazi and Kitschelt have proposed a link between allegedly stable value orientations and voting for the Extreme Right.[12] Both authors interpret the success of the Extreme Right as part of an authoritarian-materialistic "backlash" against the Green and Left-Libertarian parties that emerged from the New Social Movements of the 1970s.[13]

If there is a correlation between one's social position on the one hand and one's personality traits and value orientation on the other, these approaches should go some way towards identifying the electoral base of the modern Extreme Right. And indeed, ever since the first studies on the social bases of the original Nazi movement were published, social scientists have suspected that the working class, the lower middle-classes and particularly the so-called "petty bourgeoisie" exhibit stronger authoritarian tendencies than other social groups.[14] This alleged link between class (and, by implication, formal education) was made explicit by Kitschelt, who argued that the very nature of jobs in certain segments of the private sector predisposes their occupants towards a mixture of market-liberal and authoritarian ideas that was at one stage promoted by the *National Front* in France and the *Freedom Party* in Austria.[15]

A second strand of the literature is mainly concerned with the effects of social disintegration, i. e. a (perceived) breakdown of social norms ("anomia") and intense feelings of anxiety, anger and isolation brought about by social change. Allegedly, this mental state inspires a longing for strong leadership and rigid ideologies that are provided by the Extreme Right. A classic proponent of this approach is Parsons in his early study on the Nazi supporters. More recently, these ideas have returned in the guise of the "losers of modernization" hypothesis, i. e. the idea that certain segments of Western societies feel that their position is threatened by immigration and globalization and therefore turn to political parties which promise to insulate them from these developments.[16]

Interestingly, the losers of modernization hypothesis identifies more or less the same social groups – (unskilled) workers, the unemployed and other persons depending on welfare, parts of the lower middle classes – as the main target of Extreme Right mobilization efforts.

10 See Adorno et al., The Authoritarian Personality.
11 See Altemeyer, The Authoritarian Specter; Lederer/Schmidt, Autoritarismus und Gesellschaft; and Meloen/Linden/Witte, A Test of the Approaches of Adorno et al.
12 See Ignazi, The Silent Counter-Revolution; and Kitschelt, The Radical Right in Western Europe.
13 See Inglehart, The Silent Revolution.
14 See e. g. Parsons, Some Sociological Aspects of the Fascist Movements.
15 See Kitschelt, The Radical Right in Western Europe, pp. 4–7.
16 See Scheuch/Klingemann, Theorie des Rechtsradikalismus in westlichen Industriegesellschaften, for the original, rather complex approach; and Betz, Radical Right-Wing Populism in Western Europe, for a modern and more streamlined take.

A third class of accounts draws heavily on theories from the field of social psychology. In this perspective, group conflicts are the real cause of support for the Extreme Right. Unlike the two aforementioned approaches, this strand is relatively heterogeneous. At one end of the spectrum, it includes classic theories of purely emotional, hardly conscious scapegoating.[17] In this perspective, ethnic minorities including immigrants provide convenient targets for the free-floating aggression harbored by a society's underclass. These minorities are at the same time a) suitably different from and b) even more power- and defenseless than the members of this group.

At the other end of the spectrum, theories of Realistic Group Conflict that can be traced to the early work of Sherif/Sherif emphasize the role of a (bounded) rationality in ethnic conflicts over scarce resources like jobs and benefits.[18] This idea is especially prominent in more recent accounts.[19]

Theories of "ethnic competition",[20] "status politics",[21] "subtle", "modern", "symbolic" or "cultural" racism[22] and social identity[23] cover a middle ground between these two poles, while the notion of "relative deprivation" - the idea that one's own group is not getting what they are entitled to in comparison with another social group - provides a useful conceptional umbrella for these somewhat disparate ideas.[24]

Again, no matter what specific concept from this research tradition is applied, the usual suspects emerge: those social groups who deem themselves threatened by immigration and related processes. But not all members of these groups vote for the Extreme Right. Rather, the Extreme Right vote shows a considerable degree of variation both between and within countries in Western Europe. Some of the differences between countries might be explained by differences in the social composition of the respective societies. However, these differences cannot explain the huge differences in Extreme Right support between otherwise reasonably similar countries: Norway is hardly more deprived than its neighbor Sweden. By the same token, it is difficult to imagine that the authoritarian underclass in Austria is six or seven times larger than its counterpart in neighboring Germany. Moreover, personality traits, value orientations, group membership and even social and economic position change slowly, if at all, whereas support for the Extreme Right often exhibits a great deal of variability within countries.

One factor that is often overlooked, perhaps because it seems too obvious, is the core variable of the social-psychological model of voting, i. e. party iden-

17 See e. g. Dollard et al., Frustration and Aggression.
18 See e. g. Sherif/Sherif, Groups in Harmony and Tension.
19 E. g. Esses/Jackson/Armstrong, Intergroup Competition.
20 See Bélanger/Pinard, Ethnic Movements and the Competition Model.
21 See Lipset/Bendix, Social Status and Social Structure.
22 See Kinder/Sears, Prejudice and Politics.
23 See Tajfel et al., Social Categorization and Intergroup Behaviour.
24 See Pettigrew, Summing Up.

tifications. Historically, Western European parties of the centre left and the centre right have been able to absorb considerable authoritarian potentials in their respective societies, and even today, some voters who might otherwise be lured by the Extreme Right are simply not available for those parties because they are still firmly attached to one of the more established parties.[25] Similarly, ties to other organizations, notably churches and trade unions, are likely to reduce the probability of an Extreme Right vote. This implies that the ongoing processes of de-alignment in Western European societies will increase the potential for right-wing mobilization, everything else being equal.[26]

However, varying degrees of de-alignment are not the only differences between Western European societies that can help to explain levels of support for the Extreme Right. Moreover, party identifications are also supposed to be stable over time. Therefore, processes of de-alignment and re-alignment cannot explain short-time fluctuations of Extreme Right support within the same country.

These insights have triggered interest in a fourth, additional perspective that has come to the fore in recent years and aims to complement the three major approaches. In Winkler's original survey of the literature, this emerging perspective was presented under the label of a "political culture" that constrains the posited effects of individual factors on the Extreme Right vote. However, since the mid-1990s, interest in a whole host of other, more tangible contextual factors has grown tremendously, and it is now widely believed that the interplay between group conflicts and system-level variables can help explain the striking differences in support for the Extreme Right over time and across countries. Building on previous work by Tarrow and Kriesi and his associates,[27] Arzheimer/Carter have argued that these factors should be subsumed under the concept of "political opportunity structures", which compromise short-, medium- and long-term contextual variables that amongst them capture the degree of openness of a given political system for political entrepreneurs.[28] As it turns out, however, the concept of "opportunities" for new political actors might be too narrow: Many context factors like unemployment or immigration will not only provide the political elite with an incentive to mobilize, but will also have a direct and possibly more important impact on voters' preferences. Empirically, it is not possible to separate these two causal mechanisms since we have no reliable information on the mental calculations made by (would-be) politicians. Therefore, it seems reasonable to subsume the notion of opportunity structures under the even more general concept of contextual factors.

Over the last fifteen years or so, studies have looked at a whole host of such contextual variables, including but not limited to:

25 See Arzheimer/Carter, Christian Religiosity and Voting.
26 See Dalton/Flanagan/Beck, Electoral Change in Advanced Industrial Democracies.
27 See Kriesi et al., New Social Movements and Political Opportunities in Western Europe; Tarrow, Power in Movement.
28 See Arzheimer/Carter, Political Opportunity Structures, p. 422.

1. Opportunity structures
   a) In a strict sense: political decentralization and electoral thresholds[29]
   b) In a wider sense: positions of other parties,[30] media coverage[31] and "discursive opportunity structures"[32]
2. Variables related to the Extreme Right parties themselves
   (e. g. availability of "charismatic leaders", policy positions, reliance on populism, party sub-type)
3. Macroeconomic variables: unemployment, growth, and their trends
4. Other political variables: immigration figures

All accounts of the role of contextual variables assume - sometimes explicitly but more often implicitly - some sort of multi-level explanation in the spirit of Coleman's ideal type of sociological explanations.[33] Put simply, these explanations assume that changes at the macro-level (a declining economy, rising immigration figures, a new anti-immigrant party) bring about changes in individual preferences, which lead to (aggregate) changes in individual political behavior, i. e. an increase in electoral support for the Extreme Right. Since different groups in society have different prior propensities to vote for the Extreme Right, and since they react differently to changes in the social and political environment, both micro and macro information are required to fully model and understand the processes that transform latent or potential support for the Extreme Right into real, manifest votes.

II. Data

All empirical analyses of the nexus between the social and the political require data that fall into two broad categories: aggregate (macro) data which provide information on the behavior and properties of collectives (electoral districts, provinces, countries...), and micro data, which relate to individuals and are typically based on standardized interviews. Both categories can be further subdivided by including additional dimensions:

29 See e. g. Carter, The Extreme Right in Western Europe.
30 See Arzheimer, Contextual Factors and the Extreme Right Vote; Arzheimer/Carter, Political Opportunity Structures; and Lubbers/Gijsberts/Scheepers, Extreme Right-Wing Voting in Western Europe.
31 See Boomgaarden/Vliegenthart, Explaining the Rise of Anti-Immigrant Parties; How News Content Influences Anti-Immigration Attitudes.
32 See Koopmans/Muis, The rise of right-wing populist Pim Fortuyn; Koopmans/Olzak, Discursive Opportunities; Ter Wal, The Discourse of the Extreme Right; and Wimmer, Explaining Xenophobia and Racism.
33 See Coleman, Foundations of Social Theory.

1. Macro data
   a) Source: census data, electoral results, macro-economic and government data
   b) Temporal coverage: cross-sectional vs. longitudinal data
   c) Geographical coverage: one, few or many countries
   d) Level of aggregation: wards, constituencies, subnational units or the whole country

2. Micro data
   a) Source: national opinion polls vs. comparative multi-national studies
   b) Temporal coverage: cross-sectional, trend and panel studies
   c) Geographical coverage: one, few or many countries
   d) Level of aggregation: individual cases vs. aggregated survey results

The analytical leverage of the data depends on these sub-dimensions as well as on the reliability of the information and the level of detail they provide. As a result of technological progress and huge individual and collective investments into the infrastructure of social science research, the quality and availability of comparative data on the electorates of the Extreme Right in Western Europe have vastly improved over the last decade. Consequentially, scholars of the Extreme Right are nowadays in a much better position to analyze the social base of these parties than fifteen or even five years ago.

Nonetheless, they still face some awkward trade-offs. Generally speaking, micro-level data is preferable to macro-level data, especially if the level of aggregation is high. After all, aggregate measures are usually restricted to human behavior but provide no information on the motives behind the aggregated actions.[34]

Moreover, aggregation discards individual information. Therefore, inferences from correlations at the macro-level to the behavior of individuals are plagued by the infamous ecological fallacy unless the aggregates are homogeneous.[35] This is most easily illustrated by an example: At the level of the 96 departments of metropolitan France, there is a sizable positive correlation between the number of foreign-born persons and the vote for the *National Front*. It is, however, highly unlikely that immigrants have an above-average propensity to vote for the Extreme Right. Rather, the aggregate correlation reflects a mixture of a) the below-average propensity of immigrants to vote for the *National Front*[36] and b) a hostile reaction of other voters to the presence of immigrants. Without individual-level data, it is not possible to disentangle these two effects.[37]

34 Aggregated survey data are a somewhat degenerated special case.
35 Robinson, Ecological Correlation and the Behavior of Individuals.
36 This is illustrated by very low levels of support for the "Front National" in those departments around Paris that have the highest shares of immigrants.
37 See the exchange between Arzheimer and Carter, How (not) to operationalise subnational political opportunity structures; Kestilä/Söderlund, Subnational Political Opportunity Structures; and Kestilä-Kekkonen/Söderlund, Rejoinder.

A famous historical example for the perils of aggregate correlations concerns two time-series that moved in sync: electoral support for the NSDAP and the unemployment rate in Weimar Germany. Their positive relationship suggests that the unemployed turned to the Nazi party as their economical situation declined.[38] However, at lower levels of aggregation (Länder and Kreise), the relationship between unemployment and the NSDAP vote was actually negative. Presumably, the unemployed were less likely to vote for the NSDAP while those who (yet) had a job had a higher propensity to support the Nazis that further increased as the economy deteriorated.[39]

So why would anyone want to base their analyses on macro data? As it turns out, quite often there is no alternative because (comparable) surveys were simply not conducted at some point in time relevant to the intended analysis, at least not in all countries that are supposed to be studied under a given design. The United Kingdom is a point in case. Until recently, the parties of the Extreme Right in this country were so weak that it was next to impossible to study their supporters by means of survey data.

Moreover, survey studies suffer from a number of limitations of their own: Even seemingly simple questions do not translate well into other languages, interviewers are tempted to take shortcuts, respondents might not be able (or willing) to accurately recall past behavior and might be too embarrassed to admit to racist feelings and (presumably) unpopular opinions, and so on. As a result, survey data are often plagued by relatively high levels of systematic and random error. Macro data on the other hand are usually collected by government agencies and are therefore highly reliable. In summary, researchers are forced to choose between richness and reliability, in-depth and "broad picture" perspectives, theoretical adequacy and data availability.

But not all is bleak. (Relatively) recent initiatives in the collection, dissemination and processing of survey data have gone a long way to improve the situation of the subfield. The European Social Survey[40] with its module on immigration (2002/2003) provides a pan-European, state-of-the-art perspective on the hearts and minds of the voters of the Extreme Right. Similarly, the Mannheim Trend File[41] represents a major effort to harmonize and document the multitude of Eurobarometer surveys that have been collected in the EC/EU member states since the early 1970s. Finally, electoral support for the Extreme Right is now often analyzed by means of statistical multi-level models,[42] which allow for the joint analyses of micro and macro data, thereby alleviating some of the problems outlined above.

38 See Frey/Weck, Hat Arbeitslosigkeit den Aufstieg des Nationalsozialismus bewirkt?

39 See Falter/Zintl, The Economic Crisis; and Falter et al., Arbeitslosigkeit und Nationalsozialismus.

40 See http://www.europeansocialsurvey.org.

41 See http://www.gesis.org/en/services/data/survey-data/eurobarometer-data-service/eb-trends-trend-files/mannheim-eb-trend-file.

42 See Arzheimer, Contextual Factors and the Extreme Right Vote; and Lubbers/Gijsberts/Scheepers, Extreme Right-Wing Voting in Western Europe.

III. Findings

While men were always overrepresented amongst the French *National Front*'s voters, it is well documented that its electoral base has changed considerably over time.[43] Initially, the Front appealed primarily to the petty bourgeoisie, but it quickly transformed itself into a non-traditional workers' party. In between, it managed to attract occasional support from segments of the middle classes. The Front has been dubbed the "master case" of a successful New Right Party, and its strategies have been adopted by other parties of the European Right.[44]

Therefore, it seems at least plausible that other parties of the right have followed a similar trajectory of "proletarianization".[45] At any rate, it seems safe to assume that new, relatively unknown parties rest on relatively fluid and less than well-defined social bases, whereas older parties that have competed for votes in three or four consecutive elections build a more consolidated electoral base, often with a distinct social profile.

As it turns out, the electorates of most parties of the Extreme Right do indeed consist of a clearly defined social core that is remarkably similar to the French pattern. The most successful of these parties - the *Freedom Party* in Austria, the Norwegian *Progress Party* and some others - have regularly managed to attract votes from beyond this core so that their profile became less sharp, whereas those that project the most radical political images (e. g. the German NPD or the British BNP) were bound to frighten off the middle classes and have therefore been unable to achieve this feat. This not withstanding, a very clear picture emerges from three decades of national and comparative studies of the Extreme Right.

1. Socio-demographics

1.1 Gender

Most national studies have found huge differences in the propensity of men and women to vote for the Extreme Right, even if other factors such as occupation, education and age are controlled for. While findings vary across time, parties, countries and details of operationalization and model specification, men seem to be roughly 40 % more likely to vote for the Extreme Right than female voters.[46] Even amongst the voters of the Norwegian *Progress Party* and the *Danish People's Party* (which have been both led by women for the last four/fifteen years

43 See Mayer, The Front National in the Plural; and Mayer/Perrineau, Why Do They Vote for Le Pen?

44 See Rydgren, Is Extreme Right-Wing Populism Contagious?

45 See Oesch, Explaining Workers' Support for Right-Wing Populist Parties in Western Europe.

46 See Givens, The Radical Right Gender Gap.

respectively), about two thirds are male.[47] An important exception from this general observation, however, is the Italian *National Alliance*, which appeals to both men and women. This somewhat unusual finding seems to coincide with the party leadership's attempts to re-define the Alliance as a Christian-conservative party that eventually paved the way for the AN's merger with *Forza Italia* in 2009.

Comparative studies that rely on various data sources confirm this general pattern.[48] A whole host of explanations for this phenomenon have been proposed in the literature, spanning a multitude of approaches from psychoanalysis to rational choice. Common arguments include that

- some parties of the Extreme Right (like the Interwar Right) still project images of hyper-masculinity that are intrinsically off-putting for women;
- women are moving towards the left of men in most post-industrial societies;[49]
- women are inherently conservative and therefore more likely to be offended by the Extreme Right's radicalism and more likely to identify with parties of the centre-right.

Related to the last point is a methodological argument: If effects of conformism and social desirability are stronger in women, they might simply be less likely to admit that they support the Extreme Right in an interview situation. However, analyses of the "German Representative Electoral Statistics", a special sub-sample of ballot papers that bear marks which record the gender and age-bracket of the elector, have shown that the gender gap is real, at least in Germany. Moreover, gender effects do not completely disappear when attitudes are controlled for. As Betz noted more than fifteen years ago, the magnitude of the right-wing voting gender gap is and remains "a complex and intriguing puzzle".[50]

1.2 Education

Like gender, education is a powerful predictor of the Extreme Right vote in Western Europe. Virtually all national and comparative studies demonstrate that citizens with university education are least likely to vote for the Extreme Right. Conversely, the Extreme Right enjoys above average levels of support in lower educational strata.

This relationship is neither perfect nor necessarily linear. Some parties of the Extreme Right – most notably the Austrian *Freedom Party* – have managed to attract considerable numbers of graduates in some elections. Moreover, there is scattered evidence that the Extreme Right is even more popular amongst those

47 See Heidar/Pedersen, Party Feminism.
48 See Arzheimer, Contextual Factors and the Extreme Right Vote; and Lubbers/Gijsberts/Scheepers, Extreme Right-Wing Voting in Western Europe.
49 See Inglehart/Norris, The Developmental Theory of the Gender Gap.
50 Betz, Radical Right-Wing Populism in Western Europe, p. 146.

with middle levels of educational attainment than in the lowest educational strata, although differences between these two groups are rarely statistically significant. By and large, however, the statistical association between educational attainment and right-wing voting is remarkably strong.

There are basically three types of explanations for this relationship. A first approach claims that citizens with higher levels of educational attainment for various reasons tend to hold more liberal values than others[51] and are therefore less likely to support the authoritarian policies of the Extreme Right.

A second argument holds that supporters of the Extreme Right are primarily motivated by ethnic competition.[52] Since immigration into Western Europe is mostly low-skilled, it poses a threat only to those with low to medium levels of attainment. In fact, low-skilled immigration might be seen as a benefitting graduates, as it might bring down wages in some sectors of the service industry (e. g. childcare or housekeeping), thereby increasing their ability to purchase these services.

Third, graduates might be more susceptible to effects of social desirability, which would lead them to under-report support for the Extreme Right. This attainment-specific bias would result in overestimating the effect of education.

1.3 Class and age

Social class is a notoriously complex concept, but voting studies usually rely on either some variant of the classification developed by Erikson/Goldthorpe/Portocarero[53] or some simple typology that pits the "working class" against one or more other broadly defined occupational groups. Either way, class (in this sense) is closely related to formal education.

As outlined above, many parties initially appealed primarily to the so-called "petty bourgeoisie" of artisans, shopkeepers, farmers and other self-employed citizens. As this group has been subject to a constant and steady numerical decline in all European societies, the Extreme Right has been forced to broaden its social base. Nowadays, non-traditional workers, other members of the lower middle classes and the unemployed form the most important segment of the Extreme Right's electorate. Conversely, managers, professionals, owners of larger businesses and members of the middle and higher ranks of the public service are the groups least likely to vote for the Extreme Right. This chimes with the effect of educational attainment, although both variables are not perfectly correlated and operate independently of each other.

Apart from the effect of class, many studies demonstrate an effect of age, with younger (<30) voters being more likely to vote for the Extreme Right. Presum-

51 See Weakliem, The Effects of Education on Political Opinions.
52 See Bélanger/Pinard, Ethnic Movements and the Competition Model.
53 See Erikson/Goldthorpe/Portocarero, Intergenerational Class Mobility.

ably, this age group is less firmly attached to the established parties, has a more intensive sense of ethnic competition, is subject to lower levels of social control and more prone to experiment with their vote.

1.4 Social ties and other socio-demographic factors

Various studies have looked at the respective effects of other socio-demographic factors, often inspired by a variety of disintegration, reference-group or cleavage theories. For rather obvious reasons, trade union membership is often a strong deterrent to right-wing voting. Slightly less self-explanatory is the negative effect of church attendance, which contradicts earlier American findings. As Arzheimer/Carter demonstrate, this effect is mostly due to pre-existing party loyalties that tie religious voters to Christian/Conservative parties.[54]

Other alleged factors include household size and marital status, which are both interpreted as indicators of social isolation and anomia. The effects of these variables are, however, weak and inconsistent.

2. Attitudes

Especially during their early years, parties of the Extreme Right were often seen as vehicles for "pure", allegedly non-political protest.[55] To be sure, the parties of the Extreme Right have very mixed roots,[56] and attitudes such as distrust in and disaffection with existing parties and Euro-Skepticism have strong effects on the probability of a right-wing vote. Yet, as immigration emerged as their central issue during the 1980s, anti-immigrant sentiment arose as the single most powerful predictor of the right-wing vote.

Anti-immigrant sentiment is a complex attitude, and there is no consensus as to which sub-dimensions it entails and how it should be operationalized. Just as not all parties and politicians of the Extreme Right are extremists, not all immigration skeptics are xenophobes or racists.[57] But what ever their exact nature is, concerns about the presence of non-Western immigrants go a long way towards understanding support for the Extreme Right. While not all citizens who harbor such worries do in fact vote for the Extreme Right (many support parties of the Centre Left or Centre Right), there are next to no right-wing voters

54 See Arzheimer/Carter, Christian Religiosity and Voting.

55 See Van der Brug/Fennema, Protest or Mainstream? for a highly critical assessment of this thesis.

56 Anti-tax movements in the case of the Scandinavian Progress Parties, regionalism for the Leagues in Italy and the "Vlams Blok/Belang" in Flanders, a social movement to improve local infrastructure for the Dutch LPF and Liberalism for the Austrian Freedom Party, to name just a few.

57 See Rydgren, Immigration Sceptics, Xenophobes or Racists?

who have a positive view of immigrants and immigration. Even if the "single-issue thesis"[58] of right-wing support does not paint an accurate picture of these parties and their voters, it is difficult to overstate the importance of immigration for the modern (post-1980) Extreme Right.

Finally, identifications with either a party of the Extreme Right or another party compromise another important class of attitudes that help to understand and predict the Extreme Right vote. As outlined above, party identifications are often ignored in models of right-wing voting, presumably because their likely effects are self-evident. This is, however, a grave mistake, as this omission can seriously bias the estimates for other variables and ignores the fact that many right-wing parties have consolidated their electoral base over the last decades.

3. Contextual factors

Since the mid-1990s, contextual (mostly system level) factors have aroused a great deal of interest as they were increasingly seen as key variables for explaining the huge variation in right-wing support. Some technical issues notwithstanding, the analysis by Jackman/Volpert was groundbreaking in many ways.[59] In an aggregate study that spans 103 elections held in 16 countries between 1970 and 1990, Jackman/Volpert analyze the impact of various economic and institutional variables on the Extreme Right vote. Their main results are that the Extreme Right benefits from high unemployment, PR voting and multi-partyism, whereas high electoral thresholds are detrimental for the Extreme Right.

Later studies have elaborated on these findings by dealing with some of the technical and conceptual problems,[60] using aggregated survey data,[61] and considering a mediating effect of the welfare state.[62] Around the turn of the century, the view that immigration (usually operationalized by the number of refugees or asylum seeker applying or actually taking residence in a country) has a substantial positive effect on right-wing voting was firmly established, whereas the effects of inflation and of (aggregate) unemployment appeared to be much less consistent.

The useful study by Lubbers/Gijsberts/Scheepers represents another important step forward, as these authors were the first to model right-wing voting in a multi-level perspective that combines individual-level and system-level predictors.[63] From a methodological point of view, multi-level modelling is currently the most appropriate approach to the research problem. The study by Lubbers

58 Mudde, The Single-Issue Party Thesis.
59 See Jackman/Volpert, Conditions Favouring Parties.
60 See Golder, Explaining Variation.
61 See Knigge, The Ecological Correlates of Right-Wing Extremism.
62 See Swank/Betz, Globalization, the Welfare State and Right-Wing Populism.
63 See Lubbers/Gijsberts/Scheepers, Extreme Right-Wing Voting.

et al. was also important because they complemented their model with political factors, namely characteristics of the Extreme Right parties.

This approach was taken one step further again by Arzheimer/Carter, who include various measures for the ideological positions of other parties as well as institutional characteristics, unemployment and immigration rates into a comprehensive model of "opportunity structures" for the Extreme Right.[64]

As it turns out, immigration and unemployment work in the expected direction, though their effect is moderated by welfare state interventions that insulate vulnerable social groups from their impact. Moreover, the established parties have a substantial impact on the success of their right-wing competitors: If they publicly address issues such as immigration, the Extreme Right benefits presumably because it gains some legitimacy and relevance in the eyes of the public. If, however, they simply ignore the issues of the Extreme Right, these parties seem to suffer.[65]

The studies discussed in this section provide a detailed and nuanced account of the interplay between social, economic, institutional, political and individual factors required to transform the Extreme Right's electoral potential into actual votes. There is, however, a rather large elephant in the room: the media. If, as Arzheimer argues, party manifestos (that are usually of little relevance for the general public) have a sizeable impact on the right-wing vote, it is reasonable to assume that media effects of agenda setting and priming are even more important. Country-level studies for the Netherlands and for Germany demonstrate that this is indeed the case.[66] There are, however, no comparative studies on media effects (yet) because the necessary data are not available.

IV. Summary and outlook

Conceptual and data problems not withstanding, Political Sociology has come up with a clear image of the "typical" voter of the Extreme Right: male, young(ish), of moderate educational achievement and concerned about immigrants and immigration. While some parties of the Extreme Right have been remarkably successful in making inroads into other strata, this group forms the core of the right-wing electorates in Western Europe, making the Extreme Right a family of non-traditional working class parties.

As the size of this group is largely stable and roughly similar across countries, the interest in contextual factors that may trigger the conversion of potential into manifest support has grown during the last decade. While immigration, unemployment and other economic factors emerge time and again as variables

64 See Arzheimer/Carter, Political Opportunity Structures.

65 See Arzheimer, Contextual Factors and the Extreme Right Vote.

66 See Boomgaarden/Vliegenthart, Explaining the Rise of Anti-Immigrant Parties; How News Content Influences Anti-Immigration Attitudes.

that play a central role, recent studies demonstrate that political factors, which are (up to a degree) subject to political control and manipulation, act as important moderators.

The most glaring omission so far is the lack of comparative studies on the impact that media coverage of immigrants and immigration policies has on the prospects of the Extreme Right. Another area where more research is needed concerns the effects of smaller spatial contexts on the right-wing vote. After all, social, political and economic conditions vary massively at the sub-national, e. g. across provinces, districts, towns and even neighborhoods. It stands to reason that citizens rely on these local conditions, which have a massive impact on their everyday lives, to evaluate politicians, parties and policies at the national level. This approach has been fruitfully employed at the national level.[67] Comparative studies, however, have been hampered by vastly different subnational divisions and a lack of comparable micro- and macro-data. New initiatives for the geo-referencing of survey data and the pan-European harmonization of small-area government data will hopefully help us to overcome that impasse in the future.

67 See Kestilä/Söderlund, Local Determinants of Radical Right-Wing Voting; and Lubbers/Scheepers, French Front National Voting.

Dimensions of Ethnic Prejudice and Extreme Right-Wing Voting

Guillaume Roux

I. Introduction

This chapter deals with contemporary forms of ethnic prejudice in Western Europe and their relation to extreme right-wing or anti-immigration voting. Western European ethnic prejudice has previously been acknowledged a multidimensional phenomenon.[1] Understanding contemporary attitudes designated by such terms as "racism", "prejudice" or "xenophobia" thus implies to find out their different empirical dimensions. This even more since the forms or dimensions of ethnic prejudice are expected to vary throughout time, according to basic changes in salient facts and issues related to ethnicity.

Is racism in its historical, restrictive, biological acceptation - the one of a natural hierarchy among human races - still relevant as far as the contemporary, Western European public is concerned? What about the perception of Islam and Islamic minorities, a controversial, increasingly salient issue in the European context? To answer these questions we start by commenting a number of raw results (pooled samples provide answers to significant items), throwing some light on Western European contemporary opinion towards ethnic minorities and related issues. We then ask ourselves whether these different opinions belong to one single core prejudiced attitude, or break into several dimensions: to which extent does the general public distinguish between different dimensions or issues when it comes to ethnicity, and what do these dimensions consist in (exploratory factor analysis)?

In a third step, throwing light on the contemporary forms of ethnic prejudice may help deepening our understanding of extreme right-wing voting and its causes. Such a vote has been consistently shown to be associated with racist or

1 See Coenders/Scheepers, The Effect of Education on Nationalism; Coenders, Nationalistic Attitudes; Verberk, Attitudes towards Ethnic Minorities. For different perspectives, see also: Coenders/Scheepers/Sniderman/Verberk, Blatant and Subtle Prejudice; Kleinpenning/Hagendoorn, Forms of Racism; Pettigrew/Meertens, Subtle and Blatant Prejudice.

prejudiced attitudes.[2] However, empirical research has been less concerned with the way different forms or dimensions of ethnic prejudice may differently affect extreme right-wing voting. Negative attitudes towards immigration and migrants are a well-known, acknowledged factor of an extremist, exclusionary electoral behaviour. Nevertheless, it remains unclear whether some other dimensions of ethnic prejudice - i. e. public attitudes towards ethnicity issues other than migration and migrants - are susceptible to affect the decision to vote for an extreme right-wing party (multiple regression analysis).

From an empirical point of view, our analyses are based on the unpublished "Group-Focused Enmity" (GFE) European survey which was directed by Wilhelm Heitmeyer, University of Bielefeld, in 2009. This survey - conceived by international specialists of prejudiced attitudes from different disciplines and entirely devoted to the theme of ethnocentrism - includes numerous questions inviting to explore the various dimensions of ethnic prejudice (exploratory factor analysis). It also provides a specific indicator of "exclusionary" voting intentions, allowing to test whether these dimensions do affect the propensity to vote for the extreme right (multiple regression analysis).

II. Western European opinion towards minorities and migrants: Basic statements

The GFE survey includes an exceptional diversity of items related to ethnic prejudice and the perception of ethnic minorities. Before seeing in what way these items correlate and break into different dimensions, a simple look at the raw answers (frequencies) may reveal instructive. Indeed, independent from inter-items correlations, it is not without importance to state whether the majority of the interviewees agree, for example, that "Employers should have the right to hire only [country natives]" and "Some races are more gifted than others", or if these opinions only concern a small minority. In other words, it matters to know whether different prejudiced opinions or ideas are more or less accepted in contemporary Western Europe.

The answers of the general public to different questions about ethnicity often seem contradictory, and they may lead to confusion or indecision when it comes to interpretation. Here, we begin by mobilizing a theoretical frame aimed at understanding some fundamental logics of public opinion as far as ethnicity is concerned.

2 See notably Billiet/Witte, Attitudinal Dispositions; and for European comparisons Lubbers/Scheepers, Euroscepticism and Extreme Voting; Lubbers/Gijsberts/Scheepers, Extreme Right-Wing Voting.

1. When general principals conflict with stereotypes: Myrdal's notion of "dilemma"

Myrdal's seminal historical work "An American Dilemma" (1944) provides some original, fundamental statements about the complex logics of public opinion concerning racial and ethnic matters. Even if they were inspired by a specific historical context (the United States during the first half of the twentieth century), Myrdal's ideas apply to other historical geographical contexts.[3]

According to Myrdal, as far as racial attitudes are concerned, the big historical movement in the US - and, we would add, Western democracies in general - is the one towards racial equality. He argued that the principles of individual equality - including racial or ethnic equality - were accepted and even sustained by the largest part of the general public at the time of his writing. On the other hand, however, negative stereotypes about racial and ethnic minorities were still vivid, and so were a number of fears or "perceived threats" associated with these minorities. As a consequence, the general public often faces a "dilemma" when it comes to specific opinions, in particular when it has to decide whether it supports or opposes a given policy aimed at implementing racial equality. On the one hand, the principles of racial equality command to support such a policy. But on the other hand, a number of stereotypes and perceived threats lead to fear its consequences, commanding to oppose it.

When it comes to the context of contemporary Western European societies, what Myrdal tells us is that public opinion cannot be expected to always be "coherent", but shall always reflect a number of conflicts or contradictions. In particular, the level of general values or principles has to be distinguished from the one of stereotypes, and more specific opinions that often express the feeling of a threat.

2. Western European opinion and ethnicity: General principles and values

The following analyses and results concern all Western European countries included in the GFE survey, i. e. six countries: France, Germany, Great Britain, Italy, Portugal, and the Netherlands *(N = 6,026)*.[4] In this section, we deal with global means applying to the whole sample (pooled dataset, all six countries together). These six countries are diverse in terms of geographical position

3 For a major recent work applying the ideas of Gunnar Myrdal, see Schuman/Steeh/Bobo/Krysan, Racial Attitudes in America.

4 The survey was conducted in October-November 2008. It was developed by an interdisciplinary research team of psychologists, sociologists, educational and politcal scientists: Nona Mayer & Guillaume Roux (France), Andreas Zick, Beate Küpper, Hinna Wolf, Wilhelm Heitmeyer, Ulrich Wagner (Germany), Antal Orkeny (Hungary), Jorge Vala, Cicero Preira & Alice Ramos (Portugal), Pawel Boski (Poland), Bo Ekkehammer (Sweden), and Miles Hewstone & Katharina Schmidt (UK). As far as means for the pooled sample (Western Europe) are concerned, results are based on weighted data to take into account the relative size of the population in each country.

(South and more Northern Europe) or historical tradition (massive immigration old or recent; Republican or multicultural tradition; historical *jus soli* or *jus sanguinis* conception of citizenship). Nevertheless, global means applying to these six countries cannot be considered representative of Western European opinion in general and, even less, the European Union. To that extent, the means and results which we present are only indicative, what does not mean that they are not instructive and, sometimes, striking. International comparison, or juxtaposition of the means of the different countries, remains beyond the scope of this paper. Nevertheless, when the variance of mean differences between the different countries is very high, this shall be mentioned in a note.

Let us now look at general principles related to ethnicity matters. Does the general public support – at the level of global principles and values – fundamental political options such as ethnic equality, ethnic diversity and anti-racism? Racism in its most restrictive, historical meaning, i. e. "biological racism", clearly contradicts the principle of racial or ethnic equality. As can be seen in table 1, the GFE survey includes two questions about the idea of a natural hierarchy between different human races, namely "biological racism": "Some races are more gifted than others", and "There exists a natural hierarchy between blacks and whites".

Previous opinion pools and longitudinal data for contemporary democracies – for both the United States and Western European countries – tended to show that "biological racism" was increasingly and massively rejected.[5] Here, the two

Table 1: Public reaction to racist opinions (biological racism) (%)

	"Some races are more gifted than others"[6]	"Natural hierarchy between blacks and whites"[7]
Strongly agree	10	6
Somewhat agree	28	26
Somewhat disagree	25	28
Strongly disagree	36	40
Total	100	100
N	*2,870*	*4,873*

5 For the US, see Schuman/Steeh/Bobo/Krysan, Racial Attitudes in America. In Europe, it is currently admitted that more radical, blatant opinions towards ethnic minorities have been largely rejected in recent decades. See notably Pettigrew/Meertens, Subtle and Blatant Prejudice.

6 DK ("Don't know" answers) = 4 %. Max. (Maximal national mean) (Agreement) = 57 % in Portugal (thus strongly deviating from the mean), Min. (Minimal national mean) = 25 % in France. Note that the question was part of a split procedure (asked to a half sample).

7 DK = 2 %. Max. (Agreement) = 46 % in Portugal, Min. = 19 % in Italy. The results do not include France, for which the question was asked the reversed way: "There is no natural hierarchy between blacks and whites" (N = 987, DK = 2 %): Strongly disagree (19 %), Somewhat disagree (20 %), Somewhat agree (22 %), Strongly agree (40 %).

opinions reflecting biological racism are indeed rejected by the majority of the population (61 % disagree that "some races are more gifted", and 68 % disagree with the idea of a black-white hierarchy). Nevertheless, it is surprising and maybe even striking that such a large minority agrees with these two racist, "old-fashioned" opinions (38 and 31 %, respectively). How can we interpret these results?

In the traditional view of biological racism, the idea of a racial hierarchy implied the refusal, and even the dread of racial mixing (i. e. the possibility that people from different races could engage into intimate relationships and have children together). This proscription has even been considered one of the core or fundamental motives behind biological racism.[8] A question from the GFE survey asks whether interviewees would agree that their child "marry an immigrant", and most of all, whether they agree that "Blacks and whites should not get married". The answers to these questions help interpreting the previous results (Tables 2 and 3).

Table 2: "Accept that child marry an immigrant"[9] (%)

Yes	87
No	13
Total	100
N	*5,639*

Table 3: "Blacks and whites should not get married"[10] (%)

Strongly agree	3
Somewhat agree	7
Somewhat disagree	28
Strongly disagree	61
Total	100
N	*4,918*

Even if a substantial minority (about one third of the interviewees) accepts the idea of a racial hierarchy, the opposition to one's child marrying an immigrant and, most of all, the opinion that blacks and whites should not marry obtains much less support (13 and 10 %, respectively). Thus, even if the idea of

8 See Schuman/Steeh/Bobo/Krysan, Racial Attitudes in America; Apostle/Glock/Piazza/Suelzle, The Anatomy of Racial Attitudes.

9 DK = 1 %. Max. (Agreement) = 17 % in Great Britain, Min. = 5 % in Portugal.

10 DK = 2 %. Max. = 18 % in Portugal, Min. = 5 % in the Netherlands. The results do not include France, where the question was asked the reversed way: "It's not a problem if blacks and whites get married" (N = 1,000, DK = 1 %): Strongly disagree (6 %), Somewhat disagree (8 %), Somewhat agree (18 %), Strongly agree (68 %).

Table 4: "An employer should have the right to employ only native [country] people"[11] (%)

Strongly agree	6
Somewhat agree	10
Somewhat disagree	38
Strongly disagree	46
Total	100
N	*5,961*

racial inequality is far from having disappeared, it now appears relatively disconnected to its historical consequence or fundamental motive, the refusal and even the dread of ethnic marriage and mixing. This leads to a contrasted conclusion about the current state of biological racism. It reveals unexpectedly high, a rather striking and maybe worrying result. On the other hand, it seems that the very belief in a racial hierarchy does not have the same meaning or consequences that it historically had, and thus cannot be totally confounded with previous, historical racism.

Beside the belief in a racial hierarchy, one of the more important political matters – as far as general values are concerned – is the question whether the principle of equal rights and equal treatment is now accepted. From this point of view, interviewees were asked if "An employer should have the right to employ only native [country] people". This clearly breaks the principle of equal treatment in the field of employment.

As Table 4 shows, only a small minority of the interviewees (16 %) support the opinion favourable to national preference in the field of employment. Nevertheless, when the question is asked a bit differently, public support for national preference is more widely supported: 43 % of the interviewees agree that "When unemployment is high, there should be more rights to a job for *[country natives]*" (results not presented[12]). This may be imputed to the fact that the question evokes the threatening situation of "high unemployment", and refers to a preferential treatment ("more rights") rather than a strict exclusion ("employ only natives"). It may also be outlined that the criterion for unequal treatment here is nationality – a legal criterion – rather than race or ethnicity. In any case, the fact that a big minority (43 %) agrees with an opinion that opposes the principles of equal treatment in modern democracies remains noticeable.

The minority sustaining different versions of ethnic and racial equality and discriminations thus appear, in several cases, strikingly substantial. This means

11 DK = 1 %. Max. (Agreement) = 22 % in Great Britain, Min. = 10 % in France.
12 N = 5,885. DK = 2 %. Max. (Agreement) = 58 % in Portugal, Min. = 25 % in the Netherlands.

Table 5: Public opinion towards religious and cultural diversity in [country] (%)

	"Many religions better"[13]	"Same customs better"[14]
Strongly agree	16	12
Somewhat agree	42	32
Somewhat disagree	30	40
Strongly disagree	12	15
Total	100	100
N	*5,810*	*5,929*

that the more old-fashioned, traditional forms of ethnic prejudice still have some supporters in Western European democracies. But on the whole, coherent with previous research on that theme, a majority - more or less huge according to the issue at stake - appears to sustain the general principles of ethnic and racial equality and equal treatment.

Let us now look at a different topic, the extent to which ethnic, religious, and cultural diversity is considered a good thing for a given country, or tolerance and support for cultural diversity. Interviewees were asked whether "Many different religions is better for a country", and whether "same customs and traditions is better for a country".

The majority of the interviewees' support the general principle of cultural and religious difference within the nation-state: 58 % agree that many different religions is better for a country, and 55 % disagree that having the same customs and traditions is better.

Now are these different values and principles reflected in more specific, concrete opinions? What about negative attitudes and stereotypes for different ethnic groups, and the perception of a threat related to ethnic issues? In the next section, we shall pay much attention to public opinion towards Islam and Islamic minorities, as the GFE survey includes many questions related to this contemporary, controversial, crucial topic as far as ethnicity is at stake in Western European societies.

13 DK = 4 %. Max. (Agreement) = 66 % in France and Germany, Min. = 43 % in Portugal (all other national means > 50 %).

14 DK = 2 %. Max. (Agreement) = 63 % in France and Germany, Min. = 38 % in Portugal (all other national means > 50 %).

3. Attitudes towards groups, perceived threat, and stereotypes

3.1 Negative attitudes towards immigrants and perceived threat

According to Myrdal, the fact that the general public tends to supports basic principles of ethnic equality does not necessarily imply that negative attitudes and stereotypes associated with ethnic minorities, as well as a number of "perceived ethnic threat", have disappeared or are not even widespread.

Overall, the majority of the interviewees (53 %) agree that there are "Too many immigrants in [country]" (Table 6). This can be related to a number of stereotypes about immigrants and ethnic minorities that were not directly measured in the GFE survey but have been well shown in previous research.[15]

Table 6: "Too many immigrants in [country]"[16] (%)

Strongly agree	19
Somewhat agree	35
Somewhat disagree	31
Strongly disagree	16
Total	100
N	*5,856*

When it comes to explaining such negative attitudes, a growing academic literature focus on "Perceived ethnic threat" and the way it favours ethnic prejudice and the exclusion of migrants.[17] In this literature, an important issue is whether prejudice stems from perceived threat in the field of economy – i.e. a threat concerning the material standards of living – or in the field of culture, traditions and values, i.e. perceived threat about the norms sustaining national cohesion.[18]

Several questions of the GFE surveys allow comparing the two sources of perceived ethnic threat – namely economic and cultural threat. Questions concerning a given source of threat were asked two times: the first version referred to a threat on the country or the whole society, whereas the second referred to a threat on the interviewee himself or his personal interests. The aim of this partition was to find out whether the interviewees' first concern was for their own living standards or the situation of the country itself.

15 See notably Coenders, Nationalistic Attitudes; European Monitoring Center on Racism and Xenophobia, Attitudes towards Minority Groups.
16 DK = 3 %. Max. (Agreement) 60 to 62 % in Portugal (60 %), Italy (60 %) and Great Britain (62 %), Min. = 40 % in France (all other national means < 50 %).
17 See Quillian, Prejudice as a Response to Perceived Group Threat; Scheepers/Gijsberts/Coenders, Ethnic Exclusionism; Sniderman/Hagendoorn/Prior, Predisposing Factors and Situational Triggers; Wagner/Christ/Pettigrew/Stellmacher/Wolf, Prejudice and Minority Proportion.
18 Sniderman/Hagendoorn/Prior, Predisposing Factors and Situational Triggers.

Table 7: Perceived ethnic threat: economic and cultural, country and personal level (%)

	Economic threat		Cultural threat	
	Country	Personal	Country	Personal
	"Immigrants threaten economy in [country]"[19]	"Personal financial situation"[20]	"Way of life and values"[21]	"Personal way of life and values"[22]
Strongly agree	7	4	10	4
Somewhat agree	20	10	23	11
Somewhat disagree	44	40	40	40
Strongly disagree	29	46	28	45
Total	100	100	100	100
N	*5,871*	*5,963*	*5,916*	*5,963*

For each question, only a minority declares to perceive a threat. But overall, 44 % of the interviewees perceive at least one source of threat. Furthermore, the general perception of an ethnic threat does not limit itself to the precise sources of threat reflected by these four questions. For example, some interviewees may not feel that immigrants threaten the economy, but may perceive some forms of ethnic threat (related, for example, to insecurity, not measured in the survey). This would be coherent with the fact that a majority agrees, there are "Too many immigrants in [country]". Also note that only 31 % of the interviewees declare that "the relationship between immigrants and non-immigrants" might improve in the future, while 35 % declare that they might "stay about the same", and 34 % - quite a substantial majority - that they might "get worse" (results not presented). Answer to our four questions may thus not lead to underestimate the perception of an ethnic threat - whatever its source - in Western European societies.

We also see that in both the economic and cultural domain, the perception of a threat is always greater when it refers to the whole country, rather than the interviewees' specific situation. This confirms the results of former studies on that issue. Most of all, the more important source of perceived threat reveals to be cultural rather than economic: one third of the interviewees (33 %) agree that immigrants are threatening the way of life and values in their country (versus 27 % when it comes to economic threat in the country). National cultural change

19 DK = 3 %. Max. (Agreement) = 42 % in Great Britain, Min. = 18 % in the Netherlands.
20 DK = 1 %. Max. (Agreement) = 23 % in Great Britain, Min. = 8 % in the Netherlands.
21 DK = 2 %. Max. (Agreement) = 41 % in Great Britain, Min. = 26 % in Portugal.
22 DK = 1 %. Max. (Agreement) = 19 % in Great Britain, Min. = 10 % in Germany.

thus appears to be the biggest concern related to immigration, coherent with the findings of Sniderman et al. for the Netherlands.[23]

In Western European societies, cultural issues related to immigration are most of all issues about migrants of Islamic tradition, and the so-called "integration" of Islam in modern democracies. The former results thus invite to focus on public attitudes towards Islamic minorities, and issues related to the place of Islam in Western societies.

3.2 The perception of Islam and Muslims

Interviewees were asked whether they think that there are "Too many Muslims in [country]":

Table 8: "Too many Muslims in [country]"[24] (%)

Strongly agree	16
Somewhat agree	25
Somewhat disagree	41
Strongly disagree	17
Total	100
N	*5,215*

A substantial minority (41 %) agrees that there are "Too many Muslims" in their country. This is less than the number of people declaring that there are "Too many immigrants" (53 %). On the other hand, while the "Too many immigrants" opinion may refer to a variety of groups and motives, the "Too many Muslims" one explicitly focuses on religion, as Muslims are nothing but a religious group. It is thus, in a way, a harsher statement, one that designates a religious affiliation as problematic in a given country.

A potential source of Islamophobia identified in the academic literature is the fear of Islamic terrorism, notably after the attack of September 11. Two questions were aimed at measuring this fear: "I am scared of a possible Islamic terrorist attack in [country]", and "I am scared of becoming the victim of terrorists" (Table 9).

According to Table 9, 34 % of the interviewees are scared of personally being victims of terrorism, and half of them (50 %) declare to fear a possible Islamic terrorist attack in their country. The fear of Islamic terrorism thus appears to have great salience in European societies and may explain negative attitudes towards Muslim minorities. Nevertheless, this does not mean that the European

23 Sniderman/Hagendoorn/Prior, Predisposing Factors and Situational Triggers.
24 DK = 12 %. Max. (Agreement) = 50 % in Italy, Min. = 28 % in Portugal.

Table 9: Perceived threat related to Islamic terrorism (%)

	"Scared of Islamic terrorism in [country]"[25]	"Scared of being a victim of Islamic terrorism"[26]
Strongly agree	19	13
Somewhat agree	31	21
Somewhat disagree	31	37
Strongly disagree	19	29
Total	100	100
N	*5,841*	*5,847*

public does confound Islamic terrorists with Muslims minorities at large, nor think that Muslims in general do support Islamic terrorisms. Indeed, only 31 % of the interviewees agree that "Muslims perceive terrorists as heroes" and 21 % that "The majority of Muslims find terrorism justifiable" (the question has been asked differently in France: 23 % disagree that "the majority of Muslims find terrorism *not* justifiable").

The main other explanatory factor for these attitudes is the perception of Islamic religion itself, and negative stereotypes associated to the so-called "Islamic culture". The GFE survey asked whether "Islam is a religion of intoler-

Table 10: Opinion towards Islam and the "Muslim culture" (%)

	"Islam is a religion of intolerance"[27]	"Muslim culture fits well into [country]"[28]	"Muslims' attitudes towards women contradict our values"[29]
Strongly agree	18	5	37
Somewhat agree	36	31	41
Somewhat disagree	33	45	16
Strongly disagree	13	18	6
Total	100	100	100
N	*4,393*	*5,517*	*5,615*

25 DK = 2 %. Max. (Agreement) = 61 % in Portugal, Min. = 38 % in the Netherlands.
26 DK = 2 %. Max. = 59 % in Portugal, Min. = 17 % in the Netherlands (all other national means < 50 %).
27 DK = 10 %. Max. (Agreement) = 63 % in Portugal, Min. = 46 % in the Netherlands. The results do not include France, for which the question was asked the reversed way: "Islam is a religion of tolerance" (N = 901, DK = 6 %): Strongly disagree (21 %), Somewhat disagree (31 %), Somewhat agree (32 %), Strongly agree (16 %).
28 DK = 7 %. Max. (Disagreement) = 50 % in France and Portugal, Min. = 16 % in Germany.
29 DK = 5 %. Max. (Agreement) = 82 % in Great Britain and Italy, Min. = 76 % in Germany.

ance", "Muslim culture fits well into [country]", and "Muslim attitudes towards women contradict our values".

As Table 10 shows, the majority of the interviewees share negative views of Islam and the "Muslim culture": 54 % of the interviewees agree that "Islam is a religion of intolerance", 63 % disagree that "Muslim culture fits well into [country]", and 78 % declare, "Muslims' attitudes towards women contradict our values". Complementary analyses (not presented) show that the opinion according to which there are "Too many Muslims in [country]" is strongly related to these negative attitudes towards Islam and the Islamic culture.[30]

In other words, negative attitudes towards Muslim minorities - a central, contemporary aspect of ethnic prejudice - are strongly related to widely shared majority negative opinions about Islam and the "Islamic culture". This statement highlights the cultural component of ethnic prejudice, as well as the role of the Islamic issue and its supposed "incompatibility" with the norms and values of Western democracies.

Let us now see whether the different opinions towards ethnicity are the simple expression of one core single prejudiced attitude or racism, or if contemporary prejudice reveals more complex and break up into several, distinguished dimensions.

III. The dimensions of ethnic prejudice in Western Europe

Do the different opinions towards ethnic minorities and related issues belong to one single core prejudiced attitude? Or do they break into several dimensions showing that the European public distinguishes between different issues as far as ethnicity is concerned? Previous research has illustrated the multidimensional feature of European attitudes towards ethnicity.[31] The diversity of issues covered by the GFE survey allows paying attention to potentially emerging crucial dimensions in the context of contemporary Europe. We thus take into account, in particular, attitudes towards Islam and Islamic minorities.

From a methodological point of view, we start by identifying several groups of indicators, conceptually related and theoretically expected to belong to the same dimension. Here again, we do not aim at comparing different countries, but rather at identifying the dimensions emerging at a broad, aggregated Western European level. Whether each specific country shows specific features or departs from the general model remains beyond the scope of this research.

30 It (negatively) correlates at .40 with the opinion that "Muslim culture does not fit into the Western world", and .44 with the opinion that "Islam is a religion of intolerance" (the correlation with the idea that "Muslim attitudes towards women contradict our values" being very modest, i. e. 0.20).

31 See Coenders/Scheepers, The Effect of Education on Nationalism; Coenders, Nationalistic Attitudes; Verberk, Attitudes towards Ethnic Minorities.

Therefore, to start, we distinguish between four potential dimensions of ethnic prejudice or European attitude towards ethnic otherness:

1. Biological and blatant, "old-fashioned" racism

We first consider the historical form of ethnic prejudice, i. e. racism in the meaning of a fundamental, rigid hierarchy between different ethnic groups, whether it is based on biological beliefs or other considerations. As seen previously, this "old-fashioned" type of racism or ethnic prejudice still has some relevance in the European public. We take into account the following indicators:

- *Agree that one's child marry an immigrant*
- *Some races are more gifted than others*
- *Natural hierarchy between blacks and whites*
- *Blacks and whites should not get married*
- *Some cultures are superior to others*

2. Attitudes towards immigration and migrants

In the European context, immigration is a crucial issue when it comes to ethnicity matters. Immigration and migrants belong to the main targets of racist discourses and may constitute a specific dimension of contemporary prejudice. The following indicators aim at measuring related attitudes:

- *How many immigrants* [country] *should allow to come here?*
- *We need immigrants to keep the economy going*
- *Immigrants are a strain on the welfare system*
- *Immigrants enrich culture*
- *Feeling like a stranger because of immigrants*
- *Too many immigrants in* [country]

3. Attitudes towards cultural diversity

Our first results outlined the salience of cultural considerations as regard to contemporary prejudice in Western Europe. The following items aim at measuring the rejection of cultural as well as religious diversity, as a potential dimension of contemporary prejudice. Note that these indicators refer to cultural diversity at the level of values or general principles, without targeting any specific group, culture, custom, religion or issue.

- *Immigrants should adopt the* [country's] *culture*
- *Immigrants should maintain their culture*

- *Immigrants should maintain their culture and adopt the* [country's] *culture*
- *Many different religions better for a country*
- *Same customs and traditions better for a country*

4. Attitudes related to Islam and Islamic minorities

As our previous results have shown, the perception of Islam, Islamic minorities and the so-called "Islamic culture" appear as crucial, salient issues as far as cultural diversity in Western societies is concerned. The following indicators aim at measuring attitudes towards Muslim minorities and Islam:

- *Muslim perceive terrorists as heroes*
- *The majority of Muslims find terrorism justifiable*
- *Muslim culture fits well into* [country]
- *Muslim attitudes towards women contradict our values*
- *Islam is a religion of intolerance*
- *Muslims are too demanding*
- *There are too many Muslims in* [country]

To find out the different dimensions of ethnic prejudice, we adopted the following strategy: First, we performed separated analyses of each set of indicators. Principal factor analysis with Varimax rotation was retained as the suitable technique allowing some clear, distinguished dimensions to emerge. Applied to each group of indicators above, it led to eliminate a number of questions: when an item's commonality was below 0.7 or when – in the case of several factors – an item had substantial loadings on several dimensions.

In a second step, all remaining indicators were included in one single factor analysis. Here again, items with low Commonality, weak loadings (below 0.6), or substantial loadings on more than one dimensions were cancelled. As for the number of factors, we adopted the "elbow criteria" (scree plot test): four factors emerged with substantial eigenvalues, with a clear drop from the fifth factor (whose eigenvalue was below 0.65).[32] We thus retained the following factorial solution:

As a criterion aimed at avoiding "double loadings" (i. e. substantial loading of an indicator on more than one factor), we checked that the loading of an item on the factor in which it participates was more than 0.35 points higher than its loading on any other factor. Furthermore, we made sure that the loading of any item making up a factor was at least 0.35 higher than the loading, on this same factor, than items making up another factor.

We nevertheless tolerated slight exceptions to this rule. Indeed, the loading of the item "Too many immigrants" is 0.46 on the factor *Perception of Islam* (F1

32 Eigenvalues are respectively 3.2 (F1), 1.2 (F2), .93 (F3) and 0.85 (F4). Inter-factors correlations remain moderate (i. e. range from – 0.2 between F1 and F2, to 0.34 between F1 and F4).

Table 11: Empirical dimensions of ethnic prejudice (factor analysis)

	Factor 1	Factor 2	Factor 3	Factor 4
	Perception of Islam and Muslims	Old-fashioned racism	Attitudes twds cultural diversity	Attitudes twds immigrants
Islam is a religion of intolerance	0.92	-0.24	-0.29	0.27
Muslims are too demanding	0.79	-0.28	-0.31	0.58
Some races are more gifted than others	-0.23	0.86	0.25	-0.33
Some cultures are clearly superior to others	-0.22	0.88	0.25	-0.25
Many different religions better for a country	-0.31	0.20	0.83	-0.29
Same customs and traditions better for a country	0.20	-0.28	-0.80	0.34
Feeling like a stranger because of immigrants	0.31	-0.31	-0.32	0.92
Too many immigrants in [country]	0.46	-0.36	-0.47	0.85

column), a difference of only 0.33 points with the item "Muslims are too demanding" which makes up the factor (whose loading is 0.79). The same problem appears with this same item ("Too many immigrants") on the factor *Attitudes towards cultural diversity* (F3 factor; difference with the item "Same customs and traditions better" is only .33). Furthermore, the loading of the item "Muslims are too demanding" is 0.58 on the *Attitudes towards immigrants* factor (F4 column), a difference of only 0.30 point with the item "Too many immigrants".

The fact that and item from the *Perception of Islam* dimension tends to have a substantial loading on the *Attitudes towards immigrants* dimension, and vice-versa, is in itself instructive. It is important to note that concerning the perception of Islam dimension, only the "Muslims are too demanding" item is concerned. The other item making up the dimension, "Islam is a religion of intolerance", does not have a substantial or close to substantial loading on the *Attitudes towards immigrants* dimension. Thus when the perception of Islam itself – the Islamic religion – is concerned, there is no confusion with the attitudes towards immigrants. This means that future research should make up more items about the Islamic religion itself, allowing a better and more distinct measurement of the *Perception of Islam* dimension.

Second, the fact that the item "Muslims are too demanding" tends to load on the *Attitudes towards immigrants* dimension shows that the perception of Muslim and related issues, and the perception of Immigrants in general are not isolated from each other. On the other hand, they remain isolated enough to make up two distinct separate dimensions.

Let us now comment on the different dimensions we found and their implications for the sociological understanding of contemporary racism in Western Europe. First, we should not over-interpret the order of dimensions, especially the fact that *Perception of Islam* is the first dimension (*i. e.* the one accounting for the greater part of the data variance). Indeed, the order may vary with the adding / subtracting of a few items. On the other hand, the fact that *Perception of Islam* makes up the first dimension can be seen as a confirmation of its importance in contemporary attitudes towards ethnicity or racism. Even if an increasing number of academic studies deal with the perception of Islam or "Islamophobia", it has seldom been shown to constitute a distinct - whereas central - dimension of ethnic prejudice in Western societies.

We must insist on the fact that the dimensions do deal with perceptions of Islam - namely a religion - rather than the perceptions of Muslims themselves - namely a group or ethnic minority in Western societies. From this point of view, it must be noted that the item "Too many Muslims", if added to factor analysis, would have resulted in confusion between the *Perception of Islam* and *Attitudes towards immigrants* dimensions.

The next dimension, *Old-fashioned racism*, does not strictly refer to racism in its biological meaning of a natural hierarchy between pre-supposed "human races". This is only the case for one of the items making up the dimension "Some races are more gifted than others". The other indicator, "Some cultures are clearly superior to others", does not refer to a biological distinction any more, but a cultural one. This means that from the point of view of the European public, what makes much sense is not the classical biological/cultural distinction (or more precisely: prejudice sustained by biological/cultural justifications and beliefs), but rather the very existence of a hierarchy (at all) between different groups,[33] no matter whether it is based on natural or cultural distinctions.

Thus, this dimension expresses the very belief that a hierarchy can be installed among human groups and - as a consequence - individuals belonging to these groups. Consequently, this belief blatantly contradicts the modern value of individualism, which implies that each individual has unique specificities that do not reduce them to their belonging to a given group, and a unique value that cannot be reduced to a unique criterion or yardstick. This by contrast to the past: the past of slavery and official state racism sustained by the belief in biological inequalities; and the past of colonialism and the belief in the cultural infe-

33 It seems reasonable to consider that "culture", in the second item ("some cultures are clearly superior"), can be heard as "cultural groups" (or even more safely: implying that some cultural groups are strictly superior to others).

riority of certain nations or countries. Our results, in line with former studies, showed that these beliefs - which are also some forms of ethnic prejudice - tended to be widely rejected or at least, only endorsed by a minority of the European public (though wider, according to our first results, than we would have expected). In other words, they are blatant and most of all old, "old-fashioned" forms of racism.

Far from having disappeared, this old-fashioned racism remains a dimension of contemporary prejudice. On the other hand, as previously shown, the belief in a racial hierarchy does no more imply a fear or refusal of interracial marriage, a fundamental distinction with the historical expression and belief system of biological racism.

The next dimension, *Cultural diversity*, has to do with the fact of religious and cultural plurality within the nation-state, at the very level of general principles. This means that the indicators making up this dimension do not deal with any specific issue - such as Islam and related debates - but rather the acceptance of cultural diversity as a general value. In line with the work of Myrdal, the distinction between the endorsement of general principles and the endorsement of opinions or specific positions on concrete issues following from these principles is something we consider of fundamental relevance. Indeed, both do not necessarily coincide. This means that the general principles which the individuals claim to endorse are not *systematically* applied when it comes to opinions about specific issues. One possible interpretation of this gap is that the general principles are only falsely or hypocritically endorsed. But this was not the interpretation of Myrdal: his contribution was rather to consider why - in the case of ethnic or racial issues - the individuals had some motivations not to apply, in a number of cases, the principles they hold (in a number of cases, the principles are actually applied). This is the case when in some situations, the application of the principles is perceived as a threat on the individuals or the society's interests, this being related to a number of negative stereotypes about ethnic minorities.

This is partly illustrated by the fact that we find two distinct dimensions, *Perception of Islam* on the one hand and *Cultural diversity* on the other. Whereas the majority of the European public supports the general principle of cultural diversity, most interviewees hold negative perceptions of Islam and consider that "Muslims are too demanding" (first part of the paper).

The last dimension, *Attitudes towards immigrants*, is a classical one, expressing the fact that immigration and migrants are central topics and concerns when it comes to ethnicity matters in the European context. Here, the focus is on the acceptable amount or proportion of immigrants that a society can accept.

IV. Dimensions of ethnic prejudice and extreme right-wing voting

Now that we have identified different distinguished dimensions of contemporary racism in Western European societies, we can consider whether public attitudes related to each dimension do affect the electoral decision to vote for the extreme right. Previous research has identified ethnocentrism, xenophobic and racist attitudes as crucial factors when it comes to extreme right-wing voting.[34] Expectedly, the more citizens hold anti-immigrant and immigration attitudes, the higher their propensity to vote for extreme right-wing parties - whose opposition to immigration generally is one of their political program's key if not its main issue.[35] However, much less, attention has been paid to other contemporary forms of ethnic prejudice, and the way attitudes related to various dimensions may differently affect the propensity to vote for the extreme right.

The GFE survey does not include any question about past voting or voting in the last election, allowing measuring actual effective voting for an extreme right-wing party. To approximate interviewees' propensity to vote for such a political party, we consider the following statement: *"I would only vote for parties which want to reduce the influx of immigrants".*[36]

As a proxy for the propensity to vote for the extreme right, the focus of this question ("parties that want to reduce the influx of immigrants") suffers from being too large and too narrow at the same time. Indeed, an interviewee can plan to vote for the extreme right for a reason other than "reduce the influx of immigrants". Reversely, an interviewee can plan to vote for a party that will "reduce the influx of immigrants", but does not belong to the extreme right (a moderate right-wing party holding a restrictive position towards immigration).

On the other hand, the indicator has several advantages. First, the propensity to vote for a party that will "reduce the influx of immigrants" is certainly very close to the one to vote for the extreme right. In addition, it can plausibly be argued that many interviewees identify such a party with an extreme right-wing party. This being said, the question has the advantage of not mentioning the extreme right, thus being less exposed to "politically correct" answers (interviewees feeling close to an extreme right-wing party, but not daring to admit this socially undesirable position). As a result, the proportion of interviewees agreeing that they would only vote for a party which will "reduce the influx of immigrants" is rather substantial (32 %), a highly desirable situation as far as statistical analysis is concerned (also note that no answers are not higher that 5 %).

34 See notably Billiet/Witte, Attitudinal Dispositions; and for European comparisons: Lubbers/Scheepers, Euroscepticism and Extreme Voting; Lubbers/Gijsberts/Scheepers, Extreme Right-Wing Voting.

35 Mudde, Populist Radical Right Parties in Europe.

36 "Strongly agree" (12 %), "Somewhat agree" (20 %), "Somewhat disagree" (37 %), "Strongly disagree" (31 %). DK = 5 %. Max. (agreement) is 53 % in Great Britain (all other national means below 40 %), Min. 17 % in Portugal.

So as to evaluate the relation of ethnic prejudice's dimensions to extreme right-wing voting, we thus include the aforementioned indicator as the dependent variable in a multiple regression statistical model. More precisely, we adopt a two-step strategy. First, we run a model with voting as the dependent variable, and the different dimensions of ethnic prejudice (i. e. public attitudes on these different dimensions) as the independent variables. This model is aimed at finding out whether these dimensions affect the propensity to vote for the extreme right, and whether the effect of each dimension is a proper one (i. e. not simply reflecting the effect of another dimension; in other terms, the effect of each dimension is the effect controlled for the one of the other dimensions in the model).

In a second step, we consider the previous model with supplementary independent or control variables. Indeed, it can be suspected that the effect of a given dimension of ethnic prejudice simply reflects the effect of another known key variable of extreme right-wing voting. More precisely, we control the effects of the first model for the main previously identified variables as far as extreme right-wing voting is concerned, namely authoritarianism, political attitudes (left-right identification), and education level.[37] Only if the (hypothetical) effect of a particular dimension of ethnic prejudice resists control for these variables, we can consider having found out new variables of extreme right-wing voting, or at least provided a deeper understanding of the way ethnic prejudice – in its different components or dimensions – does affect the propensity to vote for the extreme right.

Table 11 shows results of the first model, with extreme right-wing voting as the dependent variables, and the four dimensions of ethnic prejudice as independent variables.[38] The method used is multiple linear regression (testing for multinomial regression revealed that linear regression was adapted to the data structure).

As shown in Table 11, three out of four dimensions of ethnic prejudice have a significant, proper effect (i. e. an effect that holds even controlled for the other dimensions in the model) on extreme right or anti-immigration voting. The only dimension which shows no significant effect is *Old-fashioned racism*, which seems to confirm its "old-fashioned" feature, to the extent that it does not impact one of the most salient contemporary political phenomena related to ethnic prejudice, namely extreme right-wing voting.

As for the other dimensions of ethnic prejudice, *Attitudes towards immigrants* is the one that shows the stronger effect on our dependent variable (comparing the standardized beta coefficients, third row of the table). That attitudes towards

37 Billiet/Witte, Attitudinal Dispositions; and for European comparisons: Lubbers/Scheepers, Euroscepticism and Extreme Voting; Lubbers/Gijsberts/Scheepers, Extreme Right-Wing Voting.

38 Interviewees' scores on the two questions making up each dimension have been summed up in an additive scale. Pearson's R correlations between these two questions were .50 (F1), .53 (F2), .33 (F3) and .61 (F4).

Table 12: Effect of ethnic prejudice's dimensions on extreme right-wing voting (multiple regression analysis)

	B	Beta (standardized)	Sig.
Intercept	.53		.00
Perception of Islam and Muslims	.07***	.10	.00
Old-fashioned racism	-.01	-.02	.24
Attitudes twds cultural diversity	.09***	.13	.00
Attitudes twds immigrants	.30***	.53	.00
Adjusted R^2		*.45*	

***p < .01, ** p < .05, * p < .1 (two-tailed)

immigrants do strongly affect extreme right-wing voting was a rather expected result, even more that we use, as our dependent variable, a question explicitly mentioning the goal of "reducing the influx of migrants". This result is coherent with previous literature on that theme. It can be reminded that extreme right-wing parties have been analyzed as single-issue parties – i. e. parties promoting one single issue, namely the reduction – if not suppression – of immigration. Even if this point of view has been discussed,[39] the fact remains that immigration is generally one of the main – if not the main – issue promoted by parties at the far right of the political spectrum.

A less expected, more original result is the fact that two other dimensions of ethnic prejudice significantly affect extreme right-wing voting. The striking fact here is that they do so even controlled for *Attitudes towards immigrants* (i. e. with the latest in the same model as an independent variable). In other words, it is not because they are related to *Attitudes towards immigrants* that *Perception of Islam and Muslims*, and *Attitudes towards cultural diversity* do affect extreme right-wing voting (this at the highest level of significance, i. e. below .000).[40] This means that we are measuring here is the very effect of attitudes towards Islam and Muslims on the one hand, and cultural diversity on the other hand, and not ethnic prejudice or attitudes towards ethnic minorities in general.

What we learn from this result is that apart from the very fact of disliking (or holding negative attitudes towards) immigrants, some individuals shall vote for an extreme right or anti-immigration party for the very reason that they hold negative perceptions of Islam and Muslims. So what some authors would name Islamophobia is not only one of the contemporary dimensions of ethnic prejudice in Western European societies. It also became one of the roots or causes of extreme right-wing voting. The same is true for attitudes towards cultural

39 Mudde, The Single-Issue Party Thesis.
40 Statistical testing for multicollinearity does not show any risk (remind that inter-factor correlations were relatively moderate).

diversity, meaning that beyond their attitudes towards immigration and migrants themselves, some individuals shall favour the extreme right for the very reason that they oppose the idea of a religiously and culturally diverse country.

At this stage, nevertheless, the picture is still incomplete. This means, from a statistical point of view, that our model remains underspecified. Indeed, one cannot discard the possibility that the aforementioned variables shall not show any significant effect any more if one add the main, previously identified variables of extreme right-wing voting. Table 12 shows the results from a regression model with the same variables as the previous one, plus authoritarianism,[41] left-right identification,[42] and education level[43] as control variables.

Table 13: Effect of ethnic prejudice's dimensions plus control variables on extreme right-wing voting (multiple regression analysis)

	b	Beta (standardized)	Sig.
Intercept	.74		.00
Perception of Islam and Muslims	.05***	.08	.00
Old-fashioned racism	.00	.00	.93
Attitudes twds cultural diversity	.09***	.12	.00
Attitudes twds immigrants	.26***	.46	.00
Authoritarianism	.07***	.11	.00
Left-right identification	-.06***	-.11	.00
Education	.00	.03	.16
Adjusted R^2		*.47*	

***p < .01, ** p < .05, * p < .1 (two-tailed)

As expected after previous research, authoritarianism as well as left-right identification does significantly affect extreme right-wing voting: the more one is authoritarian, the more one identifies with the right of the political spectrum, and the more chances one has to vote for the extreme right. The effect of education level is not significant maybe imputed to the number of attitudinal variables in the model (furthermore, based on previous research, the effect of education, though often substantial, is not one of the strongest ones as far as extreme right-wing voting is concerned). Unsurprisingly, the effect of *Old-fashioned racism* remains insignificant with new controls in place.

41 We use an additive scale, based on the following items: "School should primarily provide pupils with a sense of discipline" and "To maintain public order, stronger action should be taken against troublemakers" (Pearson's R = .47).

42 "With regard to politics, people sometimes speak of 'the left' and 'the right'. Where would you place yourself on a scale where 0 represents the far left and 10 represents the far right".

43 Interviewee's age when leaving school.

But the important fact here is that the effect of the three dimensions of ethnic prejudice –*Perception of Islam and Muslims, Attitudes towards cultural diversity,* and *Attitudes towards immigrants* – remains significant at a .000 level. This confirms that these variables have a proper effect on extreme right-wing voting.

V. Conclusion

This study aimed at throwing light on the contemporary forms of Western European ethnic prejudice and their relation to extreme right-wing voting, based on the recent, unedited GFE survey.

First results (descriptive statistics) are in line with the core historical statement of Myrdal about the implementation of basic principles favourable to ethnic and racial equality. The majority of the European public opposes the historical biological version of ethnic prejudice, i. e. racism in its strict acceptation (belief in a natural racial hierarchy). Nonetheless, a significant minority still holds racist opinions, showing that the more blatant, "old-fashioned" versions of ethnic prejudice have not disappeared in European societies. On the other hand, we showed that such attitudes do not have the same implications that they used to have in the past: only a small, much more reduced minority opposes inter-racial marriage. The more extreme forms of biological racism thus seem to have lost most of their relevance in public at large.

The idea of a "national preference" in certain domains such as employment does not refer to racial, biological hierarchies, but rather the legal distinction between citizens and the non-citizens of a given country. The majority of the interviewees accept the idea of equal treatment, i. e. oppose national preference, coherent with the legal dispositions of modern democracies. Nevertheless, a significant minority supports national preference, particularly in the case of a perceived threat (high unemployment).

Still considering general principles, most interviewees consider cultural diversity within the nation-state as a better option than homogeneity. However, coherent with Myrdal's notion of dilemma, the broad acceptance of principles of ethnic equality, equal treatment and cultural difference does not prevent from other widespread, negative attitudes towards ethnic minorities and migrants. Thus, the majority of the interviewees consider there are "Too many immigrants" in their country. This statement can be related to a number of fears and stereotypes associated with immigration and ethnic otherness. Amongst these "Perceived ethnic threats", fears concerning the impact of ethnic otherness on culture or "Cultural threat" are more widespread than fears about the economy. This appears as central to understand the contemporary forms of ethnic prejudice and their roots in Western Europe.

Furthermore, even if most interviewees support religious and cultural diversity in principle, negative views of Islam and Muslim culture are much widespread throughout Western European public, and even majority. This can be seen as an important source of concern regarding public opinion, since it means that negative perceptions of the growing important Muslim minority are rooted in common and probably enduring social representations and stereotypes.

Going beyond descriptive statistics, we then confirmed the multidimensional feature of contemporary attitudes towards ethnicity. Four dimensions emerged from selected items, namely *Perception of Islam and Muslims, Old-fashioned racism, Attitudes towards cultural diversity* and *Attitudes towards immigrants*. The *Attitudes towards cultural diversity* dimension confirms that general principles about ethnic and cultural diversity must be distinguished from attitudes towards ethnic groups themselves. The *Old-fashioned racism* dimension shows that traditional, "blatant" racism has not disappeared. On the other hand, it appears as distinct from other attitudes or issues, such as the very *Attitudes towards immigrants* themselves. The emergence of a *Perception of Islam and Muslims* dimension is a key result, which confirms the crucial, growing importance of Islam-related issues in the European societies and public.

These dimensions are even more important that they have a significant, distinct or proper effect on the propensity to vote for an extreme right-wing party (at the exception of *Old-fashioned racism*). This remains true after controlling for the main, previously identified individual factors of extreme right-wing voting, thus confirming the specific effect of these dimensions or attitudinal factors.

These different results can be discussed in several ways. First, our analyses are limited to the pooled sample of the six Western European countries included in the GFE survey. It thus leaves open the issue of national specificities as regard to the forms of ethnic prejudice and their relation to extreme right-wing voting. These specificities may partly depend on each country's political debates as far as ethnicity is concerned, as well as the specific strategies and discourses of national extreme right-wing forces. Furthermore, new data collection with indicators comparable to the ones that have been selected may allow confirming our results for the whole Western European population. As far as Eastern European countries are concerned, we would expect to find different results and dimensions, due to different national histories, immigration traditions, established minorities, and political debates.

The Victorious Parties - Unity in Diversity?

Patrick Moreau

I. Global framework

Our study shall analyze the parties successful at the European elections of June 2009. But this selection cannot give an account of the strength of the far right-wing parties from the Atlantic Ocean to the Ural Mountains. Powerful right-wing parties like the Norwegian *Progress Party* (*Fremskrittspartiet* - FrP, 2009 parliamentary elections: 22.9 %, 41 MPs) or the *Swiss People's Party* (*Schweizerische Volkspartei* - SVP, 2007: 29 %, 62 MPs) did not participate.

The large number of publications enables us to define the crucial elements of the success of far right groups in the West. Positions, strategies, and forms of organization can be identified which have made a party attractive for the voters at a certain point or on the long run:

- a profile of political competence and of credibility of the future realization of the program;
- proposition of a generous (even incoherent) programmatic alternative and open perspectives enabling strong identification and a high level of political commitment (militancy, financing);
- nationalism;
- use of the myth of a "golden age" to be recovered;
- political positioning critical of or against the system in order to collect and organize every variety of dissatisfaction with or rejection of the parties in power, the political elites, and the concepts of governance;
- preference of plebiscitary or direct democracy based on the (binding) referendum of citizens' initiatives; criticism of the representative democracy;
- appeal to the people ("the humbly born") against the elites ("the upper crust") presented as a homogeneous and destructive group;
- aggressive populism ("tell the truth"), verbal incitement, and provocation as a calculated breach of "political correctness";
- denunciation of genetic miscegenation and/or the national, European or "white" demographic collapse;
- xenophobic agitation and campaigns on the stop of immigration (trans-European, post-colonial or linked with globalization, and with the international conflicts);

- communitarianism, refusal of multiculturalism, of melting pot as well as of the integration of aliens; rejection of the principle of family reunification; restriction of access to the respective nationality;
- expulsion/repatriation of unemployed aliens, criminals, and "economic refugees";
- discourse on the dangers of acculturation for the members of the respective nation as well as for the aliens (ethno-pluralism);
- preference of nationals and exclusion from or restriction of benefits of the social welfare system to aliens;
- authoritarian program ("everybody in his place" in a strong state), refusal of the "ideology of human rights", priority of "duties" to rights;
- ideology of security ("self-defense" against national and international crime, homeland enemies, and terrorists), reinforcement of the police and its rights;
- discrediting aliens as criminogenic;
- request of repression (reform of criminal law, introduction of harsher penalties, death penalty) of pedophiles, drug traffickers, terrorists, etc.;
- appeal to moral rehabilitation (against the dissolution of morals, homosexuality, etc.);
- economic program: mixture of anti-bureaucratic and anti-taxation notions, and topics like the national social security systems, the rejection of privatizations, and economic protectionism;
- hostility to the European integration accused of building one centralized state;
- headed by a strong and/or charismatic leader backed by well-known, respectable, and/or popular personalities, and a part of the elites;
- the object of attention of the media (including negative campaigning).

On many levels, the continuity of the programs and forms of organization of the winners of 2009 is obvious. Are we therefore facing a "crusade for closed societies" confining itself to a dualist view of a never changing world divided in eternal friends and foes?

II. The 2009 European elections

Our study concentrates on 13 parties which won MEP seats at the June 2009 European elections: *Freiheitliche Partei Österreichs* (FPÖ), *Vlaams Belang* (VB), Ataka, *Dansk Folkeparti* (DF), *Perussuomalaiset/True Finns* (PS), *Front National* (FN), *Laikos Orthodoxos Sunagermos* (LAOS), *Jobbik Magyarországért Mozgalom* (Jobbik), *Lega Nord* (LN), *Partij voor de Vrijheid* (PVV), *Partidul România Mare* (PRM), *Slovenská Národná Strana* (SNS); *British National Party* (BNP). The *Bündnis Zukunft Österreich* (BZÖ) (Alliance for the Future of Austria) is a special case: It did not pass the 5 % barrier and does not hold a direct seat. But it was granted one in the context of the implementation of the Lisbon Treaty.

Before turning to the nature of these parties, their history, modes of organization, and programs, we need to assess their electoral power in 2009 and compare it with the preceding or following national elections. We have to keep in mind the profound differences existing between a European election with a 5 % barrier and the same election procedure in every country and the highly different conditions at the parliamentary elections in the various countries.

The successful parties in terms of their 2009 electoral strength can be classified in three groups: four weak parties close to the 5 % barrier (SNS: 5.5 %, BNP: 6.2 %, FN: 6.3 %, FPÖ: 6.4 %), a medium group of four between 7 and 10 % (LAOS: 7.1 %, PRM: 8.6 %, PS: 9.8 %, VB: 9.8 %) and a group of five strong parties between 10 and 17 % (LN: 10.2, *Ataka*: 14.1, *Jobbik*: 14.8 %, DF: 15.3 %, PVV: 17 %). A comparison of the results of the national parliamentary elections immediately preceding or following (see table 1) does not show any continuity. Parties like the FPÖ and the BZÖ suffer a profound drop between 2008 and 2009. Others progress strongly (BNP, *True Finns*). Some parties remain at a strong electoral level of about 15 %. The election results since 1990 do not reveal general tendencies either. The formations analyzed here have all experienced electoral success as well as the loss of votes.

An East-West differentiation supplies hardly any new information. Of the 13 parties (without the BZÖ), four come from the post-communist world, nine from "old" Europe. They come from half of the member states of the European Union and send 36 members to the European Parliament.

Table 1: Results of the winning parties of the 2009 European elections and of the national elections since 1990

		1990	1991	1992	1993	1994	1995	1996	1997	1998	1999
FPÖ (Austria)	%	16.6				22.5	21.9				26.9
	D	33				42	40				52
BZÖ (Austria)	%										
	D										
VB (Belgium)	%		6.6				7.8				9.9
	D		12				11				15
VB (Flemish Parliament)	%										
	D										
Attaka (Bulgaria)	%										
	D										
DF (Denmark)	%									7.4	
	D									13	
PS (Finland)	%		4.8				1.3				1.0
	D		7				1				1
FN (France)	%				12.4				14.9		
	D								1		
LAOS (Greece)	%										
	D										
JOBBIK (Hungary)	%										
	D										
LN (Italy)	%					8.4		10.1			
	D					117		59			
PVV (Netherlands)	%										
	D										
PRM (Romania)	%			3.9				4.5			
	D			16				19			
SNS (Slovakia)	%										
	D										
BNP (Great Britain)	%			0.1					0.1		
	D										

III. Categorization

Is it possible to classify these wining parties according to their character and nature? Each of them is embedded in its own country's history. Its electoral success depends on the specific conditions within its political system and correlates with economic, social, and ethnic national indicators. However, common characteristics can be found (see: summary tables at the end). Still, four categories can be distinguished:

- *The "Dinosaur Parties"*: *The Freedom Party of Austria* (FPÖ) and the French *Front National* (FN) belong to this category. Having existed for decades and having enjoyed impressive electoral successes, their organizations are very well-structured. They have gathered various currents wrestling with the his-

2000	2001	2002	2003	2004	2005	2006	2007	2008	2009	2009 E	2010	2011
		10.0				11.0		17.5		6.4		
		18				21		34		2		
						4.1		10.7		4.6		
						7		21		1		
		11.6					12.0			9.85	7.7	
		18					17			2	12	
				24.2					15.3	11.96		
				32					21	2		
					8.1				9.4	14.14		
					21				21	3		
	12.0				13.3				13.9	15.3		
	22				24				25	2		
			1.6				4.1			9.79		19.0
			3				5			1		39
		11.3		2.2			4.3			6.34		
										3		
									5.6	7.15		
									15	2		
						2.2				14.77	16.7	
										3	47	
	3.1					4.6		8.3		10.2		
	30					23		60		9		
						5.9				17.0	15.5	
						9				4	24	
19.5				13.0				3.2		8.65		
84				48						3		
						11.7				5.55	5.1	
						20				1	19	
	0.2				0.7					6.2		
										2		

tory of their respective nations (FPÖ: German National/Austrian nationalist members; FN: Pétainists, French veterans of the Algerian War, Pieds-Noirs / "Black-Feet",[1] Christian fundamentalists, integral nationalists, and national revolutionaries; they rally around charismatic leaders: Haider/Strache, Le Pen). The *British National Party* (BNP) is a white power group which has gone through a phase of strategic modernization. It belongs to this category in spite of important differences concerning the questions of violence and contacts with extreme right subcultures (Skinheads, neo-Nazis). The *Popular Orthodox Rally*, a xenophobe religious party, constitutes a separate category.

1 French citizens of various origins who lived in French Algeria before Algeria's independence.

But it has been developing towards a party resembling the FN. The question of cooperation with democratic parties is resolved in different ways: The FPÖ had already been in government power with the conservative ÖVP in 2000. The FN tried to form alliances, at least on the regional level, with the democratic right but remains an anti-system party. LAOS pursues an identical strategy. The BNP is clearly hostile towards the British political system.

- *The Nordic model:* The *Danish People's Party* (DPP) and the *True Finns* party (PS) constitute another sub-group to which the Dutch *Party of Freedom* (PVV) could also be added, but cautiously. The organizational differences are strong: DPP and PS are centralized parties while the PVV is a party without members. Nevertheless, they share their ideological basis: the intention to cooperate with the established parties, the acceptance of democracy and the rule of law, the key role of anti-Islam and anti-immigration positions, the assertion of their respective national identity combined with hostility towards a Brussels-dominated Europe, and the intention to preserve the welfare state. Their strategy is to exert pressure on the democratic parties to make them tighten their anti-migration policy and revise the general frame of the European Union.
- *Regional parties:* The *Vlaams Belang* (VB) and the *Lega Nord* (LN) are very similar phenomena because of their regional deep-rootedness (Flanders and Northern Italy). Typologically, both parties are semi-loyal of their political systems. Their organization resembles that of the FN and the FPÖ.
- *Eastern European parties:* They (*Movement for a Better Hungary, Slovak National Party, Greater Romania Party, National Union Attack*) share a pronounced anti-Romani racism and anti-Semitism, a more or less strong acceptance of violence, and the hatred of democracy and the rule of law.

1. The "Dinosaur Parties"

1.1 Austrian Freedom Party

The far right in Austria has been strong, especially the FPÖ. Its progress in the 1980s, its accession to power in a coalition government in 1983 and in 2000, and finally the rise to its present strength according to the polls as well as at various regional elections in 2009/2010 calls for a detailed examination of the reasons of this deep-rootedness.

Austria is clearly a prosperous country. It has overcome the 2008/2009 economic crises and the tensions linked with the crisis of the Euro. In January 2009, Austria's 4 % unemployment rate had been the lowest within the EU. At the end of the 2009 crisis, unemployment slightly increased to 4.4 % and has remained stable since.[2]

2 See Statistika Austria, Mikrozensus-Arbeitskräfteerhebung 2011.

One of the key issues is immigration. In 2010, 7,480,146 Austrian citizens and 895,144 foreigners lived in Austria.[3] Illegal immigration is estimated at 4 %. The political parties insist on the limitation (the conservative ÖVP and the social-democratic SPÖ) or stop of immigration (BZÖ, FPÖ). Only the *Green Party* is cultivating its multi-cultural profile supporting immigration and defending the right of asylum. Like in Denmark (see below), the democratic parties have aligned themselves to positions of the far right which also reflect the collective feelings of the Austrians.

In an EU study on value change in Austria, the results are conclusive and clear: Austrians are less and less interested in politics and trust neither political institutions nor parties. Increasingly, democracy itself has become the subject of direct criticism. Market economy is losing acceptance. A small but growing group is fundamentally opposed to the system as a whole. Respondents voice their "distance" or even hostility towards everything "foreign", be it states like Turkey, the EU or persons (migrants, asylum seekers, temporary workers, etc.). Micro-solidarity, for example within families, remains strong. But meso-solidarity has noticeably weakened. "Jealousy-induced individualism and hostility to foreigners" are becoming more and more prominent.[4]

Interest in politics has changed over the last 20 years. In 1999, 69 % of the respondents had been interested in politics; in 2008, the number dropped to 46 %. Since 1999, Austrians have lost trust in institutions. While anonymous institutions like the health system (72 %), police (70 %), or the legal system (62 %) are highly accepted in 2008, political and social institutions (parties 14 %, trade unions 26 %, parliament 28 %, EU 26 %, etc.) are at the low end of the scale. Between these two extreme poles, there is a group of institutions with relatively low values, like press 34 % or church 36 %. Compared to 1999, surprisingly, every single institution has lost acceptance except the army and the press. On the whole, "political institutions" have suffered the most significant loss, followed by the education system (-22 %). With only -4 %, the legal system and the police have remained relatively stable.[5]

In 2008, only 50 % of the respondents are satisfied with the functioning of democracy, only 4 % are very satisfied. By contrast, 35 % are rather dissatisfied and 11 % very dissatisfied. Compared to 1999, the percentage of satisfied citizens (73 %) has decreased by one third. Satisfaction with democracy has decreased in every category. The least satisfied are the FPÖ clientele (36 %), the non-denominational (48 %), supporters of "ban immigration" (9 %), and unhappy persons (-20 %). Proponents of a ban on immigration show the highest loss of satisfaction (-51 % compared to 1990). They are followed by right-wingers (-42 %), churchgoers (-31 %), persons without a formal school-leaving qualification (-30 %), and the non-denominational (-24 %).

3 See http://www.statistik.at/web_de/statistiken/bevoelkerung/bevoelkerungsstand_und_veraenderung/bevoelkerung_im_jahresdurchschnitt/023142.html.
4 See Friesl/Polak/Hamachers-Zuba (Eds.), Die Österreicher innen, p. 208.
5 Ibid., p. 216.

In 2008, 83 % favor a democratic system (1999: 93 %), 88 % are convinced that democracy is the best of all systems (1999: 94 %). "Anti-democrats" are a tiny minority. Still, acceptance of counter-models is rising. 21 % of the population can imagine a leader/a strong man at the head of the state who flouts parliament and elections (1999: 15 %), 5 % can even imagine this very well. 51 % think experts can handle government tasks and decide what is necessary for the public weal. 6 % consider a military dictatorship acceptable (1999: 1 %).

Is Austria facing a strong authoritarian temptation? The most striking difference concerns the protection of the freedom of opinion. Between 1999 and 2008, acceptance of this goal drops by 32 points (1990: 59 %; 1999: 63 %; 2008: 31 %). This may be considered a consequence of the perception of external and internal threats and dangers. Facing Islamic terrorism, the Austrians accept the limitation of the freedom of opinion of the "foes of freedom".

Since 1990, individualism has grown, while authoritarianism has remained as stable as micro-solidarity, the mega value par excellence. Xenophobia has increased by +10 %. The decline of macro-solidarity has been disconcerting (13 % in 2008).

Table 2: Mega values (indices: fully agree/agree) in %

	1990	2008
Individualism	55	76
Authoritarianism	30	30
Xenophobia	45	55
Micro-solidarity	70	72
Macro-solidarity	18	13

Source: EVS 1990–2008, p. 232.

Between 1990 and 2008, the balance of the values freedom and equality has severely shifted. The desire for equality has increased 10 % (1990: 28 %) while freedom has lost 12 % (1990: 60 %). These stark figures hide a dual development: Clearly, those who do not share the wealth demand its fairer distribution. 43 % of the low-income earners belong to this egalitarian group. Some former defenders of freedom have revised their position in the wake of the crisis. Thus, in 1990, 68 % of the university graduates preferred freedom. In 2008, the number has dropped to 51 %.

The pollsters' conclusion is important for other European countries, too: "If solidarity diminishes and individualism as well as the wish for more equality rise, the suspicion suggests itself that the demand for equality may not only be the expression of a sense of justice but also of envy".[6]

6 Ibid., p. 255.

If the Austrian society is dominated by "social envy" (Haider used the topic of "jealousy about food"), competition between different population groups (natives and migrants) shall perforce intensify. Modern Austria is a multi-cultural society. Immigrants settled in several waves. Presently, the country appears to be suffering from collective xenophobia. The acceptance of xenophobic statements has risen between 1999 and 2008, for example concerning the lifestyle of foreigners as well as their repatriation.

Table 3: Xenophobic statements

		1999	2008
Foreigners should adapt their life-style a little more to that of natives	Agreement	72	80
	Neither - nor	16	12
	Disagreement	9	6
In case of a shortage of jobs, foreigners should be sent home	Agreement	46	49
	Neither - nor	24	22
	Disagreement	26	27
Foreigners should be forbidden all forms of domestic political activity	Agreement	44	43
	Neither - nor	20	20
	Disagreement	30	30

Source: EVS 1999-2008, p. 259.

Xenophobia is nourished from three different sources: economic concerns, cultural reasons, and the issue of internal and external security. In 2008, 69 % believed criminality to have risen because of the foreigners, 66 % consider them a threat to the social systems, and 48 % are convinced they take the Austrians' jobs away. 65 % think there are too many foreigners in Austria, 52 % do no longer feel at home. The correlation between a high educational level and tolerance has continually weakened. This demonstrates the deterioration of the situation: The elites, too, have become xenophobic.

Who are the bogeymen? Considering the development between 1999 and 2008, Romani people, Muslims, migrants, and Jews have increasingly become victims of ostracism.

Systemically, the EVS study shows that the classical assumption of a close correlation between "losers of modernization" and xenophobia is applicable to Austria only in a very limited way. The most important factors are frustration and fear of modernization of society.

Besides this general context, further aspects contribute to the rootedness of the far right. Since 1945, Austria has had 27 governments, 17 of which were SPÖ/ÖVP coalition governments. The SPÖ was the sole party in power from 1970 to 1983, and the ÖVP from 1966 to 1970. From 1983 to 1987, the far right (FPÖ) was in a coalition government with the SPÖ, and from 2000 to 2006,

Table 4: Who would you not like to be your neighbor? (Simplified table)

People from which group would you not like to be your neighbor?	1999	2008	Difference 99-08
Romani people	25	32	+7
Muslims	15	31	+16
Migrants/foreign workers	15	23	+7
People with a different color of skin	7	18	+12
Jews	8	18	+11
None of the above mentioned	10	8	-2

Source: EVS 1999-2008, p. 265.

with the ÖVP. This ménage à trois situation is the central dilemma of Austrian politics.[7] The long-term continuation of Grand Coalitions has led to a gridlock perceived by voters as being caused by the *Proporz* system. This is an oppressive clientelism often forcing citizens to join one of the two big parties in order to launch a professional career. To a great extent, Jörg Haider's success at the polls since 1986 resulted from his declared intention to end this system.

Between 1983 and 1999, the FPÖ election results improved steadily. In 1999, more than a quarter of the votes went to Haider's party. An internal crisis led to the split of the FPÖ whose present chairperson is Heinz-Christian Strache. In April 2005, the BZÖ was founded and chaired by Haider until his death in 2008. Both parties together brought the national populist right back to its 1999 level: They won 28 % in the 2008 general elections.

Heinz-Christian Strache was often referred to as "young Haider's clone". Since 2005, Strache has made the most of his "young leader" physique.[8] His (seemingly) very natural style is pleasing and achieves its goal: he is popular, sexy and (thanks to his trendy clothes) attains a credibility and political aura that seems to be a welcome contrast to the "old politician" style. His talents as a communicator are undisputable. Between 2006 and 2008, he took control and consolidated the post-Haider FPÖ and its finances. He restructured its supporting and activist organizations and led a non-stop campaign meticulously echoing the voters' collective concerns about Europe and immigration. Structurally, Haider's death in 2008 left the field open for Strache.

With its 2008 election program, "Our promise to Austria", the FPÖ clearly focused on societal and security issues. Immigration was the party's flagship theme for the 2008 and 2009 elections.[9] The FPÖ advocated "a humane and consequential return" of foreigners to their homelands, particularly criminals and "parasites of the social system". Referring to Muslims, the FPÖ announced

7 See Pelinka, Vom Glanz und Elend; Dachs/Gottweis/Gerlich, Politik in Österreich.
8 See Horaczek/Reiterer, HC Strache.
9 See "Österreich im Wort", available at: www.FPOE.at\fileadmin\Contentpool\Portal\wahl08\FPÖ-Wahlprogramm_NRW08.pdf.

its intention to ban "politico-religious victory symbols" like minarets, and to penalize violations of "constitutional norms" like "violence against women, abuse of freedoms of the press and of speech, as well as cruelty to animals". The latter is the traditional expression for ritual slaughter of the European far right.

The FPÖ demanded obligatory language tests for immigrant pupils and the expulsion from school of children flunking them; a separate social security system for foreigners (including healthcare) financed exclusively by immigrants holding jobs; expulsion of long-term unemployed migrants; protection of the labor market by a national preference system. To put it bluntly: This program is an epitome of xenophobic, security-conscious, nationalist, and anti-European protest populism. It deliberately targets the social strata most discontent with - or most threatened by - Austria's economic and social situation.

Some aspects of the FPÖ's organization deserve special attention. The present membership is estimated at about 50,000. This does not include sympathizer groups in the party's supporting organizations. They comprise representations of young people, women, students, liberal professions, employers, teachers, the self-employed, university graduates, seniors, etc. Today, the FPÖ is Austria's third largest parliamentary force at the national and regional levels (Parliament: 37 seats, Federal Council: 9; regional parliaments: 69). To finance its political activities, the FPÖ had 7,192,471 € at its disposal in 2009.

At the September 2008 general elections, the ÖVP obtained 26 % of the vote (-8.3 % compared to 2006), the SPÖ 29.3 % (-6 %) and the *Greens* 10.4 % (-0.1%). The FPÖ's results jumped up 11 points to 17.5 %. The 10.7 % of the BZÖ marked an increase of 6.6 %.[10] The FPÖ suffered a defeat at the European elections (6.4 %).

Interest in the 2009 European elections was quite limited in Austria like in all EU member states. As a result, the turnout was low (46 %).[11] In Austria, the "List Martin" (17.7 %, 3 seats) is critical of the EU but it is neither extremist nor xenophobic. The result of the SPÖ was bad (23.7 %, 4 seats), that of the ÖVP mediocre (30 %, 6 seats).

Concerning the economy, the FPÖ electorate voices its negative judgment of the Austrian membership of the EU.

28 % of the younger voters elected the ÖVP and made it the strongest party within this age group. The results of FPÖ (19 %) and the *Green Party* (14 %) were also above average.

Like in 2008, the preferred party among the workers is the FPÖ, and to a lesser extent the BZÖ. At the European elections, the FPÖ profited from the economic crisis, too: Voters hit by the crisis, e. g., by staff reductions, short-time

10 See Hofer/Toth (Eds.), Wahl 2008; on the 2006 general election, see Plasser/Ulram (Eds.), Wechselwahlen.

11 See ISA, Wahltagsbefragung und Wählerstromanalyse Europawahl 2009, available at: http://www.sora.at/images/doku/wahlanalyse_sora_isa_grafiken.pdf; Analyse der EU-Wahl 2009, available at: http://www.sora.at/de/start.asp?b=556; Wählerstromanalyse EU-Wahl 2009, available at: http://www.sora.at/de/start.asp?b=554.

work, or loss of income, elected the FPÖ twice as much as the labor force not affected.

Migration and the issue of the accession of Turkey to the EU were dominating motives of the FPÖ electorate.

Table 5: The financial crisis of the EU: For Austria, the membership brings ... (EU 2009 in %)

	Rather more advantages	Neither - nor	Rather more disadvantages	Don't know
SPÖ	60	18	19	4
ÖVP	66	14	17	4
MARTIN	49	18	28	5
FPÖ	23	14	60	4
Total	49	19	28	5

Source: SORA.

Table 6: Voting behavior according to sex, age, and profession (EU 2009 in %)

	SPÖ	ÖVP	MARTIN	Grüne	FPÖ	BZÖ
Men	23	32	15	9	15	5
Women	25	28	22	10	11	4
- 35 years old	22	28	14	14	19	3
35-59 years old	23	30	20	10	10	6
60 years and older	29	33	21	2	10	4
Workers	17	29	17	5	24	7
Employees	26	30	14	15	9	4
Retired persons	31	32	22	1	10	4

Source: SORA.

Table 7: Voting behavior regarding the economic situation (labor force hit by staff reductions, loss of income or short-time work) (EU 2009 in %)

	SPÖ	ÖVP	MARTIN	Grüne	FPÖ	BZÖ
Hit by the crisis	14	36	13	10	23	2
Not hit by the crisis	23	30	17	12	12	6

Source: SORA.

Table 8: Electoral motives FPÖ (EU 2009 in %)

Loyal voter	28
Defends my interests	68
Defends Austria's interests in the EU	50
Important issues	75
Top candidate	26
Electoral advertisement	12
Against accession of Turkey to the EU	81
Against immigration	88
Rectifying of evils	60

Source: SORA.

In 2008/2009, the FPÖ rallied many anti-establishment voters worried about the future, disoriented by economic tensions, critical of the political system and the construction of Europe, and opposed to the ÖVP-SPÖ grand coalition and immigration. Each of these issues is currently relevant. This is the reason of the FPÖ's electoral triumph in September 2009 in Lower Austria and in October 2010 in Vienna.

Analyzing the 1999-2008 period, it is evident that the FPÖ (the BZÖ, too) has been able to attract voters of the type "losers/winners of modernization". Strong xenophobia among the population correlating with a high number of immigrant residents, criticism of the political elites and parties but also of social inequalities, support the theory of victims of modernization. But other voters have joined this group. The theory of the FPÖ and BZÖ being backed by winners of modernization/welfare state chauvinists is supported by the fact that in Austria, we observe an extensive welfare state system, a very low unemployment rate, and a strong (but weakening) commitment to and bond with church (Catholicism in all of Austria except Carinthia with a protestant majority). Among the institutional factors, we observe a blockage of the system also affecting trade unionism due to the *Proporz.* The discontent with the political system and the erosion of the parties in power in grand coalitions has induced an increasing socio-economic and socio-cultural change since the 1970s: The traditional parties' core groups diminished. Ideological patterns (working class culture, rural milieu) and ideologically induced culture of interpretation started to break down. This resulted in the electorate's affective and organizational destructurization.

Since 1986, the FPÖ has always adapted its program to the prevailing public opinion. The topics of protection of the social achievements (healthcare, pension systems, etc.), of immigration and criticism of the EU have developed into *the* key issues of Austrian politics. The clear messages of Strache's FPÖ and his strong charismatic personality have made the party win over (again) the "welfare state chauvinists". This turnaround to welfare state chauvinist economic and social politics has made the FPÖ a serious competitor of the SPÖ for the support of the industrial workers and many mobile voters at odds with the traditional political milieus.

1.2 The Front National

France is a prosperous country. Still, it has experienced economic problems, and a high unemployment rate (2008: 7.9 %), especially among young people. The integration of immigrants (foreign-born population: 2008: 8.56 %) whether French citizens or not has caused problems. These aspects have accompanied the political and electoral history of the *Front National* (FN).

In 1972, the project of the FN was the unification of the French "extreme right" and its re-integration into the political arena on every level (local, regional, national parliaments, and presidential elections).[12] Le Pen, former airborne officer, deputy elected on the Poujadists' list in 1956, supporter of French Algeria, became its head. Then, he was the most uncontroversial and brilliant personality of the extreme right.

Four phases can be distinguished in the FN history. Between 1972 and 1982, it established its organization. Repeated splits let the FN remain a fringe group. At the 1981 general elections, it received a meager 0.18 %. The party seemed doomed to eventual disappearance.[13] Between 1982 and 1986, the FN enjoyed its first electoral take-off due to the concurrence of two political phenomena, i. e., the erosion of the left in government and the disenchantment with its economic and social performance. The 1984 European elections ended with a triumphant FN (10.95 %, 10 MEPs). Proportional representation was introduced at the March 1986 general elections. The FN reached 9.65 % and 35 MPs. On April 24, 1988, Jean-Marie Le Pen won 14.37 % at the first ballot of the presidential election. Due to the return to the majority voting system, at the June 1988 general elections, the FN won 9.66 % of the vote but only one MP, Yann Piat. It was practically excluded from all alliances.[14] Between 1988 and 1998, the FN consolidated electorally. At the June 18, 1989, European elections, the party won 11.73 % and 10 MEPs. At the December 1989 general by-election, Marie-France Stirbois was elected MP (first ballot: 42.5 %, second ballot: 61.3 %) in the 2nd constituency of Eure-et-Loir. The FN did not only strengthen electorally. It also consolidated its internal structures (local associations, higher

12 See Boissieu, Chronologie du FN, available at: http://www.france-politique.fr/histoire-fn.htm; some important studies: Camus/Monzat, Les droites nationales; Camus, Le Front national; Mayer/Perrineau, Le Front national à découvert.

13 Some of the numerous publications: Martin, Le vote Le Pen; Mayer, Ces Français qui votent FN; Cuminal/Souchard/Wahnich/Perrineau, L'électorat de la protestation de Jean-Marie Le Pen, pp. 64–67.

14 There was only one mutual agreement on withdrawal and endorsement in Bouches-du-Rhône between the right (Jean-Claude Gaudin) and the FN.

party schools, scientific advisory board, security group, etc.), and - on the model of the *French Communist Party* - created a glacis of close or very close satellite organizations (youth, veterans, trade unionists, etc.) still active today.

The fourth period began in 1999 and is particularly complex. General secretary Bruno Mégret supported the creation of an alliance with the liberal parties and the conservative right. Le Pen rejected this strategy. In January 1999, Mégret broke away from the FN, taking with him more than half of the party's cadres. In October 1999, he founded the Mouvement national républicain (National Republican Movement - MNR) which failed to attract the NF electorate. This split weakened the party considerably concerning its local, regional, and national roots. It also stopped the FN's electoral dynamics for some time. At the 1998 European election, the party received a meager 5.69 %. At the 2001 cantonal and local elections, FN and MNR together reached no more than 10 %. The FN and its leader did certainly not expect a breakthrough at the 2002 presidential elections. Le Pen profited from the disunity of the left and the extreme weakness of Lionel Jospin, the socialist candidate. The presidential election changed into a battle of the "republican front" against Le Pen. He did not win additional voters and finished with only 17.79 % at the second round. The FN did not profit from the great publicity feat in the wake of this election but began to lose ground (2002 general elections: 11.34 %, 2004 European elections: 9.8 %). The 2007 presidential (10.44 %) and general elections (4.29 %) ended with a serious setback. This decline was accompanied by a grave internal crisis. The resignation of cadres and various splits ended with a quasi-defeat at the 2009 European election (6.34 %). In 2007 and in 2009, a part of the former NF electorate supported Nicolas Sarkozy. His ideological offers seemed - at least for some time, as the 2011 polls show - more in tune with their interests.

Nicolas Sarkozy's victory at the 2007 presidential election and at the 2009 European elections seemed to have killed the FN. In January 2011, Jean-Marie Le Pen passed the chair to his daughter Marine Le Pen. This replacement marked the beginning of a thematic and ideological modernization (refraining from revisionism, strengthening of the social profile, etc.). Presently, the FN seems to be able to profit from the disaffection of the working and lower classes with President Sarkozy's politics.

The party's weltanschauung has remained practically unchanged from the beginning.[15] Immigration remains a central mobilizing element of the FN. It is described as a machine to impoverish France and destroy its culture. The FN policy is based on "the rejection of communitarianism and the reassertion of the principle of secularism". A policy of reversing migration is given high priority. To discourage immigration, the FN intends to restrict various social welfare and family benefits "to true Frenchmen" and to enact a law of "national preference" of the social services. France is to leave the Schengen area and to withdraw from

15 See Rémond, Les Droites en France; Winock (Ed.), Histoire de l'extrême droite en France; Lecoeur, Un néo-populisme à la française; Rémond, Les Droites aujourd'hui.

the treaties transferring the competences of immigration, asylum, and visa laws to the European Union. Foreign multiple offenders are to be deported.[16]

Security issues, too, have always been on the agenda. They belong to the topics explaining Sarkozy's 2007 breakthrough among the FN electorate as well as the reflux observed at the 2011 polls. The FN deplores the insufficient "means provided for the police and the judiciary". The party insists in harsher punishment of crimes and offences. It wants to reintroduce "death penalty for the most serious crimes" (pedophiles, terrorists, child murderers, etc.). The party demands a clampdown on gang and organized crime.

The further FN program turns around some basic principles: solidarity (between the sexes, generations, the poor and the rich, etc.),[17] moral rearmament and the fight against cultural decadence,[18] defense of the birth-rate and the families,[19] preservation of traditional - especially rural - ways of life, preservation of nature and the protection of the small farmers, defense of social achievements (healthcare,[20] retirement benefits).

The FN's socio-economic program is anything but revolutionary. It claims to be a corrective of liberalism and of the negative effects of globalization. It is "social" and in touch with the underprivileged Frenchmen/women it wants to protect. But it does not favor the redistribution of the riches from top to bottom. There is no trace of anti-capitalism, but rather of Colbertism based on a strong and incentive state as the sovereign guardian of political and economic rules. The FN wants to "protect the national market with well-reasoned protectionism (produce French, buy French)", and "gain international acceptance for other mechanisms than the ultra-liberal swapping". It intends to restore the role of the Banque de France as an independent statutory monetary institution, and return to the Franc and the gold standard. The French ought to profit from a massive relief of fiscal and social dues, and the reduction of public spending by prohibiting budget deficits.[21] These are in fact conservative demands reminding of Gaullism. The FN characterizes itself as "left on social issues, right on economic issues, and enrooted in the French nation".

In the field of institutions, the FN plans to bridge the gap separating the people from the elites. It intends to "create the national referendum by popular initiative", introduce single ballot proportional representation at general,

16 See the entry on "Immigration" on the FN homepage: http://www.frontnational.com/?page_id=1095.
17 See the entry on "Solidarité": http://www.frontnational.com/?page_id=1179.
18 See the entry on "Culture": http://www.frontnational.com/?page_id=1155. The FN demands to end the public funding of associations it considers "infiltrated" by communists.
19 See the entry on "Famille - enfance": http://www.frontnational.com/?page_id=1116.
20 See the entry on "Sécurité sociale": http://www.frontnational.com/?page_id=1106.
21 Ibid. p. 117.

European, regional, and local elections, and amend the Preamble of the Constitution by the "principle of national preference".[22]

Finally, there is the question of identity and nation. In her analysis of the FN doctrine, Magali Balent[23] shows the ultimate reference to the nation. This community sharing common roots is based on ethnicity and submitted to immutable laws of nature. These laws must be accorded absolute respect otherwise decadence is unavoidable. Man belongs to a nation by birth and cannot elude it. It is the most superior form of human framework.[24] Every people has the right to its own national territory and to a Nation state. For this reason, the FN supports the Palestinians and the Serbs in the case of the Kosovo. It considers the "New World Order" - with the European Union, various international organizations, the military imperialism, and cosmopolitan ideology promoted by the USA - the deadly enemy of the nations.[25]

According to the FN, the white world is interlocked with Christianity. This is why threats to Western identity have a religious dimension, too. Besides the US, Islam is a major enemy. It is denounced as a conquering religion, violently anti-European, and with a "totalitarian core". The attacks of September 11, 2001, are considered a declaration of war to the West. The danger of Islam is a demographic one, too, because of the high birth rate of the Muslim world.

The concepts of nation and peoples are accorded central importance in the FN's discourse. Still, it postulates the natural inequality of the peoples because of the different abilities and talents of their respective members. This is a form of "modern racism".[26] It ranks the civilizations of the Third World and the Muslim nations at the bottom of the pyramid. Its top is occupied by Western civilization because of its intellectual aptitudes.[27]

Who votes FN? Nonna Mayer and Pascal Perrineau show that the FN electorate has renewed and diversified at every election since its first electoral successes.[28]

22 See the entry on "Fonction publique et institutions": http://www.frontnational.com/?page_id=1174.

23 See Balent, La "vision du monde" du Front national: Quel devenir après le départ de Jean-Marie Le Pen? Note de recherche n°XXV, available at: http://www.cevipof.com/fr/les-publications/notes-de-recherche/bdd/publication/729.

24 See Balent, La "vision du monde" du Front national, p. 7.

25 This anti-Americanism seems to be inherited from GRECE (Groupement de recherche et d'études pour la civilisation européenne), a school of thought of the "New Right" many of whose former members joined the FN in the 1990s. See Taguieff, Sur la Nouvelle droite.

26 See Balent, La "vision du monde" du Front national, p. 10.

27 Ibid.

28 See Mayer/Perrineau, Le Front national à découvert; id., Les comportements politiques; Mayer/Boy (Eds.), The French Voter Decides.

Table 9: The demographic structure of the FN 1988–2007

	Presidential 1988	Presidential 1995	Presidential 2002	Presidential 2007
Total	15	15	17	11
Sex				
Male	18	19	20	12
Female	11	12	14	9
Age				
18–24	14	18	13	10
25–34	15	20	17	10
35–49	15	16	18	11
50–64	14	14	29	12
65+	16	10	15	9
Occupation				
Farmer	10	10	22	10
Managers	19	19	22	10
Mid-level executive	14	4	13	7
Low-level employee	14	18	22	12
Worker	17	21	23	16
Jobless	17	28	20	11
Sector				
Private	16	16	20	12
Public	14	14	14	11
Education				
Primary school	15	17	24	13
Secondary school	17	20	21	13
A-levels	13	12	15	8
A-levels+2	10	13	11	3
University degree	9	4	7	4
Catholic affiliation				
Devoutly practicing	13	8	12	5
Sometimes practicing	13	13	18	10
Not practicing	16	19	20	12
Non-denominational	10	14	15	12

At the first ballot of the 1988 presidential election, Le Pen arrived at the top among small traders and artisans. His results among workers were good. In 1995, he enjoyed a breakthrough among workers und unemployed persons disappointed by the left, and in 2002, in rural and agrarian milieus and among employees (22 %) and workers.[29]

The distinctive characteristics of the FN electorate were the same in 2007.[30] Its "'ethnocentric' vision of society" was combined with a repressive attitude. Like in 2002, Le Pen was successful among voters with low levels of education (13 %). His results were worst among academics, teachers, and students (below 5 %). In 2007, 12 % of the male but only 9 % of the female electorate voted FN.[31] Nonna Mayer detects a negative correlation between the support of the extreme right and the affiliation with the Catholic community and its values, like at former elections.[32] Workers are the professional category with the best FN results: 16 %.

Finally, considering the winning conditions of the FN, we have to turn to the personality of Jean-Marie Le Pen. He was a popular tribune and a great communicator. But verbal slips cost him a lot of sympathy. Still, the FN's enrooting in French history and the crises of the political system (the erosion of the parties in power) are evident. The FN has been capable to exploit economic crises and social tensions resulting from insecurity, immigration, and the failure of immigration policies. It has always collected winners and losers of modernization. The FN is a very efficient "anti-system" party pointing out the ideological weaknesses of the socialist and communist left, but also of the conservative camp. In 2009, it suffered something of a failure at the European elections. But in 2011, it has returned to the political arena.

1.3 The British National Party

The *British National Party* (BNP) was founded by John Tyndall in 1982.[33] It had split off the *National Front*. Its current leader is Nicholas John "Nick" Griffin, born March 1, 1959. Griffin graduated from Cambridge University with an honors degree in law.[34] An ideologist rather than a tribune, Griffin is not a charismatic leader.

29 Source: Mayer, Les votes Le Pen du 21 avril 2002 au 22 avril 2007, available at: http://www.cevipof.msh-paris.fr/PEF/2007/V1/rapports/VotesLePen_NM.pdf; Mayer, Ces Français qui votent le Pen.
30 See Mayer, Les votes Le Pen.
31 Ibid.
32 Ibid.
33 On the history of the NF and BNP, see the online bibliography of the British Library, available at: http://www.bl.uk/reshelp/findhelpsubject/socsci/topbib/bnp/bnp.pdf. The "National Front" has remained an electorally marginal party on the national level.
34 See the entry on "Nick Griffin" at: http://en.wikipedia.org/wiki/Nick_Griffin; see also: http://chairmans-column.blogspot.com.

In the 1970s, Griffin "began to develop ideas around the need for an elite cadre of 'political soldiers'".[35] In 1992, he was introduced to the BNP. At that point, he was a militant right-wing extremist resorting to violence, an anti-Semite, and a negationist.[36] He strongly doubted the sense of participating in elections.[37] In 1999, the electoral success of FN and FPÖ inspired him to set about changing the party's extremist image in order to make it electable.

The structures of the BNP resemble those of the FN and the FPÖ.[38] The BNP's internal structure is authoritarian. The party adheres to the leadership principle. The chairperson exercises absolute power. The number of its activists is still relatively small. It is capable to organize "political events" but it cannot "conquer the streets". On Dec. 31, 2009, the BNP claimed 12,632 paying members (1995: 700; 1999: 1,353; 2003: 5,737). Due to the electoral reinforcement and the recruiting of new members, its financial resources have considerably increased since 2003 (£: 2003: 370,420; 2006: 726,455; 2009: 1,983,947).

The BNP has developed measures designed to "cultivate a sense of collective identity among party foot soldiers": activist training sessions, summer schools, extra-parliamentary organizations (British Nationalist Youth Movement – BNYM), a student wing (Student BNP), a record label, a radio "http://www.radiorwb.co.uk" and a television station "http://bnptv.org.uk", a patriotic shop "http://www.buyexcalibur.co.uk", a trade union "http://www.solidaritytrade-union.com", an annual party festival, and an association for former servicemen. They all contribute to Griffin's goal of a "broader 'cultural offensive'". The BNP has also encouraged followers to dress well and become more "respectable". Nonetheless, it has not been able to shed its image as a refuge for members of the extreme right (skinheads).

The BNP's results at national elections have improved slightly but remained very low (1983: 0.0 %; 1987: 0.0 %; 1992: 0.1 %; 1997: 0.1 %; 2001: 0.2 %; 2005: 0.7 %; 2010: 1.9 %). The British voting system – a one ballot first-past-the-post-system – is held to be one of the major reasons of its failure. Due to this system, the smaller parties traditionally concentrate on local elections. Since 1999, the BNP has achieved good results at local elections. In 2009, it held 54 seats at local parliaments.

The European elections, however, are a different story. At the 1999 national elections, the BNP won 1 % (10,644 votes). At the 2004 European elections, it

35 See Goodwin, In Search of the Winning Formula, pp. 169–190.
36 In 1998, Griffin received a two-year suspended prison sentence for incitement to racial hatred.
37 See Goodwin, In Search of the Winning Formula, p. 176.
38 See "British National Party, BNP, Statement of Accounts Year Ended 31 December 2009", available at: http://www.electoralcommission.org.uk/party-finance/party-finance-analysis.

received 4.9 % (808,200 votes).[39] The 2009 European elections confirmed the 2004 trend: Proportional representation enabled the BNP to mobilize successfully (2009: 6.34 %, 1,091,682 votes). Matthew J. Goodwin's essay "In Search of the Winning Formula" evaluates the BNP's political and electoral strong points and weaknesses very clearly.[40] Griffin's election brought about a more "media-friendly" approach, a more professional electoral strategy and a programmatic revision. But the party was not able to effectively mobilize its potential electorate. This failure was "not due to lack of demand for policies and ideas associated with the extreme right but rather supply factors, such as the characteristics of the party itself (i. e. its ideology, strategy, organization, and leadership), as well as the reaction of other political actors".[41]

Which is the political position of the BNP in 2009? Griffin intended to make the BNP a mass movement. To this end, it had to "'forget about racial differences, genetics, Zionism, and historical revisionism' and instead keep things 'simple'".[42] The BNP scapegoats the same groups as the other "new" and successful European radical right parties: Immigrants, ethnic minority groups, and asylum-seekers are presented as a "threat" to national identity, a major cause of crime and social unrest, and a burden on the welfare state and local resources.

The BNP has turned to anti-Islamic nativism. After 9/11, the party started its "Campaign against Islam" characterized as the "New Crusade for the survival of Western civilization and an attempt to counter the Islamification of Britain". Islam has been accused of intolerance, slaughter, looting, arson, and the molestation of women. The BNP permanently tries to scientifically prove the inability of this religion to conform to Western and British values referring to academic studies like Samuel Huntington's "The Clash of Civilizations".

How do modern voters perceive the BNP? Recent data indicate that "despite attempts at 'modernization' the BNP has been unable to shed its 'pariah' status".[43] Few voters consider the BNP a "normal" player in the political process. Still, a growing number of people consider electing the extreme right.[44]

Three aspects play a central role in the electoral mobilization for the BNP, ethnic nationalism, xenophobia, and the hostility towards the elites.[45] Public support of multiculturalism in Great Britain is "rather thin".

39 See Margetts/John/Weir, The Latent Support for the Far Right in British Politics, the BNP and UKIP in the 2004 European and London Elections, paper presented to the 2004 Elections, Public Opinion and Parties Conference, Oxford, 10–12 September 2004, available at: http://www.governmentontheweb.org/sites/governmentontheweb.org/files/Far-Right-Paper-EPOP-2004.pdf.

40 See Goodwin, In Search of the Winning Formula, pp. 169–190.

41 See Copsey, Contemporary British Fascism; Eatwell, The Extreme Right and British Exceptionalism, pp. 172–192; Goodwin, The New British Fascism.

42 Ibid.

43 See Goodwin, In Search of the Winning Formula, pp. 183–184.

44 Ibid.

45 See Ford, Who Might Vote for the BNP?, pp. 145–168.

Table 10: Ethnic nationalism and national pride in Britain (white respondents only). National identity: how important are the following to being truly British? (answers 'very' or 'fairly') (in %)

	All	Working class
Statements about being British		
Being born in Britain	73	81
Living most of one's life in Britain	72	76
Having British ancestry	50	59
Citizenship and Britishness		
People who do not share British customs and traditions are not truly British	53	57

Source: Ford, Who Might Vote for the BNP?, p. 151.

The table shows the widespread public support for birth and long-term residence as criteria for being British. A significant minority is willing to go even further and impose religious or racial criteria for Britishness. Especially the white working-class prefers a more ethnic understanding of national identity. Presently, xenophobic hostility focuses on immigrants and Muslims.

According to this table, "immigrants and asylum seekers are regarded by a majority of the British public as economically and socially costly, undercutting British workers, draining government resources, and encouraging crime and social disorder".[46] Especially the working classes harbor strong anti-immigrant sentiments. Muslims, too, are the object of intense public aversion. Here again, working-class members voice the most intense hostility.

78–84 % of the respondents call for the reduction in immigration. More than 70 % Britons support draconian measures like those regularly postulated by the BNP, e. g., the total stop of immigration, the denial of benefits to migrants (58 %), and even measures to encourage repatriation. In this case, too, the working class support is the strongest.

The Britons' dissatisfaction with their existing party political elite is evident. The voters do not fundamentally question and challenge democracy. Nevertheless, they are dissatisfied with the existing parties (5 %), and 70 % do not consider them capable of or interested in representing their opinions. Ford is not surprised "that the BNP devotes so much attention to attacking the political status quo: the populist extreme-right message that the 'system is broken' commands a great deal of public support".[47]

Who are the supporters of the extreme right?[48] Seven out of 10 supporters of the extreme right are male. The BNP finds its strongest support among the

46 Ibid., p. 152.
47 Ibid., p. 163.
48 See Goodwin/Ford/Duffy/Robey, Who Votes Extreme Right in Twenty-First Century Britain, pp. 191–210.

Table 11: Xenophobia in contemporary Britain: hostility to Muslims and immigrants (simplified table) (in %)

Attitudes to immigrants and Muslims	Agree	Working class agree
Immigrants		
Government has been dishonest about the scale of immigration (2007)	80	81
Government spends too much money assisting immigrants (2008)	64	71
Immigration is making Britain a more dangerous place in which to live (2008)	60	64
Most asylum seekers contribute nothing to the British economy and are a drain on resources (2008)	59	62
There are too many immigrants in Britain (2008)	59	63
Parts of the country don't feel like Britain any more due to immigration (2008) White respondents only	58	62
Muslims		
British Muslims more loyal to Muslims abroad than to other Britons (2003) White respondents only	62	68
Muslims need to do more to integrate into British society (2008)	56	54
Britain is in danger of losing its identity if more Muslims come to live here (2008)	48	57

Source: Ford, Who Might Vote for the BNP?, p. 153.

working class: "Unskilled manual workers and the residual class of those who are dependent on state benefits", i. e., the lower classes at the economic bottom rung.[49]

The organized electoral extreme right, as represented by the BNP, is clearly "enjoying increased support". However, the authors warn "not to overstate this 'success'". Compared to extreme right parties elsewhere in Europe, the BNP has "so far proven unable to enter the national legislature, and internally there remain questions over the absence of strong and charismatic leadership, the party's weak financial resources and a tendency to internal conflict".[50]

49 Ibid., p. 200.
50 Ibid., p. 207.

Table 12: Demographic data of BNP supporters (simplified table)

	% of adult population 2002-2006	% of BNP support
Male	47	69
Female	53	31
Age		
15-24 years	13	11
25-34 years	15	14
35-54 years	34	39
55 years +	38	36
Social class		
Higher non-manual	20	11
Lower non-manual	29	19
Skilled manual	21	32
Semi-/unskilled manual and residual	29	38
Working status		
Full-time	38	45
Not-full-time	62	55
Property		
Owner/mortgage	70	68
Local-authority rented	21	24
Privately rented	8	7
Other	1	1

Source: Ford, Who Might Vote for the BNP?, p. 198.

1.4 Popular Orthodox Rally

The *Popular Orthodox Rally* (LAOS) was founded and led by journalist Georgios Karatzaferis a few months after his expulsion from the center-right *New Democracy* in 2000.[51] Born in 1947, Georgios Karatzaferis is a media specialist. In 1983, he was offered a scholarship by the German Konrad-Adenauer-Foundation. In 1994, he obtained an honors diploma from the London School of Journalism. He is an excellent communicator and speaker with a charismatic personality.

51 See the entry on Wikipedia on "Georgios Karatzaferis": http://en.wikipedia.org/wiki/Georgios_Karatzaferis.

Initially, LAOS encountered severe political problems. But in 2004, it won the support of the *Party of Hellenism*[52] and the *Hellenic Women's Political Party*. In 2005, LAOS managed to absorb the nationalist *Hellenic Front*.[53] In spite of its attempt to "moderate" its political style, LAOS has attracted extreme nationalists. They joined the party and some of them were elected MPs. At the 2007 general elections, LAOS won 10 seats. Four of its MPs are said to belong to the "nationalist bloc".[54] As for its organization, LAOS is a strongly centralized party.

LAOS considers itself a political actor pursuing the project of patriotic "popular liberalism" combined with social solidarity. LAOS can be defined as a Christian (Orthodox), nationalist, xenophobe, anti-Semitic, anti-Islamic, homophobe, anti-system, and anti-globalization party.

Its ideology is based on the idea that after the decline of "real existing socialism", the classification of political parties and ideologies in left, right, and center does not exist any longer. Parties may only approve of or oppose globalization. LAOS violently opposes liberal globalization. It is convinced that the Greeks need to concentrate on their common interests and values. This implies that geographically or culturally, Turkey does not belong to Europe and its accession to the European Union must be prevented.[55] LAOS also wants to ban immigration from outside the EU and to expulse illegal immigrants. The Albanian immigration is presented as the most dangerous one for Greece. Until 2010, LAOS was not involved in acts of anti-immigrant violence. But in 2011, party members seem to have participated in the "hunt" of Albanians.

LAOS opposes both the European Constitution and the Lisbon Treaty. It strives for a Europe of nation states. It demands the strengthening of Greek relations with Russia and Serbia, the immediate withdrawal of all international troops from the Kosovo, and the return of this province to Serbia. LAOS is anti-Semitic,[56] anti-Zionist, revisionist, and negationist, and very critical of the United States denounced as the major supporter of globalization. Its program is highly security-oriented (more drastic police security measures, ban of protests like the 2008 riots). The party claims to defend the vested social rights (retired persons) and demands drastic tax cuts for individuals and small businesses. The

52 The "Hellenism Party" (Greek: Κόμμα Ελληνισμού) founded in 1981 was a nationalist party. Its electoral results always remained very weak (1996: General elections: 0.18 %; 1999: European el.: 0.26 %; 2000: National el.: 0.09 %).

53 Founded in 1994, the "Hellenic Front" (Greek: Ελληνικό Μέτωπο) was a nationalist party. At the 1999 European elections, the party won 0.12 % of the vote; at the 2000 general elections, it won 0.18 %. The result of the 2004 general elections - a meagre 0.09 % - led to the dissolution of the "Hellenic Front". See the entry on Wikipedia on "Hellenic Front": http://en.wikipedia.org/wiki/Hellenic_Front.

54 See "With Á Hard Group of Five on National Issues", 18 September 2007, available at: http://www.ethnos.gr/article.asp?catid=22767&subid=2&pubid=133138.

55 See "The Program of LAOS", available at: http://www.laos.gr/laos.asp?epilogi=%27pdf/PROGRAM_LAOS.pdf%27&page=laos.

56 See "Greece 2008/2009", available at: http://www.tau.ac.il/Anti-Semitism/asw2008/greece.html; "Greece 2009", available at: http://www.tau.ac.il/Anti-Semitism/asw 2009/greece.html.

powerful Greek left (*Kommounistikó Kómma Elládas* - KKE; *Synaspismos*) is the reason for LAOS' strong anti-communism.

At the March 2004 general elections, LAOS failed the 3 % barrier (2.2 %). But at the June 2004 European elections, it won 4.2 % (1 MEP). It suffered a small loss at the September 2007 general elections (3.8 %) but gained 10 seats. At the 2009 European elections, LAOS made further electoral progress (7.13 %, 2 MEPs). At the October 2009 general elections, the party scored 5.63 % and 15 seats.

Kostas Gemesis names several reasons for the 2009 electoral breakthrough of LAOS.[57] In December 2008, for nearly two weeks, Greece suffered the worst riots of the post-authoritarian period. The killing of a teenager by a police officer in Athens triggered an outbreak of terrible violence. After these shocking events, the country was more or less paralyzed until the June 2009 European elections.[58] The *Panhellenic Socialist Movement*, PASOK, the biggest opposition party, launched its "Europeanization" manifesto with the slogan "We vote for Europe - We decide about Greece". The electoral campaign of *New Democracy* (ND), governing party since 2004, had no catchy slogan and was extremely bad. Expecting ND's electoral collapse, LAOS concentrated on winning over right-wing and Euro-skeptic voters from ND and focused almost exclusively on foreign policy issues.

PASOK won the election (36.34 %, 8 seats) increasing its share of the vote by 2.6 % compared to 2004. ND suffered a crashing defeat (32.29 %, 8 seats) losing more than 10 % of its 2004 vote and 3 seats. Among the small parties, LAOS (7.15%, 2 seats) and the *Ecologist Greens* (3.49 %, 1 seat) were the winners. ND was in a most difficult position. It had been harshly punished for its poor government record. Its chairman Constantine Karamanlis knew he could not continue to run the country with a slim parliamentary majority when the Greek economy was in deep water. An early general election date was set for October 2009.

The 2009 general elections ended with a rather moderate victory of PASOK (43.92 %, 160 seats). The true winner of the election, however, was LAOS. It had strengthened its electoral base (5.63 %) and won the 15 seats it had hoped for. Its success is the result of an effective appeal to the voters opposed to immigration and disappointed by the mainstream parties. Shortly after the election, though, the skyrocketing public deficit forced the new government to take unpopular measures. Under European pressure, Papandreou introduced a far-reaching austerity program. Rather surprisingly, LAOS offered at least tacit support of the government. In 2011, LAOS has changed its position: It is critical of Papandreou hoping to profit from the wide-spread hostility of the EU. The issue

57 See Gemesis, Winning Votes and Weathering Storms: The 2009 European and Parliamentary Elections in Greece, available at: http://www.keele.ac.uk/kepru/wp/paper32.pdf.

58 Ibid.

of immigration continues to play an important role.[59] LAOS might also increase its importance due to the growing xenophobia of the Greek population.

Finally, the party profits from the disalignment of the political system, the financial crisis, and from the austerity program imposed on Greece by the EU. It is attractive for nationalist and xenophobe voters and/or those who consider the future of their country imperiled.

2. The Nordic model

2.1 Danish People's Party

The *Danish People's Party* (DPP) founded in October 1995 is a split of the *Progress Party* (PP)[60] initiated by its present chairperson Pia Kjærsgaard. To distinguish itself from the PP, the DPP effected an internal purging and became a highly centralized party with a very strong leadership. It does not tolerate factions within its ranks. In 1998, the DPP had 2,500 members (10,000 in 2010).

Since the 1997 local elections, the DPP has enjoyed an electoral take-off. It gained 7.4 % and 13 MPs at the 1998 general elections.[61] Further electoral progress in 2001 (22 MPs, 12 %) made the DPP the country's third strongest political power.[62] Even though it could have ensured the majority, the DPP preferred to support a minority government headed by Anders Fogh Rasmussen, leader of the *Liberal Party* (*Venstre*) in coalition with the *Conservative People's Party*. In return for the support of the DPP, Rasmussen's government introduced tougher restrictions on non-ECA immigration. The topic of immigration has remained the DPP's domain. Thus, in May 2011, it pushed through the re-introduction of Danish border controls to stop cross-border crime and illegal immigration.

The DPP program mirrors several political tendencies: right-wing populism, national conservatism, social conservatism, and euro-skepticism. According to Pia Kjærsgaard's definition in the introduction to the program of October 2002, the DPP wants "to assert Denmark's independence, to guarantee the freedom

59 See Public Issue 2011, available at: http://www.publicissue.gr/1388/immigration-2010.

60 The "Fremskridtspartiet" ("Progress Party") was founded by Mogens Glistrup in 1982. In the 1980s, Glistrup added a new ideological feature: the stop of immigration from Islamic countries. In 1973, the party enjoyed an electoral breakthrough followed by its decline in the 1980s: 1973: 15.9 %, 28 seats; 1975: 13.6 %, 24; 1977: 14.6 %, 26; 1979: 11.0 %, 20; 1981: 8.9 %, 16; 1984: 3.6 %, 6; 1987: 4.8 %, 9; 1988: 9.0 %, 16; 1990: 6.4 %, 12; 1994: 6.4 %, 11; 1998: 2.4 %, 4; 2001: 0.6 %, 0.

61 See Borre, Critical Issues and Political Alienation in Denmark, pp. 285-309; Krogstrup, Immigration as a Political Issue in Denmark and Sweden, pp. 610-634; Mauthe, Erfolgsbedingungen für Rechtspopulisten; Rydgren, Explaining the Emergence of Extreme Right-Wing Populist Parties, pp. 474-502.

62 In 2010, besides 25 MPs (of 179), and 2 MEPs, the DPP holds 19 seats (of 205) at Regional Councils and 186 (of 2,468) at Municipal Councils.

of the Danish people in their own country, and to preserve and promote representative government and the monarchy". This is why the "country's internal and external security" must be strengthened. Danish society is characterized as a strong community. The state plays a central role: It is "bound to render support to those Danes who are in need, and bring them security and peace of mind". The DPP calls for more direct democracy. The passage "The Danish Evangelical Lutheran Church is the church of the Danish people" presents Christianity as an "integral part of Danish life [...] a ground stone and given guidance to the people". "Danish independence" is claimed to be the primary objectives of Danish foreign policy. This is why the DPP opposes the European Union. The Danish membership of NATO and UN, though, is accepted.

Internal security requires "coherence between crime and punishment". The necessary resources need to be allocated to crime prevention and investigation. "Danish people's history, experience, beliefs, language, and customs" must be "preserved and strengthened". The DPP insists in Denmark's not being an immigration country. It will "not accept transformation to a multiethnic society". Denmark "belongs to the Danes". An "efficient social and healthcare system" and the protection of families are mandatory. The DPP emphasizes the importance of manual as well as intellectual labor for maintaining the "dynamism of the country", and of an education system "allowing for individual abilities, talents, and interests". Danish prosperity is coupled with regulatory capitalism. Denmark's prosperity is presented as "the result of enterprise, businesses, and the cooperation of hard-working individuals. Society needs entrepreneurs and must let people know that hard work and ability pay".[63]

A series of programmatic documents detail this program.[64] The fight against islamization relies on the cultural assimilation of immigrants. On the European level, the DPP calls for the complete stop of immigration from non-Western countries. It opposes the accession of Turkey to the EU and supports Israel in its conflict with Hamas as well as the US-led War on Terrorism. It favors higher defense expenditure and pursues a harsh anti-Beijing line endorsing the international recognition of Taiwan. The DPP supports sanctions against totalitarian (primarily Islamist and communist) regimes and dictatorships. In spite of its xenophobic aspects, the DPP program appears to be radical, but not extremist.

What are the reasons of the political breakthrough of this radical right party? They are certainly specific to Denmark but they also apply to the political situation in other countries like Austria.[65] The political system in Denmark is a stable and well-functioning parliamentary democracy. According to the polls, 70 %

63 See http://www.danskfolkeparti.dk/The_Party_Program_of_the_Danish_Peoples_Party.asp.

64 See http://www.danskfolkeparti.dk/Principprogram.asp; http://www.danskfolkeparti.dk/Arbejdsprogram.asp; http://www.danskfolkeparti.dk/M%C3%A6rkesager.asp.

65 See Rydgren, Explaining the Emergence of Radical Right-Wing Populist Parties, pp. 474–502; Meret, The Danish People's Party, the Italian Northern League and the Austrian Freedom Party.

of the voters declare a high or average political interest. Almost 90 % are satisfied with the functioning of democracy on the whole. The system is characterized by compromise and consent of the political parties.

The economic situation is sound, the unemployment rate low (2008: 3.4 %). Inflation is under control and the number of foreigners small (2008: 5.5 %). A priori, these conditions seem to counter the political success of a party like the DPP on the long term.[66] The system of social security is (still) excellent. Trade unions are strong and consensual social actors (union members 2006: 75 % of the workers). In 2009, the Danish society is characterized by affluence and an overwhelming feeling of belonging considering religion, culture, and the social sphere.

These indicators suggest that the phenomenon DPP might be classified a problem of affluent radicalism of a "winners of modernization" electorate. But the conditions of the DPP's success are more complex. The first important aspect is the ideological convergence of the Danish parties and the erosion of the Danish party-system since the early 1970s. The breakthrough of the *Fremskridtspartiet* in 1973 and the following national elections indicated this.[67] The *Social Democrats* were one of the losers of this development. Their influence on the trade unions and the working class began to shrink. The DPP, like other national-populist parties in Europe, offered this escheated electorate a political option.[68] The defense of social achievements and of the welfare state was the DPP's ideological bridge to the unions and workers.

In spite of their positive perception of democracy, since 1995, the majority of the voters had become increasingly apprehensive of the threat to the welfare state and its being jeopardized by immigration. The DPP was the *only* party to treat this topic and made it its trademark. There were further conflictual political issues: the balance of powers of the political authorities and the market, the level of financing of the social services by tax revenues and private provision, the extent and the nature of privatizations and public tenders, the political integration more or less passed from Denmark to the EU, and the fight against crime. The DPP programs offered radical answers considering immigrants but otherwise compatible with the programs of the conservative and liberal parties. This enabled the DPP support of minority governments but also helped further its public acceptance.

The DPP took advantage of its excellent strategic position: It presented itself as one of the driving forces of the country's economic success. Its proclaimed Euro-skepticism enabled it to criticize all measures considered problematic (e. g., the massive EU aid for Greece in 2010/2011) because it was not a member of the government. This way, the DPP was able to exploit the latent or pronounced discontent of some electoral groups like workers looking for authori-

66 See http://www.oecd.org/statisticsdata/0,3381,fr_33873108_33873309_1_1_1_1_1,00.html.

67 See Steffen, Die Parteiensysteme Dänemarks, Norwegens und Schwedens, pp. 67-108.

68 See Mauthe, Erfolgsbedingungen, p. 38.

tarian political solutions, young people afraid of the future, retired persons, and small craftsmen.[69] “While the Fremskridtspartiet had been elected largely for protest reasons, the voters of DPP are ‘normal’ voters who prefer the DPP for ideological or thematic (issue-voting) reasons [...]. Considering values, the electorate is definitely right-wing. On the economic scale, however, it moves to the left. These voters are the most unanimous supporters of higher expenditure on nursing care and old-age pensions”.[70]

To make its political profile a Christian and social one was an intelligent ideological and strategic decision of the DPP. Denmark is a country with a strong Christian-Protestant tradition and character. The DPP also wanted to distance itself from the *Fremskridtspartiet* and from the classic extreme right and to prevent Nazi or anti-Semitic right-wing extremists from joining its ranks. Even though the party is clearly Islamophobic – in 2006, during the Muhammad cartoons controversy it profited from this – it rejects and condemns every form of violent action.

Due to this political profile, the media that had fought the Fremskridtspartiet adopted a relatively neutral position towards the DPP. The vote for this party became commonplace. Presently, the majority of the voters accept the DPP’s highly critical attitude of immigration to Denmark. Furthermore, the conservative and liberal parties no longer try to exclude the DPP from political competition. Instead, following the requirements of the survival of minority governments, they have partly adopted the lines of DPP arguments.

Finally, the DPP’s success depends on several factors: The traditional milieus, especially the social-democratic one, and working class culture dissolved. The loss of ideology of the great traditional parties left an intellectual vacuum, which neither the Danish *Communist Party* nor the red-green groups could fill. The DPP was able to occupy two niches: the fight against immigration (presently linked with the hostile line against political Islam) and the criticism of the EU; and the protection of the social welfare state required by the majority of the voters.[71] Furthermore, Pia Kjærsgaard is a chairperson with charisma, capable of communicating with voters. She is perceived as a sort of antithesis of the political elites. Systemically, due to its ability to formally introduce an anti-immigrant policy and its social commitment, the DPP has profited from its popularity among winners as well as losers of modernization. The political system has reorganized and adjusted itself to this phenomenon: The governing parties paid for their remaining in power with authoritarian concessions.

69 An analysis by the trade union SiD after the 2001 election stated that among unskilled workers aged under 40, 30 % elected DPP and only 25 % the “Social Democrats”. See Rydgren, Explaining the Emergence of Radical Right-Wing Populist Parties, pp. 474–502.

70 See Mauthe, Erfolgsbedingungen für Rechtspopulisten, p. 40.

71 See Borre, Critical Issues and Political Alienation in Denmark, pp. 285–309.

2.2 The Freedom Party

The Netherlands, too, are a prosperous country with a remarkably low unemployment rate (2008: 2.8 %). The foreign population exceeds the 10 % threshold (2010: 1,390 million, 10.9 %). In addition, illegal immigration is important. Among the legal and illegal migrants, the number of Muslims is very high (850,000 in 2006). In 2010, 53,000 Dutch Muslims declared themselves deeply orthodox. [72]

Until the end of the 1970s, the Netherlands were characterized by tolerance and a strong pillarization.[73] This particularism/sectionalism had political, social, and denominational reasons. In the Dutch socio-political system, religiously, socially, and culturally defined groups coexisted side by side. The Calvinist, Catholic, socialist, and liberal pillars had their own particular social organizations (congregations/parishes, educational institutions, banks, chambers, etc.). Politics were regulated by the elites' consensus and will to compromise. For the Dutch political parties, ideological issues lost their importance. At the same time, the pillarization and the far-reaching party political consent broke up. The polder model had depended on them.[74]

The established parties intensified their fight for the political center. Campaigns became highly personalized while the significance of political programs for the electoral decision diminished.[75] Due to economic prosperity and low unemployment rates, neither the polder model nor multiculturalism had ever been challenged during the 1980s/1990s. The global economic crisis of the early 21st century and the rise of the unemployment rate to 4.7 % in 2005 changed things. The polder model became the object of criticism. A growing number of voters considered the traditional parties a political clique divorced from the citizens. The impression of a blockage of the political system increased because three established parties had ruled the country in coalition governments for decades. A new political actor capable to lift the "Hague cheese cover" was eagerly hoped for.

He appeared at the Second Chamber elections in 2002: Off the cuff, Pim Fortyun won 17 %. His and Theo van Gogh's assassinations speeded up the transformation of the political system. While tolerance declined, exclusion and

72 See "53,000 moslims streng orthodox", available at: http://www.parool.nl/parool/nl/266/RELIGIE/article/detail/1016174/2010/09/24/53-000-moslims-streng-orthodox.dhtml.

73 See Cuperus, Vom Poldermodell zum postmodernen Populismus: Die Fortuyn-Revolte in den Niederlanden, available at: http://www.renner-institut.at/download/texte/cuperus_d.pdf; Oberlechner, Strukturelle Versäulungen in Österreich und den Niederlanden: Gemeinsamkeiten, Unterschiede, Auswirkungen, available at: http://www.oezp.at/pdfs/2005-2-06.pdf.

74 "Polder model" is the term of the formal cooperation of employers, trade unions and independent government appointed members at the economic council (Sociaal Economische Raad). See Lucardie, Das Parteiensystem der Niederlande, pp. 331-350.

75 See Reuter, Rechtspopulismus in Belgien und den Niederlanden, pp. 155.

the fear of "strangers" living on Dutch soil grew. The population became increasingly certain of being threatened by terrorism and concerned about the risks for the social welfare state. There was a growing popular discontent with the insufficient capability to solve political problems. Voters in search of a way to voice their dissatisfaction decided to vote for Pim Fortuyn, and later for Geert Wilders.

Undeniably, Wilders' charisma supported the breakthrough of the new radical right. Geert Wilders was born in 1963. The son of a Catholic family left the Catholic Church when he came of age. In 1981, he worked at a Moshav in Israel. After his return, he started studying law at the Open University of Amsterdam. In 1989, Wilders joined the *People's Party for Freedom and Democracy* (*Volkspartij voor Vrijheid en Democratie* - VVD). The VVD had initially been a liberal party by and by drifting toward the nationalist right. From 1990 until 1998, Wilders worked as a speechwriter for its parliamentary group. In 1995, not an MP, he still became a member of a study group on Hungary dealing with this country's joining of the EU. He passionately embraced the case of the Hungarian minorities living in neighboring countries like the Czech Republic and Romania and supported the idea of a Greater Hungary. On July 31, 1991, he married his Hungarian wife Krisztina in Budapest. At the 1998 and 2002 general elections, he was elected a Member of the Dutch Parliament on the VVD list. In the wake of serious political discord, Wilders left the party in September 2004. The VVD favors Turkey's EU membership. For Wilders, this is completely out of the question.

Wilders formed a one-man-group Groep Wilders in Parliament. In 2005, he founded the *Freedom Party* (*Partij voor de Vrijheid* - PVV).[76] The PVV is the first and only party without members in the Dutch Parliament. It does not receive public funding granted only to parties with at least 1,000 members. The parliamentary group of the PVV, however, does receive public funds (1.1 million €).

The PVV program focuses on four main issues: Euro-skepticism, anti-Islamism, cultural conservatism, and national liberalism.[77]

The PVV is not a classic nationalist party. Geert Wilders prefers to cast it as a "patriot" movement. He does not place the nation state at the forefront of political and social values. The name of his party indicates the central reference value, namely the concept of freedom: "Freedom (Vrijheid) is seen by Wilders in its negative - the individual must be free from the state - and sovereigntist - the Netherlands must be free from Europe - dimensions".

The PVV criticizes "the political and cultural elites, and multiculturalism, and sides with the middle and working classes, without stooping to use the collectivist and homogeneous concept of 'people', which he eschews in favor of the more liberal concept of 'citizens'".[78] Wilders' conception of politics sets "the

76 See "Alleen Wilders lid PVV", available at: http://vorige.nrc.nl/binnenland/article1790538.ece/Alleen_Wilders_lid_PVV. This article presents an organizational diagram of the PVV.

77 See Pas, Où en est la droite? Les Pays-Bas, available at: http://fondapol.fr.

78 Ibid., p. 12.

corrupt elite against the virtuous people". He advocates the "return of authority" (state, police, and judiciary), and opposes economic globalization and cultural diversity. Wilders considers economic policy "secondary to the fight against the [...] Islamization of the West".

The 2006 program, distributed again at the 2009 European elections, was captioned with the slogan "The Netherlands to be proud again!". It stated that "the political elite in the Netherlands systematically ignores the interests and concerns of citizens". Wilders' goal was to make the Netherlands "a strong and vital country" again, with a powerful economy, "proud of its own identity".[79] The program proposes a massive reduction of bureaucracy. The PVV demands higher sentences for crimes and offenses, life imprisonment after three violent crimes, the maximum penalty for attempted crime; re-education camps, zero tolerance, immediate removal of non-Dutch criminals from Dutch soil. The PVV wants to focus on better education, the protection of the family and parenting. A new Article 1 of the Constitution is to confirm the predominance of Judeo-Christian and humanist culture in the Netherlands. It postulates a 5-year-stop of non-Western immigration, and a quota of no more than 5,000 immigrants per year. A quinquennial moratorium on building new mosques and Islamic schools, the closing down of radical mosques, the prohibition of foreign funding of mosques or foreign governments' influence on them, the inadmissibility of foreign imams as preachers, and the obligation to speak Dutch at prayers and worship are among the requirements. Furthermore, the PVV wants to revoke the right of non-Dutch inhabitants to vote at local elections, to abolish dual citizenship, and to refuse medical care to illegal immigrants except in emergency. Naturalization ought to be restricted to persons without a criminal record who have lived and worked in the Netherlands for ten years. The PVV demands the ban on burqas in public and the promotion of voluntary repatriation.[80]

Wilders demanded reforms of the political system, i. e., more direct democracy and mandatory referenda. The latter ought to be held on (1) Turkish EU membership, (2) the Euro, and (3) whether the West Indies ought to remain part of the Kingdom. Mayors as well as the Prime Minister must be elected by the people. Wilders wants to abolish the Senate, reduce the number of MPs from 150 to 100, and stop public subsidies for political parties.

The PVV demands to stop taxing pensions, and higher payments to retired persons under 65. It claims higher investments in roads, no tolls, higher speed limits, and new nuclear power plants. Wilders' radical Euro-skepticism is evident: The PVV demands to stop new accessions to the EU, the Schengen agreement on visas, the new European constitution, and the transfer of national political power to Brussels but its reclamation to national parliaments instead. Wilders wants to abolish the European Parliament as well as the European

79 See "Verkiezingspamplet", available at: http://www.pvv.nl/index.php?option=com_content&task=view&id=788&Itemid=139.

80 Ibid.

Commission. If Turkey becomes a member, the Netherlands ought to leave the EU. He intends to increase military efficiency and supports the fight against international terrorism.[81]

For the June 9, 2010 general elections, Wilders presented a very similar program with much the same demands dedicating even more attention to the question of Islam. "Eradicating Islam should be the primary target of Dutch foreign policy".[82] The chapter "Voting for the fight against Islam and mass immigration"[83] characterizes Islam as "above all a political ideology, a totalitarian doctrine based on dominance, violence, and oppression". Wilders insists that there is no moderate Islam even though there are moderate Muslims. The Koran "separates humankind in Muslims and inferior non-Muslims. Islam is accused of anti-Semitism, and the Jihad presented as an obligation of every Muslim. Wilders decries the position of women and homosexuals in Islam and denounces its sexism. A political ideology, Islam should not enjoy the privileges of a religion. The PVV demands a ban on the public funding of "Islamic media".

It is difficult to classify Wilders' programs. The lack of racism (in the sense of a hierarchy of the races), his unconditional support of Israel, and his pro-Americanism are striking. The total rejection of Muslims is a leitmotif, but still the PVV holds libertarian positions: It supports abortion rights, euthanasia, embryo selection, and female and homosexual empowerment.

Both, Fortuyn and Wilders have doubtlessly profited from the continuing convergence of the established parties. Decisive political differences between traditional parties have been leveled; the socio-economic left-right scheme (polder model) has weakened. Personalized election campaigns could not compensate the lack of programmatic profile of the established parties. The long-time taboo of topics like immigration, multiculturalism, and integration paved the way for the New Radical Right. Its offer seemed attractive to the losers of modernization.

2.3 The "True Finns"

The *Perussuomalaiset/True Finns* (PS) were founded in 1995 as the successor party of the *Finnish Rural Party* (*Suomen maaseudun puolue* - SMP). The SMP had flourished at elections during the 1970s and 1980. In the 1990s, it suffered a rapid decline mostly because of its participation in coalition governments.[84] Its electoral base consisted of small farmers and unemployed persons from the

81 Ibid.
82 See "Verkiezings Programma, Kiezen voor islambestrijding en tegen de massa-immigratie", http://www.pvv.nl/index.php/visie/verkiezingsprogramma.html, p. 13.
83 Ibid., pp. 13, 15.
84 The SMP results at general elections: 1962: 2.2 %, 0 seats; 1966: 1.0 %, 1 seat; 1970: 10.5 %, 18 seats; 1972: 9.2 %, 18 seats; 1975: 3.6 %, 2 seats; 1979: 4.6 %, 7 seats; 1983: 9.7 %, 17 seats; 1987: 6.3 %, 9 seats; 1991: 4.9 %, 7 seats; 1995: 1.3 %, 1 seat.

poorer Central and North of Finland. The True Finns have taken up many issues of the SMP's 1992 program.[85] The SMP was deeply rooted in groups focused on social and Finnish identity issues, but without extremist leanings.

The SMP's electoral collapse was followed by a wave of resignations. Looking for a political perspective, cadres, among them Timo Soini and Raino Vistbacka, decided to found the PS. The party was officially registered on October 13, 1995. At its first party congress in November 1995, Raino Vistbacka, the only MP of the SMP, was elected chairperson of the party with Timo Soini the party secretary.

The party owed its success largely to the organizational and rhetoric talents of Timo Juhani Soini, its chairperson since 1997. Born in 1962, he studied political science at the University of Helsinki finishing his studies as a Master of Social Sciences with a master thesis on populism in 1988. Soini is a devout Roman Catholic, a rare exception in protestant Finland. The PS does not have any distinctive features. It owns a website "www.perussuomalaiset.fi" and a news magazine.[86] In 2011, it has about 5,000 members, a youth organization counting about 1,300 members,[87] and a women's organization.[88] Its relations with the press are normal; the PS is not considered an extremist party.

In its 2009 electoral manifesto,[89] the PS calls itself "an anti-EU party" because the present system of the EU is stated not to be functioning in practice and the "supra-national EU" is considered anti-democratic. The PS prefers "sovereign nation states and intergovernmental cooperation", and opposes the transfer of more powers to the EU and its bodies. It demands a referendum on the EU constitution and rejects the Turkish EU membership.

The party supports "genuine democracy and the Nordic welfare state where welfare services are guaranteed for everybody and supplied largely by the public sector". It opposes the privatization of public services. Its top priority is the protection of the community of Finns. PS is in favor "of a responsible national immigration policy based on the principle 'when in Rome do as the Romans do'". The family is considered a key element of the stability of the Finnish society. It needs special protection in order to solve the problem of the present demographic change. The preservation of Finnish culture and identity is essential. PS ascertains the basic interests of Finland, namely to support free trade and cross-border cooperation. But it insists in the right to determine the social structures of its own country. Like its predecessor SMP, PS emphasizes the important role of agriculture and the protection of small famers, the "necessity

85 For the party program, see "Finnish Farm Party Program" (Adopted by the "Finnish Rural Party", the party conference in Helsinki on July 31 to August 1, 1992), available at: http://www.fsd.uta.fi/pohtiva/ohjelma?tunniste=smpyleis1992.
86 See http://www.perussuomalaiset.fi/perussuomalainen-lehti.
87 See http://www.ps-nuoret.net.
88 See http://ps-naiset.perussuomalaiset.fi.
89 See "True Finns EU Election Manifesto 2009", available at: http://www.fsd.uta.fi/pohtiva/ohjelma?tunniste=pseuvaaliohjelma2009.

of national self-sufficiency", and the preservation of nature. National interests are given priority, but the PS does not propose a policy of autarky.

In the election programs of the 2007 and 2011 general and the 2009 European elections,[90] there are additional indicators of the concept of identity as well as more detailed explanations on immigration. PS wants to abolish Swedish as a mandatory subject and grant more financial support of all cultural activities promoting the Finnish identity. The limitation of immigration is no less than the rejection of the Schengen Agreement, EU obligations, and the Geneva Convention. PS proposes thorough and efficient integration, "cultural compatibility" as a criterion, a quota system limiting immigration from profoundly different societies, and the introduction of language and educational level criteria if necessary. Extremist religious organizations must be prevented from taking roots in immigrant communities and the free practice of religion of moderate religious authorities facilitated. PS insists on a ban of religious courts, tight control of establishing fundamentalist religious schools, and the prohibition of the financing of religious authorities by countries like Saudi Arabia. PS wants to stop the abuse of asylum seekers' programs by trafficking networks, and prevent cultural or ethnical ghettos. Foreign criminals are to be expelled.[91]

Considering its international policy, PS favors non-alliance or neutrality and opposes accession to NATO. It is clearly pro-Israel and pro-American. PS wants to reduce foreign aid. In the politico-economic field, PS postulates nuclear energy, progressive taxation, and the protection of the welfare state and health care. Unemployment must be reduced by increased public investment in infrastructure and industry, especially heavy industry.

Just like Wilders' PVV and the Danish DPP, PS combines the topic of Finnish identity with strong social concerns. All three parties address the fear that things are not as they were, that the combination of immigration and EU membership poses a threat to the traditions of the Nordic way of life. Uncontrolled immigration is presented as a cultural and economic risk for the wellbeing of the community. Besides the strong Islamophobia, however, there is no "hard" racism like in the 1930s, and no authoritarian temptation. Instead, there is the adhesion to the national bond, to a Europe of nations, culture, and Heimat. Conservatism surfaces in the will to preserve and strengthen families, and in security concerns. Traditional left-wing positions are present, too: criticism of liberal capitalism, the rejection of privatizations, the protection of the welfare state, and interventionist measures to support agriculture and heavy industries.

90 See "True Finns rp's Parliamentary Election Manifesto 2007. Justice, Prosperity and Democracy in Europe!", Party Council, Ikaalinen, 13 August 2006, available at: http://www.fsd.uta.fi/pohtiva/ohjelma?tunniste=psvaali2006; "True Finns rp's Parliamentary Election Manifesto 2011", available at: http://www.fsd.uta.fi/pohtiva/ohjelma?tunniste=psvaaliohjelma2011.

91 See http://certifiedcontent.net/anti-spam-movement/true-finns-far-right-partyimmigration-finlands-2011-elections-projected-results.

What are the reasons of the PS' breakthrough in Finland? Since the 1990s, the Finnish economy suffered from quite a high unemployment rate (2008: 6.4 %). Immigration is weak with 3.8 % foreign-born in 2007, and about 4 % in 2011. Since 1919, Finland has been a parliamentary democracy. The Finnish system of proportional representation gave rise to a multiparty system and frequently led to the formation of coalition governments. For a long time, three big parties dominated the political landscape: The *Social Democratic Party* (*Sosialidemokraattinen Puolue*) was supported by the urban working class and small farmers. For decades, it was the strongest party in Finland. Most voters of the *Centre Party* (*Keskusta Puolue*) came from the agrarian milieu. The business community and urban professionals are the strongest supporters of the *National Coalition Party* (*Kansallinen Kokoomus*). The *True Finns* were the last to arrive in the political arena. Nevertheless, they have progressed at every national or local election (General elections: 1999: 1.0 %, 1 MP; 2003: 1.6 %, 3 MPs; 2007: 4.1 %, 5 MPs; 2011: 19.1 %, 39 MPs).[92]

The 2007 general elections led to profound political changes in Finland. After having largely dominated Finish politics, the *Social Democratic Party* suffered a serious setback (21.4 %) while the *Centre Party* advanced (23.1 %), and the *National Coalition Party* (22.3 %) celebrated a breakthrough. The latter formed a new government coalition in 2007 and sent the *Social Democrats* to the opposition benches. PS won 4.1 % and 5 MPs (of 200).

At the 2009 European elections, PS formed an electoral alliance with the *Christian Democratic Party* (*Kristillisdemokraatit* - KD). The alliance received 14 % and 2 seats, one of which went to the PS. The 2011 elections changed the balance of power. It ended with the triumph of PS (19.1 %, 39 seats) and the defeat of the established parties (*National Coalition Party*, 20.4 %, 44 seats; *Social Democratic Party* 19.1 %, 42 seats; *Centre Party*: 15.8 %, 35 seats).

The formation of a government coalition including the *True Finns* failed because they rejected the EU's financial support of Portugal and Greece. In this context, the future of PS is uncertain. It profited from the misalignment of the political system and represents the popular opposition to Europe. PS succeeded gathering numerous voters defecting from the *Social Democrats*, workers, farmers, and young people, too. Some victims of modernization had already supported the party in 2007. This phenomenon became even more pronounced in 2011. Furthermore, PS attracted Finns hostile to immigration (welfare chauvinists) in spite of the fact that immigration in general and especially Muslim immigration remains at a very low level.

The success of the Nordic model has not only been impressive in the countries analyzed here but also in Norway where the *Fremskrittspartiet* reached 22.9 % and 40 seats in 2009, and Sweden (*Sverigedemokraternan*: 2010: 5.7 %, 20 seats). The Oslo attacks committed by a fanatic might create problems for

92 PS strongly progressed at local elections: 1999: 0.9 %, 138 seats; 2000: 0.7 %, 109 seats; 2004: 0.9 %, 106 seats; 2008: 5.4 %, 442 seats (of 10,412).

these winning parties. Andrew Berwick's manifesto "2083 - A European Declaration of Independence" was clearly inspired by the Islamophobic positions of these formations. At the next elections, the Nordic and Dutch voters will have to take the Norwegian attacks into consideration. They might decide to abstain or change their political preference.

3. The regionalist parties

3.1 The Lega Nord

In the 1980s, many regionalist movements and parties were established in Northern Italy. This process must be considered in view of the structural discrepancy ("questione meridionale") between the North and the South of Italy existing since the 19th century.[93] Since 1945, support and help for the development of the South have multiplied and intensified. However, the divide between the powerful and rich industrialized North and the rural and economically depressed South continues to exist. This inequality caused a debate on the issue of the federalization of the country.

The centralism of the Italian state, and later the European integration provoked the so-called "re-territoralization". This process caused a renewal of the importance of the regions and the emergence of regionalist movements. The most important one was the Lega Lombarda founded by Umberto Bossi, Carlo Leoni, and Roberto Maroni. It stressed the ethnic and cultural particularities of the Lombardy and the Lombard people and demanded the autonomy of the region. At the 1987 general elections, the Lega Lombarda celebrated its first minor success (Parliament: 186,255 votes, 0.48 %, 1 MP; Senate: 137,276 votes, 0.42 %, 1 Senator - Umberto Bossi).

To increase their prospects of success at the 1989 European elections, the Lega Lombarda, Liga Veneta, Piemont Autonomista, Union Ligure, Liga Emigliano-Romagnola, and the Alleanza Toscana formed an electoral alliance, the Lega Lombarda - Alleanza Nord (636,242 votes, 1.83 % nationwide, 8.1 % in Lombardy, 2 MEPs). The autonomist Leghe held their first common congress at Segrate from December 7-9, 1989. In the next 3 years, these movements united and formed the *Lega Nord* (LN). Umberto Bossi, former head of the Lega Lombarda, became its chairperson.

Umberto Bossi, born in 1941, is a charismatic leader and an excellent orator. Bossi has been politically active since the 1960s. For a short time, he was a member of the *Communist Party*. Bossi had always been convinced that the LN needed organizational roots in order to have a successful political future. Since

93 Some important publications: Biorcio, La Padania Promessa; Diamanti, Bianco, rosso, verde ... e azzurro; Ignazi, Partiti politici in Italia; Pallaver, Die Lega Nord und die Konstruktion Padaniens, pp. 111-125.

the foundation, he multiplied its central ports in society using an organizational model similar to that of the *Communist Party*. Besides supporting and friendly structures, he made the LN's local enrooting (mayors, elected councilors, see infra) one of the most efficient bases of communication with the voters. In contrast to his main competitor, i. e., Sergio Berlusconi's *Forza Italia*/PDL, the LN is a party with a tight organizational structure of staffers and reliable members. Since the end of the 1990s, it has won numerous new activists. At the time of the 2009 European election, it had an estimated 100,000-130,000 members.[94]

A gigantic system of symbols, structures, and rituals was created, among them a flag for Padania invented by the LN ideologists. In addition, the LN created its own media, fake institutions, and a network of associations.

The non-existing state of Padania established its parliament "http://www.parlamentodelnord.biz". The LN publishes the daily "La Padania", "http://www.lapadania.com", and communicates by Radio "Padania Libera", "http://www.radiopadania.net" and TV "Tele Padania", "http://telepadania.portals.twww.tv". The "Padanian associations" gather activists of the movement. A comprehensive list of these structures can be found on the site "http://www.associazionipadane.com". It names 12 social organizations, six cultural associations, three formations dedicated to security and touristic issues, five sports clubs, and five miscellaneous ones.

The wish to defend the interests of the North and to oppose Roman centralism would probably not have been sufficient to ensure the parliamentary survival of the LN. A corruption scandal ("Tangentopoli") had induced a great loss of confidence in the established parties. The collapse of the traditional political system left a vacuum new political groups like LN have occupied to this day.

The LN celebrated its first big electoral success at the 1992 parliamentary elections (8.6 %). The 1993 reform of the electoral law introduced the direct election of mayors. This resulted in the strengthening of LN, which had demanded this reform for years. In the following years, many LN representatives were elected mayors, especially in smaller Northern Italian towns. At the 1993 local elections, the party received 38.8 % of the vote in Milan and provided the mayor.

In 1993, Silvio Berlusconi created the new party *Forza Italia* (FI). It severely threatened the LN's electoral strength. The talented populist agitator Berlusconi addressed the citizens disappointed by the political class and the established parties and encouraged them to speak up (again) against the Roman parties of the past. Defending neo-liberal policies, he advocated the retreat of the state, tax relief for employers, and the reduction of bureaucracy. All of these issues were also referred to by Bossi. The FI's strength was its national implantation while Bossi refused any cooperation with (even regionalist) parties of the South.

94 The official membership: 1992: 112,400; 1993: 147,297; 1994: 167,650; 1995: 123,031; 1996: 112,970; 1997: 136,503; 1998: 121,777; 1999: 123,352; 2000: 120,897; 2001: 124,310; 2002: 119,753; 2003: 131,423.

At the 1994 national elections, Bossi was forced to form an electoral alliance (called *Polo della Libertà*) with Berlusconi's FI in order to secure a strong representation of the LN in parliament.[95] The election ended with a slight loss of votes of LN (8.36 %). However, due to its alliance with Berlusconi, it held 17 seats in parliament. The LN was in a difficult strategic situation. Associated with power and appointing ministers from its own ranks, the party was forced to give up its fight against "Rome". The party changed from a fighting league ("Lega di lotta") into a governing league ("Lega di governo"). Internal tensions were stifled by Bossi who made full use of his leadership. The FI's growing strength in the polls translated into corresponding results at the 1994 European elections. While the LN reached 6.6 %, the FI received 30.61 % and 27 MEPs. Bossi realized that he was trapped. Therefore, in December 1994, he provoked the fall of Berlusconi's government. Until the 1996 elections, together with the center-left parties, LN supported Lamberto Dini's technical government.

In 1995/1996, the issue of federalism lost its mobilizing power for the LN because every party proposed reforms. The LN decided on a headlong rush and demanded the independence of the Northern regions. It changed its name from "Lega Nord - Italia federate" (Northern League - Federalized Italy) to "Lega Nord - Per l'indipendenza della Padania" (Northern League - For Padania's independence). Thus, LN had isolated itself within the political system.

At the 1996 parliamentary elections, LN run against the two alliances Ulivo and Polo delle Libertà and celebrated the biggest victory of its history (10.1 % on the national level, 20.5 % in the North, 59 MPs). Between 1996 and 1998, the LN kept up its political isolation in principle but acted quite pragmatically supporting the center-left government's efforts to make Italy fulfill the Maastricht criteria and introduce the Euro.

Bossi was facing a strategic dilemma of whether or not to leave his isolation. The electoral battle for the 1999 European elections ended with a defeat (4.49 %, 4 MEPs). In 2000, Bossi decided to form an alliance with FI. One year later, both parties ran under the roof of the center-left alliance Casa della Libertà together with the Unione dei Democratici Cristiani e Democratici di Centro (UDC) and the *Alleanza Nazionale* (AN). The 2001 parliamentary elections brought about another LN defeat (3.94 %, 30 MPs). However, Berlusconi needed the LN votes for his governing majority and offered it three ministerial posts, one of them to Bossi.[96] Thus, for several years, LN was weakened by its participation in government.

At the general elections of April 9/10, 2006, Prodi's center-left alliance L'Unione won a comfortable majority in Parliament. LN - in spite of its alliance with the regionalist Southern party *Movimento per le Autonomie - Alleati per il Sud* (MpA) - remained below the 5 % barrier (4.58 %, 26 MPs).

95 In the South, Berlusconi formed an alliance with Gianfranco Fini's MSI (Polo del Buongoverno). Bossi had refused to run together with the MSI.
96 Umberto Bossi became Minister for Institutional Reform.

On January 28, 2008, Prodi submitted his resignation. At the 2008 general elections, LN, led by Bossi with a strong hand, was back on the political stage in its Northern strongholds (8.3 %, 60 MPs). The poor results of the Prodi government, general dissatisfaction with the political class, and the conflictual fusioning of *Alleanza Nazionale* and *Forza Italia* to *Popolo della Libertà* were the decisive factors. The electoral transfers show the LN drawing almost one million of votes to the detriment of FI and AN.[97] The sociography of the LN electorate illustrates its roots in every social sphere: merchants and artisans - 13.5 %, workers - 11.3 %, employers - 10.5 %, civil servants - 7.5 %, housewives - 5.8 %, retired persons - 6.6 %.[98] Corresponding with its electoral success, the LN received four ministerial posts. Umberto Bossi became Minister for Reform.

Until the 2009 European elections, Bossi and his team successfully submitted proposals concerning internal security issues and restrictive immigration regulations. The voters were evidently grateful and turned the European elections into a great success of the party (10.2 %, 9 MEPs). The June 2009 regional and local elections, too, ended with excellent results. The number of LN mayors rose from 202 in 2004 to 363. Nevertheless, this process of reinforcement stopped in 2010. Especially at the 2011 local elections, the LN suffered from its alliance with Berlusconi. The scandals and the crisis of the alliance *Popolo della Libertà* due to the breaking away of many former AN MPs give the impression that the Italian political system may be on the eve of a new transformation. The Berlusconi era is most likely nearing its end. Bossi has to find a political line enabling the LN to stem the tide and resist the progress of the left in Northern Italy.

Marta Machiavelli analyzed the idea of Padania which besides various "territorial projects" has always been at the bottom of LN's politics and ideology.[99] LN postulates the existence of a "Padanian people or nation" whose culture was destroyed and whose rights were stolen by the ethnic majority of the "Southerners". One discovers a double ideological construction: the strangers (the South, but also non-Italian immigration) and the Padanians. This is a difficult attempt; the LN concedes a "deficit of identity": "no common language in Padania (as in Catalonia), no religious specificity (as in Ireland), no political unity in the past".[100] LN ideologists collect and invent cultural and historic elements to be classified "Padanian". These "Pandanian elements" in turn need to be presented to the voters with the help of Padanian associations and by mobilizing the public and the media. Marta Machiavelli speaks of a strategy of the "daily plebiscite" in favor of Padania to enable the Padanian project to domi-

97 See Pallaver, Die Lega Nord, p. 122.
98 Ibid.
99 See Machiavelli, La Ligue du Nord et l'invention du "Padan", available at: http://www.ceri-sciencespo.com/publica/critique/article/ci10p129-142.pdf.
100 Ibid.

nate Northern Italy culturally and politically. It is a form of right-wing Gramscism.

The construction of a Padanian identity also requires the "production of the stranger", i. e., Southerners, but also migrants regardless of their origin. Marta Machiavelli quotes Umberto Bossi who suspects the arrival of migrants to be a "global conspiracy" orchestrated by the United States against "the peoples", "an Islamic conspiracy against Christianity, a conspiracy of the Vatican lacking seminarians, a conspiracy of big business (supported by the right-wing parties) looking for cheap labor, and a conspiracy of the left on the lookout for new proletarians susceptible to giving them their vote".[101] Quite rightly, she stresses that the LN is "the only Italian party to explicitly use the xenophobe discourse" and that it thoroughly exploits this issue.[102] To escape the accusation of racism, LN turns to ethno-pluralism and the thesis of the necessity to "respect cultural diversity".

The Padanian model is that of a Europe of peoples, consisting of regions, and fighting the "Islamic invasion". The major form of resistance is culturalism as suggested by Samuel Huntington. According to LN, it is impossible for secularism and Islam to co-exist because the Islamization of Europe implies the destruction of the Christian cultural references. Islam is presented not only as a religion but also as an intolerant and blood-thirsty Weltanschauung. Therefore, Muslim immigrants are invaders who need to be fought. Bossi invokes the "right of cultural self-defense" as a "natural reaction" facing migration.[103] This explains the LN's reconciliation with Christian fundamentalist currents, especially those inspired by Mgr Lefebvre. On the other hand, in accordance with the theoretical approach of GRECE, LN affirms true racism to be found in the "destructive thought and action of globalism aiming to build a global, Anglophone, and totalitarian village on the ruins of the peoples with the tool of a global commercial subculture".[104] The political implications are evident: All individuals are fundamentally conditioned by their ethnic or national affiliation. Assimilation is impossible.[105]

During the 2009 European election campaign, LN quite visibly leaned towards the ideology of cognation and active xenophobia. Even though there is much evidence of violent racist acts of LN members against immigrants, it is also clear that Bossi's project refrains from the type of violence used by the fascist party. Based on the theses of the New Right, his approach is a meta-politi-

101 Ibid., see Bossi/Vimercati, Processo alla Lega.
102 The "National Alliance", a party with a fascist past, has moved towards conservatism and turned away from racism even though its discourse of illegal immigration is still a very harsh one.
103 Ibid.
104 Ibid. See also Mussa (Ed.), Padania, identità e società multirazziale.
105 See Taguieff, Face au racisme.

cal and cultural one. This explains the LN's everyday political pragmatism concerning its alliances with Berlusconi's party and the AN.[106]

To sum up, the phenomenon of the LN can only be understood in the context of the collapse of the Italian political system which is unique in Europe. The emergence of new post-communist, post-fascist, right-wing populist, ecologist, and regional actors enabled the LN to enroot itself in Northern Italy because it responded to the desire of a large population group for a new and modern Italy. Typologically, the LN is very close to the Austrian FPÖ, the Swiss SVP, and the French FN. This holds true for the organizational principles, the key role of the head of the party, and security, anti-migration, anti-European, anti-globalization, and anti-American issues. Like FN or FPÖ, the LN is elected by employers as well as workers and businesspersons. In the North, it can be considered a people's party. It obviously shares certain programmatic aspects (a mix of neo-liberal positions, social regionalist concepts and theses of the New Right) with FPÖ and FN. But there are also differences: While the LN has always clearly dissociated itself from fascism, neither FPÖ nor the FN have done this, at least originally. Objectively, the Italian extreme right plays practically no role in politics. This is why the LN can spread its national-populist, security-centered, and xenophobe message with the specific intellectual construction of an imaginary Padanian nation opposed to the Italian one.

3.2 Vlaams Belang

For decades, Belgium has been torn by strong economic and social tensions coupled with a language dispute between Walloons and the Flemish people. A high unemployment rate (2008: 7.8 %), the economic imbalance between rich Flanders and the economically severely depressed Wallonia, strong legal (2008: 13 %) and illegal immigration, a very pronounced xenophobia among the population,[107] and wide-spread discontent with the established parties and the political elites promoted the emergence of a powerful extreme right. Until 2004, this latter was embodied by the *Vlaams Blok* and since then by its political heir, the *Vlaams Belang* (VB). Even though Belgium is suffering from a multifaceted crisis, the welfare state is still solid, with influential trade unionism in spite of its extreme fragmentation.

The Belgian political landscape has some unique features. The crucial phenomenon is the linguistic conflict and its effects on the political system. Since the end of the 1970s, there have been no national political parties in Belgium

106 See Lega Nord, Manifesti, available at: http://www.leganord.org/ilmovimento/manifesti.asp.

107 See Maddens/Billiet/Beerten, National Identity and the Attitude towards Foreigners in Multi-national States, pp. 45–60.

except on the extreme left.[108] The history of the *Vlaams Blok* and its successor *Vlaams Belang* can only be understood in the context of the Flemish movement uniting almost every social and political trend of the Flemish society. Flemish nationalism is only one of its aspects.[109] The Flemish movement organizes itself in different political and institutional projects. Some of them strive for a federal structure within the frame of the Belgian state. Others plead for the independence of Flanders and the end of Belgium. In the past, Flemish right-wing extremism was always linked with Flemish nationalism. But since 2007, the elections in Flanders have shown these two currents to be different.

The Flemish movement was originally a linguistic response to the francization of Belgium after the independence of the country in 1830. In the 1930s, the economic crisis and the rise of the European fascisms affected Flemish nationalism in an anti-democratic and authoritarian way. In October 1931, the Verbond der Dietse Nationaal-Solidaristen - Union of Diets National Solidarists was founded, and two years later the Vlaams Nationaal Verbond, VNV (Flemish National Union) which was inspired by German national socialism and later collaborated with the occupying power.[110] After the defeat of the German Reich, this collaboration and the fact that some Flemish nationalists had joined the Waffen-SS and fought on the Eastern front were heavy burdens. Radical and anti-Belgian Flemish nationalism was discredited and disappeared from the official political scene. It survived in networks of former collaborators and combatants at the Eastern Front who had founded the Verbond van Vlaamse Oud-Oostfrontstrijders in 1951. But there was no organized political representation of Flemish nationalism. Its first and foremost action was historical (revisionism); collaboration was redefined as one aspect of the fight for Flemish emancipation. The networks strived for the political and ideological rehabilitation of their supporting the Germans during the war.

In the 1950s, another variation became dominant: cultural nationalism expressing itself mostly in the linguistic battle and the emphasis on Flemish culture. In 1954, the federalist and democratic Christelijke Vlaamse Volksunie was founded which later changed to the *Volksunie* (*People's Union* -VU) dissolved in 2001.

In the post-war period, several militant organizations were set up: in 1949, the fascist militia VMO (Vlaamse Militanten Orde - Flemish Militants Order), and in 1976, the forward thinking cell Were Di, the activist group Voorpost, the Nationalistische Studentenvereniging (Nationalist Student Association - NSV). They had only a few hundred members but they supplied the first members of the *Vlaams Blok* and especially the necessary cadres. In December 1978, the party was founded by Karel Dillen (1925-2007). He was an "ideological link" between the pre-war and the post-war periods.

108 See Dujardin/Dumoulin/Gérard/Van den Wijngaert (Eds.), Nouvelle Histoire de Belgique.
109 See Gijsels, Le Vlaams Blok; Govaert, Les griffes du lion.
110 See "Collaboratie in Vlaanderen", available at: http://www.go2war2.nl/artikel/584.

The *Vlaams Blok* was a right-wing extremist party.[111] Its organizational structures reminded of "dinosaur parties" like the FN. It was rigidly controlled and centralized. Karel Dillen was chairman for life until he stepped down voluntarily in 1996. His successor Frank Vanhecke remained chairman of the successor party *Vlaams Belang* until 2004. As for the membership, the party had about 12,000 members in 1999 and 17,544 in 2002.

In the 1990s, the party celebrated one victory after the next. It received its best score at the 2004 elections of the Flemish Parliament (24.2 %, 32 seats). On the national level, it only competed in the Flemish part of Belgium and in Brussels. In 2003, it received 11.7 % and 18 seats at the Chamber of Representatives.[112] When the party changed its name, the *Vlaams Blok* had 3 MEPs (2004), 18 seats at the Belgian Chamber (2003), 5 senators (2003), 32 MPs at the Flemish Parliament (2004), 54 seats in regional councils (2000), 461 local councilors in 163 communities (2000), and 73 seats in the new councils of the district of Antwerp (2000).

The *Vlaams Blok* disbanded on November 14, 2004, and was re-founded with the new name *Vlaams Belang* shortly after a decision of the Belgian Court of Cassation: On November 9, the court had pronounced several associations linked with the *Vlaams Blok* guilty of racism and sentenced them to heavy fines. This verdict endangered the public subsidies of the *Vlaams Blok*. For this reason, the party changed its name and modified its statute and program erasing all legally incriminating phrasings.[113]

The 2009 membership of the *Vlaams Belang* is not known. In 2006, the party gave the figure of 22,350 members - to be considered with caution. The members are organized in five provincial governments, 20 regions, and 198 local bodies.[114] The party has its highest degree of organization in the province of Antwerp and in the Brussels-Capital Region. Bruno Valkeniers, the chairman, is its central figure. However, tensions run high within a party torn between traditionalists and reformers.[115] Furthermore, the chairman, a lawyer, is not as strong a personality as his predecessors and his charisma seems limited. Filip Dewinter (whip of the VB group at the Flemish Parliament) and Gerolf Annemans (whip of the VB group at the Chamber) are the strong personalities besides the chairman.

To finance its activities, the party receives membership dues and state subsidies. The federal public endowment (election period beginning 2010) amounts to 1,601,522.60 € (Chamber and Senate). The VB groups of the Chamber and

111 See De Waele/Rea/Delwitt, L'extrême droite en France et en Belgique; Witte/Scheepers, En Flandre, pp. 95-113; Mudde, Extremismus in den Niederlanden und in Flandern, pp. 242-256.

112 See Billiet/Witte, Attitudinal Dispositions to Vote for a "New" Extreme Right-wing Party, pp. 181-202; Swyngedouw, National Elections in Belgium, pp. 62-75.

113 See Cour de cassation (Belgique), Arrêt P.04.0849.N, 9 November 2004, available at: http://jure.juridat.just.fgov.be/pdfapp/download_blob?idpdf=F-20041109-13.

114 See http://www.vlaamsbelang.org/12.

115 See http://resistances.be/vbzizanie04.html; http://resistances.be/vbdeclin.html.

of the Senate receive 1,167,067.11 €. The party has the reputation of using its means in ways differing strongly from the other Belgian parties. It has practically no expenditures for technical staff or a study center. While the PS declares about 90 full-time job equivalents and the Francophone ecologists about 15, the *Vlaams Belang* only confirms two. Most of the available resources are invested in permanent campaigns (billboards and pamphlets). They continue between elections and all year round. This is the only party to apply this strategy in Belgium.

The ideological offer of the *Vlaams Blok* was rooted in national solidarism embodied by an authoritarian state and unchallenged historical revisionism.[116] Still, the success of the party depended on other topics and on its protest strategy. There are three key issues: the will to give Flanders the Flemish independence (with Brussels its capital), the denunciation of pro-Belgian elites and traditional parties, and finally, the outright rejection of immigration. These issues have been kept on the agenda of the *Vlaams Belang*, but the tonality and intensity have changed.

The *Vlaams Blok* considered the Flemish nation an ethnic community with members genetically linked by blood. This nation cannot be escaped from nor joined. The Flemish state is the essence of the nation. It is based on organic and hierarchical principles. Ethnic homogeneity is imperative and makes independent Flanders a white nation. The authoritarian state is responsible for the well-being of the people. Political pluralism, stateless liberalism, and Marxism are enemies of the Flemish nation by nature. This vision implies the elimination of the parliamentary system because conflicts of interest fought out there contradict the general interest. Every citizen has a clearly defined place in state and society. His/her individual rights are accorded but secondary to the collective right which ranks first. In exchange, the state protects its ("true" Flemish) citizens and is committed to offering them a high standard of living and social benefits. Solidarity between the social spheres, sexes, and age groups is the ultimate principle. The Flemish model is a society with conservative morals and strong ties with church, family, and children. Deviations are not accepted. Solidarism and the principle of national preference entail a regulation of the economic system. The elimination of social conflicts strips trade unions of their legitimacy.

Immigration, especially of Muslims, is presented as a machine to kill the peoples. Its stop is considered a necessary first step to be followed by the foreigners being returned home. The party was hostile against the liberal EU and demanded a Europe of nation states in the body of a confederation of independent nations but with close ties in the fields of economy, military, and security.

After the foundation of the *Vlaams Belang*, supplementary conflict lines were added to the party program.[117] The party has not only taken to a pronounced

116 See Spruyt/Borstels, Stel dat het Vlaams Blok.
117 See Ivaldi/Swygedouw, Rechtsextremismus in populistischer Gestalt, pp. 121–143; Swygedouw/Ivaldi, The Extreme Right Utopia in Belgium and France, pp. 1–22.

anti-establishment populism, but also welfare chauvinism and latent Christian traditionalism. Flemish traditionalism has been fading into the background. In 2009, *Vlaams Belang* is an Islamophobic party with strong security, ecological, morally conservative, and economically liberal overtones. It is concerned about a social policy benefitting only "true" Flemish people. The language of the present program was toned down and resembles Danish or Dutch programmatic texts.[118]

The party strives for an independent Flemish state with Brussels its capital. It insists in the stop of immigration due to former difficulties of integrating foreigners with a Muslim background. Islam is denounced to be incompatible with basic Western values like the "equality of men and women, freedom of speech, and the separation of church and state". For aliens and immigrants who "reject, ignore or fight" assimilation, a "return policy" must be developed. The local vote for foreigners should be abolished.[119] As for internal security, the party advocates "prevention", "firm reaction", and harsher sentences. "Zero tolerance" must be the basic principle. Police presence must be reinforced.[120]

The economic policy of the *Vlaams Belang* is liberal but the state remains in control of economic life. The party strives for fiscal autonomy of Flanders and wants to lower the tax rate.[121] Social security must remain "a task of the government". Privatization must be stopped. Every citizen must have free access to all social services. Retirement pensions must be "solid" and the Flemish state must enable and support its citizens to "purchase their homes. To this end, inheritance tax, registration fees, and VAT should be further reduced".[122] Families form a "bond of solidarity between generations, between past and future".[123]

The Dutch language is affirmed to be "an essential part of the cultural and national identity". It must be the obligatory "administrative and court language". Moreover, Dutch ought to be a full and official working language of the EU.

The *Vlaams Belang* wants to operate existing nuclear power plants and prepare the construction of the next generation of them. The party professes its interest in ecological topics and opts for waste separation and recycling. Nature reserves are to be protected and expanded.[124]

With regard to the institutions, the party supports referenda, for example on voting rights for foreigners, the legalization of drugs, or the accession of Turkey to the EU.[125] For obvious legal reasons, the *Vlaams Blok* was careful to avoid the impression of being an anti-Semitic party: It did not want to run the risk of

118 See "Het programma van het Vlaams Belang", available at: http://www.vlaams-belang.org/21.
119 See "Immigratie: Europa voor de Keuze", ibid.
120 See "Veiligheid en justitie", ibid.
121 See "Een beter vlaanderen voor een lagere prijs", ibid.
122 See "Een sociale politiek", ibid.
123 See "Respect voor het leven", ibid.
124 See "Milieu, ruimtelijke ordening en mobiliteit", ibid.
125 See "SOS democratiesos", ibid.

being banned. The *Vlaams Belang*, in the wake of its de facto reorientation towards an Islamophobic political line, decided to make Israel and the Jewish communities allies of its fight against the Islamization of Europe. At Antwerp, for example, the contacts between the party and the Jewish community are very close. Geert Wilders wants to create a sort of "International" of the anti-Islam parties. In December 2010, he visited Israel together with Heinz-Christian Strache, chairperson of the *Freedom Party of Austria* (FPÖ), Filip Dewinter of the *Vlaams Belang*, René Stadtkewitz of the German party *Die Freiheit* (*Freedom*), and Kent Ekeroth of the national and anti-Islamic *Sweden Democrats* party. The group met with Jewish settlers on the West Bank, discussed "strategies against Islamic terror", and visited the Knesset. During the trip, the delegation issued the "Jerusalem Declaration" (linguistic errors and mistakes: sic): "After the totalitarian systems of the 20th Century have been overcome, the human race currently looks for a new global totalitarian threat: fundamentalist Islam. We see ourselves as part of the worldwide struggle of the defenders of democracy and human rights against all totalitarian systems and their accomplices. We are at the forefront of the fight for the Western democratic community of values. [...] We reject cultural relativism, which tolerated under the pretext of respect for other cultures and traditions that people, especially non-Muslim minorities restricted in parts of the Muslim cultural sphere in their right to liberty, equality and participation are. [...] We are committed to the humanistic ideals of the Enlightenment, an absolutely necessary historical phase of development, Islam has not yet passed. Terror, no matter by whom and for what purpose it is applied to reject completely [...] Israel is the only real democracy in the Middle East [...] Without any restriction, we are committed to the existence of the State of Israel within secure and internationally recognized borders. Similarly, the right of Israel to defend itself against any aggression, especially against Islamic terror to accept".[126]

At the 2007 general election, the party stagnated at its 2003 level obtaining 12 % and 17 seats in the Chamber. The European elections ended with its defeat. Compared to 2004, it lost almost 300,000 votes and dropped to 15.9 % among the Flemish electorate (-7.3 %). Two competing Flemish parties celebrated fair results: The *Nieuw-Vlaamse Alliantie* - N-VA (9.88 %, 1 seat) and the *Lijst Dedecker* (7.28 %, 1 seat). Both formations belong to the democratic camp. But each of them occupied some ideological topics of the *Vlaams Belang*. The N-VA argues for a Flemish Republic that must be a member of a European confederation and combines both left and right-wing policies.[127] It is concerned with ecological issues while its economical outlook is a liberal one. The *Lijst Dedecker* was founded in 2007. At the general elections on June 10, 2007, it received 6.5 %. In a moderate way, it brought forward a series of issues also essential to the *Vlaams Belang*: opposition to the accession of Turkey to the EU, introduc-

126 See "Jerusalem Declaration", available at: http://britishfreedom.org/jerusalem-declaration.
127 See http://www.n-va.be/standpunten-n-va.

tion of direct democracy with binding popular referendums, total freedom of opinion.[128]

At the 2010 general election, the *Vlaams Belang* suffered a defeat (-4.2 %, 12 seats in the Chamber). The analysis of the electoral transfers shows that the *Nieuw-Vlaamse Alliantie* profited from the weakening of the VB. The *Lijst Dedecker*, however, could not confirm its electoral 2007 and 2009 breakthrough (*Lijst Dedecker*: 150,577 votes, 2.31 %, 1 seat; *Nieuw-Vlaamse Alliantie*: 1,135,617 votes, 17.40 %, 27 seats).

Which are the motives and reasons for the *Vlaams Belang* vote? According to Frédéric Falkenhagen, it is an expression of the fear of precarious material conditions, weak social integration, a xenophobe attitude, fears of immigration and the future, dissatisfaction and distrust of the elites, and of the established political parties and powers.[129] In 2009/2010, the *Vlaams Belang* is an ethno-regionalist interclassist party with a diverse and heterogeneous social base. Almost every social class is represented.

Table 13: Sociology of the VB voters (in %)

	VB
Self-employed persons	6
Middle class, managerial staff	-
White-collar middle class	21
Middle-aged housewives	8
Blue-collar retired persons	16
Precariat	27
Students	9
Atheists	11

Source: Falkenhagen, Les électorats ethno-régionalistes en Europe occidentale.

Strikingly enough, higher employees with managerial functions avoid the *Vlaams Belang* while 21 % of the clerical workers belong to its electorate. Its biggest electoral group is the precariat (27 %) which one can assimilate with the working class.

The regional and European elections of June 7, 2009, were analyzed in view of the voters' motives.[130] This survey reveals that the financial crisis, social secu-

128 On the positions of the List, see http://www.ldd.be/nl/onze-standpunten-762.htm.

129 See Falkenhagen, Les électorats ethno-régionalistes en Europe occidentale : Etude comparée en Bavière, Ecosse, Flandre et au Pays de Galles, Doctorat de Science Politique, Paris 2010, available at: http://ecoledoctorale.sciences-po.fr/theses/theses_en_ligne/f_falkenhagen_scpo_2010/thesef_f_falkenhagen.pdf .

130 See Deschouwer/Delwit/Hooghe/Walgrave (Eds.), Les élections régionales du 7 juin 2009.

rity, and unemployment were key issues in Flanders. In Flanders, 32.9 % considered the financial crisis the most important issue (36.8 % of the VB electorate). VB voters are worried by crime (16.8 %, Flanders: 8,2 %), social security (12.6 %), and unemployment (10.5 %). Immigration (8.4 %) and state reform (5.3 %) register astonishingly low.[131] Belgium has plunged into a permanent political crisis since the collapse of the Leterme government on April 19, 2010. The situation seems blocked in the long run because the two communities have difficulties living together.

Continuing its anti-migration line, the *Vlaams Belang* is still in troubled waters. Structurally, one of its chances is the possible crisis of the Euro. The support of Greece is a problem many voters are worried about. On the other hand, since the electoral rise of the N-VA, the *Vlaams Belang* has been suffering from aggravating internal tensions and a relevant electoral decline. It has lost its hegemony on the nationalist Flemish discourse, and is left with nothing but its Islamophobia. To maintain the control of a party losing influence, VB fundamentalists led by the tandem of Filip Dewinter and Gerolf Annemans, neutralized and totally defeated their "pragmatic" adversaries. The latter had defended the idea of forfeiting the cordon sanitaire isolating the party in the political arena for more than 20 years. They wanted to reach agreements with other formations and form government coalitions in order to share power, at first on the local, later on the regional levels. This strategy had been applied by Gianfranco Fini in Italy. It enabled the foundation of a new populist and democratic right-wing party, the *National Alliance* (*Alleanza Nazionale*). Filip Dewinter and Gerolf Annemans, however, have been relying on the historical ideological heritage of the party and a strategy of "wait and see".

In the context of the present crisis, the future of the *Vlaams Belang* depends on the future institutional "success" on the federal level of Bart De Wever's N-VA. If the N-VA does well, the VB might enter a phase of permanent decline. Dewinter has placed a bet: He has decided to wait for the return to electoral strength of the *Vlaams Belang* after the arrival of the first former supporters disappointed by the N-VAs measures in government. This strategy resembles that of the FN and the "Marine Le Pen effect" menacing the re-election of President Nicolas Sarkozy. Hoping for a "glorious future", led by Filip Dewinter, the VB has decided to stay true to its demagogical, Islamophobic, and anti-establishment style. Due to the lack of a populist alternative on the left, it will continue to seduce a fringe of the electorate of the working and middle classes disappointed by the political elites and the established parties.

131 Ibid.

IV. Eastern Europe: A different right wing?

To understand the situation in Eastern Europe, we have to look at the past. After the change from the former people's democracies to liberal democracy and market economy, several groups emerged that were at the same time populist, ultranationalist, and xenophobic. They formed parliamentary factions and sometimes supported government coalitions whose ideological coherence was not always evident (especially in the case of Slovakia). This is how the names of the following parties slowly became known: *Slovak National Party*; *Greater Romania Party* in Romania; *National Union Attack* in Bulgaria, the *League of Polish Families*, *Self-Defence of the Republic of Poland*, or *Jobbik - Movement for a Better Hungary*.

The electoral results of these parties have differed widely. In Poland, for example, the *League of Polish Families* enjoyed a breakthrough followed by rapid decline. Finally, there are countries that have so far - at least until 2009 - escaped the phenomenon of radicalization, for example, the Baltic countries and Slovenia. The electoral situation has definitely been profoundly different.

1. Case studies - East

In this volume, the situation in Bulgaria and Romania is presented.[132] There are strong similarities with Hungary: the formations there are right-wing extremist. The SNS, by contrast, seems to differ typologically even though the parties show common aspects.

1.1 The Slovak National Party

Slovakia is a small country with 5.4 million inhabitants, among them a strong Hungarian minority. It has a classic parliamentary and multiparty system. No party can expect to be the only winner of elections. For this reason, since 1993, the number of coalition governments has multiplied.

At the general elections of June 17, 2006, the *Social Democratic Party* (*Smer - sociálna demokracia* - SMER) chaired by Roberto Fico came out ahead with 29 % (+15 % compared to 2002). The strong breakthrough (11.7 %) of the *Slovak National Party* (*Slovenská národná strana* - SNS) was the decisive fact of this election marked by very low participation (54 %). Appointed Prime Minister, Robert Fico decided to form a government coalition with the SNS and the *People's Party - Movement for a Democratic Slovakia* (*Ľudová strana - Hnutie za demokratické Slovensko* - ĽS-HZDS). The populist right wing party of former Prime Minister Vladimir Mečiar (from 1994 to 1998) had received

132 See Meznik/Thieme, Against all Expectations, in this volume.

8.8 % of the vote. This left-right government gave rise to many questions in Europe because of the xenophobe positions of the SNS (especially concerning the Hungarian and Romani minorities) and the authoritarian excesses of Vladimir Mečiar's government between 1994–1998.

The 2006 elections were largely a referendum on the liberal economic reforms introduced by Dzurinda's Christian-Democratic administration since 1998: the 19 % flat tax for individuals and companies alike, the privatization of several State corporations, and the abolition of free healthcare. These measures of "consolidating" public finances caused strong anxieties in the lower social strata. Besides a considerable unemployment rate, in 2008, the average Slovak had to live on less than 900,000 crowns (242 €) per month in spite of the steadily growing cost of living and the expensive partly privatized health insurance. SMER, with its slogan "A more social Slovakia" promised to put an end to Dzurinda's reforms.

Dana Huranova's analysis of the 2006 elections[133] is also valid for the 2009 European elections. They took place in a sound economic situation nevertheless characterized by increasing collective anxieties about the future. From 2008 to 2009, the economic situation deteriorated strongly: The growth rate dropped almost 10 % from 6.2 to -4.7 % while unemployment rose from 9.5 % to 12 %. The public deficit nearly tripled from -2.3 % to -6.8 %, while public debts increased from 27.7 % to 35.7 %.[134]

The SMS won 5.55 % and 1 MEP. The Slovak society was pervaded by a feeling of deception by politics. This is indicated especially by the shockingly low turnout (19.64 %). This is an "electoral sanctioning of a government which has not reacted to the expectation of the population to correct the negative social effects of the economic transformation".[135] Huranova considers the profound political changes in Slovakia in 2006 the consequence of "the discontent of the populations the majority of them feeling left behind on their own by a transition and reforms which only a tiny fringe was able to profit from".[136] Social problems are extremely important: 50 % of the respondents list unemployment, 31 % name the quality of healthcare, 29 % poverty, and 27 % the living standard. The issues democracy (4 %), environment (5 %), and women's rights (4 %) play hardly any role. In April 2006, 46 % of the Slovaks judged the development of their society favorable. 50 % were convinced it was bad.[137]

Concerning the EU, the study concludes that "the Euro-optimism [...] does not compensate the disappointment by politics". A very large majority of Slovaks is in effect pro-European. In 2006, more than 60 % considered Slovakia's EU membership "a good thing". 71 % affirm that this has been advantageous to the

133 See Huranova, L'opinion publique et la société civile en Slovaquie, available at: http://www.ceri-sciencespo.com/archive/july07/mem_dh.pdf.
134 See http://portal.statistics.sk.
135 Ibid., p. 22.
136 Ibid., p. 2.
137 Ibid., p. 10.

country (53 % of all Europeans). The distrust of policymakers and the lack of alternatives explain the low participation of the Slovak voters. The country has suffered from a phase of "democratic depression".[138] Founded in December 1989, the SNS profited from this general situation. Chaired by Ján Slota, it has been an important actor within the political system since Slovakia's independence on January 1, 1993. Slota is a charismatic but very controversial party leader. He has a past as a petty criminal and seems to have been an informer of the communist political police. The SNS functions like the democratic formations. Most right-wing extremists who dream of man-hunting violence against minorities organize themselves outside the party in paramilitary formations. The political borderlines between extremist activists and SNS-members may sometimes be blurred. But the party - as an organizational body - is not involved in the violent anti-Romani actions. It contents itself with verbal provocations.[139]

The electoral program of the SNS "We are Slovaks. A Slovak Government for Slovak People"[140] shows a "national, Christian, and social" political orientation. Apart from the pronounced hostility towards the Hungarian minority and the established political elites, this document presents an interventionist, Christian fundamentalist, and conservative view of the world. Extremist political positions do not appear there but rather in ordinary everyday statements of the SNS.

According to the party, the country is afflicted by "poverty" and growing "social insecurity". This in turn has caused the "cultural and spiritual devastation of the society" and led to a "deep moral crisis of Slovakia". A growing number of citizens have lost their "linkage with family, town, nation and state, enterprise, national or state institutions". The political class is considered corrupt and in a "servile subordination to external influence". It is the "historical aim and duty" of the SNS "to rid Slovakia of material, social, and spiritual decline". The nation state must be defended. The party wants to change the EU "into a community of independent and sovereign states".

The Slovaks are called upon to re-discover their roots and identity in order to "counterbalance the risks of globalization of the culture and the creation of the global pseudo-values". Christianity is presented as the moral orientation.[141] A strong state is needed for "directing the economic policy on setting the priorities and on setting a goal-directed allocation and grouping of bank, capital and public sources, and sources of the European Union to strengthen the regional cohesiveness of Slovakia by means of the economic, social and cultural development".[142]

138 Ibid., pp. 17-18.
139 See Mudde, Racist Extremism in Central and Eastern Europe.
140 See "Election programme of the Slovak National Party", available at: http://www.sns.sk/wp-content/uploads/2010/03/sns_program_english.pdf.
141 Ibid., pp. 38-39.
142 Ibid., pp. 3-4.

On the international scene, the SNS opposes the EU membership of Turkey, and is highly critical of the USA and the State of Israel. But there is no proof that its anti-Zionism includes a virulent anti-Semitism. The SNS has many anti-Semitic members but it does not make anti-Semitism one of its ideological reference points.[143]

This hyper-nationalist program is a sort of Slovak-style hardcore Gaullism. The façade cracks in everyday life: Violent hostility against the Romani people, anti-homosexual standpoints and statements are sometimes accompanied by perceptible sympathy of the fascist past and its leader Josef Tiso, who was executed as a war criminal.[144] But still, these indicators do not suffice to make this party a hard right-wing extremist formation like *Jobbik*.

The SNS' participation in government became a trap for the party. In 2010, it declined massively (from 11.73 % to 5.07 %, from 20 to 9 seats). The 2006–2010 period was especially interesting because the cooperation of a left party with nationalist and xenophobe formations could be observed. To this day, this "red-brown" experience has remained unique in Europe, and chances are slim that it shall be repeated.

1.2 Jobbik

The breakthrough of the Hungarian extreme right can be explained by the economic crisis and the austerity of the cure imposed on the country by the Socialist government in 2006. After its 2006 fiscal slippage, Hungary had to freeze salaries, cut the civil servants' 13th monthly salary, and raise the VAT. Hungary and Greece had committed the same mistake: consuming without saving. In 2008, the global crisis hit Hungary. The Forint, the Hungarian currency, was devalued. 1.7 million Hungarians (i. e., 1 in 5 inhabitants) found they were trapped by foreign currency loans with mechanically increasing repayment rates. Having had to resort to an IMF credit of 20 billion €, Hungary found itself put under surveillance. The Hungarian voters were to punish the government for its economic errors.

After the collapse of communism in Hungary, the nationalist extreme right tried to organize itself. The Hungarian *Justice and Life Party* (*Magyar Igazság és Élet Pártja* – MIÉP) led by the writer and journalist Istvan Csurka[145] (born 1934) enjoyed a modest political breakthrough in 1994 (1.58 %), and an electoral one in 1998 (5.47 %, 14 MPs). MIÉP's ideological offer consisted of aggressive and revanchist nationalism, deep anti-communism, anti-capitalism denunciating the

143 See Roth, Antisemitism and Racism, available at: http://www.tau.ac.il/Anti-Semitism/asw2008/slovakia.html.

144 See Kopanic, The Legacy: The Tiso Plaque Controversy, available at: http://www.ce-review.org/00/11/kopanic11.html.

145 For Csurka's biography, see http://www.doksi.hu/faces.php?order=DisplayFace&id=403.

liberal globalization, and radical anti-Semitism/anti-Zionism. In 1998, the right-wing conservative party FIDESZ (*Hungarian Civic Union/Fidesz – Magyar Polgári Szövetség*) came into power (28.18 %). Under its leader and Prime Minister Viktor Orbán, it formed a governing alliance with the smaller *Hungarian Democratic Forum*, and the *Independent Smallholders' Party*. It also established a tactical alliance with the MIÉP group in Parliament. Formally, MIÉP remained a member of the political opposition. But it supported FIDESZ at votes. This alliance provided positions in the media and administration for MIÉP members. It lost political credibility and collapsed at the 2002 national (2.2 %) and 2004 European elections (72,203 votes, 2.3 %).[146] FIDESZ lost the 2002 elections in a very close race: Its 41.07 % were surpassed by 42.05 % of the *Hungarian Socialist Party* (*Magyar Szocialista Párt*). At the 2006 national elections, FIDESZ won 42.03 % but still remained on the opposition benches.

After the defeat of FIDESZ and the decline of MIÉP, students of the Right-Wing Youth Association (*Jobboldali Ifjúsági Közösség – Jobbik*), nationalist MIÉP cadres, but also FIDESZ members considered the foundation of a new party much more radical politically, but just as economic and social. Finally, in October 2003, the party *Jobbik* (*Jobbik Magyarországért Mozgalom/Movement for a Better Hungary*) was founded. Dávid Kovács became its chairperson remaining in office until 2006. His successor is Gábor Vona. Vona's motto is "Order, prosperity, awakening. It is but a question of willpower". Born on August 20, 1978, Vona is a charismatic leader, a good orator, and communicator. He studied history and psychology at the Loránd-Eötvös-University, worked as a teacher for a short time, then went into business and has been working as product manager.[147] Vona lists two especially formative points of his family's history: He was born into a farming family repressed by the communist regime. This explains his profound anti-communism. The second point is the death of one of his grandfathers in a battle against the Red Army during the Second World War. Thus, he explains the devotion to his country the continuation of his family "tradition".

Chaired by Vona, *Jobbik's* electoral successes were impressive. Hostile to the EU, the party boycotted the 2004 European elections. For the spring 2006 elections, it ran in an electoral alliance with MIÉP named MIÉP-*Jobbik* Third Way Alliance of Parties. But the alliance missed the 5 % barrier (2006: 2.2 %). *Jobbik* enjoyed a breakthrough at the 2009 European elections (14.77 %, 3 MEPs), and at the 2010 general elections (16.67 %, 47 seats).

Since its foundation, *Jobbik* has built a tight organization dominated by the chair. Meanwhile, it is working efficiently everywhere in the country. *Jobbik*'s success can only be understood against the background of the nostalgia of Greater Hungary. A true nationalist subculture has existed and paved the way for *Jobbik*. Among others, there are bikers' clubs, fans of certain soccer clubs

146 See Tóth/Grajczjar, The Emergence of the Extreme Right in Post-socialist Hungary.
147 See Gábor Vona's official biography on the web: http://www.jobbik.hu/node/6380.

and of "national rock". Music plays an extremely important role. "National rock" has been popularized by the extreme right radio and TV station "Pannon" "http://www.pannonrtv.com/PannonRTV/news.php". Every year, its fans attend the Magyar Sziget festival, a sort of nationalist Woodstock on the banks of the Danube some miles from Budapest. At this concert, *Jobbik* and Magyar Gárda (Hungarian Guard) activists are omnipresent.

The Hungarian Guard was founded on April 25, 2007, as a non-armed paramilitary group with Vona its president. The symbolism and style of the guard imitate the *Arrow Cross Party - Hungarist Movement* (*Nyilaskeresztes Párt - Hungarista Mozgalom NYKP*), a Hungarian national socialist party.[148] The number of its co-opted members wearing a uniform is not known (2007: 630 members, more than 4,000 candidates).[149] The guard has been mostly firing up emotions against the Romani people in Hungary. It has multiplied the number of provocative rallies through villages and quarters lived in by Romani people. On December 16, 2008, the Metropolitan Court of Budapest disbanded the organization.[150]

The 2006, 2009,[151] and 2010 programs of *Jobbik* incriminate Hungary's enemies: communists, the post-communist elites, international companies, big business, cosmopolitism, globalization, political liberalism, corrupt politicians, the EU, and the axis "Tel Aviv-Washington-Brussels". This anti-elites and anti-system discourse echoes the disappointment of the lower classes more than 20 years after the fall of the communist regime, the rise of Euro-skepticism 6 years after joining the EU, and the rejection of a political class the young people consider cynical and corrupt. This ideological offer does not only answer the expectations of a part of the lower classes. It is also compatible with the ultra-nationalism with strong anti-Semitic features existing in Hungary since the 1920s. The increasing strength of *Jobbik* depends on this double anchor, but also on the rise of a new and young generation of politicians who have successfully linked nationalist ideology with today's collective frustrations. Young people, including students, think they are living in a blocked society without a future. *Jobbik* attracts them because it is the only party leading an anti-establishment discourse in a country where the extreme left does not exist.

At the European election campaign, the party characterized itself as "a high-principled, conservative, radically patriotic, Christian party with the fundamen-

148 See Szöllösi-Janze, Die Pfeilkreuzlerbewegung in Ungarn.

149 See "Interview mit Gábor Vona, Chef der Ungarischen Garde: 'Árpádflagge ist kein Pfeilkreuzler-Symbol'". In: Budapester Zeitung, 17 September 2007, available at: http://www.budapester.hu/index.php?Itemid=26&id=607&option=com_content&task=view.

150 See "Gericht löst Garde auf". In: Der Standard, available at: http://derstandard.at/1227288986751. The court argued that the activities of the Guard were directed "against the human rights of minorities as guaranteed by the Hungarian Constitution".

151 See "Jobbik 2009 Program", available at: http://www.jobbik.hu/sites/jobbik.hu/down/Jobbik-program2009EP.pdf; "Jobbik 2006 Short Program", available at: http://www.jobbik.hu/rovatok/egyeb/a_jobbik_2006-os_rovid_programja.

tal goal of protecting Hungarian values and interests". Its presumed radicalism is that of a "shift of paradigm, of the point of view necessary in every field".[152]

The party proposes two types of measures: The first is anti-capitalist or a corrective of capitalism, the second - classified as "moral rearmament" - is the fight against decadence. Concerning economic and social issues, *Jobbik* proposes a 90 % tax rate on the profits of foreign banks, and the ban of the purchase of land by foreigners. Hungarian industries are to be protected and supported by the state. The population must have access to healthcare. The system of education has to be reformed from a national point of view.

Jobbik pleads for the Hungarian state to focus on Christian values, families, and authority. It wants to combine moral and religious education and opposes abortion and homosexual marriage. The party presents itself the only defender of Hungarian families and is homophobe. It declares left-wingers and liberals, journalists, and the media enemies of Hungary. These "traitors" work for occult powers and the Jews and need to be neutralized. The media as well as the administration must be purged politically.

Jobbik's program is directed specifically against the about 700,000 Romani people (about 7 % of the population) living in Hungary. The "Romani problem" is presented as an ethnical and economic one. The key word is "gypsy criminality". According to *Jobbik*, the non-integration of the Romani people legitimizes their social exclusion and discrimination.[153]

The party is also anti-American, anti-Zionist, and anti-Semitic. Since 2003, its discourse has relied on the old anti-Semitic prejudice of the interwar period. Banks and media are said to be in the hands of the Jews. After having used communism to dominate Hungary, they have now perpetuated their control supported by multinational companies and banks from the East Coast of the US. This anti-Semitism spreads all the more easily because after 1990, there has never been a true national debate on the history of the country since 1920. Still, Vona seems to have realized the dangers of this anti-Semitism isolating the party among the other formations of the extreme right. Strache's FPÖ, for example, refuses any contact. In 2009, *Jobbik* distanced itself from holocaust deniers among its supporters who had demonstrated in front of the German embassy in Budapest. Afterwards, it called the Shoah a "tragic event from which lessons are to be drawn".[154] But the phrasing remains vague, and *Jobbik* has not solved its problem of anti-Semitism.

152 See "Vona: What Do We Mean by Radicalism?", available at: http://www.jobbik.com/hungary/3138.html.

153 See the interview with Krisztina Morvai "Aperçu du parti hongrois Jobbik", available at: http://fr.altermedia.info/general/apercu-du-parti-hongrois-jobbik_30098.html.

154 Quotes taken from: "Ungarns Parteien zur Europawahl 2009 - Teil 7: Jobbik", available at: http://www.pesterlloyd.net/2009_22/0922jobbik/0922jobbik.html; "Holocaustleugnung und offener Rassismus in Ungarn", available at: http://www.pesterlloyd.net/2009_17/0917holocaust/0917holocaust.html.

One of *Jobbik*'s major claims links nationalist dialectics with Hungarian foreign politics. *Jobbik* wants the revision of the demarcation of the 1920 Treaty of Trianon.[155] In 2007 and 2008, the Hungarian Guard had symbolically crossed the Hungarian-Slovak border and occupied Slovak territory. In its nationalist agitation, *Jobbik* denounces this treaty in terms reminding of those used by the German extreme right against the Treaty of Versailles in the days of the Weimar Republic. Besides these claims of a "Greater Hungary", *Jobbik* insists in an ethnic revision of the European borders.

Jobbik differs from the other extreme right European parties in the question of international relations. Its positions remind of Haider's FPÖ in 2002. *Jobbik* is the only European extreme right party supporting the idea of the rapprochement of Turkey and other Muslim countries. It considers the Turkic countries (Turkey, Kazakhstan, Azerbaijan, Uzbekistan, Kyrgyzstan, and Turkmenistan) "cousins" and an "ancient civilization which is a branch of the same tree, sharing the heritage of the Huns". The strengthening of the relations with Turkey is considered an economic and cultural chance. This implies for *Jobbik* to refrain from anti-Muslim and anti-Turkish propaganda. A part of its membership advocates the idea of Turkey's accession to the EU and suggests a referendum to be held together with the next European elections.[156]

Jobbik believes in a "multi-polar world". Márton Gyöngyösi, MP and vice-president of *Jobbik*'s committee on international affairs, declared his party's intention of an opening towards Russia and the Slavonic peoples.[157] The opening towards the East is matched by its highly critical position of Hungary's membership of the EU. *Jobbik* favors a "European co-operation" within the framework of a Europe of nation states. It rejects the present political union as a "centralist, bureaucratic alliance of states".

The 2010 general elections remolded the political landscape. Viktor Orbán and FIDESZ returned to power with a "super-majority" of two thirds of the seats in Parliament. This enables Orbán to change the constitution. The Hungarian left was completely annihilated. The *Hungarian Socialist Party* MSZP won only 59 of 386 seats in Parliament. Victor Orbán's new government has to deal with manifold challenges. This could increase *Jobbik*'s popularity. One of FIDESZ's electoral promises was to put an end to the policy of austerity imposed in 2006. Orbán must reconcile this promise with the budgetary rigor required

155 The Treaty of Trianon determined that Hungary lost two thirds of its territory shrinking from 325,411 km^2 before the war to 92,962 km^2 after the signing of the treaty. The treaty also decided on the separation of roughly 3.2 million Hungarians from their mother country. See Romsics, Der Friedensvertrag von Trianon.

156 See "Interview with Gábor Vona about Turkey, China and the Zionist Lobby", available at: http://www.hungarianambiance.com/2010/11/interview-with-gabor-vona-about-turkey.html.

157 See "Márton Gyöngyösi, Member of the Hungarian Parliament: 'Le radicalisme du Jobbik est contagieux'", 2 January 2011, available at: http://fr.novopress.info/75633/marton-gyongyosi-depute-hongrois-%C2%AB%C2%A0le-radicalisme-du-jobbik-est-contagieux%C2%A0%C2%BB.

by the International Monetary Fund (IMF) and the EU. The international institutions expect Hungary to continue its unpopular efforts to arrive at a 3.8 % budget deficit. The question of Hungarian minorities living in neighboring countries (primarily in Romania, Slovakia, Serbia, and the Ukraine) is also a delicate one. Orbán needs to get to grips with Hungarian nationalism and the imperatives of European cooperation with Hungary's neighbors. On the other hand, he considers *Jobbik* a political enemy to be fought with constitutional weapons which could imply legal steps against the party. One of the first is the ongoing inquiry of the financing of *Jobbik*.

2. An overview of the East

Comparing the programs of the winning parties in the post-communist world, it becomes evident that all radical parties share key programmatic lines centering on the rejection of elites (of communist origin, imported from the Diaspora, or graduates from the present universities). The original distrust of the Western social and economic model has changed with the modernization of the economies. Under the impact of the 2008/2009 crises, it has developed into a radical opposition to globalization and capitalism. The rejection of communism (its bureaucratic variation of the real existing socialism) as well as political liberalism (hyper-liberalism as well as social liberalism) marks the view of the world of those groups. The opposition to the EU has also intensified, especially concerning its extension to Muslim countries (Turkey, but also Bosnia). *Jobbik* is an exception in this case. These parties claim to defend the social classes who did not profit from the change of system (retired persons, workers, unemployed, but also young people without hope of finding a job according to their qualification).

Endemic corruption, the relative ineffectiveness of public decision making, and the political and economic predominance of the oligarchies brought about a weariness of parliamentary democracy which has lately changed into an authoritarian temptation. The parliamentary systems, the parties, and the political elites are denounced as the most anti-national elements.

Even if the communism of before 1989 has completely lost its attraction, certain nostalgia makes itself felt for the minimal material security offered by the communist regime. The right-wing extremist groups promise the redistribution of the national riches "stolen by the oligarchs", and the reestablishment of a social system protecting "the people" from the effects and costs of globalization.

The topic of homeland security is also very present. It is presented as a problem to be solved by reinforcing the police and making a lax justice "toe into line". All this is accompanied by a "moral rearmament of the people". Everywhere, the Romani people are presented as a criminogenic population.

The offer of the return to national identity constitutes the central port of the different social classes approached by these groups dealing with the glorification of the national past, an intolerant concept of the nation based on ethnos, religion (Catholics against Orthodox Christians), and language. The historical models are irredentist, like Greater Romania or Greater Hungary, and accompanied by territorial claims aiming at the integration of minorities living outside the present borders. Between 1991 and 2009, the situation has changed from a vague hostility towards "ethnic minorities" (Hungarian, Turkish, Slovak, Romanian, Ukrainian, etc.) to a serious discussion of "ethnic cleansings" and transfers of populations. This phenomenon is also present in the Baltic countries towards non-Baltic people, especially Russians. A certain fascination of the Orthodox (Bulgaria, Romania) or Catholic Church (Poland) can be observed. They are considered guardians of national identity and a force of resistance to Western materialism and moral decadence.

"Sick" elements must be excluded from the "healthy" national body: homosexuals, pedophiles, but also people corrupting morals and family. The discussion of exclusion extends to ethnic minorities and is coupled with a pro-birth and biologist (healthy and athletic youth) and ethno-cultural (popular art against decadent art) line.

On this level, we discover the major differences of these forms of right-wing populism and their Western counterparts: The anti-immigration aspect is practically nonexistent, except for some rather marginal discourses of "the Chinese invasion" or "Negro dealers". The notion of an "internal enemy" replaces the dangers of migration. But in the East and in the West, the source is the same: the longing for national identity.

Two further ideological lines of the extreme right make for a great deal of their attraction in those countries. They do not exist – or at least not in the same form or intensity – in Western Europe: anti-Semitism (including "anti-Semitism without Jews") and racism directed against the Romani people. The hostility, even hatred of minorities, like the Turkish one in Bulgaria, or the Hungarian one in Slovakia, has developed over the years. In the 1990s, it was most of all a cultural incompatibility. But meanwhile, it has taken on the form of classic racism. The majority of right-wing extremist groups are also anti-American and anti-Zionist, as well as hostile towards NATO. Radical Polish and Baltic right-wing groups, however, are pro-American and pro-NATO because of their hostility towards Russia.

Furthermore, in the East there is a high level of racist and anti-Semitic violence. The present movements often emphasize the historical continuity between them and their predecessors from before 1940. In the West, this is only the case with parties or small groups of Falangists, Italian fascists, or the German NPD.

A significant part of the population has reacted to these topics, especially when confronted with serious economic and social problems. But on the long run, these issues do not seem to be sufficient to guarantee the permanent growth of the extremist forces, much less their taking over power.

The charisma of the leaders is an important feature. The specificity of the individual trajectory often consists of communist commitment as a youngster and the further development to the extreme right (Corneliu Vadim Tudor in Romania, Volen Siderov in Bulgaria). Their personal history enables these "leaders" to play on several political stages. Wherever charismatic political personalities are lacking (Baltic countries) or have disappointed (the Kaczyński brothers in Poland), the extreme right weakens.

With regard to the electoral system, the relative instability of the political systems and the multiplication of actors (parties split) make new formations appear and compete with the extreme right on numerous topics. The Slovak SMER is a left populist party and a good example. We also observe the "radicalization" of democratic conservative parties like FIDESZ, or the movement of the Kaczyński brothers until 2007.

Finally, the number of marginal groups on the right of the existing parties (skinhead and neo-Nazi groups, paramilitary formations) is growing. They are often very violent and worry voters who are concerned about solutions of existing problems rather than hoping for a nationalist revolution.

It is also an irony of history that the economic crisis of 2008/2009 finally (momentarily?) broke the dynamism of the extreme right in the countries of the post-communist world with the exception of Hungary. Even if voters tried to send an anti-capitalist/anti-globalization message, they still tended to put more trust in the established parties, just like in the West. The central question is how long this trend will last in view of the economic effects of the "crisis management" on the populations and of their sometimes violent reactions, like in Latvia.

Further factors are also benefiting this political trend: There is a lack of historical memory work necessary to justly appreciate the national past (especially the period of 1930-1945, but also the time of real-existing socialism). The policy of the EU and of international financial institutions like the World Bank gives rise to the (often justified) feeling of increasing inequalities. The phenomena of clientelism and clanism obstructing life in the democratic system are also important issues in favor of the extreme right. For all these reasons, the extreme right has a future as a protest force against the liberal societal and ideological model in post-communist countries.

V. Comparison

In Western and Eastern Europe alike, large population groups adhere to the New Radical Right (NRR) parties, wherever their ideological roots. The diversity and intensity of this support may well remind of the 1930s, but the context is completely different: The historical fascisms and national socialism were ideologies aiming at the destruction of democracy and the building of a national, völkisch, and racialist "new order". By contrast, most of the NRR groups present themselves as "normal" actors of the political system embracing democratic values. While this "democratic pretension" needs to be verified in the West, in Eastern Europe these parties are clearly extremist.

Due to their specific character, i. e., the European dimension and the proportional representation with the 5 % barrier, the 2009 European elections constituted a political "event" strongly differing from national, regional, and local elections. The non-participation of powerful parties like the SVP (*Swiss People's*

Table 14: Attitude of the parties toward the political system

Country	Party	fascist/ national-socialist anti-system party	non-fascist anti-system party	semi loyal right-wing party	predominantly loyal right-wing party
	The "Dinosaur parties"				
Great Britain	BNP	+-	+-	+-	-
France	FN	-	+-	+	-
Austria	FPÖ	-	+-	+-	+-
Greece	LAOS	-	+-	+-	-
	The Nordic model				
Finland	PS	-	-	-	+
Denmark	DF	-	-	-	+
Netherlands	PVV	-	-	-	+
	Regionalist parties				
Belgium	VB	+-	+	+-	+-
Italy	LN	-	+	+-	-
	Eastern European parties				
Slovakia	SNS	-	-	+	+
Romania	PRM	+-	+-	-	-
Bulgaria	Ataka	+-	+-	-	-
Hungary	Jobbik	+	+-	+-	-

Explanation: + feature present; - feature absent; -+ feature partly present.

Party) makes them an incomplete account of the real strength of the New Radical Right. This fact has to be kept in mind in order to be able to deduce the existence of a "winning formula".

Comparing the results of the European and national elections since the 1990s, a rupture becomes apparent in the beginning of the 21st century. Until then, in spite of numerous sociological definitions and analyses, the extreme right-wing parties had rather a clear-cut, generally extremist, racist, often anti-Semitic, and anti-system profile. They were "pariahs" confined to the fringes of the system. The ostracism of the democratic parties legitimized itself and depended on the "flaws" of the "fascist", "neo-Nazi", and sometimes violent and racist enemy.

Things changed - at least in the West - with the emergence or change of parties like Jörg Haider's FPÖ and BZÖ, and the breakthrough of the *Lega Nord*, the *Dansk Folkeparti*, the *True Finns*, or Wilders' *Partij vor de Vrijheid*. The populist and xenophobe right has refrained from violence and dissociated itself from the extremist scenes (skinheads, paramilitary groups, etc.). Thus, these parties became powerful political actors using hybrid strategies, mixing the practice and discourse of fundamental opposition to the "system" and to the elites in power with the participation in and association with them. Their considerable success at national, regional, and local levels has enabled them to act like this. The NRR managed to establish themselves in the political systems for several reasons. Their leaders had understood that they could not become permanent actors of the political systems without respecting its formal rules. The extremist aspects (violent action, historical or neo-Hitlerite benchmarks, anti-Semitism and negationism) were dropped as counter-productive or even dangerous (risk of ban). One of the last big parties to abandon negationism was the FN. Marine Le Pen turned against her father on this issue in 2011.

Facing this phenomenon, the extreme left/the left and the liberal and conservative right have reacted differently. To simplify strongly, on the left, and especially in communist parties with extreme left wings, anti-fascism has continued to consider the emergence of the NRR and xenophobe populisms an expression of the connection "fascism-capitalism" according to Dimitrov's theses. Lately, social democratic and socialist parties have begun to reconsider this problem, their recent analyses focusing on globalization and its effects. Still, they have remained intellectually helpless facing the "proletarization" of the xenophobe populist vote in France or Austria, for example.

The conservative parties have been just as scared by the electoral breakthrough of the NRR. The liberal parties have gambled on the return to the political normality of the past after the return to the economic optimum. The conservative parties - very often together with the Social Democrats - have been hunting for their defected voters and abstentionists who have returned to voice their discontent with the present economic and social politics and the de-politization of the mainstream parties ("the flavorless hotpot" of democracies). In order to win back the voters, the democratic parties have started to usurp the issues of security, and later of immigration. Under pressure of xenophobe populisms, a process of overbidding has begun, and even (in Denmark, the Netherlands, Austria, etc.) a virtual alignment on the hard line. In 2009, the defeat seemed to be complete. The radicalized voters often preferred the original over the copy (except in France where the Sarkozy effect still played a role at the European elections).

On the lookout for a new ideological battering ram, the conservative parties – the French *Union pour la démocratie française* (UDF), the German CDU/CSU[158] and the Austrian ÖVP rediscovered the nation and its correlate, namely identity. The central question concerns those who are "exogenic" due to immigration or "non-integration". France is a symptomatic example, but the Netherlands or Denmark act very similarly. Like at a chess game, the moves of the democratic parties have made the extreme right-wing formations position or reposition themselves.

The BNP is a prisoner of the British political system. But it has begun to change. Still, it remains a white power group in spite of its semantic and strategic modernization, deeply mired in a backward-looking British nationalism and dragging the millstone of nostalgia around its neck. But there are xenophobe and Islamophobic populist formations (Denmark, the Netherlands, Finland) who – except for these mobilizing issues – consider themselves democratic parties. They may aim at sharing power in a coalition government, supporting minority governments, or – as a soft opposition – "correcting" government decisions concerning social and immigration issues.

In the intermediate position (Austria, France, Italy, Belgium, in spite of regionalist elements of *Lega Nord* and *Vlaams Belang*), there are ideologically radical parties which still want to participate in government. Of these three categories, the first one of the BNP type can only hope for a future if it undergoes a long process of modernization. The second category has been flying from one triumph to the next, while the third experienced different destinies. The *Lega Nord* has participated in government but lost ground at the May 2011 local elections. The *Vlaams Belang* seems to be declining. The *Front National* under its new chairperson Marine Le Pen appears to win back the voters lost in 2007. The FPÖ enjoys an increase of its electoral power and might return to power in a coalition government with the conservatives of the ÖVP.

158 In spite of the absence of a powerful xenophobe populist party, the concept of a "Leitkultur" (dominant German culture) was the object of extremely intense discussions in Germany.

Table 15: Strategic profile

Country	Party	Ability to form an alliance with democratic parties	Legalistic orientation	Great importance of street protest	Connections to militant scenes	Great importance of a strategy of cultural hegemony
	The "Dinosaur parties"					
Great Britain	BNP	+-	+-	+	+	+
France	FN	+-	+	+-	+-	+-
Austria	FPÖ	+	+	-	+-	+-
Greece	LAOS	+	+	+-	?	?
	The Nordic model					
Finland	PS	+	+	-	-	+-
Denmark	DF	+	+	-	-	+-
Netherlands	PVV	+	+	-	-	-
	Regionalist parties					
Belgium	VB	+	+	+-	+	+-
Italy	LN	+	+	-	-	+
	Eastern European parties					
Slovakia	SNS	+	+	-	+-	+
Romania	PRM	+-	+-	+	+	+-
Bulgaria	Ataka	+	+-	+	+	+-
Hungary	Jobbik	-	+-	+	+	+

Explanation: + feature present; - feature absent; -+ feature partly present.

We have to assess the political impact beyond the correction or tightening of immigration policies of the xenophobe populist right of the Danish or Finnish type. Are they capable to impose basic ideological changes on the left and right-wing democratic parties within their national political system and on the European level? We cannot answer this hypothetic question yet. But the popularity of the ideologemes of the Danish, Belgian, or Dutch xenophobe populists has been increasing. The Danish model - the re-introduction of border controls in June 2011 - is met with approval from France, Austria, and Germany. It seems to confirm this hypothesis.

Which are the supporting ideologemes? In our case studies, we have highlighted some theses that are attractive for voters who have so far abstained or come from every political orientation to join the NRR.

Table 16: Programmatic profile

Country	Party	anti-homo-sexual	anti-Semitic	anti-Islamic	anti-Roma	neo-pagan	anti-clerical
	The "Dinosaur parties"						
Great Britain	BNP	+	-+	+	-+	-	-+
France	FN	+	+-	+	+	-+	-
Austria	FPÖ	-	+-	+	+-	-	-
Greece	LAOS	+	+	+	+	-	-
	The Nordic model						
Finland	PS	-	-	+	-	-	-
Denmark	DF	-	-	+	-	-	-
Netherlands	PVV	-	-	+	?	-	-
	Regionalist parties						
Belgium	VB	+	-	+	+	-	-
Italy	LN	-	-	+	+	+-	+
	Eastern European parties						
Slovakia	SNS	+	+	+	+	-	-
Romania	PRM	+	+	+	+	-	-
Bulgaria	Ataka	+	+	+	+	-	-
Hungary	Jobbik	+	+	-	+	-	-

Explanation: + feature present; - feature absent; -+ feature partly present.

The NRR groups criticize the inability of the elites and mainstream parties to listen to the people and their needs. In the West, democracy is not fundamentally challenged (no appeal to dictatorship) but it is denounced as blocked. The proposed model is that of a direct democracy letting the people decide. Left parties as well as liberal or conservative formations are accused of permissiveness and of imperiling the traditions and the identity of the community. Multiculturalism is the major enemy. Foreigners are presented as not assimilable. The NRR do not demand programs to promote integration. Tolerating pockets of exogenous cultures (ethno-pluralism) is out of the question. Instead, it is precisely the (peaceful) eradication of the unfamiliar, a sort of ethnic purification to be achieved by sending the "others" – especially non-Europeans – back to the countries of their origin. The intensity of this rejection may vary: Wilders, who has a Hungarian wife, has no problems with pizzerias while Bossi wants to send Southern Italians back home. Jean-Marie Le Pen's FN still believed in the value of "blood" making – if shed – an authentic Frenchman. Strache thinks the German language and culture and the deep roots in the "Heimat" make it possible to know who is an Austrian.

Country	Party	Christian	Christian fundamentalist	anti-capitalist	revanchist	strongly euro-skeptic
	The "Dinosaur parties"					
Great Britain	BNP	-	-	+-	-	+
France	FN	+	+-	+-	-	+
Austria	FPÖ	+-	+-	+-	-	+
Greece	LAOS	+	+	+-	-	+
	The Nordic model					
Finland	PS	+	-	+-	-	+
Denmark	DF	+-	+-	-	-	+
Netherlands	PVV	+-	-	+-	-	+
	Regionalist parties					
Belgium	VB	+	-	+-	-	+
Italy	LN	-	-	+-	-	-
	Eastern European parties					
Slovakia	SNS	+	+	+-	+-	+-
Romania	PRM	+	+-	+	+	+-
Bulgaria	Ataka	+	+-	+	+	+
Hungary	Jobbik	+	+-	+	+	+

Explanation: + feature present; - feature absent; -+ feature partly present.

Jean-Yves Camus holds that "one of the principal innovations of the formations of this new type is the construction of a political program of exclusion based on the values developed by the philosophy of Enlightenment".[159] But the notion of a party of a new type is valid only in the West and refers to a small group of parties (Denmark, Finland, Norway - the latter is not treated here). Wilders' PVV without members is most certainly the newest type. *Front National* and FPÖ, however, are classic member parties with an apparatus, even though the modernization of their structures is evident.

Camus' analysis of the Scandinavian and Dutch xenophobe populisms is relevant. They demand political and religious tolerance facing an Islam presented as a totalitarian ideology. They call for the defense of the equality of the sexes, women's rights including abortion, and the rights of homosexuals. There is no urgent appeal to moral conservatism and no return to what Germans nickname the "3K" (Kinder, Küche, Kirche - children, kitchen, church) even though there is concern about the demographic decline. The xenophobia of these formations

159 See Camus, La notion d'identité divise les droites, p. 4.

Table 17: Offer profile

Country	Party	Strong charismatic leadership	Effective campaigning	Attractive programmatic offer
	The "Dinosaur parties"			
Great Britain	BNP	-	+	+-
France	FN	+	+	+-
Austria	FPÖ	+	+	+
Greece	LAOS	+	+	+-
	The Nordic model			
Finland	PS	+	+	+
Denmark	DF	+	+	+
Netherlands	PVV	+	+	+
	Regionalist parties			
Belgium	VB	+-	+	+
Italy	LN	+	+	+
	Eastern European parties			
Slovakia	SNS	+	+	+
Romania	PRM	+	+	+
Bulgaria	Ataka	+	+	+
Hungary	Jobbik	+	+	+

Explanation: + feature present; - feature absent; -+ feature partly present.

and their Weltanschauung concerning the question of identity is essentially but not exclusively Islamophobic and shows their intolerance.[160]

The anti-migration aspect and the hostility towards Islam are not really new in Europe and would not have been sufficient for the present breakthrough of the NRR. The lower and middle class voters rallying around PVV, FN or FPÖ are driven by a second preoccupation, namely, the preservation of their social achievements, and the limitation of the European integration and liberal globalization perceived as threatening. The NRR has been devoted to a "social" discourse with its voters demanding stronger state control of the economy in order to preserve the achievements of the welfare state. The mainstream parties are accused of promoting an uncontrolled market anti-social by nature (accumulation of capital benefitting the rich, de-localization and unemployment, destruction of historical industrial structures, decline in salaries, precariousness). Here, we find the discourse of "those up there" against "us down here".

160 For an analysis of the Islamophobia in Europe in 2011, see "Common Concerns About Islamic Extremism: Muslim-Western Tensions Persist", available at: http://pewglobal.org/2011/07/21/muslim-western-tensions-persist.

Polls show that the working class (especially skilled workers) has become a supporter of the NRR. It seems to have abandoned communism and the left. The polls also show that the NRR has developed modules for communicating with the "proletariat". Lacking internal documents, we cannot say when the NRR realized its chances in the neo-proletarian milieu. The majority of the extreme right of the 1990s was anti-state, anti-bureaucratic, anti-fiscal, and economically quite liberal. Artisans, farmers, soldiers, and policemen were preferred partners. If these social spheres continue to vote FPÖ or FN, the (relatively) new development of the 21st century is the radicalization of the working class vote. In answer to this, the NRR has changed its profile into a (vaguely) left one.

This strategy has a double advantage: It is embarrassing for the social-democratic left, which has problems defying the critique of both communists and the NRR of having turned into the social-liberal representative of wealthy, well-educated urban voters profiting from globalization. The conservative parties have quite the same problems: All over Europe, they, too, supported the economic modernization and the transition to a post-industrial society, which led to the disappearance of industrial structures (heavy industry, coal mining, and textile industry) inherited from the 19th century. The conservatives are also embarrassed by the capacity of the NRR to seize the issues of security, of the value of work (a scheme which is also present at the left), and of the fossilization of the elites (the lack of renewal from the basis, from the people). In view of the present debates in Austria, France, and Germany concerning future presidential or general elections, one might assume the mainstream parties to be in a tight spot ideologically. The NRR parties offer a community-based model of "We together". Not only is it linked to the nation, but it is also enrooted locally and regionally ("Heimat", the linguistic regions). The mainstream parties do have to make some choices unless they want their electoral capital to keep eroding. The battle of the identity has begun and nobody knows the winner yet.

What happened within the political systems? The parties analyzed here profit from the de-alignment of the population from the established parties in the East and in the West. Their success, for example in Denmark or Austria, depends on their capability to articulate key issues of their ideology and introduce them into practical politics (immigration, defense of the welfare state, identity). There are special cases, regionalist parties like the *Vlaams Belang* or the *Lega Nord*. They add regionalist nationalism to these issues. The British example, articulated around a white power racialist position, remains a marginal case. In the East, the economic, social, and psychological context of post-communism, the instability of the political systems, and the lack of loyal standing voters are the reasons for the extreme right to be represented on the political stage by strong electoral parties (Bulgaria, Romania, Hungary, Slovakia), but also by forms of extremist militancy (militia, guards, skinheads, etc.).

Do the contexts in the East and West differ? Prima facie, the communist heritage seems to be the dominant factor with its attendant corruption, state capture of the ex-communists, collective disorientation and the voters' fear of the future. But one could also interpret the phenomenon of post-communism as a form of standardization of the political systems towards a common model for Europe: the change into a participatory democracy with free elections, the existence of a constitutional state, and the introduction of market economy lead to a continuing rapprochement of East and West. Due to the shortness of the post-communist period – two decades only, the phenomena of electoral and everyday protest (anti-Romani racism) are much more radical or extremist in the East than in the West.

Table 18: Opportunity profile

Country	Party	Strong center parties*	Strong right-wing populist alternative**	Depolarized party system***	Strong left-wing populist party****	(Dis)favorable initiating events
	The "Dinosaur parties"					
Great Britain	BNP	+	-	-	-	+
France	FN	-	-	+	-	+
Austria	FPÖ	-	-	+	-	+
Greece	LAOS	-	-	-	+-	+
	The Nordic model					
Finland	PS	-	-	+	-	+
Denmark	DF	-	-	+	-	+
Netherlands	PVV	-	-	+	-	+
	Regionalist parties					
Belgium	VB	-	+	-	-	+
Italy	LN	-	+	+	+	+
	Eastern European parties					
Slovakia	SNS	-	+	+	+	+
Romania	PRM	-	-	+	-	+
Bulgaria	Ataka	-	-	+	-	+
Hungary	Jobbik	-	+	+	-	+

* Growing percentage of votes of center-right and center-left parties.
** Growing percentage of votes of a right-wing populist alternative.
*** National government coalition of center-right and center-left parties
**** Growing percentage of votes of a left-wing populist alternative.

Besides the difference of intensity, is there a general explanation? Since the 1990s, Anthony Giddens has studied the impact of globalization on individuals, societies, and political systems.[161] He shows the processes of globalization to be so complex that they do not only induce change on the political and social level, like the success of right or left-wing populist parties. They have also provoked local and individual transformations. "Globalization is not a single process but a complex mixture of processes, which often act in contradictory ways, producing conflicts, disjunctures, and new forms of stratification. Thus, for instance, the revival of local nationalisms and an accentuating of local identities are directly bound up with globalizing influences, to which they stand in opposition".[162] In the light of this analysis, the success of parties like FPÖ and PVV, but also of *Jobbik*, are considered reactions to changes of the meso- and micro-levels. In this context, Wilders' offer of a Dutch identity, or Bossi's of a Padanian one is able to reach various social spheres (workers, lower classes, voters with a low level of education) having a hard time to adjust to globalization. In the 1990s, Herbert Kischelt,[163] too, presented a hypothesis to be tested in the face of the present situation: "The rise of the (New Radical Right) is no 'single-issue' phenomenon concerned only with immigration. To the contrary, the themes of racism and cultural intolerance are embedded in broader right-authoritarian political dispositions that are prominent among identifiable social groups. The postindustrialization of the occupational structure, precipitating a decline and restructuring of employment in the manufacturing sector and an expansion of personal service occupations, together with the growth of the welfare state that encompasses many personal service jobs have led to the rise of a dominant political division at the level of public opinions between left - libertarians - and right - authoritarians. Whether or not this cleavage is articulated and represented by existing or by new parties depends on the strategic behavior of the established moderate leftist and rightist parties. The strategic convergence of such parties and their alternation or coalition in government facilitates the rise of new more extreme parties with left-libertarian or right-authoritarian constituencies".[164]

Uwe Backes' contribution shows that this model does not explain the reasons of the defeat of the NRR in the East and in the West in the long term (Spain for example) or in the short one (Poland). Post-industrialization and the effects of globalization occur at different times in the East and in the West. Traditional milieus have disintegrated everywhere. The speed of this phenomenon has accelerated or slowed down the emergence of the NRR. Neither the solidity (the Netherlands, Denmark) nor the collapse of the welfare state (in the East, free healthcare and nursery systems and more or less full employment disappeared) alone explain this phenomenon. Certainly, the perception of a threat to the wel-

161 See Giddens, Beyond Left and Right.
162 Ibid., p. 5.
163 See Kitschelt, The Radical Right in Western Europe.
164 Ibid., p. 257.

fare state worries and later mobilizes voters. Mobilization intensifies as soon as the debate turns to the role of immigration as an accelerator of this danger.

Another aspect seems to be central: the convergence and de-ideologization of the established parties. The great coalitions or left-right minority governments as well as the acceptance of liberal globalization and its socio-economic implications (privatization, disappearance of civil servants, threat to social achievements, retirement benefits) by the conservative as well as the social-democratic camp stand for this. The voters have difficulties distinguishing the democratic left from the democratic right. This promotes the acceptance of the clearly more ideologized discourse of the NRR and leads to new and sometimes unexpected electoral decisions (Wilders' breakthrough in 2006, for example). It is somewhat astonishing that the established parties have not tried to re-occupy their specific ideological fields since the NRR actors have been present on the political market. Debates on the values of the left or the nature of conservatism have only been reinforced at the end of a longer or shorter period of intense rapprochement of the democratic parties. They try to neutralize the NRR by falling back on the largest possible majority consensus in the parliamentary, social, and often media fields (the phase of ostracism of the NRR).

This policy of containment has obviously failed in the West. The propriety of the democratic parties is to remain in power at the price of coalitions. To this end, they are forced to reduce the frictions with partner parties and concentrate on governance. This strategy could "work" if there were no regional or international crises of the system like in 2008/2009. Even in rich countries like Austria and Denmark, the economic problems induced many voters to consider this consensual governing fragile, threatened, and incapable of working on the long run and within the frame of the EU. Fear of the future and the visible rise of collective pessimism have paved the road and consolidated the NRR.

The media, too, play an important role in this process. For evident reasons, the ostracization was a failure in the West. If Jean-Marie Le Pen is somewhat repulsive because of his revisionist positions, Pia Kjærsgaard or Geert Wilders do not in the least remind of Hitler. Since Marine Le Pen has been the FN's chairperson, her strategy of smiling and distancing herself from the historical theses of her father has made the party surprisingly more acceptable and accepted in 2011 than in 2009. In the East, the NRR leaders are much closer to their historical "brethren". They are able to operate with media largely favoring the freedom of expressing even the most radical theses ("freedom of speech") as a form of rejection of the intellectual and media oppression in communist days.

There is yet another effect favoring the NRR. Since there are no deep basic conflicts among the mainstream parties, they have used the only possible strategy to distinguish themselves: the personalization of the election campaigns. But the chairpersons of many democratic parties are apparatchiks, often without charisma, and poor communicators. This is obvious in Austria or Denmark. Their NRR competitors are excellent communicators capable of "speaking the truth" and with evident charisma. Wilders, whom we were able to watch in Germany, is a model of this type even when speaking in a foreign tongue. One must have witnessed Strache's meetings and TV appearances to know how efficiently these NRR leaders denounce the elites as being "deaf and dumb" to the people's worries.

In the context of the dealignment of the political system, the present winning parties profit from the influx of protest voters and losers of modernization. This vote is essential for their appearance on the political market but insufficient for their establishment on the long run. This can be achieved with the additional influx of winners of modernization driven by fear of the future or by the wish to preserve an identity presented by the NRR parties as threatened by immigration, the EU, and the elites in power. The topic of (regional or national) identity combined with a highly affirmative social discourse is presently the most important argument. The democratic parties seem largely disarmed facing this semantic hegemony.

The Unsuccessful Parties – Ideologies, Strategies, and Conditions of the Failure

Uwe Backes

This contribution focuses on the far right-wing parties having had little success in the last European elections. In line with Patrick Moreau, success shall be defined as the ability to gain parliamentary mandates. The different barriers in the various member countries complicate the comparison somewhat. Yet there must be a threshold somewhere. For this reason, a significant point to be included for the evaluation of the conditions for success is the question whether the failure is connected to an upward or a downward trend in winning popular support.

The analysis is divided into four parts. The first part will briefly highlight the prospects of the different parties in the run-up to the elections. The second part will analyze the programmatic similarities and differences of the parties. The third part will consider the most important elements of their strategic approaches. The last section will deal with the reasons for their failure. Socio-economic and cultural framework conditions which are the subject of other contributions in this volume will mostly be ignored.The main focus will remain on the profile of offers and the (continuously moving) opportunity structures on the political market.

The investigation of this contribution will consider a broader field of right-wing parties, thus not limiting itself to those formations which may be understood as strictly "right-wing extremist" in reference to the clear-cut rejection of fundamental constitutional values and procedures in the manner they have found their way into the Treaty of Lisbon on the European level (Art. 2: "The Union is founded on the values of respect for human dignity, freedom, democracy, equality, the rule of law and respect for human rights, including the rights of persons belonging to minorities. These values are common to the member states of a society in which pluralism, non-discrimination, tolerance, justice, solidarity, and equality between women and men prevail"[1]). This way, more light can be shed on the interim zone between open democracy enmity and, for the most part, radical, though loyal to the system, critique of the system toward the

1 Consolidated Texts of the EU Treaties as Amended by the Treaty of Lisbon, Norwich 2008, p. 5 (Art. 2).

liberal democratic status quo. In no way does this deal with a merely academic issue but with a central problem for the existence and the degree of consolidation of the democratic constitutional states.[2]

I. Election expectations

The group of parties not successful in respect to the above definition is heterogeneous in view of the expectations in the run-up of the European elections. Several parties had regularly been so weak in previous national elections that they could hardly expect to be successful in the European elections (see Table 1). Still it must be admitted that in comparison to the national elections the increased desire to experiment at European elections and the voters' leanings toward protest has sometimes led to surprises. The Belgian-Francophone *Front National* (FN)[3] was founded under the impression of the election successes of the French in 1985. In the previous legislative periods, it was represented with a seat in the two chambers of the Belgian Parliament due to the Belgian voting system (proportional representation without barring clause). However, due to the low number of Belgian seats in the European Parliament (22) and the technical blocking effect (the mathematical relation between valid votes and the mandate number comes to a theoretical hurdle of approximately 4.5 %) connected with this fact, the FN could hardly count on any chances.[4] Former FN General Secretary Carl Lang's *Parti de la France* (PDF) was created in the wake of the protest against the surrender to Le Pen's daughter Marine assuming the party leadership. The PDF was just being built up and ran for the first time, it competed with the "mother-party" of Jean-Marie Le Pen. His FN had been represented in the European Parliament for several legislative periods. It had weakened, yet its reentry seemed plausible.[5] As for the German formations, a failure at the five-percent-hurdle was foreseeable, particularly since the *Nationaldemokratische Partei Deutschlands* (NPD), the most successful electoral power, which had been active since 1964 already, did not participate. Instead, although (only halfheartedly) supported by the NPD, the organizationally extremely weak *Deutsche Volksunion* of the Munich publisher Gerhard Frey (DVU; organized as a party since 1987), participated in the elections after having reached a strategic election agreement, the so-called "Germany Pact" ("Deutschland-Pakt"). The *Republikaner*, represented in the European Par-

2 Cf. Backes, Political Extremes, pp. 175–192.

3 Cf. Coffé, Do Individual Factors, pp. 74–93; Mielants, The Long-term Historical Development, pp. 313–334; Rochtus, Extremismus in Belgien, pp. 35–50; Swyngedouw, Country Report Belgium, pp. 59–79.

4 Cf. for the systemic conditions of the elections: The European Elections: European Parliament/Directorate General for International Policies (Ed.), EU-Legislation, National Provisions and Civic Participation. Study, Brussels 2009.

5 Cf. Backes, Extremismus in Frankreich, pp. 131–148; Camus, Der Niedergang, pp. 165–175.

Table 1: Score in the European elections 2009 and the last national parliamentary elections:

Country	Party	European elections 2009	Highest score in the national parl. elections	Last national parl. elections
Austria	Bündnis Zukunft Österreich (BZÖ)	4.6	10.7	10.7
Belgium	Front National (FN)	1.3	2.3	2.0
Germany	Deutsche Volksunion (DVU) Die Republikaner (REP) Nationaldemokratische Partei Deutschlands (NPD)*	0.4 1.3 –	0.1 1.9 4.3	0.1 0.4 1.5
France	Le Parti de la France (PDF)	0.1	–	–
Italy	Fiamma Tricolore - Destra Sociale (FT) Forza Nuova (FN)	0.8 0.5	2.4 0.7	2.4 0.3
Poland	Samoobrona Rzeczpospolitej Polskiej (SO) Liga Polskich Rodzin (LPR), Libertas Polska**	1.5 1.1	11.4 8.0	1.5 1.3
Portugal	Partido Nacional Renovador (PNR)	0.4	0.2	0.2
Slovenia	Slovenska Nacionalna Stranka (SNS)	2.9	10.0	5.4
Sweden	Nationaldemokraterna (ND) Sverigedemokraterna (SD)	0.04 3.3	0.1 2.9	0.1 2.9

* No candidacy of its own; support of the DVU in the so-called "Germany-Pact".
** LPR- application on the lists of the "Libertas Polska".

liament from 1989 to 1994 (REP; founded in 1983), were just as hopeless. Above all, this caused a splintering of the electoral potential on the far right.[6] The Italian right-wing parties found themselves in a similar situation on the other side of the occasional government parties *Alleanza Nazionale* (AN) and *Lega Nord* (LN).[7] Under the leadership of party leader Luca Romagnoli, the *Movimento Sociale - Fiamma Tricolore* (MS-FT), founded by the traditionally loyal Neo-fascists around Pino Rauti in the middle of the 1990's, formed an election alliance with the newly founded *La Destra* of the former AN-health minister Francesco Storace. However, they remained far below the four-percent-hur-

6 Cf. Jesse, Wahlen 2009, p. 110.
7 Cf. Caldiron, La destra plurale, pp. 80-89; Gallagher, Exit from the Ghetto, pp. 64-86; Höhne, Der Sieg der Demokratie, pp. 89-114; Ignazi, Legitimation and Evolution, pp. 333-349; Köppl, Extremismus in Italien, pp. 197-212; Newell, Italy, pp. 469-485; Padovani, The Extreme Right, pp. 753-770; Tarchi, The Far Right Italian Style, pp. 35-50.

dle. The splinter party *Forza Nuova* (FN), founded by the former active members of the organization Terza Positione, received an even weaker result. Due to the results in previous national elections, the chances of the Portuguese *Partido Nacional Renovador* (PNR; founded in 1999) and the Swedish *Nationaldemokraterna* (ND; founded in 2001) were judged similarly weak.[8]

Initially, another group of far right parties was not considered entirely without chances. This applied particularly to the *Bündnis Zukunft Österreich* (BZÖ) founded by the FPÖ-politician Jörg Haider of Carinthia in 2005. It had won 10.7 % of the votes at the National Assembly Elections in August 2008.[9] The death of the charismatic party chairman in a car accident several months later fundamentally changed the conditions of the alliance and essentially contributed to its comparatively weak results at the European elections. The BZÖ did not fail because of the statewide four-percent-hurdle but due Austria's low number of mandate (technical blocking effect approx. 5.8 %). Due to the increase in the Austrian number of mandates as a result of the Treaty of Lisbon coming into effect, the BZÖ was later awarded an additional mandate.[10] The two Polish parties, *Samoobrona Rzeczpospolitej Polskiej* (SO) and *Liga Polskich Rodzin* (LPR), which had occasionally belonged to the PiS-led government in 2006, remained entirely without representation. With their arguments they had essentially contributed to their own instability and carried off a devastating defeat in the advance re-elections in 2007. Incidentally, in contrast to the LPR, the political chameleon SO had only limited validity as a far right party since it shows a curious mixture of right and left programmatic elements.[11] Due to the importance of its national vote, the *Slovenska Nacionalna Stranka* (SNS), founded in 1991, actually also belongs to the more hopeful formations with a continuous parliamentary representation since 1992.[12] However, the technical blocking hurdle in Slovenia is especially high (approx. 14 %) so that, viewed realistically, the party could hardly entertain any hopes of a representation in Brussels. In contrast, the expectations of the *Sverigedemokraterna* (SD) looked more favorable. They showed an upward trend and were able to triple their votes from 1.1 to 3.3 %.[13]

8 Cf. Jalali/Pinheiro, Extremismus in Portugal, pp. 299–312; Zúquete, Portugal, pp. 179–198; Freitag/Thieme, Extremismus in Schweden, pp. 329–343; Lööw, Country Report Sweden, pp. 425–462.

9 Cf. Heinisch, Right-Wing Populism in Austria, pp. 40–56; Lux/Sommersguter, Das Jörg-Haider-Experiment, pp. 39–82.

10 However, the legal translation into practice took many months and had also not yet occurred in May 2011 so that the BZÖ top candidate Ewald Stadler remained Europe-political speaker in the Vienna National Assembly for the time being.

11 Cf. Moroska, Prawicowy populism a eurosceptycyzm, pp. 207–320; Moroska/Sroka, Extremismus in Polen, p. 292; Moroska/Zuba, Two Faces of Polish Populism, pp. 123–147; Pankowski, Die Liga der Polnischen Familien, pp. 147–163; id., The Populist Radical Right in Poland; Thieme, Hammer, Sichel, Hakenkreuz.

12 Cf. Bugajski, Political Parties of Eastern Europe, pp. 662–664; Mareš, Extremismus in Slowenien, pp. 361–375; Trplan, Slovenia, pp. 245–246.

13 Cf. Freitag/Thieme, Extremismus in Schweden; Lööw, Country Report Sweden; Widfeldt, Party Change as a Necessity, pp. 265–276.

Nevertheless, even overcoming the four-percent-hurdle would not have sufficed in view of the technical hurdle of 5.5 % (18 mandates). The Riksdagen-Elections of September 2010, where they entered the National Parliament with 5.7 % of the votes for the first time, proved that the party was advancing.

II. Programmatic profile

All the parties mentioned here mostly assign themselves to the "national camp" while professional observers locate them at the right wing of their respective party systems. In this respect, only the Polish SO, which is particularly difficult to classify, is a problematic case.[14] As, however, the occasional alliance of the flamboyant populist grouping with the LPR shows, its left actionist elements do by no means exclude an alliance with far right formations. A fundamental system-critical attitude and a profound Euroscepticism present a link. Beyond that, the unusual saturation with left and right program elements is seen as an East- and Eastern Middle-European specificity.[15] Nonetheless, revolutionary social program elements are also found in the NPD and the Italian FN. In a modified form, they are readopting a synthesis of right and left as well as nationalist and socialist ideas already known from the interwar period. Thus, this phenomenon is not only found in the post-communist party systems, regardless of its coming into effect there in an especially striking form.

A systematic comparison of the ideologically programmatic profile calls for extensive differentiations, also in regard to other points. As Table 2 shows, neither the historic classification to certain traditional strains, nor the kind of system critique voiced, draws an entirely uniform picture. Only few far right formations are ideologically closely connected to the fascisms of the interwar period.[16] They still apply the most to the Italian FN and the German NPD. Both of them, typically, tried to form a combine of right extremist groupings (European National Front), which less traditionally loyal formations avoided.[17] Even the Italian FT, which developed from the protest against the distancing from the fascist era that the MSI-majority around Gianfranco Fini felt to be too extensive, preferred to join a somewhat more pragmatically-acting alliance of European far right parties under the leadership of the French FN (Alliance of European National Movements). The Portuguese PNR also approached this as other formations of the alliance occasionally showed a liking for the authoritarian political world of forms (in this case that of Salazar's Estado Novo[18]). All the formations, also those more closely oriented toward the role models of the

14 Cf. Grün/Stankiewicz, Spielarten des polnischen Rechtsradikalismus, pp. 170-199; Pankowski/Kornak, Poland, pp. 156-183.
15 Cf. Thieme, Hammer, Sichel, Hakenkreuz.
16 Cf. Hlousek/Kopecek, The Far Right, pp. 181-202.
17 Cf. the contribution of Petra Vejvodová in this volume.
18 Cf. Jalali/Pinheiro, p. 308.

Table 2: Attitude of the parties toward the political system

Country	Party	Fascist/national socialist anti-system party	Non-Fascist anti-system party	Semiloyal right-wing party	Predominantly loyal right-wing party
Austria	BZÖ	-	-	-	+
Belgium	FN	-	+	-	-
Germany	DVU REP NPD	-+ - +	-+ - -	- -+ -	- -+ -
France	PDF	-	+	-	-
Italy	FT FN	+ +	- -	- -	- -
Poland	SO LPR	- -	- +	+ -	- -
Portugal	PNR	-	+	-	-
Slovenia	SNS	-	-	-+	-
Sweden	ND SD	-+ -	-+ -	- +	- -

Explanation: + feature is present; - feature is absent; -+ feature is partly present.

interwar period, experienced a certain ideological modernization and, like the German NPD, argued on the basis of ethno-pluralism, thus distancing themselves at least in official statements from a conventional ethno-centrism (with a hierarchy of peoples and nations).[19]

Considering the attitude of the parties on the fundamental values and rules of procedure of democratic constitutional states, several groups can be distinguished. A first group connects the close orientation on authoritarian/totalitarian role models of the interwar period with a clear anti-system attitude. This applies to the German NPD and the two Italian formations, the FT and the FN. Also parties like the Belgian FN, the German DVU, the French PDF, the Polish LPR, and the Swedish ND that show a greater distance to the historic fascisms, yet simultaneously strive for a fundamental system transformation, are anti-system parties in line with Juan Linz's well-known typology.[20] The parties of the first as well as the second group can be called right-wing extremists. In comparative research, those of the third and the fourth groups are frequently considered "radical right parties"[21] as they represent a decidedly "right"/"right-wing

19 Cf. Backes, Das ideologisch-programmatische Profil der NPD, pp. 301–316.
20 Cf. Linz, The Breakdown of Democratic Regimes, pp. 32–33.
21 Cf. for example Minkenberg, Die neue radikale Rechte; Mudde, Populist Radical Right Parties; Norris, Radical Right.

populist" position but appear more discriminating and reserved in their system critique. Parties, like the German REP for years, in which camp fights are carried on between the more moderate and the more radical wing groups, and which have different attitudes toward the constitutional democratic fundamental norms, can be considered "semi-loyal". The same goes for parties like the Slovenian SNS and the Swedish SD, whose originally harsh anti-system attitude has softened over the years, having undergone an - incomplete - acculturation process. The most advanced on this path seems to be the Austrian BZÖ, even if the party has continued to make a stand against the "system parties"[22] and has violated the ethos of fundamental human equality in its anti-immigration campaigns at times. It is often not easy to decide in which direction the scales tilt in the area of tension between verbal radicalism and political pragmatism.

Is it possible to reduce the parties mentioned to a common ideological, programmatic denominator? All of them, on the basis of a concept of culturally homogenous nation states, seem to adopt an excluding attitude toward certain minorities who, in part, have lived in the territory of the nation state or have, in part, newly immigrated. Here, most of the formations emphasize the ethnic affiliation assumed to be homogenous and therefore argue on the basis of ethnopluralism since ethnicities are considered equal amongst themselves. In contrast to Alain de Benoist's concept, they embrace to the idea of the nation state. Sometimes, the definition of ethnos implicitly transgresses its boundaries as, for instance, in the case of the German NPD (the German Germanic ideology or the "White Power" in the Anglo-Saxon realm). Yet, this aspect is rarely expressed explicitly.

The re-homogenization politics of the selected parties show different degrees of rigidity. Whereas the DVU chairman Gerhard Frey, in office until the end of 2008, emphasized that the citizenship acquired a long time ago was to be respected,[23] the NPD also includes "passport-Germans" into their repatriation program of foreign citizens.[24] Nonetheless, even for the NPD, the exclusion concerns non-European immigrants foremost. The much more moderate Swedish democrats (*Sverigedemokraterna*) exclusively expound the problems of non-European immigration and, therefore, are even supported by first-generation European immigrants.[25] Since 9/11, Muslim non-Europeans (with Turkey as a geographically largely non-European country) are considered the major problem group by most of the far right parties. Nevertheless, particularly some of the formations orienting themselves on the role models of the interwar period have adopted a differing attitude toward this issue: In their own country, Muslims are considered a threat, yet, outside of the country, even Islamists are valued as potential partners against "American Zionist globalism".[26]

22 BZÖ (Ed.), Programm des Bündnis Zukunft Österreich, p. 9.
23 Cf. Frey, Wer hat Angst vor David Odonkor?, p. 6.
24 Cf. Kailitz, Die nationalsozialistische Ideologie, pp. 337-353.
25 Cf. Lööw, Country Report Sweden, p. 447.
26 Cf. Dantschke, Zwischen Feindbild und Partner, pp. 440-460.

The parties distinguish themselves also concerning the attitude displayed toward minorities who are long-time residents. Anti-Semitism is not found in all formations. The Swedish SD even emphasizes Muslim anti-Semitism in order to demonstrate its irreconcilability with the national culture.[27] In a similar way, the German REP chastise "imported anti-Semitism" in order to demonstrate their constitutional loyalty and to warn against the dangers of Muslim immigration simultaneously.[28] Wherever anti-Semitism is more openly articulated, it shows itself foremost in the form of anti-Zionism with considerable overlappings to the forms of argumentation prevalent in the extreme left. Thus, the Italian FN organized a convention focusing on "Peoples and Traditions against Banks and Major Powers" in April 2009. Among the major European extreme right parties represented were the French *Front National* (FN) and the *British National Party* (BNP).[29]

In the Western European formations, an anti-Roma attitude is hardly present. However, in many Eastern and Eastern Middle-European formations, it constitutes the center of the enemy concept. So, typically, the Slovenian SNS rejects specific legal norms for the protection of the Roma minority.[30] Generally, the anti-discrimination law is seen as an attack on the established liberal rights of the majority of the population. So, the French PDF demands the dissolution of the Haute autorité de lutte contre les discriminations et pour l'égalité (HALDE), functioning as "ideological police"[31] in France.

Besides the different positions in minority questions, the ideological program distinguishes itself by its attitude to religious issues which, traditionally, used to be very important on the right side of the political spectrum. Here, two extreme positions can be spotted in the selected parties. At one end, there is the German NPD, in which neo-paganism is more strongly rooted than in the other parties mentioned, even though it is likely that Jürgen Rieger, the exponent of the Germanic "believers of a kind community" who passed away in October 2009, has left a delicate gap. The *League of the Polish Families*, one of the two organizations classified as Catholic fundamentalist, is located at the other end. Here, the fight against abortion and deviating life styles such as homosexual relationships plays a much larger role. Furthermore, the definition of cultural homogeneity is rather of a religious than an ethnical nature so that even anti-Germanicism erupts more strongly from the aversion to Protestantism than to Germandom. This may be one of the most important reasons why the LPR is not a part of the different supra-national alliance structures. Between the two

27 Lööw, Country Report Sweden, p. 447.
28 "Republikaner fordern Sofortprogramm gegen Antisemitismus", REP-Pressemitteilung no. 45/2009, 21 September 2009.
29 Cf. The Steven Roth Institute for the Study of Antisemitism and Racism, Country Report Italy 2009, available at: http://www.tau.ac.il/Anti-Semitism/asw2009/italy.html, last accessed 20 October 2010.
30 Cf. Rotter, Slovenia, p. 535.
31 Le Parti de la France, Les principes et les valeurs, p. 4.

Table 3: Programmatic profile

Country	Party	anti-homo-sexual	anti-Semitic	anti-Islamic	anti-Roma	neo-pagan	anti-clerical	Christian	Christian-funda-mentalist	anti-capitalist	revanchist	strong Euro-sceptic
Austria	BZÖ	-	-	-+	-	-	-	+	-	-	-	-
Belgium	FN	-	+	-	-	-+	-	+	-	-+	-	-+
Germany	DVU	-	+	+	-	-	-	-+	-	-	+	+
	REP		-	+	-	-	-	-+	-	-	-+	-+
	NPD		+	-+	-	+	+	-	-	+	+	+
France	PDF	-	+x	+	-	-	-	-+	-	-	-	+
Italy	FT	-	+	+	-	-	-	+	-	+	-	+
	FN	+	+	+	-	-	-	-	+	+	-	+
Poland	SO	+	-	-	-	-	-+	+	-	+	-	+
	LPR	+	+x	-	-	-	-	+	+	-+	-	+
Portugal	PNR	+	-	-	-	-	-	-+	-	-+	-	+
Slovenia	SNS	-	-	-	+	-	+	-	-	-+	+	-+
Sweden	NS	-	+	+	-	-+	-	-	-	+	-	+
	SD	-	-	+	-	-	-	-	-	-	-	-+

Explanation: + feature is present; – feature is absent; -+ feature is partly present.

extremes, there are many variants in religious questions. Christianity is mostly at least emphasized as a pillar of European identity (aside of others). Actually, the Italian FN approaches the Polish LPR when it declares war on laizism in an outline of the future state and recommends raising Roman Catholicism to the level of a "state religion".[32] This is matched by unrestrained polemics against same sex matrimony, which is denounced as equivalent to the "adoption of children by sodomists".[33] Such comparisons raise the question of how profoundly Christian values have been internalized here. Also with regard to other groups, there is a strong impression that referring to Christianity is primarily used as a means for erecting barriers against foreign influences (particularly Islam).

Parties such as the Italian FN and the Polish LPR decidedly refer to Christianity: They do not spare with criticism of capitalism and plead for a state that is strong socio-politically, too. In this respect, the FN surpasses the LPR by aligning itself with the model of fascist corporativism and favoring a society formed upon the pattern of professional and societal associations. The striving toward autarky and the attempt to isolate oneself from global markets, is widely congruent with the concept of a "spatially-oriented economy" ("raumorientierte Volkswirtschaft") developed by the NPD. Also, the moderate far right-wing parties do not at all subscribe to the market radicalism spread by populist bureaucracy and social state critics of the seventies and the eighties. It had become unfashionable long before the outbreak of the worldwide financial and economic crisis. Of course, their catalogues of socio-protectionist measures are not embedded in socio-revolutionary programs either. The BZÖ consistently pleaded for the "reduction of taxation and tax quota", also under the threat of the global financial- and economic crisis. It ardently supports state interventions when faced with the "fundamental impairment of the international competition". Still, it appears to have the strongest market-liberal orientation.[34]

The BZÖ even sees the "EU called to task when it comes to confronting these negative developments with international agreements and control measures".[35] This shows that it has hardly anything to do with a fundamental Euroscepticism. In fact, considering the European policy of the far right-wing parties, it is necessary to differentiate between their various forms as Sofia Vasilopoulou suggested in an enlightening contribution. With regard to the BZÖ, it is more than doubtful whether the party can even be attributed the mildest form of "Euroscepticism". According to Vasilopoulou, this is the case when a party accepts the European status quo as the political arena for political action, excluding, however, the future deepening of the integration ("compromising Euroscepticism").[36] However, the BZÖ can definitely imagine a further deepening of the integration for a "core of members whose cooperation in all political fields will

32 Forza Nuova, Manifesto politico di opposizione, p. 12.
33 Ibid., p. 5.
34 BZÖ (Ed.), Bündnispositionen, p. 6.
35 Ibid.
36 Cf. Vasilopoulou, Varieties of Euroscepticism, pp. 3–23.

become even more intense".[37] For this reason, the party does not appear on the author's list. Of all the parties discussed here, the FT and the LPR are attributed to a tough "rejecting Euroscepticism".[38] According to the author's opinion, these parties are "wholeheartedly against all aspects of European integration". The NPD and the Italian FN can also rightfully be attributed to this group as they have been developing visions of European cooperation that radically break with the theory as well as the practice of European integration in the last few decades. A somewhat milder form ("conditional Euroscepticism"), according to Vasilopoulou, exists when parties take as a basis "that the principle of cooperation in Europe at a multilateral level is to an extent beneficial to the national state, but for them unification is detrimental to the interest and the sovereignty of their country".[39] They reject any further deepening of integration and demand a radical reform of the European institutions aiming at the strengthening of national interests. The French PDF, the Belgian FN, and also the Swedish SD may be attributed to this group.

III. Strategic profile

Looking at the strategic orientations of the selected parties, they center on the issue in which way election politics (the striving for the maximization of votes in elections with the aim of mandates in parliaments and the possibility of political influencing is linked to other strategic options. Here, first of all, those parties must be mentioned that almost entirely concentrate on election politics while simultaneously making a special effort to prove their capability to form alliances to the established center-right parties. In this respect, the Austrian BZÖ, which, as a secession from the FPÖ, was linked to the Christian-Democratic ÖVP in a coalition government, has gone furthest. - Due to the dissociation from the FPÖ, the BZÖ has ostentatiously emphasized its interest in alliances to the other parties. The more the programmatic profile of the far right-wing party violates the basic norms of the fundamental consensus carrying the system, the less such an attitude is bound to meet with the approval of the potential allies of the democratic spectrum. However, sometimes the "cordon sanitaire" consistently practiced by countries like Belgium and Germany is penetrated by the need for electoral agreements (as in France between the two ballots). Nevertheless, this requires a certain potential for forming coalitions in regard to the power reached. This potential is indicated by the percentage of votes as well as by a minimal ability to compromise. But due to the system of proportional representation valid in all the countries, this issue does not play a role in the European elections.

37 BZÖ (Ed.), Bündnispositionen, p. 5.
38 Cf. Vasilopoulou, Varieties, p. 11.
39 Ibid., p. 7.

Most of the parties examined here do not have any realistic options to participate in coalitions on the national level. But they still follow a legalistic course. Among them, there are also formations like the German NPD and the Italian FN that connect pronounced ideological dogmatism with a clear anti-system attitude. In consolidated democracies, violent ways for overcoming the system are frequently not understood to be target-oriented. The legalistic tactics of the national socialists in Germany in the early 1930s show that the "liberal system" can be overcome by its own means.

One part of the legalistically oriented parties, however, pursues active "street politics", wants to flank the electoral parliamentary strategy by creating extra-parliamentary pressure. Provocative scenes in the public eye attract media attention and arouse mobilization effects. It is not surprising that this combination is to be found in formations ideologically rather strongly oriented on the role models of the interwar period like the German NPD and the Italian FN. However, besides this long-running issue, i. e., the rehabilitation of the historic role models, social protest topics (NPD: against the labor market reforms "Hartz IV"; FN: the inhospitability of living quarters) have come to the fore more strongly during the last decade.[40]

Due to their provocative appearances in public, the NPD and the Italian FN have also become attractive to militant groupings (in Germany, those with an NS-affinity and skinheads; in Italy, skinheads and soccer-"ultras"). They try to use these groupings as recruiting reservoirs. However, on the basis of the much greater vitality of militant scenes alone, the NPD was essentially more successful than the Italian formations (the German authorities for the protection of the constitution estimated that there were approximately 14,000 "Neonazis" and "violent right-wing extremists" at the end of 2009[41]). For the Eastern German states this may be called a symbiosis of the NPD with militant youth scenes. There is a parallel to this in Sweden where the ND cultivates intensive contacts with a "race ideological subculture" ("White Power").[42] The Polish LPR was primarily connected to militant scenes (skinheads, national revolutionary groupings) by the all-Polish youth (Młodzież Wszechpolska, MW) that was important to street mobilization.[43] The rude farmers' protest of the SO, on the other hand, was carried by its own powers in which the flamboyant movement with its crossing of barriers also attracted the youth scene.[44]

Finally, it is of interest whether the selected parties are making a special effort toward strengthening their cultural and intellectual influence. Here, the yield is rather modest on the whole. On the one hand, the formations must be mentioned that make an effort toward cultural support from their intellectual periph-

40 Cf. Steglich, Erfolgsbedingungen der extremen Rechten, pp. 55–74; Ministero dell' Interno (Ed.), Rapporto sulla criminalità, p. 406.
41 Cf. Bundesministerium des Innern (Ed.), Verfassungsschutzbericht 2009, p. 53.
42 Cf. Lööw, Country Report Sweden, p. 448.
43 Cf. Pankowski, The Populist Radical Right in Poland, pp. 116–124.
44 Cf. Moroska/Sroka, Extremismus in Polen, p. 294.

Table 4: Strategic profile

Country	Party	Alliance ability to established democratic parties	Legalist orientation	Great importance of street protest	Connections to militant scenes	Great importance of a strategy of cultural hegemony
Austria	BZÖ	+	+	-	-	-
Belgium	FN	-	+	-	-	-
Germany	DVU	-	+	-	-	-
	REP	-	+	-	-	-
	NPD	-	+	+	+	+
France	PDF	-	+	-	-	-
Italy	FT	-	+	+	-	+
	FN	-	+	+	-+	+
Poland	SO	+	-+	+	-	-
	LPR	+	+	+	+	+
Portugal	PNR	-	+	-	-	+
Slovenia	SNS	-	+	-	-	-
Sweden	ND	-	-+	+	+	-
	SD	-	+	-	-	-

Explanation: + feature is present; - feature is absent; -+ feature is partly present.

ery, for example the German NPD ("Dresdener Schule"), although their success is rather modest. On the other hand, the *League of Polish Families* deserves being mentioned in this context as well due to its close relationship with Catholic integrism. The support of the party by Father Tadeusz Rydzyk and his popular radio station "Radio Maria" founded in 1991 with its conservative Catholic, nationalist, and anti-liberal agenda was decisive for its political breakthrough.[45] Admittedly, this cultural spectrum is worlds removed from the neo-Pagan, anti-Christian-based thought of the "nouvelle droite" and its diverse European offshoots. Yet, in another way, this also goes for all the other formations (including the francophones) that share very little with the political concepts of de Benoist and his followers.[46] Hence, there are no intellectual forums in which representatives of both worlds (the intellectual "new right" and the far right parties) work together continuously.

Efforts attempting to reach "cultural hegemony" can, however, also gain expression in another way than in the classical realm of intellectual theoretical work. An outstanding example is the Portuguese PNR. It has undertaken great efforts to credibly stylize itself as the only savior of national identity. So, for

45 Cf. Lange/Guerra, The League of Polish Families, p. 134.
46 Cf. Bar-On, Where Have All the Fascists Gone?, pp. 165-176.

example, the party designed its own calendar with events of national importance. It honors the First of May as the day of the Portuguese worker, celebrates the day of death of the poet of the great discoveries, Luís Vaz de Camões, on 1 June, and on 1 December conducts rallies and parades in remembrance of regaining Portugal's independence from Spain in the year 1640.[47]

IV. Success profile

Turning to the conditions for failure, several dimensions are to be examined: general ones, only slowly changing social, economic, cultural, and political institutional framework conditions, partially quickly changing opportunity structures, the offers by the parties, and the demand from the population. Since demand and general framework conditions are the subject of other contributions in this publication, the following considerations focus on the parties' offer and the opportunity structures.

Far right parties are even more in need of energetic leadership than other party families in order to be successful. It is not difficult to name charismatic personalities in the history of European parties who were able to snatch voters from the established parties at least occasionally and to encourage non-voters to go to the ballot-box using attractive topics and considerable marketing expertise: Pim Fortuyn, Mogens Glistrup, Jörg Haider, Jean-Marie Le Pen, Ronald Schill, and Franz Schönhuber are names often connected with surprising successes of mobilization (but also sudden failures). Their sometimes forms and methods of populist speech were copied at home and abroad.

However, a glance at the list of the parties to be examined shows that a number of them lack charismatic leadership. Sometimes, the individuals at their top are able to develop some internal integration power but are unable to develop effective recruitment beyond their own close clientele due to the lack of rhetorical brilliance and/or little personal charisma. This applies to the long-term chairpersons of the German NPD (Udo Voigt) and the REP (Rolf Schlierer) as well as for the old (Gerhard Frey) and the new (Matthias Faust) DVU chairperson. Carl Lang, an experienced party organizer, yet not a tribune, was at the head of the French PDF. Considering the BZÖ, it was the fatal accident of party founder Jörg Haider that essentially contributed to the disappointing results on the European level.[48] Due to the fights lasting for years around party founder Daniel Féret, who, in addition, was legally prosecuted in regard to forged elections during the European elections in 2004,[49] the Belgian FN was paralyzed

47 Cf. Zúquete, Portugal, p. 185.
48 At least for a considerable part of the sympathizers, the top candidate Ewald Stadler seems to have been the reason for the election. Cf. Plasser/Ulram, Analyse der Europawahl 2009, p. 29.
49 "Un an ferme pour l'ex-président du FN". In: Le Soir, 2 June 2008.

as it were. Even though the chairperson of the Portuguese PNR was attested a certain expertise in the "dialectic" presentation of radical measures, he nonetheless lacked the charisma to mobilize a broader protest clientele. Furthermore, he did not run in the European elections.[50] Even where there was an attractive leadership personality available on the national level, for the most part, the second-rate personnel competed at the Europeans. This applies, for instance, to Zmago Jelinčič, the "Slovenian Le Pen", who attended to his national mandate and put forward less attractive personnel. The largely unknown Liane Hesselbarth ran for the German DVU whereas Matthias Faust, the designated successor of the long-time party chairperson Gerhard Frey, kept to the background. The REP handled this in a similar way by having the North-Rhine-Westphalian state chairperson Ursula ("Uschi") Winkelsett run again. She had already failed in 2004. The same went for the other formations from Italy, Portugal, and Sweden. The Polish farmer tribune Lepper did not run in the European elections, and the LPR ran under a foreign flag, the national list of the European party *Libertas* of the Irishman Declan Ganley formed a short time before the election.

Considering some of the parties concerned, due to their staff as well as their financial and organizational weakness, one could hardly speak of a successful election campaign. In this respect, the only exceptions were the BZÖ and the Swedish SD. Yet in contrast to the BZÖ, the SD was on the upswing, even though the party failed due to the high hurdle. The Slovenian SNS also played a special role. For some time, it was represented in the national parliament, but it weakened as a result of party splitting. The situation of the other groupings appeared even more uncomfortable. The financially strong party founder of the DVU had stopped his support in January 2009. In contrast to the DVU, the NPD, which relinquished its own application, had an experienced election campaign troupe, yet held back its own strength in spite of the verbal support by the DVU. The REP added to further electoral fragmentation and was in a state of dissolution in many state associations. The candidacy came too early for the French PDF in order to effectively participate in the election campaign. The Belgian FN and the Italian FT were strongly weakened by internal arguments and split-ups and the Polish formations by their occasional, scandal-involved government participation.[51]

On closer examination of the programmatic offer of the parties, ideological dogmatism paired with strategic radicality is probably the most important failure. Piero Ignazi's findings of the 1990's[52] seem to continue to hold true: too much closeness to the formations of the interwar period, an aggressive militant attitude toward the liberal democratic system, and, moreover, even the closeness to violent strategies for overcoming the system diminish the chances for

50 Cf. Marchi, Partido Nacional Renovador, pp. 57–80.
51 Cf. Lange, Populismus in den neuen Mitgliedsländern, p. 24.
52 Cf. Ignazi, Extreme Right Parties.

Table 5: Offer profile

Country	Party	Strong charismatic leadership	Effective election campaign organization	Attractive programmatic offer
Austria	BZÖ	-	+	+
Belgium	FN	-	-	+
Germany	DVU	-	-	-+
	REP	-	-	+
	NPD	-	-+	-
France	PDF	-	-	+
Italy	FT	-	-	-+
	FN	-	-	-
Poland	SO	+	-	+
	LPR	+	-	-+
Portugal	PNR	+	+	-+
Slovenia	SNS	+	-	+
Sweden	NS	-	-	-
	SD	+	+	+

Expanation: + feature is present; – feature is absent; -+ feature is partly present.

competition. The German DVU and NPD parties, the Swedish ND, and the two MSI-secessions in Italy clearly substantiate this thesis. The stronger parties in the group of the unsuccessful (such as the BZÖ and the Swedish SD) are marked by a certain programmatic flexibility in this respect and seem to be more able than others to perceive changing moods in the population and to adapt their program accordingly. Being "populist" formations, they stir up resentments against minorities and encourage the widespread clichés of the unworldliness and the distance to the people of "those in power".

As we have seen, the selected parties are still widespread, ideologically as well as strategically. A greater distance to the anti-democratic movements of the interwar period and a higher degree of ideological programmatic flexibility do not always constitute sufficient factors for success. Moreover, the offer needs to be connected with the demand, which, on the one hand, depends on the general socio-economic and political-cultural framework conditions of the party competition and, on the other hand, on the often rapidly changing opportunity structures.

Non-established parties only receive a chance if the established ones show weaknesses, and political niches and spaces for opportunity open up this way. This is why we must first examine whether system-supporting center-right and center-left parties have lost their influence on the voters. Comparing the results of the 2009 European elections with the ones of 2004, the picture is inconsistent. In some countries (Austria, Belgium, and Germany), the center parties decisively lost influence. In other countries, the moderate left lost voters whereas the moderate right was able to gain votes. This went for Italy, where Berlusconi's *Partito della Libertà* won the election. The situation in Poland was similar with the *Platforma Obywatelska*'s (PO) strong increase in votes. Also in Slovenia, the addition of the mandate number of the two moderate right formations represented in the EVP fractions, *Nova Slovenija* (NSi) and *Slovenska Demokratska Stranka* (SDS), gained votes whereas the moderate left lost in importance.

The depolarization of the party system makes room at the wings. The Austrian consociational democracy with its frequent coalition governments of the two largest democratic parties, the ÖVP and the SPÖ, offers a classic example. Their new government coalition has raised the chances for right-wing populist formations since 2008. The same goes for Belgium, where the large democratic parties often cooperate in broad coalitions, at last under Prime Ministers Herman van Rompuy and Yves Leterme. In Germany, this constellation is less frequent. Nonetheless, the second great coalition (CDU/CSU and SPD, 2005 to 2009) has without a doubt contributed to the strengthening of the political wings on the federal state level. However, this applies more to the (extreme) left than to the (extreme) right. The Portuguese cohabitation of the conservative state president Cavaco Silva with socialist prime minister Sócrates shows that a great coalition is not a sufficient prerequisite for right-wing parties to become stronger. There existed no cohabitation in France at the time of the European elections in 2009. The last one was some years ago; furthermore, cohabitations have become more improbable in Paris due to the constitutional reform of the year 2000 (adaptation of the election periods of the state president and the National Assembly). In Poland, there can be no mention of cohabitation in the years 2007 to 2010 (PiS state president, PO prime minister) because the mandate holders belonged to different parties but not far more different camps with a significant ideological programmatic difference. In addition, the far right parties were weakened on account of their recent government participation.

The few successful right-wing parties had to face strong populist competitors in some countries. In Austria, this concerned the right side of the political spectrum, where the FPÖ and the Eurosceptic Hans-Peter Martin were able to win. The same applied to France, where the party of Jean-Marie Le Pen entered the European Parliament again, even though weakened. Italy literally appeared as the El Dorado of right-wing populism with a respective prime minister at the top and the LN, especially strong in Northern Italy, its competitor. In Poland, the victory of the moderate right *Prawo i Sprawiedliwość* (PiS) of the Kaczynski brothers deprived the far right parties of a part of their basis, and in Portugal the PNR was confronted with the immigration and Eurosceptic moderate right of the *Partido Popular* (CDS-PP). In Germany, the "national camp" was splintered; in addition, there as well as in Portugal, there was populist competition from the left wing especially in the realm of criticism of the establishment, the EU, and of the negative consequences of the (neo-liberal) globalization. In

Table 6: Opportunity profile

Country	Party	Strong center parties*	Strong right-wing populist alternative**	Depolarized party system***	Strong left-wing populist party****	(Un-) favorable key events	Militant democracy	Cordon sanitaire	Strong counter-mobilization
Austria	BZÖ	-	+	+	-	+	-+	-	-+
Belgium	FN	+	-	-	-	-	-+	+	+
Germany	DVU	+	-	+	+	-	+	+	+
	REP	+	-	+	+	-	+	+	+
	NPD	+	-	+	+	-	+	+	+
France	PDF	+	+	-	+	+	-	+	+
Italy	FT	+	+	-	+	-	-	-+	+
	FN	+	+	-	+	-	-	+	+
Poland	SO	+	+	+	-	+	+	-	-
	LPR	+	+	+	-	+	+	-	-+
Portugal	PNR	+	-	+	+	-	+	+	-+
Slovenia	SNS	+	-	+	-	-	-	+	-
Sweden	ND	-	+	+	-	-	-+	+	+
	SD	-	-	+	-	-	-	+	+

Explanation: + feature is present; – feature is absent; -+ feature is partly present.
* Growing share of votes of center-right and center-left parties.
** Growing share of votes of a right-populist alternative.
*** National coalition government from center-right and center-left parties.
**** Growing share of votes of a left-populist alternative.

Sweden, the Euro-sceptical *Junilistan* lost much ground, yet most likely contributed to the weakening of the SD.

Political opportunities are in part the consequence of changing objective conditions (leadership competence, membership numbers, financial power, etc.). However, they depend to a considerable degree on their public perception. According to objective measures, a party can be in relatively good condition. But if it transmits the opposite image to the public, the appearance is sometimes more important than reality. Not only do structural factors play an important role in the creation of perceived reality but also situational ones. So, aside from the competition with the FPÖ, the death of the central figure, Jörg Haider, in the wake of the 2009 European elections is an important factor to explain the relative failure of the BZÖ. For the NPD, the consistent weakening of economic potency as the result of fraudulent finance manipulations, faulty account statements, and the loss of important financial backers have lately added to the failure. Political failure in leadership responsibilities is a further point. It applies to both Polish formations, whose escapades during the PiS-led government may essentially explain the rapid decline of popular support.

One last important complex defining the opportunity structures concerns the way state institutions, established actors, and civil society deal with far right parties, whether they become subject to a strong marginalization pressure or are able to fill the political space more or less undisturbed in a far-reaching free play of forces. A first factor is the state's handling of right-wing parties. In some of the countries of interest, right-wing extremist parties can be banned. They have to live with the threat of being banned. This typ of a "militant democracy" exists in Germany, Poland, Portugal, and Slovenia.[53]

For the selected parties, the statutory regulations had hardly any relevance in practice. The only banning proceedings (in Germany against the NPD) failed due to the intensive observation (intermediaries in party committees) of the security authorities,[54] which, however, does not exactly express a lack of official vigilance. It appears to be pronounced all over Europe beyond the German framework on the basis of historic experience with the right wing of the political spectrum. Even where banning legally operating organizations is unknown, the scope of action of actors disloyal to the system can be restricted, for example, by regulations in the party financing (most of all: Belgium[55]) or, to a large extent, in the realm of "hate crimes"[56] by applying the meanwhile anchored antidiscrimination law. However, by their very nature, these instruments are the less relevant the "softer" the appearance of the right-wing parties operating in a democratic gray zone (as in Poland and Slovenia) is.

This partly explains the missing or rather existing "cordon sanitaire". Hardened right-wing extremist parties do not only have to expect legal sanctions much sooner. They are also met with less acceptance as partners of an alliance by the established parties. In some countries (such as Germany, Belgium, Portugal, and Sweden), the rejection of the established parties remained complete even though some of the actors (REP in Germany, PNR in Portugal, SD in Sweden) passed through a moderation process.

Particularly this does not apply to Austria: on the one hand, the BZÖ is more moderate than all the other formations examined here and, on the other hand, "challenging the gray zone, that is, the rightist populism with its xenophobic, sometimes racist, sometimes revisionist aspects, would lead the Austrian polity into deep water as this brand of rightist elements [...] also exists in the two moderate mainstream parties".[57] Here, the close link of the problem with the political culture of the relevant countries becomes evident - a complex that is thoroughly examined in other contributions to this publication.[58]

53 Cf. Jesse/Thieme, Extremismus in den EU-Staaten, pp. 437-439; Jesse, Demokratieschutz, pp. 449-474.
54 Cf. Flemming, Das NPD-Verbotsverfahren; Weckenbrock, Die streitbare Demokratie.
55 Cf. Swyngedouw, Country Report Belgium, pp. 59-79.
56 Cf. OSCE/ODIHR (Ed.), Hate Crimes in the OSCE Region.
57 Pelinka, Country Report Austria, p. 43.
58 Cf. the contribution of David Art in this volume.

Another aspect besides the constitution militancy and the restrictive behavior of the established parties concerns the extent of societal anti-mobilization. It is not easy to estimate as comparative data are missing. In the Eastern countries Poland and Slovenia, it appears rather weak, most likely also due to the relative weakness of the organized civil society as a late result of the communist rule. Considering this, it must be taken into account that the right-wing parties in question are for the most part to be classified as the "soft" type. The strong anti-mobilization in Germany and Sweden, on the other hand, might be attributed to the accord of an at least regionally successful right extremist election mobilization with strongly accentuated militant scenes (groups with an NS-affinity, skinheads, race-ideological underground). In any case, the "anti-fascist" groupings active in all the countries can count on broader social support. However, "anti-fascism" gets out of hand in a partially violent way in both countries[59] so that the attacked "rightists" can sometimes credibly stylize themselves as victims of political violence. The coincidental structure and the dynamics of interaction of right-wing actors can be truly understood only when the behavior of the hard-boiled antagonists is taken into consideration. In contrast to Sweden and all the other countries examined, Germany, essentially as a long-term result of the cultural break of the years 1933 to 1945, is marked by the accord of constitutional militancy, "cordon sanitaire", and strong anti-mobilization, which considerably lessens the chances for success of the right-wing parties.

V. Conclusion

Failure has many fathers. There are numerous factors encouraging and an equally high number counteracting it. Offer, request, and coincidental structures form a complex independent interaction framework of continuous mobility within which it seems difficult to name individual decisive factors. Individual factors hindering success can be compensated by others and, in the reverse, a party can be successful when an element that encourages success comes into play at a decisive moment: The German REP was successful in Berlin in 1989 due to provocative xenophobic election advertisement helping it gain sudden fame. Of course, it is easier to reach success momentarily than consistently. If a party is unable to distinguish itself from its competitors by an attractive offer, failure seems preprogrammed.[60] Still, the making of an "attractive offer" highly depends on the situation and its interpretation. Accidental factors may play a decisive role. Therefore, it seems hardly possible to establish a "losing formula" valid in every case.

59 Cf. Backes/Mletzko/Stoye, NPD-Wahlmobilisierung; Lööw, Country Report Sweden, p. 458.
60 Cf. for Germany: Steglich, Rechtsaußenparteien in Deutschland.

Of course, another question is how failure becomes consistent with a certain probability. This might be the case when a party is not able to adapt a competitive profile and offer to the conditions on the political market in order to create the requirement for using a "window of opportunity" under favorable framework conditions. As the curves of the electoral success of the discussed parties show, however, at least some of them might be able to succeed, if not on short notice then at least in the medium or long run.

Radical Right-Wing Populist Parties in Office – A Cross-National Comparison

Sarah L. de Lange

I. Introduction

In early February 2000, all eyes were on Austria. After thirteen years of grand coalition governance, the *Sozialdemokratische Partei Österreichs* (SPÖ) and *Österreichische Volkspartei* (ÖVP) went their separate ways and the ÖVP decided to ally with the radical right-wing populist *Freiheitliche Partei Österreichs* (FPÖ) instead.[1] On 4 February 2000, the first "black-blue" government was inaugurated, and six FPÖ ministers assumed office. The international community was outraged and the member states of the European Union imposed bilateral sanctions on Austria to express their discontent with the composition of the new government. Although the FPÖ was not the first radical right-wing populist party (RRWP) to assume office in post-war Western Europe – the *Alleanza Nazionale* (AN) and the *Lega Nord* (LN) had taken up government responsibility in Italy in 1994 – the government participation of the party constituted the transgression of a political taboo in the minds of many commentators, politicians, and scholars. Prior to 2000, the mainstream right had only sporadically allied with the radical right. Contrary to the mainstream left, which had invited green parties to assume office in the 1980s and 1990s, the mainstream right had always shun away from the radical right. At the time, RRWPs were seen as political pariahs, and many mainstream right parties feared that cooperation with these parties would be frowned upon. In this respect, the formation of the Austrian ÖVP-

1 The "war of words" about an appropriate terminology to describe parties like the FPÖ is still ongoing. Mudde, The War of Words; Mudde, The Populist Radical Right in Europe. This article employs the term RRWPs because of its distinctive capacities and because the term strikes the right balance between exclusiveness on the one and inclusiveness on the other hand. Zaslove, Alpine Populism, Padania and Beyond, p. 66. To define the ideology of RRWPs, this article follows Betz, who argues that these parties are "right-wing" in their "rejection of individual and social equality and of political projects that seek to achieve it", "radical" in their "rejection of the established socio-cultural and social-political system", and "populist" in their "unscrupulous use and instrumentalization of diffuse public sentiments of anxiety and disenchantment" and "appeal to the common man and his allegedly superior common sense". Betz, Radical Right-Wing Populism in Western Europe, p. 4.

FPÖ government in 2000, and the reformation of this government in 2003, constitute a turning point in Western European politics.

In recent years, the number of RRWPs participating in government coalitions with mainstream right parties rose. In 2001, the AN and the LN participated in the Casa della Liberta, a pre-electoral coalition led by Silvio Berlusconi, that proved victorious in the elections being held the same year. Shortly after these elections, the Italian RRWPs were invited by Berlusconi to join his government coalition again, an invitation that the *Forza Italia* (FI) leader extended once more in 2008. In 2001, two Scandinavian RRWPs, the Danish *Dansk Folkeparti* (DF) and the Norwegian *Fremskrittspartiet* (FRP), were successful in their respective national elections as well, and they subsequently became government support parties. Although they did not formally join the government coalition, the parties provided the mainstream right with the necessary support to guarantee the survival of their minority governments.[2] In Denmark, this new government formula proved so successful that the right-wing minority government is still in office today, and still relies on the DF to pass the annual budget and major pieces of legislation. In 2002, the *Lijst Pim Fortuyn* (LPF) made its electoral breakthrough in the Dutch national elections. Its landslide victory made the party incontournable during the coalition negotiations and it assumed office only five months after being founded (see Table 1).[3]

This overview raises important questions about the government participation of RRWPs. Most of these questions focus on those RRWPs that have successfully made the transition from pariah to power. Why the AN, DF, FPÖ, FRP, LN, and LPF? What sets these parties apart from other RRWPs, such as the Belgian *Vlaams Belang* (VB) or the French *Front National* (FN)? Are they more

2 RRWPs that support minority governments are de facto coalition members, because they participate in "a more or less permanent coalition that ensures acceptance of all or almost all government proposals". De Swaan, Coalition Theories and Cabinet Formations, p. 85. Precondition to count support parties as coalition members is that the support provided by the party to the minority government "takes the form of an explicit, comprehensive, and more than short-term commitment to the policies as well as the survival of the government". Strøm, Minority Government and Majority rule, pp. 60–61. The relationship between the support party and the minority government is thus structural in nature and formalized by a written or oral agreement that is made public. Under these conditions "what are formally minority governments have relationships with their 'support' parties that are so institutionalized that they come close to being majority governments". Bale/Bergman, A Taste of Honey Is Worse Than None at All?, p. 422. On these grounds, the DF and the FRP are counted as government parties.

3 Although the "Schweizerische Volkspartei" (SVP) has been in government the period under study and has been widely recognized as RRWP since the early 1980s, the party is not included in this study. McGann/Kitschelt, The Radical Right in the Alps; Skenderovic, Immigration and the Radical Right in Switzerland. Strictly speaking, Switzerland cannot be qualified as a parliamentary democracy and coalition formation in this country does not occur along the same lines as in other Western European countries. Instead, Switzerland is ruled through a system of co-governance, which brings together the parliamentary parties in a collective executive body named the Swiss Federal Council.

Table 1: Radical right parties in public office in Western Europe

Country	Cabinet	Mainstream party	RRWP	Year
Austria	Schüssel I	ÖVP	FPÖ	2000
	Schüssel II	ÖVP	FPÖ	2003
Denmark	Rasmussen I	V, KF	DF*	2001
	Rasmussen II	V, KF	DF*	2005
	Rasmussen III	V, KF	DF*	2007
Italy	Berlusconi I	FI, CCD-UDC	AN, LN	1994
	Berlusconi II	FI, CCD-UDC	AN, LN	2001
	Berlusconi III	FI	AN, LN	2005
	Berlusconi IV	PdL	LN	2008
Netherlands	Balkenende I	CDA, VVD	LPF	2002
Norway	Bondevik II	KRF, V, H	FRP*	2001

* RRWP acts as support party to minority government.

successful? Less radical perhaps? Most of these questions have been answered, and it has been demonstrated that RRWPs are more likely to govern the larger their seat share and the smaller their policy distance to the prime minister party.[4] In this chapter, I wish to turn around the telescope and focus on the mainstream right parties that have decided to govern with RRWPs instead.[5] Why do these parties govern with RRWPs? Why do they find them attractive coalition partners? And do the benefits of governing with RRWPs outweigh the costs? As the formulation of these questions already suggests, this contribution adopts a rational choice approach. It departs from the assumption that parties behave as rational actors in the electoral and the coalition formation process. Following Müller and Strøm, this behavior characterizes parties as office-, policy-, and vote-seekers.[6] Office-seeking parties value office and more specifically cabinet positions and will try to obtain as many ministerial portfolios as possible. Policy-seeking parties aim to influence policy-making, either by contributing to the coalition agreement, by taking up specific cabinet portfolios, or by influencing policy-making from the opposition benches. Vote-seeking parties try to maximize the share of votes they receive in elections. Although office, policy, and votes are clearly distinct, political parties will often pursue a combination of these three party goals.

In this chapter, I will sketch the contours of my theoretical framework and demonstrate that mainstream right parties in Austria, Denmark, Italy, the

4 De Lange, From Pariah to Power.
5 For a similar, but less formalized analysis see Bale, Cinderella and her Ugly Sisters.
6 Müller/Strøm, Policy, Office, or Votes?

Netherlands, and Norway were motivated by a combination of office, policy and votes when they decided to govern with RRWPs. In other words, are RRWPs attractive coalition partners to mainstream right parties because they are instrumental in the realization of those parties' goals? More specifically, RRWPs are more attractive coalition partners than other parties because they give mainstream right parties better chances to maximize their control over office, policy, and votes. I will conclude with a comparative outlook to Eastern Europe, where RRWPs have also governed in recent years.

II. Parties between office, policy, and votes

Parties are rational actors seeking to maximize office, policy or votes, or a combination of these objectives.[7] As Strøm argues, "we can fruitfully think of vote seeking, office seeking, and policy seeking as three independent and mutually conflicting forms of behaviour in which political parties can engage".[8] Office, policy, and votes correspond closely to the three arenas in which parties compete: the executive arena, the legislative arena, and the electoral arena.

The office-seeking party seeks to win control over the executive in order to maximize its access to the spoils of office, which are the "private goods bestowed on recipients of politically discretionary governmental and subgovernmental appointments".[9] These private goods usually take the form of cabinet portfolios, but can also entail patronage appointments in and outside the legislature (e. g. in the judiciary, the civil service, parastatal agencies, and sub- and supranational government institutions).[10] The latter addition is crucial because it implies that support parties can also share in the spoils of office. Even office-oriented coalition formation theories can thus shed light on minority governments and the role support parties play in their survival.

The model of the policy-oriented parties assumes that "considerations of policy are foremost in the minds of the actors and that the parliamentary game is, in fact, about the determination of major government policy".[11] Parties are expected to have policy positions on which they campaign in elections and which they seek to realize in the legislative and executive. If parties are unable to change policy in the direction of their most preferred position, they will attempt to prevent changes in the opposite direction. An important way to realize pol-

7 Müller/Strøm, Policy, Office, or Votes? Some scholars distinguish a fourth party goal, which is either internal cohesion or intraparty democracy maximization. Cf. Harmel/Janda, An Integrated Theory of Party Goals and Party Change; Luebbert, Comparative Democracy; Sjöblom, Party Strategies in a Multiparty System.
8 Strøm, A Behavioral Theory of Competitive Political Parties, pp. 570–571.
9 Ibid., p. 567.
10 The spoils of office can also be less tangible, for example in the form of public recognition and media exposure.
11 De Swaan, Coalition Theories and Cabinet Formations, p. 88.

icy objectives is to assume office since this gives parties a vote in the cabinet decision-making, and control over government portfolios, and hence over policy-making.[12] However, it is also possible for parties to bring about policy changes through legislative procedures. Moreover, policy payoffs are public goods that benefit parties in government and opposition alike, and it is therefore conceivable that parties realize policy objectives by remaining passive.[13] The ways in which policy-seeking parties can achieve their goals are thus manifold.

The model of the vote-seeking party is derived from the work of Downs, who claims "parties formulate policies in order to win elections, rather than win elections in order to formulate policies".[14] The idea that political parties are first and foremost vote maximizers has always been widely accepted in the study of electoral competition, but is less prominent in the coalition formation literature. Generally speaking, vote-seeking behavior is qualified as an instrumental party goal, i. e. it is normally interpreted as a means to achieve either office or policy influence. This has already been acknowledged by Downs, who underlines that "[party] members are motivated by their personal desire for the income, prestige, and power, which come from holding office [...]. Since none of the appurtenances of office can be obtained without being elected, the main goal of every party is the winning of elections. Thus, all its actions are aimed at maximizing votes".[15] In a similar fashion, he stresses, "the more votes a party wins, the more chance it has to enter a coalition, the more power it receives if it does enter one, and the more individuals in it hold office in the government coalition. Hence vote-maximizing is still the basic motive underlying the behavior of parties".[16]

In recent years, the idea that *the* office-seeking party, *the* policy-seeking party, or *the* vote-seeking party does not exist has become widespread. The vast majority of political parties seek to satisfy more than one goal simultaneously, which has led to attempts to come to an integrative theory of competitive party behavior.[17] These theories take account of the fact that 1) parties compete in different arenas; 2) parties have to reconcile short- and long-term interests; and 3) parties can pursue goals for intrinsic and instrumental reasons. These analytical observations are closely linked with each other.

An integrative theory of competitive behavior starts with the acknowledgement that government formation, taking place in the parliamentary and executive arena, is nested in a more elaborate pattern of political competition, which

12 Cf. Döring, Parliaments and Majority Rule in Western Europe; Döring/Hallerberg, Patterns of Parliamentary Behaviour.
13 Laver/Schofield, Multiparty Government, p. 53.
14 Downs, An Economic Theory of Democracy, p. 28.
15 Ibid., p. 34.
16 Ibid., p. 159.
17 Cf. Laver, Party Competition and Party System Change; Laver/Budge, Party and Coalition Policy in Western Europe; Müller/Strøm, Policy, Office, or Votes?; Narud, Voters, Parties and Governments; Sened, A Model of Coalition Formation; Sjöblom, Party Strategies in a Multiparty System; Strøm, A Behavioral Theory of Competitive Political Parties.

also encompasses the electoral arena in which parties compete for votes.[18] Coalition building is then part of a cyclical process of elections, parliamentary and executive majority construction, legislative activity, after which new elections are scheduled. The cyclical nature of this process requires parties to be future-oriented and to make trade-offs between short- and long-term interests. At times, they will have to forgo immediate benefits because the pursuit of these benefits interferes with a party's long-term ambitions. This also relates to the fact that the pursuit of an objective is not necessarily motivated by intrinsic considerations; it might also be part of an instrumental strategy, i. e. a means to an end rather than an end in itself. In short, "to the extent that the actor at the same time strives towards several goals that are interdependent – for instance, so that all goals cannot at the same time be optimized, a weighing of one against the must be made".[19]

To give only one example in which these elements surface: policy realization requires parties to please voters, and form, and maintain agreements with other parties over a sustained period.[20] However, in the legislative arena, parties are forced to water down their positions in order to make policy compromise possible, while in the electoral arena, parties have to mark policy distances to maintain a distinguishable profile for the voter. Changes in party positions between the electoral and legislative and/or executive arena are risky because voters prefer reliable and responsible parties.[21] To satisfy the two conditions necessary for policy realization is thus not an easy task, especially since competition in different arenas can ask for different strategies, and strategies employed in one arena can have a contradictory effect on the realization of objectives in another.[22]

In other words, parties often face trade-offs that impose themselves when the realization of one goal (e. g. office) is incompatible with the realization of another (e. g. votes). Although office and votes are notoriously difficult to reconcile, potential trade-offs between office and policy, and policy and votes present themselves at times. In the end, most trade-offs boil down to contrast between the satisfaction of short-term interests on the one and the realization of long-term objectives on the other hand and are particularly pronounced when parties have to decide whether they want to govern, and if so, which parties they want to govern with. Government participation is attractive to parties because 1) when participating in government, they obtain a share of the spoils of office, most notably portfolios; 2) when controlling portfolios, they are able to influence government policy, an objective they also realize on a more general level through their contribution to the coalition agreement which constitutes the cor-

18 Cf. Austen-Smith/Banks, Elections, Coalitions, and Legislative Outcomes; Laver/Shepsle, Coalitions and Cabinet Government; Strøm, A Behavioral Theory of Competitive Political Parties; Tsebelis, Nested Games.
19 Sjöblom, Party Strategies in a Multiparty System, p. 31.
20 Cf. Lupia/Strøm, Coalition Governance Theory.
21 Downs, An Economic Theory of Democracy, pp. 103–109.
22 Narud, Voters, Parties and Governments.

nerstone of government policy; 3) government participation can have positive effects on a party's future electoral results, since it can deliver the policy promises made during the election campaign and demonstrate its reliability and authority. However, government participation can also entail negative consequences because of which parties can decide to prefer opposition to government. The benefits of government participation can be insufficient to satisfy a party, and a potential coalition agreement can entail policy compromises a party is unwilling to make, either on principle, or because the party fears electoral punishment if it does not keep its electoral promises.[23]

In the remainder of this chapter, I will demonstrate that those mainstream right parties having governed with RRWPs have always had multiple coalition alternatives to choose from during the coalition formation process, even though some of these alternatives might not have been actively explored. These alternatives can be divided into two groups, one consisting of coalitions with mainstream left, centre, and right parties, and the other one consisting of coalitions with mainstream right parties and RRWPs.[24] If forced to choose between the two, mainstream right parties display a clear preference for the latter as they do not face trade-offs between office, policy, and votes in these coalitions. When governing with other mainstream parties, mainstream right parties will realize only some of their office-seeking aspirations and very little of their policy- and vote-seeking aspirations. In such coalitions, they are likely to be the junior coalition partner having to make serious policy compromises and incur substantial electoral costs. When governing with RRWPs, on the other hand, they are likely to obtain the prime ministership, making only limited policy compromises and winning back votes lost to their radical right-wing populist competitors in previous elections. I will demonstrate the validity of these claims using quantitative data. First, I will focus on the office and vote benefits mainstream right parties can expect from their collaboration with RRWPs, by using election results to show why RRWPs are more attractive coalition partners than other mainstream parties. Then I will concentrate on the policy benefits mainstream right parties expect to receive from this collaboration, using the results of expert surveys to establish that RRWPs also have more attractive policy positions.

23 Retrospective voting is an important determinant of electoral behavior, and it has been demonstrated that incumbency effects are often negative because voters judge that the discrepancy between promises and performances is too large as a consequence of which parties loose reliability and hence support. Lupia/Strøm, Coalition Governance Theory; Rose/Mackie, Incumbency in Government; Strøm, Party Goals and Government Performance; Strøm, A Behavorial Theory of Competitive Political Parties; Strøm/Müller, Political Parties and Hard Choices.

24 The seat distributions presented in Tables 2a to 2e reveal that in none of the countries in which RRWPs have risen to power, a centre-right government would have had a parliamentary majority.

III. Explaining why mainstream right parties govern with RRWPs - an office- and vote-oriented approach

Electoral dynamics have an important impact on the composition of government coalitions as they determine parties' bargaining power in the coalition formation process. There is ample evidence that the larger the party, the stronger its bargaining power, and the greater the likelihood that it will govern.[25] And indeed, those RRWPs having participated in government coalitions in recent years are among the most successful members of the RRWP family in Western Europe.[26] The FPÖ, for example, commanded 26.9 % of the seats in the Austrian parliament when it was invited to take part in the coalition negotiations by the ÖVP in 2000 (see Table 2a).[27] The DF won 1 % of the seats in the Danish Folketinget in 2001, 13.3 % in 2005, and 14.3 % in 2007 (see Table 2b). When the AN and LN participated in the Berlusconi I cabinet in 1994, they controlled 17.3 % and 18.6 % of the seats in the Italian Camera dei Deputati. In 2001 their seat share had declined considerably (to 15.7 % and 4.8 % respectively), but they remained important actors in Italian politics (see Table 2c). The LPF equally turned out to be one of the largest Dutch parties after the 2002 elections gaining 17 % of the seats in the 2002 elections (see Table 2d). And the FRP was victorious in the 2001 elections to the Norwegian Storting, obtaining 14.6 % of the seats (see Table 2e).

However, the reason why RRWPs are particularly attractive coalition partners, is connected to the fact that they are small enough to be dominated by the mainstream right. In this respect, they are much more attractive coalition partners for Christian-democratic, conservative, or liberal parties than social democratic parties. Although RRWPs have grown rapidly in most Western European countries, they remain relatively small to comparative standards. Within their respective party systems, RRWPs usually rank as third or fourth largest party. Thus, the FPÖ has always been smaller than the *Österreichische Volkspartei* (ÖVP) and *Sozialdemokratische Partei Österreichs* (SPÖ), the DF has always been smaller than the *Socialdemokratiet* (SD) and *Venstre* (V), the AN and LN have always been smaller than the *Democratici di Sinistra* (DS) or the *Partido Democratico* (DP), and the FRP has always been smaller than *Det Norske Arbeiderparti* (DNA) and *Høyre* (H). What is particularly noteworthy is that most RRWPs control fewer seats than those social democratic parties which mainstream right parties could potentially govern with as well. In 1999, for example, the SPÖ remained the largest party in the Austrian Nationalrat with 33.2 % of the seats, despite having lost a considerable number of voters to the

25 Dumont/Bäck, Why So Few, and Why So Late?; Mattila/Raunio, Does Winning Pay?
26 De Lange, From Pariah to Power.
27 Of course, the FPÖ was decimated in the following elections and its seat share dropped to 9.5 %. For this reason, the formation of the Schüssel II cabinet is a bit of an anomaly. It can be argued, however, that by this time ties had already developed between the ÖVP and FPÖ, reducing the transaction costs of the reformation of "Schwarz-Blau".

FPÖ over the years (see Table 2a). In Denmark, SD won 29.1 % of the seats in 2001, 25.8 % in the 2005 elections, and 25.7 % in the 2007 elections (see Table 2b). The Italian mainstream left, represented by the DS in 1994 and 2001 and the PD in 2008, controlled 19.8 %, 21.7 %, and 34.4 % in the successive elections (see Table 2c). And in Norway the DNA remained the largest party in the Norwegian parliament after the 2001 elections (see Table 2e). The only exception to this rule is the Dutch *Partij van de Arbeid* (PvdA), which lost a considerable number of seats in the 2002 elections and came in third, following the LPF (see Table 2d). Because these social-democratic parties are relatively large, they are less attractive coalition partners for mainstream right parties than RRWPs. They can less easily be dominated and are less likely to accept a small or weak set of cabinet portfolios as pay-off for their government participation.

The Austrian case illustrates this point quite clearly. The SPÖ-ÖVP governments that assumed office between 1986 and 1999 have always been described as grand coalitions, whereas the ÖVP-FPÖ governments that assumed office in 2000 and 2003 have been described as small coalitions. While the ÖVP was the junior partner in the grand coalitions, it was the senior partner in the small coalitions. Consequentially, the pay off it received in the small coalitions was far greater than that in the grand coalitions. In the latter coalitions, the SPÖ appointed the prime minister and obtained the majority of cabinet portfolios. By switching allegiances, the ÖVP found itself in the driver's seat for once and was able to claim the prime ministership and a number of high profile ministerial posts, such as the Ministry of Foreign Affairs and the Ministry of Interior.

Table 2a: Austria

		Percentage of seats (change since last elections)	
1999	Die Grünen	7.4	(+ 3.8)
	Sozialdemokratische Partei Österreichs	33.2	(- 3.3)
	Österreichische Volkspartei	*26.9*	*(n. c.)*
	Freiheitliche Partei Österreichs	*26.9*	*(+ 6.2)*
2002	Die Grünen	10.0	(+ 2.0)
	Sozialdemokratische Partei Österreichs	36.5	(+ 3.4)
	Österreichische Volkspartei	*42.3*	*(+ 15.4)*
	Freiheitliche Partei Österreichs	*9.5*	*(- 16.9)*

Parties in italics formed coalition government.

Table 2b: Denmark

		Percentage of seats (change since last elections)	
2001	Enhedslisten - De Rød-Grønne	2.4 %	(- 0.3)
	Socialistisk Folkeparti	6.4 %	(- 1.2)
	Socialdemokratiet	29.1 %	(- 6.8)
	Radikale Venstre	5.2 %	(+ 1.3)
	Kristeligt Folkeparti	2.3 %	(- 0.2)
	Venstre - Danmarks Liberale Parti	*31.3 %*	*(+ 7.2)*
	Konservative Folkeparti	*9.1 %*	*(+ 0.2)*
	Dansk Folkeparti	*12.0 %*	*(+ 4.6)*
2005	Enhedslisten - De Rød-Grønne	2.4 %	(+ 1.0)
	Socialistisk Folkeparti	9.2 %	(- 0.4)
	Socialdemokratiet	25.8 %	(- 3.3)
	Radikale Venstre	9.2 %	(+ 4.0)
	Venstre - Danmarks Liberale Parti	*29.0 %*	*(- 2.2)*
	Konservative Folkeparti	*10.3 %*	*(+ 1.2)*
	Dansk Folkeparti	*13.3 %*	*(+ 1.3)*
2007	Enhedslisten - De Rød-Grønne	2.3 %	(- 1.2)
	Socialistisk Folkeparti	13.1 %	(+ 7.0)
	Socialdemokratiet	25.7 %	(- 0.3)
	Radikale Venstre	5.1 %	(- 4.1)
	Liberal Alliance	2.9 %	(+ 2.8)
	Venstre - Danmarks Liberale Parti	*26.3 %*	*(- 2.8)*
	Konservative Folkeparti	*10.3 %*	*(+ 0.1)*
	Dansk Folkeparti	*14.3 %*	*(+ 0.6)*

Parties in italics formed coalition government.

Table 2c: Italy

		Seat share	Change in vote share
1994	Rifondazione Communista	6.2 %	+ 0.7
	Democratici di Sinistra	19.8 %	+ 0.4
	Federazione dei Verdi	1.7 %	- 0.8
	Movimento per la Democrazia - La Rete	1.0 %	+ 1.0
	Alleanza Democratica	2.9 %	+ 2.9
	Partito Populare Italiano	5.2 %	- 27.5
	Partito Socialista Italiano	2.2 %	- 12.4
	Patto Segni	2.1 %	+ 2.1
	Südtiroler Volkspartei	0.5 %	n. c.
	Lista Pannella - Riformatori	1.0 %	n. c.
	Centro Cristiano Democratico - Cristiani Democratici Uniti	*4.3 %*	*+ 5.5*
	Forza Italia	*17.0 %*	*+ 15.7*
	Lega Nord	*18.6 %*	*+ 9.9*
	Alleanza Nazionale	*17.3 %*	*+ 11.9*
2001	Rifondazione Communista	1.7 %	- 3.8
	Partito dei Communisti Italiani	1.4 %	n. c.
	Democratici di Sinistra	21.7 %	- 5.1
	Federazione dei Verdi - Socialisti Democratici Italiani	1.3 %	+ 0.1
	La Margherita	13.7 %	- 2.7
	Südtiroler Volkspartei	0.5 %	n. c.
	Centro Cristiano Democratico - Cristiani Democratici Uniti	6.5 %	+ 0.6
	Nuovo Partito Sociale Italiano	0.5 %	+ 0.5
	Forza Italia	*30.6 %*	*+ 9.4*
	Alleanza Nazionale	*15.7 %*	*+ 1.5*
	Lega Nord	*4.8 %*	*- 3.4*
2008	Partito Democratico	34.4 %	+ 2.0
	Italia dei Valori	4.6 %	+ 2.1
	Südtiroler Volkspartei	0.3 %	n. c.
	Unione dei Democratici Cristiani e di Centro	5.7 %	- 1.1
	Movimento per l'Autonomia	*1.3 %*	*+ 1.1*
	Popolo della Libertà	*43.8 %*	*- 1.2*
	Lega Nord	*9.5 %*	*+ 3.8*

Parties in italics formed coalition government.

Table 2d: Netherlands

		Percentage of seats (change since last elections)	
2002	Socialistische Partij	5.9 %	(+ 2.4)
	GroenLinks	7.0 %	(- 0.3)
	Partij van de Arbeid	15.1 %	(- 13.9)
	Democraten66	5.1 %	(- 3.9)
	Leefbaar Nederland	2.4 %	(+ 1.6)
	ChristenUnie	2.5 %	(- 0.6)
	Christen Democratisch Appèl	*27.9 %*	*(+ 9.5)*
	Volkspartij voor Vrijheid en Democratie	*15.4 %*	*(- 9.3)*
	Staatkundig Gereformeerde Partij	1.7 %	(- 0.1)
	Lijst Pim Fortuyn	*17.0 %*	*(+17.0)*

Parties in italics formed coalition government.

Table 2e: Norway

		Percentage of seats (change since last elections)	
2001	Sosialistisk Venstreparti	12.5 %	(+ 6.5)
	Senterpartiet	5.6 %	(- 2.4)
	Det Norske Arbeiderparti	24.4 %	(- 10.7)
	Kristelig Folkeparti	*12.4 %*	*(- 1.3)*
	Venstre	*3.9 %*	*(- 0.5)*
	Fremskrittspartiet	*14.6 %*	*(- 0.7)*
	Høyre	*21.2 %*	*(+ 6.9)*

Parties in italics formed coalition government.

In most Western European countries, the growth of RRWPs has gone hand in hand with the decline of mainstream parties. While election by election RRWPs grew larger, mainstream parties got smaller. In order to curb their electoral losses, many mainstream parties have sought ways to take the wind out of the sails of RRWPs; giving these parties government responsibility has become a popular way to achieve this.[28] Several scholars have pointed out that this vote-

28 Similar strategic calculations can explain the government participation of green parties. Dumont/Bäck conclude that "the willingness of the main party of the left to include Green parties in government seems indeed to increase when the latter are seen as electoral opponents who would continue to win votes in the opposition if the main party of

seeking strategy has been at the heart of many mainstream right parties' decision to cooperate with the radical right. Heinisch argued that many mainstream parties believed that "public office will [...] deflate the hyperbole that has accompanied their meteoric rise".[29] Downs made a similar statement believing that "incumbency will give the pariah the rope with which it will ultimately hang itself".[30]

Let me return to the Austrian case to illustrate their claims. From 1986 to 1999, the FPÖ increased its vote and seat share at almost every election it contested: 9.7 % in 1986, 16.6 % in 1990, 22.5 % in 1994, 20 % in 1995, and 26.9 % in 1999. The votes cast for the FPÖ came from both the ÖVP and SPÖ, each of which lost roughly one-third of their votes between 1986 and 1999. However, in 1999 the electoral situation of the ÖVP was far more precarious than that of the SPÖ. Although the party won as many seats as the FPÖ, it lost its position as second Austrian party to the RRWP. This made the party realize that it was now or never and that it had to take immediate action if it wanted to turn the electoral tide. Wolfgang Schüssel, leader of the ÖVP at the time of the 1999 elections, has always been quite honest about the ÖVP's desire to regain votes lost to the FPÖ. He justified the ÖVP's cooperation with the FPÖ by stating that "trying to marginalize the FPÖ had not worked and that the only way to contain Haider was to bring the FPÖ in a position where they had to exercise governmental responsibility".[31] Other students of Austrian politics also point at the importance of the ÖVP's vote-seeking strategy for the formation of "Schwarz-Blau" and concluded, "the parties' politicians voluntarily admit that their objective of integrating the FPÖ into government was also to undermine the 'opposition reflex', i. e. the FPÖ's capacity to attract voters who cast their vote rather 'against' the government than in favour of the opposition".[32]

Similar considerations have been observed in other countries where RRWPs have become fully-fledged cabinet members, such as Italy and the Netherlands. In the latter country, the severe electoral losses of the incumbent parties in the 2002 earthquake elections were generally seen as evidence of voter dissatisfaction with the "purple" government coalition in which liberals and social democrats had worked together for eight years in spite of their ideological differences. At the start of the coalition formation process, most leading politicians interpreted the election results as a clear demand for political change. CDA-leader Jan Peter Balkenende stated "the results of the elections held on Wednesday 15 May 2002, show that the Dutch population has a clear desire for change", while his *GroenLinks*-colleague Paul Rosenmöller concluded "the large gains of the CDA and LPF and the fact that these parties together with the VVD have

the left were to be the only party of the left in government (due to the negative electoral effect of incumbency)". Dumont/Bäck, Why so Few, and Why so Late?, p. 53.

29 Henisch, Success in Opposition – Failure in Government, pp. 99–100.

30 Downs, Pariahs in their Mids, p. 6.

31 Heinisch, Populism, Proporz, Pariah, p. 229.

32 Ahlemeyer, The Coalition Potential of Extreme Right Parties in Western Europe, p. 119.

become the three largest parties of the country point in one direction. The voter wants the pendulum to swing to the right".[33] Minutes of the parliamentary debates that took place during the 2002 coalition negotiations demonstrate that most mainstream parties believed the election results reflected a clear preference on the part of the electorate for a government coalition of CDA, LPF, and VVD.[34] Although there is little that suggests that the CDA and VVD actively sought to neutralize the electoral success of the LPF by giving the party governmental responsibility, they clearly took electoral dynamics into consideration when they invited the party to join their government. Of course, in the Scandinavian countries in which RRWPs have been support parties electoral dynamics play a slightly different role. Support parties face fewer challenges than cabinet members do, as they are not forced to appoint capable ministers and junior ministers and do not have to take full responsibility for policy compromises. For this reason, they are less likely to suffer from negative incumbency effects in the elections that follow their participation in government. Hence, the DF and FRP have continued to thrive in recent elections, while the FPÖ and LPF have collapsed electorally after having been in office.

IV. Explaining why mainstream right parties govern with RRWPs - a policy-oriented approach

By governing with RRWPs, mainstream right parties do not only realize their office and vote objectives. In coalitions with RRWPs, it is also possible for mainstream right parties to influence policy more easily than in coalitions with other mainstream parties. An assessment of the policy positions of the various parties and the policy ranges of the various coalition alternatives explains why this is the case.

Political parties have a clear preference for government coalitions that are ideologically connected and compact. The most common way to establish whether coalitions meet these criteria is by estimating parties' positions on the left-right dimension and calculating the policy ranges of (potential) coalitions based on these positions. When the policy ranges of the government coalitions that included mainstream right and RRWPs are calculated and compared to those of alternative coalitions that did not form, it becomes apparent that the former are ideologically far more compact than the latter.[35] In other words, in

33 Kamerstukken 61855, Tweede Kamer der Staten-Generaal, Vergaderjaar 2001-2002.

34 Handelingen 7434A02, Tweede Kamer der Staten-Generaal, Vergaderjaar 2001-2002; Kamerstukken 61855, Tweede Kamer der Staten-Generaal, Vergaderjaar 2001-2002.

35 To calculate parties' policy positions on the left-right dimension, experts' placements of these parties on the left-right scale, ranging from 1 (left) to 20 (right), have been used. Benoit/Laver, Party Policy in Modern Democracies, p. 230. The mean positions experts attributed to parties on these scales have been standardized using the standardization formula advocated by Carter, The Extreme Right in Western Europe, pp. 113-114.

each of the countries in which government coalitions between mainstream right and RRWPs have been formed, the distances between these parties are significantly smaller that that between mainstream left, centre, and right parties.

In Austria, for example, the distance between the ÖVP, on the one hand, and FPÖ, on the other, was 16 points on a scale ranging from 1 to 100. This distance was much smaller than the one between the ÖVP and the SPÖ, which could have formed an alternative coalition that would also have been connected. The policy range of this alternative coalition (29 points on a scale ranging from 1 to 100) would have been almost double that of the black-blue coalition (see Figure 1). In Denmark the contrast between the policy range of the Rasmussen governments (01), on the one hand, and that of any alternative coalition on the other (39), is ever more striking (see Figure 2). In Italy, the distance between the mainstream right and the populist radical right is also considerably smaller than that between the mainstream right and the mainstream left. The various Berlusconi governments have a policy range of 24 points on the left-right dimension, while any alternative coalition would have had a policy range of at least 50 points on the same dimension (see Figure 3). In the Netherlands, the distance between the most left- and the most right-leaning party in the Balkenende I government is 21 points on the left-right scale, whereas the distance between the parties included in any alternative coalition would have been at least 41 points (see Figure 5). And in Norway, the policy range of the Bondevik II government is 29 points, compared to 46 points for any alternative coalition (see Figure 5). Thus, each of the government coalitions including RRWPs is more ideologically compact than any alternatives that were available at the time of the formation of these coalitions, suggesting that at least part of the reason why they were formed lies in their ideological coherence.

However, it is often argued that Western European political spaces are not uni-dimensional, but multi-dimensional.[36] As a consequence of changing voter preferences and the emergence of green and RRWPs, a second dimension, often referred to as the cultural dimension, has developed in recent years.[37] The extremes of this dimension are formed by the libertarian pole, associated with a preference for libertarian cultural policies focussing on cultural egalitarianism and individual freedom, and the authoritarian pole, associated with a preference for authoritarian cultural policies focussing on authoritarianism, cultural

36 Cf. Benoit/Laver, Party Policy in Modern Democracies; Kitschelt, The Radical Right in Western Europe; Kitschelt, Diversification and Reconfiguration of Party Systems in Postindustrial Democracies; Kriesi et al., Globalization and the Transformation of National Political Space; Warwick, Toward a Common Dimensionality in West European Policy Spaces.

37 Kriesi et al., Globalization and the Transformation of National Political Space. Other scholars refer to this dimension as the GAL-TAN dimension or libertarian-authoritarian dimension. Marks et al., Party Competition and European Integration in the East and the West; Kitschelt, The Radical Right in Western Europe; Kitschelt, Diversification and Reconfiguration of Party Systems in Postindustrial Democracies.

inegalitarianism, and traditionalism.[38] As a result of "the ethnicization of politics", parties' positions on the issues of immigration and integration have become most indicative of their positions on the cultural dimension.[39] Not surprisingly, these two issues are very salient in the programs of RRWPs.

In the previous section it was noted that in most cases the policy distances between mainstream right and RRWPs on the right left-dimension were particularly small at the time of the formation of government coalitions between these parties, especially when compared to the policy distances between mainstream left and right parties. On the cultural dimension, however, the distances between mainstream right and RRWPs are often much larger than those between mainstream left and right parties.[40] In Austria, for example, the distance between the ÖVP and FPÖ on the cultural dimension (26 on a scale from 0 to 100) is larger than that between the ÖVP and the SPÖ (24) (see Figure 1). Similarly, in Denmark the policy range of the Rasmussen governments on this dimension (23) is significantly larger than that of any alternative coalition, which would have included most mainstream parties (19). Also, in Italy and Norway the distances between mainstream right and RRWPs on the cultural dimension (55 and 59 respectively) are greater than those between the mainstream left and mainstream right (47 and 19 respectively). Only in the Netherlands, the opposite is the case. In 2002 the policy range of the Balkenende I government was smaller than that of any alternative coalition (36 versus 42), which can be explained by the fact that Dutch VVD is one of the most monoculturally-oriented mainstream parties in Western Europe.

On the basis of parties' positions on the cultural and the left-right dimension, two-dimensional spaces can be constructed visually representing the distances between mainstream right and RRWPs in Austria, Denmark, Italy, the Netherlands, and Norway. The party positional configurations of the Austrian, Danish, Italian, Dutch, and Norwegian spaces are very similar to those discussed by Kitschelt and Kriesi et al.[41] Most left-wing parties (e. g. green parties and socialist or social-democratic parties) can be found in the lower-left quadrant, suggesting that these parties combine a more multicultural appeal with a state-oriented appeal, whereas most right-wing parties (e. g. Christian-democratic,

38 Kitschelt, The Radical Right in Western Europe; Kitschelt, Diversification and Reconfiguration of Party Systems in Postindustrial Democracies.

39 Kriesi et al., Globalization and the Transformation of National Political Space, p. 924.

40 To calculate parties' policy positions on the cultural dimension, experts' placement of these parties on the immigration scale, ranging from 1 (favors policies designed to help asylum seekers and immigrants integrate into [insert country's] society) to 20 (favors policies designed to have asylum seekers and immigrants return to their country of origin), have been used. Benoit/Laver, Party Policy in Modern Democracies, p. 229. The average positions experts attributed to parties on these scales have been standardized using the standardization formula advocated by Carter, The Extreme Right in Western Europe, pp. 113-114.

41 Kitschelt, The Radical Right in Western Europe; Kitschelt, Diversification and Reconfiguration of Party Systems in Postindustrial Democracies; Kriesi et al., Globalization and the Transformation of National Political Space.

conservative, liberal, and RRWPs) can be found in the upper-right quadrant, suggesting that these parties combine a more monocultural appeal with a more market-oriented appeal.

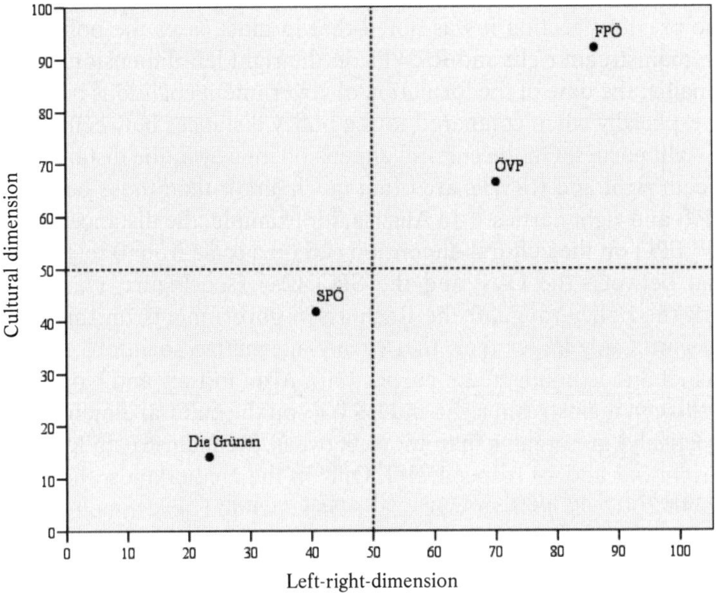

Figure 1a: The multi-dimensional space in Austria

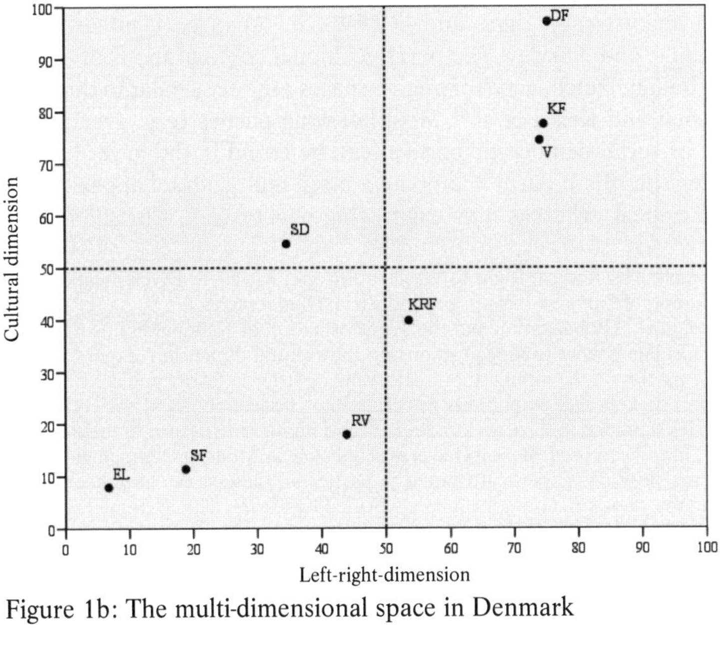

Figure 1b: The multi-dimensional space in Denmark

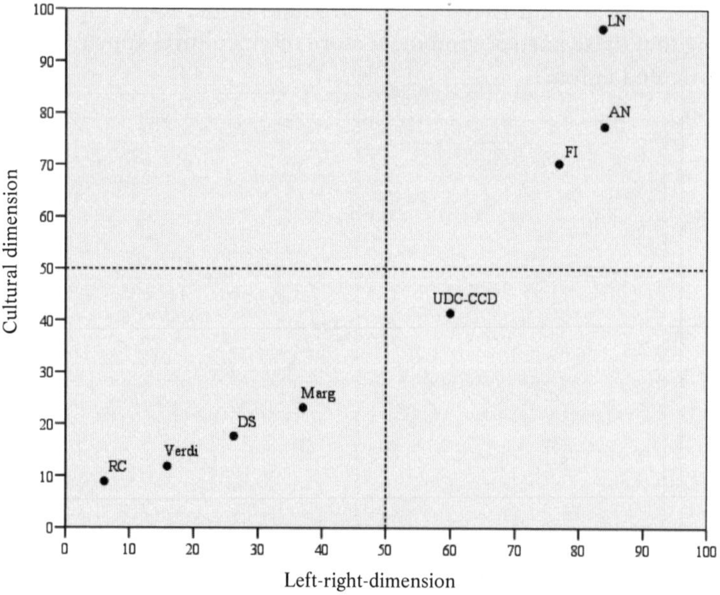

Figure 1c: The multi-dimensional space in Italy

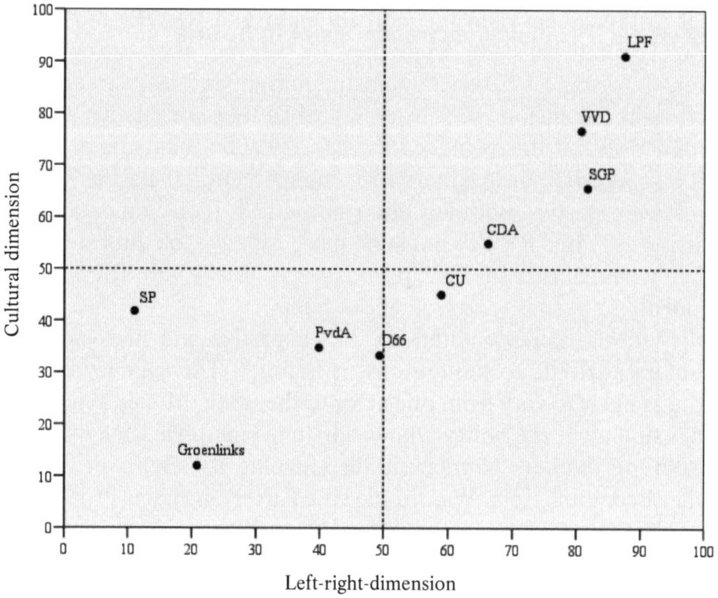

Figure 1d: The multi-dimensional space in the Netherlands

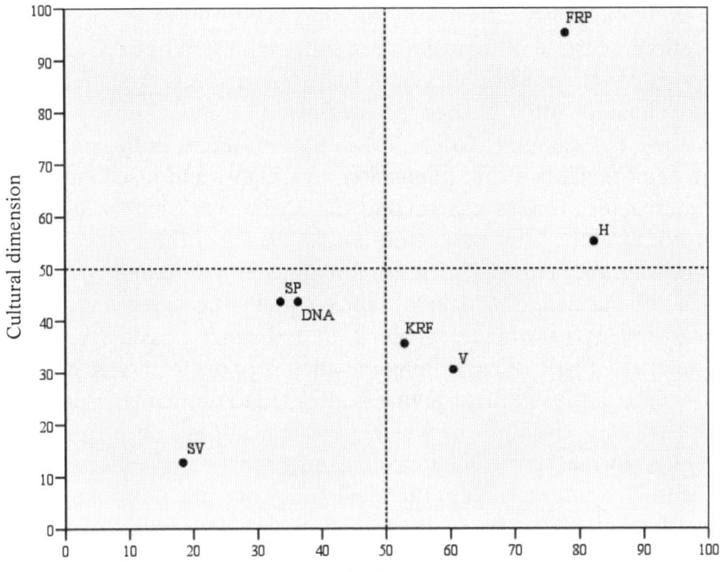

Figure 1e: The multi-dimensional space in Norway

However, the figures highlight the existence of an interesting puzzle. They show that distances between mainstream right and RRWPs on the left-right dimension are relatively small, while they are substantial on the cultural dimension. Inversely, distances between mainstream right and mainstream left parties on the left-right dimension are substantial, while they are relatively small on the cultural dimension. If this is indeed the case, why do mainstream right parties favor RRWPs as coalition partners over mainstream left parties? I will argue that mainstream parties, both left and right, attach more importance to socio-economic issues, while RRWPs attribute more salience to cultural issues.[42] This can explain why mainstream right parties prefer to ally with RRWPs, since it is possible for these parties to logroll about policy.

In policy terms, salience refers to the "cognitive and motivational importance", actors attribute to dimensions or issues.[43] The saliency of issues and dimensions is likely to vary from one actor to the other. Müller and Jenny argue: "Allerdings sind nicht alle policy-Dimensionen in einem Parteiensystem von gleicher Bedeutung. Weiters können sie für einzelne Parteien von höchst unterschiedlicher Bedeutung sein. Was für die eine Partei ein vitales Problem ist, kann für eine andere Partei unter 'ferner liefen' klassifiziert sein".[44] In a similar fashion Laver and Hunt note that "different parties do indeed attach different

42 Benoit/Laver, Party Policy in Modern Democracies.
43 Stokes, Spatial Models of Party Competition, p. 169.
44 Müller/Jenny, Abgeordnete, Parteien und Koalitionspolitik, p. 141. See also Sjöblom, Party Strategies in a Multiparty System, pp. 170 ff.

weights to the same policy dimensions" in most Western European countries.[45] The implications of these observations are far-reaching. When parties attribute different levels of salience to policy issues and dimensions, this affects the perceptions they have of other parties' policy positions, and of policy differences and similarities. For example, when parties have different policy positions and "when one actor weights a first dimension very highly and a second not at all, while another actor weights the second dimension very highly and the first dimension not at all [...] the two actors might even feel there is no difference between them in policy terms".[46] The combination of multi-dimensionality of the policy space and variable dimensional saliency and issue saliency creates a particular environment in which logrolling is a distinct possibility. The term logrolling refers to a type of bargaining in which support for policy proposals is exchanged based on the importance that is attached to particular issues. In other words, it refers to a situation in which parties negotiate on a quid pro quo basis.[47] In more formal terms, the logrolling deal represents a policy agreement in which "actor A agrees to accept the ideal policy of actor B on one dimension in exchange for actor B's agreement to accept the ideal policy of actor A on another dimension".[48] It differs fundamentally from other types of policy agreements, which are based on the "split-the-difference" principle.

Thus, even though mainstream right parties and RRWPs might take up quite different positions on immigration and integration issues, they are unlikely to experience these differences as problematic. After all, mainstream right parties do not attach great importance to these issues and are therefore willing to give RRWPs free rein of these issues. However, reaching policy compromise with mainstream left parties is much more difficult for them, as socio-economic issues, on which the mainstream left and mainstream right take markedly different stances, are salient for both.

Let me illustrate this principle by returning to the Austrian example. Issue and dimensional salience play important roles in Austrian politics, and especially in the coalition formation process that took place after the 1999 elections. At the time of these elections, the four Austrian parliamentary parties attributed different levels of salience to the issues that were important in the election campaign. Socio-economic issues and cultural issues, such as immigration and integration, or law and order, appeared particularly salient during this campaign. The prominence of economic and financial issues can be explained by the budgetary crisis Austria was confronted with in the late 1990s, while cultural issues were put on the agenda by the FPÖ, on the one hand, and *die Grünen*, on the

45 Laver/Hunt, Policy and Party Competition, p. 82.
46 Ibid., p. 80.
47 Logrolling, a practice common in the U.S. Congress, usually refers to the trading of votes by members of parliament to obtain the passage of legislation of interest to individual members of parliament. The practice relies on differential patterns of salience of issues or dimensions.
48 Laver/Hunt, Policy and Party Competition, p. 80.

other. The ÖVP and the SPÖ attached most importance to socio-economic issues, calling for budgetary reforms (the ÖVP) and labour market reforms (the SPÖ). For the FPÖ and *die Grünen* cultural issues were particularly relevant at the time of the 1999 elections, with the former campaigning for more restrictive immigration policies and the latter for better protection of the environment as well as human and women's rights.[49]

Not surprisingly, the coalition negotiations between the ÖVP and SPÖ were unsuccessful because the two mainstream parties were unable to compromise on socio-economic issues. More specifically, the SPÖ was unable to sell the austerity measures it had agreed to during the negotiations, including a transfer of the Ministry of Finance from the SPÖ to the ÖVP, to its auxiliary organizations. The ÖVP and FPÖ found it much easier to reach a policy compromise. The coalition agreement between these parties is characterized by logrolling. According to Ahlemeyer "the ÖVP gave almost free rein to the FPÖ in terms of immigration policies - as part of a quid pro quo between the two partners".[50] In return, the FPÖ supported an extensive economic reform program to which the ÖVP was strongly committed. This deal was attractive for several reasons. First, it allowed the ÖVP and FPÖ to realize the policy at the core of their policy programs. Second, it allowed the parties to please their electoral constituencies. Roughly, 47 % of the FPÖ voters listed the FPÖ's immigration position as the main reason for their support of the party. Similar considerations played a role after the 2002 elections, when the ÖVP engaged in mutual coalition negotiations with *die Grünen* and the FPÖ. These two parties are situated on opposite ends of the political spectre and differ especially when it comes to their positions immigration issues. The ÖVP offered each party free reign in the domain of immigration policy. It appeared willing to revoke measures taken by the black-blue coalition when it negotiated with *die Grünen*. At the same time, the ÖVP gave the FPÖ control over the immigration policy when the incumbent parties decided to renew their government coalition.[51]

In sum, the formation of the Schüssel I and II cabinets demonstrates that it has been much easier for the ÖVP and the FPÖ to reach a policy agreement than for the SPÖ and the ÖVP. The reason for this difference extends beyond the simple explanation that the policy differences between the ÖVP and the SPÖ are greater than between the ÖVP and the FPÖ. A comprehensive explanation

49 The question of European integration was less salient at the time of 1999 elections, since the requirements for participation in Euro as laid down in the Stability Pact had already been met, and the question of enlargement had not yet gained momentum. Religious issues appeared secondary at the time of the 1999 elections as well, even though family policy was quite prominent in the electoral campaign. Although the ÖVP and FPÖ agreed on the importance of these issues, they made different policy proposal. The former party proposed an extension of maternity leave, while the latter party proposed the introduction of the children cheque. Heinisch, Populism, Proporz, Pariah; Müller/Jenny, Abgeordnete, Parteien und Koalitionspolitik.

50 Ahlemeyer, The Coalition Potential of Extreme Right Parties in Western Europe, p. 98.

51 Ibid., p. 114.

also includes the observation that the nature of the policy differences between the ÖVP and the SPÖ differ from those between the ÖVP and the FPÖ. Where the SPÖ and the ÖVP take divergent positions on the same dimension, the ÖVP and the FPÖ take divergent positions on different dimensions. In the former situation, the only solution is policy compromise, which requires that mainstream right parties abandon their preferred policy positions. In the latter situation, parties have the possibility to logroll in which event they can realize part of their preferred policy positions. The policy preferences they see included in the government agreement under this scheme are normally at the core of their policy programme. The cost-benefit calculations in this situation are thus more positive for mainstream right parties than making a conventional policy compromise.

V. A comparative outlook

Western Europe is not the only region in which RRWPs have governed in recent years. In several Eastern European countries, RRWPs have also made the transition from pariah to power. Table 3 demonstrates that they have assumed office in Estonia, Poland, Romania, and Slovakia. In Estonia, the *Eesti Rahvusliku Sõltumatuse Partei* (ERSP) was invited to participate in a government coalition in 1992 by *Isamaa-Mõõdukad,* a conservative party, and gratefully accepted this invitation. The same happened to the Polish *Liga Polskich Rodzin* (LPR), which was invited to govern by the national conservative *Prawo i Sprawiedliwość* (PiS) in 2006. In Romania, the *Partidul România Mare* (PRM) and *Partidul Unității Naționale a Românilor* (PUNR) briefly governed in the first half of the 1990s. Finally, in Slovakia the *Slovenská národná strana* (SNS) assumed office in 1992, 1994 and again in 2006.[52]

Table 3: Radical right parties in office in Eastern Europe

Country	Cabinet	Mainstream party	RRWP	Year
Estonia	Laar I	Isamaa-Mõõdukad	ERSP	1992
	Tarand I	Isamaa-Mõõdukad	ERSP	1994
Poland	Kaczyński I	PiS, SO	LPR	2006
Romania	Văcăroiu I	PDSR, PSM	PRM, PUNR*	1993
Slovakia	Mečiar II	HZDS, ZRS	SNS	1992
	Mečiar III	HZDSm ZRS	SNS	1994
	Fico I	Smer, HZDS	SNS	2006

* RRWP acts as support party to minority government.

52 Mudde, Populist Radical Right Parties in Europe, p. 280.

The composition of the government coalitions in which the Eastern European RRWPs have participated is quite different from that of the government coalitions in which their Western European counterparts have participated. Most importantly, the government coalitions have been more ideologically diverse, with a number of RRWPs collaborating with left-wing parties. Examples include the Polish LPR, which governed with the social populist *Samoobrona Rzeczpospolitej Polskiej* ("Samoobrona"), the Romanian PRM and PUNR, which joined the social-democratic *Partidul Democrației Sociale in România* (PDSR) and the social populist *Partidul Socialist al Muncii* (PSM) in office in 1995, and the SNS, which allied with the communist *Združenie robotníkov Slovenska* (ZRS) in 1992 and 1994 and with the social populist *Smer - sociálna demokracia* ("Smer") in 2006. Ishiyama has succinctly described these alliances as red-brown coalitions, since they bring together various types of former communists and nationalists.[53]

Although the composition of the government coalitions in Eastern Europe clearly differs from that of the government coalitions in Western Europe, their formation can still be explained by the office-, policy-, and vote-seeking behavior of the parties that have teamed up with the RRWPs. However, the dimensionality of Eastern European political spaces, as well as positions parties take up in these spaces, differs from that of Western European political spaces.[54] In Central and Eastern Europe, parties tend to combine left-wing, state-oriented appeals with authoritarian appeals and right-wing, market-oriented appeals with libertarian appeals. Thus, most parties are either located in the upper-left quadrant or the lower-right quadrant of the political space. RRWPs are often the exception to this rule. Like their radical right-wing brethren in Western Europe, they are located in the upper-half of the political space, on the authoritarian extreme of the cultural dimension. In terms of their position on the left-right dimension, the picture is slightly more complex, with some Eastern European RRWPs placed more to the left of this dimension and others more to the right. This means that these parties are often located closer to left-wing parties than to right-wing parties, especially when their respective positions on the cultural dimension are taken into account. In the countries in which this is the case, RRWPs are thus more attractive coalition partners to the left than for the right.

53 Ishiyama, Strange Bedfellows.
54 Benoit/Laver, Party Policy in Modern Democracies; Kitschelt et al., Post-Communist Party Systems; Marks et al., Party Competition and European Integration in the East and West.

VI. Conclusion

Since the late 1990s, many RRWPs, both in Eastern and Western Europe, have made the transition from pariah to power. To explain their government participation, it is essential to investigate why other parties find it attractive to govern with these parties. Mainstream right parties in Western Europe prefer RRWPs to mainstream left parties as coalition partners because they are "cheap" coalition partners which can easily be dominated and with which coalition agreements can be concluded without too many difficulties. Thus, RRWPs are ideal coalition partners for mainstream right parties because they enable these parties to realize office, policy *and* votes. This is unique as parties usually face trade-offs between these goals when assuming office. Parties in Eastern Europe govern with RRWPs for similar reasons. Hence, the apparent differences between East and West, exemplified by the different compositions of the government coalitions in which RRPWs have participated, disguise important similarities in incentives for mainstream parties to ally with RRWPs.

Let me conclude with a number of more general observations. Debates about the government participation of RRWPs have often had a strong normative component. Many commentators and scholars have investigated whether the rise to power of RRWPs has had negative consequences for the stability of governments or the quality of democracy. They have examined whether RRWPs in power have fundamentally changed immigration and integration policies and curtailed minority rights. Although these debates are certainly important, they should not distract from the fact that the interactions between mainstream and RRWPs are part of the broader process of party competition and cooperation, in which strategic considerations often prevail over normative consideration. To understand why mainstream parties no longer treat RRWPs as political pariahs, it is necessary to analyze how the success of these parties has transformed the competitive and cooperative dynamics in Western European party systems. The rise of RRWPs has shifted the balance of power in Western European parliaments to the right and has therefore provided some mainstream parties with new coalition alternatives. In many cases, these new coalitions are more attractive than old alliances because their formation is less costly for mainstream parties. Governing with RRWPs provides mainstream parties with significant shares of cabinet portfolios, substantial influence over policy-making, and a chance to win back voters lost to their radical right competitors in previous elections.

Against all Expectations - Right-Wing Extremism in Romania and Bulgaria

Michael Meznik / Tom Thieme

I. Introduction

Who compares the development of right-wing extremism in Bulgaria and Romania in the past ten years, will gain an astonishing insight - at least at the level of political parties. There have been a number of analogies in both states after the collapse of communism (end of the national-communist systems, extended transformation of systems and joining the EU in 2007) and opportunity structures in the East Balkans which were similarly favorable for right-wing extremism (insufficient processes of coming to terms with the past, insufficient democratic consolidation among elites and population, economic backwardness compared to other East Central European states). However, as far as chronology is concerned, the development of right-wing extremist parties happened in diametrically opposite ways. In Romania, several right-wing extremist parties were elected to the parliament already in the 1990s. They took over government responsibility, and were sometimes able to strongly root their anti-democratic ideas of society in the political discourse. In the year 2000 the *Party of Greater Romania* (PRM) became the second-strongest power of the Romanian party system with 19.5 % of the votes, and its chairman, Vadim Tudor, reached the final ballot for presidency. In Bulgaria on the other hand, the rise of right-wing extremist parties started very belatedly, as late as in the year 2005. Since then, the situation has turned to the opposite. Currently, in Romania (right-wing) extremist powers are not represented in the national assembly, while in Bulgaria the right-wing extremist alliance ATAKA supports Prime Minister Bojko Borisov's centre-right coalition. These different tendencies raise the question why right-wing extremism has developed in such contradictory ways in the past 20 years despite similar prevailing conditions.

Scientific literature provides different approaches at an explanation of the specific causes and ways of appearance of right-wing extremist phenomena. Most of them are in accordance to each other but only describe one direction of the developments (success or abstinence).[1] For the time being, there are no

1 See Rechtsradikalismus in Transformationsgesellschaften. In: Osteuropa, 52 (2002) 3/5/7/8, pp. 247-335, 612-630, 885-913, 1056-1062.

convincing answers to the question of why in some countries there have developed strong right-wing extremist movements during or after system transformation, whereas other countries are or seem to be resistant against such phenomena. Among the attempts at an explanation, the approach by Minkenberg/Beichelt on the case of Romania is somewhat plausible. They understand Romanian right-wing extremism as a result of system transformation,[2] which, however, cannot be true to the same extent for the later case of Bulgaria. Explaining the latter by the theory of a so-called "post-EU-accession syndrome" - as Attila Ágh[3] does in the case of the development of extremism and populism in Hungaria - is not convincing for two reasons. On the one hand, right-wing extremism in Romania declined conspicuously after the country's accession to the EU. On the other hand, the currently most successful right-wing extremist party in Bulgaria, ATAKA, does not fundamentally reject the EU. This contribution is meant to find out if instead the inner nature of right-wing extremist attempts in the fields of ideology, strategy, and organization proves to be more convincing in respect of their success or failure.

Literature for a comparative analysis of right-wing extremism in Romania and Bulgaria is ambivalent, and this is obviously appropriate to the explosive nature of the problem. There are a number of publications on Romania and the success of right-wing extremist parties at the end of the 1990s,[4] whereas there have been only very few studies on their decline since the mid-2000s.[5] In contrast, publications on right-wing extremism in Bulgaria were a rarity until about 2005,[6] and only with the establishment of the right-wing extremist formation of ATAKA there was an increase of research interest in Bulgarian right-wing extremism at the party level.[7] In both states, studies on non-party and rather subcultural right-wing extremism are still research desiderata.[8]

The contribution presented here attempts to provide explanations for both development paths of right-wing extremist phenomena by the example of the Southeastern European states of Bulgaria and Romania. At first, the framework conditions under which such forces may be successful (or not) shall be determined. In this context, historical roots of right-wing extremist movements, the significance of respective political cultures, and additionally minority problems in the individual states will be discussed. The analysis of right-wing extremist organizations differentiates according to party and non-party right-wing extremism.

2 Beichelt/Minkenberg, Rechtsradikalismus, pp. 247-262.
3 Ágh, Hungarian Politics, pp. 68-81.
4 See a. o. Carey, Post-Communist Right Radicalism; Shafir, The Mind, pp. 213-232; Marginalization or Mainstream? pp. 247-267; Grün, Rechtsradikale Massenmobilisierung, pp. 293-304; Andreescu, Extremismul de Dreaptă în România.
5 See Andreescu, Romania, pp. 184-209; For an extremism-theoretical perspective, see: Adamson/Florean/Thieme, Extremismus in Rumänien, pp. 311-326.
6 See Bell, The Radical Right in Bulgaria.
7 See Ivanov/Ilieva, Bulgaria, pp. 1-29; Žečeva, "ATAKA", pp. 49-65.
8 See Country Reports Romania and Bulgaria, pp. 1-29 and 184-209; Bertelsmann Stiftung (Ed.), Strategies for Combating.

Concerning parties, the analysis of election results since 1990, possible alliances, and government participation (Section 3.1) as well as ideologic, strategic, and organizational activities are in the fore (Section 3.2). Aspects such as positions on the nation and the EU, behavior towards democratic forces, and the relationship to anti-democratic counterparts will figure prominently, just as answering the question about the nature of right-wing extremist groups. Non-party organizations will be analyzed most of all in respect of their readiness for violence, their activities, and their sub-cultural environment (Section 4).

As a conclusion, it will be about classifying the various movements, an evaluation of the potential danger of such organizations as well as about explaining the success or failure of right-wing extremist phenomena. An outlook will serve for estimating the future chances of the establishment of right-wing extremism in Bulgaria and Romania and for evaluating the results against the background of current research.

II. Framework conditions

Although Romania's farewell to communism in 1989/90 is an exception among the otherwise mostly peaceful revolutions in East and Central Europe,[9] in the cases of both Bulgaria and Romania there happened a "top-down system change", as Wolfgang Merkel pointed out.[10] The establishment of democracy was organized by reformers from the second ranks of the former communist state parties, the armies, and secret services deriving their legitimacy from the removal of Zhivkov or the shooting of Ceaușescu. Extensive personal continuities, but most of all the lack of powerful pluralist counter-elites slowed down the consolidation of the new democratic systems. Indeed, there happened the formal institutionalization of democratic constitutions and ways of procedure, but there was no consolidation of democracy based on acceptance and satisfaction. Thus, still today historic influences on these societies as well as lacking democratic influence are a fertile ground for the development and establishment of right-wing extremist organizations.

Romania and Bulgaria both look back to a long tradition of right-wing extremist movements. In Romania in the inter-war period there developed the Fascist Iron Guard under the authoritarian leadership of Corneliu Zelea Codreanu and became a mass movement.[11] In Bulgaria, the Union of Bulgarian National Legions was successful.[12] With the Red Army occupying both countries in 1944, and the start of Sovietization, nationalist associations were banned. At first,

9 On the peaceful revolutions in East Europe, see among others: Auer, Das Erbe von 1989, pp. 31-46.
10 Cf. Merkel, Systemtransformation, pp. 342-347.
11 For details see Petreu, An Infamous Past.
12 In the 1930s the Union of Bulgarian National Legions had about 200,000 members. See Meznik, Extremismus in Bulgarien, pp. 49-62, here 51.

nationalism officially disappeared. However - in Romania with the communist Party leader Ceaușescu coming into power in 1964, in Bulgaria since the late 1970s - there was a renaissance still during the socialist era.[13] To secure their power in these even more backward countries in comparison to Eastern Central Europe (not to speak of Western Europe), the regimes instrumentalized so-called "national values". This way they supported an atmosphere of prejudice towards foreigners, which is still present in the mentalities of the populations. The range of rejection reaches from latent prejudices to manifest hostility and is even found in the midst of society. In Romania it is most of all directed against the Hungarian minority; in Bulgaria it is the Turkish minority whose members were subjected to forced assimilation in the late 1980s. The Roma minorities are discriminated against in both countries.[14]

There is no anti-extremist consensus in Romania and Bulgaria. Although - according to their constitutions - anti-democratic parties are banned, politically and socially it is not clear what must be considered extremist or democratic at all. While civil society developments led to a spread of democratic ideas in the East Central European region already before 1989, the regime conflict in South Eastern Europe is considered to have not been solved (yet). On the other hand, there were no oppositional counter-elite during the radical change of 1989/90 that would have been morally entitled and able to provide the rooting of democratic-cultural principles. Accordingly, in Romania and Bulgaria, anti-democratic rhetoric is neither discredited nor a sole feature of extremist parties. The latter are not principally excluded from government coalitions. In many fields of civil society the will as well as the resources to work against ethnically-nationalistically legitimated political mobilization are lacking.

These days, the national-communist heritage of the two countries does not only characterize societal conflicts and the opportunity structures of right-wing extremism but it also results in an image of the anti-democratic actors which - according to classical left-right categories - cannot be clearly classified. Right-wing extremist parties referring to a country's nationalist traditions cannot ignore the communist era. The establishment of a spiritual continuity from the pre-war and inter-war periods to the socialist era cannot be imagined without referring to national communism during the Cold War. Also the "cleavage" (post) communist vs. anti-communist is little helpful. It results in a split of the party systems - not of the political extremisms, which belong to the same historic continuity. Neither in the societies under discussion nor in international

13 On the development of Bulgarian nationalism see in general: Todorova, The Courses and Discourses of Bulgarian Nationalism, pp. 55–102. In Claudia Weber's opinion, the turn towards Bulgarian nationalism happened as early as in the mid-1950s. See Weber, Geschichte und Macht, pp. 77–90.

14 See Hausleitner, Wettlauf der Patrioten, pp. 599–626.

relevant literature,[15] there is a consensus on the kind of political extremism to which most of the actors of the anti-democratic spheres must be attributed.

III. Right-wing extremist parties

3.1 Election development

In the 1990s, right-wing extremist parties in Romania were frequently successful during elections. Although after the confusing initial elections on May 20, 1990, none of them was elected to parliament, a number of phantom parties and splinter groups were able to join the constitutional assembly following in the wake of the *National Salvation Front* (FSN), among them some clearly anti-democratic groups. Between 1990 and 1992, there emerged political parties from many of these associations. After the parliament elections of 1992, two right-wing extremist parties entered Romania's Chamber of Deputies and Senate. *Romanian National Unity* (PUNR) and the *Party of Greater Romania* (PRM) achieved 7.7 % and 3.9 % respectively. After the election they became coalition partners of the post-communist *Party of Romania's Social Democracy* (PDSR), before - after internal quarrels on the treaty on cooperation with Hungary - this alliance changed its official cooperation into a formal cooperation agreement. It was valid until the end of the four-year legislature in 1996.[16]

Taking part in the government resulted in different consequences for the two parties. For the PUNR, the 1996 elections marked the beginning of its fall. It achieved 4.3 % of the votes and lost more than three per cent compared to 1992. Even an election alliance with two other right-wing extremist parties (see Table 1) in the year 2000 could not stop the decline of this party. With 1.4 %, the PUNR clearly failed to overcome the minimum level of nine per cent for three-party-alliances, which was applied for the first time.[17] The party never recovered from this defeat and from being excluded from parliament. In 2004, it achieved 0.5 % of the votes. For the elections of 2008, the party did not run anymore as an independent party. Two years earlier, it had joined the *Conservative Party* (PC).[18]

The *Party of Greater Romania*, on the other hand, survived its period as a government party without damage. It was the only party of the voted-out coalition to improve its result in the elections of 1996, compared to four years pre-

15 On different conceptions and classifications see Minkenberg, Die radikale Rechte, pp. 305-322; Grün, Rechtsradikale Massenmobilisierung, pp. 293-304; Meznik, Extremismus in Bulgarien, pp. 49-62.

16 See Andreescu, Extremismul, p. 30.

17 For details see Autengruber, Die politischen Parteien.

18 See Central Election Office of Romania, Results of the Romanian parliamentary elections 2004 and 2008, available at: http://www.bec2004.ro/ und http://www. becparlamentare2008.ro/ last accessed 4 October 2010.

viously, although only slightly (4.5 %). The actual rise of the PRM started as an opposition party. As with all elections in Romania (with the exception of 1992), in 2000 the government parties were punished. With 19.5 %, the PRM achieved an unpredicted record.[19] In the presidential elections of the same day, PRM chairman Corneliu Vadim Tudor reached the final ballot, however, he was clearly defeated by the later head of government, Ion Iliescu (33.2 %).

Although the PRM had developed into the collective party of the nationalist camp by that time, its election results were on the decline from then on. In the parliament elections of 2004, the party lost more than 5 % (12.9 %) compared to 2000, Tudor lost more than 15 % in the presidential elections. In 2008, there followed the low point of the PRM's history. The introduction of elements of direct election to Romania's election system resulted in signs of breaking in the party, which had vainly litigated against the new law. Being isolated from all other parties, with 3.2 % the PRM achieved its worst result ever at the national level.[20] However, this was not the party's end. With 8.7 % of the votes in the European elections of 2009, the PRM experienced a quick and unexpected comeback. Since then its showpiece, Tudor, has been a member of the European Parliament.[21]

Table 1: Results of right-wing extremist parties at parliament and European elections in Romania since 1992 (in %)*

	Parliamentary elections					European elections	
	1992	1996	2000	2004	2008	2007	2009
PUNR	7.7	4.4	1.4	0.5	–	–	–
PRM	3.9	4.5	19.5	12.9	3.2	4.2	8.7
PNG	–	–	0.2	2.2	2.3	4.9	–

* Results for the Chamber of Deputies of the Romanian parliament.
Source: Central Election Office of Romania, compilation by the authors.

Other right-wing extremist parties were not able to benefit from the weakness of the PRM. The *Party of the New Generation* (PNG), founded by George Becali in the year 2000 with the intention to use it as a foundation of this billionaire's ambitions to become president, did not become really established. Although since the year 2000 elections the PNG has been able to gradually improve its results (2000: 0.2; 2004: 2.2; 2008: 2.3 %),[22] each time it clearly failed to achieve the five per cent minimum required for parliament. After his temporary success in the European elections of 2007 (4.9 %), Becali also had

19 See De Nève, Wahlen in Rumänien, pp. 281–298, here pp. 285–287.
20 See Gabanyi, Die Parlamentswahlen in Rumänien 2008, pp. 64–75, here 72.
21 See Europäisches Parlament (Ed.), Ergebnisse der Europawahl 2009 in Rumänien, available at http://www.europarl.europa.eu/parliament/archive/elections2009/pdf/RO%20Elus.pdf last access 20 September 2010.
22 See Nohlen/Stöver (Eds.), Elections in Europe.

to postpone his intention to become president of Romania. In 2004, he achieved 1.8 % in the first round of the election; in 2009, it was 1.9 %. Given its lack of success and hopelessness, for the European elections of 2009 the PNG ran on the PRM ticket. Just like Vadim Tudor, the PNG's chairman Becali was also elected to the European parliament, where he must be satisfied with being an MP.[23] However, this way he enjoys parliamentary immunity, as in Romania several legal proceedings have been taken against him.

In Bulgaria, until the parliamentary elections of 2005 - despite many attempts - all right-wing extremist parties had by far failed to be elected to the national assembly. Attempts by parties such as the *Bulgarian Democratic Forum* (BDF) and the *Internal Macedonian Revolutionary Organization/Bulgarian National Movement* (VMRO-BND), which tried to ideologically connect to pre-socialist traditions of active right-wing extremist movements, became a failure. Apart from the four per cent minimum required for being elected to parliament, this was most of all due to the logics of political debating during the first decade of transformation. The predominant confrontation between the BSP, the successor to the former communist state party, and the oppositional collective movement *Union of Democratic Forces* (SDS) supported the development of a "bipolar" party system[24] and weakened extremist parties. Only as a part of the SDS, candidates from right-wing extremist parties (most of all from the BDF) were able to send individual MPs to the national parliament during the 1990s.

The vacuum resulting from the declining significance of the opposition communist vs. anti-communist was at first filled by populist forces in 2001. This way, individual representatives of right-wing extremist parties, running on the tickets of more extensive election coalitions, achieved mandates, most of all the VMRO. Finally, in the 2005 elections the ATAKA coalition, which had initially developed as a heterogeneous alliance of both right- and left-wing forces under Volen Siderov, achieved 8.1 % per cent of the votes.[25] Despite some internal quarrels following soon after which resulted in individual MPs leaving the parliament faction, Siderov and ATAKA were once more able to do clearly better in the following presidential elections in 2006 (21.5 % in the first round) as well as the elections to the European parliament in 2007 (14.2 %).

Although in the parliament elections of 2009 ATAKA was only doing slightly better (by 1.3 % to 9.4 %), this election result meant a clear cut. The triumph of the conservative law-and-order party GERB under Sofia mayor Bojko Borisov (39.7 %) once again resulted in the ruling post-communists being removed from office, and for the first time there was a minority government tolerated by right-wing extremist ATAKA. As for Borisov both the post-communist election alliance "Coalition for Bulgaria", which came second, and the *Movement for Rights and Freedom* (DPS), the parliamentary representation of the Turkish

23 See Gammelin, Sternchen, Stars und Extremisten.
24 See e.g. Karasimeonov, The Party System in Bulgaria, pp. 39–57, here 45.
25 On individual election results compare here and in the following Riedel, Das politische System Bulgariens, pp. 677–728, here 698–699.

Table 2: Results of right-wing extremist parties at parliamentary and European elections in Bulgaria since 1994 (in %)

	Parliamentary elections					European elections	
	1994	1997	2001	2005	2009	2007	2009
VMRO*	-	-	3.6	5.2	4.1	1.9	2.3
ATAKA	-	-	-	8.1	9.4	14.2	12.0

* since 2001 as part of changing election and party alliances.
Source: Official Election Office of Bulgaria, compilation by the authors.

minority, coming third, were out of question as coalition partners. Bulgaria's "new strong man" decided for a minority government together with the party alliance Blue Coalition, tolerated by ATAKA. For the time being, its top man Siderov has supported the Borisov cabinet without reservations.

3.2 Organization, ideology, and strategies of right-wing extremist parties

While right-wing extremism in Romania was mostly split up (mostly regionally) after 1990, the *Party of Greater Romania* had risen to become the country's central power by the end of the 1990s. Anyway, there were more common grounds than differences between PUNR and PRM. Both parties were in ideologic and personal continuity both with the fascist and the national-communist dictatorships. They were considered hostile towards minorities, and were essentially influenced by central leaders. Still today, the PRM's chairman is Ceauşescu's former "poet laureate", Corneliu Vadim Tudor. Right from the beginning, he was the undebated leader of the party. In the 1990s, it constantly gained supporters. Until its peak in 2000, the number of members - allegedly - rose to 155,000.[26] The personal connections between the PRM and the former secret service, Securitate, are an open secret.[27]

Tudor's ideology is to the same extent based on the ideas of the dictators Antonescu and Ceauşescu. The PRM adores Marshal Antonescu as a national hero and a holy warrior against Bolshevism. With his nationalist-Bolshevist course, Ceauşescu is said to have directly followed the tradition of Romanian fascist movements. The merits of both in connection with Romania's independence are uploaded with conspiracy theories - the Romanian nation is said to be threatened by its Hungarian and Jewish minorities.[28] Most of all anti-semitism

26 There are no reliable data on the membership rates of Romanian parties. Neither are membership fees raised nor registrations listed, and thus there is no leaving a party or being excluded. The number of inactive members cannot be estimated. Furthermore, the parties' local or regional branches play only an insignificant role. On the organization of Romanian parties and their role in the party system, see Oltenau, Rumänien, pp. 147-166.
27 See Shafir, The Mind, p. 214.
28 See Grün, Rechtsradikale Massenmobilisierung, pp. 297-299.

works as an element connecting all historic breaks and is used to explain all historic achievements and mistakes. A Holocaust - on this, Ceauşescu, Tudor, and many Romanians agreed - has never happened in Romania.

Right from the beginning, Tudor has defined the PRM's political course as well as its change. In the 1990s, he rejected Romania's democratization and propagated the erection of a military dictatorship according to the historical model. The party program - just as ideologic references - is a mixture of nationalist and socialist claims. The PRM calls itself a centre party, as its economic policy, as claimed by the party, is left-wing and its minority policy right-wing. Its ideas of the nation are characterized by its belief in the particularity of the Romanian people. Orthodox denomination is considered the essential criterion of ex- and inclusion. The PRM instrumentalizes the economic difficulties of the transformation process and thus increases an uploaded ethnic consciousness of society.

Tudor has extended the nationalist discourse by social topics such as poverty, corruption and unemployment. He claims that enemies of the Romanian nation are responsible for this: the political elites, the Gypsies, Hungarians, Jews, and homosexuals. Accordingly, the PRM supports a number of so-called "pro-Romanian" measures. It supports the nationalization of foreign, Jewish, and Hungarian private property, and it rejects the privatization of state enterprises. It demands the restoration of the Romanian army, and it demands the abolition of essential minority rights, as the latter are said to be a kind of positive discrimination towards the Romanian majority population.[29] Due to its combination of nationalist and communist programmatic elements, the PRM addresses, most of all, those who have suffered losses in the course of the system change. However, the addition of right-wing and left-wing extremist positions has nothing to do with coming closer to the democratic centre.

Strategically and organizationally, the PRM is completely oriented at Vadim Tudor. He is said to be charismatic as he led the party towards its successes in the 1990s. However, he is also responsible for its decline after 2000. The German-Romanian winner of the Nobel Prize in Literature, Herta Müller, describes Tudor's political style as "sometimes rough, then scholarly, sometimes vulgar, then religious, sometimes sentimental, then railing, [...] always strictly militaristic and openly racist".[30] Tudor demands unconditional loyalty from his functionaries and still today decides staff questions in an authoritative manner. His self-staging shows features of the personal cult of the Ceauşescu era. Although there are local branches of the party, they do not serve for an inner-party development of opinion but for providing funds for election campaigns and for supporting the leadership. Tudor's exceptional standing with the PRM

29 See Roger, Les parties anti-système dans la Roumanie post-communiste, pp. 101-136.
30 Müller, Vor der Diktatur ist nach der Diktatur, available at http://www.tagesspiegel.de/kultur/literatur/Herta-Mueller-Nobelpreis-Rumaenien;art138,2918734 last accessed 27 September 2010.

results most of all from his activity as the editor of the nationalist weekly "România Mare" since 1990. By help of this nationwide-known paper he was not only able to spread his party's political message but at the same time to stage himself as its undebated showpiece and mouthpiece. Gabriel Andreescu sees the essential strong point of Tudor and the PRM in the fact that they are able to produce and distribute their own mass media.[31]

The year 2000 meant a cut for the PRM. The party won almost 20 % at the parliamentary elections, and Tudor made it to the final ballot for presidency. However, as EU representatives had made unmistakably clear to Romania's political elite that a party such as the PRM would endanger the country's European integration process, Tudor was without any real option at the peak of his election success. Support for him declined. This led to an inner-party change of strategy. To be able to (co-)rule in the future, the party had to become more moderate or at least had to look respectable. At the beginning of 2004, Tudor spoke of a spiritual experience that had fundamentally changed his attitude towards Judaism. He explained that he had been an anti-semite, but that God had opened his eyes, and from then on, he loved Jews as much as he had hated them in the past.[32] Tudor followed up his words with action. In Transsylvania he funded a memorial in honor of Israel's murdered Prime Minister, Yitzhak Rabin. At Aushwitz the former Holocaust denier Tudor, heading a PRM delegation, laid a wreath and confessed that Romania's Jews had been exterminated.[33] However, the seriousness of his regret may be doubted, not only because Tudor's change of course happened so abruptly and the reasons he gave were so implausible. Not everybody in the PRM follows Tudor's course. Still today, in the party paper of the same name there appear anti-semitic and minority-hostile publications.[34] Apart from anti-semitism, Tudor's thinking seems to be characterized rather by continuity than by change.

Tudor's moderateness or legalistic tactics were punished by the voters. As the PRM was no longer a visible alternative to the democratic parties, in the face of a lacking coalition option many Romanians saw no reason why they should vote them. Tudor became a victim of his own vanity. Still in the 1990s, he gained popularity as the defender of Romanian national interests, his political competitors only being able to run in his tracks. Due to the prospects of joining the EU, suddenly Tudor himself was perceived as a danger for Romania's future. Tudor did not want to play the role of a political outsider; he could not stand social exclusion. For the time being, his (alleged) reformation has speeded up the PRM's loss in significance.

31 See Andreescu, Extremismul.

32 See Oancea, Mythen und Vergangenheit - Rumänien nach der Wende, unpublished dissertation thesis, Munich 2005, under: http://edoc.ub.uni-muenchen.de/4577/1/Oancea_Daniela.pdf, pp. 113-114, last accessed 28 September 2010.

33 See ibid., p. 114.

34 On this topic see the online archive of the PRM party magazine "România Mare", available at http://www.romare.ro/ last accessed 24 September 2010.

Since being elected into parliament in 2005, ATAKA under Volen Siderov has been the most important power of party right-wing extremism in Bulgaria. Considering ATAKA right-wing extremist is based on Siderov's activity as a publicist as well as on his scandalous media appearances in the election campaign of 2005. In the context of his own TV program, he led a xenophobic hate campaign against the Turkish population and, most of all, the Roma minority.[35] Statements found among party documents and the positions supported by the party since 2005 were the reason for different, contradicting attempts at a classification: among others, ATAKA has been called "right-wing extremist", "populist" and, particularly because of its demand for the renationalization of privatized enterprises, a "left-wing extremist" power.[36] A look at the "20 Points",[37] published during the election campaign of 2005 and valid still today - a kind of catalogue of demands where ATAKA articulates typical nationalist as well as social-political and anti-elite positions - illustrates how difficult it is to classify this party. The heterogeneity of demands does not only reflect election-strategic calculations but also the structure of ATAKA, which was originally started as a coalition, developed from a pragmatic alliance of right-wing and left-wing extremists.[38] The least common denominator in this context was the nation and concerns in respect of its further existence. Within the party, there is a fierce debate on the kind of nationalism as being supported by Siderov and ATAKA.[39] Essential points of the program are resentment towards the Turkish minority and its political representation as well as thus connected demands for an end of the Turkish-language news programs on state TV and a ban of the "unconstitutional ethnic DPS party". An integral part of ATAKA's nationalism is the identification of "enemies of the nation", which are found most of all among the Roma population as well as among external powers such as the US, NATO, and international financial institutions. Siderov considers Roma a criminal "privileged" minority "terrorizing" the majority population and, due to a high birthrate, threatening with pushing away the native population.

35 Siderov is the author of two books that must be counted among the genre of anti-Semitic world conspiracy literature. In his TV program, he repeatedly presents the Bulgarian nation as the victim of criminal "Gypsy terror". ATAKA's essential slogans for election campaigns were "No to Turkeyzation! No to Gypsization!" as well as "Let's take Bulgaria back!".

36 See Žečeva, "ATAKA", p. 50.

37 See 20 točki na Partija ATAKA, available at http://www.ataka.bg/en/index.php?option=com_content&task= view&id=14&Itemid=27 last accessed 14 September 2010.

38 The coalition was formed of Siderov's ATAKA, "Defence"-Union of Patriotic Forces, "Fatherland"-Movement of National Rescue, The Bulgarian "National-patriotic Party", and the "Zora" Political Circle.

39 Meanwhile there is a debate between Siderov and those forces as having left the coalition, in the context of which the latter accuse him of an "opportunistic" kind of nationalism which is used only to maximize votes, and against which they claim their own "authentic nationalism". In the course of this debate there have been publications aiming at providing evidence that Siderov has betrayed the original goals of the coalition. Nejčev et al., Volen Siderov.

Given the generally high degree of support for accession to the European Union among the Bulgarian population, the attitude towards the EU is somewhat more differentiated. Demands only aim at changing those regulations of the accession treaty that are unfavorable for Bulgaria. EU membership is not rejected in principle; rather ATAKA attempts increased networking with other extremely right-wing forces in the EU parliament.

ATAKA's attitude towards democratic forces has changed since its first appearance in 2005. The initial attitude of fundamental opposition against the "corrupt elite" - including the demand to bring "national traitors" to court - has been replaced by a pragmatic way of dealing with political opponents since one has joined the parliament. One exception is the unchanged rejection of the DPS, particularly of its leading circle around the party's chairman, Ahmed Dogan, who is accused to once again have submitted Bulgaria under "the Turkish yoke".

Meanwhile ATAKA is provided with regional party structures, and in the last municipal elections in 2009, it achieved above-average results in some cities on the Black Sea coast. In this context, the principle of total opposition has been given up on in some municipalities where ATAKA joined alliances with other right-wing (as well as democratic) forces.[40] After ATAKA's unexpectedly good results in the national elections as well as the elections to the European parliament, its long-term establishment in the party system seems to be realistic. This raises the question about the preconditions for the party's success and the motivations for voting it. Protest against the established political class, which is frequently and beyond party lines stigmatized by corruption scandals, is one important reason. Apart from such anti-establishment reflexes and from Siderov's appearance,[41] also social-populist demands are a motivation for many voters. For example, ATAKA demands to give the health and educational systems as well as social security and general welfare priority above foreign-political obligations such as those towards the EU and NATO. Although the average voter of ATAKA[42] does not belong to the poorest classes, since 1990 they have suffered from a severe decline in status and are afraid of the new competition resulting from accession to the EU. In this context, the ATAKA electorate is united by a distinctive feeling of being losers, which is supported by their social status, the (alleged) sell-out of Bulgarian enterprises in favor of foreign investors, social security, or just by the belief that in the course of the transformation the "Bulgarian way of life" has been lost. That is where ATAKA's essential slogan

40 See Žečeva, "ATAKA", p. 64.

41 In public, Siderov does not only present himself as a defender of the interests of the common people and a relentless fighter for Bulgaria. He also always tries to symbolically connect to historic models - e. g. when new party members are welcomed, this is staged as a pathetic ritual with references to Vasil Levski, the predominant figure of the Bulgarian fight for independence in the 19th century. Another example is his stylized portrait on the pages of the "ATAKA" magazine suggesting a similarity to Vasil Levski.

42 Cf. Ivanova, Strah i žažda za văzmezdie.

starts out from: "Let us take Bulgaria back!" Moreover, its irreconcilable attitude towards the DPS results in votes. Many Bulgarians consider the minority rights of the Turkish population to be exaggerated and criticize the clientelism spreading around this party. ATAKA is believed to be the only reliable force, having never been a coalition partner of the "Party of Turks" and thus being able to take the position of a pro-Bulgarian "corrective".

Apart from the different time of establishing, there are many parallels between the Romanian PRM and ATAKA to be found. Both parties connect to the nationalism of the pre-communist era, but at the same time to the era of real existing socialism. From this, there results a mixture of positions from both extremist antipodes, which can be proven for most anti-democratic parties in post-communist Europe.[43] With Vadim Tudor and Volen Siderov, both parties are headed by undebated leaders skilfully using their nationwide popularity and their influence on the media for "great" appearances where they stage themselves as the patron saints of their nations which are said to be threatened by enemies from the inside and the outside. And at the same time, both parties and their leaders must be attributed for some years a clear (although strategically motivated) process of moderation. The pragmatic reason for this is most of all that they want to be elected. This will not be successful by powerless radical opposition and attitudes of clearly rejecting the system but rather by being a moderate alternative to the system, although this way Tudor has lost many sympathizers in Romania.

IV. Non-party right-wing extremism

In Romania and Bulgaria, the lines between right-wing extremist parties and non-party associations are blurred. This is on the one hand due to the social significance of right-wing extremism. Racist and system-hostile positions are found in almost all parts of society and thus also with mass organizations. In Romania, to this there belongs the so-called cultural organization of Vatra Românesca as well as some lines of Romania's Orthodox Church. They communicate an exclusive and sometimes intolerant way of understanding the nation to their millions of followers. Most of all in respect of the combination of Orthodoxy and nationalism, the positions of right-wing extremist forces and the official Church line are similar. The Romanian state, they say, is owned by the Romanians, and a Romanian is who is a member of the Christian-Orthodox Church. Gabriel Andreescu calls the Association of Christian-Orthodox Students in Romania the "maybe most powerful organization of Orthodox fundamentalism".[44]

On the other hand, in both countries many former followers of the anti-system parties are organized by non-party organizations. Among them there count

43 See in detail Thieme, Hammer, Sichel, Hakenkreuz.
44 Andreescu, Romania, pp. 191–192.

associations such as the Romanian collective movement The New Right-Wing (Noua Dreaptă - ND) and the *Bulgarian National Union* (Bulgarski Nacionalen sajuz - BNS), founded in 2001. The ND supports a militant nationalist ideology in connection with Christian Orthodoxy as a source of the spiritual unity of all Romanians. It considers itself a successor organization of the Fascist Iron Guard. According to the movement's original name (Legion of Michael the Archangel), its followers call themselves neo-legionnaires. The group recruits its mostly young activists around football grounds and in the environment of the Hooligan scene. Noua Dreaptă claims to have more than 6,000 members. Although - according to the numbers of people taking part in their demonstrations - we may suppose that actually it is just some hundred followers, the group is present in most regions of Romania and is well-known for its provocative actions. By way of mass poster actions, the publication of a magazine of the same name, as well as by its well established Internet presence Noua Dreaptă succeeds with being perceived nationwide.[45] It is considered violent and organizes para-military training camps for its members. Also in the field of international right-wing extremism Noua Dreaptă is a well-known figure. In 2003, it was one of the founding members of the European National Front, and it maintains intensive relations to right-wing extremist associations a. o. in Germany, France, Italy, Spain and East Central Europe. The *National Democratic Party of Germany* (NPD) is one of its closest partners.[46]

With respect to both organization and topic, Noua Dreaptă meets all criteria of a militant right-wing extremist organization. Due to its close relations to the Christian-Orthodox Church and its strict interpretation of the faith, the appearance of the New Right-Wing looks mystical or even messianic. On September 13th each year, it organizes a memorial march in honor of the founder of the Legion, Corneliu Codreanu. By way of services and gospels, the Orthodox Church is very much included into the memorial celebrations. The movement demands the status of official heroes for all nationalists who - as it claims - have sacrificed themselves for God, the nation and the Romanian fatherland. Noua Dreaptă calls "Romania's spiritual and cultural resurrection" its holy mission.[47] All Romanians, it says, are entitled to live in one united state. Thus, the foremost goal is to achieve the reunion of Romania and Moldavia to one Greater Romanian state. On its homepage the New Right-Wing shows the outlines of a Romanian-Moldavian united state against the background of the Romanian tricolor.[48]

45 For details see the homepage of Noua Dreaptă, http://www.nouadreapta.org last accessed 1 October 2010.

46 In 2004, ND Secretary General Claudiu Mihutiu took part in the so-called NPD Summer University. In 2005, as a guest he represented the NEW Right-Wing on the 40th anniversary of the National Democrats. In this context, obviuosly Noua Dreaptă places great value on its appearance towards the outside. On its homepage, the New Right-Wing reports about its activities in detail.

47 Ibid.

48 See ibid.

The manifest of Noua Dreaptă consists of a close connection of nationalist and religiously fundamentalist positions. For example, there is the demand for raising and educating the young people in the "spirit of a Christian nation".[49] Furthermore, the New Right-Wing claims that since 1989 there has been an offensive of sects against the Orthodox Church, threatening the spiritual unity of the Romanian people. It rejects any kind of religious freedom. The danger of a cultural pollution by foreign - most of all Western - cultures is said to result in social injustice, foreign capitalism and individualized materialism. Noua Dreaptă's hostility towards foreigners and minorities - just as with all right-wing extremist associations in Romania - aims at Hungarians and Roma, but also at Bulgarians. Due to their historic experiences, it is claimed, these ethnic groups do not share the same values, which is said to make coexistence impossible.[50] ND wages a morally reasoned and Church-supported campaign most of all against homosexuals. On May 28, 2009, about 50 ND followers demonstrated against the first gay parade in Bukarest. Under the slogan "For normality, against homosexuality" they demanded the re-criminalization of homosexuality and thus the end of Romania's moral decline. In this respect, however, the ND is hardly different from the "liberal" parliament party *Partidul Conservator* (PUR) and the official Church line. The model of society the ND strives for may be characterized as a kind of Christian-Orthodox theocracy.

The *Bulgarian National Union* is the most important non-party organization of the extreme right-wing in Bulgaria. It is provided with a nationwide organizational structure, and since 2006 it has been politically represented by the Guard (Gvardija) movement which is registered according to the political parties act. It calls itself the "organization of nationally conscious Bulgarians" with the goal to "realize the heritage of the forefathers and to start the resurrection of the Bulgarian nation".[51] BNS nationalism is different from Romanian nationalism - such as SD - by strongly focusing on an "Aryan" proto-Bulgarian identity and thus rejecting all Orthodox traditions.[52] The transition after 1989 is called a "democracy of hypocrites", in the context of which a "treacherous elite has become rich at the expense of the common Bulgarian worker and [...] steals the future of our children". One important part of the BNS's system opposition, apart from fundamental criticism of "treacherous politicians", is the rejection of parliament as a "place where corruption and collective irresponsibility become

49 See the ND program, available at http://www.nouadreapta.org/obiective.php last accessed 4 October 2010.

50 See Andreescu, Romania, p. 190.

51 This as well as the following quotations come from a section of a programmatic text of the BNS, headlined "Our Fight", available at http://bg.bgns.net/Za-nas/Borba.html last accessed 6 October 2010.

52 The connected reference to important Bulgarian ruling families from the time before Christianization is expressed by the symbols of the BNS. The family name chosen by its chairman, Bojan Rasate, is originally the name of a son of Tsar Boris I., under whom Bulgaria was Christianized in the 9th century. The historic Rasate wanted to revoke Christianization. His father punished him for that.

manifest as well as an order where the talented and respected personality is only the executive of an incompetent majority".

The BNS claims to be the "patriotic" defender of "traditional Bulgarianism" and attacks all "enemies" of the nation, the Roma minority and sexual minorities.[53] The peak of mobilization against the Roma was the establishment of a National Guard in the summer of 2007, which was supposed to protect the Bulgarian population against alleged "Gypsy terror". As in Romania, the connection to violent military groups is obvious. To the BNS organization, there belongs a sports association (Edelweiss) as well as an association, which collects funds for Bulgarians in need. Furthermore, BNS chairman Bojan Rasate has his own TV program at a private channel where he comments on the current political situation. The organizational structure reflects the strategic openness of this collective movement: By way of the sports association and its local structures, the BNS connects to a variety of right-wing extremist groups, whereas the claim for social justice is supposed to become credible by way of charity actions. In his TV program as well as his appearances with mainstream media, Rasate presents himself as a strict but prudent critical observer of the current political situation, while always being obliged to the people.[54] The BNS may best be characterized as a group developing a catchy program from the racist ideology of an "Aryan" identity and from populist-nationalist, social-political and anti-elite positions.

Apart from BNS, there is a variety of right-wing extremist splinter groups in Bulgaria, however without being provided with an apparatus, which could be compared to that of the National Union. None of them shows the latter's public presence, and many of them are restricted to a most of all virtual existence on the Internet. In contrast to Romania, however, there is no Skinhead movement in the actual sense in Bulgaria. Instead, there are reports on individual ad hoc groups of young people defining themselves as Skinheads, which are held responsible for attacks on immigrants and minorities. Skinheads appear also in the milieu of football fan clubs in big cities as well as in the environment of right-wing extremist parties - mostly functioning as security men - without being lastingly integrated into fixed organizational structures.[55]

53 In the summer of 2008, the BNU started a poster campaign under the slogan "Be intolerant! Be normal!", on which the participants of a gay parade were confronting a nuclear family.

54 Among this there also counts the massive presence of the BNU symbol and the BNU web address in the public space of the capital, Sofia, which was achieved by way of extended graffiti campaigns.

55 See Ivanov/Ilieva, Bulgaria, pp. 13-14.

V. Conclusion

As reasons for right-wing extremism in the post-communist states in Europe, the relevant literature often illuminates a list of factors. Among them, there are the numerous difficulties due to the multi-dimensionality of the transformation processes, (objective and subjective) losses in status and wealth among those not benefitting from the system change, a democratic-political culture which is not sufficiently rooted in the populations as well as among the political elites, and the loss of national independence as a result of EU integration. This may be true concerning the programs and the voters of right-wing extremist parties in Bulgaria and Romania, which criticize most of all a "treacherous political class", which is said to be responsible for the national, cultural and social decline of these states. However, if the cause of right-wing extremist success is said to be most of all due to structural aspects, there is the question of why the extent and consolidation capacities of right-wing extremist organizations differ considerably, not only between Romania and Bulgaria but also in respect of East Central European states.[56] Doubtlessly, the framework conditions (lacking democratic traditions, multi-dimensional system transformation, a lack of coming to grips with the past, political culture, minority problems) improve the chances of right-wing extremist forces to become established. However, this does not explain why right-wing extremism in Bulgaria was abstinent for a long time and gained significance only shortly before the country's accession to the EU, whereas the development in Romania was rather the other way round, although the structural conditions of both states are or have been at least similar, though not identical.

The favorable opportunity structures for right-wing extremism in Southeast Europe are due both to structure and situation. In Romania, in March 1990, there were serious riots between Romanians and Hungarians in the city of Târgu Mures, in the course of which six people died. In the following, this resulted in an increase of followers of right-wing extremist parties, which instrumentalized the conflict. The situation is similar in Bulgaria, where quarrels with Gypsies peaked with the establishment of a so-called National Guard.[57] Furthermore, the loss in significance of right-wing extremist parties in Romania and the parallel rise of ATAKA in Bulgaria did not come along with a change of democratic or anti-democratic attitudes among the populations or politicians. Still, in both states there are latent conflicts between minority and majority populations. A consequent debate on the dictatorial past and the idea of one's own history is still missing.[58] The fact that the democratic parties do not keep distance from

56 For an overview see Jesse/Thieme, Politischer Extremismus, p. 443.

57 Also for Hungary (Prime Minister Gyurcsány's Speech on Lies in 2006) and Slovakia (bilateral Slovakian-Hungarian conflict in 2009), concrete incidents can be identified as having triggered off right-wing extremist mobilization and success in elections and increase the significance of situative factors as explaining right-wing extremist potentials.

58 On Bulgaria see: Meznik, Wer braucht die Vergangenheit?, pp. 79–89.

right-wing extremist organizations shows effect: The brutalization of the political climate is well on the way. Due to the moderation and (in the case of Romania) marginalization of extremist parties in the past ten years, militant groups have even gained relevance. A democratic political culture only basically exists. Thus, the declining election results of PRM in Romania cannot be explained by the democratic actors reluctantly distancing themselves from political extremism after the year 2000. By way of a populist way of appearance and moderate nationalist statements, top politicians such as Romania's president, Traian Băsescu, succeed with offering a non-extremist alternative to former PRM voters.[59] In Romania, the competition for outbidding each other in respect of popular touch and national sentiment has resulted in a kind of all party populism. The same is true for Bulgaria, where the head of government, Bojko Borisov, maintains a similar political style, but the credibility of the still rather young ATAKA party has not been very much affected by this, and (for the time being) it has been able to resist its democratic-populist competitors.

It is doubtful whether this will last. Doubtlessly, the success of many right-wing extremist parties (all over Europe) is due to central leaders such as Tudor or Siderov, who are well known across their nations and know about public relations. Just the same, however, these persons are also responsible for the decline and/or the split and/or the breakdown of such organizations, and inner conflicts are not a rarity with right-wing extremist parties. In contradicting ways, Bulgaria and Romania are ideal-typical examples of this: Since the year 2000, it seems as if the attractiveness of the (allegedly) charismatic leader Tudor is on the decline among the Romanian electorate. Among many voters with a national but not anti-democratic attitude, his often contradictory statements and unrespectable appearances resulted in a massive loss of trust. On the other hand, despite inner quarrels after the ATAKA coalition had been elected to parliament, Siderov and his party succeeded with stabilizing the party, and in the first two years of supporting Prime Minister Borisov's minority government they have mastered the balancing act between being a party of radical protest and a constructive government party.

It would be wrong to conclude from the current weakness of right-wing extremism in Romania that it will generally disappear, and to predict - in the case of Bulgaria - ATAKA's decline in the near future, due to participating in the government. Still the opportunity structures are favorable for anti-democratic actors: In Romania and Bulgaria, there is no anti-extremist consensus in the form of consequently rejecting (right-wing) extremism in politics and society, just as there is no middle class showing a positive attitude towards democracy. Even violent extremist organizations are present in the nationwide media.[60] The difficult economic and social situation has hardly improved since

59 See Gabanyi, Rumänien, pp. 56–67.

60 See the appearances of the ND chairman in the information program of Romanian TV, available at http://www.nouadreapta.org/video.php last accessed 5 October 2010.

accession to the EU, but it has rather become even more difficult as a result of the financial crisis of 2008, and increasingly societies are torn apart by the polarization between pro-European elites and more nationalist populations. Extremist organizations are very much aware of such developments. More than ever, right-wing extremist organizations work on the unity of their own camps. As the ideologic foundations of most actors are identical and hardly different from the ideas of broad (not all) parts of society, the absence of renewed extremist success would be more surprising than their return. Under such auspices, Romania's and Bulgaria's goodbye to their national heritage of the past will take considerable time.

Transnational Cooperation of the Far Right in the European Union and Attempts to Institutionalize Mutual Relations

Petra Vejvodová

One of the key characteristics of contemporary global capitalism is the proliferation of transnational structures and activities. Many studies on transnationalism and transnational activism or contentious politics have been written in recent years.[1] One of the central themes of these studies deals with the construction of an environment that is supportive of transnational activities while stimulating the creation of such relations and strengthening cooperative bonds. We begin to understand transnational relations as regular cross-border interaction between (political) actors. The academic discussion is aware of the fact that transnational ties are not associated exclusively with the state and its official institutions. Non-state actors are interested in entering transnational structures or activities as well.

The duration and quality of these mutual relations often vary. The primary motivation is the strengthening of ideological cooperation, mutual support, and international influence. However, relations are not always strictly cooperative. Actors may also enter transnational structures or activities because of potential gain. In this case, common goals or ideas are of minor importance.[2] Actors take advantage of opportunities that arise from joining formal structures.

Far right political parties are also interested in establishing international ties and introducing their respective issues to a transnational level. Nevertheless, transnational cooperation of the far right has received little attention amongst scholars. Most of the research touches upon the transnational cooperation of one specific far right subject. Transnational cooperation is studied from the national perspective, in the case study form. The research is based on a question: "Who are the main partners in abroad?". In his book "Populist Radical Right Political Parties in Europe", Cas Mudde provides a more profound insight

1 Cf. Císař, Transnacionální politické sítě; Della Porta/Tarrow, Transnational Protest; Imig/Tarrow, The Europeanization of Movements?; ibid., Contentious Europeans; Tarrow, The New Transnationalism.

2 Cf. Císař, Transnacionální politické sítě, p. 37.

into international cooperation between populist radical right wing political parties.[3] More attention is generally paid to neo-Nazi and white supremacist groups.[4]

I. The European Union as a political opportunity structure

Tarrow argues that political opportunities are very important for political action. They offer the chance for political action. Political opportunities are understood as consistent (though not necessarily permanent or formal) dimensions of the political environment. They provide incentives for action by raising expectations of success or failure.[5] Although the structure of political opportunities is primarily a conceptual tool for the study of social movements, some basic thoughts and principles apply to political parties, too. Generally speaking, the concept of a structure of political opportunity helps answering the question as to why some political actors (social movements, or in our case, far right political parties) are active and in motion.

The European Union (EU) is a very complex and systematic construction. It is also the most important structure of political opportunity in Europe (inadvertently) providing opportunities for far right political activism. The sole existence of such an organization offers the chance to define one's position and adapt one's political relation with it. The European cooperation provides opportunities and ways of cooperation which the far right political parties can use to further their common goals. The European Parliament offers the possibility to represent political opinions and ideas. Furthermore, it enables the formation of strong parliamentary blocks between parties.

At the European level, there was practically no party involvement between 1951 and 1979. There were no parliamentary EU elections to contest in. Before 1975, no regular summits set strategic priorities for the union. This began to change gradually. Since 1979, there have been direct elections to the European Parliament. Since 1990, party leaders have met regularly. The involvement of political parties in European politics has been slow to develop.[6]

The European elections have offered an important opportunity for the far right to become a participant of European politics. Elections are an umbrella under which new challenges are often formed.[7] The far right uses them to gain some power and to push issues considered to potentially increase its chances of success on the European level. Attempts at greater success are possible in the European arena after having failed on the national level. In fact, some political

3 Cf. Mudde, Populist Radical Right Political Parties in Europe.
4 Cf. Simi/Futrell, American Swastika; Greven/Grumke, Globalisierter Rechtsextremismus?
5 Cf. Tarrow, Power in Movement, pp. 71–77.
6 Cf. Leonard, Europe without Frontiers, pp. 11–12.
7 Cf. ibid., p. 78.

parties hold better and stronger positions there than in their respective countries. Furthermore, such cooperation is also prompted material aspects in terms of budgetary financing. Far right parties promote their opposition to globalization and integration; but while facing the challenges of such issues, they are also trying to benefit from their advantages.

As Cas Mudde stresses, far right international and transnational collaboration has received little academic attention. There are two views of how to judge the European cooperation between far right parties. Some scholars believe that cooperation on the international level has increased and that the first signs have become visible. They are certain to have detected traces of the rise of a "European ideology" transcending national differences. Others claim that the far right cannot be considered a political actor on the European level because of its limited level of institutionalization and its minor ability to form strong and functioning official structures. All attempts to create stable organizational structures have failed.[8]

While most far right parties are consistently critical of the European integration, many of them support some form of cooperation amongst each other, and most of them embrace the idea of a European alliance. After all, in the ideologies of radical right politics, it has been present in different forms since the end of World War II, e. g. in the European Social Movement or the European New Right. The creation of the European Parliament (EP) brought with it a new opportunity to cooperate. The foundation of political factions in the EP indicates a joint struggle to attain common goals. It offers a platform for discussion and clarification of common ideology. It is also pragmatic in terms of procuring financial support. The EP became a place where parties of the far right were able to cooperate and voice their criticism of the EU. International cooperation also offers the advantage of spreading concepts, ideas, and strategies. It may promote greater compatibility of the far right, as well as greater unity across the geographic regions. Furthermore, it empowers relatively minor players who normally have less influence. Political groups unsuccessful on the regional or state levels may be able to consolidate their positions collaborating with parties of similar ideology that are more influential.

II. The need for minimal consensus to attain cooperation

The first important attempt to unite the far right came after the EP elections of 1984. The leader of the French *Front National* (FN), Jean-Marie Le Pen, headed the grouping European Right between 1984 and 1989. It remained intact until 1991. In the second period (after the elections of 1989), it was known as Technical Group of the European Right.[9]

8 Cf. Mudde, Populist Radical Right Parties, p. 158.
9 Cf. ibid., p. 178.

During the 1990s, there was little desire for cooperation between far right parties. Jean-Marie Le Pen, however, stubbornly insisted on his idea of the European collaboration. In 1997, he announced the foundation of the European National Union (EURONAT), a far right organization without a direct relationship to the EP. The basic idea of EURONAT was to reject EU, NATO, and other attempts to create one European governmental and parliamentary unit. It can be described by the motto "Europe of national states".[10] The organizational structure was free and most activities were coordinated by Le Pen. There were plans to build a worldwide platform, known as Mondo-Nat. However, these plans were never realized.

During the 1990s, Le Pen visited Eastern European countries to promote his project. He received a fair amount of support in Central Europe. But EURONAT did not attract far right parties from Western countries. The Czech *Sdružení pro Republiku - Republikánská strana Československa* (SPR-RSČ), the Hungarian *Magyar Igazság és Élet Pártja* (MIÉP), and the *Slovenská národná strana* (SNS) connected through EURONAT. Many other European parties became members of it but some of them left this platform after a short time. Researching the history of party membership is difficult because of the short and shadowy existence of EURONAT.[11] The true purpose of EURONAT was revealed a few years later. After the EP elections of 1999, which were unsuccessful for far right parties, the level of cooperation amongst its members decreased. The founding member, the French FN, began to lose interest in continuing the EURONAT experiment. As the 2004 EP elections confirmed, membership in EURONAT did not ensure the positive results that had been expected.[12]

The transnational organization European National Front (ENF) was established in 2003. This grouping was not directly related with the EU. With the exception of the *Nationaldemokratische Partei Deutschlands* (NPD), its members are mostly minor players who do not receive many votes in national or European elections.[13] Contrary to previous cases, the ENF is not influenced by the French FN. This organization promotes a Europe of independent nations and strives to fight in the name of "European civilization". The ENF opposes immigration, the admission of Turkey into the EU, American imperialism, and globalization. The

10 Fiala/Mareš/Sokol, Eurostrany, p. 175.
11 Cf. Mudde, Populist Radical Right Parties, p. 176.
12 Ten parties that can be classified as populist or far right parties, received mandates in the EP: The FN (7), VB (3), MSI-FT (1), FPÖ (1), LPR (10), LA-OS (1), LN (4), AS (1), DFP (1), DUP (1). A membership base of 30 was sufficient to create distinct factions. The parties instead entered into other groups. Cf. Mudde, Populist Radical Right Parties, p. 179.
13 Members of the ENF are "Forza Nuova" (Italy), "La Falange" (Spain), "Renouveau Francais" (France), NPD (Germany), "Nuova Dreaptă" (Romania). In the past, members have also come from Central Europe: NOP, "Slovak National Unity", and "National Unity" from the Czech Republic.

idea of the Turkish EU membership is generally considered to be in conflict with European identity.[14]

Identity, Tradition, Sovereignty (ITS) is another political faction of the far right in the EP. It was created in January 2007, after Romania and Bulgaria had been admitted into the EU.[15] Its formation was initiated at a Vienna meeting organized by *Freiheitliche Partei Österreichs* (FPÖ) in 2005. Delegates agreed to intensify common actions, and the pan-European party was created in 2007. According to the Vienna Declaration, members announced the intention to establish a Europe of free and independent nations within the framework of a confederation of sovereign nation-states.[16] Further common interests were the rejection of Turkish EU membership, the protection of Europe against "Islamization", immigration, and American imperialism.

After the ITS' failure, four of its members (FPÖ, FN, the Bulgarian ATAKA, the Belgian *Vlaams Belang* (VB)) announced their intention to continue their cooperation in accordance with the Vienna Declaration. This was in January 2008, and it led to the formation of another party under the working name of *European Patriotic Party*. Once again, its goals were to defend a Europe of free nation states against the threats of Islamization, immigration, and the Turkish EU membership.[17]

The last and most recent example of collaboration dates from October 2009. Delegates from *Jobbik* (Hungary), *Front National* (FN, Belgium), FN (France), *Movimiento Sociale Italiano - Fiamma Tricolore* (MSI-FT, Italy), and the *National Democratic Party* (Sweden) announced the creation of the Alliance of National European Movements (AENM) in Budapest. Negotiations were also conducted with the *British National Party* (BNP, Great Britain), *Svoboda* (Ukraine), *Movimiento Social Republicano* (Spain) and the FN (Belgium). These parties became members in the first half of 2010. The last wave of expansion brought Portugal's *Partido Nacional Renovador* and Sweden's *Nationaldemokraterna* into the alliance that was to become an official European political party separate from political groups within the EP. The strategic aim is to create a corresponding political group at the EP within a short time.[18] The Alliance is based

14 Cf. Zondlak, Evropská národní fronta, available at: http://www.rexter.cz/evropska-narodni-fronta/2006/05/01/#more-223.

15 Members of the ITS came from: ATAKA (Bulgaria), PRM (Romania), FPÖ (Austria), VB (Belgium), FN (France), MSI-FT (Italy), AS (Italy), and one independent MP from Great Britain. Cf. Fiala/Mareš/Sokol, Eurostrany, p. 177.

16 Cf. Fiala/Mareš/Sokol, Eurostrany, p. 177; Mudde, Populist Radical Right Parties, p. 180.

17 Cf. BBC News, 25 January 2008, "EU Far-Right Groups to Form Party", available at: http://news.bbc.co.uk/2/hi/europe/7210036.stm; Wienerzeitung, 25 January 2008, "FPÖ to Help Form Pan-European Right-Wing Umbrella Party", available at: http://www.wienerzeitung.at/DesktopDefault.aspx?TabID=4082&Alias=wzo&cob=324360.

18 25 deputies from seven countries are needed to create a political group in the EP. In the electoral period of 2009-2014, there were enough deputies in the EP from populist and far right parties to form a group, but not all of the right wing parties intend to join

on a common goal to protect Europe from religious, economic, and financial imperialism, while opposing the EU and globalization in general. The purpose of the alliance is to "reject all attempts at creating a so called European 'superstate', it calls for a solution of the immigration problem [...], it advocates the effective protection of Europe against the new threats of terrorism, as well as political, economic, financial or religious imperialism. It calls for strong pro-family policies to reverse Europe's population decline and the promotion of traditional values in society. It also seeks a joint struggle against the destructive effects of globalization".[19] The common declaration of its members demands the "creation of a Europe of free, independent and equal nations in the framework of a confederation of sovereign nation states, refraining from taking decisions on matters properly taken by states themselves".[20]

Obviously, a few topics ensure a minimal consensus amongst European far right parties. First, there is the EU itself. Its development and evolution is scrutinized. Far right parties accuse the EU because of becoming a "superstate". It is considered restrictive of national sovereignty. The EU's liberalism and social-democratic values are also criticized. The far right parties of post-communist countries try to attract attention by comparing the EU to the Soviet Bloc, in the sense of the limitation of state sovereignty. Similar analogies have been drawn by leaders from Western European parties. Umberto Bossi, leader of the Italian *Lega Nord* (LN), has repeatedly referred to the EU as "the Soviet Union of Europe".[21] Many far right parties had been supportive of the process of European integration. But the 1992 Maastricht Treaty changed this attitude. It is considered a tangible step towards the formation of a supranational body. The German *Republicans,* for example, described the Maastricht Treaty as a "Versailles without weapons". Jean-Marie Le Pen of the French FN compared it with the Treaty of Troyes. Moreover, far right parties of non-EU members were very skeptical of the Maastricht Treaty at the time of its inception. The leader of the Hungarian MIÉP was convinced the Maastricht Treaty would lead to the disappearance of the Hungarian ethnic community as an independent entity.[22] The far right mostly considers the European Union an arena where the activities of left-wing and "pseudo-humanistic" forces lead to uncontrolled immigration or the spreading of destructive postmodern values. Their critique is also combined with harsh criticism of the democratic political representation on both national

this alliance. This is due to the persistence of differing relations, which will be addressed later on in this paper. The alliance created from the aforementioned parties so far has 8 deputies in the EP (BNP [2], "Jobbik" [3], FN [3]).

19 London Patriot, 15 June 2010, "The Alliance of European Nationalist Movement Holds its First General Assembly", available at: http://www.londonpatriot.org/2010/06/15/the-alliance-of-european-nationalist-movements-holds-its-first-general-assembly.

20 BNP, 24 June 2010, "Alliance of European National Movements Expands to 9 Parties", available at: http://www.bnp.org.uk/news/alliance-european-national-movements-expands-9-parties.

21 Mudde, Populist Radical Right Parties, pp. 160–161.

22 Cf. ibid., pp. 159–160.

and European levels. Far right parties tend to see European integration as a bureaucratic and elitist phenomenon undermining concepts and values such as the nation state, national identity, state sovereignty, and national affiliation. Furthermore, they consider the EU as a project of globalization which they oppose. From the Neo-Nazi point of view, the EU is a "Jewish project".[23]

Far right parties create a space where the voice of popular opposition and protest against developments declared anti-national are enacted. The BNP considers the withdrawal from the EU one of its top priorities in foreign policy.[24] A similar declaration was made by Jean-Marie Le Pen. The Czech *Dělnická strana* (DS) demands the restoration of Czech sovereignty and the Czech Republic's withdrawal from the European Union. It refuses to accept the transfer of competences to a multinational center in Brussels, fearing a loss of national sovereignty. The DS also refuses to accept the deepening federalization of Europe, the creation of a European government, and the institution of the European president. The party prefers cooperation among nations on an equal and mutual basis. The party document "Analysis of Membership of the Czech Republic in the European Union" was written prior to the accession to the EU. It envisions the Czech Republic to become the poorest country in the EU, a colony deprived of any rights, and the Czech people reduced to the status of poorly paid workers.[25]

Nevertheless, far right parties have made some progress at European elections. Voters in general do not see the European Parliament as a strong body and do not attach primary importance to the elections. Better results and more seats in the European Parliament ensue from low voter participation in combination with the stable electorate of the far right, and, to some extent, the experimental character of European elections.[26] While the German *Republicans* failed to enter the Bundestag, they managed to win some seats in the European Parliament of 1989. The French FN made its breakthrough at the 1984 European elections.[27]

Secondly, a very popular and significant topic is the question of immigration and the perceived threat of the Islamization of Europe. This led to a discussion on the issue of the Turkish EU membership. Immigrants from the Third World are considered the cause of all problems, e. g., unemployment or the crisis of the social systems. Cross-social issues like high criminality are turned into ethnic ones. One of the major proponents of this topic is the *Schweizerische*

23 Cf. Mareš, Transnational Networks of Extreme Right Parties. p. 10, available at: http://ispo.fss.muni.cz/uploads/2download/Working_papers/ispo_wp_2006_8.pdf, last accessed 29 June 2010.

24 Cf. BNP, 12 May 2010, "Foreign Affairs", available at: http://www.bnp.org.uk/policies/foreign-affairs.

25 Cf. Vejvodová, Aplikace teorie extremismu, p. 21.

26 In Central Europe, voters often act more courageously at European elections voting for smaller or protest parties. This is mainly due the fact that the European Parliament is perceived as a distant body with little direct influence on peoples' lives.

27 Cf. Hainsworth, The Extreme Right, p. 83.

Volkspartei (SVP) linking criminality with the presence of immigrants in a highly populist way. The problem of "Islamization" is currently under frequent discussion. Election campaigns on both European and national levels stress the alleged threat. The rejection of the Turkish EU membership has become a feature of the successful campaigns of political parties such as the French FN. Among its most important proponents are the BNP, VB, the SVP, and the Czech *Národní strana* (NS, which ceased to exist in 2009). In its platform, the BNP demands to "reach an accord with the Muslim world whereby they will agree to take back their excess population which is currently colonizing this country, in exchange for an ironclad guarantee that Britain will never again interfere in the political affairs of the Middle East".[28] The intention to cooperate was demonstrated in May 2009 in Cologne, Germany. The political movement Pro Köln organized an Anti-Islamization-Congress. Pro Köln had invited parties like the FPÖ, VB, LN, the French FN, and the Czech NS. The Belgian organization Cities against Islamization was founded in January 2008. It also stresses the threat of Muslims in Europe. Political parties such as VB and the FPÖ became partners.[29]

The third big issue of the far right on the European level is "globalization". According to the far right, globalization forms the basis of all negative phenomena like immigration and economic crises. It is perceived as a factor of the loss of identity and the destruction of traditional patterns in Europe.[30] After the 2002 French presidential elections, the German NPD praised Jean-Marie Le Pen. They considered his reaching the run-off a clear sign of the French people's turning away from their government's pro-globalization policies.[31] Far right parties regard globalization as a deliberately created instrument to destroy "Volk and Nation" and as the "denationalization" of nation states. They present themselves as the defenders of nationalism, of national traditions, and values.[32]

Every topic introduced by the far right aims at one central goal, namely: preserving the European identity. This ideology may be called "European nationalism" in continuity with the European New Right of the 1970s and 1980s. Pierre Milza describes the European nationalism of the New Right as based on the superiority of the white race. Nation as a key element has been replaced by race. Attention is focused on the strong cultural identity of the continent. Europe is described as looking for its Indo-European roots while fighting against high immigration waves.[33]

Besides ideological issues, pragmatism is an important element. Collaboration can yield positive consequences from being visible on the international level,

28 BNP, "Foreign Affairs", available at: http://www.bnp.org.uk/policies/foreign-affairs.
29 Cf. Bundesamt für Verfassungsschutz, Verfassungsschutzbericht 2009, p. 118, available at: http://verfassungsschutz.de/de/publikationen/verfassungsschutzbericht/, last accessed 29 June 2010.
30 Cf. Grumke, Die transnationale Infrastruktur, p. 23.
31 Cf. Grumke, The Transatlantic Dimension, p. 69.
32 Cf. Scharenberg, Brücke zum Mainstream, p. 80.
33 Cf. Milza, Evropa v černých košilích, p. 243.

getting easier access to other possible partners, to sharing the expenses of political campaigns. By creating a European political party or faction within the EP, parties gain access to valuable EU funds and financing. Therefore, the far right parties are highly motivated to cooperate with each other. But seeking EU money has two sides to the coin: EU funding may initiate and strengthen the institutionalization of mutual relations of the far right. At the same time, pragmatic thinking may also discourage such cooperation. Pragmatism may coax parties into joining another (usually bigger and more stable) faction instead of creating a new one whose survival is insecure.

III. The limits and obstacles of cooperation

Far right parties often speak of international cooperation. According to them European identity and European culture need to be protected in order not to be destroyed by foreign (non-European) influence. The common motivation and good starting point for the strengthening of mutual relations or even for the creation of an official structure are evident. This is why far right partnerships and alliances have quite a long history, which is also full of break-ups and unfulfilled ideals. The weakness, instability, and short life of partnerships are significant. No alliance of far right political parties lasted longer than one five-year European legislative period. The only exception is the European National Front of 2003. However, its success is relative. The ENF is still alive, albeit with a low level of activity. It exists more as a side project of the web. The existence of the ENF is more of a residual sentiment than a real organization.

All the groupings mentioned above have had internal problems based on various animosities among their members. Mutual or one-sided animosity appears to be one of the biggest problems in stabilizing far right transnational cooperation in general.

The Technical Group of the European Right suffered from ideological differences between the FN and *Vlaams Blok*. Tension was created by two types of nationalism, namely: state nationalism vs. ethnic nationalism.[34] In the EP, German *Republican* and MSI deputies demonstrated their inability to cooperate in the framework of one ideological party family. The *Republicans* joined the Technical Group in 1989 while the MSI refused cooperation because of a German-Italian dispute over the status of South Tyrol.[35]

The ENF had to handle a row with the NPD and its allies on one side and the Polish *Narodowe Odrodzenie Polski* (NOP) and its allies on the other side. Each had radically different views on history. Members from Slavic countries could not accept the fact that the NPD was gaining influence. The anti-German attitude of the NOP finally caused the break up of the ENF. The ENF had also

34 Cf. Mudde, Populist Radical Right Parties, p. 167.
35 Cf. Fiala/Mareš/Sokol, Eurostrany, p. 174.

been weakened by disputes between Czech and Polish members over Těšín/ Cieszyn. They resulted in the Central European members' leaving of the ENF. In EURONAT, there were obvious disagreements between the *German People's Union* (DVU) and the Czech SPR-RSČ concerning the Sudetenland question. Problematic relations between Slovak and Hungarian members also weakened the coalition.

ITS, the political faction of the EP, was the shortest lived as it lasted only 10 months. Its collapse was brought about by Alessandra Mussolini's remarks. The Alternativa Sociale (AS)-member referred to Romanians as "habitual law-breakers". Five Romanian MEPs subsequently withdrew from the faction. This left the ITS with only 18 MEPs: two short of the 20 MEPs needed to form a political faction in the EP.[36]

It is clear that stability and good long-term relations amongst far right groups in Europe are fragile at best. The broader the scope of the EU, the more difficult it becomes for far right parties to unify. Some parties cannot cooperate because of historical issues, e. g. in Central Europe,[37] or as became visible within the ENF. Other barriers arise from more "ideological" bases. The far right can be united in its critique of the EU, but when it comes to the question of just what Europe should look like instead, politicians are no longer unified. The type of Europe they want to arise in place of the current EU is obscure. The following questions surface: Should membership be defined by nation or by state? Which degree of integration would be desirable? Which kind of policies would be necessary to establish cooperation? The model of a Europe based on nations is preferred by parties whose ideology is founded on ethnic nationalism (Belgian VB). A Europe based on states is preferred by parties based on state nationalism (French FN). Former groups also differed: EURONAT and the ITS were based on the idea of a Europe of national states. On the other hand, the ENF promotes a Europe based on nations. Moreover, opinions differ, even concerning one policy, e. g. the question of collective security or military cooperation. Some parties, like the Austrian FPÖ, want a European army committed to partnership with NATO. Others prefer a Europe independent of NATO because they consider this alliance an instrument of the US.[38] Which are the policies to be solved together and which to be confined to the national level? These are the contentious issues of the discussions.

Nationalism is the general and common denominator of the problems mentioned above. First, nationalism causes more problems on the path to cooperation because, by nature, it defends national traditions, goods, and values. Therefore, cooperation between European far right parties faces a unique prob-

36 Cf. BBC News, 9 November 2007, "EU Far-Right Bloc Faces Collapse", available at: http://news.bbc.co.uk/2/hi/europe/7086986.stm.

37 Hungarian political party "Jobbik" demands the annulment of the Beneš Decrees and Trianon Treaty. This is unacceptable for Czech and Slovak parties.

38 Cf. Mudde, Populist Radical Right Parties, p. 169.

lem. Members of other political families (liberals, conservatives, socialists etc.) share the same values and the principles in every policy. Their respective nations or states of origin are of little relevance. Nationalism is not a central or exclusive feature of their ideologies. They share universal values. Therefore, the creation of international structures to attain their goals is much simpler. The far right is different in this respect. Nationalist political parties consider themselves the keepers of traditions specific to their country of origin. They must defend them against all other traditions. Therefore, they often stress nationalism in a chauvinist way and thus cause conflicts even among the far right party family.

History also creates barriers for collaboration. The far right uses history to define its own identity and position in the system. It simplifies by distinguishing the two categories so important to it, namely, we and the others (we and our enemies). History has witnessed numerous conflicts between various nations. Some interpretations of national histories supported by the far right inevitably come into sharp conflict with the perspectives of other nations and countries. This is especially true if they are accompanied by territorial controversies or the existence of irredentism among national minorities etc.[39] Nevertheless, cooperation is important to the far right in the contemporary world. Some political parties have been able to overcome historical disputes.

Nationalism deeply rooted in party profiles can have positive effects on the transnationalization of the far right, even if on a somewhat symbolic level. It appears in the form of visual propaganda in election campaigns. Prior to the referendum on the building of minarets, the SVP used a poster portraying a Swiss flag bearing minarets as missiles. The FN has used a very similar poster. A woman wearing a burqa is portrayed next to a map of France covered by an Algerian flag, and, once again, minarets as missiles. The Czech NS also drew its inspiration from the SVP: one of its election posters portrayed white sheep kicking out black sheep from the backdrop of the national flag.

From this perspective, the Neo-Nazi movement, for example, realizes more potential of successful transnational cooperation than nationalists. As a white supremacy movement, Neo-Nazis defend a racially homogeneous Europe. The Neo-Nazi movement is moving towards a concept of a Europe of solely white nations sharing a common space and livelihood. This may lead to what could be considered a common European identity. Neo-Nazism defends the white race against everything foreign (all non-European nations). The white race is the common denominator. The emphasis on nationality is decreasing. This concept also helps some Neo-Nazi groups to overcome their historical experience and disputes, e. g., Czech and German Neo-Nazis are able to intensify their relations and cooperate.

The element of leadership inherent to the far right also plays a very important role. Many parties are built on the charismatic leadership of strong author-

39 Cf. Mareš, Transnational Networks, p. 7.

itative personalities. The leaders of big parties with great visions of a successful international far right are intent on strengthening international cooperation. They definitely project their own ambitions into the international far right movement and build international ties according to their own ideas. They want their respective political party to be the acclaimed international leader. This yields the effect that the most successful parties are not able to cooperate because of their struggle of strong personages. For a long time, Jean-Marie Le Pen and the FN tried to assume the leadership on the European level. Some parties were not able to accept it and did not support the FN. For example, the FPÖ and FN never cooperated during the leadership of Jörg Haider. This was due to the "egoistic battles for dominance" between Haider and Le Pen.

IV. The case of Central Europe

In this paper, mutual disputes between Central European far right parties have been mentioned several times. Far right parties from this region can be described as slightly different from other parties of the far right party family. They arose out of distinct circumstances (the political transformations at the end of the 1980s and the economic transformation at the beginning of 1990s). In Western Europe, it is typical for the far right to oppose immigration from the Third World. This phenomenon is absent in Central Europe. Instead, these parties voice their opposition to ethnic minorities. Another visible and important feature effecting transnational cooperation are the very complicated regional relations resulting from the collapse of the Habsburg monarchy and the re-drawing of the European map after World War I.[40]

Regional relations complicate efforts towards transnational cooperation. Far right parties were already looking for foreign partners in Western Europe in the 1990's. This was easier than creating alliances in a region where mutual relations were very limited by opposing demands, political orientation and territorial questions. In the 1990s, the SPR-RSČ and SNS could not cooperate because of differing views on the split of the Czechoslovak federation. The SNS and MIÉP were in conflict over ethnic minorities and national boundaries. This dispute is persisting in the relation between the SNS and *Jobbik*. The MIÉP and the SPR-RSČ could not find a common language due to opposing attitudes towards Germany (the SPR-RSČ being anti-German and the MIÉP pro-German).

The relation between the Slovakian and the Hungarian far right is currently the most problematic. *Jobbik* demands the annulment of the Beneš Decrees and the Trianon Treaty, both dealing with the borders and ethnics after World War II and I. This is unacceptable both to Slovaks and Czechs. Mutual animosity

40 Cf. Kopeček, The Far Right in Europe.

affected the relationship between the SNS and the Czech NS.[41] Initially, the NS cooperated with the SNS youth wing. After the meeting between the NS and *Jobbik* in Bratislava in July 2008, the SNS leadership banned cooperation with the NS. The meeting was considered a provocation.[42] In late 1990s, the SPR-RSČ, SNS and MIÉP reconvened at EURONAT. But the explosive relationship between the SNS and the MIÉP could not be mitigated.

Hardly anything has changed by now. The far right still takes advantage of Western partners, while having no intention to build a strong regional block and to create stable partnerships. Every cooperation is on a bilateral basis, e.g. between the former DS and the *Slovenská Pospolitost* (SP). Often, it merely consists of mutual support at demonstrations and other protest events. There are few multilateral contacts in Central Europe. Where they exist, a common platform was usually created by Western partners.

For many reasons, the central European far right searches for relations in Western Europe. One motivating factor arises from the fact that far right parties tend to seek partnerships not encumbered by historical and territorial disputes. Another motivation is the pragmatic expectation of gain. Partnerships with more influential political parties can improve the respective position among others. The party expects a promotional effect. A very good relationship developed between the NS of the Czech Republic and the BNP. An NS delegation was present at the 2008 BNP meeting. The same year, BNP chairman Nick Griffin attended the NS meeting. The *National Democrats* of Sweden were also partners of the NS. The Czech *Dělnická strana sociální spravedlnosti* (former DS) fosters good relations with the German NPD, especially with its Bavarian division. Mutual visits and support at public events are crucial.

An exception in the generally poor relations among central European far right parties is the International Third Position project initiated by the British and Italian far right in 1980s. The International Third Position helped intensify and strengthen relations between the Czech *Hnutí národního sjednocení*, the Polish NOP, and the Slovakian SP at the end of the 1990s. This tripartite cooperation continued in the ENF and still is the example of the most intensive collaboration in the region. The "Nationalist Olympic games" organized by the SP in the summer of 2009 were evidence of the closeness of the Czech, Polish, and Slovak far right. The participants came from the DS, *Falanga* from Poland, and *Nuova Dreaptă* of Romania.[43]

41 The "National Party" announced the end of its existence in November 2009.
42 Cf. Hnonline.sk, 22 July 2008, "Extremizmus zavítal na Slovensko", available at: http://hnonline.sk/c1-26040300-extremizmus-zavital-na-slovensko.
43 Cf. Dělnické listy, 9 September 2009, Olympiáda nacionalistů, available at: http://www.delnickelisty.cz/olympiada-nacionalistu.

V. Near future?

The success of the *Alliance of National European Movements* remains to be seen. Presently, it is almost clear that the creation of a faction in the EP will be very complicated. All EP parties prepared to join the alliance have a total of 8 deputies. There are no other parties in the position to join. The *Partidul România Mare* and *Slovenská národná strana* announced that they do not intend to cooperate. Neither is Jobbik willing to cooperate with them because it "will not participate in any alliance with any party that is chauvinist towards ethnic Hungarians and the Romanians and the Slovaks are very strongly against ethnic Hungarians".[44] Joining with the Belgian FN precludes cooperation with the more popular VB. The Bulgarian ATAKA is moving towards the center-right. Critical points can also arise from within. Friendly relations between *Jobbik* and the BNP conflicted with different national perspectives, e. g. on agriculture. Other problems may arise from the conflict of state (French FN) with ethnic nationalism (Belgian FN). In general, strong forms of nationalism represent real threats to this project. The only strong motivations to join the alliance are the common negative view of European integration and the xenophobic fears of immigration. The unifying elements are the protest styles of the far right and generally critical attitudes. However, the history of alliances and international far right projects has shown them to be of little relevance.

44 Euobserver.com, 29 October 2009, "Jobbik, BNP move to form pan-European far right alliance", available at: http://euobserver.com/843/28888.

II.
Militant Scenes and Subcultures

Neo-Nazism in Europe

Jean-Yves Camus

The term "neo-Nazism" is generally used to describe those movements that, since 1945, have propagated an ideology based on race, anti-Semitism, and revisionism and that have generally attempted to revive the aims and actions of German national socialism. On closer inspection, however, the scientific validity of the term is questionable. The prefix "neo" seems to suggest that the doctrine has been updated to fit the period and yet "neo-Nazism" has rarely undergone modernization, often contenting itself with propagating Hitlerism as a political cult. "Neo-Nazism" is therefore simply an indication that the groups or individuals concerned existed and acted after the military and political defeat of the Third Reich. We should also ask whether the term "Nazism" itself is appropriate. In fact, it is not entirely appropriate, first and foremost because Nazism does not form an ideological bloc. The traditionalist Philippe Baillet, principle distributor of the works of Julius Evola in France,[1] emphasizes this echoing the words of Ian Kershaw: "Having been regarded for a long time as a flawless monolithic bloc - an image which provided a perfect response to the absolute loathing in which it must have been held - today, the national socialist regime looks more [...] like a form of modern feudal anarchy".[2] The term Nazi often conceals a patchwork of influences. For example, the doctrinal work "Les peuples blancs survivront-ils?", published in 1987 by the New European Order (NEO), recommends reading Hitler, Alfred Rosenberg as well as a number of raciologists. These raciologists are described by Armin Mohler as authors from the populist movement (völkische Bewegung), such as Ludwig Woltmann, Otto Reche, Walter Scheidt, Hans F. K. Günther, and Otto Hauser, who the historian of the "Conservative Revolution" describes as "perhaps the least serious of the theoreticians on race".[3] The same ideological heterogeneity is apparent in the case of the American Francis Parker Yockey, author of the cult work "Imperium" (1948). This icon of European neo-Nazism came from the *Christian Party*

1 In the mid-1970s, Philippe Baillet, then a disciple of the Italian nationalist revolutionary, Giorgio Freda, worked on the "Cahiers du Centre d'études doctrinales Evola", and on "Devenir européen" (D. E.), one of the first French neo-Nazi publications to present his works (D. E, n° 14, 1973).

2 Baillet, Pour la contre-révolution blanche, p. 63.

3 Mohler, La Révolution conservatrice en Allemagne, p. 473.

founded by the Protestant William Dudley Pelley, but also collaborated with the anti-Jewish Catholic priest Charles Coughlin.

We will thus attempt to describe how neo-Nazism, a term which we are only using as a matter of convention, is organized and disseminated in Europe, first by means of transnational networks, then by breaking new ground in methods of organization particularly under the influence of the American racist right wing. We will then paint a brief picture of the current neo-Nazi political parties and organizations, both in Western Europe and in Central and Eastern Europe where the militant wings of this movement now appear to be concentrated.

I. International neo-Nazi organizations

This term (often substituted by that of "black internationals"), widely used in anti-fascist sensationalist literature, indicates the many attempts, after 1945, to create networks for militantism and propaganda at the supra-national or even intercontinental level. However, whereas the various pre-war attempts to establish an international fascist organization benefited from Italian state support or, in the case of the Weltdienst and Fichte-Bund in particular, from the support of a fraction of the NSDAP, the post-war "internationals" are informal groupings. The grandiloquent nature of their proclamations, the staging of their meetings for the media, and the range of their contacts are simply so many ways of masking their utter marginality. The question is whether some of them actually do have a political function or whether they are simply sects, cultivating a caricature of Nazism created by what the Americans call "Hollywood Nazis". More difficult to resolve is the question as to the possible manipulation of some of these groups, formerly by way of Soviet propaganda and administrative bodies, today by the administrations of other countries, with the aim of lending weight to the theory of a possible (and totally improbable) resurgence of the Nazi peril.

Chronologically speaking, the first transnational organization (1949–54) was the European Liberation Front (ELF) founded in London by Francis Parker Yockey. With its nationalist-revolutionary position along the same lines as those promoted by Jean Thiriart in the sixties, the ELF's specialty was the propagation of neutralist ideas at the height of the Cold War. Yockey believed the "barbarism" of the Russian spirit to be less harmful for Europe than the actions of what he termed "America-Jewry",[4] which leads one to wonder about his possible role as a Soviet agent of influence. In May 1951, the inaugural meeting of the European Social Movement (ESM) took place in Malmö (Sweden), an organization with neo-fascist allegiance as demonstrated by the presence among its founders of Oswald Mosley, Maurice Bardèche, Karl-Heinz Priester from the *Deutsche Reichspartei*, and delegates from the *Italian Social Movement*.

4 Yockey, The World in Flames: An Estimate of the World Situation, available at: http://home.alphalink.com.au/~radnat/fpyockey/index.html.

The more hardline neo-Nazi faction (including representatives from the *Sozialistische Reichspartei Deutschlands*) within the ESM split away in September of the same year giving rise to the New European Order (NEO) which published "Le Courrier du continent" from Lausanne until at least 2005 and whose originator, Swiss-born Gaston-Armand Amaudruz (born in 1920), continues to keep the flame alive.[5] From the beginning, the NEO's ideology[6] was based on the writings of Amaudruz and the French-born René Binet, champions of a social Darwinism derived from eugenics and Promethean ideas, which echoed the biological racism of the novels of Marc Augier (Saint-Loup) and the Franco-Argentine anthropologist Jacques de Mahieu.[7] Organ of the NEO until the 1970s, "L'Europe réelle", is published from Brussels by a former non-commissioned officer of the Wallonian Legion, Jean-Robert Debbaudt, who has made frequent attempts to revive the electoral chances of small neo-Rexist movements without any notable success.[8] One of the NEO's characteristics is that it has disseminated a mystique about race whilst at the same time representing, in the words of one leading Belgian nationalist revolutionary, "the European extreme right in its least militant form".[9] In fact, although the NEO met about every two years until 1985 (the last time in Haguenau in Alsace), its impact stems mainly from its capacity to mobilize symbolic militant figures who personify the continuity between the post-war period and the Nazi era. These men, Amaudruz, Binet, Debbaudt, as well as the former German SS officer Priester, have a past, real or mythologized, in which they fought both physically and ideologically alongside the Nazis. It is for this reason that the Belgian movement Nation was able to say, when Debbaudt joined its ranks in 2001: "We have gained a fine symbol".[10]

Another supra-national group, the National Party of Europe, arose from the Venice Declaration signed in March 1962 on the initiative of Oswald Mosley, in collaboration with Thiriart, the German NPD, and the Italian MSI. This was not, strictly speaking, a neo-Nazi group since its written aims, which incidentally came to nothing, proposed an integrated socio-economic program along fascist-planist lines and a Europe with integrated political power run by an

5 The last criminal conviction of Amaudruz for racial discrimination as a result of his negationist writings dates back to May 2002. He was accused, among other things, of having disseminated, through the association Truth and Justice, the following pamphlet: Le procès Amaudruz: Une parodie de justice.

6 Summarized in: Amaudruz, Nous autres racistes.

7 Having worn the uniform of the Waffen-SS at the end of the war, Mahieu spent the rest of his life producing books along the lines of Jacques Bergier and Robert Charroux, seeking to demonstrate that the Vikings discovered South America. His "Précis de biopolitique" (Montréal 1969) has become a classic of the biological racism movement.

8 The first was the "Mouvement Social Belge" in 1954. In 1977, his "Front Nationaliste Populaire" won 0.2 % of the vote in the legislative elections. It is him, we owe for a brochure written together with Robert Eburie: La vérité sur le complot nazi de Bruxelles (Huizingen), Brussels, undated.

9 Interview with Hervé Van Laethem, from the Mouvement Nation, Brussels, 6 July 2009.

10 Ibid.

elected government, with national parliaments retaining only subsidiary powers. It was continued from 1960 to 1969 by the Jeune Europe movement, run by Thiriart. The affiliations with Jeune Europe are few but exist at the symbolic level. The first is the militant career of its leader who was supposed to have switched from socialism to the Amis du Grand Reich Allemand (AGRA) under the Nazi occupation and was said to have belonged, at the same time, to the Fichte-Bund, the national Bolshevik movement of Heinrich and Theodor Kessemeier based in Hamburg. The second is the name of the movement that harks back to "La Jeune Europe" magazine, published in Berlin (1942) by "Échanges culturels inter-universitaires" to defend "the fundamental idea of European unification", a subject that was also touched on by AGRA whose aim was "to orient national-socialism towards a popular socialism and to opt definitively [...] for biological materialism".[11]

The creation of the World Union of National Socialists (WUNS) in England in August 1962, brings us to the foremost "International Nazi Organization", born out of the rapprochement between the "Führer" of the *American Nazi Party*, George Lincoln Rockwell, and that of the British National Socialist Movement, Colin Jordan. The foundation charter of WUNS, the "Costwold Agreement", is written like a declaration of religious faith. It contains seven principles: "the struggle for race", the organic character of every society, the respect for the eternal laws of nature, the struggle for life, the denial of the supremacy of money, the right to the personal development of the individual, and the belief "that Adolf Hitler was the gift of an inscrutable Providence to a world on the brink of Zionist-Bolshevik catastrophe".[12] After the assassination of Rockwell in 1967, the leadership of WUNS passed to the founder of the Nationalsozialistische Deutsche Arbeiterpartei - Auslands-Organisation (NSDAP-AO), the American Gary Rex Lauck, supported by the leader of Denmark's Nationalsocialistiske Bevægelse (DNSB), the Dane Poul Heinrich Riis-Knudsen. Lauck, known under the sobriquet of "Farm-belt führer" (he is based in Nebraska), is the prototype of the leader of a sectarian cult combined with the solid capability of an entrepreneur. The NSDAP-AO is an export company for Nazi propaganda (books, posters, military memorabilia, the journals "NS-Kampfruf" and "The New Order") in twelve languages whose specialty, under the American system of freedom of expression, is to distribute the most extreme examples of national socialist literature,[13] generally banned in Europe. The disciple of an orthodox, religious form of Nazism, endowed with a physique identical to Hitler's and a fake German accent, Matt Koehl, led WUNS to a split and later lost control of it to Colin Jordan in 1995–99, following his imprisonment in Germany. Since the death of Jordan in 2009, WUNS has been re-launched by

11 On AGRA: Bruyne, Léon Degrelle et la Légion Wallonie.
12 Text available at: http://nationalsocialist.net/cotswold.htm.
13 In particular, reissues of the anti-Semitic books of Julius Streicher and Kurt Eggers, sold on the website http://www.nazi-lauck-nsdapao.com.

Jeff Schoepp of the American National Socialist Movement (NSM) who has adapted it for an audience of young skinheads by offering white power music, video games, and clothing via the website "http://nsm88records.com/theshop". With the shifting of neo-Nazi propaganda away from printed media towards the virtual universe of the internet, WUNS is now principally a network of websites, sometimes very well supplied with informative and theoretical documents (in Spain, "http://www.nuevorden.net"; in France, the website of the *French National Socialist Party*, "http://www.aime-et-sers.com") but deprived of a militant base. The most visible of the affiliated groups are Russian National Unity (RNU), the British People's Party[14] and the Italian movement Fascismo e Libertà, founded in 1991 by the MSI senator Giorgio Pisano, on the same political lines as the Salò Republic. WUNS, like the NSDAP-AO and neo-Nazism in general, has not escaped the phenomenon of "exotic" Nazism much loved by the media. This refers to the proliferation of small groups, generally restricted to a handful of members, which are situated around the world in the most unlikely of countries. WUNS also posts among its affiliates an Iranian, a Japanese, and a Brazilian *Nazi Party* which are the symptoms of a recurring phenomenon: neo-Nazism appears and disappears like a fashion, briefly used by a youth fraction to express its rejection of the accepted codes by imitating an ideology seen as the most transgressive according to the norms of Western culture.[15]

The only transnational organization to have made any ideological innovations is the Círculo Español de Amigos de Europa (CEDADE) founded in 1966 in Francoist Spain which, after 1978, under the presidency of Pedro Varela, abandoned purely Spanish political action to become a European and Latin-American group. At the beginning, at least, in the same manner as the Mexican neo-Nazi Salvador Borrego, major writer on contemporary neo-Nazism, CEDADE made innovations by including Catholicism within its doctrinal body, despite being affiliated to the NEO. It also distinguishes itself by a pronounced Wagnerian aestheticism and a marked interest in ecology and regionalism, notably in the bulletin of the French section "Projets et references", which reports the first attempts to establish a political unification of ecologists.

A special attention should finally be paid to the very specific status and role German neo-Nazism has played since 1945. On the one hand, the German neo-Nazi movement enjoys a cult status around the world, for it is believed to be in direct line with the NSDAP. This explains why German or Austrian activists such as Michaël Kühnen and Friedhelm Busse from the *Freiheitliche Deutsche Arbeiterpartei*, Christian Worch (Aktionsfront Nationaler Sozialisten), and the

14 A candidate for the BPP won 4.95 % of the votes at a local election in Todmorden, in West Yorkshire, in May 2010.

15 In the case of the Mongolian movement Tsagaan Khass, the leader claimed to have learned about Nazism as a result of its having spread through post-soviet Russia. See "Mongolian neo-Nazis: Anti-Chinese sentiment fuels rise of ultra-nationalism", in: The Guardian, 2 August 2010.

leaders of the Austrian Volkstreue außerparlamentarische Opposition (VAPO) have received a wide foreign support when they were prosecuted in their countries. On the other hand, the German movements cannot be the driving force of the neo-Nazi international gathering and militancy because of the very close watch the Bundesamt für Verfassungsschutz (BfV) is keeping on them. Finally, although the 2010 BfV report gives an estimate of 5,600 neo-Nazi activists in Germany, and this is certainly the highest figure in Europe outside of Russia, the very singular link between the present and the past of German Nazism makes it almost impossible for foreigners to duplicate or even, imitate. This is also what makes the Autonome Nationalisten and "freie Kameradschaften" almost non-exportable.

II. The transatlantic link and the emergence of white supremacism in Europe

Since the 1990s, a new neo-Nazi culture has developed in the United States made up of new organizational forms which were rapidly imported to Europe by British and Scandinavian groups, before spreading elsewhere, particularly the former Soviet Union. Classifiable under the generic label of white supremacist groups, they have their origin in the notion of "White Power" developed by George Lincoln Rockwell as a response to "Black Power", slogan of the Black Panthers. The principle demands are the separation of white and non-white populations (on American territory) and, purely and simply, the expulsion of the non-white population (on European territory), the necessity for racial awareness among "Caucasian" peoples and the belief in their genetic and civilizational superiority. Most of these movements refuse to include Jews within the definition of "white people" with the exception of American Renaissance, the creation of the American Jared Taylor, whose annual conferences have included among their speakers Bruno Gollnisch, Nick Griffin, and the Canadian revisionist Nazi, Paul Fromm. Although the supremacist movements declare themselves to be rabidly anti-Semitic, Taylor is in agreement with the French essayist Guillaume Faye who, in a book which has caused controversy within the "national camp", predicts the imminence of a racial war in which the Jews will be tactical allies against the Muslim peril.[16]

In Europe, the influence of the American culture of white power has two sides, ideological and tactical. At the ideas level, one sees in particular the emergence of the Christian Identity Movement, which revisits Christian theology by proclaiming the Aryans as the "chosen people" and portraying the Jews as the seed of Satan. Jeffrey Kaplan, in his work "Encyclopedia of White Power: A Sourcebook on the Radical Racist Right",[17] stresses the repercussions of this

16 Faye, La Nouvelle question juive.
17 Cf. Kaplan, Encyclopedia of White Power.

movement for the Swedish neo-Nazi scene which, between 1995 and 1999, entered a phase of clandestine terrorist activity by way of groups such as Vitt Ariskt Motstand (VAM), the electoral ground being occupied by the *Nationalsocialistisk front*. The World Church of the Creator (WCOTC), founded in 1973 by Ben Klassen, is based on the same template but rejects the historical accuracy of certain biblical passages, doubts the actual existence of Jesus, and expresses its credo by way of a duality between "white/beautiful/good" and "non-white/bad". According to Ben Klassen "the laws of nature are fixed, rigid and eternal"; they are only concerned with the survival of the species, not of individuals; they are based on the struggle for survival and do not allow for the hybridization of species, from which he infers the injunction against the crossbreeding of peoples.[18] In decline since the imprisonment in 2005 of its supreme leader, Matt Hale, and renamed The Creativity Movement, the sect did acquire a certain amount of visibility in Sweden during the 1990s[19] when it first used professional marketing methods to produce and distribute music from the neo-Nazi metal scene via the magazine "Nordland" and the company of the same name.[20] The WCOTC still seems to have a network of correspondents in the United Kingdom, Croatia, France, Iceland, Slovakia, and in Eastern Germany.[21]

Several themes born out of American neo-Nazism have also clustered together to form the hard core of the position held by European racist groups. The first is the belief in the imminence and necessity of a racial war between whites, on the one hand, and "mud races" (all non-whites) on the other. It is a conflict in which the white supremacists may be the victors if they train and arm themselves for a confrontation both with their ethnic enemies and with the state, every echelon of government above that of the county being regarded as illegitimate. The bible of those who believe in this scenario is the work "The Turner Diaries" by William Pierce (alias Andrew Mac Donald),[22] published in 1978 and supplemented in 1979 by the political novel, "Hunter". The emergence of the concept of the Zionist Occupation Government (ZOG) defines the ideology of European neo-Nazi activists of the time: the belief in the quasi-satanic and totalitarian nature of all forms of democratic power imagined to be in the hands of the Jews, secret masters of the world. The terrorism of which they are the harbingers is based on the model of that practiced in the United States by The

18 Cf. Klassen, Nature's Eternal Religion.

19 On this point and on Swedish neo-Nazism in general, see Lööw, Nazismen i Sverige 1980–1997.

20 This transposed the methods and content of the North American magazine "Resistance and Resistance Records" in Scandinavia, then the property of the National Alliance movement.

21 The journal of the French section, founded by the pioneer of the movement, skinhead neo-Nazi Olivier Devalez, states: "It is not the time for an armed insurrection for which we do not have the human or material resources". In: Creativité, (2002) 5.

22 Published by the National Vanguard movement in Hillsboro. The most recent book from the American racialist far right in the vein of "The Turner Diaries" is Kyle Bristow's "White Apocalypse", self-published in 2010.

Order and Bruder Schweigen[23] (1983–84). Few of the movements will actually take any action apart from Combat 18 and its dissident group the Racial Volunteer Force, both British in origin, which have branched out into Europe in conjunction with the skinhead organization Blood and Honour. The importation of American neo-Nazi ideas, accelerated by the development of the Internet, has also brought about the adoption in Europe of the supremacist credo invented by David Lane, the famous motto Fourteen Words: "We must secure the existence of our people and a future for White Children".[24] Lane's ideological viewpoint also placed emphasis on the development of female militancy, not in the style of the classic "bird" skinhead but that of the political militant engaged in defending the traditional family, the differentiation of the sexes and the female warrior. As stated by the Women for Aryan Unity (WAU), an American-Canadian movement whose European branch is based in Ireland: "Being a woman is a very difficult task. We are generally obliged to be both warrior and mother".[25]

It is, however, in its methods of organization that the imitation of American neo-Nazism produces its greatest effect, by the implementation of "lone wolf" campaigns and of leaderless resistance. The lone wolf[26] is an activist who, aware of the high degree of infiltration of the supremacist movements by the security services and the risks posed to the success of violent operations by flaws commonly present in the neo-Nazi milieu (particularly mythomania) takes action on his own or by setting up a very small cell with one or two other individuals. The activists thus have no contact with each other, are not bound by any vertical hierarchy and gain their terrorist knowledge either from their former military experience or by downloading from the Internet declassified army manuals or similar literature, derived if necessary from activist movements of the extreme left. By extension, leaderless resistance is a mode of operation that involves acting without any affiliation to a political organization, a principle developed in the 1960s by the American colonel Iulius Amoss and extended in 1983 by Louis Beam of Aryan Nations.[27] Applicable both to the Islamic Jihad Movement and to the extreme left, like the theory of the lone wolf, it is strongly disputed by the experts for whom, at least in the case of the neo-Nazis, terrorists always have a militant link to a political organization which, without giving them orders, maintains them in a climate which promotes racial violence. The British anti-fascist

23 A literal reference to a phrase from the German patriotic song of 1814 "Wenn alle untreu warden", later taken up by the Waffen-SS and by the hagiographical book about this military unit edited by Hausser/Peiper, Wenn alle Brüder schweigen.

24 Ideologue of The Order Lane (1938–2007), who professed to be an Odinist by faith, is the author of the 88 Precepts, written after his imprisonment in 1985. Document available at: http://www.jrbooksonline.com/PDF_Books/Lane/88_Precepts.pdf.

25 Presentation in the magazine "Skuld": http://homefrontmagazine.org/wau14/?page.

26 This type of campaign appears to have been first theorized by Tom Metzger, leader of White Aryan Resistance, in the 1990s.

27 Text available in English and Russian: http://www.louisbeam.com/leaderless.htm.

magazine “Searchlight” thus published a report in 2011 entitled “Lone Wolves: Myth or Reality?”,[28] which demonstrated the adherence of neo-Nazis, arrested for acts of terror in the United Kingdom, to groups such as Combat 18, Aryan Strike Force, the *British People's Party*, and indeed the *British National Party*.[29]

Still, the essential contribution of American (and British) neo-Nazism really seems to be its capacity to mobilize the militant resources of the skinhead movement, politicized on the extreme right wing, and to export this device throughout Europe. It was in the United Kingdom, in the early 1970s, where the emergence of the *National Front* attracted a section of skinheads who were, first and foremost, a part of English working class youth culture. In the early 1980s, Tom Metzger and White Aryan Resistance then systemized this change within the American context, giving the white power movement in particular the aura of an American sub-culture, highly prized, particularly in the Eastern bloc, by a youth in a phase of imitating Western codes. The racist skinhead movement has always been divided into two large transnational organizations that share both militant force and the significant financial resources provided by white power music: Blood and Honour and the Hammerskins. Founded in 1987 in the United Kingdom, Blood and Honour owes a great deal to the legendary figure of Ian Stuart Donaldson, “front man” of the band Skrewdriver and founder of the movement Rock against Communism (RAC). The group has “divisions” on all continents. In 2011, in continental Europe, its presence is divided equally between the Western European divisions and those situated in Central and Eastern Europe, some of which are “official”, others bearing the generic name without being formally recognized by the British central office, as in the case of Blood and Honour Russia. For its part, the Hammerskin Nation is divided, like bikers' clubs, into chapters. Most are located in the United States; the European presence seems to be much larger in the West than in Central Europe (one chapter only in Hungary) and non-existent in Russia. The ideological differences are weak, the structure of these movements primarily based on the type of urban tribes competing for dominion over a territory. We are nevertheless witnessing, particularly in the North-East of France, the emergence of the phenomenon of the rural skinhead, independent of the two main organizations and whose political motivation corresponds to that of the movement in general: racism exacerbated towards people of color and immigrants, the abhorrence of homosexuals and all related “perversions”, Nazi fetishism, a taste for violence as a way of life.

28 Cf. Searchlight (Ed.), Lone Wolves: Myth or Reality?

29 Until March 2011 Arthur Kemp, the most visible ideologue of British racism, author of “March of the Titans” (1999), belonged to the national leadership of the BNP.

III. The neo-Nazi political parties

The legislation in force in Europe often prohibits the expression of Nazism or fascism, particularly in Germany, Austria, and Italy. In countries whose laws authorize them to take part in elections, neo-Nazi groups have sometimes chosen to stand, not to gain election but to demonstrate publicly the fact of their existence and their way of thinking. Their results are very modest. Pioneers of the subject, the Dutch *Nederlandse Volks-Unie*, which has been standing in legislative elections since 1977, have never achieved more than 0.4 % of the vote. At the regional elections in Sjælland in November 2005, the Danish DNSB gained 0.1 % of the vote. In the Grästorp municipal elections in 2010, the Swedish *Svanskarnas party*, successor to *Folkfronten*, gained a seat with 2.8 % of the votes but its leader Daniel Höglund was ultimately unable to take it up. In the United Kingdom, in May 2010, the BPP gained 4.95 % of the vote in a town in West Yorkshire, with just 283 votes. The Greek organization Chrissi Avghi (Golden Dawn), if it can be considered neo-Nazi, is undoubtedly the one, which has achieved the greatest electoral success in Western Europe: at the European elections in 2009 its list gained 23,564 votes, that is 0.46 %. At the same election in 1999, it had collected 48,532 votes, that is 0.75 %.

The electoral incursions of neo-Nazism in Eastern Europe have hardly been any more successful. In the Czech Republic, the *Dělnická strana* of Tomas Vandras was banned in February 2010 after having obtained 25,368 votes, that is 1.07 % at the 2009 European elections. Most of the parties classed as neo-Nazi by the militant anti-fascist literature are actually linked to other ideological traditions: that of the Polish National Radical Camp in the case of the NOP (*Narodowe Odrodzenie Polski*); that of the Hungarian *Nyilaskeresztes Párt* (Arrow Cross) in the case of *Jobbik*; that of the *Pērkonkrusts* (Thunder Cross), Ustasha, the Iron Guard, that is to say, local fascism, in Lithuania, Croatia, and Romania. With the current state of the political forces, the electoral emergence of neo-Nazism is plainly impossible in Europe, where neo-Nazi violence represents a public order problem. This is particularly the case in Russia where, despite state repression, which was increased in 2011, groups are still proliferating (Slaviansky Soyuz; Russian National Unity, National Socialist Society North) which have developed a mixture of national socialism, orthodox fundamentalism, and anti-Western nationalism deviating completely from the ideological canons of neo-Nazism, but which are responsible for a significant number of homicidal acts against non-Russians, particularly those from the Caucasian and Asian republics.

IV. Conclusion

Neo-Nazism is a marginal ideology. Its content is generally far removed from that of historical national socialism which today's self-proclaimed Nazis regard more as a basis for transgression than as a structured ideology. No serious attempt has been made at all to update this political family, which has innovated only by seeking to disseminate its message by means of the Nazi esotericism of Savitri Devi and Miguel Serrano, or by way of arcane history with its fascination for the occult roots of Nazism. The real question that arises in relation to neo-Nazism does not concern its content but its function. To pose this question, which goes beyond the remit of this paper, is to contemplate the fact that neo-Nazism has largely been manipulation, firstly by the secret services of the Communist Bloc in order to give credence to the idea that Western democracies were intrinsically fascist in nature; secondly by certain police forces in their fight against the extreme left; and finally, without any doubt, by Muslim countries (currently Iran) whose state-sponsored anti-Semitism leads them to consider ultra-right movements as acceptable allies.

Holocaust-denial – New Trends of a Pseudo-Scientific Smokescreen of Anti-Semitism

Jean-Yves Camus

I. Definition

Holocaust-denial is the seemingly scientific and would-be scholarly attempt at "proving" that the genocide of the Jews by the Nazis and their allies during the Second World War did not really take place. Holocaust-deniers pretend that the genocide was invented after 1945 by the Allied powers and the Jews in order to justify the laws of exception that were used at Nuremberg to convict the Nazi war criminals, simply because they had lost the war. They also believe that the genocide is a means of culpabilizing the German people for the actions of Nazi Germany, and to legitimize the creation of the State of Israel in 1948. Their rationale is that the Jewish organizations worldwide have, with the support of the United States and the other Allied powers, blackmailed the countries where the extermination of the Jews took place in order that up to this day, Jewish communities, Jewish organizations, and Israel can unduly receive financial compensation for the wartime sufferings of the Jews.

Holocaust-denial is constantly resorting to conspiracy theories and is constantly reactivating the old anti-Jewish stereotypes of deceit, greed, and manipulation. As such, it is intrinsically anti-Semitic, and many rabid anti-Semites of the pre-World War II era have become deniers after 1945, acting as a link between two or even three generations of Jew-baiters. To name but a few whose political activity outside of Germany span from the 1930s to the last quarter of the 20th century: the Australian Eric Dudley Butler (1916–2006), the French Henry Coston (1910–2001), and the Canadian Adrien Arcand[1] (1899–1967) have promoted Holocaust-denial after having held rather conventional, Christian-inspired, anti-Jewish ideas, mixed with a fascination for national socialism. Their influence has remained to this day in the extreme right subculture of their respective countries. Other individuals have combined a pre-1940 involvement in biological racism and a later influence on the European, and even

1 On Arcand, see Nadeau, Adrien Arcand. According to the author, Arcand was probably the first Holocaust-denier, even before Bardèche, that is in 1945–46. Interview with Nadeau, Paris, 27 May 2011.

American network of Holocaust-deniers: such is the case of the little-known Robert H. Ketels from Belgium.[2] He was followed by his younger fellow citizen Claude Nancy (aka. Claude Soas) whose book "Vers un matérialisme biologique" is a favorite read in the neo-Nazi underground.[3]

Because of the legislation against anti-Semitism that now exists in most European countries, and also in order to legitimize its obvious anti-Jewish bias, Holocaust-denial has been resorting to the trick of presenting itself as "anti-Zionism". Thus it has been taken advantage of the fact that it is not criminalized to oppose the Zionist ideology and even the right of the Jewish people to settle in their own state in Israel. Furthermore, the deniers have understood that it is legally difficult to draw a clear line between anti-Semitic and non-anti-Semitic (such as Jewish Orthodox or Marxist) anti-Zionism. In 2011, the Arab-Muslim world is the region where Holocaust-denial is the most widespread. There, it exists under the cover of Islamist ideology or masked as a kind of secular Arab nationalism which denies Israel's very right to exist. Its sources are notably the pan-Arabism of the Baath party or the "pan-Syrian" ideology of Antoun Saadé.[4] It has become the official vulgate of the Islamic Republic of Iran under president Ahmadinejad and also that of important Islamist political forces such as the Muslim Brotherhood in Egypt, when its former leader Mohamed Ali Akef, was in office.[5] This form of denial also exists within Islamist movements in Western Europe.

Due to their complete disconnection from reality and to the fact that their functioning depends on a quasi-theology, as well as to their total de-legitimization of their opponents, Holocaust-deniers are like a political sect that is very similar to a network of believers (the novelist Saint-Loup called them "religionnaires") who are trying to propagate a faith. One of the major problems with Holocaust-denial is its pseudo-academic appearance. Based on the postulate according to which history permanently invites to revise former scientific results in the light of new documents, evidence, and interpretation, the Holocaust-denials claim to be an historical school legitimately opposing another they name "exterminationist", i. e., believing in the material reality of the genocide of the Jews by the Nazis. This pseudo-scientificity is demonstrated by the titles of some of their journals and organizations ("Annales d'Histoire révisionniste"; Institute for Historical Review; Collegium Humanum – Akademie für Umwelt und

2 Ketels published Le Culte de la Race blanche in 1935 and Révision des idées et Souvenirs 1914–1951 in 1953. An observer of colonial rule in Congo, Ketels was a virulent critic of race-mixing and his role as a forerunner in the "social-racist" movement is acknowledged in Amaudruz, Nous autres racistes.

3 Born in 1931, Nancy died on July 26, 2010. His book was self-published in the 1970s and re-published in 2011 under the title: Hacia un materialismo biologic: La caida del materialismo historico.

4 Saadé and Michel Aflak, the founding theoretician of Bath, were Christians.

5 Cf. Spiegel Online, Iran soll sich für Holocaust-Komitee einsetzen, 23 December 2005, http://www.spiegel.de/politik/ausland/0,1518,392182,00.html, last accessed 22 October 2006.

Lebensschutz), in their frenzy of organizing conferences, and in an obsession with academic titles. One of the major French publishing houses in this field is named Akribeia, after the Greek word that means "the scrupulousness of the scholar". In fact, a few key figures in the Holocaust-denial sect are academics - but never historians: Robert Faurisson taught French literature, Udo Walendy is a journalist and a political scientist, Wilhelm Stäglich was a judge; Germar Rudolf is a chemist; Ernst Zündel is a graphic designer, and Sylvia Stolz is a lawyer. The Briton David Irving is a writer attempting to pass as a self-taught historian. He also briefly studied physics. The Austrian Holocaust-deniers Gerd Honsik and Walter Ochensberger are full-time neo-Nazi activists. Always concerned about their respectability, Holocaust-deniers have disguised the intention of their venture by calling themselves "revisionists". For this reason, the term "revisionist" may never be used except to characterize authors who admit the material reality of the genocide of the Jews while reducing the number of the victims below the figure that is agreed upon by historians that is between 5 and 6 million victims.[6]

One of the important trends of the last decades was the emergence of what Pierre-André Taguieff called "dubitationnisme",[7] a French word meaning that one circumvents the taboo of openly denying the Holocaust by expressing doubts about its reality. This form of expression is the paradoxical though very predictable consequence of the anti-racist legislation. It is the questioning of the reality of the genocide in a more subtle way than "hardcore Holocaust-denial". Dubitationnistes say that they do not hold any preconceived idea as to the reality and scope of the genocide. They claim to be "free-thinkers" who declare the Holocaust-denial theory to be equally worthy of interest as the "exterminationist" one. The best example of dubitationnisme is Jean-Marie Le Pen's statement aired on the radio station "RTL" on September 13, 1987: "I am asking myself certain questions. And I do not say the gas chambers did not exist. I have not been able to see them myself. I have not studied the matter. But I believe it is a detail of the history of the Second World War".[8] A different expression was used by Bruno Gollnisch, an academic and one of the leaders of the *Front National*, at a press-conference in Lyon, on October 11, 2004. He first declared that he was not able to make a proper judgement on the Second World War because from an academic point of view, being a professor of Japanese Law, he could only take a stand on issues related to the Asian-Pacific theatre of war. Then he continued: "I acknowledge there were millions of casualties due to the disaster of deportation and that of the concentration camps [...]. However when it comes to the methods and scope of this disaster, I leave it to the judgement of special-

6 The number of Jewish victims of the genocide has been estimated at 5.750 million in Gilbert, Atlas de la Shoah, and at 5.1 million in Hilberg, Die Vernichtung der europäischen Juden.

7 Taguieff, La nouvelle judéophobie.

8 For a video and verbatim of the declaration, see: http://www.lepoint.fr/actualites-societe/video-le-pen-en-1987-les-chambres-a-gaz-sont-un-point-de-detail/920/0/241025.

ized historians, whose discussions ought to be free and not threatened by a communist-inspired law. The intention of the so-called Gayssot Act was to make forget the Soviet crimes".[9]

The Holocaust-denial sect is obsessed with the genocide of the Jews. Occasionally, it casts doubt on the extermination of other population groups like gypsies, political prisoners, the mentally ill, or homosexuals. But it remains focused on the question of the genocide of the Jews and the gas chambers and denies their existence. This focusing has further consequences on its view of history. For example, deniers of the genocide believe in a "Jewish conspiracy" against Nazi Germany before the outbreak of World War II. They also share a harsh anti-Zionism. This in turn is often accompanied by conspiracy theories largely inspired by the Protocols of the Elders of Zion, if not literally, at least in spirit.

There are other forms of genocide denial than those connected with the extermination of the Jews. Especially in Turkey, the official historiography never accepted the fact that in 1915, the Armenians were the victims of genocide.[10] Instead, the Turkish criminal code considers the admission of this genocide a crime. We could also name the genocide of the Tutsi in Rwanda. A whole field of research remains to be opened concerning the possible involvement of the deniers of the genocide of the Jews in denying other forms of genocide. There is at least one example of a denier of the Nazi genocide, the German citizen living in South Africa, Claus Nordbruch, who also denies the genocide of the Herero, an indigenous people of Namibia. Its extermination had been planned by the German colonizers of what was then German South-West Africa, at the beginning of the 20th century.[11] The denial of the Armenian genocide sometimes tallies with that of the Jewish genocide within the Turkish Islamist or the ultranationalist secular movements. Faurisson also denies the genocide of the Gypsies and that of the homosexuals, as well as the extermination of retarded people.[12] There is at least one - if only marginal - example of a political opponent from Rwanda living in Belgium, Boniface Rutayisire, who in August 2009, published a text accusing the Jews of being responsible for "the crimes of the genocide against the Tutsis, the Hutus, and the Congolese". Without negating the reality of the Shoah, he accuses "individuals of Jewish identity to continue

9 Gollnisch's conviction by the Lyon Court of Appeals was overruled by a decision of the Cour de Cassation, the higest judicial authority, on 23 June 2009, and he was therefore cleared of all charges. Parts of Gollnisch's statement which were the ground for his indictment are reproduced in the ruling of the Higher Court: http://legifrance.gouv.fr/affichJuriJudi.do?idTexte=JURITEXT000020821426.

10 On the Armenian genocide, see Kieser/Schaller (Eds.), Der Völkermord an den Armeniern und die Shoah.

11 The website of Nordbruch, "http://www.nordbruch.org", presents his book: Nordbruch, Völkermord an den Herero in Deutsch-Südwestafrika.

12 Cf. Faurisson, Introduction aux Ecrits révisionnistes, p. XXV. He claims those are "other myths of the second world war".

to want to show that the Jewish genocide resembles the Tutsi genocide even though that is false".[13] But this seems to be an isolated case.

II. Holocaust-denial: The origins (1944–1967)

The history of Holocaust-denial has been researched extensively.[14] This is why we shall only review it quickly, trying to establish a chronology from 1945 until today and then attempting to define its different ideological patterns: the extreme right, the extreme left, and finally, Islamism or Arab secular nationalism. This history is striking at first sight because of the short time between the discovery[15] of the genocide and its being challenged. The camps were liberated by the American, British, French, and Soviet armies between the end of November 1944 (Natzweiler-Struthof, Alsace) and May 1945 (Mauthausen, Neuengamme, Stutthof). The extermination camps (which must be clearly distinguished from the concentration camps) were liberated between July 1944 (Majdanek, a "mixed" concentration and extermination camp) and January 1945 (Auschwitz, Chelmno). The first publications re-writing the history of the war and voicing theories that question the number of victims of the Shoah, the modus operandi of the extermination, or its intentionality were published in 1948 (Maurice Bardèche, "Nuremberg ou la terre promise") and 1950 (Rassinier, "Le Mensonge d'Ulysse"), both of them in France.[16] Holocaust-denial has been exported to the United States, Great Britain, and the rest of the world since the mid-1950s. Thus, it is likely that the Arab regimes already used it for their anti-Zionist and anti-Jewish propaganda addressed to its own populations. But it is not until after the year 2000 that Islamism and Arab nationalism have used it as a tool of their external propaganda, including that targeted to the Muslim populations living abroad. In this respect, we assume that they have made successive use of it in order to consolidate authoritarian Arab regimes by exploiting the Palestinian issue. Since the beginning of the al Aqsa intifada (September 2000), they have used it in order to equate the State of Israel, its citizens, and, by extension, the Jews, to the Nazis.

13 Cf. the French version: Rutayisire, Lettre au Premier Ministre d'Israel et à autres Juifs et leurs organisations, available at: http://murengerantwari.unblog.fr/2009/08/30/lettre-au-premier-ministre-disrael-et-a-dautres-juifs-et-leurs-organisations/, last accessed 18 December 2009.

14 On the history of Holocaust-denial: Lipstad, Betrifft: Leugnen des Holocaust; Benz, Realitätsverweigerung.

15 In fact, the term "discovery" is inadequate because the existence of concentration camps had been known before the war and that of extermination camps at least since 1942. But it was only after the liberation of the camps that the complete truth became known of what had happened there, especially due to the evidence given by the survivors. For a firsthand testimonial account proving that the plan of the total extermination of the Jews had been known since spring 1942, cf. Sadovsky, Berlin 1942. It is a document of the responsible person for the hunt of foreign Jews of the Paris police.

16 Cf. Bardèche, Nuremberg ou la terre promise; Rassinier, Le Mensonge d'Ulysse.

From the very beginning, the spreading of Holocaust-denial in Germany and in Austria has been restricted by the legal arsenal existing in those countries against anti-Semitism and neo-Nazism. In Germany it appeared only very late, i. e., in the 1970s. Works were then published, such as, Heinz Roth, "Warum werden wir Deutschen belogen?" (1973), Richard Harwood, "Starben wirklich sechs Millionen? Endlich die Wahrheit" (1974), Arthur Butz, "Der Jahrhundertbetrug" (1976), Wilhelm Stäglich, "Der Auschwitz-Mythos: Legende oder Wirklichkeit? Eine kritische Bestandsaufnahme" (1979).[17] Like elsewhere, the denial of the Shoah was intertwined with the praise of national socialism. Some of its first theoreticians, for example, Thies Christophersen and Erich Kern (Kernmayr), had been members of the NSDAP.

It is necessary to understand that Holocaust-denial arose from the extreme right and extreme left at the same time - but that the members of the extreme left who became deniers of the Shoah often joined the extreme right after a time. In some respect, Maurice Bardèche (1909-1998) is the founding father of Holocaust-denial. He was a French academic who wrote in the fascist weekly "Je suis partout". He was a fellow student and later brother-in-law of the fascist writer Robert Brasillach who was executed in 1945. When Bardèche set out to dispute the Nazi crimes, his initial motivation was the de-legitimization of the victor's justice. He repudiated what he held to be a special justice of vengeance and exception, staged at the Nuremberg Trials, where the notion of "crimes against humanity" had been introduced for the first time. A collaborationist of only minor importance, Bardèche strove for the rehabilitation of collaboration, of the Vichy regime, and, finally, of European fascism.

His political attitudes may have been radicalized by Brasillach's execution which he - like the whole French extreme right - considered a crime. But he had shown anti-Semitic leanings in his pre-war writings. The publication of his book coincided with the foundation of the State of Israel. It showed an incontestable propensity for a world outlook founded on the conspiracy theory.[18] The foundation of the Jewish state fitted in as an additional confirmation of the intention of the Jewish people to dominate the world. Thus, since his first public expression, the denial of the genocide of the Jews has emphasized anti-Zionism. Anti-Zionism camouflages the anti-Semitism made inacceptable in its unadorned form by the discovery of the Nazi crimes. From 1952, Bardèche popularized it in his quarterly journal "Défense de l'Occident" which was a sort of a forum for European neo-fascism. Bardèche was followed by Paul Rassinier (1906-1967), who came from a totally different political sphere, namely from the pacifist and broadly anarchist wing of the SFIO, the French socialist party. Rassinier had become an MP in 1946 before he was excluded from the SFIO because of his theories, but he kept on writing for anarchist and pacifist publi-

17 Cf. Roth, Warum werden wir Deutschen belogen?; Harwood, Starben wirklich sechs Millionen?; Butz, Der Jahrhundertbetrug; Stäglich, Der Auschwitz-Mythos.

18 On the conspiracy theory, cf. Taguieff, La foire aux illuminés.

cations until the 1960s. He had been a member of the underground resistance and had been deported to the forced labor camp of Dora. His works convey his personal experience as well as his ideology. On the one hand, as a former inmate, his hatred focused on his former communist co-detainees whom he accused of having protected their own fold in the camps at the expense of the other, non-communist prisoners. On the other hand, like that segment of the ultra-left called the Italian left,[19] and also like the Council Communists,[20] as well as some orthodox Marxists, he considered Nazism to be basically nothing but a variation of the hated capitalism and anti-fascism. To him, anti-fascism was but a sort of smokescreen propagated by the bourgeoisie in order to quench the desire of the oppressed classes to revolt. For him as well as for his subsequent heirs in the group La Vieille Taupe[21] that gathered around Pierre Guillaume and Serge Thion, the Nazi horror and what they consider the everyday horror of capitalist oppression are of the same kind. Rassinier set off with a radical critique of the possible ideological use of anti-fascism. He challenged the number of victims of the genocide and downplayed the unique nature of the homicidal gas chambers as a means of mass annihilation, but he did not deny their existence. He also followed in the steps of the rationalist and freethinking tradition, which consists in submitting every fact to the critique of reason, beginning with certainties and dogmas.

To these hypercriticists, it is impossible that the genocide really happened because it is, strictly speaking, outside the realm of reason. They refuse to admit that hard proof of the genocide may be hard to demonstrate because it was accomplished in the utmost secrecy and organized by the executioners in such a way that there would be no documents left. They simply seem to forget that the dead cannot testify to the way they were killed. They furthermore discredit direct witnesses, that is camp survivors, because of their assumed lack of objectivity. Extreme left Holocaust-deniers always point out the inevitable incoherence, i. e., factual errors, of the recollections of the survivors, in order to discredit their substance. They are also convinced that the Shoah never happened because if Nazism is nothing but a variation of bourgeois capitalism, it ought to have exploited the deported Jews as a proletarian work force of its production machinery instead of wiping them out and thus depriving itself of a cheap labor force. They simply reject the argument that anti-Semitism was the core of Nazi theories and that the Nazis just considered the Jews as a sub-human race that

19 Orthodox Marxist current founded by Amadeo Bordiga as split of the Partito Comunista d'Italia. It insists on anti-fascism being a weapon of the bourgeoisie against the working class.

20 Anti-Leninist Marxist current inspired by Spartakism advocating an anti-authoritarian Marxism founded on a "Republic of Workers' Councils".

21 This Paris library had been founded in 1965 and was a rallying point for Council Communists. It did not deny the genocide until Pierre Guillaume, one of its former associates, aligned it on his newly espoused Holocaust-denying views, which were not shared by the majority of the former militants.

was to be exterminated in order to let the "one thousand years Reich" stay in power.

However, Rassinier quickly moved away from just reducing the number of victims. Since the mid-1950s, he supported outright Holocaust-denial and the theory of the Jewish conspiracy. His writings were edited by activists of the extreme right, in this case, by Henry Coston (1910–2001). In France, from the beginning of the 1930s until his death, Coston was the chief propagandist of the theory of the Judeo-Mason conspiracy. Since the mid-50s, Rassinier even turned to neo-Nazis, for example the German Karl-Heinz Priester, a former SS officer. Priester became his editor and succeeded, just like Bardèche, with the aggregation of all three Holocaust-denial traditions, namely the extreme left, the extreme right, and the Arab anti-Zionist. Rassinier and Coston wrote to each other regularly. They were in contact with a former aide of Goebbels who had become the responsible official of the service in charge of the foreign propaganda of Nasser's Egyptian regime, Johann von Leers (1902–1965) who assured their translation into Arabic. Until Peron's fall, von Leers had been a refugee in Argentina. A rabid anti-Semite,[22] he had published a journal for the fringe of the German community sympathetic to national socialism, "Der Weg", which was one of the first open expressions of Holocaust-denial.[23] The same configuration can be found at Rassinier's funeral: the funeral orations were held by an anarchist, Emile Bauchet, followed by the self-avowed fascist Bardèche. At that time, the Holocaust-denial movement was not as extensive as it has become after the beginning of the 1980s. It was still largely confined to circles limited by their political impact and social influence, namely, to militant neo-Nazis. Gradually, it has been exploited by Arab propaganda. We need to understand and explain what permitted this development.

III. Holocaust-denial in Western Europe: Why the growth?

In Europe and the United States, the growth of Holocaust-denial from the 1950s to the 1970s occurs within a context characterized by the Cold War, and the multiplication of conflicts between Israel and its neighbors in the Middle East (1956, 1967, 1973, the so-called Lebanon War in 1982). Furthermore, the development of a national Palestinian movement permitted the compensation of various attempts at Arab unity having collapsed. The Cold War had several consequences. On the one side, it led to the relativization of national-socialist crimes because they were compared with those of communism. It even allowed some Western secret services to use or employ people with a Nazi or collaborator's past. On the other side, in the Arab world supported by the USSR, as well as among Western supporters of the Third World so-called "freedom movements"

22 Cf. especially Leers, Die Verbrechernatur der Juden.
23 Cf. Meding, Der Weg.

and the communists, the Cold War increased the identification of Israel with the West, and also that of Israel with imperialism and colonialism.

As a consequence, the Soviet propaganda increased its challenging of the legitimacy of the Jewish State and its mobilization of anti-Zionism. This propaganda never committed itself to plain denial of the Shoah.[24] However, it evaded the specifically Jewish dimension of the Nazi genocide. Several other factors can also be identified which have doubtlessly encouraged the emergence of Holocaust-denial. The first is the gradual discovery in Europe, mostly in the 1970s, of what Nazi occupation, the ideological roots of fascism and national socialism really meant, and of the true extent of collaboration. For a long time, these topics had been obscured in the collective memory.[25] The new awareness brought about the phenomenon of Holocaust-denial as a way to alleviate the burden of culpability. The second factor is the development of the Jewish memory, with the increasing number of public accounts of their plague by survivors of the genocide who had remained silent for a long time. In a general manner, this was accompanied by the growing visibility of the Jewish communities in the Diaspora. Their representative organizations began formulating demands concerning the public commemoration of the genocide, the introduction of more stringent laws against anti-Semitism and in some cases for the long overdue financial compensations the survivors had to get in order to compensate for the properties and assets confiscated by the Nazis.[26] This last point makes deniers argue that it is impossible for Jewish communities to have been destroyed and yet be so big in numbers today.

Originally, France was the major centre of Holocaust-denial circles. After Rassinier's death, they assembled mostly around the journal "Défense de l'Occident", published until November 1982, and around the history teacher François Duprat, one of the leaders of the neo-fascist groups Occident, Ordre Nouveau, and from 1972 until his death in 1978, of the *Front National*. Duprat self-published the "Cahiers européens". He also published Thies Christophersen's pamphlet "Die Auschwitz Lüge" in 1976 and in 1978, the pamphlet "Did Six Million Really Die?"[27] by Richard Verall (alias Richard Harwood), a leader of the British *National Front*. However, those works were confined to the small

24 This would necessarily have brought about the partial rejection of the assumed role of the USSR in the fight against the Nazis.

25 In 1970, the time of Nazi occupation and collaboration became the subject of discussion in France due to Marcel Ophuls' film "The Sorrow and the Pity". The re-discovery of the past continued with the publication of Robert Paxton's book Vichy France, Old Guard and New Order, 1940–1944 in 1972. It continued with controversial debates of the French origins of fascism with the publications of Sternhell, La droite révolutionnaire; id., Neither Right nor Left; and the essay of Lévy, L'Idéologie française.

26 In France, these demands lead to the acknowledgement of the share of responsibility for the deportation of the Jews of the French State by President Chirac in July 1995. Subsequently, this leads to a decree accepted by the Jospin government (2000) organizing the indemnization of the survivors of the Shoah and their offspring.

27 On this point, cf. Lebourg, Le monde vu de la plus extrême droite.

world of the fringe extreme right. Wide media coverage of Holocaust-denial was first accomplished by Robert Faurisson, a professor at the University of Lyon and a specialist of modern French poetry. Since the 1960s, Faurisson had been interested in the topics of the gas chambers. He had not been an active militant of the extreme right. On the contrary, he insisted in having been rather close to the anti-colonialist left - but without proof. However, in June 1978, he published an article in "Défense de l'Occident", with a Holocaust-denial content. It was in fact consistent with a seldom reported event in his youth. In 1949, Faurisson attended the trial of Pierre Gallet, a leader of the Milice Française who was sentenced to death by the Paris court. This trial left an imprint on the young man's mind and was his first contact with war crimes and collaboration.[28]

Robert Faurisson became notorious on December 29, 1978 when the French daily "Le Monde" published a column by him, in which he disclosed his views. For the next three years, this text set in motion a whole mechanism of exposure of Holocaust-denial in the media, followed by replies from the scientific community denouncing Holocaust-denial as the imposture it is. The controversy coincided with the airing of the "Holocaust" drama series on French public TV, starting on February 13, 1979 and with the press campaign against the "New Right", considered by many on the left as neo-Nazism in disguise. Later on the mainstream national media allowed him to expose his views again, when he was interviewed on the radio Europe 1 on December 17, 1980. A much-heated controversy followed, during which a part of the Anarchist ultra-left campaigned in favor of Faurisson's freedom of speech, not without demonstrating its skepticism of the "official" history of the Nazi genocide, interpreted as just another mass slaughter in the long tradition of barbarity that they think is inherent with capitalism. This is why the council communist group La Guerre Sociale published the booklet "De l'exploitation dans les camps à l'exploitation des camps" and why the figurehead of the American alternative left, Noam Chomsky, wrote the preface to "Mémoire en défense contre ceux qui m'accusent de falsifier l'histoire" published by Faurisson at la Vieille Taupe in December 1980.

In fact, the methods of the Holocaust-deniers, the attitude of the scientific community concerning them, and even the ideological issues have remained the same from then until today. New emblematic figures of the movement appeared in the 1980s especially in France, like Serge Thion, Henri Roques,[29] Roger Garaudy,[30] and in the 1990s, Vincent Reynouard. Some of them have distinctive ideological features (in the case of Garaudy, a well-known past as a communist intellectual, first Stalinist, then anti-Stalinist) but basically, all of them

28 Cf. Brigneau, Mais qui est donc le professeur Faurisson?
29 Author of Roque, Die Geständnisse des Kurt Gerstein.
30 Communist philosopher who broke with Marxism and converted to Islam; Author of Die Gründungsmythen der israelischen Politik, which first appeared in the journal "Sleipnir" published by Peter Töpfer. Since 1996, it was edited by Eigner Verlag, managed by Peter Töpfer who claims to adhere to "national anarchism"; Garaudy, Die Gründungsmythen der israelischen Politik.

stick to the definition of Holocaust-denial as given by Faurisson on the airwaves of "Europe 1" and which is to be considered the manifesto of Holocaust-denial. It deserves to be quoted extensively: "Hitler's pretended gas-chambers and the pretended genocide of the Jews form one and the same historical lie which has allowed for a gigantic political and financial fraud. Its principal beneficiaries are the State of Israel and international Zionism. Its principal victims are the German people, with the exception of its leaders, and the whole Palestinian people".[31]

There are a few new patterns of Holocaust-denial that emerged after the 1980s. First of all, it is now to be found in Eastern Europe,[32] where it oscillates between pure and simple denial of the genocide and the trivialization of Nazism by comparing it with communism. This is often coupled with the rehabilitation of ultra-nationalist movements of before 1945. Also "exotic" forms of Holocaust-denial have appeared, like that of the author Aiju Kimura in Japan.[33] But the only true innovation besides the spreading of Holocaust-denial in certain Arab-Muslim milieus is the support given by some Catholic fundamentalists to Holocaust-denial.

In January 2009, Bishop Richard Williamson from the Society of St. Pius X caused a controversy because at the Zaitzkofen (Bavaria) seminary of the followers of the late Bishop Marcel Lefebvre, he insisted that there had been no gas chambers and he considerably reduced the number of Jewish victims of Nazism. This is his verbatim statement: "I do not believe that there were gas chambers [...]. I think that 200,000 to 300,000 Jews died in National Socialist concentration camps [...] but not one of them through gas chambers".[34] Officially condemned by the Society of St. Pius X, this declaration is not the only example of the denial of the genocide of the Jews in this school of thought. The French group Les Intransigeants[35] deserves to be mentioned here, as the magazine "Sans Concession" published by the French Holocaust-denier Vincent Reynouard, who claims to be a Sedevacantist.[36]

The controversy stirred up by Bishop Williamson's remarks hurt the ongoing negotiations about the re-integration of the Society of St. Pius X into the Roman

31 Cf. "Die Siege des Revisionismus", Das Papier des Prof. Robert Faurisson für die Teheraner Holocaust-Konferenz 2006, www.kreuz.net/reader/bookentry.4966.attachment1.pdf, last accessed 30 September 2009.

32 On Holocaust-denial in Middle and Eastern European states, cf. Shafir, Between Denial and "Comparative Trivialization".

33 In 1995, a widely read Japanese journal, "Marco Polo", caused a scandal publishing a Holocaust-denial article. Some months later, Kimura published the first complete book with this opinion in Tokyo. Kimura who has his own website, www.jca.apc.org/~altmedka, distributes a Japanese translation of Garaudy's book Die Gründungmythen der israelischen Politik.

34 Cf. Wensierski, Problem für den Papst. In: Der Spiegel, (2009) 4, p. 32.

35 Cf. http://intransigeants.wordpress.com, last accessed 10 April 2011.

36 On the theory of Sedevacantism see the apologetic book of Rothkranz, Die Sedisvakanzthese.

Catholic Church. It obliterated the most interesting point of the fundamentalist Catholic denial of the genocide, namely, the total lack of logic with regard to the theology of Judaism which this movement sticks to. In fact, traditional Catholic fundamentalists largely approved of the canonization of Maximilian Kolbe and Edith Stein during the pontificate of John Paul II. Father Kolbe's body was burned in a crematorium furnace at the camp at Auschwitz, and Edith Stein was gassed there because she was born a Jew. Finally, it must be noted that fundamentalist Catholicism hitches up to the theory of the deicidal people and to the concept according to which anti-Semitism is a divine punishment imposed by God in order to punish the Jewish people for its unfaithfulness. But it refuses to follow this line of argument to the end and to consider the material reality of the genocide as the concretization of this divine punishment.

Politically, the Holocaust-denial sect is practically deprived of perspectives because of the laws banning expressions of racism, anti-Semitism, and the denial of crimes against humanity. This is true especially in Western Europe, including Great Britain, which used to adhere to an extensive concept of the freedom of expression. Thus, neo-Nazism can no longer be expressed freely except in Scandinavia where the Moroccan Islamist Ahmed Rami, the founder of "Radio Islam", and the Russian-Israeli Israël Shamir have chosen to live (in Sweden). The latter presents himself as a convert to Greek orthodoxy of Jewish origin who changed from "ultra-left" anti-Zionism to an alliance with the neo-Nazis.

Repressive legislation and permanent police surveillance, often comprising measures of dispersal, prohibition of conferences, or denial of entry (cf. the case of David Irving), are executed with harsh sentences in court and completed with professional bans. Due to these measures, except for a few very small and purely neo-national socialist groups,[37] hardly any political party striving for electoral success dares to voice Holocaust-denial theories in public. But still, leaders intending to improve their parties' respectability - like Nick Griffin, chairman of the *British National Party* and member of the European Parliament[38] - have denied the genocide of the Jews verbally and in print. Yet, in most cases, turning from "soft" to open Holocaust-denial is followed by the expulsion or forced resignation of the person who uttered it. In November 2008, Senator Michel Delacroix had to resign from his position as the chairperson of the Belgian *Front National.* He was trapped by the publication of a video showing him singing "My little Jewess is at Dachau. She is in burning lime. She left her ghetto. To be burned alive".[39] The same misfortune befell the former Senator and vice-chairperson of the *Vlaams Blok,* Roeland Raes.[40] The chair of the MS-*Fiamma*

37 Thus, the Danmarks Nationalsocialistiske Bevægelse (DNSB) distributes the publications of Thies Christophersen, Mark Weber, Fred Leuchter, and Josef Turner.
38 Sentenced in 1998, according to the Public Order Act, for statements in his publication at that time.
39 Cf. Le Soir, 6 November 2008.
40 He stepped down from his post at the "Vlaams Blok" after an interview with the Dutch chain NCRV in February 2001.

Tricolore, Luca Romagnoli, had been MEP from 2004 to 2009. He did not step down after having declared on February 22, 2006: "You ask me whether the gas chambers existed. Frankly, I have no means at all to assert or to negate this question".[41] His party has now faded into oblivion.

In addition to the aforementioned persons, the star authors of the European Holocaust-denial community come from various countries. Their provenance establishes some sort of cartography of this phenomenon: Germany and Austria (with a "new wave" of deniers like Sylvia Stolz and Peter Töpfer), Belgium (the brothers Verbeke and their association Vrij Historisch Onderzoek, VHO), Great Britain (David Irving, the pro-Iran activist, Michèle Renouf), Italy (Carlo Mattogno and the Marxist Claudio Moffa), Sweden (Ditlieb Felderer, Ahmed Rami[42]), and Switzerland (Jürgen Graf,[43] Gaston-Armand Amaudruz, René-Louis Berclaz, and Bernhard Schaub).

The weight of Germany, Austria, and German-speaking Switzerland is important in the complex Holocaust-denial web. But it is not at all predominant. A new and important fact is the emergence of Holocaust-denial authors and movements in Middle and Eastern Europe. There, the denial of the genocide of the Jews seems to be mostly propagated by neo-Nazi and skinhead groups. They incorporate it into their political program without the slightest attempt at a theoretic conception. *Noua Dreaptă* (Romania), *Slovenska Postpolitost* (Slovakia), and *Bulgarski Nacionalni Soyouz*, for example, are affiliated with the neo-fascist organization European National Front.[44] *Narodowe Odrodzenie Polski* (NOP), *Nacionalni Stroj* (Serbia), and *Narodni Odpor* (Czeck Republic) belong to the same ideological vein. Few authors dedicate themselves specifically to Holocaust-denial. The diffusion of their production inevitably meets with the obstacle of the language. Still, one can name the Romanians Georges Piscosi-Denescu,[45] Ion Coja,[46] and Gheorghe Buzatu,[47] as well as the Polish author Tomas Gabisz. With some delay, Eastern-European Holocaust-deniers have appeared on the internet: The Slovak website "http://beo.sk" and the websites

41 Interview at the Italian TV chain Sky TG24.

42 A Moroccan, Ahmed Rami, whose website is called "Radio Islam" (available at: http://www.abbc2.com) offers an exemplary synthesis of Holocaust-denial, rabid anti-Semitism in the vein of the Protocols, of Nazism (he distributes Mein Kampf), and Islamism.

43 Graf's book Der Holocaust-Schwindel, 1993 ("The Holocaust Fraud"), became a classic in these circles. The author fled to Iran in fall 2000 in order to escape a prison sentence imposed by a Swiss court.

44 NPD and "Forza Nuova" are the driving forces.

45 Manager of the anti-totalitarian Romanian Library in Paris, returned to Romania. His captivating article on the penetration of Holocaust-denial writings in communist Romania can be found at: http://www.aaargh.codoh.info/roma/roma.html, last accessed 20 December 2010.

46 Former Senator (1992-96), linguist at the University of Bucharest; member of the ultra nationalist Vatra Romanească.

47 Former vice-president of the senate, elected representative of the "Greater Romania Party", historian at the University of Craiova.

of the two most important skinhead organizations (Blood and Honor, Hammerskins) convey the negation of the genocide.

Nowadays, European Holocaust-denial functions very largely through the internet. This enables deniers to put their writings at the disposal of a very large public. They evade anti-racist legislation because of the vagueness of the laws concerning the penal responsibility of the authors of e-literature. Recent court sentences in France establish the responsibility of the web providers and orders them to implement filtering measures which make Holocaust-denial websites practically inaccessible, although mirror-sites hosted in countries without such legislation can be used to circumvent the filtering.[48] Some formerly highly frequented sites have become difficult to access because the big search-engines do not reference them any longer. The freedom of expression is guaranteed in the First Amendment of the Constitution of the United States of America. Thus, the legal situation in the US still gives a lot of leeway to Holocaust-deniers who often resort to American or Eastern European (especially Russian) providers. This way, filtering processes can be easily circumvented. The decisive role of the United States in the spreading of Holocaust-denial makes it necessary to understand the currants of exchange with Europe.

IV. The process of Holocaust-denial exchange between Europe and America

The North-American denial of the genocide began with one of Rassinier's intellectual masters, Harry Elmer Barnes (1889–1968). Attracted to the isolationist milieus in the 1930s and 1940s, but originally quite "liberal" according to American standards, Barnes commanded two unique particularities: He was a renowned scholar teaching at Columbia, and, considering World War I, he had initially been a revisionist. He had actually published two books: "The Genesis of the World War: An Introduction to the Problem of War Guilt" (1926), and "In Quest of Truth and Justice: Debunking the War Guilty Myth" (1928). They questioned the imperial nature of the Austro-German war machinery and criticized some of the anti-German campaigns of the enemy countries of the Second Reich as being nothing but pure propaganda. After 1945, he started to embrace positions maintaining that the responsibility for the conflict did not lie with Hitler but with the Allies and the "Zionists". He was convinced that the magnitude of their "crimes" equaled or even surpassed those of the Third Reich. Gradually, he approached the extreme right[49] and finally bluntly adopted Holocaust-denial positions. One of his disciples, David L. Hoggan (1923–1988),

48 Sentence of the Paris Civil Court, of 20 April 2005, summoning the American hosts of the site AAARGH "to stop any release of the Website from their server(s) on French territory".

49 We list his very little known brochure: Barnes, Crucifying the Saviour of France.

followed him along this way. In 1948, Hoggan defended his doctoral thesis at Harvard in which he insisted that Hitler had not wanted the war. In 1961, it appeared in print and was entitled "The Forced War". Later, its author became a denier of the genocide who in 1969, published "The Myth of the Six Millions".

In the United States as well as in Canada, Holocaust-denial was increasing among the extreme right when another scholar, Austin J. App, published his book "The Six Million Swindle: Blackmailing the German People for Hard Marks with Fabricated Corpses" in 1973. This book is distinguished by the fact that the author listed the following eight theses which, according to him, codify the convictions of Holocaust-deniers: (1) The Nazis wanted the Jews to emigrate, they did not want to exterminate them. If they had really wanted to exterminate them, not one single Jew would have survived. (2) Not one single Jew was gassed in a German camp. (3) The Jews who disappeared during the war were on Soviet and not on German territory. (4) The majority of the Jews killed by the Nazis were killed because they were criminals, spies or subversive elements. (5) Had the genocide really happened, Israel would have opened its archives to historians instead of accusing everybody who questions its existence of anti-Semitism. (6) Every single proof of the reality of the genocide is based on misquotations of Nazi documents. (7) The burden of proof remains with the accusers. They must verify the number of 6 million victims. (8) Jewish and non-Jewish historians diverge concerning their estimations of the number of victims, which shows that they are unable to supply any proof. This intellectual approach is very much similar to Sigmund Freud's famous *witz* of the cauldron. To this day, it constitutes the "hard core" of the Holocaust-denial tale, in addition to the above mentioned dogma of Faurisson.

A supporter of Holocaust-denial since 1949, App had founded an association of Americans of German origin that was clearly pro-Nazi in 1945. His writings, together with the work of Arthur Butz, "The Hoax of the Twentieth Century", constituted the base of the propaganda launched since 1978 by what could be reasonably called the "center of international Holocaust-denial", namely the Institute for Historical Review (IHR) founded by Willis Carto and William D. McCalden, based in California. Already known for his role as an editor of Noontide Press, in 1958, Carto founded the Liberty Lobby which developed into one of the most important organs of propaganda of the extreme right in the United States. Cato largely borrowed from his spiritual mentor, the American neo-Nazi Francis Parker Yockey.[50]

From 1979 to 2004, IHR organized an annual international conference, later to be complemented by a pseudo-scholarly publication, the "Journal of Historical Review". Almost every Holocaust-denier in the whole world has participated in one or contributed to the other at least once, including Noam Chomsky who in 1985 delivered a speech on "the crisis of the Middle East and

50 On Yockey and his major work Imperium (1948), which has turned into a "bible" of international neo-fascism, cf. Koogan, Dreamer of the Day.

the threat of a nuclear war".[51] Since 1995 directed by Mark Weber and having parted ways with Carto (who has published the "Barnes Review"[52] since 1994), the IHR was a bridge between deniers on both sides of the Atlantic Ocean.[53] But Bradley R. Smith's[54] Committee for Open Debate on the Holocaust (CODOH) is a serious competitor.

When it comes to the exchange of propaganda between North America and Europe, the key personality of this galaxy is David Duke, though. He was the first to comprehend the important possibilities arising for the spreading Holocaust-denial in Central and Eastern Europe. Convinced that the future of Holocaust-denial lies there, he submitted a doctoral thesis in history at the Ukrainian private university MAUP (in Kiev) in September 2005. MAUP president Georgy Tchokin had transformed it into a stronghold of anti-Semitic ultranationalism.[55] Duke is certain that Russia "holds the key of the survival of the white race". He has travelled in this country several times[56] and has established close ties with national-communist milieus, especially with the deputy of the State Duma, General Albert Makashov, and with Alexander Prokhanov, the editor of the journal "Zavtra". Duke is the organizer as well as the guest star of the European-American Unity and Leadership Conference, officially concerned with the question of white identity. However, in 2004, Germar Rudolf, John Tyndall, and Willis Carto participated. In 2005, the conference was attended by Pedro Varela, Michèle Renouf, and Nick Griffin.

Finally, one should mention an icon of Holocaust-denial, the German-Canadian Ernst Zündel (1939), who from 2007 until 2010 was jailed in Germany after being extradited there from Canada. Since 1978, Zündel has been known as a prominent denier. In Toronto, he established Samisdat Publishers which printed his chief work "The Hitler We Loved and Why". Zündel is emblematic of a global category of Holocaust-deniers which is rarely analyzed: it is the group of persons of German origin who deny the genocide because this enables them to rehabilitate national socialism and German nationalism, to exalt the idea of the ethnic German community, and to present the German people as the collective victim of the war. In North America, there are Zündel's wife, Ingrid Rimland, Paul Fromm, founder of the Movement Canada First, Fred Leuchter, and Austin App; in Australia, Frederick Toben of the Adelaide Institute; Siegfried Ellwanger Castan in Brazil; Ditlieb Felderer in

51 Monzat, Enquêtes sur la droite extrême, p. 197.
52 Cf. http://www.barnesreview.org, last accessed 20 December 2010.
53 Michele Renouf, Faurisson, the Croatian diplomat Tomislav Sunić, Irving, and Graf were invited by IHR.
54 Cf. http://www.codoh.com/index2.html, last accessed 20 December 2010.
55 The topic of the thesis was: "Zionism as a Form of Racial Supremacism". Duke published it as a pseudo-academic book: Jewish Supremacism: My Awakening to the Jewish Question in 2001.
56 He also visited other countries: In April 2009, he was arrested and later released by the Czech police. He had been invited to Prague by the neo-Nazi group Narodni Odpor.

Sweden (born in Innsbruck, Austria), and Pedro Varela Geiss, the owner of the Libreria Europa in Barcelona, Spain.

V. Arab/Muslim Holocaust-denial: An under-estimated aspect of the problem

It is essential to avoid the confusion and the polemical debates comparing Islamism and national socialism in an abusive way.[57] However, it cannot be denied that a high amount of Holocaust-denial propaganda is available to the public in the Arab-Muslim World (including, by the way, regions like the Indian sub-continent and South-East Asia, on which there is a severe lack of research).[58] We also know that the works of the major Western Holocaust-deniers are translated into Arabic.[59] Furthermore, Middle-Eastern satellite TV channels[60] broadcast and spread the denial of the genocide in that part of the world as well as among the populations of Muslim origin in Europe. Even though Arab Holocaust-denial often includes an Islamic component, it cannot be reduced to this by far.

Nationalism and pan-Arabism hold their stakes: a movement like the Arab-European League in Belgium and in the Netherlands, is closely linked with Holocaust-denial, and the Iraqi translator of Garaudy and Graf, Jawad Bashara, is a cadre of the *Communist Party*.[61] In February 2006, as a response to the affair of the Muhammad cartoons, the League's founder Dyab Abou Jahjah, a Belgian citizen of Lebanese origin, published Holocaust-denial drawings on its website. One of them shows Anne Frank and Adolf Hitler in bed. Hitler says: "Write this in your diary, Anne".[62] We also find that Holocaust-denial may come from Middle-Eastern Christian milieus, at home as well as in Diaspora. The *Syrian Social Nationalist Party* (SSNP), founded by the Greek Orthodox Antoun Saadé, is highly appreciated by the European Philo-Arabic extreme right. This is all the more interesting because it is represented in the Lebanese Parliament where it is part of the pro-Syrian coalition of the opposition which Hezbollah also belongs to.

57 The similarity between those ideologies is defended by Küntzel, Djihad und Judenhass.

58 Among the major works written in the Middle East: Abdo, La vérité sur l'holocauste des juifs; and the works of the Jordanian Ibrahim Alloush.

59 Cf. the Arabic translation of Garaudy, The Founding Myths of Israeli Politics, appeared in 1996 at éditions Ezzaman in Rabat (Morocco) and in the same year at Kamal al-Chariat in Amman (Jordan); cf. also Thion, Vérité historique ou vérité politique?. The Publisher Dar Tlass is the publishing house of the former Syrian Minister of Defense, General Mustafa Tlass.

60 For example the chains Sahar (Iran), Al Rahma (Egypt), and al-Manar (Lebanon, Hezbollah).

61 Bashara published Critique de la raison juive occidentale. On his itinerary, cf. La Vieille Taupe, 5 (1997).

62 Teitelbaum, Salomon, vous êtes juif?, p. 235.

Nationalist Holocaust-deniers can also be found among Turkish Islamists and secular ultra-nationalists in Turkey (the MHP party) and among the Turkish communities in Europe. This denial of the genocide is specific because it is almost always accompanied by the negation of yet another genocide, namely that of the Armenians. Furthermore, this Holocaust-denial firmly believes in various conspiracy theories which depict, depending on the scenario, the United States, the Kurdish people, and Israel to be in league against Turkey. Turkish Holocaust-denial has a severe impact because journals like "Millî Gazete" and "Vakit"[63] are widely sold in Europe.

The denial of the genocide presently constitutes an important part of the official ideology of one Muslim state only, namely, the Islamic Republic of Iran. President Mahmud Ahmadinedjad has not only used it repeatedly because he feels the necessity to support the Palestinian cause. The head of the Iranian State is as deeply convinced of the European Holocaust-deniers' theories. European Holocaust-deniers were able to hold their official conference in Tehran in December 2006 because they were formally invited by the government there.[64] This was possible because of the role played by a special advisor to president Ahmadinedjad, namely Mohammad Ali Ramin, in the spreading of Holocaust-denial in Iran. Born in 1954, Ramin is a mechanical engineer presenting himself as an "expert of the dialogue of world cultures". During the 2006 conference, he participated in a discussion on the topic "The Necessity to Revise the Holocaust". A low-level politician of the presidential clan (he only ranked 52nd in the constituency of Tehran at the 2004 elections), Ramin still retains some importance because the head of state still lends him his ear. It was Ramin who suggested a declaration on the necessity of "repatriating" the Israelis to Europe, and on the "myth of the Holocaust". He was the one who conceived the idea of the Holocaust-denial conference, too. He is also president of the Society for the Defence of Muslims in the West and the founder of a group called The Cells of the Martyrs of the Velayat (velayat: the conservation of the dogma in Shiite Islam).

Among the speakers, there were many Arab-Muslim deniers of the genocide, for example, Ghazi Hussein,[65] a Palestinian living in Syria; Zaryani Abdurrahman, a Malay; T. Borshe, a Jordanian; Abou Ziad Idrissi, a Moroccan; a Tajik named Torjanzadeh, and an Iranian living in Canada, Shiraz Dossa. Most of them are left-wing nationalists, complacent with Islamism but not Islamists them-

63 Due to its Holocaust-denial and anti-Semitic contents, the sale of "Vakit" was forbidden in Germany in February 2005. In France, Zeynel Cekici, the responsible of Turkish descent of the website "www.alterinfo.net", was condemned to four months in prison with suspense by the magistrates' court of Mulhouse for incitement to discrimination, defamation, and denial of the existence of a crime against humanity in June 2009. Teitelbaum, Salomon, vous êtes juif?, p. 235.

64 The three Austrian participants in this globally broadcasted conference were Moshe Arieh Friedman, Wolfgang Fröhlich (who did not speak), and Herbert Schaller.

65 Ghazi Hussein received a law degree in Germany in 1962, became a lawyer and taught there. Two of his anti-Semitic books were translated into German.

selves - in short: "Islamo-leftists". Thus, Shiraz Dossa is an admirer of Noam Chomsky and a dedicated opponent of liberalism. He teaches at the Catholic Saint Francis University in Nova Scotia, Canada. Trying to explain how the Shoah is used by the United States to "wage war against the Muslims", the tone of his speech was clearly "anti-imperialist". Ghazi Hussein, a former legal advisor to the Syrian presidency, is a member of the PLO, which he represented as "ambassador" to Austria and to the International Atomic Energy Agency. But first of all, he is a rabid anti-Semite who published a pamphlet "Yasser Arafat and the Solution of the Zionist Crisis in Palestine" in Damascus. There, he claims that the Palestinian leader was a Moroccan Jew who immigrated to Egypt.

Finally, there is definitely an important link between German-speaking deniers and Iran. It was already known that Jürgen Graf had taken refuge in Tehran for some time. The German Holocaust-denier Gert Ittner is assumed to have lived there, too. He was a member of the neo-Nazi group Freie Nationalisten, and was sentenced in April 2005. Above all, Mohamed Ali Ramin had lived in Germany for 17 years and founded an Islamic association there, the Islamische Gemeinschaft in Clausthal e. V. He has an old friendship with Gert Frings, a NPD executive in Cologne, and also with the operators (of Turkish origin) of the Islamist website "www.muslim-markt.de" which regularly opens its columns to the extreme right. In this strange galaxy, neo-Nazis mix with militants of the extreme left, Muslim fundamentalists, and militant atheists (the Frenchmen Serge Thion and Faurisson, both participants of the Tehran Conference, and the Briton Alexander Baron). It represents the essence of Holocaust-denial in today's world. Holocaust-denial theory and ideology are elaborated in the Western world but the propaganda is mostly deployed in the Muslim world then all over the Third World. In the Spanish-speaking world though, dissemination goes the other way round. This is exemplified by the strongly "anti-imperialist"/anti-American connotation of the Argentinean left Peronist Norberto Ceresole[66] (1943-2003) whose life consisted of round trips between Latin America (Argentina, Venezuela) and Europe; or the spreading of Adrian Salbuchi's[67] articles, produced in Argentina and very popular on the websites of the anti-globalization left activists. The French former academic Maria Poumier plays a key role in the Holocaust-denial networks between Europe and Latin America, her commitment to Holocaust-denial stemming from her role of an indefatigable propagandist of the Cuban regime.[68] These anti-Western/anti-imperialist leanings of Holocaust-denial are perfectly represented

66 Cf. Ceresole, España y los judíos. Ceresole was an advisor of Haya de la Torre in Peru, later of the Venezolan president Chavez. He translated the works of Roger Garaudy.

67 Cf. Salbuchi, Acerca del "antisemitismo", http://www.asalbuchi.com.ar/2008/03/acerca-del-antisemitismo.

68 Translator of José Marti; she taught at the University of La Habanna for 10 years. Very close to the comedian Dieudonné, she ran as a candidate on the list of the "Anti-Zionist Party" at the 2009 European elections.

by the network of the French comedian Dieudonné[69] which succeeded in bringing together the political and electoral expression of anti-Semitic and conspiracy theory traditions, namely the extreme right; the anti-globalization left and pro-Iran Islamism.

VI. Conclusion

In 2011, Holocaust-denial is mostly disseminated through the internet. Legislation against racism and anti-Semitism has considerably reduced the use of printed material (newspapers, journals). Those that still exist are read by a small group of militants already convinced of the case. But the role of the internet poses a severe methodological problem to the researcher. In effect, the proliferative character of the sites makes it very difficult to establish a hierarchy of the contents and to identify the authors. This is due to the system of links that function "in a continuous loop". The traditional problem of the social sciences, i. e., the "magnifying effect", may lead the researcher to over-exaggerate the importance of research his research topic. This is due to the lack of distance of the researcher to his object because of his methods of examination. Considering the denial of the genocide of the Jews, this is clearly the case. For this reason, it is difficult to correctly estimate the real impact of Holocaust-denial.

It seems, however, that in the Western world, Holocaust-denial is more or less a sectarian phenomenon. It appears usually as an integral part of the political culture of the extreme right, and is very often nurtured by a view of the world that depends on the conspiracy theory.[70] It is also spread throughout the extreme left, but less frequently. There, it draws from an old tendency of hypercriticism equally taken up by orthodox Marxism, which does not admit a difference of nature of capitalism, fascism, and Nazism. More and more, the denial of the genocide, in every political family, feeds on absolute anti-Zionism denying the Jewish people the right to a state and turning around the scheme of the victim and the torturer - which applies to the genocide of the Jews by the Nazis - in favor of the Palestinians against Israel.

In this worldview, the Palestinian, not the Jews anymore, have become the pariahs outlawed by the nations.[71] If one ascertains that the denial of the genocide of the Jews has migrated to the Arabo-Muslim world, it is important to note that in Europe and the United States, Holocaust-denial grew after 1975, that is the year when the United Nations have voted resolution 3379 equating Zionism and racism. Even though one has to refrain from completely equalizing anti-

69 Cf. especially the website "www.lesogres.info" which is probably the most often read obsessively anti-Semitic francophone site.

70 To learn about this topic, turn to the brilliant book of Taguieff, La foire aux illuminés.

71 Thought scheme often applied in left-wing extremist and Islamist movements, in Ahamdinejad's Iran, at the Lebanese Hezbollah, and the Palestinian Hamas, even the Palestinian people in general.

Semitism and anti-Zionism, it is also true that anti-Zionism in its radical form is the principal vector of anti-Semitism at present. The demonstrations in Europe against the Israeli military operation in Gaza in 2008/2009 time and time again gave way to propaganda and newspaper articles, including in the mainstream media, which trivialize the genocide of the Jews and characterize the Israelis as "new Nazis", perpetrators of "crimes against humanity" of a genocidal nature.

The nazification of Israel and the Jews, accompanied by the denial or trivialization of the genocide of the Jews by the Nazis, lead in fact to the de-diabolization of national socialism and its allies. At the same time, the goal of this theoretical scheme is to make the triad Israel-Jews-Zionism a figure of absolute evil.

Finally, the denial of the Shoah is heavily charged emotionally, not only for the Jewish communities and the survivors of the genocide, but also for the collective memory of all the peoples who suffered from Nazi occupation. It is often shocking due to its despicable, extreme, and obscene character. But it may not be the ideology which contributes the most to relativizing the specificity and range of the genocide of the Jews. Just as much is contributed - and with a lot more apparent scientific respectability and social and political acceptability - by the more and more indiscriminate use of the term "genocide", or by the controversy on the responsibilities of the outbreak of the war, and also the acceptability of the comparison between the Nazi crimes and those committed by the communist regimes. On the long term, there is a real uncertainty about the future treatment, in history books and in the collective conscience, of such an extraordinary event, in the true sense of the world, as the Nazi genocide of the Jews.

Paramilitary Structures in Eastern Europe

Věra Stojarová

I. Introduction

The word "paramilitary" has been used in various ways although its meaning remains ambiguous.[1] For example, the "Encyclopaedia of Fascism" points to three elements of WW II paramilitarism: continuous violent propaganda, the image of the street fighter, and the presentation of paramilitary groups as mass organizations.[2] Nevertheless, the emergence of other violent non-state affiliated actors (VNSA) complicates the issue. They overlap in most cases or transform from one kind into another.

As Williams suggests, the distinguishing feature of warlords is that of the charismatic leader. Militias are very similar albeit without such charismatic leaders. Paramilitary forces are initially an extension of government forces; they come into existence with the tacit consent and often the active encouragement of government or state military forces. Insurgencies are thus defined as organized movements aiming to overthrow a constituted government through subversion and armed conflict while terrorists use indiscriminate violence against civilian targets. Yet, even where there is not a clear-cut transformation from one kind of VNSA into another, the boundaries between them are blurred. Part of the reason for this ambiguity is that terrorists, insurgents, warlords, militias, and paramilitary forces all engage to one degree or another in criminal activities.[3] Nevertheless, this classification would leave out the current nationalist and chauvinist formations arising in Eastern Europe that are not linked to the official military forces. Mareš and Stojar suggest an enlarged scope in the definition of paramilitaries: those involved in armed post-communist conflicts and the vigilante paramilitary formations (mostly with racist orientation) of political parties and

1 This paper has been undertaken as part of the Research Project "Political Parties and Representation of Interests in Contemporary European Democracies" (code MSM0021622407).
2 Cf. Blamires, World Fascism, p. 506.
3 Cf. Williams, Violent Non-State Actors, pp. 9–17, available at: http://www.humansecuritygateway.com/documents/ISN_ViolentNon-StateActors.pdf, last accessed 30 June 2010.

movements.[4] Again, a problem arises here when considering formations that are not tied to political parties. This would lead us back to the first definition although it must be kept in mind that skinheads and other violent subcultural groups will not be dealt with.

The term "extreme right" will be used throughout the text; sometimes the borders between the radical and extreme right might be unclear. Therefore, in some cases the reader will find the term "radical right".[5] It is simply impossible to draw a sharp line between the two terms and distinguish clearly between radical right and extreme right formations. Most of the formations balance between the two but can be more easily distinguished from democratic centre formations.

II. Paramilitaries in the Balkans

The paramilitary formations of the wars in Croatia and Bosnia and Herzegovina (BiH) are quite straightforward. They fit into the definition of paramilitarism as an extension of government forces, though there is some overlap with warlords or militias. Most of them were engaged in organized crime. Paramilitary formations were created under the specific situation due to the fact that neither of the war parties had fully formed armed forces. These units recruited volunteers and were formed as the armed factions of individual political parties or movements. They incorporated nationalistic idealists as well as criminals motivated by the vision of easily gained plunder. The aimed symbiosis of state and crime started at the beginning of the war when criminals were released from prison in order to join paramilitary units and do the dirty work for the state. These armed forces functioned until the state ceased to support (or tolerate) them and started to eradicate them.[6] The paramilitary organizations usually lived in symbiosis with the official armies of the recognized or self-proclaimed republics for which they opened access to the black market with weapons, oil etc.

The most famous Croatian paramilitary organizations were the Croatian Defense Forces (Hrvatske obrambene snage, HOS) and the Fiery Stallions. The HOS were formed by the right-wing radical Dobroslav Paraga in the spring of 1991 as the armed wing of the extremist Croatian *Party of Right* (*Hrvatska stranka prava*, HSP), which claimed to assume Ustasha heritage.[7] They became

4 Cf. Mareš/Stojar, Extreme Right.

5 Radical right is understood as the inter-grade between extremism and democracy as it is acknowledged in academic circles. Radicalism takes place within the parameters of constitutional democracy while extremism is behind this border and fights against state order as defined by the constitution. Extremism and radicalism are both anti-liberal and anti-constitutional. The difference is that extremism is fundamentally anti-democratic. Cf. Mudde, Politischer Extremismus, p. 89; Mareš, Pravicový extremismus, pp. 33–34.

6 Cf. Pandurević, Rat u BiH, pp. 100–107; Kanzleiter, Jugoslawiens multiethnische Kriegsgewinnler, p. 103.

7 The Ustasha ruled the Independent State of Croatia (NDH) during WW II. Their main ideology was a blend of Nazism, fascism, and Croatian ultra-nationalism aimed mainly against Serbs and Roma on NDH territory.

known for ethnic cleansing in Vukovar and Osijek as early as autumn 1991. The HOS led a more or less private war. It was not only because of them that, by the end of 1992, the number of war casualties had already reached 6,500 dead, 6,500 missing, and 20,000 injured. There were 600,000 refugees and internally displaced persons (IDPS).[8]

The voluntary guard (the so-called Tigers under the command of Željko Ražnatović Arkan) was the most famous paramilitary force on the Serbian side. Initially, the guard consisted mainly of hooligans of the Red Star (Crvena Zvezda) football team of Belgrade but then its ranks grew to thousands. The Tigers were tied to the Serbian secret service and therefore had very close links to the Milošević regime. Somewhere at the borderline between state and paramilitary was the Special Operations Unit (Jedinica za specijalne operacije, JSO) better known as the Red Berets (Crvene Beretke). Both groupings were founded by the former chief of secret police, Jovica Stanišić, and his close associate Franko Simatović. Although the unit was working directly under state command, it was mainly composed of former criminals and the mafia.[9] Other famous formations included the Serbian Chetnics Movement[10] led by Vojislav Šešelj (currently indicted by the International Criminal Tribunal for the former Yugoslavia, ICTY), the Serbian guard (military wing of the Serbian Renewal Movement - Srpski pokret obnove, SPO) and the White Eagles (Beli orlovi) of Mirko Jović.[11] These paramilitary formations were responsible for most of the ethnic cleansing in former Yugoslavia from April 1991 until the end of the war in 1995.[12] These groups were financially and logistically supported by the Serbian Ministry of Internal Affairs. The most famous members of the security forces participating in the organization of the paramilitary formations were Radovan Stojičić-Badža, Frank Simatović-Frenkija, and Mihalj Kertes (the former commander of so-called Red Berets).

Similarly to the situation amongst the Croats and Serbs, it is difficult to distinguish between the official army of Bosnia-Herzegovina and the Bosnian paramilitary formations. Groups such as El-Mudžahíd, the Green Berets (Zelene beretke) or the Patriotic League (Patriotska Liga) were usually set up as paramilitary formations but were eventually incorporated into the official army of BiH. The categorization of the army of Western Bosnia is also problematic. It was led by Fikret Abdić, who stood against the leadership of Alija Izetbegović and cooperated with the Serbs and Croats against the Bosnian army.

8 Cf. Hofbauer, Balkankrieg, p. 43.
9 The daily "Kurir" published the information that around 1,000 members of the Arkan Tigers and the Red Berets are contracted with private security companies in Iraq. Nevertheless, this seems to be rather ill founded media information. Cf. Kurir, 17/18 April 2004, p. 5.
10 The Chetnics were a predominantly Serbian and nationalist force during WW II that fought for the restoration of the monarchy.
11 The White Eagles were the pro-fascist paramilitary unit during WW II.
12 Cf. Kumar, Divide and Fall?, pp. 39-41; Lopušina, Tajne srpske policije, p. 68.

The paramilitary formations in Croatia and BiH disappeared and were dissolved. Most of their commanders were indicted by the ICTY; ordinary members were assimilated into the structures of organized crime. The perception of the former warriors in Bosnian society is problematic; it can generally be said that most of them are perceived negatively, in contrast to the official military forces. The stabilization and association process in both countries and their road towards Euro/Atlantic structures exclude the renewal of the paramilitary formations. However, we cannot talk about the full consolidation of political systems. The political scenes in both countries react very sensitively to foreign affairs while the future of Croatia and BiH does not only depend on the expansion policies of the EU member states, but also on the political situation in neighboring countries.

The case becomes more complicated when looking at the Albanian (para-) military/insurgent/militia/organized crime (OC) scene. The Kosovo Liberation Army (Ushtria Çlirimtare e Kosovës, UÇK, engl. acronym KLA) underwent turbulent development in a very short time. Keeping the Williams definition in mind, the KLA could either be categorized as an insurgent group using terrorist means being engaged in the OC, or by its self-description as a national liberation army. Moreover, the formation absorbed all anti-Serbian forces including the enverite National movement for liberated Kosovo (Levizja Kombëtare per Çlirimin e Kosovës, LKÇK) or communist *Albanian Revolutionary Party* (*Partia Revolucionare Shqiptare*, PRSH). The only unifying link was the fight for an independent Kosovo - the extreme right label would thus be more than disputable in this case as well.[13] The sister formations, Liberation Army of Preshevo, Medvedja, and Bujanovac (Ushtria Çlirimtare e Preshevës, Medvegjës dhe Bujanocit, UÇPMB) and the National Liberation Army (Ushtria Çlirimtare Kombëtare, UÇK, eng. acronym NLA) in Macedonia would probably also fall under the insurgents although they were not willing to seize power. Their rather limited goals were to change the status of Albanians, as was the case in Macedonia. Nevertheless, the aims of both formations were changing over time and initially both were fighting for the inclusion of "their territory" to Kosovo. They were somehow linked to the former KLA, which was already transformed into the political, military, and police wings. Thus, under certain circumstances, these could also be seen as paramilitary formations.

The organizations that were set up after 1999 are rather blurred. Viewed from a certain angle, they could easily be classified as extreme right paramilitary formations. The Albanian National Army (ANA) declares itself to be the successor formation of KLA, NLA, and UÇPMB while operating in Serbia, Mace-

13 Cf. Kusovać, The KLA: Braced to Defend and Control, available at: http://www.janes.com/defence/news/kosovo/jir990401_01_n.shtml, last accessed 30 June 2008; see also Stýskalíková, Případ UÇK; Lipsius, Kommunistische Parteien; Reuter, Die internationale Gemeinschaft.

donia, Albania, Kosovo, and Northern Greece.[14] The ANA declares itself to fight for the creation of a Greater Albania[15] and it is estimated to have 200 activists. It is not known who stands in its leadership.[16] Initially, the ANA was rather known as an Internet phantom, issuing statements via modern technologies. The first reference dates to 2002 and the most famous one to 2005 when it attempted to assassinate then Kosovo president, Ibrahim Rugova. The ANA's organizational structures and goals remain quite unclear. They are therefore very hard to classify, oscillating somewhere between militia, paramilitary organization, and insurgent groups using terrorist means being linked to the OC. Along with the ANA, however, there are additional formations that emerged in the region. The Army of the Republic of Ilirida was created in Macedonia in 2002. It fought for the transfer of Western Macedonia into either Kosovo or Albanian territory. The group allegedly has 200 members who swore loyalty to Leka Zogu.[17] In 2005, the Army for the Independence of Kosovo (UPK) emerged in Kosovo. It was threatening the international administration, while inciting the Kosovo parliament to declare independence. The variety of the ethnic Albanian groups can be explained by their rivalry in OC activities and the control of smuggling routes. The declared fight for Greater Albania or Greater Kosovo serves much more as a cover for OC activities striving for profit than the "liberation" of the Albanian nation.[18] All Albanian formations present a security threat to the region on local and state levels, and, most importantly, to human security. There are still a lot of weapons in the region, and border permeability and the linking of the groups to the OC facilitate the infiltration of new arms.

In Macedonia, the paramilitary force Lions (Lavovi) emerged in 2001. It was an unauthorized body of former police and military reservists sponsored unofficially by Ljube Boskovski (Secretary of State for Interior Affairs). It was not until after the conflict (in autumn 2001) that the paramilitary unit was trans-

14 The Scanderberg Division (named after the WW II formation that fought alongside Italian and German forces) in Western Macedonia, the division of Adam Jashari (one of the founding fathers of KLA) in Kosovo, the Malesia Division in Montenegro, and the Çameria Division for Southern Albania and Northern Greece.

15 The goal keeps changing. In January 2008, the leaders claimed that they were not fighting for pan-Albanian unification, but for the protection Kosovo's territorial integrity when it is threatened. Cf. B92.net, Kosovo Terror Group Issues Fresh Threats, 21 January 2008, available at: http://www.b92.net/eng/news/politics-article.php?yyyy=2008&mm=01&dd=21&nav_id=47122.

16 Bolju Dilaver, called "Leku", is frequently mentioned in connection with the ANA. Some sources state that the political wing is the National Liberation Front of Albanians led by Valdet Vardari.

17 Leka Zogu is the son of the former Albanian king, Zogu I. He denied any links to the Army of the Republic of Ilirida.

18 Cf. Jane's World Insurgency and Terrorism, (20) 2004, p. 528, available at: http://jwit.janes.com/public/jwit/index.shtml. Macedonian security expert Biljana Vankovska claims that the 2001 conflict in Macedonia also started as a war between OC gangs rather than through an escalation of ethnic crisis.

formed into the official police unit. The Lions were believed to have about 2,000 armed members, and they were actively using the threat of ethnic cleansing against ethnic Albanians. There has been much post-conflict controversy around the Lions. The head of the Macedonian Orthodox Church, Archbishop Stefan, gave medallions of Christ to the paramilitaries. The Lions' commander, Goran Stojkov, was promoted to the grandiose rank of major general. These acts were highly criticized by human rights activists. The Lions were finally disbanded in early 2003 with about half their membership being absorbed into the police.

Another paramilitary unit (often confused with the previous formation) emerged in Macedonia under the name of Macedonian Lions (Makedonski lavovi). The latter did not have links to the police or any state structure. It was a product of radical groups supported by the Macedonian diaspora around the world. The unit was rather limited in regards to personnel - there were less then a hundred people. The group did not become famous for activities during the Macedonian-Albanian conflict. It was much more a media phantom. The short duration of the armed conflict and the fact that neither Macedonian society nor state structures favored these units, meant that the group did not expand. It disappeared after a rather short time. Another smaller paramilitary group that was active in Macedonia was the Red Berets. They continued to intimidate and harass ethnic Albanian civilians even after the Ohrid peace agreement.[19]

On the Serbian side, a new extreme right paramilitary unit emerged in relation to the Kosovo case in May 2007. The Saint Tsar Lazar Guard (Garda svetog cara Lazara) was formed mainly by veterans of the Yugoslavian wars. Its leaders stated that the formation had around 5,000 members while other sources claimed that it was not more than a few hundred. The guard proclaims a new fight for the "liberation" of Kosovo (back to Serbian hands). Its radical statements include those that every ethnic Albanian should be either killed or returned to Albania. Those Serbs who disagreed with their views were also threatened.[20] The leaders were calling on the Serbian parliament to wage a war with Kosovo while calling for demonstrations. The main unrest was expected after the declaration of Kosovo independence; the guard does not seem to have public support, and its actions were stopped by Serbian and UNMIK (Interim Administration Mission in Kosovo) authorities who prevented the spread of violence.

19 Cf. Phillips, Macedonia, pp. 156–160.

20 Cf. B92.net, Czar Lazar Guard: War is Inevitable, 16 November 2007, available at: http://www.b92.net/eng/news/politics-article.php?yyyy=2007&mm=11&dd=16&nav_id=45450.

III. Paramilitaries in the post-Soviet arena

Similarly to the Balkans, many nationalist paramilitary units were formed during the disintegration of the Soviet Union. One of the most well-known, during the conflicts in Abkhazia and Southern Ossetia, were the Cossacks.[21] Quite interestingly, and despite historical enmity, the Cossacks fought alongside Chechen units against the Georgian army.[22]

A rather clear example of the extreme right in the post-Soviet arena is Russian National Unity (Russkoye Natsionalnoye Edinstvo, RNE). Its proclaimed goals are the ethnic cleansing of the "motherland", meaning especially the deportation of Jews and Caucasian minorities to Israel and the Turkic countries (e. g., Turkey, Azerbaijan). It won support with the slogan "Russia for the Russians".[23] The RNE was founded by Aleksander Barkashov in 1990, and its membership grew to 100,000 by the late 1990s. In 2000, it split into two groups: Barkashov's RNU-1 and Andrey and Yevgenny Lalochkin's RNU-2.[24] The followers usually claim to be both anti-Semitic and sympathizers of Nazism. Despite the split, the organization remains quite large. It is active not only in Russia but also in Ukraine and the Baltic states. The RNU became famous in 1993 when it took part in patrolling the residence of the Russian parliament against president Yeltsin's troops. Members wear black uniforms and berets with a red and white swastika emblem and use a straight arm salute with the greeting "Hail Russia!" ("Slava Rossii!"). New recruits, referred to as supporters ("storonniki"), traditionally serve as low-level functionaries while advanced members attain the rank of comrades in arms ("soratniki"). The latter serve the leadership of the group. The primary activities of the organization are combat training, shooting practice, and mock stormings of abandoned buildings. The combatants are trained by former Soviet officers.[25] The RNU took part in the 2001 municipal elections in Latvia but did not win a seat.[26]

The Ukrainian National Assembly - Ukrainian National Self Defense (Ukrainska Natsionalna Asamblea - Ukrainska Natsionalna Samooborona, UNA-UNSO) was created in 1990 in Lviv. Initially fighting for an independent

21 The name recalls the descendants of runaway serfs and outlaws who in the past were employed to protect the country's Southern border and were carrying policing functions in cooperation with interior ministry forces.

22 Parfitt, Armed Cossacks Pour in to Fight Georgians: Neighbours Mobilise in Anger at Tblisi's Attack on Enclave, The Guardian, 9 August 2008, available at: http://www.guardian.co.uk/world/2008/aug/09/russia.georgial.

23 Muižnieks, Latvia, pp. 111-112. The term "Russian" is understood broadly in comprising "representatives of the trinity of the Russian people: Russians, Ukrainians and Byelorussians".

24 Institute for Safety, Security and Crisis Management, 20th Century Right Wing Groups in Europe: Prone to Extremism or Terrorism? 4 July 2008, available at: http://www.transnationalterrorism.eu/tekst/publications/Rightwing%20terrorism.pdf.

25 Biznes i Baltiia cited from Muižnieks, Lativa, p. 112.

26 Russian National Unity, Encyclopedia, available at: http://en.allexperts.com/e/r/ru/russian_national_unity.htm.

Ukraine, it then stepped into regional conflicts, mainly as a nationalist anti-Russian force. They fought against Moldovan forces in Transnistria in support and defense of the local Ukrainian minority. In the Georgian/Abkhaz conflict, they joined the Georgian side against the Russian-backed Abkhaz troops. Again, during the First Chechen War, they joined the anti-Russian, Chechen separatist forces.

Among the Baltic States, Lithuania is the only country without any militaristic radical right-wing organizations. However, the *National Rebirth Party* is quite successful with 15 % of the vote. In Estonia, the Centre for Decolonization Initiative (Dekoloniseerimise Algatuskeskus, DA) targets neighboring Russia as well as the ethnic Russian citizens within Estonia.

In Latvia, extensive "russification" during the communist era and the fact that around one-third of the population is ethnic Russian (speaking little Latvian) are probable roots behind the quiet but large nationalist scene. In 1990, a movement emerged bearing the same name as a political party from the 1930s that was oriented towards fascism and anti-Semitism. It was known as Pērkonkrusts (relates to Swastika, literally translated as Perun Cross or Thunder Cross).[27] The organization became famous for its overt pro-German and anti-Russian orientation, protesting mainly on 9 May when it attempted to destroy monuments built as a commemoration of the Red Army's liberation of Latvia from German occupation.[28] Of the nine members accused in 2000, eight were found guilty of explosives charges. Seven were found guilty of destroying a monument, four of hostage taking, three of property destruction, two of false testimony, and two of appealing to the violent overthrow of the government; the sentences ranged from one-and-half years to three years in prison.[29] The Latvian National Front (Latvijas nacionala fronte, LNF) is another ultra-nationalist, homophobic anti-Semitic and anti-Russian organization that claims that "Latvia should be liberated from occupants" and that "Latvia should stipulate peaceful repatriation of occupants to their ethnic fatherland".[30]

Similarly to what we observed with regards to the Yugoslavian conflicts, the paramilitaries in the post-Soviet republics were of criminal origin. This was the case with the Kadyrovcy, a paramilitary unit of the former pro-Moscow president of the Chechen Republic, Ahmad Kadyrov. It was headed by his son and current president, Ramzan Kadyrov. According to the group leader, its numerical strength had reached 3,000 men by 2003 (according to the former President

27 Perun (Lithuanian: Perkūnas, Latvian: Pērkons) is a god of thunder in both Baltic and Slavic mythology. For the historical Pērkonkrusts, see e. g. Ezergailis, Anti-Semitism.

28 Cf. "Antisemitism and Xenophobia Today", available at: http://www.axt.org.uk/antisem/archive/archive2/latvia/latvia.htm, last accessed 30 June 2010.

29 Muižnieks, Latvia, pp. 105-106.

30 Latvian Centre for Human Rights, Integration and Minority Information Service, available at: http://www.humanrights.org.lv/html/27768.html, last accessed 30 June 2010; The Baltic Times, Extremism in Latvian Government, 22 November 2004, available at: http://www.baltictimes.com/news/articles/10974/.

Alu Alkhanov, who served from 2004 to 2007). One and a half years later, this figure had grown to 7,000.[31] The presence of pro-Moscow forces in Chechnya fighting the separatist rebels, helped Russians to withdraw some troops from the region; the Kadyrovcy were officially disbanded in 2006 despite allegations by human rights activists of crimes and human rights abuses.[32] Nevertheless, the inclusion of Kadyrovcy in this text seems to be problematic due to its pro-Russian orientation that excludes the right-wing extremism, which would presuppose Chechen nationalism.[33] Chechen village and clan paramilitary units take the form of small teams that can fight either independently or in larger formations. They employ light arms and utilize surprise attacks and quick withdrawal. The small units usually group into formations of a few hundred fighters under an independent commander with no central control and often with very little coordination.[34] The Chechen forces would probably be categorized as insurgents, similar to the ethnic Albanian formations who aim to overthrow the current government.

In Georgia, a group known as Mkhedrioni (translated usually as horsemen or knights),[35] was set up by Dzhaba Ioseliani in 1989. The leader of that unit very often referred to the armed group who fought against the Persian and Ottoman Empires and he believed himself to be an heir of this formation. The unit was meant to counteract Abhkaz and Ossetian nationalists in Georgia and the region as a whole. They got engaged in criminal activities and racketeering. They reached their peak during Georgian president Zviad Gamsakhurdia's rise to power. His power base was very uncertain, as was his control over two armed groups, Ioseliani's Mkhedrioni and the National Guard,[36] led by Tengiz Kitovani. After Gamsakhurdia took power, he ordered the disarmament of National Guard and imprisoned Ioseliani and others. Nevertheless, Kitovani assembled a group that besieged the parliament buildings, launching a coup that forced Gamsakhurdia to flee the country. The Mkhedrioni were transformed

31 Simonov, New Chechen Army Threatens Moscow, available at: http://www.axisglobe.com/article.asp?article=983, last accessed 30 June 2010.

32 See e. g. Internal Displacement Monitoring Centre, Kadyrovtsy, allegedly responsible for human rights abuse, http://www.internal-displacement.org/idmc/website/countries.nsf/(httpEnvelopes)/2A8E4FA1CBB75B01C12573300024B2DF?OpenDocument, last accessed 30 June 2010.

33 The Vostok unit, led by Sulim Yamadaev, presents a similar case. It is a Chechen paramilitary formation controlled by the Russian Ministry of Defense. Even though both fulfill the criteria of paramilitarism, they cannot be seen as being on the radical right.

34 Shultz/Dew, Insurgents, p. 139.

35 Cf. Collier/Sambanis, Understanding, p. 266; Los Angeles Times, Dzhaba Ioseliani, 76: Oft-Imprisoned Leader of Georgian Paramilitary Force, 5 March 2003, available at: http://articles.latimes.com/2003/mar/05/local/me-dzhaba5.

36 The National Guard was a proto-army that served as a basis for the future official Georgian army. Legislation that authorized the build-up of an army on the basis of conscription, was approved in January of 1991. By mid-1991, the National Guard and Mkhedrioni both had about 1,000 fighters and 10,000 associate members. Cf. Collier/Sambanis, Understanding, p. 271.

into the Rescue Corps in 1994. The group was banned after the assassination attempt on Eduard Shevardnadze, and its leaders were arrested.[37] Supporters first tried to register a political party under the name Mkhedrioni and then under the name of Union of Patriots. Both queries were refused.

IV. Current paramilitary units in Central and Eastern Europe

The present nationalist scene is rather full of small nationalist movements closely related to skinhead and other subcultural groups. These cannot really be classified as paramilitary units. They do not have the capacity and are quite limited to the organization of marches and political events.[38] Current paramilitary units in Central and Eastern Europe (CEE) devote themselves to be the safeguards of "law and order". They therefore aim to cleanse society of those they see as "disruptors" or unwanted elements. These comprise of ethnic minorities and religious groups (e. g., Roma in Central Europe, Chechens, and other, mainly Caucasian nations in Russia[39)]. In Poland and Hungary, it is mainly Jews and recent Muslim immigrants. Also targeted are homeless people, gays and lesbians, criminals, drug addicts, and leftist activists. Some organizations have made close ties to the International Third Position (ITP), a neo-fascist network founded by Italian and British nationalists. The Polish, Slovakian, and Romanian extreme right movements found their way to the ITP. The European National Front (ENF) emerged in 2003. ENF principals include the defense of culture, tradition and Christian identity against uncontrolled migration, or the potential admission of Turkey and Israel into the EU. The ENF claims to strive for an economic system based on social justice. It also claims to defend traditional family values and aims to establish a world order that is free of U.S. imperialism.[40]

In the Czech Republic, two small formations emerged that had the goal of safeguarding the rule of law against so-called socially inadaptable citizens. The Protection Corps of the Workers' Party (Ochranné sbory Dělnické strany) was founded in February 2008 as units that were to protect the leaders of the

37 Ioseliani was charged with treason and plotting the killings of several Georgian political leaders. He was sentenced to 11 years in prison. Cf. Collier/Sambanis, Understanding, p. 266; see also Los Angeles Times, Dzhaba Ioseliani, 76: Oft-Imprisoned Leader of Georgian Paramilitary Force, 5 March 2003, available at: http://articles.latimes.com/2003/mar/05/local/me-dzhaba5.

38 E. g., in Serbia we could mention the Obraz, Nacionalni stroj, Sveti Justin Filozof, Dveri, Poslednji Obracun, or Srpska Desnica movements. Cf. The Stephen Roth Institute, Republic of Serbia 2005, available at: http://www.tau.ac.il/Anti-Semitism/asw2005/serbia.htm, last accessed 30 June 2010.

39 In 2004 and 2005, the Institute for Social-Political Research of the Russian Academy of Sciences released the results of a survey in which 57 % of the respondents declared that they had negative attitudes towards the nations of the Caucasus. Cf. N-Ost, Rechtsextremismus und Antisemitismus in Mittel-, Ost- und Südosteuropa, p. 9, available at: http://www.n-ost.de/cms/images//n-ost-stipendien-doku.pdf.

40 Cf. European National Front, http://www.europeannationalfront.org/.

Workers' Party while providing security at party proceedings.[41] However, the corps became rather famous for their vigilant activities against the large Roma populations of Northern Bohemia. After the Workers' Party was banned, a new *Workers' Party of Social Justice* (*Dělnická strana sociální spravedlnosti*, DSSS)[42] emerged along with the Protection Corps of the Workers Party of Social Justice (Ochranné sbory Dělnické strany sociální spravedlnosti). They declared their readiness to remain present in regions where there is tension with Roma communities.

A second formation, the National Guard (Národní garda), is more likely to fulfill the criteria of paramilitary formation. In its charter it says, "the paramilitary-civil-defense tasks which should ensure the defense and protection of life and property of the Czech inhabitants, territorial integrity, defense and economical-political stability of the Czech republic".[43] The members wear outdated Czech army uniforms. The leader, Michal Kubík, claims that the guard was founded to provide relief in times of natural disasters, floods etc. It has around 2,300 application forms on record, mainly from former soldiers or police officers. Similarly to the first formation, the guard was founded by the radical right-wing *National Party* (*Národní strana*). Over time, it has become a rather independent formation.[44]

Attacks on the Roma community sometimes resulted in the creation of Roma safeguarding units. The most recent case was after a spring 2009 arson attack in Northern Moravia when a two-year-old girl and her parents were seriously burnt. As the incident received media and societal attention, the Roma announced the creation of units to protect the local community. Their only equipment was supposed to be cellular phones and cameras.[45] At present, it seems that the units only "patrolled" for a couple of days and that no real paramilitary organization emerged out of the situation.

After a period of considerable media attention, the *National Party* and its National Guard slumped and de facto perished in the second half of 2009. There are two more quite quaint examples of paramilitary units that cannot be added to the extreme right formations. Nevertheless, their emergence and activity runs outside of the framework of the democratic state. The first is a special emergency unit of the energy giant ČEZ[46] whose controversial crackdowns against

41 Cf. Delnickastrana, http://www.delnickastrana.cz/Sbory.htm.

42 The party is identical to the previous one. It changed only in name. The personnel remained the same. Cf. http://www.dsss.cz/.

43 Cf. Národní garda, http://www.narodni-garda.cz/files/down/radNG.pdf.

44 Cf. Národní garda, Souboj Kubíka s Bublanem. Sekundantem byla Mladá fronta Plus, available at: http://www.narodni-strana.cz/clanek.php?id_clanku=2750, last accessed 30 June 2010.

45 Cf. ČTK, Romové: Ochranné hlídky budou demonstrace monitorovat beze zbraní, 23 April 2009, available at: http://web.volny.cz/noviny/zdomova/clanek/~volny/IDC/108136/romove-ochranne-hlidky-budou-demonstrace-monitorovat-beze-zbrani.html.

46 Czech Energy Enterprise (České energetické závody, ČEZ) is the dominant producer of electricity in the Czech Republic.

fraudulent consumers of electricity from the distribution net aroused negative reactions. The activities of the unit were subsequently suspended. The formation wore black uniforms and imitated police or military units of special designation in its structure and training. Members were trained by instructors with police and military backgrounds. The second group, the Civil Guards (Občanské hlídky), were units of the populist right-wing *Public Affairs Party* (*Věci veřejné*, VV). They were formed to strike against "inadaptable persons", especially the homeless. Even in this case, it was not a typical paramilitary unit as its members were employees of the ABL security agency (Agentura Bílý Lev). The company's owner is amongst the leaders of the VV Party. In both cases, since members are company employees, the principle of voluntarism typical for paramilitary units is absent.

The Slovakian Community (Slovenská Postpolitost, SP) and New Free Slovakia (Nové Slobodne Slovensko, NSS) are two organizations which are very close to the Skinhead scene. They mainly organize protests against the Roma while part of their ideology is also anti-Semitic. When attending special rallies, the members wear black uniforms resembling those of Hlinka's troops (Hlinkova garda), those paramilitary units operating during the WW II Slovak state.[47] The Slovakian organizations are always the first ones to support Serbian nationalism. They commemorate the anniversaries of NATO attacks on the Federal Republic of Yugoslavia.[48]

In Romania, the organization with paramilitary tendencies is the New Right (Noua Dreaptă, ND), led by Tudor Ionescu. ND strives for a Greater Romania and, like most similar formations, it acts in racist, anti-Semitic ways. One of the biggest manifestations of ND power were demonstrations during the first Gay Pride Parade ever organized in Bucharest in 2007. The following statement was issued: "Saying NO to homosexuality is not a prejudice, but the manifestation of a system of values based on the Holy Scriptures and the traditional values of the Romanian family".[49] In neighboring Bulgaria, it is the Bulgarian National Union (Bulgarski natsionalen sujuz, BNS), which encompasses neo-Nazi elements and anti-Roma sentiments.

The most unique case amongst all of these groups probably is the Hungarian Guard (Magyar Gárda, MG). It was founded in 2007 with around 300 members, but by 2009 this number had grown to 3,000.[50] The guard was founded by the political party *Movement for a Better Hungary* (*Jobbik Magyarországért Mozgalom*)[51] and its members present themselves in the green-and-brown uni-

47 Cf. Milo, Slovakia, p. 217.
48 Cf. Slovenská Postpolitost, http://pospolitost.wordpress.com/.
49 Noua Dreaptă, http://www.nouadreapta.org/limbistraine_prezentare.php?idx=24&lmb=eng.
50 Cf. The European Union Times, The Hungarian Guard: Restored, Renewed and Here to Stay, 12 July 2009, available at: http://news.ronatvan.com/2009/07/12/the-hungarian-guard-restored-renewed-and-here-to-stay/.
51 Commonly known in the short form "Jobbik", literally translated as "better".

forms with emblems and insignia based on symbols used by the Hungarian fascists of WW II (*Arrow Cross Party*). The guard became an issue in politics and media, as some politicians attempted to present themselves either as supporters of this "service to the nation" or as opponents to a "nationalist threat". Several priests were also present at the inauguration of the extreme right-wing guards. The guard was commanded by Gábor Vona, head of the aforementioned *Jobbik*. Immediately after the inauguration of the guard, protests and warnings came from both the political milieu and from Jewish organizations. The Hungarian Court of Appeal ruled on 2 July 2009 that the Hungarian National Guard be dissolved because its marches had fuelled ethnic tensions while leading to the disruption of public order.[52] Nevertheless, the guard immediately called for protests and on 12 July for the restoration of the Hungarian Guard. The leadership planned an appeal to the Strasbourg European Court of Human Rights, claiming that the ruling violated the freedom of assembly and that it is not the guard itself but "Gypsy criminals, drug users, multi-national companies, Israeli acquisitions in the country and the government itself that the people find terrifying".[53]

The radicalization of the Hungarian Guard was to a certain extent suppressed by its political wing, the *Jobbik* party. It enjoyed success in the 2009 European parliamentary elections and they finished as the third largest party in 2010 Hungarian federal vote. Gábor Vona ostentatiously swore his oath in the uniform of the Hungarian guard. This move was criticized by the Hungarian president and other state personalities. One of the main topics of *Jobbik* was the 90th anniversary of the Trianon Treaty. This issue was also taken over and promoted by the right-wing *Fidesz* party. The Hungarian Guard even had an effect on the election campaign in neighboring Slovakia. Most notably, the *Slovakian National Party* used the themes of the Hungarian Guard on their billboards and posters to warn against the potential threat to Slovakia's territorial integrity.

In Slovenia, it is the National-Social Union of Slovenia (Nacional-socialna zveza Slovenija) that represents an extreme right organization with its own paramilitary units. The group Hervardi was set up in the town of Maribor on the same day that Slovenia entered the European Union (1 May 2004). By November 2006, the organization covered the whole of Slovenian territory. According to group statements, the name Hervardi was chosen in honor of the historic defenders of the Slavic principality of Carantania, which emerged in the 7th century. The group claims to defend the Slovenian nation, culture, and language. At the same time, it compares Slovenia's position in the EU to its subjugation during the Roman Empire. At the same time, Hervardi claim to stand

52 Cf. Hungary Court bans Hungarian Guard, 3 July 2009, available at: http://news. ronatvan.com/2009/07/03/hungary-court-bans-hungarian-guard/.

53 Politics, Radical Nationalists Demonstrate in Budapest, "re-establish" Magyar Gárda, 13 July 2009, available at: http://www.politics.hu/20090713/radical-nationalists-demonstrate-in-budapest-reestablish-magyar-garda.

against Italian fascism and German national socialism, as they are seen to be akin to Yugoslavian unitarism (both Serbian and Croatian), clericalism, and communism.[54] While the group claims to protect Slovenian culture, it provides its members with a kind of military training. The men wear camouflage uniforms; the organization uses a flag with the old Black Panther symbol and has its own anthem.

In Poland, the All Polish Youth combines nationalism with Catholicism. It claims to be "modern patriotism-tradition and modernity in one, upbringing its members in the spirit of national and Catholic values".[55] There are several other organizations in Poland that are openly nationalist and anti-Semitic (e. g., the National Right (Prawica Narodowa)). One group does not only direct its hatred against Jews, but it also aims to purge Poland altogether of "Judeo-Christianity".[56] As elsewhere, Roma and left-wing activists are principal targets.

V. Conclusion

The paramilitary foundations of the 1990s and the early 21st century have been either those related to the Yugoslavian and post-Soviet conflicts or to newly emerging groups that safeguard "public order". The paramilitary formations that were engaged during the wars were usually set up with the active encouragement of the governments, working closely within state structure and official army units. Some of them were later dissolved into official armed forces. They had clear structures and systems of command, wearing uniforms and using systems of rank. Others simply walked along in different camouflage outfits, demonstrating no apparent structure or hierarchy.

The only genuine extreme right paramilitary formations are probably those related to the conflicts in Croatia and in BiH. They were created under the consent of both self-proclaimed and internationally recognized states. Even though Kosovo had declared its independence in 1992, it was not recognized elsewhere until 2008. Therefore, the ethnic Albanian formations in Kosovo territory should rather be seen as insurgent groups. The same applies to all of the Caucasian guerrilla units fighting against the Russian dominance. An additional problem with the ethnic Albanian formations is that their membership did not only consist of extreme right, but also of Marxist and Enveristic persons.

It seems that there are new types of paramilitary formations emerging in Central and Eastern Europe. These units are organized, hierarchical, and sometimes uniformed. They are not necessarily tied to official government structures. Sometimes they are offshoots of political parties on the extreme right. They claim to safeguard the public order and fight against either other nations or eth-

54 Cf. Hervardi, Kdo smo, available at: http://www.hervardi.com/kdo_smo.php.
55 Polish Youth, About Us, available at: http://www.polish-youth.org/index.php?go=kim.
56 Pankowski/Kornak, Poland, p. 166.

nic groups. This is mainly the case with the post-Soviet formations that fight either for or against russification, or the CEE units set up to safeguard society from the Roma and what are seen as "social enemies": criminals, gays, lesbians, drug-addicts, alcoholics, perverts etc. Most of these formations do not wear uniforms (except for the notorious and well-known case of the Hungarian Guard) but try to arrange training for its members. Nevertheless, it seems that the paramilitary formations are at the margin of the social spectrum, do not have popular support, and do not present a threat to society. They could become a danger once they change their outlook from a purely militant one to a more family oriented one that uses softer propaganda in recruiting new members.

Vigilantism against the Roma in East Central Europe

Miroslav Mareš

I. Introduction

The security situation in East Central Europe (ECE) in the current post-communist period is characterized by ethnic tension between a part of the majority population and the Roma people. It is the fear of Roma crime that drives the politicization and securitization of this phenomenon. Some direct outgrowths of the anti-Roma activities are the different types of anti-Roma vigilantism endeavored by various actors (i. e. paramilitary groups). This paper tries to conceptualize and classify the vigilante activities against the Roma and to explain the risks connected to these activities.

Les Johnston defines vigilantism as a "social movement giving rise to premeditated acts of force - or threatened force - by autonomous citizens. It arises as a reaction to the transgression of institutionalized norms by individuals or groups or to their potential or to imputed transgression. Such acts are focused upon crime control and/or social control and aim to offer assurances (or 'guarantees') of security both to the participants and to other members of a given established order".[1]

Vigilantism against the Roma community is caused by the very real existence of Roma crime, on the one hand, and to strong racist prejudices against the Roma in East Central Europe, on the other hand. It may be motivated by the real threat of Roma crime and/or by the political misuse of this issue. Consequently, in order to understand anti-Roma vigilantism, a short analysis of the general discussion in reference to the so-called "Roma-question" in the ECE-countries (Romania, Bulgaria, Hungary, Slovakia, the Czech Republic, Poland, and Slovenia[2]) is of the essence.

Various approaches can be used for an analysis of current anti-Roma vigilantism in East Central Europe.[3] Basically, research on vigilantism has been focused

1 Johnston, What is Vigilantism?, p. 232.

2 Western European countries, South Eastern European countries (Serbia, Montenegro, Croatia, Macedonia, Kosovo, Albania, Greece) and post-Soviet countries are not included in this paper.

3 This paper was written as a part of the project "Contemporary Paramilitarism in the Czech Republic in Context of Transnational Development Trends of Political Violence in Europe" (code GA407/09/0100), founded by the Czech Science Foundation.

on geographic areas other than ECE (Latin America, the USA, Northern Ireland etc.). Hence, the data and events of the post-communist era have, as yet, not been included in this research. Nevertheless, vigilantism against the Roma has been researched outside ECE, e. g. in Great Britain.[4] Anti-Roma vigilantism is an important part of racist anti-Roma violence in ECE and was investigated there in the context of the research concerning the extreme right and racism in ECE.[5] Violence is a result of general anti-Roma prejudices and, in that respect, anti-Gypsyism and Roma-phobia are typical of the extreme and populist right in ECE.[6] Several publications have already dealt with the reactions of anti-racist movements and Roma-organizations to racist attacks.[7]

Anti-Roma vigilantism is interrelated with the rise to popularity of some right-wing extremist parties in East Central Europe (e. g. Jobbik in Hungary and the Workers Party in the Czech Republic). This rise of the extreme right activities in East Central Europe, including the violence against the Roma, is also considered a threat to the general democratic development in Europe as it carries the danger of new ethnic conflicts in the center of the continent.[8]

II. The "Roma-question" in East Central Europe

The Roma are a stateless nation that had its geographic origin in India. The number of Roma in Europe is estimated at seven to nine million people, however, the real number is not known.[9] There is a large Roma-population in the ECE-countries. The Roma are estimated to make up approx. 9 % of the population in Romania (around two million in total), 8 % in Bulgaria (700,000), 4 % in Hungary (600,000), 4 % in Slovakia (500,000), and 2 % in the Czech Republic (300,000).[10] In addition, there are several thousand Roma living in Poland and Slovenia.

The situation of the Roma in East Central Europe is characterized by many controversial issues caused by two dominant interrelated problems: anti-Roma prejudices within the majority population including anti-Roma behavior (so-called anti-Gypsyism[11]), on the one hand, and the problematic behavior of a

4 Cf. Johnston, What is Vigilantism?, pp. 220–223.
5 Cf. Mudde, Central and Eastern Europe, p. 274.
6 Cf. Mudde, Populist Radical Right Parties in Europe, p. 86.
7 Cf. Szabó, Movement and Counter-Movement Mobilization, p. 169.
8 Cf. Mayer/Odehnal, Aufmarsch: Die Rechte Gefahr aus Osteuropa, p. 16.
9 Cf. Ringold/Orenstein/Wilkens, Roma in an Expanding Europe, p. 3, available at: http://siteresources.worldbank.org/EXTROMA/Resources/roma_in_expanding_europe.pdf, last accessed 7 November 2009.
10 Ibid., p. 4; Cf. Petrova, The Roma: Between the Myth and the Future, available at: http://www.errc.org/cikk.php?cikk=1844&archiv=1, last accessed 7 November 2009.
11 Cf. Nicolae, Anti-Gypsyism: A Definiton – European Grassroot Roma Organisation, available at: http://www.ergonetwork.org/antigypsyism.htm, last accessed 7 November 2009.

large part of the Roma population, on the other hand. Tangible discrimination issues and security risks can be perceived in both.

The structural handicaps of the Roma are mostly related to poverty, discrimination on the labor market, and the segregation of Roma children in the educational process.[12] Sub-standard housing in the so-called "Roma ghettos" determines the political and cultural socialization of a large part of the Roma population. Some problems are not as important today as they once were in the past; evidently, the sterilization of Roma women is a historical issue, and only a small number of lawsuits relating to sterilization[13] have an impact on the current political discussion.

The Roma people have difficulties adapting their own traditional values and life-style to the values and life-style of the majority society. This calls forth a number of hate tirades from the latter, mostly full of pejorative and sweeping statements directed at the entire Roma population. As an example, the statement by the mayor of the Ovcha Kupel District of Sofia, Bulgaria, ought to be mentioned, here. According to the OSCE report, on 14 November 2006 he reacted to the government's plans to relocate a Roma community to his district by reportedly stating that Roma people "cannot live among [Bulgarian] citizens. [...] a Roma settlement near Bulgarian living quarters is ten times more harmful than a garbage bin".[14]

According to Cas Mudde, there are four major prejudices against the Roma among the extreme right:

- The Roma are inherently primitive;
- The Roma are inherently criminal;
- The Roma are social parasites;
- The Roma are the beneficiaries of positive state discrimination.[15]

"Criminals" and "social parasites" are probably the most frequently repeated invectives in reference to the Roma in addition to the criticism regarding the allegedly "positive discrimination" of the Roma (i.e. "affirmative action"). Lately, the denial of the Roma holocaust of World War II has been on the rise while, simultaneously, the Roma holocaust victims are being denigrated in various ways.[16]

12 Cf. Kovats, Možnosti a výzvy, pp. 14–15.
13 Several cases are mentioned in Lydia Gall, Coercive Sterilisation – an Example of Multiple Discrimination. Roma Rights, 2, 2009, available at: http://www.errc.org/en-research-and-advocacy-roma-details.php?article_id=3564&page=10, last accessed 24 June 2011.
14 Hate crimes in the OSCE Region: Incidents and Responses. Annual Report for 2006, p. 74.
15 Cf. Mudde, Populist Radical Right Parties in Europe, p. 87–88.
16 Cf. Král, Týrali Češi Cikány, nebo naopak?, available at: http://www.zvedavec.org/pohledy/2005/04/1184-tyrali-cesi-cikany-nebo-naopak.htm, last accessed 17 June 2010.

The Roma are victims of various violent attacks, including racial murder, that are, in part, committed by organized right-wing extremists, in part, by racists that come from the "ordinary population", and, in part, by members of the security forces, mainly by police officers.[17] However, vigilant violence is only one part of anti-Roma violence, overall.

The different types of discrimination as well as expectations, or rather the hope, for a better life have led to the emigration of Roma people to Western Europe and North America (especially to Canada). Some controversial effects of Roma immigration (e. g. the re-implementation of the Canadian visa for the citizens of the Czech Republic in 2009) broaden the gap between the majority population and the Roma minority.

A certain segment of the Roma is also involved in a number of unlawful practices. The misuse of social benefits, drug abuse, disturbing the peace during night hours as well as various other forms of crime are often related to Roma communities. There are only limited data and information about the actual extent of Roma crime available due to the fact that official statistics concerning Roma crime are impossible to compile during the current political climate and legal environment in East Central Europe. However, in summer 2009, Slovak Christian Democrat Vladimír Palko suggested recording Roma crime in the official statistics in Slovakia.[18]

According to Europol, Roma-organized criminal groups from Romania dominate child trafficking.[19] Czech expert Roman Kryštof separates Roma crime into external (against non-Roma people) and internal crime (within the Roma community). He focuses on the situation in the Czech Republic and Slovakia and features as the most important forms of external crime: pimping; prostitution; child trafficking; trafficking of human beings, in general; robbery; and drug-related crimes.[20]

The fear of Roma crime is one of the strongest sources of anti-Roma prejudices. This fear is also brought up in the public discussion concerning the "Roma-question" as the above-mentioned complex of issues within the coexistence of the Roma people and the majority population is called. This discussion plays an important role in the countries of East Central Europe. The basic actors of this debate are:

a) Human rights activists and Roma representatives;
b) Moderate politicians from established democratic parties seeking broad consonance;

17 Cf. Hate crimes in the OSCE Region: Incidents and Responses. Annual Report for 2006, p. 82.
18 Cf. Palko, Buďme normální, available at: http://blog.aktualne.centrum.sk/blogy/vladimir-palko-.php?itemid=551, last accessed 7 November 2009.
19 Cf. EU Organized Crime Threat Assessment, p. 21.
20 Cf. Kryštof, Romany Communities' Ways of Living in Relation to Criminality, available at: http://epolis.cz/download/pdf/materialsEN_27_1.pdf, last accessed 7 November 2009.

c) Politicians from established democratic parties employing tough "law and order"- rhetoric;
d) right-wing extremists who use anti-Roma rhetoric with the goal of winning public support and harming the democratic regime.

Anti-Gypsyism and the significance of the rise in the political self-confidence of the Roma have intensified the politicization of the "Roma-question" in recent years. Vigilantism is one of the possible forms of engaging in politics interrelated with the "Roma-question". In the following, the different types of vigilant activities and the motives for them will be described and demonstrated on particular cases.

III. "Verbal vigilantism"

The term "verbal vigilantism" as it is used in this article means verbal threats and the planning of vigilante activities. In public debates in East Central Europe, numerous threatening statements are made against Roma communities in relationship to the efforts of fighting Roma crime and delinquency. Some of the threats are actually carried out in connection with crimes committed by Roma people; sometimes, there are only threats made against Roma crime, in general.

As a typical example of generally threatening propaganda, the slogan "Final solution to the Roma-question" by the *National Party* (*Národní strana*) in the Czech Republic must be mentioned here. The party employed this wording in its 2009 propaganda pamphlet as well as in its propaganda commercial on national television before the European Elections in 2009. In this commercial, a number of negative aspects of life in a Roma community were presented. Although the official party statement of the so-called "final solution" actually referred to a voluntary departure of the Roma from the Czech Republic,[21] the expression "final solution" immediately evoked the Nazi era, thus carrying harmful potential.

Some individuals in the ECE-countries openly proposed inhumane suggestions. So, Slovak racist activist Július Sokol stated, "How to prevent a racial war? It is too late for sterilization (they are too many). Beyond this, it is no solution to aggressiveness, and it cannot stop depredation of woods, agricultural stands and plantations. The only effective and civilized solution is creation of reservations, where men and women will be segregated in order to stop population explosion. However, the EU does not permit this, is led by Jews and their Masonic lackeys".[22]

21 Cf. Gaudin, Konečné řešení otázky cikánské v českých zemích, available at: http://www.narodni-strana.cz/propag_mat/KO_RE_OT_CI.pdf, last accessed 7 November 2009.
22 Sokol, Pán predseda cigánskej (a futbalovej) vlády!

In some cases, "autonomous citizens" agreed with the racist statements made by politicians. For example, in a public meeting in 2006, Liana Janáčková, a member of the Czech Senate, who had also been the former mayor of the Marianské Hory district in Ostrava, made the following statement in respect to housing Roma people in a locality called Bedřiška: "Unfortunately, I'm a racist, I disagree with the integration of Gypsies and their living throughout the district. Unfortunately, Bedřiška was chosen, therefore, they will be there, behind a tall fence, with electricity".[23] At the same meeting, deputy mayor Jiří Sezemský commented: "Give me a license to own a rifle and permission to shoot them all, and I'll go and do it". Both Janáčková and Sezemský were supported by a large part of the Czech public.

It is important to mention that not every attempt to punish the crimes committed by Roma people can be called verbal racist vigilantism, particularly when these attempts are dealing with real criminals and occur within a legal context. It is interesting that some Roma activists also express the need for fair investigation and punishment of the crimes committed by Roma people with the goal of stopping the anti-Roma opinion that "gypsies are allowed commit crimes, and nobody can do anything about it" from spreading.

The article by Roma activist Patrik Banga from the Czech Republic is an example of such a request. He criticizes the fact that the police incriminated no-one after a massive, violent attack carried out by a Roma family against a police patrol in Lysec u Teplic in September 2009 after a man, who had been robbed by members of this family, had called the police. Banga argues that police reluctance may well be one of the reasons for the evergrowing anti-Roma prejudice.[24]

IV. Patrols, monitoring, and "prevention"

The most frequent form of vigilantism is the patrolling and monitoring the scenes of Roma crime. Patrolling and monitoring are, usually, closely connected. Patrols mainly operate in places where there is a high crime rate and/or fear of crime. They try to observe the situation and to pursue (and sometimes punish) the perpetrators. Vigilantes sometimes agree to cooperate with the police; nevertheless, they often act autonomously. They want to prevent crime by threatening the potential perpetrators.

Sometimes, ad hoc established citizens' groups that are not affiliated with any political organization carry out such vigilante activities. In some cases, the vigilantes' aim does not only extend to Roma crime. Some vigilantes aim at any

23 Romea/CTK, Czech Senator Janackova's Deputy Suspected of Racism too, available at: http://www.romea.cz/english/index.php?id=detail&detail=2007_786, last accessed 7 November 2009.

24 Cf. Banga, Útok Romů na policii v Lysci zůstává i přes svědectví bez obvinění, čí je to chyba, available at: http://www.romea.cz/index.php?id=detail&detail=2007_6860, last accessed 7 November 2009.

kind of crime and at all perpetrators. This was the case with the "Safe Nusle Organization" established in Prague in 1998, which only existed for a few months (Nusle is a district of the Czech capital). This group rejected racism and was open to all "honest citizens"; however, there were no Roma-members.[25]

In 2006, the self-announced citizens' home-guard in Ústí nad Labem, Czech Republic, established itself against the Roma in the neighborhood of the (in-)famous Matiční Street.[26] These citizens criticized the municipal government for its reluctance concerning the crimes committed by their Roma neighbors. Still, an official home-guard was never established, there. Overall, it would be difficult to assign distinct racist motives to this vigilante activity as non-Roma crime was untypical for this area, and there had been serious disputes between the Roma and other citizens in Matiční Street since the mid-1990s.[27] This street attracted the world's attention in 1998/1999, when the municipality had a wall erected between the Roma houses and the rest of the street due to all the rubbish that had collected in the Roma housing district. After domestic and international protests by the Roma and human rights activists, the wall was removed.

There is, however, an obvious racist dimension to the vigilante activities of the "White Power" youth sub-cultures. In the 1990s, racist skinhead gangs in ECE frequently presented themselves as "law and order" units. The concept of the "European Skinhead Army" propagated by the English neo-Nazi band "No Remorse" had its impact also in post-communist countries. However, this kind of propaganda was mostly the first and the last step of such activities. They carried out several violent ad hoc attacks motivated by vigilantism; however, they carried less weight than their having the opportunity of demonstrating their own aggressiveness. Any attempts to create Ku Klux Klan branches in skinhead and post-skinhead circles in the ECE countries were only a temporary phenomenon.

A more sophisticated example of skinhead vigilante activities was the patrolling by a gang that was active under the cover of the Bohemia Hammerskins at the Brno railway station in 1993/1994. In those years, a mass emigration wave of Roma people arrived in the Czech Republic from Slovakia. In the Brno incident, racist skinheads fought against Roma delinquency, sometimes even in cooperation with the railway station staff. They also terrorized the Roma before their journey to the western part of the Czech Republic.

Since the beginning of 1990, several politically active organizations were trying to make use of the potential militant youngsters presented to create more effective vigilante units on paramilitary principles. Countering Roma crime was an important task, among others, for the Movement of National Unification (HNS) in the Czech Republic, for the Slovak Community (SP) in Slovakia, par-

25 Cf. Veber, Bezpečné Nusle: sdružení pro poctivé lidi bez rozdílu, available at: http://ib.ctkcz, last accessed 8 October 2009.

26 Cf. Cesarová, Lidé z Matiční chtějí zřídit domobranu, pokud jim město nepomůže, available at: http://ib.ctkcz, last accessed 8 October 2009.

27 Cf. Roček, Zeď (The Wall), p. 13.

tially also for the New Right (ND) in Romania and other groupings in the ECE countries.

The new era of paramilitary vigilantism began in 2007 with the founding of the Hungarian Guard, the Magyar Garda (MG), initiated by the political party *Movement for a Better Hungary, Jobbik.* The Hungarian Guard had more on their task-list than merely vigilantism, mostly in the context of international relations in East Central Europe (e. g. it was prepared for the potential defense against a Slovak or Romanian military attack on Hungary).

However, anti-Roma vigilantism also was an important part of MG activity. In announcing the MG on 12 November 2007, an individual who went by the pen name Corvinus wrote the following on the international neo-Nazi server www.stormfront.org: "The Magyar Garda's plan is to secure the villages and towns where the gypsy minority is causing trouble, murder, threatening and basically any criminal activity. They said they go to any town for request to help them with the gypsy problems!"[28] In fact, the MG operated in potentially dangerous localities. For example, 80 MG guards patrolled the Hungarian village of Kiskunlacháza in September 2009 after the brutal Roma attack on a 14-year-old girl.[29]

The Hungarian Guard has over one-thousand members. It is also a very important political force. According to a public opinion poll, 9 % of the Hungarian population support the MG.[30] Despite the ban of the organization in 2009, it continues to exist, even without legal registration. It is an important instrumentof the *Jobbik* party's political marketing strategy. This party won 14.7 % of the votes and three mandates in the European election in 2009 and, then, 16.67 % of the votes and 47 mandates in the parliamentary election in 2010. Csanád Szegedi, a member of the European Parliament (EP), wore the uniform of the MG during his first appearance in the EP in Strasburg (in protest against the MG ban in Hungary).[31]

The Hungarian Guard was an inspiration also for political parties in other ECE countries. Most likely, only the National Guard (NG) in Bulgaria was established in summer 2007 without having been significantly influenced by the MG. The National Guard in the Czech Republic, which was also established in November 2007 on the initiative of the Czech *National Party,* was probably more strongly inspired by Hungary (strategically, not ideologically). Interestingly, the representatives of the NG and the MG and their mother parties met in

28 Corvinus, Hungarian Guard helps on Gypsy infestations, available at: www.stormfront.org, last accessed 12 November 2007.

29 Cf. TASR via Security and Society, Rómovia v Maďarsku zbili mladú ženu – objavilo sa 80 gardistov, available at: http://security.sk.cx/?q=node/2711, last accessed 29 September 2009.

30 Cf. SITA via Security and Society, Maďarskú gardu podporuje každý jedenásty Maďar, available at: http://security.sk.cx/?q=node/2306, last accessed 29 September 2009.

31 Cf. Czipke, Hungarian Guard uniform-wearing Jobbik MEP mistaken for French Hanuman, available at: http://www.politics.hu/20090729/hungarian-guard-uniform-wearing-jobbik-mep-mistaken-for-french-handyman, last accessed 7 November 2009.

Bratislava in July 2008,[32] but due to disputes over the so-called Beneš decrees from the post-war period (they were drafted in reference to the German and Hungarian population of the former Czechoslovakia), the cooperation did not continue.

According to the leader of the NG, Michal Kubík, the main functions of this organization are to protect party meetings, to help in case of national disasters, and to be a "bulwark" against what he called "uncooperative minorities and immigrants whose interest- governing bodies are placed above those of orderly Czech citizens".[33] However, the NG's activities are very limited.

Two non-uniformed members of the NG patrolled outside a school in Karlovy Vary in June 2008, where a gang of Roma children had attacked pupils. One of the guards was the father of a pupil.[34] In April 2008, the NG also announced patrolling the National Memorial Terezín (a World War II Nazi Concentration Camp) after perpetrators of Roma origin had stolen the tombstones of Jewish victims buried there. The Memorial's director flatly refused any help by the NG.[35] The alleged major reason for the Terezín activity was to show that the *National Party* observed the traditions of anti-Nazi fight (its nationalism has anti-Pan-Germanic aims). However, despite the attention by the media, the NG activity did not lead to any significant increase in voters for the *National Party.*

Establishing the Protection Corps of the *Workers' Party* (OS-DS) in the Czech Republic in 2008 proved to be more successful. First, they were on duty in Janov, a quarter of the North Bohemian town of Litvínov on 4 October 2008. Thirteen members of the OS-DS tried "to observe" Roma crime, but they were stopped by a Roma group armed with sticks. One Roma used a racial slur against one of the female guards. This attracted the media. Later, not only the DS but also hard-core Nazi organizations such as the National Resistance (NO) and the Autonomous Nationalists (AN) misused the situation in Janov for their own strategic purposes (see chapter VII).

The OS-DS also operated in several localities in Northern Bohemia in the first half of the year 2009. In these localities, the OS-DS carried off a significantly higher result (around 5 % - 8 % more) in the European Election than in the previous elections.[36] However, the average result came to only 1.07 % of the votes. As a result, the DS became the most successful far right party in the Czech

32 Cf. Jobbik, Czech National Party and Jobbik to Meet in Pozsony, available at: http://www.jobbik.com/plugins/p2013_news, last accessed 23 July 2008.

33 Alda, Guard up as Nationalist Paramilitary Launches, available at: http://www.narodni-strana.cz/clanek.php?id_clanku=2604, last accessed 7 November 2009.

34 Cf. Holec, Pěst lidu, available at: http://www.reflex.cz/Clanek32868.html, last accessed 8 November 2009.

35 Cf. Idnes.cz, Národní garda chce hlídat Terezín, available at: http://zpravy.idnes.cz/narodni-garda-chce-hlidat-terezin-jsou-to-nackove-odmitl-to-reditel-1fi-/domaci.asp?c=A080422_130119_domaci_jw, last accessed 8 November 2009.

36 Cf. Mareš, National and Right-Wing Radicalism in the New Democracies: Czech Republic. pp. 10–11, available at: http://www.ivo.sk/buxus/docs//rozne/extremizmus_studie/Tschechien.pdf, last accessed 16 June 2010.

Republic since the year 2000. It was, however, banned by the Czech Supreme Administrative Court in February 2010. One of the reasons that led to the ban was the existence of the OS-DS. According to the court, the OS-DS illegally replaced state bodies.[37]

The successor party of the DS, the *Workers' Party of Social Justice* (DSSS), established a new vigilante organization in May 2010, the Civic Patrols of the DSSS (Občanské hlídky DSSS). They effected their first action in the village of Ředhošť in June 2010, where tensions and clashes between some Roma families and people from the majority population had escalated a few days prior.[38]

Following the OS-DS model, the Slovak community also started such "monitoring raids" on Roma settlements in summer 2009. The first of them was an anti-Roma protest in the village of Sariske Michalany in August 2009, where two youngsters from a Roma settlement had allegedly beaten up a 65-year-old man at the village's football stadium the weekend before.[39] There, right-wing extremists clashed with the police.

During their meeting, Marian Kotleba, the leader of the SP, announced that the new nationalist party had been established in Slovakia. As an independent candidate for the district, administrator Kotleba won 10.03 % of the votes in the regional elections of the Banskobystricky district in November 2009. However, the new *People's Party, Our Slovakia* (*Ľudová strana Naše Slovensko*), won only 1.33 % of the votes in the parliamentary elections in June 2010.[40]

V. Lynching and pogroms

Some vigilante actions are aimed against real or alleged perpetrators of crimes with the goal of punishing them. The illegal force used in the "self-protection" against theft could be called the first step of lynch justice. According to Christo Ivanov and Margarita Ilieva,in Bulgaria, there is a consistent pattern of civilian anti-Roma violence and pervasive practices such as "shooting and stabbing perpetrated by farmers, owners, and guards resulting in serious injury and death".[41] Homeless Roma people and drug addicts are subject to lynch justice due to the mixture of racial motives and the "law and order" policy of the extreme right. For example, in May 2007, a group of young members of the local Nazi gang,

37 Cf. Nejvyšší správní soud, Pst 1/2009-348, available at: http://www.nssoud.cz/main.aspx?cls=anonymZneni&id=22047&mark=, last acessed 17 June 2010.

38 Cf. Česká tisková kancelář, Far Right Renews Vigilante Patrols against Roma. available at: http://www.praguemonitor.com/2010/06/09/far-right-party-renews-vigilante-patrols-against-roma, last accessed 17 June 2010.

39 Cf. Stanková, Police Disperse Anti-Roma Protesters, available at: http://spectator.sme.sk/articles/view/36177/2/police_disperse_anti_roma_protesters.html, last accessed 17 June 2010.

40 Cf. Ľudová strana naše Slovensko, Ďakujeme všetkým našim voličom a podporovateľom, available at: http://www.naseslovensko.org/, last accessed 17 June 2010.

41 Ivanov/Ilieva, Bulgaria, p. 18.

the White Rebels Clan, started beating up a 26-year-old homeless Roma drug addict in the South Moravian town of Hodonín. Afterwards, one of the attackers doused the victim with toluene, took out a lighter, and set the man on fire.[42] He died from his injuries.

The entire family of a Roma perpetrator may become the target of lynch justice. For example, in the early 1990's, a group of "ordinary citizens" attacked the house of a Roma family in the Western Bohemian town of Klatovy between 21 February and 23 February 1991. Some members of this family were allegedly involved in criminal activities. During the clashes, 21-year-old Roma Emil Bendík was killed.[43]

The entire Roma population of the locality is often a target for punishment. In such cases, the term "pogrom" might apply. One of the most (in-) famous cases was reported from Romania in 1993. According to the Human Rights Watch Report, "On September 20, some Romas in the town of Hadareni were attacked by a large mob. During the violence, three Romas were killed. One Romanian, who was stabbed by a Roma male during the violence, also died. In addition, thirteen houses of Romas were set on fire and destroyed, and another twenty-five were partially or seriously damaged. Reports indicate that the police were slow to arrive on the scene of the violence and did little or nothing to intervene or to protect the Romas who were being attacked. The Romanian government responded more severely in the Hadareni case by, among other things, dismissing the county police chief and taking disciplinary action against two local police officers".[44]

Such cases are also typical for present-day East Central Europe, but the consequences are not as tragic. In 2006, the European Roma Rights Center reported about one of these incidents in Slovenia:

"On 29 October, a group of around 30 Roma from Decja vas near the village of Ambrus in the municipality of Ivančnaa Gorica, including a number of children, were evacuated to the Postojna refugee center, a former military barracks, in order to protect them from local non-Romani citizens. This action was apparently undertaken as a result of a conflict that had arisen from an incident which had occurred approximately one week prior, in which a non-Romani man had reportedly been attacked by the inhabitants of the settlement. He later required emergency medical treatment. Following the attack, on 23 October, non-Romani villagers met and openly called for violence against the local Roma. Police were reportedly present at the meeting, which was broadcast on national television, but failed to intervene. Following the meeting, the entire local Romani community fled from their homes into the forest. They spent several nights hiding in the forest in fear of retribution by non-Romani residents who had threatened them with a

42 Cf. Smyčková/Franek, Burning a Roma to Death Not Seen as a Racist Crime, available at: http://aktualne.centrum.cz/czechnews/clanek.phtml?id=514859, last accessed 7 November 2009.

43 Cf. Mareš, Terorismus v České republice, p. 140.

44 Human Rights Watch, Human Rights Watch World Report 1994: Romania, available at: http://www.unhcr.org/refworld/docid/467fca90c.html, last accessed 7 November 2009.

range of actions, including death. On 28 October, the Roma attempted to return to their homes under police protection. However, approximately 200 non-Romani residents objected to the return of the Roma and, by threatening violence, demanded that the authorities resettle the Romani community living there to a more suitable location 'for security and ecological reasons'."[45]

Lynching can be carried out by ideologically non-profiled groups of ordinary citizens as well as by extremist groups. In 1993, in the Czech town of Písek, a regional group of skinheads organized a raid against the Roma of the town, mostly against Roma drug addicts. The leader of this skinhead group supported the Calixstines (Kališníci), a Czech nationalist ideological trend inspired by the Hussite Movement of the first half of the 15th century (a calix was this movement's symbol). During the raid, a group of young Roma drug addicts was driven away to the river, where attackers threw rocks at them. One of the Roma, 17-year-old Tibor Danihel, was killed. The attackers were later sentenced for murder.[46]

VI. Terrorism

Vigilante terrorism can be defined as the organized and strategically planned use of excessive vigilante violence with the goal of threatening a significantly higher number of people than only the direct victims of terrorist attacks or terrorist campaigns. Vigilantes use particular terrorist acts to threaten members of the enemy entity that, from the terrorist's point of view, are defined as deviant and criminal. Some cases of lynch justice can simultaneously be termed terrorism.

In ECE it is often difficult to apply the concept of vigilante terrorism to anti-Roma violence, mostly due to the lack of strategic planning, unclear motivation (the element of threatening is only sometimes significantly stronger than the element of vengeance), and, sometimes, the questionable intensity of violence. However, a different point of view is taken from the position of an "independent observer", on the one hand, and that of the victims of so-called "low intensity threats", on the other hand. If threats are played down or denied by the governmental security officials, the victims feel even more violated.

A case that took place in Poland is of special interest. According to Rafal Pankowski and Marcin Kornak: "In early December, 2000 Roma families living on Zakonnic Street, Piastowska Street, and Rybacka Street in the town of Brzeg were subject to repeated harassment by gangs of Nazi-skins who invaded the area under the cover of night, sprayed racist graffiti on the houses, tried to kick in doors, and broke windows. The police were called several times but failed to arrive in time to arrest the perpetrators. Speaking to the local press, police offi-

45 European Roma Right's Centre, Slovene Authorities Capitulate to Mob, available at: http://www.errc.org/cikk.php?cikk=2653, last accessed 7 November 2009.
46 Cf. Mareš, Terorismus v ČR, p. 167.

cers downgraded the attacks to bogus stories invented by the Roma themselves".[47]

Many arson attacks were committed against Roma housing in ECE, but there are no statistics available for the entire area. An evaluation of the motives for such attacks is also impossible in many of the cases. A series of arson attacks in the Czech Republic is being investigated. According to the police, the perpetrators of an attack against a Roma house in Vítkov, in which a two-year-old Roma girl was burned over 80 % of her body, are known. They are members of neo-Nazi structures in Silesia and Northern Moravia. In those areas, several other unexplained arson attacks were committed.[48] If the same group committed them, it would be more than likely that the attacks had a terrorist character. However, neither the group's name, or their program, nor any relevant statements concerning the attacks are available.

In a similar case, a most brutal series of attacks, in which shotguns and hand-grenades were used, was committed in Hungary in 2008–2009. In nine different attacks, six Roma were killed (including a father and his five-year-old son, who were shot dead when they were running from their house). The Hungarian police arrested a group of four suspected perpetrators at the end of August 2009 that, according to the police, were members of neo-Nazi structures.[49]

VII. Vigilantism during ethnic riots

A new arena for various vigilante activities in East Central Europe are the ethnic or rather inter-ethnic riots, in which Roma rioters fall in with a specific unit of organized or non-organized vigilantes. In 2004, Eastern Slovakia was struck by a series of looting by Roma people (in shops and supermarkets). In her reaction to the riots, the leader of the right-wing extremist Slovak community, Marian Kotleba, stated: "Slovaks have the right to use guns for the protection of their lives and property".[50] However, due to the prompt pacification of the Roma riots by the Slovak police and the army, neither any organized nor any non-organized vigilantes were sent into action.

A similar situation was reported from Bulgaria in 2007. As a result of Roma protests after clashes between the Roma and racist skinheads, the leaders of the Bulgarian National Unity (BNS) announced that the National Guard (NG)

47 Pankowski/Kornak, Poland, p. 174.

48 Cf. Albert/Redlová, Racism in the Czech Republic, p. 23, available at: http://cms.horus.be/files/99935/MediaArchive/national/Czech%20Republic%20-%20SR%202008.pdf, last accessed 8 November 2009.

49 Cf. Koning, Roma Killings Expose Social Tensions in Hungary, available at: http://www.spiegel.de/international/europe/0,1518,645369,00.html, last accessed 8 November 2009.

50 Kotleba, Vyhlásenie Slovenskej pospolitosti k cigánským rabovačkám, available at: http://pospolitost.org/, last accessed 8 November 2009.

should be sent in to combat Roma delinquency. However, after the minister of the interior clearly refused this kind of action, the operation by the National Guard was stopped.[51]

In 2008 and 2009, riots were provoked by the Czech neo-Nazis in relationship to previous "monitoring patrols" (see chapter IV), mostly in Litvínov-Janov on 18 October 2008 and 17 November 2008 and (without prior patrolling by the OS-DS) in Přerov on 4 April 2009. Human-rights-activist Gwendolyn Albert gives a concise description of their strategy:

> "During the last year and a half, the Workers' Party has perfected a formula: it sends its 'patrols' to towns with large Roma ghettos to 'monitor' the situation, which usually means meeting with local residents to ask them about their grievances in respect to their 'inadaptable' neighbors. The party then claims it has been 'invited to address the situation', and an individual related to the party then convenes a public demonstration in the town, which usually involves a march through the Roma quarter. Members of hard-core neo-Nazi organizations, usually the National Resistance and the Autonomous Nationalists, then show up in support armed with blades and other weapons (gun violence has yet to become part of the formula). In cases, where they can make advance preparations, they even cache weapons and material such as smoke bombs along the route of the march. The intention is to provoke the Romani community to violence: Delighted onlookers were captured on video in various towns urging these attempted pogroms".[52]

This strategy of the Czech neo-Nazis is also popular in ECE and might serve as a model to extremists of other countries.

VIII. Reactions to vigilantism

Anti-Roma vigilantism causes a number of reactions by state institutions as well as non-state institutions and organizations on the local, regional, national, European, and international level. It is possible to see the measures against vigilantism in a three-dimensional way. First, there are the actions aimed directly at the vigilantes; second, there is the general counteraction by the extremists, and, third, there is the general policy supposed to benefit the Roma population.

The reaction of the Roma and their supporters sometimes aim at creating their own self-defense home-guard structures against extreme right vigilantes. For example, in the Moravian town of Ostrava in summer 2001, the right-wing extremist home-guard operated at the same time as the Roma home-guard whereas the police tried to prevent clashes between them.[53] In March 2009, in the Hungarian district Györ-Moson-Sopron, it was announced that a Roma guard were being established in reaction to the local activities of the Hungarian

51 Cf. Human Rights First, 2008 Hate Crime Survey, p. 116, available at: http://security.sk.cx/?=node/2029, last accessed 9 November 2009.
52 Albert, Hatred is the Cheapest Fuel, p. 31.
53 Cf. Mareš, Terorismus v ČR. p. 234.

guard.[54] In some cases, Roma patrols or home-guards are prepared to cooperate with the police, as seen in the proposal for establishing patrols in the Czech Republic after the arson attack in Vítkov in spring 2009 (see chapter VI).[55] However, such activities are temporarily limited.

State security forces are employing new tactics in dealing with the vigilantes, and state institutions are trying to apply legislative measures to the vigilantes, including banning vigilante organizations (such as the Hungarian guard in 2009, or by including the discussions respective the illegal character of the OS-DS in the government's proposal for banning the *Workers' Party* in the Czech Republic as of September 2009).

In general, anti-extremist concepts and statements in reference to the issues of vigilantism and paramilitarism are sometimes discussed on the European level. For example, the EP resolution of 13 December 2007 on combating the rise of extremism in Europe states that the EP "seriously concerned the resurgence in Europe of extremist movements and paramilitary groups and parties, some of which even have governmental responsibilities, which base their ideology, political discourse, practices, and conduct on discrimination, including racism, intolerance, incitement to religious hatred, exclusion, xenophobia, anti-Semitism, anti-Gypsyism, homophobia, misogyny, and ultra-nationalism, whereas several European countries have recently experienced hatred, violent events, and killing".[56]

Various activities for supporting the Roma population are included in governmental as well as non-governmental concepts (one of the most important is the 2005–2015 decade of Roma inclusion). As for the Roma, solving the controversial aspects might prove to be a very important element in the discursive considerations against racist, right-wing extremist, and other vigilante propaganda.

IX. Conclusion

The Roma are the main victims of racist violence in East Central Europe. Cas Mudde wrote: "It seems justified to postulate that the level of racist extremist violence in Central and Eastern Europe is on average higher than in Western Europe".[57] This conclusion by Mudde from the year 2005 was written after the racist wave in the 1990s, but before the "strategic" new growth of vigilantism at the end of the first decade of the new century. Despite the fact that vigilante violence against the Roma is on the rise also in Western Europe (e. g. in Italy and

54 Cf. TASR via Security and Society, Maďarsko – Rómovia chcú vlastnú gardu, available at: http://security.sk.cx/?=node/2029, last accessed 9 November 2009.

55 Cf. Cyril Koky to Miroslav Mareš (e-mail), 23 April 2009.

56 European Parliament resolution of 13 December 2007 on combating the rise of extremism in Europe, available at: http://www.europarl.europa.eu/sides/getDoc.do?type=TA&reference=P6-TA-2007-0623&language=EN, last accessed 9 November 2009.

57 Mudde, Central and Eastern Europe, p. 275.

in Northern Ireland), East and Central Europe remain the essential areas of anti-Roma violence. The number of vigilante attacks and actions is only one of the important elements for evaluating this threat. The quality and the strategic planning of vigilantism are important additional factors.

Self-defense activities by ordinary citizens merely have a temporal character. At times, such activities are proportional reactions to the actually existing problems of the locality (home-guard patrols etc.). These very real problems may also lead to excessive, unlawful violence from ordinary citizens, in which individuals, families as well as Roma settlements may become targets. Such activities can burden the inter-ethnic relationships in a region for a long time (as in Hadareni). Nevertheless, if the activities only occur in an isolated and discontinuous way, they carry only limited potential for a change in the regime order.

The strategic use of violence by the right-wing extremist organizations is a significant threat to the peaceful coexistence of the Roma and the majority population. To separate vigilant and non-vigilant violence is especially difficult as the Roma are viewed as "criminals" from a racist point of view. Both the "legal" paramilitary order units of the "new type" of political parties as well as new forms of terrorism and violent riots are perceived emotively from the point of view of the Roma as well as from that of human rights activists and antifascists. Yet, the extreme right activities enjoy the support of a part of the majority population (especially in the neighborhood of "Roma ghettos"), of some of the members of the security forces, and of established politicians.

The non-governmental organization "Human Rights First" wrote about this problem: "The persistence of anti-Roma violence and discrimination by ordinary citizens occurs in the context of abusive patterns of treatment of Roma by police and public authorities. Private violence seeking the expulsion of Roma families and communities sometimes occurs in tandem with official efforts to achieve the same ends. The prevalence of racist anti-Roma rhetoric even by the highest public authorities in some countries further exacerbates the problem. Some of the principal developments in Europe regarding racist violence against Roma involve this combination of public and private prejudice".[58]

The situation in East Central Europe can be improved in a long-term perspective by countering the racist prejudices in this area as well as by providing systematic solutions to all the problematic issues of the "Roma question" with the assistance of domestic, European, and international state and non-state institutions and organizations. However, the present economic crisis and the negative developments in the political culture could have a negative impact on the security situation in the ECE countries, particularly in regard to the government, society, economics, and crime. The worst scenario (at least in some regions), outside of an effective state control, would be a development toward latent violent and armed interethnic mass conflicts staged by brutal paramilitaries and gangs targeting the civilian population.

58 Human Rights First, 2008 Hate Crime Survey, p. 111.

Turkish Extreme Right-Wing Movements – Between Turkism, Islamism, Eurasism, and Pan-Turkism

Stéphane de Tapia

I. Roots and frames of reference of nationalist Turkish movements

The forms and manifestations of Turkish nationalism – including its most extremist forms – can be compared to European nationalisms. The functioning of the ruling bodies of its parties and groups, its messages and behavioral patterns associate it with and link it to other European nationalisms. Still, the knowledge of its historical roots and ideological references is important and even vital for a better understanding of its manifestations and contradictions. In Turkey, the latter are often violent, heated, and vociferous – contrary to its discreetness and quietness among the immigrants' body in Europe. There, they often go unnoticed except during major crises like the racist crimes in Mölln and Solingen in Germany in 1993,[1] or when internal Turkish problems are deflected concerning a specific section of the emigrant population, like the Armenian, Cypriot, or Kurdish questions.

The first part shall therefore explain the roots and the ideological frames of reference of this extremist nationalism. Without this information, it is difficult to comprehend the discourse and the (particularly rich and colorful) iconography. In the second part, we shall describe and analyze the little we know of the manifestations of this nationalism that is offended in the immigrant milieu in Europe. There are numerous excellent studies on nationalism and extremist political parties and movements in Turkey. However, with very few exceptions, analyses of the situation in Europe are rare and fragmentary.

Turkey, the huge country of 780,000 km² and more than 76 million inhabitants, is European (by its history, population, its political and economic commitment) as well as Asian (by its geography, its ethno-historical origins, and its religious affiliation). But what do Europe and Asia stand for in a context where the

1 Several Turkish immigrants were the victims of two cases of malicious arson. Hundreds of thousands of Turks carrying thousands of flags participated in the demonstrations in the streets of German cities. They deeply impressed the German population as well as the government, which became aware of the underlying power. In those days, young people of Turkish background organized the hunting of skinheads and Republikaner (the leader of this party, Franz Schönhuber, needed police protection).

Turkish republican nation state is largely the heir to a multi-ethnic and multi-denominational Empire which, at the peak of its power, extended from the city walls of Vienna to the Russo-Ukrainian borders (through Tatar allies), beyond the Caucasus (through Circassian and Chechen allies) to the borders of the Caspian and the Red Sea, from the Sahara to the borders of the kingdom of Morocco? Turkey was a bridge as well as a crossroads since the high antiquity, well before the arrival of Central Asian nomads. Their Altaic language and Muslim confession prevailed (very gradually in both cases). Turkey is an immigration country, and an emigration and transit country at the same time. It is an immigration country due to its role as a refuge for all Muslim populations who fell prey to what is nowadays known as "ethnic cleansing" (from 1691, the loss of Hungary, to 1989, the last massive exodus of Turks from Bulgaria). It is an emigration country considering the expulsion or – to put it more modestly – "exchange" of populations (Armenians, Greeks from Anatolia and the Black Sea, Assyro-Chaldeans, around the cataclysmic year 1915) and, more recently, of populations swept along by the international movement of working migration of the second half of the twentieth century. More than seven million Turkish people have already participated in this emigration (including re-migration) movement. Differing in extent, it is present in Western and Eastern Europe, in North America (rarer in Latin America), the Middle East, Russia and Central Asia, and Oceania.

1. Some necessary and useful definitions

The agony of the Ottoman Empire was a long one. Turkey returned to what was called the "concert of nations" in the nineteenth and early twentieth century at first due to the influence exerted by the founder of the republic, Atatürk (between 1923 an 1938), and later by his successors in the 1950s and 1980s. During these three transitional periods of Turkish political life, ideologies followed each other and were modified – but always based on a defensive nationalism that was shaped by the successive retreats of the Empire until its disappearance in 1923/24. Each ideology seems like a sometimes desperate attempt to face exterior (colonial and imperial) aggressions, and the disintegration of the Empire due to the blows dealt by nationalisms rising from the West to the East (Greek, Serb, Bulgarian, Romanian, Albanian, Arab, Armenian, Kurdish). Every ideology conceived and constructed with (or in opposition to) the politicians in charge or the intelligentsia, responds to a particular moment of modern and contemporary Turkish history. But these ideologies did not disappear when another transformation followed. They combine, change, and rise again to react to what is conceived – accurately or not – an external or internal aggression against which Turkishness (*türklük*) is affirmed as the Turkish identity.

It is necessary to define some notions that have been on the minds and have bothered the intellects (and sometimes still do) in Turkey and elsewhere

(Crimea, Idel-Ural, Azerbaijan, Turkestan, etc.). Often, these trends are born in Russia before they become established in Turkey. Quite often, they appear to be defensive reactions to Western (including Russian) aggressions or expansions. With the fall of the USSR, they can be re-exported from Turkey to their countries of origin, or rise from the ashes of the long Soviet repression.

Pan-Islamism can be defined as an attempt of self-defense against the increasingly aggressive and efficient imperialist and colonialist West. Due to his position and office as Caliph, the representative of Allah and commander of the believers, the Ottoman Sultan tries to gather all Muslim peoples. But he very quickly comes up against the hostility of the Arab peoples and their leaders. They try to shake off the Ottoman yoke even if this implies forming an alliance with the European infidels.

Ottomanism is another attempt to gather the peoples against the European imperialism/colonialism, this time within the Ottoman Empire. Ottomanism liberates itself from Islam and attempts to unite Muslims, Christians, and Jews living in the same country while promoting reforms in the sense of modernization or even a certain democratization. One of its results is the constitutional movement of 1908. Numerous Greek and Armenian deputes were elected, and the peoples of the Empire form a close union - but not for very long.

Pan-Touranism developed after European scholars had discovered - especially Hungarians and Russians (quite often with Tatar roots) - Turkic roots in Central and High Asia, and comparable linguistic structures of the Finno-Ugric (especially Finnish and Hungarian) and Altaic languages (Turk, Mongol, Manchu-Tungus groups). It led to three nationalisms, respectively pan-nationalisms: Finish, Hungarian, and Turkism/pan-Turkist.

Pan-Turkism and Turkism: What is Turkishness (*türklük*)? Pan-Turkism is derived from the pan-Touranian revelation and the new scientific approach (linguistics, history, ethnography, sociology, etc.). To a large extent, it echoes other nationalist movements (pan-Slavism, pan-Germanism) which attempt to unify all the peoples who supposedly share the same origin to build a modern nation and a nation state. This, too, is a self-defensive reaction largely due to the failure of other political philosophies. But Tatar and Turkistanian influences are obvious.

Turkism is to the Turk nation state what Stalinism is to Trotskism: the revolution in one sole country. Enver Paşa was a pan-Turkist at heart - he is said to have died in Central Asia attacking a Soviet unit on horseback in the Fergana Valley. The future Atatürk is much more of a realist and aims at creating a modern Turkey. In fact, Enver as well as Mustafa Kemal are followers of *türkçülük*, pan-Turkism, or Turkism, depending on the context which is a distinction of the level more than one of nationalist logic. Atatürk embraces it, and gladly receives pan-Turkic, reformist (i. e. sometimes revolutionary) Russian intellectuals. But he still keeps them under close surveillance. Many of them will become professors, or deputes, and shall play an eminent role in the definition of Turk nationalism. But they will never be permitted to create an anti-Soviet base in Turkey.

Eurasianism (Russian: *evrijastsvo*/Turkish: *avrasyacılık*) and *Neo-Eurasianism*: An original way in Turkey – or the local adaptation of the rejection of the occident? Eurasianism is a Russian geopolitical school before knowing its Turkish, Azerbaijani, or Kazakh versions. It was "invented" by anti-communist, rather modernist intellectuals with expert knowledge of the Turko-Mongol historiography. Among them, there were historians like Vernadsky and geographers like Savitsky. The present Russian currant is called Neo-Eurasianism (Lev Gumilev, Aleksandr Dugin, Sergey Panarin, etc.) in order to differentiate it from the founding fathers of the 1920s to 1930s. Clearly leaning more towards fascism, strangely enough, Neo-Eurasianism sparks the interest of many left-wing Turk intellectuals who are completely destabilized by the disappearance of the socialist ideologies and their non-acceptance by the Europeans. Nowadays, the works of the Eurasists and Neo-Eurasists are translated into Turkish, and Russian theoreticians like Sergey Dugin are frequently invited to Turkey. There, both Eurasianisms discuss the same topics: the superficiality and the duplicity of the West with reference to the true values of the East. Doubtlessly, the crucial point is the definition of the role of the leader: the Russian orthodoxy or the Sunnite Turko-Tatar Islam.

2. Turkic roots of Turkism and pan-Turkism

The extension of the Turkophone population in Eurasia is enormous, reaching from the Balkans to Northern Siberia. The diversity of political und legal situations of the about 40 recognized Turkophone peoples cannot really hide the fragility of the Turkophone area, which is much less compact than the Arabophone or even the Iranophone area. Thus, it is not surprising that the peoples considered did not easily conceive themselves as stemming from the same linguistic family and – metaphorically speaking – as members of a possible political community.

Ismail Gasprinski and the journal Tercüman; the precursor: Crimean Tatar, teacher, educationalist and journalist, Ismail Gasprinski (from the village Gaspra, 1851–1914) strongly emphasizes education, its democratization and prevalence as well as the necessity to reform the teaching of languages as well as the position and situation of the autochthonous Muslims in the Russian Empire. Thus, he is one of the innovators and pioneers of Muslim reformism (*usul-i cadid/Jadidism*) that will spread throughout the whole Volga region and in Central Asia.[2] Its influence in Turkey is equally important. Nevertheless, the Ottomans analyzed the possibility of reforms to save the Empire and its role within the international community.

2 There is a rich literature about apparition of Turkic reformism and subsequent nationalist movements. See for instance: Bennigsen/Lemercier-Quelquejay, Les Musulmans oubliés; and Bennigsen/Lemercier-Quelquejay, Le Soufi et le Commissaire.

Tatar, Azerbaijani, and Central-Asian immigration to Turkey: Turk nationalism is born on the banks of the Volga River: Very early, Caucasian and Central Asian Turko-Tatars had to face the Russian expansion, which was often subtle and pragmatic, but sometimes fierce and forcing assimilation.[3] Thus, the Tatars - living in a diaspora-like situation - were the great initiators of the cultural, linguistic, religious, and also political and institutional reform which helped the Turkic peoples in Russia regain their dignity and autonomy as well as their independence. Most likely, Sultan Galiev is the last avatar of this reformist trend in the wake of nationalism. The complete works about this public figure that disappeared during Stalin's regime have meanwhile been translated into Turkish.[4] Between 1890 and 1920, a great number of "Russian Muslim" intellectuals emigrated to Turkey and other countries such as Poland, France, or Germany. They played an important role in the definition of Turkish nationalism (Yusuf Akçura, Mehmet Emin Rasulzade, Ali Hüseyinzade Turan, Ahmet Ağaoğlu, Sadri Maksudi Arsal, Zeki Velidi Togan, to name a few).[5]

The influence of the Turkologists: scientific discourse and discovery of the Asian roots: Russian (like Radlov or Thomsen), Hungarian, and Western travelers and scientists discovered epigraphic stelae written in ancient Turkish, archaeological sites, and Buddhist manuscripts confirming the Chinese medieval annals. This was an important contribution towards the recognition of the origins of the Turkic peoples, first of all Ottoman, and the birth of turkology as historical and linguistic science. The texts of the stelae at Orkhon, the Mongol creek giving birth to the river Amour, with their direct, emotional, and surprisingly modern style have thus become the credo of Turkish nationalists.[6]

3. The "naturalization" of Turkish nationalism

Under the combined influence of international politics and the Russian Muslim intellectuals, Turkish Ottoman nationalist thinkers appear. They attempt to resist the divestiture of the empire. Yet, they are fully conscious of the necessity to react and profoundly reform the state as well as society. This is considered the only way to prevent the dismemberment of the Empire whose complete military, political, and economic decline is obvious. This development gave rise to Ottoman Turkists, writers and poets, high civil servants, officers, journalists, and essayists, like Ziya Gökalp who is considered the father of Turkish sociology.

3 Cf. Kappeler, La Russie.

4 Sultan Galiev (1892–1940) was a fellow traveler of the Bolsheviks. He was an influential representative of the Muslim peoples of Russia before he was demoted (progressively since 1922), neutralized, and finally executed by the NKVD under poorly known conditions in Moscow at the Lefortovo prison in 1940 for "bourgeois nationalism". He was rehabilitated in 1990. Cf. Bennigsen/Lemercier-Quelquejay, Sultan Galiev.

5 Cf. Bezanis, Volga-Ural Tatars in Emigration; Bezanis, Soviet Muslim Emigrés; Copeaux, De la mer Noire à la mer Baltique; or Copeaux, Le mouvement prométhéen.

6 Cf. Copeaux, Espace et temps de la nation turque.

The after-effects of the liberation movements of the Ottoman minorities against the background of the European colonial expansion: The European expansion on the Southern Coast of the Mediterranean (Great Britain, France, Italy) and on the Western and Northern Coast of the Black Sea (Austria, Russia) forced the Ottoman Empire to pull back. Each military withdrawal is a prelude to the independence of a new State (Greece, from 1830 to 1912, Romania, Bulgaria, and Serbia in 1878, Albania in 1913), of the protectorate of a region (1882: Egypt, 1878: Cyprus, 1860: Lebanon), or of its direct colonization by Europeans (1930: Algeria, 1912: Tripolitania), and even the annexation of a region (1775-1783: Crimea, 1784-1859: North Caucasus). Each territorial withdrawal caused a massive wave of Turkic-Muslim refugees often expelled under terrible conditions by the leaders of the newly independent countries.[7] While the fate of the Christian victims of conflicts and of Ottoman violence has quite rightly moved and concerned the Europeans, they have rarely denounced the "ethnic cleansing" of Muslim victims (many of whom are not ethnically Turkish: Bosniaks, Albanians, Caucasians, etc.). The most nationalist Turkish elements can often be found among these segments of the population.

Intellectual responses, ideological responses at first Ottoman, then Turkish: At this point, the above described ideologies from pan-Islamism to Eurasism interfere. The Ottoman intellectuals did not succeed in conceiving a viable solution - or rather: history moved too fast. It went slowly at first, but after the defeat at the second siege of Vienna (1683), the withdrawal became faster and faster. The national demands of the peoples sometimes conquered several centuries ago (six centuries in some regions of Greece and Bulgaria) eventually became interesting for the central regions (Greeks of the Aegean, Armenians, Kurds). Also, instead of the very general Ottoman answers (pan-Islamism, Ottomanism), more viable as well as more radical responses were finally opted for (Turk nationalism). Due to their geo-political extension and their more global character, pan-Turkism and Eurasism (expanding rapidly at present) are in an intermediary position.

Shilly-shallying between Turkism (Mustafa Kemal Atatürk) and pan-Turkism (Enver Paşa): The end of the Empire and the emergence of the republic brought about the necessity to build a nation state of the modern Western/European type. Mustafa Kemal Atatürk and Enver Paşa were not only men with entirely opposite characters but also with strongly contradicting ideas about the future of Turkey. Because of the First World War, however, their latent conflict never really broke out. Atatürk decided to resist in Anatolia and to re-found Turkey on a new basis while Enver Paşa went to Central Asia to fight the Red Army. He was convinced to play a serious political role there and to "recreate" a Turk

7 The refugees ("Muhacir" in the Ottoman and later the first republican period, "Mübadil" for the exchanged population from Greece, more recently "Göçmen", according to the official terminology of the movement) constitute a significant part of the present Turkish population. Between 1775 (from the Crimea) and 1989 (from Bulgaria), there were at least 7.5 million of refugees.

state. The option "Turkism in one sole country" led him on to pan-Turkic ideas. They have been largely used as a contribution to the creation of a national history, of a national language purified from Arab and Persian elements, a national Turkish identity, strictly controlled externally, and - as demonstrated by the case of Hüseyin Nihal Atsız[8] - resolutely fighting the vaguest attempts of political autonomization.

4. The influence of European fascism (1930-1960)

There are numerous examples of authoritarian regimes in Europe in the 1930s. As a reaction to the Soviet revolution, they all developed an openly conservative nationalist discourse sometimes mixed with revolutionary accents (following the example of the German National Socialism). Turkey cannot escape this current but refuses to be a part of it. Permanently referring to the incontestable personality of Atatürk (who died in 1938), its one-party government successfully carries out a number of basic reforms while keeping the nationalist line prevailing since 1908 with at first the Committee of Union and Progress, and then Mustafa Kemal's *Republican People's Party*. The most democratic tendencies often confront the most fascist ones (in the European sense of the term). The attraction of Germany was still strong (like in Iran, too, in those days) in spite of the cataclysmic experience of the First World War. In the 1940s, Istanbul became the hub of international espionage: The pro-Nazis tried to tie Turkey closer to Germany. But Atatürk's successor, İsmet İnönü, former liegeman of the president, remains cautious (just like Francisco Franco). Because of its declaration of war on Germany in 1945, Turkey becomes one of the founders of UN, NATO, OECD, and the Council of Europe. It also benefits from the Marshall Plan.

4.1 Hüseyin Nihal Atsız: A change of direction of Turkish nationalism (1905-1975)

Hüseyin Nihal Atsız, a fascistic intellectual, writer, poet, and Turkologist acclaimed by the extreme right but rejected by the University (1933), is a key figure for the comprehension of the extremist nationalist movements. This nationalism, however, is a major transverse element of Turkish political life.[9] His activism during the 1930s and 1940s, i. e. at the time of the rapid development of fascist ideologies including German National Socialism, his noncon-

8 Cf. Copeaux, Espace et temps de la nation turque; Bezanis, Volga-Ural Tatars in Emigration; or Bezanis, Soviet Muslim Emigrés.

9 Cf. Yerasimos/Seufert/Vorhoff (Eds.), Civil Society in the Grip of Nationalism; and Copeaux, Espace et temps de la nation turque.

formist ideas, but also the ostracism he was received with by prominent intellectuals, led to his dismissal as a teacher and a court trial charging him with racism and pan-Turanism in 1944. This made him the ideal victim, the misunderstood hero of young people at odds with authority, the uncompromising spiritual master of nationalists rebelling against the establishment.[10] He shall have an exceptional disciple, namely, Hüseyin Feyzullah, a young Cypriot officer better known as Alparslan Türkeş.

His life is rather chaotic, punctuated with expulsions and court trials, and it is marked by distinct opinions: His first expulsion from the Military Medical Academy (1925) was followed by one from the University of Istanbul (1933) where he had worked with great historians well-known for their Turkist or pan-Turkist beliefs (for example Mehmet Fuad Köprülü, Zeki Velidi Togan and Abdülkadir İnan, the latter two of Bashkirian origin). The great 1944 court trial – more than 30 defendants, among them Zeki Velidi Togan and Alparslan Türkeş charged with racism and pan-Turanism – could not stop him. Condemned to six years and six months in prison, his sentence is reduced to one and a half years, finally he is amnestied.

He launches several journals and is a prolific writer using many genres (pamphlets, poetry, novels, historical studies, articles, etc.). He has a certain influence while remaining marginal but relatively protected: Every sentence is reduced if not amnestied by military authorities or the Court of Appeal (*Yargıtay*), read: the current President of the republic. In spite of all his expulsions and sentences, he often holds public positions on a moderate level (high school or secondary high school professor or librarian), none of which stops his extreme activism. With Atsız, pan-Turkism has taken a new shape: it is limited to Turkey and becomes openly fascist, racist, and xenophobe. Turkey is the only possible sanctuary of Turkist ideas since the USSR and China have turned communist. Constructing their respective version of socialism, both of them suppress even the vaguest hint and desire of independence, i. e. of autonomy of the peoples who had been conquered by their respective imperial predecessors. Due to its special services (Amt Ausland/Abwehr des OKW), Germany succeeded in bringing three personalities to the fore who were strongly influenced by its proper methods (Alparslan Türkeş, Sadi Koçaş, Tekin Arıburnu; all three of them officers holding posts abroad). From this, the paramilitary commandoes of the Grey Wolves will emerge.

10 This idea is shared by many right-wing parties, for example the French Front National.

4.2 Hüseyin Feyzullah from Cyprus who became Alparslan Türkeş (1917-1997)

Born in Cyprus in 1917, Hüseyin Feyzullah turns into Alparslan Türkeş due to the influence of his teachers who were active supporters of pan-Turkism.[11] Being a student at the Military School of Kuleli (Istanbul) in 1933, he meets Hüseyin Nihal Atsız and contributes to the pan-Turanist journal "Orhun" (with Atsız being the editor-in-chief).[12] He becomes interested in Nazi ideas and together with 250 officer cadets receives a scholarship of nine month in Germany. He is then appointed to the rank of a colonel and participates in several missions abroad (1955-1957 at the Pentagon, School for Atomic and Nuclear Technology in Germany, then again back to Washington a liaison-officer in the position of a regimental commander). Having participated in the first coup d'état of the post-Kemalist era on May 27, 1960, he became secretary of the Prime Minister, General Cemal Gürsel, and then leaves for India as a military attaché. He begins acting his true part in civilian politics in the end of 1963 creating nationalist associations and founding his first political party, the CKMP - *Cumhuriyetçi Köylü Millet Partisi/Republican Peasants' Nation Party* whose president he became in 1965.

This is the beginning of a long political career. In 1969, the CKMP becomes the MHP - *Milliyetçi Hareket Partisi.* But all the tools exist to this very day: The Grey Wolves (*Bozkurtlar*) regroup under the name of Idealists (*Űlkücüler*). Their organization is based on models of *Hitlerjugend* and *Schutzstaffeln*. The ideological pillars are represented by the doctrine of the "nine spheres" (*dokuz ışık*): nationalism/*milliyetçilik*, idealism/*ülkücülük*, moralism/*ahlakçılık*, scientism/*ilimcilik*, "societalism"[13]/*toplumculuk*, agrarism/*köycülük*, liberalism et individualism/*hürriyetçilik ve şahsiyetçilik*, ideology of development and populism/*gelişmecilik ve halkçılık*, industrialism and mechanization/*endüstricilik ve teknikcilik*.[14] This is indeed a government program. It may seem contradictory but it recalls the six arrows (*altı ok*) of Kemalism: republicanism/*cumhuriyetçilik*, populism/*halkçılık*, nationalism/*milliyetçilik*, laicism/*laiklik*, government control/*devletçilik*, revolutionarism/*devrimcilik*. At least two of these principles are shared by CHP and MHP: nationalism and populism, but quoting Karl

11 Cf. Aslan/Bozay et al., Graue Wölfe heulen wieder, pp. 68-69.

12 Orhun/Orkhon is the river giving birth to the Selengge, which in turn is a tributary of the Siberian river Amour. At the river Orkhon, steles have been found proving the size of the first Turk Empire. In this region, the important person Gengis Khan made his appearance.

13 I hope this neologism shall be excused. The literal translation ought to have been socialism, but in Turkish, this term does not mean the same thing.

14 Cf. Aslan/Bozay, Selbstethnisierung als Barriere zur gesellschaftlichen Partizipation: Die Leitkultur der Grauen Wölfe (Bozkurt): Eine Aufklärungsschrift, Gewerkschaft Erziehung und Wissenschaft Stadtverband, 2007, pp. 159-160, available at: http://www.gew-koeln.de/02/aktuell/themen/selbstethnisierung.pdf.

Binswanger and Fethi Sipahioğlu, Kemal Bozay emphasizes[15] how it does indeed remind very much of the discourse of "Mein Kampf".[16]

5. The emergence of the MHP, a major actor on the political scene in Turkey

The MHP will undergo many changes, oscillating between highly important roles and commanding a sizeable electorate: It participates in government coalitions (from 1975–1977, with Erbakan and Feyzioğlu, in 1980 with Demirel, from 1999–2002 with Ecevit). It takes up its role of a (sometimes violent) opposition (1978–1980), at times forming a direct alliance with the military and the secret services (like MİT – *Millî İstihbarat Teşkilâtı*/National Intelligence Organization, or JİTEM – *Jandarma İstihbarat Terörle Mücadele*/Gendarmerie Intelligence and Fight against Terrorism Organization), supporting the paramilitary Kurdish organization of the Village guards (*Köy korucuları*), or – in contrast – being pursued by the military regime (after the coup d'état of September 12, 1980: Together with 600 party members, the President is brought to trial). Like all other parties, the MHP is banned. Yet, it profits most from the Turkish migrant community in Europe. This latter provides shelter for the most active party members.

The party is organized around a leader (*Başbuğ*: an old medieval central Asian title, which is historically – but rarely – attested to in Turkish historiography. Into German, it is often translated with "Führer"!).[17] Its discipline is quasi-military. The young idealists rally in training camps (in 1968: almost 100,000 in 34 sites. At the same time, the extreme left is initiated to urban guerrilla, the proletarian revolution, and rural insurgence!). Martial arts like Karate, Kung Fu, and Taek-Won-Do, the latter brought back from Korea between 1950 and 1955, are copiously taught. The teachers are often former soldiers sympathizing with or members of the party. At certain points, the secret services and indirectly – by way of Turkish services – the CIA play an important role (financing, logistics, armament, cadres).[18] The power of the party rises, at first between 1960 and 1970, and again between 1990 and 2000. After the death of its founder Alparslan Türkeş (1997), there was an evident change of practice as

15 Cf. ibid., p. 160.
16 Study of Binswanger and Sipahioğlu, 1988: Türkisch-islamische Vereine als Faktor deutsch-türkischer Koexistenz, München. We find that nowadays, the Turkish translation of Hitler's "Mein Kampf" is present in every bookstore, not only in nationalist or fascist ones after some European hesitation concerning the Turkish EU-membership. For several years, it has been a best seller!
17 "Başbuğ" is a rare title among the numerous khans ("kan, qan"), "beg","yabgu", "tegin", "shad", "tarkan", "tchor", "tutuk", "ataman" (adopted by the Cossacks) of the heroic epoch. The "çavuş" seems to have been an important person, a low sergeant of the Turkish army or, still lower, a Maghrebian legal assistant.
18 Cf. Aslan/Bozay (Eds.), Graue Wölfe heulen wieder, pp. 101–132.

well as discourse. This was due to the influence of the new "president-başbuğ" Devlet Bahçeli, an academic of Turkmen origin (in the Turkish sense of the term) whose organizing abilities are well known. But the party is also a victim of its own success and finds itself split in two: Due to the very direct influence of Turgut Őzal, a new party is formed where the Islamic affiliation plays a bigger role, namely, the *BBP - Büyük Birlik Partisi/Great Union Party* of Muhsin Yazıcıoğlu. Őzal used to be the leader of the Idealists and had thus collaborated very closely with Alparslan Türkeş!

6. Recent developments and ideological differences: MHP and BBP

The responsible persons of the coup d'état of September 12, 1980, applied the ideas of the most conservative right immediately. They shook up Turkish internal policy not only by banning all parties and imprisoning their leaders - preceding coups d'état had done the same - but because it led to a much more serious repression than the former ones, reintroduced Islam intensely (while reaffirming the principles of Atatürk and of secularism) as a defence and shield against socialism and communism. This coup attacks the foundations of the extreme right, but very ambiguously because (except for the responsible persons barred for some time) nationalist ideas or rather: the Turko-Islamic synthesis became the credo of the new regime. In 1982, this regime proposed a rather conservative constitution (contrary to that of 1963). Present-day Turkey has still not succeeded to dispose of it in spite of numerous readjustments made by the present AKP government. For the nationalist right, there are two major consequences: The return to Europe, but also to underground activities, and furthermore, the re-Islamization of the entire political landscape with a split of the MHP provoked from outside.

6.1 "Pernicious effects" of the 1980 coup d'état: "Mafia-like" machinations and re-Islamization

A great part of these machinations follow the 1980 coup d'état when a significant number of the "idealists" find themselves imprisoned with ordinary prisoners, among them some godfathers of the Turkish mafia. The "idealists" often lost their jobs or their parallel function for certain secret services of the state. These machinations are also a result of the fact that these activists live on the fringes of society. They are often in close contact with various traffickers and dealers of different objects (arms, drugs, forged documents, prostitution, and all other forms of crime). This is neither new nor original: All over the world, relations of secret services with the underworld are often ambiguous. On the other hand, it has often been written that between 1908 and 1922, the members of the organization *Osmanlı Mahsus-i Teşkilât*/Ottoman special organization of the Committee of Union and Progress (among other activities, the armed branch of the operations to eliminate the Armenians of the Empire around 1915) were often recruited in prison for the "dirty work". And since 1965 - but on the base of former services - Turkey has created the secret police branch MİT - *Millî İstihbarat Teşkilâtı*[19] whose methods closely remind of those of the Ottoman police.

One remembers the rather strange case of Mehmet Ali Ağca and especially the procrastination of the European police and judiciary in order to analyze the personality and the political ideas of the young Turkish man who had attempted to kill Pope John Paul II who retained severe after-effects of this attempt on his life. Yet, Ağca was immediately recognized by Turkish witnesses. They stated that he had been searched for the political murder of the left-wing journalist Abdi İpekçi. They claimed that he benefitted from the complicity of the police with the Grey Wolves in Turkey and in Europe (just like Abdullah Çatlı, who died much later, in 1996, in a car accident), and that he had been seen and met in Strasbourg and Paris. Like many others, Abdullah Çatlı and Alaettin Çakıcı are such shady figures. Some of them, like Abdullah Çatlı, are buried with the honors accorded to national heroes and with the responsible persons of the majority of the democratic parties being present. Their curriculum vitae is complex and can be resumed like this: young activist right-wing extremist student accused of numerous murders and acts of torture (against left activists in the late 1970s), member of the secret services against the Kurdish guerrilla (between 1980 and 2000), friend of gangsters known in the underworld and in the show business. Bozay and Mumcu name numerous cases of activists some of whom were brought to Europe for shelter (the most prominent ones), others imprisoned in Turkey where they got to know members of the "mafia". After their release, they were without a job and did not find any other means of making a living than by trafficking drugs, arms, prostitution, etc. Sometimes they were used again - by the police and the secret services in East Anatolia.[20]

The re-Islamization noted by all commentators is described in depth by Copeaux, Bora/Can as well as Bozay. It is based on the development of the *Democratic Party* of Adnan Menderes since the 1950s as well as on the measures taken by the military government since September 1980 - with the exception of Kenan Evren - favoring a "moderate Islam" as a means of defense against communism and socialism (and due to this fact very widely supported by the American administration).[21] It depends on the resuming of the increasingly open activities of the conservative Brotherhoods, *tarikat*, and "neo-tarikat" (Naqshibendi, Süleymancı, Nurcu, among them the powerful group of Feth'ul-

19 See http://www.mit.gov.tr

20 Cf. Bozay, "... Ich bin stolz, Türke zu sein!"; and Mumcu, Silah Kaçakçılığı ve Terör.

21 Cf. Copeaux, Espace et temps de la nation turque; Bora/Can, Devlet, Ocak, Dergâh; and Bozay, "... Ich bin stolz, Türke zu sein!".

lah Gülen active in Turkey, Central Asia, and among the emigrants)[22] forbidden in 1925. However, the re-Islamization was also supported by conservative intellectuals as described by Copeaux and Güvenç/Şaylan/Tekeli/Turan.[23] If the *tarikat* (brotherhoods) are definitely an expression of the classical Anatolian or Balkan Islam, the discourse of the "neo-tarikat" is a much more political one.

It is the triumph of the "Turko-Islamic synthesis" (*Türk-İslam Sentezi*) conceived and planned by the Club of Intellectuals (*Aydınlar Ocağı*). This synthesis glorifies and promotes a very nationalist and Turkic view of Islam considered to have attained its true expression with the Ottomans and the Turkic people. The Arab or Iranian contributions are reduced to insignificance or negated. Accordingly, the Turkic peoples created the most accomplished form of Islam due to their intrinsic qualities. And it is the duty of Kemalist Turkey to re-discover this authentic and ideal synthesis.

6.2 The BBP: An almost successful attempt of taking over external control

Muhsin Yazıcıoğlu (1954–2009), born in Sivas (Şarkışla), is a former person responsible of the youth organizations. He is chosen by Turgut Őzal to create a new party still considered right-wing extremist but much more influenced by Islam. The BBP – *Büyük Birlik Partisi/Great Union Party* clearly aims at the re-Islamization of the Turkish nationalist right wing. Its founder was a former responsible of the Idealist Youth, a movement very close to Alparslan Türkeş, which is shown repeatedly by photos diffused via internet. The movement splits up. But the BBP and its youth organziations (*Nizam-i Alem Teşklâtları*: the Organizations of the World Order, renamend *Alperen Ocakları*: Homestead of the Heroic Saints, the latter's connotation being clearly more religious and more Turkish while the first expression is typically ottoman) will finally be more successful in Europe than in Turkey. This is proven by elections: their results are rather disappointing. Muhsin Yazıcıoğlu died in 2009 in a helicopter accident sometimes considered to have been an assassination attempt. He was honored with a state funeral where almost all leaders of political parties – including the left ones – were present even though his role as an organizer of right-wing extremist terrorist militia is known. A poem written in prison is presented by all the media in a continuous loop. The BBP fully participates in the Turko-Islamic synthesis and – in Turkey as well as in Europe – is able to lean and rely on the Süleymancı who very discretely built many places of worship in Europe.

22 Having already founded several associations offering educational and academic support in Pantin, Paris, and Bischheim, this group has recently opened a private junior high school in Villeneuve Saint Georges.

23 Cf. Copeaux, Espace et temps de la nation turque; and Güvenç/Şaylan/Tekeli/Turan, Türk-Islam Sentezi.

6.3 Devlet Bahçeli: Organizing abilities, new style, integration into parliamentary life

Devlet Bahçeli was born in Osmaniye near Adana in 1948. He comes from an old well-to-do farming family of Turkmen origin. His father was a member of the CHP. His family is known by the traditional name of the lineage, i. e. Fettahoğulları. As a student, he already distinguishes himself by his organizing abilities and his nationalist ideas. He meets Alparslan Türkeş and founds several organizations (he is one of the founders of *Űlkü Ocakları* and of ŰMİD-Der, the university wing of the party) linked with MHP or MÇP (intermediate formation following the ban on MHP; but this new party subsequently reuses its initial name). After the death of Türkeş (1997), he is elected president of the MHP and even becomes deputy prime minister from 1999 to 2002 in an alliance with the *Social Democrat* Ecevit.

Devlet Bahçeli was an economist who had pursued his academic career at the same time being an ardent political activist. Until the last months (in the fall of 2009, following Barack Obama's trip to Turkey, the tone changes radically considering the policy of more openness towards the Kurds and Armenia) he shapes a new style. The organizations persist, but the verbal excesses are banished. The party joins the government and supports the AKP in power. Violent incidents are avoided and party members, responsible persons on the national level, as well as members of parliament are often invited to participate in TV debates.

II. Forms of nationalism existing among the immigrants in Europe

We have to admit that we know very little about Turkish right-wing extremist movements within the Turkish migrant community in Europe (in spite of its presence for more than four decades) or elsewhere (USA, Australia, Russia, Central Asia, etc.). They are often quoted and succinctly described, sometimes with some faults of appreciation or of analysis; but they do not attract - or even spurn? - research. They intrigue the journalists who already have a tendency to demonize or exaggerate the effects of the movement. The permanent feature of the latter seems to be its discretion except in exceptional cases (demonstrations for a Turkish Cyprus, against the PKK, reactions to racist crimes in Germany or to various facts touching the question of "Turkish identity").[24] The article of Antakyali (1992) or the thesis of Rigoni (2001) go further in their analyses.[25] While the Turkish situation is precisely known, the European situation would well deserve additional information or a research taking a deeper look into it.

24 Cf. Manço/Manço (Eds.), Turcs de Belgique; and Bozarslan, Une communauté et ses institutions.

25 Cf. Antakyali, La droite nationaliste; and Rigoni, Mobilisations et enjeux des migrations turques en Europe.

But still, a German researcher of Turkish origin, Kemal Bozay (with Fikret Aslan 1997, 2005), has published important works on the subject.[26]

1. Defensive nationalism of migrants

The situation in Turkey differs somewhat from that of the emigration: In Turkey, it is mostly a question of the fight against the enemy within Turkey (the Marxist Left, the minorities who are foreign agents or spies); in the emigration, Turko-Muslim identity has to be defended against acculturation, integration, or worse, assimilation. The language, the Islam (Turkish and thus not comparable to the Arab one), values (among them the authoritarian patriarchal values: father is the boss) need to be defended against the aggressions of the host society which is resented as assimilationist: Among other things, a central aim is to keep children from acculturating, *dejenere olmadan,* to save them from "degenerating". Some parents go as far as to send their children back to Turkey when the reach adolescence.[27]

These feelings of distrust of and distance from the host societies are not the privilege of the extreme right, of active members, and supporters of the MHP and the BBP. In reality, they are shared by very many immigrant groups, from the religious right wing to the left-wing laicist kemalists, including nationalist Kurds. For all of them, including the extreme right, it is therefore important to maintain good contacts with the local authorities in order to be accepted as representatives of a united and closely-knit Turkish community capable to negotiate on equal footing and to promote the values of Turkishness still unknown in the host society. Nothing disturbs them more than the Turkish-Arab hodgepodge resulting from the fact that the nuances of Islam are hardly known to the European mind. The intercultural and interreligious dialogue is systematically sought, and with a certain success, by the way: Towns and cities often play the game - but without assessing the stakes of their Turkish collaborates.

2. Europe - the extension of the Turkish political contradictions

The emigration of about seven million Turkish citizens to Europe in general and to Germany in particular is a major social fact. The actual number of emigrants is estimated around three to four million today. The difference is quite considerable and due to the return to the native country. This phenomenon is barely realized (or recognized), according to the German research office Isoplan.[28]

26 Cf. Aslan/Bozay, Graue Wölfe heulen wieder; or Bozay, "... Ich bin stolz, Türke zu sein!".
27 Cf. Establet, Comment peut-on être français?
28 On December 31, 1999, Germany alone had registered 3,528,850 entries and 2,334,261 exits of Turks returning to their home country between 1960 and 1999. At

Migration itself has been studied extensively. There are several thousands of reference works in every language (Turkish, German, English, French, Dutch, etc.). This emigration started in the years 1950 to 1960 and constituted a wide specter of migration. It largely resulted from economic imbalance and political crises. Every coup d'état (1960, 1970, 1980) resulted in the departure of opponents generally from the left and/or minorities like Kurds and Alevi. However, this departure was also - and this is less known - an exit gate for the young *ülkücü* members and the most exposed leaders of the organization when the MHP was banned like all other parties. One can speak of the sanctuarization of the Turkish migrant community facing the military and police repression.[29]

2.1 The MHP, its establishment and organization: discreet but efficient

Since 1978, the MHP has been represented by the federation called *ADŰTDF-Avrupa Demokratik Űlkücü Türk Dernekleri Federasyonu* (Föderation der Türkisch-Demokratischen Idealisten in Europa) in Germany and later in almost all European countries with Turkish immigration (Switzerland, Austria, France, the Netherlands, Belgium). Like in Turkey, local associations can create women or youth groups whose names are often neutral (German-Turkish/French-Turkish Society etc. - which does not at all mean that every group with this name is connected with the MHP). By and large, its activities are known: In 1980, it had about 26,000 members in 110 associations. 2,800 members live in North Rhine-Westphalia, the German region where the Turkish population is the largest (1992) and where 7,000 Turks participated in a Congress on Mai 22, 1993.[30]

Of up to 220 associations counted, 170 were in Germany alone. Bozay/Aslan refer to the fact that during the first years, the CSU had close and friendly connections with the MHP, which was epitomized by Alparslan Türkeş and Franz Josef Strauss. But the character of these ties was not exclusive: parties like NPD (*Nationaldemokratische Partei Deutschlands - National Democratic Party of Germany*), DVU (*Deutsche Volksunion - German People's Union*) and FAP (*Freiheitliche Deutsche Arbeiterpartei - Free German Workers' Party*) were also approached.[31] This shows the logical framework of the extreme right, which is

the same time, 2,053,564 Turkish immigrants are living in Germany according to the data raised on "Ausländer in Deutschland", electronic journal of Isoplan: 45 Jahre Arbeitsmigration nach Deutschland, available at http://www.isoplan.de/aid/2000-4.

29 Cf. Rigoni, Mobilisations et enjeux des migrations; and Bora/Can, Devlet, Ocak, Dergâh; and Bora/Can, Devlet ve Kuzgun; Cf. also Aslan/Bozay, Graue Wölfe heulen wieder; and Bozay, "... Ich bin stolz, Türke zu sein!".

30 NRW-Ministerium für Arbeit, Gesundheit und Soziales des Landes Nordrhein-Westfalen, Zentrum für Türkeistudien (Ed.): Türkische Muslime in Nordrhein-Westfalen, pp. 106-107.

31 Cf. Aslan/Bozay, Graue Wölfe heulen wieder, pp. 175-197; and Bozay, "... Ich bin stolz, Türke zu sein!".

able to organize violent racist and anti-immigrant demonstrations while at the same time having the best possible relationships with its "colleagues" who share the same values. Associations with this frame of thought may receive material, moral, or political support from heads of enterprises, and even from consulates, not to talk about Turkish secret services. Aslan/Bozay give numerous details about these complex multilateral relationships that are not necessarily clandestine. Especially in Germany, Austria, and the Netherlands, the congresses of the Federation have often been visited by diplomats working in the Consulates and Embassies.

In France, the logic of "integration" collides with Turkish concepts of allegiance to both nation and state, and the concepts of the affiliation with Islam and Turkishness. The Anglo-Saxon conception of the state is shared by countries like Germany, Austria, Switzerland, Great Britain, the Netherlands, and Flanders. It enables the Turkish nationalist or Islamo-nationalist right to develop its action and its theses within a population that is receptive because of its relative marginalization and the attacks of a certain xenophobic - here: turkophobic - fringe of the population and of the elites. The myths and the representation of the grey wolf guiding the tribe westward, the triumphant nomad riders, the Ottoman Empire at its height - victorious of all the Christian kingdoms - these are all refuges enabling the affirmation of a neglected grandeur that only needs to express itself. Newspapers, journals, and websites abundantly express it: Turkey is a great power getting back on its feet, by any means, and it will take its place again facing the Europeans. This quasi credo is permanently reinforced by the procrastination and reluctance of the EU concerning the membership of Turkey. A rising number of Turks, intellectuals as well as poorly educated ones, from the Islamist or nationalist right wing to the Kemalist secular left, threaten Europe with the worst disappointment because this Europe is completely incapable of recognizing Turkish "values". The withdrawal of the community is not a simple unilateral fact.

2.2 The BBP, split and grass-root re-Islamization

The UACTI-Union des Associations Culturelles Turco-Islamiques (Union of cultural Turko-Islamic associations), 90 associations with 1,500 members and 2,500 sympathizers in 1991, was established in Belgium at Brussels, Liège, Charleroi, Anvers, Gand, and Limbourg. It is described as a new formation of the Turkish nationalist right in the emigration.[32] A little later, it is mentioned in Germany. There, the *ATİB-Avrupa Türk İslam Birliği/TİKDB-Avrupa Türk İslam Kültür Dernekleri Birliği* (Türkisch-Islamische Union in Europa/Union der türkisch-islamischen Kulturvereine in Europa) emerges with its president Musa Serdar Çelebi, a former MHP representative in Europe. In 1992, it counts

32 Cf. Manço/Manço (Eds.), Turcs de Belgique, pp. 257-261, Table VI 268-270.

11,000 members and 110 associations.[33] Muhsin Yazıcıoğlu had decided to split. He is a former very close collaborator of Alparslan Türkeş. Considering the results of the local and national elections, the split party will be more successful in Europe than in Turkey. The split seems to have been provoked by Turgut Őzal, following the logic of control of the Turkish society by the Turko-Islamic synthesis largely supported by the American and Turkish secret services at the time when the Islam seemed to be the best possible stronghold against communism. We know the sequel (Iran, Afghanistan, Pakistan, and Turkey). Each of these countries has its own history and its own special logic. The only thing left to do is the re-Islamization from the bottom starting at school and with the education of children and women. Fifteen years later, this process is quite advanced. Due to the authority of Muhsin Yazıcıoğlu, whose organizational talents were known, by the way, Europe witnessed the (extremely discreet) appearance of the *Nizam-i Alêm Teşkilâtları* (Organizations of the World Order) nowadays changed to *Alperen Ocakları* (Homes of the Heroes) modeled after the *Űlkü Ocakları*.

2.3 Kemalism in emigration: When the inevitable personality of Atatürk is reclaimed by everybody and for everything

In spite of more and more direct criticism, especially by the Islamic milieus and by militant Kurds, and sometimes by the revolutionary extreme left, the personality of Atatürk, sometimes named the Great Leader (*Ulu Őnder*) remains indispensable and sacred. The major problem is that Atatürk (his life, his work) serves more and more to justify everything and its opposite as well - from the membership of the European Union to Eurasism, from the greatness of Turkish Islam to the defense of secularism, passing by pan-Turkism and the Turko-Islamic synthesis. To counter the rise to power of Muslim and Islamist Movements, associations of defense of the thought of Atatürk (*Atatürk Düşünce Derneği*)[34] have frequently been founded and organized in federations in Turkey and in Europe. In Europe, these associations generally seem - even if they organize demonstrations in the countries of Turkish immigration in order to popularize the historical and political personality of the founder of the republic - to lead a rather defensive dialogue internally. It is very nationalist (Turkey, Secular, one and indivisible) and has hardly any impact outside of its milieu. The lack of clarity is thus linked with diverging discourses with a nationalist connotation colliding with the European demands of integration.

33 NRW-Ministerium für Arbeit, Gesundheit und Soziales des Landes Nordrhein-Westfalen, Zentrum für Türkeistudien (Ed.): Türkische Muslime in Nordrhein-Westfalen, pp. 108-110.
34 http://www.add.org.tr.

3. Europe - sanctuary of the extreme right and basis of the recapturing of Turkey

As mentioned above, in the 1980s, Europe became the refuge of the opponents of the regime established by a military coup d'état on September 12, 1980. Several dozens of thousands of Turkish citizens tried to obtain the status of a refugee in the principal receiving countries of the Turkish emigration: Germany, France, the Netherlands, Switzerland, Belgium, and Sweden. The movement is ambiguous for several reasons: 1.) The immigration of workers is suspended between 1973 and 1974. The request for political asylum is one of the only open doors (The marriage of the following generations of immigrants will become important later). 2.) The authorities responsible for matters concerning the right of asylum are often overburdened, or quite incompetent.[35] 3.) The influx of asylum-seekers is extremely varied. They include militants of the extreme left and of the left (among them trade unionists, journalists, students, and teachers), members of minorities stigmatized by the Anatolian power (Kurds and Alevis) or simply non-Muslim minorities (Christians from South-East Anatolia; they shall later be double-locked between PKK and security forces), but also members of the extreme right (who generally pretend to be left wing militants suppressed by the police - which often supplied useful papers like true false certificates of torture!).[36]

3.1 When Grey Wolves disguise as communist victims: True refugees and New Mafiosi

Aslan/Bozay precisely describe how all of Europe turns into a sanctuary not only for the left and Islamist opposition groups, but also for the members of the MHP forbidden by the military junta and its numerous subsidiaries.[37] They list numerous facts and names of persons known in Turkey (facts reported by the press). Bora/Can also mention it but without giving a very detailed account of where their analysis of Turkey is centered.[38] The illegal MHP withdraws into the

35 As a student of the Turkish language, the author was often called to accompany asylum seekers to different places (associations, lawyers' offices, prefecture, police stations, enterprises, hospitals, etc.) to fill in forms or translate. The same happened with the associations of Turkish workers at Strasbourg in the frame of regularizations like in 1980. This was an excellent observation post for a master thesis in human sciences (geography).

36 And by experience, the author can testify that "it works"! Meetings with "idealist" members, by chance or professionally, as the representative of the regional delegation of the Fonds d'Action Sociale (Social Action Funds), at evaluations of the linguistic or professional training - another excellent observation post.

37 Cf. Aslan/Bozay, Graue Wölfe heulen wieder, pp. 133-142; and Bozay, "... Ich bin stolz, Türke zu sein!", pp. 176-210.

38 Cf. Bora/Can, Devlet, Ocak, Dergâh, pp. 410-416 among the division of the movement in Europe; and Bora/Can, Devlet ve Kuzgun, pp. 247-248.

German cities, into affiliated associations in order to shelter certain members watched or searched for by the police and justice. Later, the MHP recomposes itself at first using the acronym MP - *Muhafazakar Parti* (*Conservative Party*, 1983-1985), then MÇP - *Milliyetçi Çalışma Partisi* (*Nationalist Workers' Party*, 1985-1993), and finally resuming its original name in 1993. Emigration, by the accumulation of earned incomes and savings, is also a source of considerable financing escaping every administrative, fiscal, or legal Turkish control.

Like in Turkey, we witness the reconciliation of these activists who are used to certain violence - among them several who are wanted for murder, torture, or terrorist attacks - and the godfathers of the Turkish "mafia". Trafficking of weapons and drugs, contract killing sometimes for political reasons, sometimes for financial gain, as well as aggressive and violent intimidations are common practice of both groups. They find common interests but may also find themselves exploited by the local authorities.[39] The studies quoted above show every time how the migrant community can be integrated as space-resource literally as well as figuratively, as a source of financing and of refuge in case of problems in Turkey. Evidently, relationships between the European and Turkish police forces do exist even if it were only through the intermediary of Interpol. But sometimes they are difficult and charged with ambiguities because national interests do not always tally (fight against terrorism, trafficking, corruption, illegal immigration, etc.). Without considering these facts, it is difficult to understand how Mehmet Ali Ağca, Abdullah Çatlı (also involved in the assassination attempt on John-Paul II), Alaettin Çakıcı, Oral Çelik (involved in the murder of the journalist Abdi İpekçi), to name only the best-known agents, should have been able to move with faked identities without too many problems in Europe before taking up again their activities in Turkey at "security services" connected to the State in the fight against the PKK.

3.2 Discreet presence, abounding activity, open partnership

Turkish nationalism in Europe is most certainly more directed at internal usage than for proselyte purposes. It is a defensive nationalism which is particularly aggressive when it attacks those considered deviators or traitors of Turkishness but very respectful towards form and (interreligious, intercultural) dialogue with foreigners. This is a permanent feature to be observed at Islamic groups as well as at kemalist secularists or Alevi associations. The cleavages are often more artificial than it seems. Terms and methods of collaboration of groups considered political enemies do exist within the large right-wing family more than within that of the left-wing. It often depends on the moment and the circumstances of observation and can develop in relation to events in Turkey, above

39 Cf. Bora/Can, Devlet, Ocak, Dergâh, pp. 377-406; cf. also Mumcu, Silah Kaçakçılığı ve Terör.

all. Bozay even gives the postal addresses of associations linked to MHP and BBP in Germany and Belgium, and their names only in the Netherlands.[40] Except for those who clearly mention "idealist", they often call themselves Turkish Cultural Association, German-Turkish Association, or United Families and their activities stress young people and sports, very often Taek-Won-Do, a souvenir brought back from Korea (after the Turkish participation in the Korean War 1950-1953).

3.3 Is pan-Turkism exportable?

At different degrees, "idealism" is quite present in the Turkish migrant community. It largely depends on the massiveness and the concentration of the Turkish presence (Germany, the Netherlands) or on the existence of specific migrant networks, natives of rural or urban zones, which are strongholds of the MHP and BBP parties in Turkey (Yozgat, Sivas, the districts Emirdağ, Korgan-Kumru, etc.). In Europe, though, this ideology remains discreet, for internal use much more than for proselytizing. And if it is able to find common points with ideologies of the same family, these relationships are factual and episodic, except in high places. Just the contrary, the idealist members more often try to establish personal relationships with town and city authorities first of all, whether they are right or left. In Central Asia, the Balkans, and in Caucasia, the situation is entirely different.[41]

In a recent article (2009), Fahri Türk illuminates the recent diffusion of pan-Turkist ideas in the Turkophone area.[42] There, a certain Turkish expansionism has met with the local renaissance of pan-Turkist ideas nipped in the bud by the Stalinist regime. Here, just like in the early twentieth century, pan-Turkism is also linked with the awareness of intellectuals protesting against the Soviet power: poets (like the Uzbek Muhammed Salih or the Kazak Olcas Süleymanov), writers (indirectly the Kyrgyz Chingiz Aitmatov), historians (like the Azerbaijani Aliyev renamed Elçibey, who became President of the Republic of Azerbaijan, reminding, by the way, of the case of the Lithuanian Vitautas Landsbergis), linguists, etc.[43] find themselves at the head of the anti-Soviet protest at first, and of the opposition movement since 1992. The author lists, describes, and analyzes the parties *Müsavat* (*Equality*), *Bozkurt* (*Grey Wolf*),

40 Bozay, "... Ich bin stolz, Türke zu sein!", 2005, pp. 242-246.
41 Cf. Bora/Can, Devlet, Ocak, Dergâh, pp. 495-539.
42 Cf. Türk, Azerbaycan ve Orta Asya.
43 This democratic reform discourse, which was anti-Soviet at the very least, was often led by intellectuals. The historian Vitautas Landsbergis in Lithuania, first President after independence, reminds of Bronislaw Geremek, the Polish historian who joined Solidarnosc and later became minister, or of Abulfez Aliyev, renamed Elçibey, the first President of Azerbaijan. Central Asia and the Caucasus have encountered the same phenomena. Sometimes, there is only a short way from the protest against the USSR to nationalism.

Turan in Azerbaijan, *Alaş, Azat* (*Free*), *Republican Party of Kazakhstan, Birlik* (*Unity*), *Erk* (*Liberty*), *Vatan Terakki* (*Homeland and Progress*), *People's Party of Turkestan* an *Islamic People's Party of Turkestan* in Uzbekistan.

On the one hand, names of the 1920s reappear; on the other hand, Turkish names are adopted. The detailed lecture of this article would lead too far. We shall sum it up simply by stating that pan-Turkism is carefully kept at a distance, forcibly suppressed as soon as it grows in size by the present leaders who play, just like Atatürk in his days, the card of a shady nationalism confined to the national borders inherited from the USSR, without irredentism in spite of the existence of minorities outside the borders. Furthermore, the "repatriation" of the "brothers" in foreign countries (*Haric'dagi O'zbekler*), or of the members of the Diaspora (*oralmandar* for the Kazaks) is organized. We also retain that Turkish nationalists are often present, in Azerbaijan more than elsewhere. However, in reality their influence remains weak, on the one hand because their discourse is not adapted to the local situation and on the other hand because the governments and leaders of the republics are especially watchful and jealous of their prerogatives.

III. Conclusion

The small world of the Grey Wolves, as they are often called, referring to one of their emblems, remains impenetrable, mysterious, and disquieting. However, we think it is not that dangerous for the European civil and political societies. It organizes itself like societies in Diaspora seeking institutional contacts while limiting interpersonal exchange with the local populations at the same time. In a certain way it reproduces the Turko-Ottoman model of cohabitation between *millet* (ethno-confessional communities recognized by the Ottoman Empire) but under different circumstances: Here, it is the minority and cannot play the decisive role in politics.

There is a difference between political relations within the community and between ethnic groups. There, the jealous defense of the Turkish cultural and political identity adapts very poorly to "competition" like that of the Armenian Diaspora demanding the admission of the genocide and the condemnation of the Turkish state, or of the emerging Kurd Diaspora demanding an autonomous Kurdistan for want of being independent, or of the emergence of an Assyro-Chaldean (Christian orthodox) discussion, which also more and more often speaks of the admission of the 1915 genocide. The position towards the Alevis is clearly more subtle. Quite often, Alevi *dede*s are invited to *kurultay* at Erciyes. The Turkism of the nomad (thus Central Asian) origins of the Turkmen Alevism are emphasized. In fact, the positions of certain Alevi circles are just as nationalist and Turkic. The left and the extreme left remain the enemies to be fought even though the points of view of these latter actually seem at least quite colorless, if not totally outdated. The members of the extreme right participated in violent demonstrations (mostly in Germany and Belgium), sometimes assassinated opponents (Armenian members of ASALA, militant Kurds, members of the extreme left). In the wake of the relative re-Islamization of the members due to the split of MHP and BBP, and with the leadership of Devlet Bahçeli, the MHP starts a re-conversion which also touches the migrant community: One rather tries to become the recognized spokesperson at the intercultural and interreligious dialogue while at the same time focusing on transmitting Turkish values to the children of the immigration and on the defense of Turkishness suffering from the European assimilationism.

The BBP functions exactly along the same lines under the general leadership of Muhsin Yazıcıoğlu and Musa Serdar Çelebi, both of them former MHP cadres. But the position on re-Islamization, of the synthesis between Turkishness and Islam plays a much more important role. Some "idealists" even claim to represent their pre-Islamic Turkish roots, sometimes even rejecting Islam as an imported religion - and therefore not a Turkish one. *Űlkü Ocakları* is nowadays answered by the *Alperen Ocakları*, which are both brothers and competitors at the same time.

III.
Cultural Trends and Political Ideas

Globalized Anti-Globalists - The Ideological Basis of the Internationalization of Right-Wing Extremism

Thomas Grumke

I. International nationalists or nationalist international?

Ultranationalism - e.g. if in the construction of national belonging specific ethnic, cultural or religious criteria of exclusion are reinforced, condensed to collective ideas of homogeneity and linked with authoritarian political models - doubtlessly is one of the ideological characteristics of right-wing extremism. This could lead to the conclusion that right-wing extremists for this reason do not tend to cooperate on a long-term basis with right-wing extremists from other countries. Especially in the 21st century that is absolutely incorrect. On the contrary, more extensive international and transnational networking is taking place on the extreme right, which is more and more interlinked organizationally and ideologically.

The conditions of context for right-wing extremists are favorable in the era of globalization. That globalization aids and abets the evolution and spread of right-wing extremism has been shown.[1] Globalization processes simply frighten many people: "Thus the fear of the seemingly unmanageable is transformed into fear of something that is not quite as hopeless to fight against, in fear of crime, the antisocial, of minorities and the like, or - what amounts to often the same - a structure is seen behind the threat".[2] The processes and impositions of globalization act as humus of right-wing extremism nationally and internationally.

The recent electoral success of the right-wing extremist *Jobbik* party in Hungary may be seen as proof of the above said. In a message of greetings, the NPD leader Udo Voigt wrote on April 11, 2010: "Ideologically, there is much agreement between our countries and our two parties. [...] The Hungarian people begins on this day to defend itself effectively against the sell-out, the exploitation by globalization, imperialism and against the 'American Way of Life' with

1 See Stöss, Globalisierung und rechtsextreme Einstellungen; Grumke, Die transnationale Infrastruktur.

2 Welzk, Globalisierung und Neofaschismus, p. 38. This and the following translations of quotes are all mine, T. G.

the planned multi-cultural fusion with strangers. [...] We stand by your side! For a free Hungary, Germany and Europe!”.[3]

Hereby the central themes of contemporary right-wing extremism and even the central ideological foundation for their international cooperation are mentioned. Right-wing extremists have established their own definitions and thoughts, which will be briefly presented below in order to increase the basis for understanding the international networking of the scene. Structure follows ideology. In other words: it can not be assumed, that right-wing extremists from different countries cooperate or organize meetings and then start investigating what their common goals and ideas would be. On the contrary, there will typically be - unless there are e. g. economic interests involved - cooperation only because of ideological consensus and/or common political goals.

II. The ideology of international right-wing extremism

1. Pan-Aryan Weltanschauung

Michael Kühnen, who like no other has influenced the German extreme right, coined the phrase: “The system does not have flaws, it is the flaw” as well as the demand for the “fight against foreign infiltration”,[4] the volkish motivated “fight against environmental destruction” and for a “cultural revolution against Americanism”.[5] Here, in the mid-1980s Kühnen already formulated what are today central elements of internationally active right-wing extremists.

In his greetings for the book “Alles Große steht im Sturm” (roughly meaning: “All great things are exposed to strong resistance”), published for the 35th anniversary of the NPD and the 30th anniversary of Junge Nationaldemokraten (JN), the founder and then leader of the West Virginia based National Alliance, Dr. William L. Pierce,[6] set forth his ideological parameters for international cooperation: “Nationalists in Germany, in Europe and also in America are facing the common enemy of all people, the international monopoly capital that wants to deal the death blow to all historically grown nations in favor of a multicultural ‘melting pot’. Our fight against the attempts for world domination and economic imperialism by multinational corporations will be hard and full of privations – but the goal of Volksgemeinschaft - finding back to its roots -will be worth to take on this hard fight and all troubles that come with it”.[7]

3 “NPD freut sich über den Wahlerfolg der Jobbik-Partei”, press release of the NPD of 11 April 2010, available at: http://www.npd.de/html/714/artikel/detail/1228, last accessed 14 April 2010.
4 The original phrase is “Kampf gegen die Überfremdung” which is to be understood both in a cultural and in a biological/racial sense.
5 Kühnen, Lexikon der Neuen Front (1987), available at: http://www.nazi-lauck-nsdap-ao.com, last accessed 10 May 2003.
6 William Pierce died from cancer at the age of 68 on July 23, 2002.
7 In: Apfel (Ed.), Alles Große steht im Sturm, p. 23.

This statement, which can be seen as paradigmatic for internationally active right-wing extremists, shows clearly, that the "fight" is no longer just for the defense of one's nation from outside enemies, but for more. Crucial internationally operating activists like Pierce define nationality not by citizenship or geography, but by race. Worth defending and protecting is not the nation as such, but rather the seriously endangered "white race" (endangered by "infiltration" and "race-mixing"), which is under massive attack in their ancestral nations by the "international capital" that has no traditions, history nor scruples. Openly or thinly veiled, this "international capital" is portrayed as Jewish dominated. The result is a hard to digest brew of long existing anti-Semitic or volkish theories and argumentations as well as alternative ingredients like "international (racial) solidarity", "anti-imperialism" and "foreigners out".

The result is a so-called pan-Aryan Weltanschauung, which - not any more slavophobic like Hitlerian NS-ideology - explicitly includes Eastern Europe and Russia as a part of the "white world". Only with this in mind it can be understood, when World War II is described as a "fratricidal disaster".[8] David Duke even puts his hopes on Russia in preventing what he calls the "relentless and systematic destruction of the European genotype" because "our race faces a world-wide genetic catastrophe. There is only one word that can describe it: genocide".[9]

To repeat: internationally cooperating right-wing extremists are not flag-waving patriots, but markedly fundamental enemies of pluralism, free democracy and all its representatives. The idea of ZOG (= Zionist Occupied Government) meanwhile dominates the right-wing extremist discourse and is universally accepted as the description of what is seen as puppet governments of global (Jewish dominated) financial interests in Europe and North America. Principal goal is the preservation (or purity) of the "white race", which consequentially results in the total rejection of any form of immigration, understood as "foreign infiltration" in a racial and cultural sense.

This falls into line with a virulent anti-Americanism, which indeed has to be described more accurately as anti-"American system" though. The influence of American based investment and media firms including "Wall Street" is criticized as imperialistic and degenerating for the race and all nations.

Anti-Semitism acts as the vital, internationally compatible ideological glue. The word Jew does not even have to be mentioned openly, right-wing extremists from both sides of the Atlantic know exactly whom the "One Worlders" are and what "New World Order" or "East Coast" mean. This ideology is transported through internationally recognized and established codes, symbols and writings. This includes among other things the "14 words" of American right-wing terrorist David Lane ("We must secure the existence of our people and a

8 Ibid.

9 Duke, Is Russia the Key to White Survival?, available at: www.davidduke.com, last accessed 20 April 2010.

future for White children") or William Pierce's "Turner Diaries" (published under the pseudonym Andrew McDonald) from 1978, about which the author gloated after a trip through Europe: "*Every* nationalist in Europe has heard about 'The Turner Diaries'".[10] The book has been translated into many languages and is available now in German under the title "Die Turner Tagebücher", translated by "German enthusiasts".[11]

In this novel, which has rightfully been called a right-wing extremist bible, the "Aryan revolution" starts out with a bomb attack on FBI headquarters and climaxes in the so-called "Day of the Rope", on which tenth of thousands are hanged by the street sides with signs around their necks saying "I betrayed my race". After a nuclear civil war and a "mopping-up period" (i. e. the killing of all "non-whites"), the entire world at the end of the novel is "Aryan". It is designative that violence is portrayed here more as the cure than as the malady and deliberately promoted and defended. This all-out positive position on political violence - as the only solution to the problem of what is seen as fundamental oppression of the "Aryan race" by ZOG - is inherent in a growing number of internationally active right-wing extremists. Violence is regarded though as no less than the forced last resource in the fight for survival.

"In this fight, every opponent of today's America is objectively our ally, even if tomorrow he will become our enemy", writes the extremist Swiss veteran Gaston Armand Amaudruz in his preface to the NPD-volume "Alles Große steht im Sturm".[12] The former chairman of the *British National Party* (BNP), John Tyndall, writes in his preface in the name of his party: "The same enemies, the same political and social problems, the same method of resolution for these problems and definitely also a common future. All this interconnects the nationalist parties of Europe".[13]

The above mentioned central ideological elements pan-Aryan racism, anti-Semitism and (revolutionary) enmity towards the system in a political, cultural, social and economic sense lead a growing number of top right-wing extremists to the conclusion: "Cooperation across borders will become increasingly important for progress - and perhaps survival - in the future".[14]

2. Anti-globalism

Globalization is a central theme of propaganda and agitation for right-wing extremists world wide. In addition, extreme right critics of globalization intertwine social and cultural issues and in turn ethnicize them. Their counter is a

10 "Report from Greece". In: National Alliance Bulletin, (1998) 11, p. 12.
11 "Die Turner Tagebücher in Print". In: National Alliance Bulletin, (1998) 12, p. 1.
12 Amaudruz, Preface, p. 15.
13 Ibid., p. 22.
14 "Report from Greece". In: National Alliance Bulletin, (1998) 11, p. 10.

re-nationalized, racial order - no less than the reconstruction of an ethnically defined national volkish community.

At this point, definitions from the "Little Dictionary of basic political concepts",[15] which is widely circulated among right-wing extremists, are used as examples. Under the entry "globalization", we read, "Globalization is the tendency of international capitalism, if possible to create uniform conditions for profit-enhancing production of labor forces, exploitation of raw materials and the monopolistic marketing of goods". This development has "caused the destruction of independent regional and national life and business forms".[16] In turn, "internationalism" is seen as "the counterpart of nationalism". It is the attempt to "dominate the world's peoples, their economy and their traditional ways of life, to transform and exploit them for profit's sake".[17] Globalization, as right-wing extremists understand it, therefore is an instrument of domination of all nations with the goal to destroy their idiosyncrasies and autonomy in the name of profit. The U.S., regarded as a center of globalization, is considered a significant risk as "internationalism and globalization, and the imperialism of the western 'values' in the wake of the U.S. threaten the sovereignty of nations to a great extent".[18]

To that extent, the process of globalization from an extreme right point of view threatens not only the national economy, but - more importantly - the national culture, identity, and tradition for the worst. MTV, McDonald's and other "American pabulum" consumed by young people in the right-wing extremist thinking are instruments of a carefully planned controlled culture destroying internationalist "globalism". This, in turn, is the opposite of the desired drive for self-sufficiency.[19] In contemporary right-wing extremism, the term "globalism" plays a central role and in this context most frequently stands for the power of ahistorical and faceless big business, for "American cultural imperialism" and a "multi-racial genocide", allegedly sought "from Washington, Wall Street and Hollywood". According to that ideology, there is a kind of monopoly in the U.S., particularly on the east coast (as a synonym for a Jewish hegemony).

By the initiated "inundation policy" Germany is supposed to be weakened, and with the constant reference to the crimes of the past, demoralized and humiliated. In terms of concepts and content, one has to distinguish between the process of globalization and "globalism". In the tract "12 Theses on Globalism" created by the Nationaldemokratischer Hochschulbund (NHB), the Student Association of the NPD, which is widely circulated in the right-wing movement, the differentiation is clear: "globalization is the process used by the globalists to achieve their goals". More specifically: "The migration flows delib-

15 This and the following quotes: Deutsche Stimme-Verlag (Ed.), Taschenkalender des Nationalen Widerstandes 2006, available at: http://www.ds-versand.de.
16 Ibid., entry "Globalisierung".
17 Ibid., entry "Internationalismus".
18 Ibid., entry "Souveränität".
19 Ibid., entry "Autarkie".

erately caused by the globalists lead to the uniformity of the markets, their products and their communication as well as to the destruction of grown languages and cultures".[20]

Right-wing extremists thus see the process of globalization as a deliberately controlled destruction of cultures, traditions and values (and, ultimately, of nations and peoples) by the above-described powerful "globalists". In internationally understood right-wing extremist codes "globalists" are also "East Coast", "globalism" is also "New World Order" (NWO), and governments and elites involved in this "globalization plan" are the "Zionist Occupied Government" (ZOG). ZOG, it is firmly believed, is a hidden Jewish world conspiracy, in which all the democratic governments, banks, media and many others are secretly controlled by Jews and must be fought at all costs. And against such a powerful enemy, "white patriots" can only be fighting together!

Another bogey is the "One World" (or "New World Order"), which in the "Little Dictionary of basic political concepts"[21] is called a "delusion", that is "fed by the belief in a homogeneous humanity without ties and traditions". In this context, two more enemy provisions are made, the United Nations and human rights: "the tool of imperialism to create the 'One World' is the 'United Nations'. The ideological limed twig on the global enforcement of the 'Western values' are 'human rights'".[22]

According to right-wing extremist logic, "the individual stands above a specific group in the name of human rights, selfish self-interests trump the alleged interests of the ethnic community".[23] "The need of the hour", says Karl Richter, since 2009 Deputy NPD national chairman and member of the Council of the City of Munich, "is a sustained and resolute stand against everything that is currently praised by the big brothers: globalization, human rights, multiculturalism, the liberalization and atomization of all areas of life".[24]

Who these "big brothers" are remains unclear, of course. Much more informative on this are the submissions in the NPD brochure "Arguments for candidates and officials. A handout for the public debate", in which the question "Why does the NPD so strongly reject globalization?" is answered as follows: "Globalization is the planetary spread of the capitalist economic system under the leadership of the Great Money. This has, despite by its very nature being Jewish-nomadic and homeless, its politically and militarily protected location mainly on the East Coast of the United States".[25] Moreover it says in the

20 Nationaler Hochschulbund, 12 Thesen zum Globalismus, available at: http://www.npd-goettingen.de/Weltanschauung/12_Thesen_zum_Globalismus.html, last accessed on 21 April 2010.
21 This and the following quotes: Deutsche Stimme-Verlag (Ed.), Taschenkalender des Nationalen Widerstandes 2006, Riesa, n. pag.; available at: http://www.ds-versand.de.
22 Ibid., entry "Eine Welt".
23 See Pfahl-Traughber, Globalisierung als Agitationsthema, p. 41.
24 Richter, Der Chaoskanzler, p. 1.
25 NPD, Argumente für Kandidaten, p. 19.

brochure: "Encouraged by modern communication technologies and mass media, cultural Americanization attacks the organically grown identities of peoples and is working on a consumerist and uniformed people".[26]

Globalization - in a right-wing extremist context - in sum stands for the power of international big business, for American cultural imperialism and for a "multi-racial genocide" or a "race destroying debris field", sought by "Washington, Wall Street and Hollywood", as the chairman of the *British National Party* (BNP), the MEP Nick Griffin, put it in an interview with the NPD paper "Deutsche Stimme" in 2002.[27]

III. The network of international right-wing extremism

In the 21st century, a transnational network of right-wing extremists is being formed, which is supported by a collective identity and an internationally compatible ideology. The collective identity is that of a white man a) in the sense of ethnicity and b) in terms of cultural belonging to a decidedly Western culture. The compatible ideological elements are the re-nationalization and re-ethicizing of politics and the volkish opposition to a parliamentary-democratic system.[28]

If right-wing extremists want to be more than the sum of national rallying points of protest against social change, progressive discourse and multiculturalism, if they really want to achieve their fundamental objectives politically, then they must also think and act globally and appear as a transnational actor. Richard Stöss rightfully notes, "The degree of interconnection of national right-wing extremists, the question in particular, whether they manage to overcome national and international conflicts, can be an important indicator of political viability, and thus the potential threat right-wing extremists actually pose".[29] Although often at odds in their own countries, at least on an ideological level something like a transnational extreme right has evolved - more to the point: an international of nationalists. Agreeing on a common enemy, a more and more defined infrastructure with regular events, fixed communication platforms and a lively exchange of goods and ideas has developed over recent years.

The ideological foundation for a transnational cooperation of the extreme right is laid. Irrespective of the different context structures, mobilization and agitation strengths of each national right-wing scene, cross-border networking of the extreme right even reached the European Parliament years ago. On November 17, 2004, the NPD chairperson Udo Voigt visited the European Parliament in Strasbourg on invitation of then-MEP Alessandra Mussolini. It also came to other meetings and informal discussions with the Chairman of the

26 Ibid.
27 Freiheitsrechte der Völker zurückfordern: Interview mit Nick Griffin. In: Deutsche Stimme, March 2002, p. 3.
28 See above; or in greater detail: Grumke, Die transnationale Infrastruktur.
29 Stöss, Zur Vernetzung der extremen Rechten, p. 2.

National Front, Jean Marie Le Pen, *Forza Nuova* and the *Lega Nord*.[30] In a press statement to these meetings apart from the usual leitmotifs, the strict rejection of EU membership of Turkey and the summoning of an international solidarity of the nationalists were included: "In the political struggle against alienation, globalization and the mitigation of the American economic imperialism, it was agreed, as in the rejection of an accession of Turkey to the EU. After intensive discussions, we came to an agreement to cooperate more intensively in particular in Europe in the future. The MEP Alessandra Mussolini assured the party leader of the NPD her support for national German concerns in the European Parliament".[31]

What still seemed the exception at that time is now the rule. It belongs to normality today that regular right-wing dates as the "Rudolf Hess Memorial", May 1 ("Labor Day") or the commemoration of the bombing of Dresden take place with massive international participation. With the same matter of course, German right-wing extremists take part in events, demonstrations and concerts of their "comrades" abroad.

Today, all right-wing extremists in Western industrialized countries are facing almost identical challenges. The enemy is not organized nationally but globally. Accordingly, more and more right-wing extremists are looking to a transnational network to fight against the seemingly overwhelming (Jewish) conspiracy. In the course of this development, networking has become tighter, contacts abroad have intensified, and communication channels have improved, altogether making for a permanent exchange of information and lively event tourism.

The number of internationally attended right-wing meetings, events, and demonstrations are on the increase. This results in a complex web of cooperation, which is illustrated in the examples highlighted in this paper.

Pan-Aryanism, the ideological basis for this network, is essentially a modern anti-modern ideology. Guided by the internationally famous "14 Words" of the American right-wing terrorist David Lane ("We must secure the existence of our people and a future for white children") and the fundamental opposition to ZOG, right-wing extremists globally have a common counter-myth, which overrides all other ideological differences. Trans-nationally co-operating right-wing extremists are not simply flag-waving patriots, but very fundamental enemies of pluralism, parliamentary democracy and its representatives. This identity-oriented resistance is de facto the globalization of hatred and in Western and Eastern Europe alike a battle for the parliaments and civil society.

30 "NPD-Parteivorsitzender zu Gast bei Alessandra Mussolini in Straßburg", press release of 21 November 2004, available at: http://www.npd.de.

31 Ibid.

IV. Right-wing extremism in the 21st century – the globalized anti-globalizers

The re-nationalization and re-ethnicization propagated by the extreme right is both a fundamental alternative to the dominant neo-liberal globalization as well as to the social-ecological version ("Global Governance") and must be taken seriously. The increasing reflexive modernity, i. e. the quickening pace of social and political change, also benefits the mobilization of the extremist right.

In the 21st Century, a deeper internationalization – or better: transnationalization – of right-wing extremism, especially in an ideological but also in a structural sense, is apparent. It may seem paradoxical, but the "nationalist resistance" is not necessarily from one's own country. Right-wing anti-globalists "globalize" – and to make it even more complicated – a unifying ideological element is the struggle against "globalism". The extreme right responds to the demands of "globalism", which are diagnosed by it: "the trend towards liquefaction [...] is met with a re-homogenization of identity and a reaffirmation of supposed certainties".[32] "Globalism" and the social question have become new campaign and propaganda issues for right-wing extremists. At the same time, right-wing extremists regard themselves executor of the will of the people, who are irritated by how quickly the processes of globalization progress.

It should be noted in conclusion: Today, right-wing extremism can be described as an international, modern and multifaceted phenomenon.[33] Opposition to globalization and the defense of social justice – however understood – per se is neither left nor right in the 21st century. Right-wing extremists react "to the loss of traditions and boundaries of identity, accelerated by globalization and de-nationalization".[34] The right extremists are not just "regular" critics of globalization, but anti-globalists, their approach is not progressive-democratic, but volkish-extremist. The ideological arsenal of the People (the Volk) and the nation is extended by the extreme right by ideas such as globalization, (anti-)capitalism, imperialism and identity, and thus made internationally compatible.[35] Both because of their internal structural conditions as well as external factors – particularly a "cultural resonance" with parts of the population[36] – the right-wing extremist movement can be marginalized simply by external repression or the hope that it will implode one day. Unlike suspected by some authors, the right-wing extremist movement in Germany is not a "painful

32 Scharenberg, Plädoyer für eine Mehrebenenanalyse, p. 663.
33 See Minkenberg, Die neue radikale Rechte; see Greven/Grumke, Globalisierter Rechtsextremismus?.
34 Scharenberg, Plädoyer für eine Mehrebenenanalyse, p. 662.
35 See Grumke, Die transnationale Infrastruktur.
36 See Grumke, Die rechtsextremistische Bewegung, pp. 488–490.
37 Ohlemacher, Schmerzhafte Episoden.
38 Scheuch/Klingemann, Theorie des Rechtsradikalismus, p. 12–14.

episode"[37] but rather a "normal pathology of Western industrial societies".[38] Right-wing extremists live, like all fundamentalists, in a hermetically sealed ideological counter-world. So the question is: How can a free society accept a declaration of absolute enmity without betraying its own liberal democratic ideals?

Intellectual Right-Wing Extremism – Alain de Benoist's Mazeway Resynthesis since 2000

Tamir Bar-On

I. Introduction

Alain de Benoist (b. 1943) is considered the leading intellectual of the French nouvelle droite (New Right – ND). Today the ND is also known as the European New Right (ENR) due to its pan-European and transnational influence. The ND is a metapolitical "school of thought"[1] with a right-wing Gramscian perspective, which distanced itself from neo-fascist and extreme right-wing political parties and violent, extra-parliamentary subcultures of the extreme-right. The ND achieved the height of its notoriety in the late 1970s when de Benoist won France's most prestigious literary prize from the Académie française in 1978 for "Vu de droite" ("Seen from the right").[2] In the same period, the ND doyen was invited to write in "Le Figaro", an influential centre-right Paris daily and France's oldest newspaper. Owing to his youthful attachment to pro-French Algeria ultra-nationalist circles and Conservative Revolution (CR) thinkers of the inter-war era, French and foreign critics on the liberal-left accused its leader of crypto-fascist tendencies into the 21st century.[3]

CR connotes non-Nazi fascisms of the inter-war era. CR thinkers combined German ultra-nationalism, defense of the organic folk community, technological modernity, and socialist revisionism, which valorized the worker and soldier as models for a reborn authoritarian state superseding the egalitarian "decadence" of liberalism, socialism, and traditional conservatism. CR thinkers included Carl Schmitt (the Nazi crown jurist), Arthur Moeller van den Bruck (inventor of the term "Third Reich"), and Ernst Jünger (ultra-nationalist war veteran who penned "The Storm of Steel", his hymn to World War One soldierly virtues). The term CR was popularized by the Swiss-born Armin Mohler, who wrote a doctoral thesis under Karl Jaspers in the late 1940s. Mohler called the CR thinkers the "Trotskyites of the German Revolution".[4]

1 The term used by Duranton-Crabol, Visages de la Nouvelle droite.
2 Benoist, Vu de droite.
3 See Griffin, Foreword: Another Face? Another Mazeway?
4 Griffin (Ed.), Fascism, p. 352.

De Benoist insisted the ND offered a new political paradigm beyond outdated categories such as right and left, or fascism and anti-fascism.[5] In the post-communist period after the fall of the Marxist-Leninist Soviet Union in 1991 and the post-9-11 "war on terror", the ND leader turned increasingly more anti-capitalist, anti-liberal, and anti-American. De Benoist's worldview is a synthesis of two main political tendencies: CR + New Left (NL) = ND.[6]

As the principal transnational messenger of ND ideas, de Benoist helped spread ND ideas to numerous European countries through like-minded intellectuals, journals, think-tanks, and conferences. It is generally acknowledged that de Benoist assisted the French ultra-nationalist milieu in its turn towards a pan-European perspective, while also giving the ND more legitimacy by distancing it from Vichy collaboration, fascism, and Nazism. As the political climate shifted in France and Europe towards greater support for neo-liberal and extreme right-wing political movements and parties in the 1980s and 1990s,[7] ND ideas spread throughout the continent. Paradoxically, the star status of the ND leader declined in France after the victory of the French *Socialists* in the 1981 presidential elections and as some former ND supporters such as Pierre Vial, Yvan Blot, and Jean-Yves Le Gallou joined Jean-Marie Le Pen's anti-immigrant political party, the *Front National* (FN - National Front).[8]

The purpose of this paper is to examine ND ideas in the first decade of the 21st century principally through the prism of its leading intellectual, Alain de Benoist. I focus on de Benoist's writings since 2000 and especially "The French New Right in the Year 2000", the ND's official manifesto for the new millennium, which first appeared in ND journal "Éléments" in 1999.[9] The manifesto was penned by de Benoist and Charles Champetier, a former head of the youth wing of the ND. The manifesto also re-appeared in 2000 as "Manifeste pour une renaissance européenne. A la découverte du GRECE. Son histoire, ses idées, son organisation".

In his entry for "Alain de Benoist" in "World Fascism: A Historical Encyclopedia" (2006), Bastow writes: "He has moved from fascism in more recent years".[10] In contrast to Bastow's position, I want to argue that de Benoist never worked from an explicitly fascist tradition per se, but simultaneously never fully exited extreme right-wing political space in the new millennium. The thesis of this paper is that despite de Benoist's "opening to the left", ecological, and direct democracy influences in the first decade of the 21st century, the ND thinker never definitively left the extreme right-wing milieu. De Benoist startles with his anti-capitalist mantra inspired by the American and French NL or his synthesis

5 See Benoist, The End of the Left-Right Dichotomy.
6 See Bar-On, The Ambiguities of the Nouvelle Droite; id., Where Have All the Fascists Gone?; id., Fascism to the Nouvelle Droite.
7 Ignazi, Extreme Right Parties in Western Europe, pp. 22–26.
8 McCulloch, The Nouvelle Droite in the 1980s and 1990s, pp. 158–178.
9 Benoist/Champetier, La Nouvelle Droite de l'an 2000.
10 Bastow, Alain de Benoist, p. 88.

of modern, "post-modern" and anti-modern themes, yet he remains more fundamentally indebted to European extreme right-wing traditions which reject central tenets of the Enlightenment project. I use Roger Griffin's notions of "mazeway resynthesis" and "alternative political modernism" to situate de Benoist's contemporary worldview.[11]

De Benoist's continued anti-egalitarianism, rejection of the Rights of Man and representative democracy, as well as valorization of pagan elite rule, makes him more primordially a man of the right than left. Right and left might be categories that are not as useful in an age of "communism in ruins",[12] but the fact that the ND leader still rejects administratively-imposed equality based on the model of the 1789 French Revolution definitively separates him from pro-egalitarian liberal, centre, centre-right, and left-wing political movements and parties.[13] Moreover, in rejecting the allegedly "abstract" Rights of Man, de Benoist unambiguously ties himself to extreme right-wing traditions which have a long historical lineage dating back to the 18th century: counter-revolutionary monarchists, integral nationalists, Vichyites, "non-conformists",[14] CR thinkers, fascists, and contemporary extreme right-wing parties.

II. Alain de Benoist - the ND's principal messenger

In this section, I provide a brief sketch of ND leader Alain de Benoist and demonstrate how he has been the main agent of spreading ND ideas beyond France in a transnational spirit. De Benoist has also been responsible for restoring an aura of credibility to the extreme right-wing milieu and turning French ultra-nationalists into avid pan-Europeanists and radical ethnopluralists. De Benoist was born on December 11, 1943 in Saint-Symphorien, France. He is an intellectual, philosopher, and political commentator who was the most visible face of the French ND at its height of mass media attention in the 1970s. He had ultra-nationalist, pro-French Algeria tendencies at the beginning of his career in the 1960s. Along with about 40 other ultra-nationalists, in 1968 de Benoist helped create the Groupement de recherche et d'études pour la civilisation européenne (GRECE - Research and Study Group for European Civilization), the ND's main think-tank. He is the editor of three ND journals

11 Griffin, Modernism and Fascism.

12 For example, Versluis writes: "Left and Right no longer seem to have any clear, widely accepted reference points or definitions, and political actors themselves have not helped matters". Versluis, What's Right?, p. 153.

13 For Norberto Bobbio, the left broadly stands for equality and the right inequality. See Bobbio, Left and Right, pp. 60–79.

14 A term popularized by Jean-Louis Loubet del Bayle in: Les non-conformistes des années 30, Paris 1969. Non-conformists were French thinkers of the 1930s, including Emmanuel Mounier, Alexandre Marc, and Robert Aron, who sought for a "third way" between communism and capitalism, while rejecting liberal democracy, parliamentarism, and fascism.

founded in three different decades: "Nouvelle École" (1969), "Éléments" (1973), and "Krisis" (1988). Moreover, de Benoist was the director of several publishing collections, including "Éditions Copernic" (1977-81), "Éditions de Labyrinthe" (since 1982), "Éditions Pardès" (1989-1993), and "L'Âge d'Homme" (since 2003).

Given de Benoist's writing production of over 50 books and thousands of articles in areas as diverse as philosophy, cultural anthropology, arts, sports, and political affairs of the day, encyclopaedic-like knowledge, exposure and prestige, the French intellectual was able to spread ND ideas beyond a narrow elite circle. While the star status of de Benoist faded after the ND's mass media storm in 1979, it briefly returned in 1993 and 1994 when 40 and later 1500 European intellectuals warned in "Le Monde" of the "danger" of ND ideas, particularly its attempts to unite with disgruntled leftists in a post-Cold War era.[15]

In recent years, de Benoist has toured Europe to promote his ideas. In 2009, he appeared on the television program "France Culture" and engaged in a dialogue with the ND-influenced editor of Berlin's "Junge Freiheit" (Young Freedom), Dieter Stein, on the merits of the term "nouvelle droite". In 2007, de Benoist made television appearances on "Europe 1", while in 2005 on Spain's "Tele Madrid". From 2007 to 2009, de Benoist made regular appearances on "Radio Courtoisie". In 2008, de Benoist was interviewed by Milan-based conservative newspaper "Il Giornale".

De Benoist's principal writings have been translated into many European languages.[16] In the new century, de Benoist published a work on Carl Schmitt and just war theory in Italian as "Terrorismo e 'guerre giuste' Sull'attualità di Carl Schmitt" (Guida, Napoli 2007). A controversial book accused of right-wing revisionism by leftist critics, "Comunismo y nazismo: 25 reflexiones sobre el totalitarismo en el siglo XX (1917-1989) ('Communism and Nazism')", was published in Spanish in 2005 (Ediciones Áltera, Barcelona) and in the same year in Croatian as "Komunizam i nacizam: 25 ogleda o totalitarizmu u XX stoljeću" (Zlatko Hasanbegovic, Zagreb). "Jézus és testvérei Gondolatok a vallásról és a hitrõl" (Europa Authentica, Budapest) appeared in Hungarian in 2005. "Manifesto per una rinascita europea" (Nuove idee, Roma), or "Manifesto for a European Renaissance", appeared in Italian in 2005. "On Being a Pagan" appeared in English in 2005 (Ultra, Atlanta). A critique of liberal capitalist globalization, "Kritik der Menschenrechte: Warum Universalismus und Globalisierung die Freiheit bedrohen" (Junge Freiheit, Berlin), appeared in German in 2004. De Benoist's most famous work "Vu de droite" published its newest edition in 2002, sold more than 25,000 copies worldwide, and was translated into Italian, Portuguese, German, and Romanian.[17]

15 See The Appeal To Vigilance. In: Le Monde, 13 July 1993.

16 For the full list of translations see Alain de Benoist's website, http://www. alain-debenoist. com, last accessed 31 May 2010.

17 Benoist, Preface à la nouvelle édition de "Vu de Droite" (2002), http://www.alain-debenoist.com/pdf/preface_nouvelle_edition_vu_de_droite.pdf, last accessed 31 May 2010.

De Benoist's ideas have been disseminated throughout Europe by other ND intellectuals, many with roots in the extreme-right or neo-fascism: Marco Tarchi in Italy, Michael Walker and Troy Southgate in England, Robert Steuckers in Belgium, Luc Pauwels and Marcel Rüter in Holland, Javier Esparza in Spain, Aleksandr Dugin and Aleksandr Panarin in Russia, Bogdan Radulescu in Romania, and Pierre Krebs and Armin Mohler in Germany.[18] "The New Right in the Year 2000" was translated into English, German, Italian, Spanish, Dutch, Danish, and Hungarian by ND or ND-friendly journals, including "Telos" (USA), "Junge Freiheit" (Germany), "Diorama letterario" (Italy), "Hespérides" (Spain), "TeKos" (Holland), and "Nomos" (Denmark).

Today the ND's influence can be felt on diverse publications such as "Telos" and "The Occidental Quarterly" (USA), "The Mankind Quarterly and The Scorpion" (United Kingdom), "Punto y coma" and "Hespérides" (Spain), "Neue Anthropologie" (Germany), and "Maiastra" (Romania). According to Minkenberg, the ND is intellectually close to the German Neue Rechte, the New Right in the United Kingdom, Nieuw Rechts in the Netherlands and Flanders (Belgium), Forza Nuova in Italy, Imperium Europa in Malta, and New Right forces in the USA connected to Paul Weyrich and the Free Congress Foundation.[19] In 2005, the self-proclaimed "National Anarchist" Troy Southgate, who rejects the Anglo-American New Right and supports de Benoist's ND, launched the New Right in London and eventually its journal "New Imperium". Peunova and Shekhovtsov point out how ND geopolitical ideas, interpreted by Aleksandr Dugin and political philosopher Aleksandr Panarin (1940–2003), have influenced the Russian New Right, and found the ear of key Russian political elites.[20] De Benoist's website provides translations of his works in eight European languages: French, English, German, Italian, Spanish, Dutch, Polish, and Czech. There are also websites for GRECE and "Éléments",[21] as well as an Internet presence for numerous ND journals from "Junge Freiheit" in Germany to "Diorama letterario" in Italy. An ND variant of Wikipedia, Metapedia, was created by ND supporters to disseminate ND ideas worldwide.

It can be argued that the entire European extreme right-wing political spectrum from the Italian *Lega Nord* (Northern League – LN) to *Vlaams Belang* (Flemish Interest) in Belgium have been influenced by the politically correct language (i. e. anti-totalitarian, anti-racist, post-fascist, and pro-democracy) of the ND. If three extreme right-wing political parties, the MSI and LN in Italy and

18 In the 1980s, Marco Tarchi was an activist with the Italian neo-fascist "Movimento Sociale Italiano" (MSI – Italian Social Movement), while Michael Walker was an organizer in central London for the "British National Front" (BNF).

19 See Minkenberg, The Renewal of the Radical Right.

20 See Peunova, An Eastern Incarnation of the European New Right; Shekhovtsov, Aleksandr Dugin's Neo-Eurasianism; The Palingenetic Thrust of Russian Neo-Eurasianism.

21 For GRECE's site, including articles from "Éléments", see http://www.grece-fr.net/accueil.php, last accessed 31 May 2010.

the *Freiheitliche Partei Österreichs* (Austrian Freedom Party - FPÖ), participated in national coalitions in Italy (1994, 2001, and 2008) and Austria (2000) respectively, this hints at the cultural shift in values against liberalism, multiculturalism, and the mainstream political class. The ND helped engender this pan-European cultural shift in the 1980s and 1990s. Working from a Gramscian perspective, which seeks to win hearts and minds in a long-term struggle within civil society, de Benoist reasons that one day ND ideas will be the ruling ideas of Europe. It is only different political circumstances that might allow key European elites and the mass public to convert to ND ideas, as they did en masse to "third way" political ideologies throughout Europe in the inter-war years.[22]

De Benoist has served as the key messenger of ND ideas within France and throughout Europe, as well as the USA, Canada, Australia, New Zealand, and Latin America. For example, "Disenso" is an Argentinean journal edited by Alberto Buela, which is influenced by ND ideas. "Disenso" is distributed throughout Latin America. The ND's manifesto has been disseminated to Australian and New Zealand nationalist circles,[23] as well as sympathetic circles in the USA through the publication of Michael O'Meara's, "New Culture, New Right: Anti-liberalism in Postmodern Europe" (2004).[24] O'Meara, like Tomislav Sunic before him, has written a sympathetic portrayal of the ND as a fellow traveler.[25] De Benoist indirectly criticized Sunic in a 2009 interview in which he lamented that the title of Sunic's 1990 book on the ND gave away the ND project.[26] The title is "The European New Right: Against Equality and Democracy." In recent years, de Benoist continues to reject equality, but support direct rather than representative variants of democracy. De Benoist continued the project GRECE had begun in 1969 of avoiding "outdated vocabulary" (i. e. openly pro-racism, pro-colonialism, pro-collaboration, and pro-fascism), which was ironically influenced by French neo-fascists such as Dominique Venner (b. 1935) and Maurice Bardèche (1907–98).[27]

III. A New Right, leftist Right, New Left, or Old Right in new clothes?

In the 21st century, de Benoist baffled many of his critics with his vehement rejection of liberal capitalist globalization, as well as sympathy for ecological and NL movements. Extreme right-wingers, Catholic nationalists, leftists, liberals, and mainstream conservatives were all troubled by de Benoist's intellectual migra-

22 See Bar-On, Understanding Political Conversion and Mimetic Rivalry.
23 See New Right Australia/New Zealand, http://newrightausnz.blogspot.com, last accessed 2 June 2010.
24 O'Meara, New Culture, New Right.
25 See Sunic, The European New Right.
26 See Benoist, The European New Right Forty Years Later. p. 64.
27 See Bar-On, Where Have all the Fascists Gone?, p. 36.

tions.[28] Some FN supporters viewed de Benoist as a crypto-communist, while Catholic nationalists rejected his virulent pagan anti-Christianity. Leftists and liberals said he was a fascist in disguise,[29] while mainstream conservatives thought he was too revolutionary and excessively critical of neo-liberalism, the West, and the USA. Some wondered if de Benoist was not re-inventing the NL legacy of the 1968ers?[30] Is de Benoist today part of the New Right, leftist Right, Old Right, or NL?

De Benoist's strategy in the 21st century is continued affinity for extreme right-wing and CR authors, as evidenced by his massive four-volume work on the French right and far-right milieu and "Beyond the Rights of Man" (2004).[31] In a series of writings and interviews in the new century from 2003 to 2005, de Benoist continued to defend CR authors such Schmitt and Jünger, anti-modernist fascists such as Evola, the "heroic" ultra-nationalist Maurras, French fascist leader George Valois, and revisionist accounts of Vichy collaboration.[32] De Benoist often ignored or severely downplayed the real historical links to fascism of the aforementioned thinkers. In 2002, on the 25 anniversary of the publication of his "Vu de droite", de Benoist reiterated what he wrote in 1977, namely, that the "greatest" danger in the world today is the "progressive disappearance of diversity from the world," which he added includes biodiversity of the natural world and cultures and peoples.[33] De Benoist associates diversity with inequality as positive in contrast to the projects of modernity, Enlightenment, and liberalism, which valorize the notion of equality. Equality, de Benoist insists, is equivalent with global capitalist homogenization, universalism, and the disappearances of rooted cultural differences at the "end of history". In rejecting administrative equality, de Benoist remains a man of the right more than left.

At the same time, de Benoist sought to co-opt NL, ecological, "anti-racist," and democratic ideals in the spirit of the times.[34] His aims remain the same as they were in the early 1980s: destruction of liberalism, socialism, social democracy, capitalism, and communist resurgence, all rooted in a Judeo-Christian worldview, which was thoroughly egalitarian and destructive of natural hierarchies and cultures and the need for elite rule.[35]

In the new century, the ND continued to borrow the notion of the "right to difference" from the French Socialists to provide ideological ammunition for

28 On de Benoist's intellectual migrations from the 1960s to 1980s, see Taguieff, Sur la nouvelle droite.
29 See, for example, Griffin (Ed.), Fascism, pp. 1-12.
30 See Piccone, Confronting the French New Right.
31 Benoist, Au-delà des droits de l'homme; id., Bibliographie générale des droites françaises (four volumes).
32 See Bar-On, Where Have all the Fascists Gone? pp. 201-202.
33 See Benoist, Préface à la nouvelle édition (2002). In: id., Vu de droite. Available at http://www.alaindebenoist.com/pdf/preface_nouvelle_edition_vu_de_droite.pdf, last accessed 1 June 2010.
34 See, for example, Benoist, Demain, la décroissance!
35 See Benoist et al., La Cause des peuples, pp. 167-184.

contemporary extreme right-wing political parties such as the French FN, the Italian LN, and *British National Party* (BNP). These extreme right-wing political parties claimed they were not racist but culturally protective of both "home" and "host" cultures in wishing to end non-white, non-European immigration.[36] These extreme right-wing political parties called their liberal opponents "racists" since they sought to promote liberal capitalism and multiculturalism, which were allegedly destructive of rooted European national or regional cultures. This inversion strategy of turning multicultural, anti-racism into a form of racism was borrowed from the ND.

What was most shocking about the ND's ideological makeover in the new millennium under de Benoist is that he rejected the pillars of the right: the nation-state and nationalism. De Benoist claimed that the French state was destructive of regional identities (i. e. Basque, Breton, Corsican, or Occitanian) buried by the notion of the "one and indivisible" French republic. Old rightists such as Charles Maurras (1868–1952) similarly attacked the French revolutionary state born in 1789, which allegedly destroyed local, regional, and linguistic cultures in the process of constructing the French nation-state and republicanism. The new goal of the ND would be a "Europe of a Hundred Flags". This "Europe of a Hundred Flags" would be a pan-European empire with a hierarchical, authoritarian, corporatist, and pagan orientation, cleansed of immigrants and bent on preserving ethnic homogeneity within the "authentic," historic regions of Europe.[37] While it is true that fascists and Nazis generally rejected the conception of the nation as proposed by the ND, the goals of empire, authoritarian corporatism, and internally homogeneity are shared with fascists of the inter-war years. Also, early post-war neo-fascists like Bardèche already called for pan-European fascism. Moreover, it is instructive how the ND re-interpreted the "right to difference" in a pan-European framework in order to promote a "multiculturalism of the right," which aims at conserving the "authentic" regions of Europe against the onslaught of non-European immigrants.

The goal of a pan-European empire, which rejects the pro-capitalist and technocratic European Union (EU) of today, provided the ND with an ideological reformulation that could increase the transnational thrust of ND ideas. It is no accident that contemporary extreme right-wing parties such as the FN have called for pan-European unity and a geopolitical pole of confrontation against the USA and other potential world powers. This is the same position as the one of the ND leader. De Benoist even promoted radical anti-Western regimes to challenge the USA's global hegemony and its promotion of liberalism worldwide. In short, the stance of the ND and most extreme right-wing political parties is the same: Support for pan-European unity, but rejection of the contemporary capitalist EU.[38]

36 See Shields, The Extreme Right in France from Pétain to Le Pen, pp. 237–244.
37 See Bar-On, Fascism to the Nouvelle Droite; Spektorowski, Ethnoregionalism.
38 See Mudde, Globalisation: The Multi-Faced Enemy?

IV. "The French New Right in the Year 2000": Mazeway resynthesis

In 1999 and 2000, the ND traced its social, political and philosophical vision for the new millennium in a manifesto entitled "The French New Right in the Year 2000".[39] The manifesto is split into three sections: 1) Predicaments (a critical analysis of the contemporary period); 2) Foundations (outlining the ND's view of man and the world); and 3) Outlooks (positions on current issues and debates). In the manifesto's "Introduction", the ND claims to be a metapolitical force seeking to represent "the excluded middle" in relation to dichotomies such as tribalism and globalism, nationalism and internationalism, liberalism and Marxism, individualism and collectivism, progressivism and conservatism. This position of representing the "excluded middle" harkens back to a populist tradition of winning the hearts and minds of the "silent majority" against the corrupt political and economic elites of Europe.[40] The middle position also appears moderate in relation to the extremes of right and left, although not all ND positions in the manifesto are moderate as in their rejection of representative democracy and immigration. The ND claims it seeks a new political synthesis beyond "outmoded" categories such as left and right (see "Introduction"), a tactic common to new political outfits on the right and left. The ND anticipates resistance to such a project arguing that a new synthesis is threatening for "the guardians of thought" wedded to outdated ideological orthodoxies (see "Introduction").

The manifesto in question is what Griffin would call "mazeway resynthesis" in which "old and new ideological and ritual elements - some of which would previously have been incongruous or incompatible - are forged through 'ludic recombination' into a totalizing worldview".[41] The manifesto is a pastiche of modern, anti-modern, and post-modern influences. "Incompatible" left and right-wing traditions (i. e. CR and NL) coexist with scientific and mythical worldviews, including the promotion of pagan rituals harkening back to Europe's distant past. The ND does not use the term "anti-modern" but rather the politically correct "pre-modern" in order to avoid stigmatization for the right. Around the time of the French Revolution and for many years, the right was viewed with suspicion. The right was the carrier of anti-modern values and associated with the political players that rejected the republican values of the 1789 French Revolution: Church, regions, aristocracy, and monarchy.

What is also striking about the ND manifesto is the disproportionate concern with the preservation of rooted ethnic communities, as well as the desire to create direct democracies based on ethnic criteria of membership. There is hardly any section in the manifesto that does not express preference for rooted, homo-

39 In this section, I will quote from the English translation of Benoist/Champetier, La Nouvelle Droite de l'an 2000. See Benoist/Champetier, The French New Right in the Year 2000, http://www.freespeechproject.com/alain9.html, last accessed 1 June 2010.

40 See Taggart, Populism.

41 Griffin, Foreword: Another Face? Another Mazeway?, p. xiii.

geneous communities. Moreover, while de Benoist's turns away from narrow French nationalism, colonialism, and overt racism are impressive, the ND has not fully abandoned its CR influences; it rejects administrative equality, and views immigration as a "negative phenomenon" in line with extreme right-wing political parties. De Benoist ultimately desires a pan-European empire cleansed of immigrants, which paradoxically in first instance recognizes cultural differences in the public sphere. This might not be called fascism, but it is a decidedly anti-liberal, anti-egalitarian, and anti-multicultural project, which has serious doubts about Enlightenment reason and progress, aspects of modernity, and the legacy of 1789.

Living in an interregnum, a type of historical watershed between contemporary decadence and revolutionary palingenesis (rebirth) in the near future,[42] the ND insists that at the dawn of the 21st century we live at the end of modernity. The current post-modern age, argue de Benoist and Champetier, will lead to what Nietzsche called "a fixed horizon framed by myth":[43] the revival of pan-European civilization (empire) in the context of a homogeneous "Europe of a Hundred Flags". This myth will be part of a "totalizing vision of the world, which banishes pluralism, relativism, and *anomie* and at the same time subsumes mythicized elements of the past".[44]

It is important to note that the ND's ideological "mazeway resynthesis" in the manifesto is grounded not within what one scholar called "reactionary modernism",[45] but rather "a certain way of conceiving 'modernism' when it operates in the sphere of revolutionary politics".[46] As Griffin argues, it is possible to define modernism in a way that makes it applicable not just to innovative experiments in aesthetic form and style, but to any initiative in the cultural, social, or political sphere that seeks to restore a sense of sublime order and purpose to the contemporary "world", thereby counteracting the (perceived) erosion of an overarching "nomos" or "sacred canopy" under the fragmenting and secularizing impact of modernity.[47]

1. Section one: Critique of modernity and theorizing modernity's demise

In section 1, clause 1 of the manifesto entitled "Modernity", the authors offer a radical critique of modernity and theorize about modernity's demise. De Benoist and Champetier attack the Judeo-Christian tradition and its liberal, universal offshoot, which "attempts by every available means to uproot individuals from

42 Concept of "spherical time" borrowed from Armin Mohler, Jünger's former press secretary. See Griffin (Ed.), Fascism, pp. 351–354; Modernism and Fascism; Foreword: Another Face? Another Mazeway?, pp. xii-xvi.
43 Quoted in Griffin, Foreword: Another Face? Another Mazeway?, p. xiv.
44 Ibid.
45 Herf, Reactionary Modernism.
46 Griffin, Foreword: Another Face? Another Mazeway, p. xii.
47 Ibid.

their individual communities" and to eradicate diversity from the planet. The ND authors imply that various European ethnic and regional communities have been undermined by a "foreign" Judeo-Christian tradition, which attacks Europe's polytheistic, pagan religions of the past. Modernity alone is not responsible for the decline of European ethnic groups, but also 2000 plus years of Christianity and its precursor Judaism. However, Christianity was unique because "it became the religion of the way out of religion". As modernity undermined traditional religions, as well as caused fear and egoism due to the "primacy of money" (capitalism), the loss of collective meaning, and the turn from countryside towards industrial production, moderns did not lose their need for meaning. Political projects based on the desire for freedom or equality such as liberalism and socialism failed to liberate humanity, while also engendering totalitarian horrors such Stalinism, fascism, Nazism, as well as genocide and wars. The acceleration of the "end of ideologies" phenomenon in the post-Cold War, "post-communist" context simultaneously fuels a political crisis and crisis of meaning.

The ND views the 20th century as the end of modern times and the beginning of the post-modern era. The new millennium is marked by the "dictatorship" of liberal globalization and capitalism, but also a return to "tribes" and "networks", the politics of group identities, ecological and quality of life concerns, a turn away from elitism, and generalized social violence. The "New Class" managing liberal globalization still lacks answers for both our political problems and the search for meaning in an age when "God is dead!". Using ideological "mazeway resynthesis", de Benoist and Champetier insist that in this century we will turn away from modernity, using "premodern values" in a postmodern synthesis:

Having nothing new to say and observing the growing malaise of contemporary societies, the agents of the dominant ideology are reduced to the clichés-ridden discourse so common in the media in a world threatened by implosion - implosion, not explosion, because modernity will not be transcended with a grand soir (a secular version of the Second Coming of Christ), but with the appearance of thousands of auroras, i. e. the birth of sovereign spaces liberated from the domination of the modern. Modernity will not be transcended by returning to the past, but by means of certain premodern values in a decisively postmodern dimension. It is only at the price of such a radical restructuring that anomie and contemporary nihilism will be exorcised.

In his work on the German New Right, Woods points out that the ND "is engaged in a political and cultural response to Modernity".[48] What de Benoist and Champetier most fear is "the domination of the modern": the Enlightenment, the emancipatory potential of reason in human history, capitalism, industrialization, rampant egoism, democratic politics, liberal values, multiculturalism, feminism, globalization, egalitarianism, the turn away from the sacred, and

48 Woods, Germany's New Right as Culture and Politics, p. 21.

the demise of meaning structured through rooted, homogeneous ethnic communities. Historically, these fears are shared with counter-revolutionaries such as Joseph de Maistre (1753–1821), integral nationalists such as Charles Maurras, anti-modern Traditionalists such as Julius Evola (1898–1974),[49] Vichyites, nonconformists, CR thinkers, and fascists of various types.

The ND position in respect of modernity is influenced by the CR's revolutionary and palingenetic mindset, as well as "mazeway resynthesis" combining modern, anti-modern, and post-modern influences.[50] Although the ND tactically rejects the violence of inter-war fascists and Nazis, like them they promote an "alternative political modernism" and embody the characteristics of a "revitalization movement" with de Benoist its European prophet.[51] The ND leader views the current period as an interregnum, a temporary stage between the current age of black decadence, meaninglessness, and nihilism associated with capitalist globalization, and eventual pan-European rebirth along elitist, revolutionary, ethnic lines. There is a possibility of ending the interregnum and the "dictatorship" of capitalist values worldwide where everything has a price and nothing has a value, de Benoist and Champetier insist. One hears Nietzschean and Evolian calls in the manifesto for "heroic" European elites determined to supersede the modern world and restore the scared canopy of meaning destroyed by an alienating modernity. Current political, economic, and culture elites fail to understand "the malaise of modernity",[52] while explosive global revolutions on a grand scale are no longer plausible after 20th century totalitarian disasters. The current liberal capitalist system will fall through implosion and thousands of sovereign political spaces "liberated from the domination of the modern". The ND seeks a revolutionary, new secular pan-European state in which a new age is born, a spherical conception of time arises against linear liberal time, and a myth of "common origins" for Indo-European civilization returns. Modern, "premodern", and post-modern values will be synthesized in a new pan-European imperial (yet not imperialist) civilization, which respects the "common origins" of its historic regions and nations against the homogenizing steamrollers of the nation-state, globalization, and liberal multiculturalism. The ND project will supposedly resolve the political crises of Europe from the democratic deficit to immigration and ecological concerns, as well as its spiritual crisis born of modernity's de-sacralization of the world.

For the authors of the manifesto, there is no possibility of returning to a mythical past or "golden age", but instead modernity will be superseded by returning to "premodern" values in a post-modern spirit. As belief in liberal and socialist progress myths fade due to post-modern influences, the fall of communist regimes in Europe, and the rise of a socially destructive neo-liberalism, new

49 For an elucidation of the Italian philosopher's Traditionalist worldview, see his 1934 text Revolt Against the Modern World.
50 Griffin, Modernity, Modernism, and Fascism, pp. 9–24.
51 Griffin, Modernism and Fascism; Bar-On, Understanding Political Conversion, p. 246.
52 Term from Taylor, The Malaise of Modernity.

myths are required for Europe. Jünger insisted that ultra-nationalism was the unifying myth, which could undermine the nihilism of the inter-war years and the loss of faith in progress spawned by modernity.[53] De Benoist and Champetier similarly seek the return of a European myth of "common origins" in this period between the modern and post-modern. They desire the restoration of a hierarchical, elitist, pagan, aristocratic, and roots-based Indo-European civilization, buried by the avalanche of the Judeo-Christian tradition and the loss of meaning associated with modernity. The anomie and nihilism of the modern world will be "exorcised" by a return to pagan, "premodern" values without a complete return to the Europe before the emergence of modernity.

There is an inherent "alternative political modernism" in the ND's project. Modern technology, communications systems, economic prowess, and state forces will be marshaled in serving "premodern values" in a post-modern direction. Each generation requires its new myths of mass hope in order to tackle its contemporary problems. While the right has historically tried to conserve traditions of the past, those traditions worth preserving change depending on political circumstances: Christianity, monarchy, nation, race, Europe, the West, or liberal democracy. The right has also changed its positions based on the twists and turns of the left. For de Benoist, a right that always remains Christian, monarchical, racist, imperialist, or neo-liberal is a right that has no values and does not understand that the key values of the right must be preserving the world's cultural diversity and stopping egalitarianism, the killer of rooted cultural diversity worldwide. Examples of right-wing movements that were modernist yet served anti-modern values included CR thinkers and the "Action française" under Charles Maurras. Like CR thinkers or counter-revolutionary monarchists, the ND argues that in order to conserve what is worthwhile, the right must sometimes turn revolutionary. The ND reasons that as destructive modern, liberal, and capitalist values become impregnated worldwide, a revolutionary stance is even more imperative in order to preserve Europe's historic regions, nations, and cultures.

For the ND, the worst aspects of modernity change depend on political circumstances. In section 1, number 3, "Liberalism: The Main Enemy", the traditional right-wingers will be surprised that liberalism and not communism is the main enemy. For the ND, this change from a primary anti-communism to a primary anti-liberalism predated the fall of communist states after the fall of the Berlin Wall in 1989.[54] The authors reject liberalism and Marxism as mirror, materialistic, and "totalitarian" ideologies: "In almost all respects, liberalism has only realized more effectively certain objectives it shares with Marxism: the eradication of collective identities and traditional cultures, the disenchantment of the world, and the universalization of the system of production". Liberalism and Marxism are viewed as universal, moralizing ideologies and enemies of ethnic

53 See Woods, Germany's New Right as Culture and Politics, p. 21.
54 See Duranton-Crabol, Visages de la Nouvelle Droite, pp. 227–229.

groups worldwide. Yet, liberalism is the main enemy today since it is the dominant planetary model after the official fall of the Marxist-Leninist Soviet Union in 1991 and hence a greater danger to rooted ethnic communities around the globe.

2. Section two: The ND's "premodern" conception of man

In section 2 of the manifesto, de Benoist and Champetier trace the philosophical foundations of the ND's "premodern", anti-egalitarian conception of man. Modernity is held responsible for undermining "natural" inequalities between human beings. In clause 1, "Man: An Aspect of Life", the authors claim that modernity has attempted to "deny any human nature" and the modern world consequently spawned false utopias, which led to totalitarianism and concentration camps. In a passage that would make the egalitarian liberal-left shiver, de Benoist and Champetier allude to an older biological concept to defend ethnic communities: "To the extent that life is generated above all through the transmission of information contained in genetic material, man is not born like a blank page".

Yet, for the ND biology interacts with culture: "He [man] can construct himself historically and culturally on the basis of the presuppositions of his biological constitution, which are his human limitations". Claiming to be anti-reductionist, "the New Right proposes a vision of a well-balanced individual, taking into account both inborn, personal abilities and the social environment. It rejects ideologies that emphasize only one of these factors, be it biological, economic, or mechanical". The absence of the word culture might be purposeful, while the biological focus is a holdover from the ND's fixation with biology and scientism in the 1970s as supposedly rational, biological explanations for radical differences between ethnic groups and the naturalness of elite rule. This biological position is generally downplayed in new ND publications, for obvious reasons related to the odious biological and racial anti-Semitism of Nazism and the fascist and Vichy race laws.

In clause 2, "Man: A Rooted, Imperiled, and Open Being", the ND highlights its main obsession with rooted ethnic or cultural communities. In a crucial passage echoing French counterrevolutionary Joseph de Maistre in which he said that he never met human beings before, de Benoist and Champetier attack the "abstract" notion of humanity: "From the sociohistorical viewpoint, man as such does not exist, because his membership within humanity is always mediated by a particular cultural belonging".

Instead the authors promote a radical cultural ethnopluralism: "All cultures have their own 'center of gravity' (Herder): different cultures provide different responses to essential questions. This is why all attempts to unify them end up by destroying them. Man is rooted by nature in his culture". It is from this radical, Herderian ethnopluralism that the ND argues for the flowering of hundreds of "homogeneous" communities within the framework of a "heterogeneous" world. De Benoist and Champetier attack the notion of universal laws or rights in a world of diverse cultures. Such a drive for universalism is equated with totalitarianism and the West. Humans are concretely rooted in a time, place, and culture, while different cultures have competing answers for multiple problems. Universal human rights are a sham based on the ethnocentric worldview of the West. Humans are not good or bad, while tragedy is a fact of human existence in contrast to the progressive view of human nature of liberalism and socialism, which posit a universal, peaceful "end of history".

In clause 3, "Society: A Body of Communities", the authors argue that "Membership in the collective does not destroy individual identity; rather, it is the basis for it". For the ND, the most important collective form of belonging is the *ethnos*: people of the same race or nationality who share a distinctive culture. The authors argue, "modernity has not liberated man from his original familial belonging or from local, tribal, corporative or religious attachments". In the modern world with a capitalist market favoring the strongest bureaucracies and states, which call for total obedience, the search for life meaning is denigrated and individualism rises. De Benoist and Champetier write: "The great project of modern emancipation has resulted only in generalized alienation. Because modern societies tend to bring together individuals who experience each other as strangers, no longer having any mutual confidence, they cannot envision a social relation not subject to a 'neutral' regulatory authority". The authors continue: "Only a return to communities and to a politics of human dimensions" would undermine the lack of social bonds, reification caused by capitalism, and the proliferation of abstract juridical regulations of the state, supra-national organizations, and corporations, which invade all aspects of our modern lives.

In clause 4, "Politics: An Essence and an Art", we are told that political life must serve "values" rather than science or technological imperatives. The illusion of the modern world, the authors argue, is that politics can be neutral. The political conception that the ND theorists favor is of the "good" more than the "just": a right-wing more than left-wing conception. Against Bodin, Hobbes, and the notion of the all-powerful Leviathan-like state, de Benoist and Champetier favor a federation of organic communities and multiple allegiances along Althusian lines.[55] This is a far cry from the fascist penchant for an all-powerful state, party, and leader imposing a unitary conception of national sovereignty on the nation. It is in this desire for a federation of ethnic communities and multiple allegiances (sovereignties) that the authors unite "pre-modern", "tribal" forms of belonging with post-modern sensibilities that express anguish about the ability of the modern state and ideologies to emancipate humanity.

55 German Calvinist political philosopher Johannes Althusius (1563–1648) considered one of the early federalists. See Benoist, The First Federalist: Johannes Althusius. Available at: http://www.alaindebenoist.com/pdf/the_first_federalist_althusius.pdf, last accessed 1 June 2010.

In clause 5, "Beyond the Marketplace", the model of the economy favored is "premodern" in the spirit of the Hungarian intellectual Karl Polanyi (1886-1964) in which "the economic was embedded and contextualized within other orders of human activity". The economic realm throughout human history was cursed, the authors argue, because of the damage it could cause to a society through abundance, unlimited technological prowess, or the "dictatorship" of money. De Benoist and Champetier insist that capitalist and communist models of development will not be sustained. The 21st century will be an era of "decommodification", ecological balance, and respect for harmony and nature. If the economy is at the centre of our lives in a capitalist society, the ND economic model will be an economy in the "service of people", regions, or communities. The economic realm would be subordinated to political and military realms.

In clause 6, "Ethics: The Construction of Oneself", the authors argue that modernity has supplanted traditional ethics, whether the aristocratic "will to excellence" or traditions of popular classes. The ancient, pagan, tripartite hierarchical model of politics ought to be restored to Europe. Permanent values should be restored against the main value of modernity, the desire to earn more money, viewed as a symptom of nihilism. Human rights are seen as a "strategic weapon of Western ethnocentrism", liberal democracy hides the nihilism of capitalism, and all we desire in a liberal society is more rights without corresponding duties.

We are in the hour of the Nietzschean "last man", warn the authors, and only Appolo and Dionysius can rescue us from total nihilism, relativism, and decadence. Apollo and Dionysius were both sons of Zeus in ancient Greek mythology. Apollo is considered the god of the Sun, music, and poetry. Dionysius is the god of wine, ecstasy, and intoxication. The authors use the two figures to symbolize opposites that are not necessarily rivals: the individual versus collective, light versus darkness, or civilization versus primitivism. Liberal Western societies have supplanted traditional ethics by stressing a moralistic view of the world based on material and utilitarian conceptions of life and a unitary conception of the just. In short, the modern world will be superseded by recalling the European past in a post-modern spirit. We can only supersede modernity by accepting it in part, while synthesizing elements of the "pre-modern" past and the inherent doubts of post-modernists in an age where emancipatory "grand narratives" are no longer relevant. In a fragmented age of differing values and political projects, rejection of the political, social, and cultural aspects of modernity will flower in thousands of regional and national communities worldwide.

In clause 7, "Technology: The Mobilization of the World", the authors note that technology should be regulated by non-technological imperatives. Modernity has created a technological explosion with ramifications in science, medicine, industry, and governments. Yet, the technological explosion of the 20th century alone, insist the French authors, has seen more changes than the last 15,000 years of history, including cloning, artificial procreation, and genetic fingerprinting. Moreover, the technological explosion has led to the disappearance of ethical, symbolic, or religious codes of meaning. Technology has created a "technoscience" whose reason for being is merely more transformation of the world without thinking of the consequences of the "will to technology". Rejecting both technophobia and technophilia, the ND calls for a questioning of the idea that each societal problem needs more technological solutions. Political authorities should guide technological decisions.

In clause 8, "The World: A Pluriversum", the ND valorizes diversity and is not even afraid to use the politically incorrect notion of "race": "Diversity is inherent in the very movement of life, which flourishes as it becomes more complex. The plurality and variety of races, ethnic groups, languages, customs, even religions has characterized the development of humanity since the very beginning". "The true wealth of the world is first and foremost the diversity of its cultures and peoples", the authors insist. Note the use of race, as biology before, which is not completely omitted from the ND's culturalist notion of the homogeneous *ethnos*.

In a key passage from the same section, de Benoist and Champetier claim to reject the proselytizing, ethnocentric zeal of the West, which de Benoist once radically defended in the notion of French Algeria: "Homogenizing universalism is only the projection and the mask of an ethnocentrism extended over the whole planet".

The authors see hope in the new century as modernization is becoming increasingly disconnected from Westernization: "New civilizations are acquiring modern means of power and knowledge without renouncing their historical and cultural heritage for the benefit of Western ideologies and values". Presumably communist China and North Korea, Bolivarian Venezuela under Hugo Chávez, the indigenous socialism of Evo Morales in Bolivia, the Islamic Republic of Iran under Ahmadī-Nežād, the anti-globalization movement, ecologists, traditionalists, "third way" ultra-nationalists, revolutionary leftists, and the ND are all candidates to challenge Westernization, liberalism, and the USA. There are reverberations here of Evola's elitist, pagan, fascist call to arms against the mercantile values of the West. De Benoist has recently called for a radical schism between rooted traditional, regional or national European values, on the one hand, and the homogenizing ethos of Westernization promoted by the liberal capitalist USA, on the other hand.[56]

De Benoist and Champetier, however, reject Fukuyama's "end of history" thesis, endorse Huntington's idea of a "clash of civilizations", and attack the USA as the greatest world danger for cultural and civilizational pluralism. Using Schmittian language, the authors argue that a new "Nomos of Earth" is emerging in international relations. That is, a "multipolar world of emerging civilizations" will challenge the USA as the world's sole remaining superpower. Like Huntington, de Benoist sees the main civilizational conflict as the "West" and

56 Benoist in Sylvain, European Son, p. 27.

"the rest", or seven main civilizations resisting the dominant liberal capitalist model of the West.

In clause 9, "The Cosmos: A Continuum", the ND invokes what Griffin has called a "mythical palingenetic" worldview by arguing the ND "believes the return of the sacred will be accomplished by the returning to some founding myths". This founding myth will be centred on a regional or national *ethnos* within a pan-European, federal framework. The myth will challenge the "disenchantment of the world" and the turn away from the sacred spawned by modernity. "The French New Right is imbued with a very long memory: it maintains a relation to the beginning that harbors a sense of what is coming", adds the manifesto. This would mean a "long memory" for pagan Indo-European origins buried by the Judeo-Christian tradition and its modern, egalitarian liberal and socialist secular derivatives. Rejecting liberal and socialist variants of progress and linear time, the authors view present and future but "permanent dimensions of all lived moments". In this cyclical variant of time, past and future are present in the present, actual time. Modern, anti-modern, and post-modern currents of thought are fused in order to supersede modernity, its egalitarian ethos, and its linear, progressive vision of time. "Mazeway resynthesis" is also an integral part of section 2 of the manifesto, which stresses the ND's anti-modern impulses, including politically incorrect biological arguments about preserving rooted cultures.

3. Section three: A revival of hundreds of homogeneous ethnic communities

In Section 3 of the manifesto, the Positions section, which highlights the ND's stances on current issues, seven of the thirteen positions are directly related to a preservation of homogeneous ethnic, cultural or regional communities. The aim of this section is to inspire the flowering of hundreds of internally homogeneous communities connected to "premodern" values, which challenge the cultural and political aspects of modernity and the greatest carrier of modern values, the superpower USA. If some insist that the ND is now the NL, they might reconsider how there is lots that is old in the ND. While there is a serious attack on the nature of global capitalism, there is no real concern for offering a concrete program that would rectify social injustice, material inequalities, and the billions of miserable people around the planet that live in permanent states of unemployment, underemployment, or poverty.

In position 1, "Against Indifferentiation and Uprooting; For Clear and Strong Identities", the authors invoke capitalist globalization as the bogeyman responsible for the acceleration of ethnic conflict. As the authors write, "modernity encouraged questioning identity", while it "has not been able to satisfy the need for identity". Modernity, de Benoist and Champetier imply, questioned identity by claiming that Europe's rooted regional identities were anti-progressive relics of the past. In the modern world, we are viewed as universal political subjects destined for a multicultural heaven in the context of liberal or socialist forms of governance. Nationalism was further destructive of ethnic and regional identities by assimilating local languages, cultures, and traditions. Rejecting the idea of a "citizen of the world", the manifesto calls for a radical, pro-"Third World" ethnopluralism and "the struggle against Western imperialism".

Stressing the "primacy of differences" against universalist utopias, which undermine traditional identities, the authors embrace what ND thinker Guillaume Faye called the "cause of peoples" against the liberal "New Class". This "New Class" refers to the elite political, economic, and cultural leaders of the current global order. This "New Class" is global, multinational, liberal, and hyper-capitalist. Faye, like de Benoist and Champetier, consider the "New Class" ethnocentric and neo-imperialist because they prop up a dominant Western, capitalist model and impose it on all cultures and civilizations. The "New Class" is attacked as the destroyer of strong identities worldwide: native religions, indigenous cultures, Europe's historic regions, and traditional ethnicities and their languages. Yet, difference, or "the right to difference", cannot be used to exclude, which is a disingenuous claim if we later read position 3's arguments "against immigration".

In position 2, "Against Racism; For the Right to Difference", the ND claims to take a radical "anti-racist" position. The ND co-opts the insights of anti-racist groups like SOS-Racisme, which entered the French political scene in the early 1980s in conjunction with the rise of the anti-immigrant FN. The manifesto claims that people cannot be blamed for being racist if they choose their own ethnic groups in marriage to others: "The term racism cannot be defined as a preference for endogamy, which arises from freedom of choice of individuals and of peoples. The Jewish people, for instance, owe their survival to their rejection of mixed marriages". The Jewish example is purposefully provocative as rates of mixed marriages are rising in Jewish communities worldwide, while perhaps cultivated to appeal to some anti-Semitic sectors of the extreme-right. If people cannot be blamed for racism, the implication is that the liberal, multiculturalist "New Class" is held responsible for sowing the seeds of racism by allegedly seeking to abolish cultural differences in an egalitarian, homogeneous liberal order.

However, racism is officially rejected in the manifesto in the spirit of the times: "Racism is an erroneous doctrine, one rooted in time". But the twist is that "anti-racism" is a disguised form of racism: For the ND, race should not be jettisoned as a concept and both racism and anti-racism should be rejected: For the New Right, the struggle against racism is not won by negating the concept of races, nor by the desire to blend all races into an undifferentiated whole. Rather, the struggle against racism is waged by the refusal of both exclusion and assimilation: neither apartheid nor the melting pot; rather, acceptance of the other as Other through a dialogic perspective of mutual enrichment.

Claiming to support "true" multiculturalism based on a "dialogic perspective of mutual enrichment", the ND merely co-opted the pro-multicultural discourse of the liberal-left in order to appear anti-racist and win supporters in a decidedly anti-racist age. But the ND has not abandoned racism, even if it says it has. In position 3, "Against Immigration; For Cooperation", we see the ND repairing its ties with the traditional, far right-wing milieu, which in the 1980s thought it was becoming crypto-communist as it had been critical of Le Pen's FN and flirted with the left and NL. In line with most extreme right-wing parties, immigration is seen as a negative process for Europe today: "By reason of its rapid growth and its massive proportions, immigration such as one sees today in Europe constitutes an undeniably negative phenomenon". The anti-capitalist mantra is different from the FN, which directly blames immigrants for all of France's ills, although similar to sectors of the Italian MSI: "The responsibility for current immigration lies primarily, not with the immigrants, but with the industrialized nations which have reduced man to the level of merchandise that can be relocated anywhere". Yet, the restrictive immigration calls in the manifesto are similar to the FN. Both FN and ND argue that restricting immigration will benefit immigrant and host societies alike since both will be able to maintain homogeneous ethnic communities: "Thus the New Right favors policies restrictive of immigration, coupled with increased cooperation with Third World countries where organic interdependence and traditional ways of life still survive, in order to overcome imbalances resulting from globalization".

Immigrants are too numerous and will not all of a sudden leave Europe. Thus, the authors propose a "communitarian model" of recognizing collective cultural identities in the public sphere. In a triumph of ethnic over civic republican belonging, the authors argue: "This communitarian politic could, in the long run, lead to a dissociation of citizenship from nationality". This "multiculturalism of the right" recognizes public differences in order to exclude immigrants from public life through normal parliamentary channels or the mechanism of referenda.

In position 4, "Against Sexism: For the Recognition of Gender", the ND claims to be against sexism in a modern vein, but liberal and socialist feminists will view "differentialist feminism" as an attack on egalitarian feminism and a return to anti-modern values.

In position 5, "Against New Class; For Autonomy from Bottom Up", the ND thinkers sound either like new leftists or old rightists. Globalization has produced the worldwide domination of Western elites through the media, transnational firms, and international organizations. Elites are detached from the concerns of citizens, the "New Class" has no social responsibilities, and there is greater need for shared values and meaning between the lower classes and elites. Local communities rather than corporations, the New Class elites, or EU bureaucrats must ultimately decide on the fate of their communities. There are the simultaneous decentralist influences of the 1968ers and the anti-Jacobin, anti-statist old rightists such as Maurras, who rejected the "dictatorship" of modern values and the individualist impulses of the legacy of 1789.

In position 6, "Against Jacobinism; For a Federal Europe", the nation-state so dear to fascists and the extreme-right in general is rejected as outmoded: "The nation-state is now too big to manage little problems and too small to address big ones". Belonging will be European and federal in nature as "the future belongs to large cultures and civilizations capable of organizing themselves into autonomous entities and of acquiring enough power to resist outside interference". Federalism would allow for the protection of strong regions, nations, and historical cultures, while allowing Europeans to "rediscover their 'common origins'".

It is significant that Europe as a federalized, sovereign power bloc would be tied with Russia against the USA, the key representative of liberalism. This is certainly part of a larger attempt to weaken the USA as a global superpower, while the alliance with Russia has historical echoes of the Nazi-Soviet Non-Aggression Pact of 1939 and the National Bolshevist tendency in Germany led by Ernst Niekisch (1889–1967) that sought to unite a re-spiritualized, worker-centred Germany and Stalinist Soviet Union in order to destroy the "materialism" of Western civilization. The desire to unite with Russia in a federal Europe would be based on the anti-bureaucratic principle of subsidiarity, but centralism is required in creating a single currency and bank, as well as common diplomatic, military, and science and technology policies for a unified Europe. It is unclear how the pan-European centralist thrust of the manifesto would not overwhelm the desire to respect political decisions at the lowest levels possible.

In position 7, "Against Depoliticization; For the Strengthening of Democracy", the *demos* (people) and *ethnos* are united in a manner, which valorizes homogeneous forms of community belonging, while rejecting the modern, US and French democratic revolutions and the communist revolutions in the East: Democracy did not first appear with the Revolutions of 1776 and 1789. Rather, it has constituted a constant tradition in Europe since the existence of the ancient Greek city and since the time of ancient German "freedoms". Democracy is not synonymous with the former "popular democracies" of the East nor with liberal parliamentary democracy today so prevalent in Western countries. Nor does democracy refer to the political party system. Rather, it denotes a system whereby the people are sovereign.

In a key passage, after "abstract" equality in the liberal mode is rejected, the authors unite *ethnos* and *demos* in a decidedly pre-modern manner: "The essential idea of democracy is neither that of the individual nor of humanity, but rather the idea of a body of citizens politically united into a people". "People" here does not imply all the people (*demos*), but a circumscribed, homogeneous people along rooted ethnic lines. Is this not a disguised form of racism? Is this not partly an anti-modern project, which pines for the age before modernity, capitalism, liberalism, egalitarianism, immigration, and multiculturalism supposedly destroyed rooted European regions, nations, and communities? In fairness to de Benoist, he has defended the right of Muslims to wear their Islamic garb in public space, but perhaps as a tactic to infuriate Europeans by telling them they have "lost" their rooted European cultures.[57] The implication is that Muslims in Europe maintain their own rooted cultures far away from home, while the French or Europeans allow their rooted cultures to be destroyed through demographic swamping, unfettered immigration, capitalism, and US cultural influences. De Benoist's aim is a "multiculturalism of the right", one that recognizes public cultural differences in order to restrict immigration and give preference to white Europeans and their historic regions and nations.

In an attempt to split the people from what the ND considers the pro-globalization New Class of politicians, media, and CEO's, the procedure of the referendum is invoked in order to allow the people the possibility to return to the *ethnos* and "counteract the overwhelming power of money" in political life. The nationalist right certainly has a history of appealing to the people above the "corrupt" politicians, political parties, and power of industrialists. De Gaulle utilized the referendum to end French colonialism in Algeria. In 1961, de Gaulle organized a referendum on self-determination. About 75 % of the French population accepted it. In 1962, the Evian Accords ended the Algerian War and granted independence to Algeria. In another referendum in respect of the Evian accords, nearly 91 % of mainland France supported it. The implicit argument of the ND is that in the new millennium France has become the colony of uncontrolled immigration, the new Algeria is mainland France, and perhaps the "common sense" of the people united in the framework of an *ethnos* can vote to democratically reverse this "ethnocidal"[58] project destructive of Europe's pagan past and historic regions and nations.

In position 8, "Against Productivism; For New Forms of Labor", the ND calls for the "imperative gradually to dissociate work from income. The possibility must be explored of establishing a fixed minimum stipend or income for every citizen from birth until death and without asking anything in return". The ND rejects modernity's totalizing, punishing, and de-humanizing conception of labor, which has not stopped cycles of mass unemployment, technology getting rid of workers, or the rich from getting richer and the poor poorer. The liberal capitalist model of labor is a form of pseudo-emancipation: "It is modernity which, through its productivist goal of totally mobilizing all resources, has made of work a value in itself, the principal mode of socialization, and an illusory form of emancipation and of the autonomy of the individual ("freedom through work")".

Positions 9–12 of the manifesto highlight the ND's "left-wing" or ecological concerns: "Against the Ruthless Pursuit of Current Economic Policies; For an

57 See Benoist, Sur le foulard Islamique, available at: http://www.alaindebenoist.com/pdf/sur_le_foulard_islamique.pdf, last accessed 1 June 2010.

58 A term distinctive from genocide inspired by French ethnologist Robert Jaulin (1928–1996) used by ND thinkers to connote the destruction of the culture of a people. See, for example, Faye, Le système à tuer les peuples.

Economy at the Service of the People" (9); "Against Gigantism; For Local Communities" (10); "Against Megalopolis; For Cities on a Human Scale" (11); and "Against Unbridled Technology; For an Integral Ecology" (12). An economy in the "service of the people" would have strict international environmental laws, the IMF, World Bank, and corporations would be severely restrained by local economies, Third World debt would be forgiven, and cooperatives, mutual societies, and non-profit organizations would be integrated into the economy. The economy cannot be calculated by quantifiable figures alone such as Gross Domestic Product, but it must be an economy in the true service of local people, regions, and communities rather than outsiders (i. e. capitalists, "New Class", EU bureaucrats, immigrants, etc.).

In position 10, the ND rejects the gigantism of the welfare state, large corporations, and state bureaucracies out of touch with ordinary people: "Only responsible individuals in responsible communities can establish a social justice which is not synonymous with welfare". Rejecting the state and capitalism's gigantism, the authors paint a return to "premodern" communities, values, and festivals in a pagan spirit, which smashes the linear rhythms of modernity. Pagan festivals connote European revival and renewal - the sense of a new historical beginning for Europe.

In position 11, the authors call for the end of massive cities and a return to eco-friendly cities of a human scale, as well as the expansion of rural areas. In position 12, the ND calls for an "integral ecology" and the rejection of technology for its own sake. There are limits to growth, Western models of growth are a failure, and harmony and ecological considerations must be restored. We might also need to de-industrialize, fine polluters, and renew resources if we are to survive as a species.

Finally, position 13, "For Independence of Thought and a Return to Discussion of Ideas", is the ND's call for unlimited free expression. It is part of the ND's Gramscian strategy to win hearts and minds to suggest that the liberal "New Class" is dogmatic and the ND is a victim of "thought control". The ND supports "a return to critical thinking and strongly supports total freedom of expression". The ND also calls for "new syntheses" and a "common front against the disciples of Trissotin, Tartuffe, and Torquemada". If you dare accuse the ND of racism or of quasi-fascist tendencies, perhaps you are the racist or fascist! The ND constantly cries out that it is the victim of thought control, or a "new inquisition". As the ND speaks out against "hegemonic" worldviews such as liberalism, democracy, capitalism, the Rights of Man, and the egalitarian, "progressive" legacy of modernity, they claim they are persecuted for their positions. Those that dig deep and look for ND connections to CR thinkers or fascism just have ideological axes to grind. In contrast to the dominant liberal-left intelligentsia of Europe, ND ideas have provoked such a sharp reaction because ND thinkers are visionaries with a genuinely new political paradigm. As a result, ND thinkers insist the Old Left, Old Right, and traditional conservatives are scared because the ND challenges their outdated categories. ND voices are allegedly silenced and marginalized by "New Class" intellectuals, guardians of the inhumane global capitalist order.

Yet, the ND has not been marginalized. Europe has increasingly heard its thinkers. The political parties and people have heard the ND message and its leading prophet. The message is more than ever appealing because it promises a reborn European empire able to once again be a dominant geopolitical player in the international arena. The ND promises a Europe that is demographically assertive against other regions of the world. It promises a Europe with a restored pride for its historic regions and nations. Most importantly, it promises a hierarchical Europe "liberated" from the excesses of modernity by looking backwards to the glorious, "pre-modern", pagan Indo-European past. Yet, this is not merely a nostalgic project in a totally anti-modern, traditionalist spirit. The ND's project is imbued with the spirit of post-modernism, which expresses existential anguish about "grand narratives" such as liberalism. It simultaneously harkens back to a glorious European past and looks forward towards a mythical future, which will not negate the technological advances of the modern world. In short, the ND project is a variant of "alternative political modernism" and its worldview is a veritable "mazeway resynthesis" consisting of modern, anti-modern, and post-modern influences.

V. Conclusion

This paper has sought to trace an aspect of intellectual right-wing extremism in the 21st century, namely, the worldview of ND leader Alain de Benoist. De Benoist has transformed a narrow nationalistic French metapolitical movement into a pan-European New Right project seeking to smash the modern revolutionary heritage of 1789. I sought to argue that in the new millennium, despite the ND's "opening to the NL", direct democracy, and ecological influences, the ND worldview never definitively exited extreme right-wing political space. The ND has never worked from an explicitly fascist tradition. Yet, some of its main theoretical influences such as Evola and CR thinkers seriously influenced and participated in Nazi and fascist projects. I also argued that in the ND worldview homogeneous ethnic belonging trumps concern for modern, representative democracy. Democracy is valorized in order to revive homogeneous ethnic belonging. The Italian LN, a federalist, anti-immigrant party, is one concrete model of a political outfit that mimics ND ideas.[59]

I used "The French New Right in the Year 2000" to highlight the ND project for the new century. I suggested that the ND's manifesto is a synthesis of modern, anti-modern, and post-modern influences. I used Griffin's notions of "mazeway resynthesis" and "alternative political modernism" to situate de Benoist's worldview. For the ND, the fall of European civilization began with

59 See Zaslove, The Dark Side of European Politics; Alpine Populism, Padania and Beyond.

Christianity and its modern, egalitarian secular offshoots liberalism, social democracy, socialism, and communism. The demise of European civilizations and its period of decadence accelerate with liberal republican revolutions of the 18th century and continue with socialist totalitarianism in the Soviet Union, the "dictatorship" of capitalist values, and the triumph of an alienating modern, "totalitarian" life devoid of spiritual meaning. Globalization, multiculturalism, and feminism accelerate modern egalitarian values, which further destroy Europe's rooted historic regions, nations, and pagan past. The new millennium represents the end of modernity and the possibility of overcoming the hated effects of modernity: egalitarianism, egoism, the triumph of global capitalism, the demise of traditional rooted communities, and the loss of the sacred. Heroic elites like the ND must prepare Europe for a turn away from the dominant, modern, liberal capitalist model.

The modern will be paradoxically defeated using modern technological and economic means and returning to shared "common origins" in an ethnically-based pan-European framework, which restores Europe to a new period of major player in world history. Fear of the cultural effects of the modern world is combined with a valorization of the technological and economic aspects of modernity.[60] Modern, anti-modern, and post-modern values will unite to supersede the era of liberal modernity. Thousands of sovereign cultural and regional entities will reject the dominant liberal model, which is a destroyer of rooted cultures via universalist anti-racism, the human rights discourse, and multiculturalism. Europe's doors will be closed to immigrants for the benefit of rooted cultures worldwide, as the former "Third World" and Europe will cooperate to defeat Western civilization.

The underlying dread that the ND highlights is related to doubts about the merits of liberalism, democracy, multiculturalism, and key aspects of modernity. However, there will be no going back to a "golden age" that can never return, but only a "mazeway resynthesis" consisting of modern, anti-modern, and post-modern influences. Europeans were once masters of their political destinies and owners of colonies. However, on the geopolitical front, there is a sense that the modern world brought with it a retreat from history against rising powers: the USA, China, Japan, India, the Muslim world, and Latin America. Europeans must return to their vocation as major players in world history by embracing elitist, hierarchical societies. Demographically, the ND insists the situation is tragic for Europeans as white Europeans no longer have children, while Asians, Latin Americans, Africans, and Muslims reinforce their own world status through numbers and "invade" Europe through uncontrolled immigration. Politically, the ND underscores doubts about the welfare state, the way it is too generous for "non-native" Europeans and immigrants, and unrepresentative bureaucratic and statist liberal democracies. Spiritually, although the ND rejects the Judeo-

60 See Habermas (Ed.), The New Conservatism, pp. 36–37.

Christian tradition and its thinkers are largely agnostic, they call for a return to the sacred and the canopy of meaning destroyed by the processes of modernity.

In conclusion, the discourse of the ND in respect of modernity poses challenges for the liberal-left related to the struggle over different notions of community and the ability of extreme right-wing discourses to mutate in the post-war era. First, the ND's pro-communitarian discourse straddles pro- and anti-multicultural positions by valorizing the "right to difference" of various communities, yet dreading multiculturalism as a form of "ethnocide". Second, the ND, in conjunction with far right-wing parties like the FN and fascists in another epoch, are willing to work within the liberal democratic framework in order to seek its demise. Yet, they must work with other political forces, which might be on the neo-liberal right and reject their anti-capitalist, anti-egalitarian worldview. This matters little to the ND as they seek the general metapolitical transformation of the European body politic and "Zeitgeist". Third, the ND is a cultivated, sophisticated right that the left generally fails to acknowledge and is light years away from the brutal violence of the squadristi or brownshirts. Fourth, fascism was able to mutate in the post-war years and, for Griffin, one intellectually impressive strand was the ND. This raises questions of definitional issues over what constitutes fascism, whether it was epochal, and whether fascism is about core ideological goals and tactical and organizational framework.[61]

Finally, the ND in combination with anti-immigrant parties like the FN, has been instrumental in shifting the European discourse against cultural aspects of modernity (i. e. alienation, egoism, rampant materialism and hedonism, cultural pluralism, and the decline of community), liberalism, immigration, immigrants, minorities, and multiculturalism. The vociferous voices against Turkey's entrance into the EU across the political spectrum, the Swiss referendum questioning the construction of new minarets in 2009, and the French government's bill in 2010 banning the Islamic veil in public places speak volumes about the cultural shifts in the European body politic. In addition, 2008 saw the creation of the French extreme right-wing party *La nouvelle droite populaire* (NDP), which includes former GRECE secretary-general Pierre Vial. Its campaigns have included "Non aux minarets" (No to minarets) and support for European parliamentary candidates, which firmly reject the Islamicization of France and Europe. According to the ND's own metapolitical logic pioneered by de Benoist, the times are changing. Ultimately, the ND waits for the day a new rights framework is erected throughout Europe. In this new political framework, the collective rights of historic European ethnic groups trump individual rights and the rights of immigrants. Rights in the liberal sense would be subordinated to the duty of protecting homogenized European ethnic communities seeking to abolish "humanity's condition of homelessness"[62] caused by modernity.

61 Cf. Payne, A History of Fascism: 1914–1945.
62 Griffin, Foreword: Another Face? Another Mazeway?, p. xvi.

Memory Politics in Western Europe

David Art

Over the last decade, the legacies of past atrocities have emerged as salient political issues across advanced industrial democracies. From Australia to Canada, victim groups have demanded redress for systematic violations of human rights committed by the state or by members of society. Public debates over historic injustices have produced a variety of different outcomes, such as official state apologies, reparations, and the creation of national holidays to remember the victims. At the same time, they have also produced denials and backlashes, fueled far right political forces, and generally become enmeshed in partisan political conflict. This should not strike observers as surprising, for debates about past atrocities raise issues central to contemporary politics: national identity, the treatment of minorities and immigrants, and the legitimacy of radical right politics in democratic states are just some of the topics at the heart of "dealing with" history. The past, in short, has become a field of political contention, albeit one that has only recently become an object of study by political scientists.[1]

Europe provides a fascinating laboratory for examining the relevance of the past to contemporary politics. Across Europe, the Second World War in particular has only become more politically salient as distance to it increases. The exculpatory narratives of the war that reduced Nazism, fascism, and wartime collaboration to a small - and unrepresentative - group of national political elites have unraveled over the last several decades. The tales of nations united in resistance that served as the symbolic foundations of both the postwar French and Italian states have been challenged. In Austria, the consensus that the state had been "Hitler's first victim" eroded during the presidential campaign of Kurt Waldheim in 1986. More recently, politicians and academics in Switzerland and Sweden have been forced to revise the widely accepted view of their states as neutrals who kept their hands free of Nazi atrocities. The Dutch have questioned the "Anne Frank" narrative that long shaped their historical memory of the war years, and have begun to confront the fact that 75 % of Dutch Jews were sent to the death camps, a figure higher than in any other part of occupied Europe. For reasons of space, this paper focuses only on cases in Western Europe, but

1 There are some important exceptions; see Booth, Communities of Memory, pp. 249-263; Bermeo, Democracy and the Lessons of Dictatorship, pp. 273-291.

it is important to note that countries in Central and Eastern Europe – most notably Poland – have also been the sites of intense public debates about the Second World War as previously hegemonic anti-fascist narratives have eroded.

One reason for the collapse of the European "founding myths", as one scholar has referred to them, is the end of the Cold War.[2] In the early postwar period, the United States was willing to overlook the extent of wartime collaboration or support for fascism in its search for allies in the war against communism. With this imperative no longer operative, claims by victim groups, which might have been quietly buried in the past, have been supported by the US government. Certainly, other factors have played a role as well. The impending disappearance of the generation of survivors has arguably forced governments into quick action in the realm of reparations. Progress in historical scholarship, coupled with the discovery of voluminous archival materials in the former Soviet Union and Eastern Europe, has radically changed our understanding of the period. More controversially, the growing importance of the Holocaust for Jews, particularly in the United States, has led to increased claim making against those who persecuted Jews, as well as those who profited from such persecution.[3]

But one of the most important reasons for the return of history has been the resurgence of the far right in Western Europe. This is not because such parties like the *French National Front* (FN), the *German Republicans* (REP), or even the *Italian National Alliance* (AN) actually represent a revival of fascism. Rather, they belong to an emerging party family that falls under the rubric "extreme-right", "right-wing populist" or "radical-right".[4] Their defining feature is nationalism, and they have all appealed to racial stereotypes and xenophobia.[5] Although mainstream parties throughout Europe have often done this as well, far right parties have made draconian immigration policies central to their program and engaged regularly in a radically xenophobic political discourse.

Yet even if the claims of a resurgent fascism are misplaced, the very fact that they are being made is important in and of itself. Political elites across Europe have – to varying degrees and to varying success – tried to fend off the right-wing populist challenge by linking these parties to a fascist or collaborationist past. At the same time, many far right parties have woven apologetic interpretations of the Second World War into their contemporary political identities, thereby transforming history into a partisan political issue. For these reasons, the process of "dealing with the past" and the electoral success of far right par-

2 The term "founding myths" is from Judt, The Past is Another Country, pp. 83–118.
3 On this point, see Novick, The Holocaust in American Life.
4 I use the terms "right-wing populist" and far right interchangeably in this paper. In so doing, I align myself with those scholars who view populism as one of the defining features of this new party family: Betz/Immerfall (Eds.), The New Politics of the Right; Rydgren, Radical Right Populism in Sweden, pp. 27–54.
5 On the debate over the definition of the radical right, see Eatwell, The Rebirth of the "Extreme Right" in Western Europe?, pp. 410–414; Mudde, The War of Words, pp. 225–248. An expert survey conducted by Lubbers appears in Norris, Radical Right: Parties and Electoral Competition.

ties cannot, I argue, be separated. As of yet, however, scholars have largely failed to link the two.

The purpose of this paper is to begin to explore the connections between memory and the far right, and at the same time contribute to the growing debate concerning the cross-national variation in support for right-wing populist parties. One of the most puzzling aspects of the far right phenomenon has been its divergent trajectory in advanced industrial societies over the last several decades. Far right parties differ not only in terms of their electoral support (see Table 1), but also in terms of their integration into the political system. They have become members of national coalition governments in Austria, Italy, the Netherlands and Switzerland. In Denmark and Norway, current governments rely on support from far right parties. In Belgium and France, the far right is strong but so-called "cordon-sanitaires" have kept it out of political office. In Germany, Sweden, and Wallonia, far right parties have been either electorally insignificant or have collapsed after a single electoral success. In the Netherlands, Geert Wilder's *Party of Freedom* (PVV) may avoid collapsing like previous incarnations of Dutch right-wing populism, like the List Pim Fortuyn and the Center Democrats, but it is too soon to tell.

Table 1: Successful and unsuccessful radical right parties as of July 2009*

Party	Country	Outcome
Austrian Freedom Party (FPÖ)	Austria	Success
Belgian National Front (FNb)	Belgium (Wallonia)	Failure
British National Party (BNP)	Great Britain	Failure
Center Democrats (CD)	Netherlands	Failure
Danish People's Party (DF)	Denmark	Success
German National Party (NPD)	Germany	Failure
German People's Union (DVU)	Germany	Failure
List Pim Fortuyn (LPF)	Netherlands	Failure
National Alliance (AN)	Italy	Success
National Front (FN)	France	Success
New Democracy (ND)	Sweden	Failure
Northen League (LN)	Italy	Success
Progress Party (FrP)	Norway	Success
Republicans (REP)	Germany	Failure
Sweden Democrats (SD)	Sweden	Failure
Swiss People's Party (SVP)	Switzerland	Success
Vlaams Belang (VB)	Belgium (Flanders)	Success

* Success is defined as winning 5 % of the vote in three successive national parliamentary elections.

Why has the far right been strong in Denmark and weak in Sweden? Why has the far right been a powerful force in Austrian politics but a marginal player in Germany? Scholars have attempted to explain such cross-national variation with reference to differences in patterns of immigration, unemployment, or electoral rules.[6] There is a great deal of scholarly debate over the significance of these variables, and a consensus on any one has yet to emerge.

This paper sketches out an ideational explanation for the divergent development of the far right in three European states: Germany, Italy and France. The far right has been electorally weak and politically marginalized in Germany. In France, the far right has done well in elections but has been prevented, by a combination of electoral institutions *and* political party strategies, from wielding political power. In Italy, the far right is not only electorally strong but has been become a party of government. My central claim is that ideas about the wartime past, specifically ideas held by elites from mainstream political forces, have played a central role in the different trajectories of these parties.[7] While I am not claiming that ecological correlates and electoral institutions do not matter, I argue that the success or failure of postwar far right parties need to be understood in the context of the political-cultural environment in which these parties find themselves. While a much richer evidentiary base is obviously needed to make the argument compelling, the goal here is simply to demonstrate that it is plausible.

The rest of this paper proceeds as follows. The first section offers a cross-national comparison of how 10 different European states have come to terms with the wartime past. This exercise in classification is necessary both to provide some concrete indicators for a "fuzzy" subject, and to provide a basis for future comparative work. The second section lays out in greater depth the connection between this process and far right parties. The third section focuses on Germany and argues that the "culture of contrition" that evolved during numerous critical public examinations of the Nazi past has kept far right political parties weak and marginalized.[8] The fourth section turns to France, a case that has shown marked variation in the extent of dealing with the past over time. Before Vichy became a salient political issue in the late 1980s, the National Front was able to rise quickly and consolidate itself in French politics. Since then, the French political establishment has used history as a weapon against the far right, justifying its current marginalization with reference to the "lessons of history". The fifth section turns to Italy and argues that the necessary condition for the

6 On immigration as the central variable in the success of right-wing populist parties, see Knigge, The Ecological Correlates, pp. 249–279: Golder, Explaining Variation, pp. 432–466; Gibson, The Growth of Anti-Immigrant Parties; On the relationship, see Jackman/Volpert, Conditions Favouring Parties, pp. 501–521; Golder, Explaining Variation; Norris, Radical Right; and Carter, Proportional Representation and the Fortunes, pp. 125–146.

7 I treat the cases of Germany and Austria more fully in Art, The Politics of the Nazi Past.

8 I borrow this phrase from Wilds, Identity Creation, pp. 83–102.

regeneration of the far right was a change in elite ideas about the fascist past and the legitimacy of the MSI during the transformation of the Italian party system. The sixth and final section discusses how the past has become an important issue in the politics of the European Union and European Integration. I argue that contrition and an ongoing critical examination of historical complicity is becoming a pan-European value.

I. Comparing contrition

How can one compare the process of dealing with the past across European countries? There are several possible indicators that allow researchers to compare the extent and level of dealing with the past across cases. These are best presented as responses to three different questions.

First, to what extent have official state representatives recognized the crimes of previous regimes and condemned them or apologized for them? Second, for how long have political elites and the general population critically discussed wartime behavior, and how politically salient have these debates been? Third, have elites converged around a particular interpretation of the fascist, collaborationist, or "neutral" past, or do different historical interpretations still compete in the marketplace of ideas? Below I treat each of these variables (also summarized in Table 2) in turn.

1. State recognition

State recognition of past complicity varies enormously across countries. At one pole are states like Turkey, whose representatives have repeatedly denied the existence of the Armenian Genocide. Germany occupies a unique position at the other end of the spectrum; its official representatives have not only apologized for past atrocities but have turned contrition into a form of statecraft. Most states - including the states of Western Europe - fall somewhere in between these two poles. Yet the timing and nature of official recognition of atrocities committed during the Second World War still differ markedly across them. Of the three original fascist states, Germany was the first to acknowledge responsibility for genocide by offering restitution to the state of Israel in the early 1950s. Since then, German presidents (the head-of-state) have offered numerous apologies to countries and groups that suffered under Nazism. Austria, the other surviving successor state of the Third Reich, only offered an apology in 1991, and this was delivered by the Prime Minister (the head of government) rather than the head-of-state (President).[9] Italy has yet to offer an official apol-

9 It was also in the context of a speech on Yugoslavia to which foreign journalists were invited but Austrian ones were not. Interview with Therezija Stoisits (Greens), Member of Parliament, 5 July 2002, Vienna.

ogy either to the victims of Italian aggression in Africa and the Balkans, or to the domestic victims of fascism.

Of the states with collaborationist pasts, France became the first to offer an official apology for complicity in Nazi crimes when President Jacques Chirac, the head-of-state, did so in 1995. In 1999, the Norwegian government issued an official apology to Norwegian Jewry. In 2000, Dutch Prime Minister Wim Kok extended an apology to all the victims of the Nazis. The Belgian Prime Minister Guy Verhofstadt apologized for the government's role in the deportation of Jews in 2002. In 2003, Danish Prime Minister Anders Fogh Rasmussen offered the first public condemnation of collaboration, although he stopped short of issuing an apology. Of the two neutral states under analysis, the Swiss President apologized for the country's role in laundering Nazi gold and for turning back Jewish refugees, in 1997 and 1999, respectively.[10] Sweden's Prime Minister Goran Persson first publicly recognized the "political and moral responsibility for what Swedish officials did - or failed to do - during the war years" in 2000 but did not issue an official apology.[11]

2. Public debates

The duration and intensity of public debates about the past are another source of variation among the cases.[12] In Germany and the Netherlands, public discussions of national complicity began in the 1960s. In France and Austria, such debates date from the mid 1980s. In all the other cases under consideration, public deliberation about past atrocities was virtually absent until the middle of the past decade. The timing of such debates influences the extent to which members of the population have rejected the pleasant postwar founding myths that had previously dominated political discourse and school curricula. Whereas Germans have been exposed to critical historical examinations of their past for forty years, Belgians and Danes are only beginning to change their attitudes about their states' pasts.

The intensity of public debates also differs markedly across Western European states. In Austria, France and Germany, public debates about the past have been quite salient in both politics and the media. I have therefore coded them as "high". In the Scandinavian states and in the Netherlands, public

10 I do not include the Portuguese case in this essay, for three reasons. First, Portugal lacks a right-wing populist party since the Portuguese People's Party is really a national conservative party. Second, debates about the extent of collaboration during the period of "neutrality" have really not unfolded in Portugal. Third, as in Spain, discussions of Portugal's wartime past are inextricably linked to a domestic fascist regime. That being said, I do agree with scholars who argue that memories of a recent authoritarian experience have prevented the emergence of the far right on the Iberian Peninsula.

11 The Independent, 27 January 2000.

12 For a theoretical discussion of public debates, see Art, The Politics of the Nazi Past.

debates about the past have been rather low volume affairs. Belgium and Switzerland each received a score of "medium". These codings reflect my substantive knowledge of the cases, but the results of a Lexis-Nexis search for each state using equivalent search terms should improve our confidence in them.[13] It Italy, public debate about fascism was muted for a long period, but the political salience of history has risen markedly in the past couple of years as Berlusconi and his coalition partners have tried to undermine Italy's official antifascist consensus. The current mayor of Rome, for example, refused to condemn fascism as an absolute evil in an interview with the "Corriere della Sera" newspaper during a trip to Israel in September 2008.[14] In the same month, Defense Minister Ignazio La Russa defended fascist soldiers who defended their homeland against the Anglo-American landings during the 65 anniversary of Rome's resistance to Nazi occupation. The left has protested vigorously against what they see as an attempt to rewrite history and some have even warned that the immigration policies of the *Lega Nord* (Berlusconi's current coalition partner) and the self-defense militias the party appears to support constitute a revival of fascism.

3. Consensus or disagreement

The presence or absence of an elite consensus regarding historical interpretation is the final, and most crucial, variable in the overall process of "dealing with the past". By consensus, I mean that elites from across the political spectrum (with the possible exception of the far right) have accepted the fact that their states were complicit, to varying degrees, in wartime violations of basic human rights. This elite consensus can be the product of intense public debate. In Germany, France, and the Netherlands, politicians have converged around an interpretation of the past, after years of discussion, which recognizes crimes against humanity and assumes responsibility for them. In the three Scandinavian

13 To get a more objective measure of the salience of the memory of the Second World War in the politics of 10 European states, I conducted a Lexis-Nexis guided news search of major international newspapers using the following search terms in the full-text of articles: Country name (variable), Second World War, and Memory. To correct for the fact that large countries (such as Germany) received more coverage than smaller ones, I divided the total number of articles for each country by its population according to the CIA's world factbook. I assumed that the percentage of irrelevant articles produced by the search were equal across countries. This produced the following results: France 57.2, Norway 47.1, Germany 45.1, Austria 44.3, Switzerland 37.9, Belgium 33.9, Denmark 31.3, Sweden 23, Italy 20.7, the Netherlands 19.3 %. This rank ordering is mostly consistent with my subjective coding of the cases based on my knowledge of them. The major difference concerns Norway, which ranks second in the Lexis-Nexis search but which I have coded as "low". My suspicion is that the relatively small number of articles (217) may have contained a high number of irrelevant hits.

14 At the same time, Alemanno has also supported the construction of a Holocaust museum in Rome.

countries, where debates about the wartime past emerged later and have been of lower intensity, politicians have largely updated their historical interpretations of their respective nation's past. Of the three, Swedish elites have made the most extensive attempt to change mass attitudes in line with this new consensus. In 1997, Prime Minister Perrson launched an extensive Holocaust education campaign that involved publishing and freely distributing a book about the Holocaust and Sweden's wartime behavior. Over 800,000 copies of this book, titled "Tell Ye Your Children," have been published, making it the most widely distributed book in Swedish history after the Bible.[15]

It is important to note that public debates can also produce polarization. In Austria, a long-standing public debate about Austrian complicity in Nazi crimes has not produced an elite consensus, but rather enduring polarization between those who recognize a high degree of Austrian complicity and those who view Austria as primarily a victim of Nazi aggression. In Switzerland, many politicians have resisted changing their previous attitudes about Swiss neutrality in light of recent debates over Nazi gold and the sealing of borders to refugees. Similarly, as I suggested above, Italian politicians still offer radically different interpretations of the fascist experience, and history has become a battle ground in contemporary partisan politics.

Belgium offers an especially interesting case of elite conflict over history, for the rifts in this debate have been superimposed on the broader dispute between the Walloons and the Flemish. Many Walloons contend that Flemish nationalists have a highly collaborationist past, and it is a historical fact that thousands of Dutch-speaking Belgians did fight on the German side, in large part to promote the interests of their language group.[16] The Flemish, for their part, argue that the postwar punishment of collaborators was overly harsh and used primarily to suppress postwar Flemish nationalism. Some Flemish politicians, and not only those from the former extreme-right *Vlaams Bloc*, have sought amnesties for the "victims" of postwar justice. The Wallonians have denounced such initiatives, and have forced government officials with links to groups working on behalf of collaborators to resign. Since the late 1990s, the past has become a persistent issue in Belgian partisan politics.

15 Interview with Paul Levine, co-author of "Tell Ye Your Children". 25 May 2005, Stockholm.

16 It should be noted that the Nazis found collaborators in both Flanders and Wallonia. In Flanders, the Nazis installed the nationalist "Vlaams National Verbond" (VNV) before replacing them with a smaller group named De Vlag. In Wallonia, a right-wing Catholic movement named The Rexists were appointed to posts in the government.

Table 2: Comparative contrition

Country	Form of complicity	First official recognition of complicity	Beginning of public debate	Intensity of debate	Elite consensus?	Theme for the far right?
Germany	Fascist State	1952 (apology)	1960s	High	Yes	Yes
Austria	Fascist State	1991 (apology)	1980s	High	No	Yes
Italy	Fascist State	NONE	1990s	High	No	Yes
France	Collaboration	1995 (apology)	1980s	High	Yes	Yes
Netherlands	Collaboration	2000 (apology)	1960s	Low	Yes	No
Belgium	Collaboration	2002 (apology)	1990s	Medium	No	Yes
Norway	Collaboration	1997 (apology)	1990s	Low	Yes	No
Denmark	Collaboration	2003 (condemnation)	1990s	Low	Yes	No
Switzerland	"Neutrality"	1997 (apology)	1990s	Medium	No	Yes
Sweden	"Neutrality"	2000 (condemnation)	1990s	Low	Yes	Yes

II. The far right and the Second World War

What is the connection between historical memory of the Second World War and the recent development of the far right? It is important to note that the past has clearly not been significant for some right-wing populist parties. Far right parties in Scandinavia and the Netherlands have not made the defense of national history into a political issue. The late Pim Fortuyn, for example, clearly and consistently condemned Nazism, as has Geert Wilders. Members of the far right *Danish People's Party* identify explicitly with the Danish resistance movement rather than with Nazi collaborators.[17] It would also be misleading to claim that the electoral success of the far right can be explained primarily with reference to their historical interpretations. Most Austrians, for example, did not vote for Jörg Haider because of his apologist interpretations and qualified defenses of Nazism, although this certainly helped mobilize his extreme right base.[18]

The links between the far right and the past are more complicated, yet certainly consequential. Many far right parties intertwine apologetic narratives of the war years with an essentialist view of national identity, opposition to immigration, and rejection of cosmopolitan values. As the self-proclaimed defenders of the national from the pressures of European integration and globalization, these parties aim to protect the history that constitutes their respective nations.

17 Interview with Jesper Langballe (DV), Member of Parliament, 17 May 2005, Copenhagen.
18 Cf. Art, The Politics of the Nazi Past.

They have represented their societies as the victims of international conspiracies to degrade their pasts and identity. They have downplayed the crimes committed in their state and denied that anything can be gained by forcing their populations to "work through" or "come to terms with" a past that belongs to a disappearing generation. In Austria, Jörg Haider (FPÖ) skillfully rode the chauvinist reaction against international censure of Austria's wartime behavior following the Waldheim debate in 1986. Christoph Blocher, the leader of the far right *Swiss People's Party* (SV), mounted a similar attack against international critics and domestic traitors after the Nazi gold story broke in the mid 1990s. In France, Le Pen has described a critical examination of the Vichy regime as an affront to the nation's honor. And in all of these countries, right-wing populists have decried the "politically correct" histories disseminated by elites out of touch with the values and historical memories of ordinary people. History, in short, has become another rhetorical weapon in a populist attack on the political and intellectual establishments.

The past also matters to the extent that mainstream political parties, and the media, have used history as a weapon against the far right. Again, it does not matter whether or not far right parties actually possess the ideological baggage of fascism for them to be effectively linked with it. But as I argue below, history can only be an effective weapon where there is an elite consensus renouncing the state's wartime behavior and a commitment to eliminate any vestiges of support for it. This elite consensus has been the most solid, and politically important, in Germany.

III. Germany: The culture of contrition

In the immediate postwar period, it seemed scarcely unimaginable that Germany would later become *the* internationally recognized model of a society that has critically examined its shameful past and turned contrition into a form of statecraft. Leaders from across the political spectrum in the late 1940s and 1950s generally portrayed Germans as the victims of a small clique of Nazi fanatics who had hijacked the German state. The *Christian Democratic* Chancellor Konrad Adenauer's "founding myth" of postwar Germany was designed to avoid alienating the millions of Germans who had embraced Nazism. Although *Social Democrats* spoke more explicitly about German complicity than *Christian Democrats*, they were unwilling to challenge Adenauer's policy of rapidly reintegrating former Nazis into German politics and society through broad amnesties. Although Adenauer did recognize Germany's moral burden by paying reparations to Israel, the Nazi past was nearly altogether absent from German political discourse in the first several postwar decades.[19]

19 On early efforts to deal with the Nazi past in Germany, see Herf, Divided Memory; and Frei, Adenauer and the Nazi Past.

This began to change in the 1960s when the ideological cleavage between the German right and left widened. A series of trials, including the Eichmann trial in Israel, and parliamentary debates about removing the statue of limitations for crimes against humanity raised the salience of the Nazi past in contemporary politics. Members of the leftist Student Movement pointed out the ideological and personal continuities between Nazi Germany and the Federal Republic, and used them as a weapon against the political establishment. The anti-authoritarian New Left that grew of out of the student movement, and later coalesced into the *Green Party*, defined itself as a reaction to the Nazi past.[20] The right, for its part, drew parallels between the student movement and the radicalization of the left that contributed to the collapse of Weimar. When some fringe movements of the New Left turned to terrorism in the 1970s, conservatives argued that this was a consequence of a "false mastering of the past" which had destroyed traditional political values, such as patriotism.[21] Conservative politicians and intellectuals called for Germany to develop a "normal" national identity, which involved redefining Germany's relationship with its history. While not denying the crimes of Nazism, conservatives emphasized the positive sides of German history and claimed that the left's obsession with the years 1933-1945 was hampering Germany's political development.

This simmering debate between right and left reached a new peak in the mid -1980s. Two factors contributed to the explosion of public debate about the Nazi past. First, upon coming to power in 1982 Chancellor Helmut Kohl identified "normalization" of the Nazi past as one of his central goals. Second, the passing of several forty-year anniversaries related to the Nazi past - and particularly the fortieth anniversary of Germany's capitulation on May 8, 1945 - gave Kohl the opportunity to stage-manage several commemorations consistent with his preference to "allow the past to pass away". The visit by President Reagan and Kohl to the Bitburg cemetery, where former members of the Waffen-SS were buried, was to mark the symbolic end of the Second World War.

Yet things did not go as planned, in large part because Kohl miscalculated the degree of opposition within German society toward putting the past to rest. By the early 1980s, members of the Student Movement had come to occupy important positions within politics and the media. The German public had also been exposed to a powerful, if maudlin, reminder of the Nazi past in the form of the Hollywood mini-series "Holocaust", which millions of Germans watched in 1979.[22] If Kohl had hoped to normalize German history, his actions had the unintended effect of transforming the Nazi past into a salient political issue for the German left.

20 Cf. Markovits/Gorski, The German Left: Red, Green and Beyond, pp. 18-21. As Green politician Joschka Fischer once remarked, "most of us became Greens precisely because of German history". In: Die Zeit, 7 February 1985.

21 Alfred Dregger (CDU), quoted in Dubiel, Niemand ist frei von der Geschichte, p. 156.

22 On this point, see Markovits/Noveck, Germany, pp. 428-32.

Public deliberation about the Nazi past was intense, and the details of that debate cannot be reproduced here. The important point is that the balance of political forces adopting "contrite" positions toward the Nazi past shifted fundamentally as a result. To put it simply, the left won. Bitburg created a public relations fiasco that rendered conservatives wary of trying to normalize the Nazi past. Moreover, several important figures within the *Christian Democratic* camp, particularly President Richard von Weizsäcker and CDU Party Chairman Heiner Geissler, publicly sided with those politicians and intellectuals who demanded that contrition for the Nazi past remain a central duty for all Germans. A discernable shift occurred within intellectual circles as well. When Ernst Nolte published an article challenging the notion that the Holocaust was a unique event, and was thus comparable to other atrocities such as Stalinism and genocide in Cambodia, the philosopher Jürgen Habermas wrote a passionate rebuttal. This "Historians' Debate" ("Historikerstreit") was carried out in the pages of Germany's prominent newspapers and weeklies for several years, and nearly every German intellectual of any stature participated in it.[23] In the end, Nolte stood virtually alone.

As politicians and elites reached a consensus, contrition became the only publicly acceptable position for politicians to take regarding the Nazi past. Contrition became, in other words, the cornerstone of what I refer to as "political correctness-German style". Like race in the United States, the Nazi past has become the "third rail" in German politics, and politicians who have challenged the contrition discourse have seen their careers ended within a matter of days.[24] At the same time, German politicians are expected to participate in ceremonies marking critical events in the Holocaust (such as the Pogroms of November 9, 1938, and the liberation of Auschwitz on January 27, 1944) and to demonstrate contrition in relations with other foreign countries, especially Israel and Poland.

What is the relationship between the rise of the culture of contrition and the fortunes of right-wing populism in Germany? The *Republicans* (REP) emerged during the height of debates about the Nazi past in 1983, and rejection of the contrition narrative was always a central element of its members' political ideology. The party's leader, Franz Schönhuber, had lost his job as a radio announcer in Bavaria after he published a book defending his record in the Waffen-SS. During speeches at the REP first party congress, party founders called for an end to "mastering the past" and for Germans to develop a healthy national identity. The very first page of the 1987 party program laments that

23 On the Historians' Debate, see Maier, The Unmasterable Past.

24 An example was the former President of the Bundestag Philipp Jenninger (CDU). On November 9, 1988, Jenninger delivered a speech commemorating the 50th anniversary of Pogromnacht (also referred to as "Kristallnacht") before the German Bundestag. Although Jenninger was clearly not attempting to defend ordinary Germans who participated in attacks on Jews, a combination of poor speechwriting and oratorical skills gave the impression that he was. SPD and "Green" parliamentarians left the room in protest, and CDU politicians convinced Jenninger to resign the next day.

"the war propaganda of the victorious powers has entered our history books, and our youth must believe their exaggerations and falsifications to a large degree because an objective history is not possible".[25] In-depth interviews with REP politicians revealed that many joined the party specifically because of the party's defense of Germany's wartime history. The rise of the REP was thus, in part, a by-product of the public debate about the Nazi past.

But the REP failure to reproduce the gains of other right-wing populist parties across Western Europe was also intimately connected with the results of that debate. After initial breakthroughs in several state elections in the late 1980s and the early 1990s, the REP won only 2.5 % in national parliamentary elections in 1994 and quickly became politically irrelevant. During its brief heyday, however, the party received enormous attention from German political parties, the media, and civil society. When the REP captured 7.5 % in the West Berlin state election in 1989, all of these forces immediately focused on the meaning of the REP for German democracy. The overriding consensus was that right-wing populism represented a threat that needed to be repulsed.

The "culture of contrition" both structured political and social actors' reactions to a new far right party and provided them with weapons for combating it. For parties and intellectuals on the left, it was patently unacceptable for a party with a revisionist reading of the Nazi past to consolidate itself in Germany. *Social Democrats*, *Greens*, trade unionists, and a variety of groups from civil society organized to battle the REP at every opportunity. This entailed organizing protests during REP campaign events and meetings, harassing REP politicians and party members, and blocking public and private venues for REP political activity. While some have deemed this behavior "helpless antifascism", these acts of disruption, repeated hundreds of times across Germany, had a large cumulative effect. As I detail in depth elsewhere, they undermined the REP ability to recruit capable party members and perform many of the necessary tasks of political organization.[26]

Although the German right was less involved in protest activity, its response was no less consequential for the development of the REP. The CDU/CSU could have conceivably agreed to cooperate with the new party, particularly because the REP went to great pains to represent themselves as "national conservative" and thus potential coalition partners. There were indeed isolated politicians within the *Christian Democratic* camp who argued for this course. Yet the overwhelming response within the CDU/CSU was that anything short of complete delegitimation and marginalization of the REP was politically impossible. Kohl's drive to make Germany a "normal" nation had paradoxically turned contrition into a pillar of German political culture. Not only would overtures to the REP reignite charges that *Christian Democrats* were attempting to bury the Nazi past, but many (perhaps most) German conservatives believed that right-wing pop-

25 Die Republikaner, Parteiprogramm (1987).
26 These arguments are extended in Art, Reacting to the Radical Right.

ulism was a dangerous and politically illegitimate force in the successor state of the Third Reich.[27]

In contrast to many other parties on the right in Western Europe, the CDU/CSU adopted a strict and comprehensive policy of "marginalization" (Ausgrenzung) toward the far right. Ausgrenzung prohibited personal contact with REP politicians, reliance of REP votes to pass legislation, and support for any REP candidate or proposal. This occurred at every political level. Even party members in communal parliaments, which are not normally known for their ideological battles, were instructed to vote against the most mundane proposals of REP politicians, such as the installation of a traffic light, on principle. Critically, the central justification for this policy was based on the CDU/CSU's dramatic change of position regarding the Nazi past. The CDU party chairman Heiner Geissler justified Ausgrenzung on an internal party report that found that the REP were not a possible coalition partner because they sought to downplay the Nazi past.[28] Edmund Stoiber, the leader of the CSU, also grounded Ausgrenzung in part on the REP's "irresponsible dealing" with the past and the party's similarity to Nazi demagoguery.[29]

By preventing the REP from forming coalitions, by protesting against them, and by generally using the rhetorical weapons of the German "lessons of history", political elites in (West) Germany created insurmountable problems for the REP. The particular way in which Germans have confronted the Nazi past has thus proved to be a powerful constraint on right-wing populism. It must be emphasized that this was not the inevitable result of Germany's Nazi past, for even this past has no inherent meaning. As noted above, German elites held different views about the years 1933–1945 over the postwar decades. It was through the process of public debate that the "culture of contrition" became a requirement for German politicians from both right and left. As a final note, this culture only prevails in the former West Germany where such a public debate was possible. In Eastern Germany, very different patterns of memory prevailed and the far right has found much more hospitable terrain.[30]

IV. France: The shadow of Vichy

For nearly five decades, the myth of the French nation united in resistance against foreign occupation was a central, and uncontested, part of French political culture. The construction of this narrative began immediately after the end of the Second World War. Charles De Gaulle and his followers consciously exaggerated the scope of the internal Resistance to include everyone except a small

27 This point emerged in dozens of in-depth interviews by the author with CDU and CSU politicians conducted in 2001–2002 in Berlin, Stuttgart, and Munich.
28 Cf. Stöss, Die Extreme Rechte in der Bundesrepublik, p. 215.
29 Cf. Jaschke, Die Republikaner, p. 59.
30 For an analysis of the far right in Eastern Germany, see Art, The Wild, Wild East.

band of traitors.[31] French men and women, the majority of which had been neither resistors nor collaborators, were invited to identify with the Resistance, which was presented as "an abstraction, an achievement not of the résistants but of the nation as a whole".[32] The Gaullists maintained that "True France" had never ceased to exist during the Occupation and was embodied in the Resistance. Vichy was a "parenthesis", an aberration in French history, and Gaullists categorically denied that Vichy had any connection with French society or with French political traditions.

The *French Communist Party*'s (PCF) narrative of the war years was similarly exculpatory. The party glorified its role in the Resistance, which it conceived as a national insurrection, the culmination of a revolutionary struggle that had begun with the French Revolution, and continued in the Revolution of 1848 and the Paris Commune of 1871. The PCF lauded the French people, and specifically the French working class, for their heroic role in this national insurrection. Like Gaullists, communists maintained that the nation had rejected fascist ideology and resisted, either passively or actively, from the beginning of the occupation.

The view that France had been a nation of resistors was thus shared by both the French right and left. It was only in the 1990s that this hegemonic discourse unraveled, and that the question of French complicity in the Holocaust became the subject of public debate. Although it is true that Marcel Orphus' 1968 film "The Sorrow and the Pity" had challenged the heroic wartime narrative, and that the historian Robert Paxton's 1973 book "Vichy France" radically altered the historiography of the Vichy era, these critical examinations of French complicity hardly penetrated beyond a rather narrow intellectual circle.[33]

The rise and consolidation of the *National Front* occurred before Vichy became a salient issue in French politics. In 1983, the FN managed an electoral coup in by-elections in Dreux, an economically depressed city on the outskirts of Paris. But perhaps more important than the showing itself (the FN only gained 9 % of the vote) was the fact that the center-right formed a join list with the extreme right party in order to defeat the left. Neither the FN's xenophobia, nor its open defense of the Vichy regime, appeared to rule it out as a potential alliance partner. To be sure, conservative politicians took different positions on the legitimacy of the FN. While Jacques Chirac, then the mayor of Paris, ruled out any deals with the FN, other politicians, such as Charles Pasqua and Raymond Barre, were ambiguous. Pasqua famously noted in 1988, for example, that the mainstream right shared the same values as the FN. Many conservative voters were also sympathetic toward cooperating with the radical right. Even

31 Stanley Hoffman writes that de Gaulle was a firm believer in "pedagogical sublimation" and was fully aware of the mythical nature of his narrative of the war years. Hoffman, foreword to The Vichy Syndrome, by Rousso, viii.

32 Rousso, Vichy Syndrome, p. 71.

33 In fact, France's most prestigious publisher, Gallimard, rejected Paxton's book for publication.

after Le Pen had referred to the gas chambers as a "minor detail" in the Second World War, nearly one-third of mainstream right sympathizers supported electoral deals with the FN.[34]

The French left was also complicit in the rise of the FN. When Le Pen complained that he was not receiving enough media attention in 1982, Mitterrand convinced the leaders of France's three public television channels to increase their coverage of the party.[35] In 1986, Mitterrand's government changed the electoral rules for the 1986 presidential and parliamentary elections, replacing the two-ballot majoritarian system with proportional representation. The FN, which had captured 9.7 %, gained 35 seats in the National Assembly. This bolstered the party's national profile and endowed it with legitimacy.

During the 1980s, the link between the Vichy past and the FN was rarely made. Mitterrand himself had good reason not to bring up the Vichy past. As a young man, the President had been a junior minister in the Vichy regime before switching over to the Resistance. As President, Mitterrand repeatedly refused to apologize on behalf of the French state for the persecution of Jews. Before his death, he reiterated that "France was not responsible" for crimes committed by a "minority of activists who seized the occasion of the defeat to take power".[36] He also played a central role in preventing the trials of several important Vichy officials, such as René Bousquet, and delaying the trials of others, such as Paul Touvier and Maurice Papon.

Table 3: The memory of World War II in France

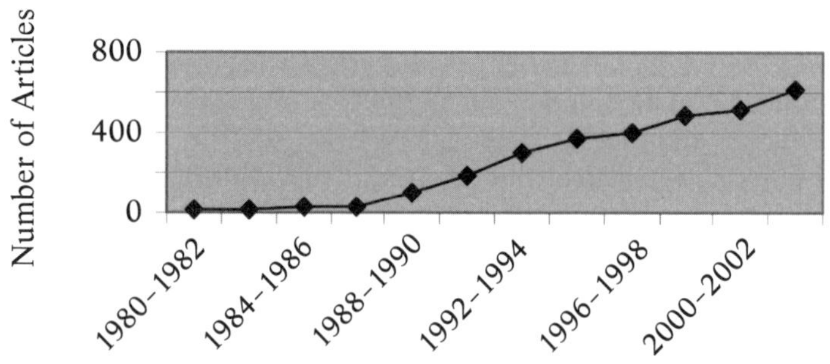

Source: The number of articles was generated from a Lexis-Nexis guided news search of major newspapers using the search terms (full text): France, Second World War, and Memory.

34 Cf. Marcus, The National Front in French Politics, p. 143.
35 Cf. Mayer, The French National Front, p. 21.
36 Le Monde, 18 July 1995.

It was only in the mid 1990s that a national debate about the Vichy past occurred. The proximate cause for it was the trial of Touvier, a member of Vichy's national militia who was convicted of committing crimes against humanity in 1994. After that, calls by Jewish groups for an official apology from the French state became increasingly strident and received greater media attention. In 1995, Jacques Chirac became the first French President to acknowledge the complicity of the French state in the Holocaust. In his address commemorating the Vél d'Hiv roundup, Chirac emphasized the domestic support for the Nazis' racial policies and programs, stating that "the criminal insanity of the occupying forces was seconded by the French, by the French state".[37] The President's speech also sparked demonstrations of contrition from other important groups in French society. For the first time ever, the French Catholic Church apologized for its silence on the Jewish deportations. France's main police union also apologized to Jews and expressed its "eternal regret" for the arrests made under Vichy.[38]

It was in this atmosphere of contrition that the trial of Maurice Papon, a Vichy civil servant charged with deporting Jews, commenced in 1997. However, the Papon trial demonstrated that contrition had not yet become a political consensus. Philip Seguin, the head of the *Rassemblement pour la Republique* (RPR) denounced the "climate of collective expiation and permanent self-flagellation" that was damaging public spirit. Other Gaullists distanced themselves from Chirac and asserted that since "Vichy was not France", France could not be held accountable for crimes against humanity. They considered the Papon trial a pretext for "throwing serious discredit on the honor of our country, on General de Gaulle, and on the Resistance". In an open letter published in the conservative daily "Le Figaro" titled "Enough! Enough! Enough!", Seguin charged that the Papon trial had become nothing less than "the trial of General de Gaulle and Gaullism" as well as "the trial of France".[39]

This defense of the Gaullist narrative was clearly motivated by partisan competition as well as by Seguin's and other politicians' fidelity to de Gaulle's legacy. Seguin nearly admitted as much when he questioned whether "this delirious atmosphere [...] does not serve an implicit objective: that of continuing to prop-up the electoral force of the National Front". French conservatives like Seguin did not want the FN to become the primary beneficiary of a backlash against the growing culture of contrition in France. For his part, Le Pen was certainly representing his party as the defender of French history, arguing that "politically organized Judaism" was becoming an insidious influence.

37 The Vél D'Hiv was the former bicycle race track where French police imprisoned 13,000 Parisian Jews before sending them to Nazi death camps. The round-up, which proceeded contrary to German orders and without the participation of German soldiers, stands as an important example of Vichy's willing collaboration in the Final Solution. Cf. Le Monde, 18 July 1995.

38 Cf. Financial Times, 1 April 1998.

39 Le Figaro, 21 October 1997.

Since the Papon trial, the French government has taken further steps to raise the salience of the Vichy past in contemporary politics and an elite consensus has emerged. On July 16, 2000, the country marked its first national day in memory of the racist and anti-semitic crimes of the French State. The month before, President Chirac had opened a permanent exhibit in the national military museum in the Invalides that documented the persecution of French Jews by their fellow countrymen and their state.[40] During the Presidential campaign of 2002, in which Le Pen effectively ended the Socialist Prime Minister's Lionel Jospin's political career by finishing second to Chirac in the first round, Chirac and elites from across the political spectrum used the Vichy past as a weapon against the far right. "In our darkest hour", Chirac reminded an audience at an election rally, "it was the leaders of the extreme right who betrayed the French people by allying themselves with the forces of evil and our nation's enemies".[41] He accused the FN of "embracing a past of shame, cowardice, and betrayal" and claimed "history has definitively disqualified them from speaking in the name of France".[42]

French elites have thus begun to embrace contrition and, like their counterparts in Germany, use history as a weapon against the far right. In contrast to Germany, however, public debates about the Nazi past occurred after a right-wing populist party had consolidated itself in the party system. It is interesting to speculate whether an earlier, critical, and sustained examination of Vichy would have constrained the rise of the FN. Of more current relevance is whether the unfolding culture of contrition in France will continue to keep the far right from wielding a greater degree of political power.

V. Italy: Mussolini's children?

Of the three cases under examination here, it is in Italy where a critical public discussion of the wartime past has, until recently, been the most limited. Although the brutality of the Italian fascist regime pales in comparison to that of the Nazis, Italians did systematically commit crimes against humanity in both Africa and in the Balkans. Yet, as one scholar notes, "Italian actions against others are still not part of the broader national consciousness".[43] As a result, there exists virtually no literature on the memory of Italian war crimes. Politicians do not discuss them. Italians, by and large, still prefer to think of themselves as victims, and the older generation in particular continues to identify with the antifascism on which the Republic was founded.

Still, an antifascist consensus - always much stronger in the North than in the South - kept the neo-fascist *Italian Social Movement* (MSI) on the margins

40 Cf. The Times, 17 July 2000.
41 The Independent, 3 May 2002.
42 The Scotsman, 3 May 2002.
43 Waltson, History and Memory, p. 183.

of Italian politics for nearly five decades. The MSI did enter into some local governing coalitions in the early postwar period, and the party consistently polled around 6 % in national parliamentary elections. Yet because the ruling *Christian Democrats* (DC) ruled out cooperation with the neo-fascists, the MSI was confined to the political ghetto until the dramatic collapse of the Italian party system in the early 1990s.

As several scholars have noted, the dramatic reversal of the MSI's fortune was primarily the result of changes in the political environment.[44] When the "Clean Hands" (*Mani Pulite*) investigation exposed the massive degree of corruption within both the DC and the PSI (the *Italian Socialist Party*), the MSI became one of the only existing political forces untouched by the scandal. But the MSI could never have taken advantage of the crisis in Italian politics had it not received the support of other political actors, particularly of Silvio Berlusconi.

Berlusconi, the media tycoon who formed his own party *Forza Italia* ("Go Italy") in 1993, overturned the MSI's status as a pariah party within a matter of months. His first important action was to express support for Gianofranco Fini, the ambitious young leader of the MSI, who was a candidate for the mayor of Rome in November 1993. Berlusconi's endorsement "If I were in Rome I would certainly vote for Fini" made headlines across Italy.[45] Although Fini did not win the elections, he placed a strong second, winning 47 % of the vote. Alessandra Mussolini, the granddaughter of the Duce, also posted a remarkable showing, winning 43 % in the second-round of the mayoral election in Naples.

The next step in the so-called "customs clearance" (*Sdoganamento*) of the MSI occurred when Berlusconi entered into an electoral coalition with Fini's newly founded *Alleanza Nationale* (AN). After his success in Rome, Fini sought to revamp the public's perception of the extreme-right and succeeded in convincing party delegates to dissolve the MSI in favor of the AN, which Fini described as "a common home of all the right".[46] Although interviews with the party rank-and file suggest that the neo-fascists had changed in name only, Berlusconi announced that he was forming an electoral alliance (The Freedom Alliance) with both the AN and Umberto Bossi's Northern League to contest the 1994 parliamentary elections. After nearly fifty years of isolation, the Italian extreme-right had come in from the cold.

Berlusconi's near monopoly of the Italian private television, which gives him the ability to "swamp the television screens with endless political commercials", was another critical factor in legitimating the AN.[47] Fini and Bossi were presented as politicians like any other, and their electoral alliances with Berlusconi brought them favorable news coverage at virtually no cost. In the event, the AN received 13.5 % of the vote in the 1994 elections, nearly tripling its total from

44 Cf. Ignazi, The Extreme Right in Western Europe; Gallagher, Exit from the Ghetto, pp. 64-86.
45 Cf. La Repubblica, 24 November 1993.
46 Bull/Newell, Italy Changes Course, pp. 72-99.
47 Cf. Statham, Berlusconi, the Media, and the New Right in Italy, p. 96.

two years earlier and earning five places in Berlusconi's cabinet. Although the AN's first foray into government was to be short-lived (Berlusconi's Freedom Alliance lasted only nine months), the party, and Fini in particular, profited enormously from the experience. By early 1995, public opinion polls showed that Fini had become the most popular politician in Italy.[48]

The AN's achievement of political respectability within a few years occurred without the party truly changing its attitudes toward the past. Fini's 1994 description of Mussolini as the "greatest statesman of the 20th century" sparked a minor uproar from the left, but did not come close to disqualifying him from public office. Nor did an interview with the newspaper "La Stampa" in which Fini said that "there are periods in which liberty is not the most important value. Fascism suppressed liberty of association for the benefit of social progress".[49] Outright praise for fascism was also common among other AN politicians. One of Fini's allies in Milan, Ignazio La Russa, described Mussolini as the historical figure he most admired. Roberto Predolin, La Russa's running mate, reserved that distinction for the Romanian fascist Corneliu Codreanu.[50] Interviews with AN rank-and-file demonstrate that historical apologia and revisionism are widespread.[51]

In marked contrast to Germany, and to France after 1995, historical memory in Italy did not preclude a far right party, and indeed a party that traced its roots directly to fascism, from forming coalitions and coming to power in Italy. This newfound permissiveness must be understood in the context of a general reevaluation of, and even certain nostalgia for, the fascist era in Italian politics and society since the late 1980s.[52] As Paul Ginsborg notes, the Italian left also played a role in this historical revisionism by speaking the language of "national reconciliation" and letting "bygones be bygones". Francisco Rutelli, the left of center Mayor of Rome, even proposed naming a square after Giuseppe Bottai, a supposedly "liberal" fascist leader.[53] Against this backdrop of revisionism, Berlusconi's contention that Mussolini had "never killed anyone" and "used to send people on vacation in internal exile" becomes more understandable.[54] And with Alessandra Mussolini regularly praising her grandfather on the Italian talk-show circuit, it is little wonder that Berlusconi's remark did not provoke the political fallout that a similar one in France or Germany would have engendered.

Interestingly, the most significant efforts to atone for the fascist past have come from an unlikely source: Gianfranco Fini has changed course dramatically over the last several years. In November 2003, Fini visited Israel and denounced fascism as an era of "absolute evil" in Italian history.[55] On the sixtieth anniver-

48 Cf. Corriere della Sera, 27 February 1995.
49 Gallagher, Exit from the Ghetto p. 76.
50 Cf. Ibid., p. 73.
51 Cf. Ignazi, The Extreme Right in Western Europe.
52 Cf. The Guardian, 10 September, 2001.
53 Cf. Ginsborg, Silvio Berlusconi, p. 155.
54 Cf. International Herald Tribune, 29 October 2003.
55 Cf. ANSA, 24 November 2003.

sary of the liberation of Auschwitz (January 27, 2005), Fini spoke of a "moral duty to transmit to future generations the memory of this atrocity which must never be repeated, in any form". He even noted that "there are some people in Italy who, either through ignorance or bad faith, tend to minimize saying that the 1938 [anti-semitic] laws did not have an important and tragic role in the persecution and extermination of the Jews".[56] It was statements like these that led Alessandra Mussolini and other hardliners to bolt from the AN.

What is one to make of Fini's contrition? As the Italian Foreign Minister, Fini has an obligation to uphold Italy's international reputation. Yet Fini's about-face has more to do with remaking his own party than limiting the damage of Berlusconi's gaffes. Visiting Israel has become the most efficient way for nationalist politicians in Europe to gain acceptability and to insulate themselves against charges of right-wing populism and chauvinism. Fini has also used history to move his party from the extreme-right to the center right in Italian politics. It is an open question whether the rank and file have followed their leader, but Fini recognized that refashioning the party as a national conservative one and cutting any lingering stigma of fascism were in the AN's long-term interests.

Over the last two years, the political salience of the war years has increased dramatically as the left has accused members of the Berlusconi government of fascist sympathies, while politicians like La Russa and Alemanno have refused to follow Fini's lead in categorically condemning fascism. The situation is similar to that in Austria, where elites continue to debate Austria's victim status. It is unclear whether this period of debate in Italy will lead to a new elite consensus, or whether the past will simply continue to be instrumentalized for partisan political purposes without a more substantive discussion that would help to counter a profound lack of historical knowledge among the general public. In any event, the lack of anything approaching a "culture of contrition" continues to provide space for both historical revisionism and far right politics in the country that first gave rise to fascism.

VI. The European dimension

Before turning to contrition as a nascent European value, let me qualify the claims I have made to this point. I am *not* contending that historical interpretations of fascism, collaboration, or neutrality have been the only important variable in the divergent development of the far right across Western Europe. Clearly, electoral institutions matter - one can only speculate about the vote-share of the *British National Party* (BNP) in a PR system as opposed to first-past -the-post. Cross-national patterns of immigration and unemployment are also clearly important in any story of variation, although it is significant that some states that have experienced both in large quantities (Germany, Sweden, the

56 ANSA, 27 January 2005.

Netherlands) have not developed strong right-wing populist parties. Conversely, some states without the combination of high immigration rates and unemployment (Norway), or without high immigration (Italy), have produced a powerful far right.

What I have argued is that ideas – in this case ideas about history – also play a central role in explaining the divergent development of far right parties in post-war Western Europe. In states with a strong or nascent "culture of contrition", the far right has been stigmatized by mainstream political forces and has been unable to consolidate itself in the party system (see Table 3). This describes the situation in Germany, and appears to pertain in both the Netherlands and Sweden, although more research on these cases in needed.

Table 4: Historical memory and far right success*

		Elite historical consensus	
		Yes	No
Far right	Strong	France	Austria
		Norway	Italy
		Denmark	Belgium
			Switzerland
	Weak	Germany	
		Sweden	
		Netherlands	

* Success here is defined as in Table 1.

In states where historical consciousness remains polarized and elites continue to offer conflicting views of the past, the far right has had a far easier time recruiting allies and has generally benefited from highly-charged public debates. Austria, Switzerland, Belgium and Italy fit this pattern. Norway and Denmark represent cases where far right parties have become strong without using history in partisan politics. In France, as I have argued, the FN consolidated itself in the party system before an elite consensus emerged that the party was unacceptable given the Vichy past.

Given the small number of cases, and the large number of variables, it is impossible to determine the effect of ideas relative to other factors. But if the reader has been convinced that ideas about the past do in fact matter, then this paper has achieved its central goal. Further work might analyze any of the cases I have touched upon in more depth, or perhaps consider the influence of historical memory on partisan politics in other cases; the United States, South Africa, and states in Central and Eastern Europe might prove particularly fruitful.

Returning to Europe, there have been significant attempts to make remembrance of past atrocities a European value. In late January of 2000, the heads of the fifteen member states of the European Union met in Stockholm for a conference on the Holocaust. When the *Austrian Christian Democrats* (ÖVP) formed a national government with the FPÖ several days later, the response from the fourteen other member states was dramatic and unprecedented. Arguing that the presence of an openly apologist political party in a governing coalition violated European norms, the EU fourteen imposed symbolic sanctions on Austria. These remained in force for over six months, during which the Austrian right railed against such discrimination but, at the same time, quickly pushed legislation through parliament that provided restitution for slave laborers and for Jews whose property was "aryanized" under Nazism. More recently, French politicians have argued that a critical examination of the Armenian Genocide on the part of the Turkish government become a prerequisite for EU ascension talks. A small diplomatic row ensued, and a Turkish government official noted angrily that "there was no such genocide, so there is no question of recognizing a genocide that did not happen".[57] Yet several months later, Turkish Prime Minister Erdoğan did call for an impartial study by historians into the deaths of more than 1.5 million Armenians between 1915 and 1923, marking the first sign of change in official attitudes toward this past.[58]

Like groups within European states, the EU has clearly been using history for political motives. In the Austrian case, it is no coincidence that the two most vocal proponents of the sanctions were Belgium and France, both of which faced domestic problems with large far right parties. The French also have a host of other reasons for keeping Turkey out of the EU for as long as possible, and clearly recognized the potential for the Armenian issue to complicate ascension talks. But the increasing use of history in politics may lead to its further institutionalization. Recently, European leaders commemorated the sixtieth anniversary of the liberation of Auschwitz (January 27, 1945) and the EU assembly unanimously adopted a resolution declaring January 27th "European Holocaust Memorial Day" across the EU. And after Prince Harry of Great Britain showed up at a costume party wearing a swastika armband, Germans called for an EU ban on Nazi symbols. Although the proposal was shelved due to concerns that it would limit freedom of expression, European leaders are currently discussing a compromise deal. As in so many other policy arenas, the institutionalization of contrition and remembrance would signal a "Germanization" of the European Union. Whether or not this would partially free Germany from shouldering the lion-share of the burden for Nazi atrocities remains an open, and potentially vexing, question.

57 The Times, 15 December 2004.
58 Cf. Los Angeles Times, 9 March 2005.

Right-Wing Esotericism in Europe

Ulrike Heß-Meining

I. Introduction

Esotericism is an ideology that finds a meaning in supernatural forces, in gods, angels, good vibrations, and that cares for Mother Nature and the environment. At first glance, this does not show many connections with ideas or persons on the extreme right. For this reason, right-wing esotericism is often overlooked by political science. Another aspect of its marginal position in science may simply be that these ideas seem too absurd to take them seriously when being confronted with them for the first time.

Historically, there has been an evident relationship of the extreme right with esoteric circles at the beginning of the 20th century, for example, the notorious Thule-Gesellschaft, which was founded in Munich in 1918 by Rudolf von Sebottendorf. The Thule-Gesellschaft promoted racist ("völkische") ideas. Some of its followers became famous members of the NSDAP, like Rudolf Hess, Hans Frank, and Julius Streicher.[1] The "Third Reich" confused anti-Semitism with mystic faith in the force of Celtic and Germanic runes. It created new symbols like the "Black Sun", a symbol of the SS at the "Wewelsburg", a castle near Paderborn which was used and reshaped by the SS, using concentration camp inmates as slave laborers.

The criteria to help identify whether an esoteric text has links to the extreme right are therefore the same as for extreme rightist thoughts in general. We will look for aggressive nationalism, anti-Semitism, racism, intolerance and the "survival of the fittest", conspiratorial theories and the promoting of violence as a normal means to solve conflicts. Especially interesting, of course, are connections with anti-Semitism, national socialist ideas or the idealization of Hitler and, as we shall see, conspiratorial theories.[2]

Since the end of the Nazi era, in different countries there have always been several publications on occult issues, telling stories of so-called Nazi-UFOs,

1 Goodrick-Clarke, Black Sun.

2 For connections of anti-Semitism, conspiratorial theories, and esotericism, see Bundesamt für Verfassungsschutz (Ed.), Argumentationsmuster im rechtsextremistischen Antisemitismus: Aktuelle Entwicklungen, available at: http://www.verfassungsschutz.de/download/SHOW/broschuere_0511_2_antisemitismus.pdf.

Arian empires in the arctic (Wilhelm Landig, a former member of the SS), Indian-Germanic cultures in South-America (Jacques de Mahieu) or Hitler being still alive but deep-frozen in the Antarctic (Miguel Serrano).[3]

Starting in the US in the 1970ies with Gary Allen's "None Dare Call It Conspiracy", extreme right Christian fundamentalists forced a worldview of conspiracies performed by powerful groups such as the Rockefellers, the Council of Foreign Relations, the Bilderbergers[4] and so on. In 1976, Des Griffin published "Descent into Slavery?", another highlight of the genre. There it says that Jews were in control of National Socialism and that the US-government was planning a Holocaust for Christians.[5]

Because of these roots in the US there is an academic discourse in English, dealing with Christian fundamentalists as well as with UFO-cults and conspiratorial theories. It scrutinizes the links of those movements to the extreme right.[6]

With reference to the classical essay by Richard Hofstadter "The Paranoid Style in American Politics", there are some publications discussing the political and cultural implications of the fast-growing conspiratorial theories in the 1990ies and the early 10s of the present century.[7] Most of these publications focus on the US or at least on English-language texts. Especially interesting as a background for our subject is Michael Barkun's "A Culture of Conspiracy", published in 2003.[8] Its content touches subjects such as the "New World Order" (NWO), the "Illuminati", UFO Conspiracy Theories, British publicist David Icke, Anti-Catholicism, Anti-Masonry, and Anti-Semitism. Although Barkun's focus of interest is US-American literature and websites, his book provides a lot of background information for a better understanding of European right-wing esotericism. Concerning Icke, it analyzes a British writer as well.

The scientific discourse in Europe regarding this subject focuses on several main characters disseminating these thoughts in Europe. In Germany, one of the big names is Jan van Helsing (alias of Jan Udo Holey); in Great Britain, it is David Icke. In the context of our debate, it is widely agreed that Jan van Helsing quite overtly diffused anti-Semitic and extreme rightist thoughts, especially

3 Gugenberger/Petri/Schweidlenka, Weltverschwörungstheorien, pp. 150–152.

4 Allegations concerning a Bilderberg Group have been based on the annual Bilderberg Meetings. Founded in 1954 by Prince Bernhard of the Netherlands its aim was to improve the relationship between Western Europe and North America by arranging meetings of influential persons from politics, economics, and the media. Due to the informal and private character of these meetings, there are no publications. The participants promise to remain silent about the meetings. This kind of organization fostered conspiratorial theories about a supposed Bilderberg Group planning a "New World Order" or even constituting a secret World Government. The official website provides further information: http://www.bilderbergmeetings.org/index.php, last accessed 3 November 2010.

5 Gugenberger/Petri/Schweidlenka, Weltverschwörungstheorien, pp. 146–147, 186.

6 Cf. Barkun, A Culture of Conspiracy.

7 See Robins/Post, Political Paranoia; Knight, Conspiracy Culture; Walker Fields, White Hope, pp. 157–176; Goldberg, Enemies Within; Fenster, Conspiracy Theories.

8 Barkun, A Culture of Conspiracy.

in the first two volumes of "Geheimgesellschaften" ("Secret Societies").[9] Concerning David Icke, Barkun demonstrates anti-Semitism in several of his texts.

Right-wing esotericism exists nearly all over Europe. The historical connection suggests a focus on Germany, which will be taken under scrutiny. The nature of the Internet, which links the flow of ideas so strongly that the origins of these thoughts become blurred, makes it difficult to be always sure to have a European sample or a source from a particular country. Given the origins of conspiratorial theories, we sometimes have to refer to the US - or cannot be sure if an article in English has its roots in Great Britain, in the United States or in any other country.

The academic discourse so far emphasizes - even in texts published after 2000 - esoteric publications from the 1990ies. The aim of the present text is therefore to show the development of extreme right esotericism since 2000 and to analyze its contents. It is especially important to evaluate the dissemination, and as far as possible, the quantity of right-wing esotericism.

II. Esoteric scenes and topics with right-wing implications

The short description of right-wing esotericism above shows that this genre includes different types.

a) Websites or texts that are obviously extreme rightist, written by admittedly extreme right-wing organizations. Examples are sites of neo-Nazi organizations focusing on esoteric topics or publications with reference to Aryan cults (e. g. Thule-Gesellschaft, Lanz von Liebenfels etc.), Germanic or Celtic roots or religion.
b) Texts, or quite often videos, with an esoteric background and a special focus on secret societies and conspiratorial thoughts that explicitly and positively mention the Third Reich, expressions of overt anti-Semitism, etc. One way to identify ideas and features of the extreme right in esotericism is the thematization of poor but powerful Nazis who managed to escape the Allies with the help of extraterrestrials or mystic forces.
c) Mainly esoteric or conspiratorial texts or videos with several references to the Illuminati, the Rothschilds or other dark powers that aim at governing the world. These texts or movies constitute a grey zone, especially on sites or in esoteric texts with references to conspiracies. Good examples are texts about the "New World Order", supposing a regime of the Illuminati, the

9 See Gugenberger/Petri/Schweidlenka, Weltverschwörungstheorien; Meining, Rechte Esoterik in Deutschland, available at: http://www.verfassungsschutz.thueringen.de/infomaterial/symposien/2002/Meining.pdf. For the influence of Jan van Helsing in France, see François/Kreis, L'ufologie radical, available at: http://www.politicahermetica.com/Conference/Ufologie.pdf.

Bilderbergers or similar constructions. These conceptions often, but not always, come along with anti-Semitic assumptions, for example, identifying Jews in the same context as the Illuminati.

These stages of involvement with extremism correspond with different scenes: neo-Nazi or other extremist groups with esoteric interests, convinced esoterics who publish – as one aspect among others – right-wing issues in their magazines or on their websites and, most important, the growing but not necessarily extremist group of conspiracists, the so-called truthers or truth-seekers.

Conspiratorial theories are indicators of extreme rightist thinking. Extreme rightists often feel persecuted by "communists", by "democrats" or by "capitalists". The most important conspiratorial theory, which historically is definitely part of extreme rightist thinking, is anti-Semitism, often linked to the notorious Protocols of the Elders of Zion. The disguise as anti-Zionism is frequently used in those texts.

There are several distinctive arguments of esotericism that incline to extreme right topics: Mystics who feel close to – not always "friendly" – supernatural forces are afraid of being followed by "them". If "they" cooperate with Israel, for example, there may easily be a link to thoughts of the extreme right.

Supernatural powers are not always associated with gods or godlike extraterrestrials. Common characters who have power over humankind are the Illuminati. These are often identified as bankers or other wealthy people – and as Jews.

Nevertheless, it is often not easy to decide if an esoteric or conspiratorial website includes extreme rightist matter. The mentioning of runes or Celtic history, for example, is not automatically connected with politics or neo-Nazis. Another example is the reference to Illuminati. There is a considerable number of texts that explicitly name prominent Jews or Jewish families as Illuminati (e. g. the Rothschilds). This is more than a hint for an anti-Semitic background of the conspiratorial theory. However, Illuminati are not always Jewish – how is it then possible to decide if there are links to right-wing extremism? And are the readers of those texts or viewers of those movies aware of this context? A certain camouflage enlarges the problem.[10] One name that is frequently used is the Rockefellers. They are accused of being agents of the "New World Order". At first glance, while knowing that the Rockefeller family is Protestant, this does not seem to fit in an anti-Semitic pattern. However, an investigation of some

10 "The fascination with secrecy and duplicity would seem to make the alien-conspiracy literature a perfect site for anti-Semitism. In fact, the connection in this case is considerably more complex. Despite the fact that overt anti-Semitism may be found mixed with allegations about aliens, it is often accompanied by strong assertions that the authors are neither anti-Semites nor racists. Rather, they claim to reject racism and to seek only to protect the interests of Jews. The result is occasionally overt anti-Semitism, but more often a refracted racism and anti-Semitism that allow those who use them simultaneously to repudiate them". Barkun, A Culture of Conspiracy, p. 140.

notorious websites, results in the impression that the Rockefellers are falsely regarded as "Jewish".[11]

III. A change in quality: The increase of the Internet in the past ten years

Even though the World Wide Web already existed in the 1990ies, the distribution of esoteric texts mainly took place through cheap copies one could get at specialized shops or from mail order-companies. Only ten years ago, interested consumers had to research these publications at obscure bookshops or mail order bookshops and esoteric fairs to get a complete picture of the situation. These shops published catalogues that had to be ordered or collected at esoteric fairs. Now, at the touch of a button, readers simply go online and choose whatever they want out of a huge variety of esoteric and right-wing editors. The most important technological change in recent years concerning the data traffic of the Internet is the high increase in speed and in the amount of data transported. This development has made it possible to easily get access to videos via the Internet.

The formation of "YouTube" in 2005 marked the beginning of a new era. Now it is common to upload movies on one's own homepage - a possibility avidly used in the esoteric as well as in the truth-seeker-scene. If one starts "Google" and enters "esotericism", besides magazines, online-shops, books, and homepages one will also find downloadable movies, DVDs that can be bought and - TV-stations. Of course, there is a variety of neo-Nazi esoteric and conspiratorial websites with downloadable material, texts as well as videos.

This obvious change in quality provided by the Internet includes an increase in the quantity of esoteric websites that also promote right-wing and conspiratorial issues. So it is easier for both, the providers of these topics and the people who may be interested, to enlarge the network of right-wing esotericism.

However, there is not only facilitation for those people who are already inclined to those ideas. It is also more likely to attract especially young people to right-wing esotericism. Youngsters use the Internet more frequently and are fascinated by subjects like conspiracies, violence, and "secrets". This explains Internet successes like "Loose Change", the infamous conspiratorial video on September 11.

Another good example is "Zeitgeist - the Movie", an American production by Peter Joseph of 2007, which swept into Europe via "YouTube" and "Google Video". The connection of this oeuvre to right-wing esotericism is proven, for example, by its ample reference to Jordan Maxwell, a notorious American eso-

11 See http://staatpreussen.com/htmlrockefeller.html; and http://allezitate.com/john-d-rockefeller/biographie, both last accessed 1 June 2010.

teric with sympathies for extreme rightist conspiratorial thinking.[12] The translation of "Zeitgeist" into German, Spanish, French, Greek, Czech, Italian, Russian, and other languages shows the importance of this conspiratorial movie as well as the documented views on "YouTube".[13] Not being bluntly extreme rightist, its topics nevertheless show a certain closeness to anti-Semitism and the conspiracy of the "New World Order". "Zeitgeist" is divided into three parts: Part 1 is an esoteric compilation about Jesus. It states that Jesus never existed and that the Christian faith is a myth with the aim to submit humankind.[14] Part 2 concentrates on the assumption that the incidents at September 11 were planned or at least enabled by the US-government. The third part deals with the more or less explicit anti-Semitic topic that the international banks as well as the Federal Reserve Bank wanted to start or at least extend the World Wars and the Vietnam War to make profit. It further assumes a secret agreement to create a "North-American Union" with the US, Canada, and Mexico as members, in order to abolish the Canadian Dollar, the US Dollar, and the Mexican Peso and to replace them by the "Amero". The movie finally suggests that the government implants a chip into every person to gain control over everybody. In 2008, a second video called "Zeitgeist Addendum" was released, being distributed in different languages. Additionally, there is an official website "http://www.zeitgeistmovie.com" and a "Zeitgeist" movement. This movie clearly shows that the medium itself influences and changes the reception of its content.

IV. Evaluation of the dissemination of right-wing esotericism

In times when only printed material could be published, it was comparatively easy to estimate the dissemination of books or magazines with esoteric content and extreme rightist thoughts. One simply had to figure out the number of copies sold. In the 1990ies, when access to the Internet was not as prevalent as now, the success of a certain kind of right-wing esotericism could always be measured with reference to the bestselling books. In 1997, when Daniel Pipes wanted to stress the importance of conspiracy theories in the US, he simply had to note the number of five million copies sold of "None Dare Call It Conspiracy"

12 See http://www.esowatch.com/ge/index.php?title=Jordan_Maxwell; http://www.jordanmaxwell.com/articles/questions/index.html, both last accessed 18 June 2010.

13 The structure of "YouTube" makes it difficult to calculate the overall views. There are different parts of the video uploaded by many users. For example, part one in English language counted 3,660,533 views, another full version over 800,000 on 29 June 2010. One statement by a mystic who calls herself Acharya on "YouTube" claims "at least 15 million views". See "Zeitgeist, Part 1 (Religion) Debunked? Acharya Responds", available at: http://www.youtube.com/watch?v=F_9ZyddjaM4, last accessed 15 July 2010.

14 One can find these allegations in various texts by authors analyzed in the following paragraphs. For an example see Icke, The Biggest Secret, p. 91.

until then.[15] Similarly, it can be stated positively that, because of the copies sold, Jan van Helsing as well as David Icke have more influence on the esoteric scene than, for example, Robin de Ruiter. All of them publish books, and one can at least guess their impact by their availability at bookstores or the number of copies sold.

If the sales rank issued by the Internet bookseller Amazon is taken as a criterion, it is even possible to get an impression of the success of relatively unknown publications: Among the books in German language sold by Amazon, Robin de Ruiter's "Die 13 satanischen Blutlinien - Die Ursache vielen Elends und Übels auf Erden" ("Worldwide Evil and Misery: The Legacy of the 13 Satanic Bloodlines") achieved sales rank 235,548 (and none of his books sells better), while David Icke's German translation of "The Biggest Secret" ("Das größte Geheimnis") sells at position 5,487, and Jan van Helsing's "Hände weg von diesem Buch" ("Don't Touch This Book") holds number 2,176 on 2 June 2010.

So how is the impact of information that is only available on the Internet to be judged? Clicks are not always counted. Even if they are, one cannot be sure if a click was intended or if the person who clicked actually read the site. There is no threshold to get information, like the prize of a book or a magazine. That makes it even more difficult to decide how seriously these rumors, for example on conspiracies of Jewish bankers, are taken and how widespread they really are. Therefore, firsthand one has to go to the contents to decide if there is any danger emanating from this part of the Internet.

The following illustration of right-wing esotericism shows websites on the very extreme right wing, including Holocaust deniers. Mostly it is not possible to estimate their influence, and it is not very probable that they find many readers. Nevertheless, these sectarian groups come out with ideas or subjects one can recognize in videos or texts that are not specifically extremely right wing, like the mentioned "Zeitgeist - the Movie".

V. Neo-Nazism and esotericism - some recent examples from the Internet

We shall first take a brief look at two websites of notorious organizations from the extreme right-wing: The Thule-Seminar designed and created by Pierre Krebs and the Deutsche-Stimme-Versand, a mail order-company, closely linked to the *Nationaldemokratische Partei Deutschlands* (NPD) in Germany.[16] As one expects from extreme rightist ideas, there is an emphasis on racism, on Nazi-symbols, and on nationalism. Both websites, however, also show esoteric symbols like the black sun or Odin's ravens.

15 See Pipes, Conspiracy, p. 17.
16 See http://www.im.nrw.de/sch/342.htm, last accessed 19 July 2010.

The Thule-Seminar highlights from the beginning a connection between extreme-rightist nationalism and the Neuheidentum (neo-paganism). It uses "Germanic" phrases and refers to Gods like "Wodan".[17]

Heller/Maegerle show the importance of neo-paganism for the foundations of the Thule-Seminar, and they assume that neo-paganism does not find a lot of sympathy on the extreme right.[18] This, indeed, is to be questioned. There are several sect-like right-wing groups that can easily be found on the Internet (like the Reichsbewegung, which we will take under scrutiny next), with different interpretations of neo-paganism, Germanic or Celtic roots, and other esoteric ideas. These extreme groups probably do not appeal to a broader public, but conspiratorial theories that highlight Illuminati and condemn Christianity (as being "Jewish") do. Therefore, it is extremely important to examine the similarities in ideological contents of neo-Nazi groups and not overtly extremist esoteric and conspiratorial websites.

There is this interesting example of the Reichsbewegung (Reich-movement) or Neue Gemeinschaft von Philosophen (New Fellowship of Philosophers), which recently came out with a website.

The Neue Gemeinschaft von Philosophen fits to the credo of Pierre Krebs and the Thule-Seminar, claiming that the Europeans must unite and search for their cultural, originally pagan roots. Although they deny being extreme rightist, in their program they emphasize the main topics of the "New Right". They disapprove cultural and ethnic diversity, fearing the "ethnic death" of the European peoples (Völker): "The intolerable conditions in the European homelands swamped by the conglomerate masses of people, the cultural and religious influences of people from all over the world were reason for serious concern. It was clear to us: If everything would continue like this, the irreversible ethnic death of European peoples would be executed within a few decades".[19]

In their program, they frequently use expressions that were part of the national socialist ideology, like "Volk" or "völkisch". They contrast "alien religious influences" against the "true European Weltanschauung". "Something had to be found that restores the identity of the European people, their higher

17 "According to its own claims, the Thule-seminar consists of a 'convent of several circles (Hugin-, Munin-, and Gunkincircle)', which participate in 'basic research projects focussing on questions of the Indoeuropean culture'. There is a 'strong cooperation with all European think tanks that stand for a ›new culture‹'. Krebs defined them as 'European synergies', 'tightly connected think tanks' and 'cells of spiritual resistance'. The Thule-seminar considers itself a 'new order' holding holy orders in the most intimate inner circle. It has its own code of honor, 'which should be the basis for a new jurisdiction in the future, and which understands to determine, who belongs to us and who does not yet deserve to carry the knot of Wotan of the ›Thule Seminar‹'". All translations by the author if not indicated otherwise, U. H.-M.
Heller/Maegerle, Die Sprache des Hasses, pp. 115–116, with reference to Krebs (Ed.), Das Thule-Seminar.

18 Cf. ibid., p. 117.

19 http://www.reichsbewegung.org/portal/index.php?option=com_content&view=article&id=99&Itemid=109, last accessed 26 February 2010, pp. 1–2.

spiritual sense of life and with it their 'völkisch' and spiritual cultural will of self-determination. Something they share as people and as Europeans and they set up against the incessantly penetrating culturally and politically strange influences! The unique outlook of Europe had to be rediscovered and called back into the consciousness of the Europeans".[20]

The "Weltanschauung" of these "true" Europeans leads us back to neo-Pagan ideas. As one could have expected in the context above, alien religious influences do not refer to Islam only. They are also directed against Christianity, and, of course, Judaism. Talking about Atlantis and the "Holy Irminsul", they claim to create a "new philosophy" that operates as "the reborn ur-European Weltanschauung" called "Kosmoterik".[21]

Although these "new philosophers" deny being right-wing, their quotations confirm ultra-nationalist convictions. The movement of the Reichsbewegung/ Neue Gemeinschaft von Philosophen qualifies as being overtly extreme-rightist by presenting a text with the title "Alles, was man zum Thema Holocaust wissen muss"[22] ("All You Have to Know about the Holocaust") with the revisionist contents one should expect.

Extremely interesting in our context is the mingling of extreme-rightist ideology with conspiratorial theory, which is programmatically described as follows: "As the truth is the basis of the Idea of the Reich, it is consequent that all Truther scenes are involved in detecting the usual big lies in all special areas and search for truth. In principle, the Reichsbewegung is the world's biggest movement of truth finding, which unites all truther scenes".[23]

The examples for conspiratorial theories on the Reichsbewegung website are therefore numerous: they refer to the NWO-topic with "Rot den Rothschild", going on with medically based conspiracies like swine flue and AIDS being created by the "secret" world government, focusing on chemtrails, the so called CO_2-climate-lie and various other subjects.

It is virtually impossible to identify the persons being responsible for this website because the writers seem to opt for an undercover strategy.[24] The only infor-

20 Ibid.
21 Cf. ibid.
22 Cf. ibid.
23 Ibid.
24 "The ultimate objective of the Reichsbewegung is a constitutional assembly. Only such a committee can decide the form, structure, and constitution of a newly potent German Empire! Contrary to various other Reichs groups (movement of the citizens of the Reich, KRRs, governments in exile etc.) which are all present in public and which even demand 'their right' of the vassal regime OMF-BRD (ha,ha,ha) and which are of the opinion that this system would obediently watch how they try to reactivate the German Reich – the Neue Gemeinschaft von Philosophen is convinced that in these times only an undercover Reichsbewegung will have a real chance. It is only with the help of conspiracy, that the structures and the decentralized organization can be built up, which cannot be the target of espionage and likely destruction. At this occasion we want to emphasize again that we are considering every action as treason, which jeopardizes the anonymity of the Neue Gemeinschaft von Philosophen".

mation the domain-research site "whois" provides is an address in Westchester, California. Obviously, the German authors try to eschew the German laws that prohibit the denial of the Holocaust and the glorification of the Nazi-regime. They use strategies of denying that they are anti-Semitic, too.[25]

The websites discussed in this chapter so far show obvious connections to the neo-Nazi scene. Additionally, one can find a multitude of websites that concentrate on some conspiratorial subject (e. g. the Bilderbergers, NWO, UFOs),[26] expressing in this context strong anti-Semitic sentiments. These conspiracy theories often do not show a colorful esoteric story like old Germanic myths or National Socialists having been saved by extra-terrestrials in the Antarctic. Instead, they have visions of hidden forces governing the world and focus heavily on conspiracies of all kinds. Although these are not classical examples of extreme right esotericism, they are potentially interesting expressions of irrationalism transporting right-wing ideas. Again, it is not always possible to estimate the dissemination and the usage of these sites. What makes an evaluation even more complicated is the fact that these websites are often, understandably, anonymous. Using the domain-based research service "whois", one mostly receives "protected" as a result for "registrant name", and as an address some city in the United States or even in South Africa. The languages used indicate European authors: besides English, one can easily find German, but also Spanish, French, and Russian.

One example, translated in all the languages named above, is "www.phumph.com",[27] headlining on the main page "The Stealthy Grip of Judaism". Its interests focus, among other topics, on the denial of the Holocaust as well as on "Hitler - Saint or Sinner?", the "Protocols of the Elders of Zion" and the Bilderberg Group. As the titles indicate, its prime content is suggesting a Jewish world-conspiracy. Another website, exclusively in German, is "www.staatpreussen.com" promising to deliver "Reports from Prussia and its Provinces and concerning the rest of the world".[28] It provides the world with news concerning a certain "Generalfeldmarschall Niklaus von Flüe Rimpler", who as "Protektor des Reichslands Elsaß-Lothringen", for example, claims a forest in Alsace.

For the original text, see http://www.reichsbewegung.org/portal/index.php?option=com_content&view=article&id=13&Itemid=25, last accessed 26 February 2010.

25 In conspiratorial as well as in esoteric sites overt anti-Semitic statements often go together with the denial of being an anti-Semite. One argumentation is that the Jews nowadays are not really Jews (but a dangerous conspiratorial group, which wants to gain the world leadership). For an example, see Neue Gemeinschaft von Philosophen, Erfindung des jüdischen Volkes, p. 1, available at: http://www.reichsbewegung.org, last accessed 26 February 2010.

26 Examples are available at: http://www.bilderberg.org/tonyhom.htm; http://www.american-show.de/neue-weltordnung-deutscher-bundesprasident-fordert-die-weltregierung, last accessed 29 June 2010.

27 Cf. ibid., last accessed 15 July 2010.

28 In German it says, "Meldungen aus Preußen und seinen Provinzen, und darüber hinaus die Welt betreffend".

Again, one main target on this site is the alleged Jewish influence. In a so-called "Judenaufstellung", it focuses on conspiratorial theories concerning Jews.

The examples listed in this paragraph share the obvious ideological orientation toward neo-national socialist views. They have in common that the objectives that are supposed to be reached are in the foreground instead of one personality. Even the "Generalfeldmarschall" is only one subject among others. The writers of these websites would like to build a new "German Reich" or to achieve a European ethnic homogeneity. By their mainly anonymous publications they do not hope to make money but to manipulate opinions. This is different with the authors presented in the following chapter.

VI. Esoteric entrepreneurs

Nowadays, esotericism is big business. According to latest estimations, the volume of sales on the esoteric market is 18 to 25 billion Euros in Germany every year.[29] The persons presented in this chapter share one common interest: they try to make a living by publishing esoteric texts, videos or websites. With the exception of Robin de Ruiter, who studied theology and history, the esoteric entrepreneurs presented here do not have any academic background. This is an interesting fact concerning the social structural background of these writers, indeed.

Their obviously economic aims have various consequences. First, they have to publish under a name, creating a "trade mark". Second, they have to be cautious with too offensive statements, not to alienate the interested public and not to come into conflict with the law, for example in Germany. These authors normally avoid close contact with parties of the extreme right, but stress health issues or concentrate on conspiratorial subjects. Whether this distance is ideological or results from economical interests is not clear. Already in 2002, Pfahl-Traughber remarked that Jan Udo Holey acts at a distance from neo-national socialist parties and considers his worldviews a "new phenomenon" within the extreme political right.[30] The esoteric focus, while omitting pagan religion or Odin's ravens, shifts very much to the various truthseeker communities. Nevertheless, the following authors make use of statements with anti-Semitic content, references to "Third Reich" issues or to conspiracy theories. More writers could be described in this chapter. The selection of the portrayed authors cannot be complete.[31]

29 See "Hinters Licht geführt". In: Die Zeit, 8 July 2010, p. 54, with reference to futurologist Eike Wenzel.
30 Pfahl-Traughber, Renaissance der antisemitisch-antifreimaurerischen Verschwörungstheorie, p. 88.
31 Other esoteric writers are e. g. Armin Risi or Trutz Hardo; See Fromm, Rechtsradikalismus in der Esoterik, pp. 149–233.

1. The "Holey Empire"

Jan Udo Holey, better known as "Jan van Helsing", is important in this context for several reasons. Born in 1967, he started as an author with his early success "Geheimgesellschaften und ihre Macht im 20. Jahrhundert" ("Secret Societies and Their Power in the 20th Century", two volumes 1993 and 1995). In 1996, he sold more than 100,000 copies of the first volume until it was confiscated through law enforcement action because of its overtly anti-Semitic content. His persistence is also remarkable. He still publishes a great deal and is active as a publisher, video producer, and even as a provider of an Internet television broadcasting channel. With the exception of "Geheimgesellschaften", one can easily purchase his books at ordinary bookshops in Germany. The titles by Holey published in the 1990ies are well documented by Gugenberger/Petri/Schweidlenka, by Goodrick-Clarke, and several others. But the spread of these ideas is going on. Via Internet, it is not even a problem to get pdf-files of "Geheimgesellschaften".[32] From time to time one can order the first two volumes antiquarian on Amazon at exceptionally high prices.

Further publications of the new decade include classical esoteric subjects like "Die Kinder des neuen Jahrtausends: Mediale Kinder verändern die Welt" (2001) and "Wer hat Angst vorm schwarzen Mann?" (2005), a book about the "black man" - Death. "Die Jahrtausendlüge: Auf der Spur des Pyramidenrätsels" (co-author Stefan Erdmann[33]) (2008) is another title referring to mysteries.

Most interesting in our context is the book "Hände weg von diesem Buch!", published in 2004, which seems to be his biggest success until now. According to Amazon, it appears in the 13th edition. Amazon provides the additional information that the German copies sold add up to 165,000.[34] It is also published in French "Ne touchez pas à ce livre" (published by the German Hesper Verlag, Saarbrücken 2009) and in English "Don't Touch This Book" (published by AmaDeus).

32 See for example http://www.der-trommler.de/staatsfeind/Die_Akte/die_akte.html, last accessed 22 June 2010.

33 Erdmann is another author writing in the "circle" of Jan Udo Holey. With AmaDeus, he publishes books like "Banken, Brot und Bomben" (two volumes 2003) or "Geheimakte Bundeslade" (2005). Jan Udo Holey is often referring to Erdmann in "Hände weg von diesem Buch". Erdmann quotes the "Prophecies of the Elders of Zion" and believes in a "New World Order".

34 See http://www.amazon.de/Hände-weg-von-diesem-Buch/dp/3980710688, last accessed 21 June 2010.
The author confirms this estimation: "Meine Bücher verkaufen sich sehr gut, zum Beispiel gingen von 'Hände weg von diesem Buch!' innerhalb von vier Jahren alleine in deutscher Sprache über 150 000 Stück über den Ladentisch. Und ich habe ja noch 9 weitere Bücher geschrieben". Van Helsing/Dr. Dinero, Das 1-Million-Euro-Buch, p. 57. "My books are selling very well. E. g. within four years 'Don't Touch This Book' sold 150,000 times in the German language alone. And I wrote 9 other books".

Again it is a book that presents Holey's anti-Semitic right-wing opinions - this time often in a more subtle way. However, there are also examples in which references are comparatively obvious. For example, Holey analyzes the meaning of the symbols on the one-dollar-bill, just like so many conspiracy theorists before him: "The 'Great Seal', the 'pyramid with the all-seeing eye', the Magen David consisting of thirteen stars above the phoenix, the phoenix itself, the state coat of arms on the reverse side of the seal as well as the original of the Star-Spangled Banner with the thirteen stripes and the thirteen stars are old and important symbols of the Illuminati. They were created as an assignment from the Rothschilds and are placed by Adam Weishaupt. But their symbolism reverts not only to Egyptian heritage but to the Andes (Ecuador) as well. Phillip Rothschild designed the Illuminati-Dollar-Pyramid, as it was revealed by his girlfriend Ann Rand in her book 'Atlas Shrugged'".[35]

"The nephew of Admiral Byrd, whom I met and interviewed in Phoenix, Arizona, confirmed that at that time his uncle had taken a plane to the North pole. There he found the entrance to an interior hollow space in which one or several high cultures resided. While sitting in their airplanes, Admiral Byrd and his co-pilot Floyd Bennett were suddenly being escorted by two flying saucers which they had also filmed. They described the insignia of sovereignty as swastikas. This was confirmed by Admiral Byrd's nephew, Harley Byrd. Let us leave that aside at this point".[36] Or, even more bluntly: "Also the 'God' Jahwe of the Old Testament could be considered a destructive, slave holding extra-terrestrial. The inevitable question arises what kind of 'God' this must be, who commands his 'chosen People' to destroy without exception other people and tribes during the Exodus. What kind of a God is this, who demands or even forces that his 'chosen People' commit genocide".[37]

He adumbrates right-wing subjects also in "Das 1-Million-Euro-Buch".[38] It was published by "Jan van Helsing" together with the anonymous co-author "Dr. Dinero"[39] in 2009. The most important aim of this book is to serve as a life-counseling feature and to earn money - for the authors. They identify the "New World Order" as a reason for the financial crisis since 2008 and state that the crash resulted from a plan envisioned long beforehand.[40]

35 Van Helsing, Hände weg von diesem Buch, p. 192.

36 Ibid., p. 159.

37 Ibid., p. 107.

38 Published in Fichtenau: AmaDeus Verlag (Nr. 3,067 in books, www.amazon.de, 6 November 2009). This is his new book, which seems to sell very well, too.

39 It seems quite probable that Dr. Dinero is identical with the "mental trainer" Frank Wilde, who advertises his book "Beweg Deinen Arsch" at the end of the Million Euro book, published by AmaDeus.

40 Van Helsing/Dr. Dinero, Das 1-Million-Euro-Buch, p. 23.
"For at least 15 years the so-called 'conspiracy theorists' warned of what we are now encountering. It is part of an all-encompassing plan to lead humanity into total control, the so-called New World Order, a new order with a new currency system without cash. The economic crisis did not fall from heaven above, and also big banks are not feable-minded - everything was planned beforehand. But leave that aside for the moment".

A genuine family business trading with esotericism evolved with the foundation of the AmaDeus Verlag. It was founded by Jan Udo Holey's mother, Luise Holey, in 1997. There his father, Johannes Holey, published his first book "Jesus 2000: Das Friedensreich naht". According to the website "www.johannes-holey.de" (accessed 6 November 2009), Jan Udo Holey inherited the publishing house some time later. From this time on books and videos of Holey father and son were edited by AmaDeus.

In 2009, father Johannes Holey nearly reached the success of his son with his book "Jetzt reichts" ("Now It Is Enough"). Amazon reports that this book is listed Number 1,870 of German books sold.[41] The book was seen on piles at several bookstores in Germany. It is both, a perfect camouflage and a perfect access to right-wing esotericism – camouflage because "soft" esoteric subjects like health problems, the danger of microwaves, and vegetarianism prevail over political chapters like "Lies in politics and economy". Access because rightist and conspiratorial ideas can be found. Without being bluntly anti-Semitic, there is a certain subtext, quoting beside esoteric texts also conspiratorial and right-wing sources. Above all, the reader is invited to watch "Secret-TV", to read magazines like "Zeiten-Schrift" or "Nexus" and to subscribe to the information of "Kopp-Exklusiv". We shall soon hear more about these publications.

Today, Jan Udo Holey refrains from disseminating openly anti-Semitic statements. However, between the lines of his publication one might recognize certain keywords, well-known to anti-Semitic and world-conspiracy thinking circles.

"Secret-TV", too, is a product of Jan Udo Holey and was founded on 1 January 2007. It operates as: "Der erfolgreichste deutschsprachige Internet-TV-Sender, der zeigt, was andere Medien verschweigen" ("The most successful TV-broadcast-station in the German language, showing what other media keep secret"). Examples of the secrets of other media are: "Die Evolutions-Lüge" ("The Evolution-Lie"), "UFO-Konferenz Washington 2007" or "Geheimtechnologien des 3. Reichs" ("Secret Technologies of the Third Reich").[42] "Secret-TV" is still available, but ended uploading new videos with 15 January 2010.[43] Thus, the structure of the family business, the "Holey Empire", again concentrates on publishing. They even run a small company, the Lieblings-Verlag, editing children's books.

41 See http://www.amazon.de, last accessed 6 November 2009.

42 See http://www.secret.tv/category/Wissenschaft__Technik_5035436.html, last accessed 9 November 2009.

43 "This offers to me the once in a lifetime chance to continue living and developing the idea of a really free broadcast. Meanwhile I am free to concentrate on new book projects. Therefore I decided to hand over secret TV to the nexworld-Team". The German version is available at: http://www.secret.tv/artikel5060950/Jan_van_Helsing_verabschiedet_sich_von_secretTV.

2. Jo Conrad

Another German author and publisher of esoteric books with contents inclining to the extreme right is Jo Conrad, born in 1958. He is the founder of the company Bignose Media.[44] On his website he distributes downloads, self-composed music, videos, and his books published by Bignose Media. Conrad is not as industrious a writer compared to Jan Udo Holey. By now he has published four books: "Zusammenhänge" ("Connections", 1998), "Ursprünge" ("Roots", 2000), "Entwirrungen" ("Disentanglements", 2001) and "Wendungen" ("Twists", 2004). According to his homepage, "Entwirrungen" is his most successful book, appearing in the ninth edition and translated into Czech. Its contents sound familiar after reading Jan van Helsing: "This book tells about the Gods of the different religions, the Kennedy-assassination, secret societies, UFOs, alternative cures, AIDS, terrorism, forbidden books, and many other things, otherwise you get only filtered information".[45]

In his books, he quotes Jan van Helsing/Jan Udo Holey and Gary Allen and refers to the "Protocols of the Elders of Zion".[46] He was a longtime collaborator of Jan Udo Holey. During recent years, he has been cooperating with "Secret-TV". The joint venture ceased in 2009, when Jo Conrad got involved with the "Fürstentum Germania",[47] an esoteric living community with leanings to the movement "Kommissarische Regierung des Deutschen Reiches" (KRR), to anti-Semitism and to the chemtrail conspiracy. Conrad contributed the anthem of the "Fürstentum Germania". This was a little too much even for Jan Udo Holey, who published an open letter concerning the break up with Jo Conrad. He states that "Secret-TV" is an independent medium and concludes that this impartiality was hurt by Conrad's commitment for the "Fürstentum".[48] However, Holey could have known long before - in 2005, Conrad gave an interview for the magazine "A.N.O.S",[49] published by the notorious and convicted NPD member Christian Deichen.[50]

44 See http://www.joconrad.de, last accessed 16 June 2010.
45 See http://www.joconrad.de/buecher.htm, last accessed 16 June 2010.
46 For more information, see Fromm, Rechtsradikalismus in der Esoterik, pp. 221-223.
47 The "Fürstentum Germania" existed only between February and May 2009 and was then evicted by the police; because of the ruinous state of the old castle it could be located.
48 This letter is quoted in "Eso-Watch: Jo Conrad" www.esowatch.com, last accessed 16 June 2010.
49 The meaning of this abbrevation is "zerschlagt die neue Weltordnung" or in Latin "anti novus ordo seclorum", Verfassungsschutzbericht Mecklenburg-Vorpommern 2006, p. 60, available at:
http://www.verfassungsschutz-mv.de/cms2/Verfassungsschutz_prod/Verfassungsschutz/content_downloads/Verfassungsschutzberichte/VS-Bericht202006.pdf.
50 See http://www.esowatch.com/ge/index.php?title=Jo_Conrad, last accessed 16 June 2010.

3. David Icke

David Icke, born in 1952, looks back to an amazing career as a soccer player, sports reporter, and speaker of the *Green Party* in Great Britain. Since 1990, when he started to hear an inner voice, he has been pursuing a new career as a mystic.

He fits perfectly to the category of "esoteric entrepreneurs", due to his various activities, including TV appearances, long lectures in esoteric circles[51] and, of course, books, which he publishes himself, for some years even at the publishing house Bridge of Love Publications[52] which is probably owned by himself, and on his website. Additionally, he sells DVDs, runs his own "YouTube"-channel and at least is connected to a television program called "Edge Media Television" which "is broadcast in the UK on the Sky platform from 6am until 10pm" "www.edgemediatv.com".

One example of his success is "The Biggest Secret", published in 1999.[53] It was also published in French in 2001 and in German in 2004.[54] The German release has reached its fourth edition in 2009. Another book is "Children of the Matrix", translated into French.[55] In "The Biggest Secret", Icke develops an extremely strange "theory" about reptile characters ruling the world, for example the British royal family transforming into reptiles, killing and eating-children.[56]

Classifying Icke as "extreme rightist", compared to Jan Udo Holey and Jo Conrad, has frequently been discussed as a prevalent controversy.[57] His books contain wild accusations against members of the former Bush government and other prominent persons whom he alleges to abuse little children and to prac-

51 He acts as a really alert businessman having sold his appearance, for example in Zurich on 14 November 2009, holds connections to "Nexus" and was obviously using the "swine-flue-vaccination conspiracy" to reach a bigger public in autumn 2009. See http://www.davidicke.com, last accessed 12 November 2009.

52 It is not entirely clear, if he owned this publishing company. One can still enter an outdated website with this name. His latest publication of April 2010 "Human Race Get Off Your Knees: The Lion Sleeps No More" is released by David Icke Books Ltd. Barkun states: "Icke's early work was issued by the British New Age publisher Gateway, which allegedly dropped him because of concerns about anti-Semitic material. His later work has appeared under the imprint of Bridge of Love Publications, which seems entirely devoted to publishing work he has written or supports". Barkun, A Culture of Conspiracy, p. 108.

53 Icke, The Biggest Secret.

54 Icke, Le plus grand secret, tome 1 et 2., and in German: Das größte Geheimnis: Dieses Buch verändert die Welt.

55 Enfants de la matrice, tome 1, 1998, tome 2.

56 Icke, The Biggest Secret, p. 462.

57 Barkun states: "While Icke has clearly sought to cultivate the extreme right, however, the effort has not been without tension, largely a product of the New Age baggage attached to his political ideas. As a result, his attitude about the American radical right seems to be a mixture of admiration and frustration". Barkun, A Culture of Conspiracy, p. 107.

tice Satanism. According to his books, those persons belong to the "New World Order" and planned the assaults on nine eleven.[58] These odd conspiratorial ideas come along with more antiquated ones like taking "The Protocols of the Elders of Zion" seriously.[59]

One article by David Icke with a striking relation to the extreme right is "Was Hitler a Rothschild?".[60] First, Icke explains to the public that he is not anti-Semitic because he only speaks against the Rothschilds for the reason that this family represents "one of the most notorious black occult bloodlines of Middle Ages Germany".[61] He disclaims being anti-Semitic by falsely stating that the Rothschild family is not Jewish but that nevertheless it was and is controlling the world and was therefore responsible for installing Hitler, too. "How strange then, that as I have documented in 'And the Truth Shall Set You Free' and 'The Biggest Secret', along with endless other researchers and scholars, Adolf Hitler and the Nazis were created and funded by [...] the Rothschilds. It was they who arranged for Hitler to come to power through the Illuminati secret societies in Germany like the Thule-Gesellschaft and the Vril-Gesellschaft which they created through their German networks; it was the Rothschilds who funded Hitler through the Bank of England and other British and American sources like the Rothschild's Kuhn, Loeb, bank which also funded the Russian Revolution".[62]

In the next passage, Icke envisions the Rothschilds' responsibility for "Hitler's war machine": "The very heart of Hitler's war machine was the chemical giant, I. G. Farben, which had an American arm that was controlled by the Rothschilds through their lackeys, the Warburgs. Paul Warburg, who manipulated into existence the privately-owned 'central bank' of America, the Federal Reserve, in 1913, was on the board of American I. G. Indeed Hitler's (sic!) I. G. Farben, which ran the slave labor camp at Auschwitz was, in reality, a division of Standard Oil, officially owned by the Rockefellers, but in truth the Rockefeller Empire was funded into existence by [...] the Rothschilds. See 'And the Truth Shall Set You Free' and 'The Biggest Secret' for the detailed background of this and other aspects of this story. The Rothschilds also owned the German news agencies during both World Wars and thus controlled the flow of 'information' to Germans and the outside world. Incidentally, when Allied troops entered Germany they found that the I. G. Farben factories, the very core of Hitler's war operation, had not been hit by the mass bombing and neither had Ford factories - another Illuminati supporter of Hitler. Other factories nearby had been demolished by bombing raids".[63]

58 Icke, The Biggest Secret; Icke, Alice in Wonderland and the World Trade Center Disaster; both titles translated into German.
59 Goodrick-Clarke, Im Schatten der Schwarzen Sonne, p. 552.
60 Http://web.archive.org/web/20030410085724/www.davidicke.com/icke/articles/hitler.html, last accessed 15 July 2010.
61 Ibid.
62 Ibid.
63 Ibid.

Icke himself states that his website has millions of visitors every week and is one of the most frequently visited websites concerning conspiracies worldwide.[64] The English Wikipedia speaks of 600,000 hits per week. Whatever the truth, the fact remains that Icke's website is made up very professionally and obviously is financially successful. It contains numerous web links and information on the events of Icke himself. Barkun confirms his profits, too.[65]

Besides being commercially successful, one might argue that these lunatic thoughts are no danger because they are so obviously historically and factually wrong. However, traces of these ideas are to be found in popular Internet sources like the "Zeitgeist" movie, for example, which presents the allegation that the EU or NAFTA are only steps towards a world government - led by Illuminati - or the denouncement of Christian religion in nearly the same words.

4. Robin de Ruiter

Another author distributing all over Europe is the Dutchman Robin de Ruiter (born in 1951) who mainly publishes in Dutch, Spanish, and German, but also in English and French. He advertises that his books appear in more than one hundred countries;[66] a commentary on Amazon speaks of him as "perhaps the most prominent European conspiracy writer after David Icke".[67]

In 1989, he started with "De 13 Satanische bloedlijnen - Wegbereiders van de Antichrist", Mayra Publications, Enschede, but he has become more productive in the past few years. Despite this long publishing history, no reference to his name could be found in any academic discussion.[68] There are several websites saying that this book is banned in France - but there is no source indicated.[69] "Worldwide Evil and Misery: The Legacy of the 13 Satanic Bloodlines", edited 2008 by Mayra publishers, seems to be a newer version of this issue. It contains heavy conspiratorial anti-Semitic ideas: "The Zionists have conquered Palestine with weapons, bombs, grenades and fighter planes. The Illuminati have helped to power and finance both Zionism and Adolf Hitler. They are at the beginning of the current state of Israel! The eventual foundation of an Israeli state in Palestine was a crucial element of the Illuminati program.

64 Icke, Alice im Wunderland und das World Trade Center Disaster, p. 665.

65 "[H]e certainly did not invent the concept of evil inner-earth reptilians, an idea that spread rapidly in the 1990s; but no one has done more to spread it. Within months of 'The Biggest Secret's publication, he claimed thirty thousand copies in print". Barkun, A Culture of Conspiracy, p. 106.

66 See http://www.marketingnewauthors.com/wwem.html, last accessed 15 July 2010.

67 Http://www.amazon.de/Worldwide-Evil-Misery-Satanic-Bloodlines/dp/9079680079/ref=sr_1_1/280-9615693-1151312?ie=UTF8&s=books-intl-de&qid=1279184589&sr=1-1, last accessed 15 July 2010.

68 For a critical evaluation in a blog, see http://www.manfred-gebhard.de/Ruiter.htm, last accessed 15 July 2010.

69 See http://www.mayrapublications.nl/, last accessed 15 July 2010.

Today, the foundation is being laid in Israel, making it possible for the world leader they will elect one day to rule the world from Jerusalem".[70]

In the Bayerische Staatsbibliothek, one of the world's largest libraries, there are titles listed like the German translation of the book "Die 13 satanischen Blutlinien" (Durach[71] 2000), "Der 11. September 2001" (Durach 2002), "Die Eingreiftruppen des Antichristen" (Durach 2003), "Die Köder des Satanskultes" (Durach 2004), "Der 11. September 2001 und andere Verbrechen gegen die Menschheit" (Frankfurt am Main 2004), "The Watchtower Society" (Durach 2006) and, together with Jenny Estrada, "Der Zweite Weltkrieg: die Schwarze Liste der US-Regierung" (Enschede 2009).

De Ruiter published two largely overlapping books about nine eleven in 2002 and 2004.[72] The title of the 2002 edition aims directly at the "occult powers behind the terrorist assaults on the US".[73] In both books, he unfolds anti-American convictions. The "conspirators" stem directly from the "13 satanic bloodlines", inclined to rule the world as the "New World Order". In some parts of this text, he has trouble hiding his anti-Semitism that is mixed with religious confidence: "Because of the great participation of those who are called Jews in a One-World-Conspiracy, many persons are considering the world conspiracy as Jewish. This is deceiving, because we find a hidden order. The One-World-Conspiracy is a religious conspiracy. At heart, this conspiracy is satanic. It is important to know that the leading families are also belonging to the leading Satanists of the world and are considering the devil as the true god".[74] This reminds considerably of Icke and concludes in the opinion: "Since the beginning of world history until our modern age the basis of our satanic conspiracy and its dogma is the conviction that one day Satan will openly govern this world".[75] The resemblance to Icke also consists of some strange allegations as, for example, Al Gore being a Satanist addicted to blood and always carrying a suitcase filled with blood with him.[76]

70 Ruiter, Worldwide Evil and Misery; quoted after http://www.kevinalfredstrom.com/wp-content/uploads/2009/02/deruiter-chapter-20.pdf , p. 36, last accessed 15 July 2010.

71 De Ruiters German publications were published in the Zambon Verlag (Frankfurt a. M.) and in the Verlag Anton A. Schmidt (Durach) in the edition "Pro Fide Catholica". While the latter inclines towards ultra religious opinions, Zambon Verlag represents a completely different direction: http://www.zambon.net/zambon-frame/zambon-frame-deu/zambon-startdeu.html, last accessed 17 March 2010.
It publishes titles like "Stalin anders betrachtet" (Author: Ludo Martens) which indicate that this publisher belongs to the extreme left. While conspiratorial thinking prevails on the extreme right, there are examples with leftists, too, e. g. Krysmanski, Wem gehört die EU? Studie im Auftrag der Europaabgeordneten Sahra Wagenknecht.

72 I am referring to the German edition: Ruiter, Im Namen der neuen Weltordnung: Der 11. September 2001 und andere Verbrechen gegen die Menschheit; Ruiter, Der 11. September 2001: Osama bin Laden und die okkulten Kräfte hinter den terroristischen Anschlägen auf die USA.

73 Cf. German title of the book, see above.

74 Cf. Ruiter, Der 11. September 2001, pp. 6–7.

75 Cf. ibid., p. 7.

76 Ruiter, Die 13 satanischen Blutlinien, p. 26.

VII. Meeting the media: publishing houses and magazines

Alongside with anonymous websites and celebrated authors, there is a third category, media magazines or publishing houses promoting esotericism, conspiratorial theories and dubious texts containing extremely right-wing tendencies. On the one hand, there are publishing companies quite overtly specialized in esotericism or conspiratorial subjects, and on the other hand there are popular science magazines aimed at a broader public, released by commercially oriented editors with no special interest in politics. The latter are not extreme rightist, but they stress subjects that highlight "secrets" and "conspiracies", thus furthering interest in conspiratorial theories.

1. The Kopp-Verlag and "Kopp-Exklusiv": "Serious journalism" meets esotericism and lots of conspiracies

The Kopp-Verlag in Rottenburg am Neckar, owned by Jochen Kopp, is a publishing company that sells books and videos by other publishers via mail order, too. According to Internet sources, it is quite successful. Kopp employed 30 persons in 2008 and sent 150,000 catalogues to its readers every month.[77] Its credo unites "truth-seeking" and provides publishing possibilities for "researchers" beyond the "mainstream".[78]

Successful titles published by Kopp include books about natural healing, e. g. curing hair loss. But the program offers for sale also titles about UFOs, "Men in Black", "Flugscheiben über Neuschwabenland",[79] conspiratorial subjects, "forbidden" archeology, esotericism, and politics. It sells DVDs, for example "Nazi-UFOs - die Verschwörung" ("Nazi-UFOs - the Conspiracy") or "Legende Tiger-Panzer - Panzer des Zweiten Weltkriegs" ("Legend Tiger-Tank - Tanks of World War II").

77 Http://www.dug-software.de/wir-ueber-uns/pressearchiv.html, last accessed 7 July 2010.

78 "It is the objective of the Kopp-Verlag to point to suppressed information, discoveries and inventions. The spreading of forbidden topics, political correctness and censorship in our society and in the media should be reviewed in books and articles that reveal hitherto suppressed facts. [...] Mainly unorthodox researchers, discoverers and inventors outside the groves of academia were and are indebted to mankind's progress. But again and again trailblazing developments run into opposition, that is being dictated by commercial and political interests. [...] It is also the objective of the Kopp-Verlag to draw the attention of the public to topics that are focused on in an exaggerated manner. These are topics that are overrated by the media and therefore divert our attention from essentially more important reports that are being treated only marginally or not at all". The German version is available at: http://www.kopp-verlag.de/Wir-ueber-uns.htm?websale7=kopp-verlag&tpl=01-aa/tpl_wir_ueber_uns.htm, last accessed 6 July 2010.

79 "Flying Saucers over Neuschwabenland". This oeuvre is about an idea we already encountered - about Nazis who escaped to the Antarctic. The authors are Heiner Gehring and Karl-Heinz Zunneck.

Using the options of the Internet, in recent years Kopp has expanded its enterprise by an information service and an additional online resource. The information service "Kopp-Exklusiv" promises: "Werfen Sie einen Blick hinter die Kulissen der Macht - und erfahren Sie, was die Massenmedien Ihnen verschweigen" ("Have a look behind the curtains of power - and learn what mass media try to keep secret").[80] What mass media hide are classical conspiratorial subjects like "Mr. Westerwelle and Mossad - is it possible to blackmail the foreign minister?" or "Barack Obama - the CIA's puppet on a string?". Esoteric subjects include "And the Turin Grave cloth is authentic after all" ("Und das Grabtuch ist doch echt").[81] This information is not cheap. One has to pay € 250 per annum for 52 issues - the reduced prize for clients is € 150.

"Kopp online"[82] is a combination of printed news and a news channel with newscast videos. The printed announcements mix esoteric ideas - such as dangers of a solar eclipse or interpretations of the I Ging - with political issues like the American oil disaster or speculations about the German politician Roland Koch. The former Prime Minister of the German Federal State of Hesse aroused suspicion because he participated in the Bilderberg Conference in 2009. The newscast program includes similar subjects. It stresses political issues, e.g. the events in Israel in July 2010. Former "Tagesschau"-presenter Eva Herman, who is no longer working for the German public television because of her controversial and heavily debated announcements concerning family politics, often reads the news.

The Kopp publishing company also provides a forum for other journalists who came into conflict with the public opinion.

2. The European dimension: "Nexus"

The bimonthly esoteric magazine "Nexus" was founded in Australia in 1986. Now it is published in Australia, France, Germany, Greece, Italy, Poland and Romania. A European release is published in English. The postal address is Amsterdam. It is therefore an impressive example of the proliferation of esoteric right-wing ideas across Europe.

It is difficult to evaluate its success because "Nexus" is distributed widely via Internet. Some articles are free to the public on the homepages in different languages. One can download the German issue of the magazine by paying online. The printed German edition is only 2,700 copies.

The subjects in the German issue of "Nexus" from January 2008 show a mixture of esoteric, conspiratorial, and neo-Nazi matters:

80 Http://www.kopp-exklusiv.de/, last accessed 9 November 2009.
81 Http://www.kopp-exklusiv.de, last accessed 15 July 2010.
82 Http://info.kopp-verlag.de/index.html, last accessed 15 July 2010.

- "Earth: Secrets of the Ice Age are melting"
- "Illuminati: Chinese Secret Societies issue an ultimatum"
- "High Doses of Vitamin B12 to Cure Dementia"
- "How Adolf Hitler's Death was Invented"
- "The Wheat-Circle Season 2007"
- "Commercial Animal Food and the Subsequent Damage"

It would be especially interesting in our context to have a look at "Hitler's Death".

The text "How Adolf Hitler's Death was Invented" was published in three parts in the German "Nexus" (2008) Nos. 14, 15, and 16 by the Australian Giordan Smith. It first appeared in the English version in October/November 2007. "Nexus" introduces Smith as an "independent academic" with "modern German History" as his special subject.[83] The story culminates in part three of the article, where the abstract states: "The British targeted the story of Hitler's suicide as a weapon of psychological warfare, to discredit National-Socialism and to break the will of resistance of the German people against the foreign occupying forces".[84]

The same "Nexus" issue also contains a story about "Hitler's secret wonder-weapons". The mixture of esotericism, conspiracies, and right-wing history makes "Nexus" a representative example of a well-established media outlet in this field.

3. Switzerland: Home of the "Zeiten-Schrift"

A quite "established" but highly controversial esoteric magazine is the Swiss publication "Zeiten-Schrift", founded in 1993. It is already well analyzed in Gugenberger et al. 1998. Publishers Benjamin and Ursula Seiler-Spielemann went online, too. They are featuring in Internet articles like "9/11 The conspiracy behind conspiracy" or "Poor Jews".[85] The English version of their homepage runs under the title "Facts are facts", which reminds of other "truth-seeking" sites.[86]

In the printed version, "Zeiten-Schrift" includes articles like "War-guilt: How Germany was forced into World War II" ("Kriegsschuld: Wie Deutschland der Zweite Weltkrieg aufgezwungen wurde").[87]

The issue (2005) 46 of the magazine includes several articles with a heavy revisionist and anti-Semitic background by Ursula Seiler, entitled "Hitler: Dunkle Geheimnisse aus seinen frühen Jahren" ("Hitler: Dark Secrets from his early years").

83 Nexus (2008) 14, p. 45.
84 Nexus (2008) 16, p. 47.
85 Http://www.zeitenschrift.com, last accessed 10 November 2009.
86 Http://www.facts-are-facts.com, last accessed 10 November 2009.
87 Zeiten-Schrift (2005) 46.

Especially in the article on Hitler's early years one finds a mixture of national socialist, extreme rightist ideology and esoteric topics like the holy lance. It is also worthwhile to analyze the context of the whole issue, which includes articles with medical-conspiratorial background "Codex Alimentarius: How the Pharmaceutical Industry tries to impede the success of dietary supplements worldwide",[88] "green" subjects like "Green thumb: nature ghosts give advise for gardening and agriculture",[89] the esoteric in Goethe's "Faust" or spirituality. All this is topped with a great deal of advertisement, bridging subjects from Feng Shui as far as to the infamous Grabert-Verlag.[90]

4. The penetration of mainstream media by conspiratorial thoughts and right-wing esotericism

Topics discussed in right-wing esotericism, for example the construct of "The New World Order", have arrived at mainstream media in recent years. There have been several examples of non right-wing esoteric fiction in the nineties, like "File X", an American TV-production, which was broadcasted around the world. Another illustration of non right-wing esotericism in fiction are the thrillers by Dan Brown, with subjects like the Illuminati, the secret bloodline of Jesus or the Free-Masons.

A new dimension since is the discussion of conspiratorial theories in non-fictional magazines (TV and print). Secret societies, the "New World Order", and dangers of conspiracies are more and more prominent topics in German language magazines and TV-productions. Titles include "Welt der Wunder"[91] ("World of Miracles"), "Galileo Mystery", and "Mysteries".

Examples of articles in "Welt der Wunder" are "Die Geheimakten von 9/11" ("Secret Files of 9/11"), issue September 2009; "Geheimakte Freimaurer: Regieren Sie wirklich die Welt?" ("Secret File Free-Masons: Do They Really Rule the World?"), issue October 2009. "Welt der Wunder" is also a TV format broadcasted on German "RTL 2", a nationwide TV channel.

"Galileo Mystery", a TV magazine, had first been aired in 2006 and was regularly broadcasted on the German private channel "Pro 7" between May 2007 and August 2009. As side production of the popular science magazine

88 Ibid., pp. 9–12.
89 Ibid., pp. 14–15.
90 This publishing-house is notorious for its revisionist and anti-Semitic books. The titles include: Brennecke, Gerhard: Die Nürnberger Geschichtsentstellung; Fritsch, Ludwig A.: Amerikas Verantwortung für die Verbrechen am deutschen Volk; Friedrich, Georg: Hitlers letzter Trumpf, among others. Available at: http://www.grabert-verlag.de, last accessed 15 July 2010.
91 "Welt der Wunder" is released by the Bauer media group, Hamburg. According to the published media data information it is published with over 300,000 copies per month in 2010. Male readers outnumber female readers by far. See http://www.bauermedia.com/518.0.html, last accessed 28 June 2010.

"Galileo", it offered subjects like "Ghost-photography" or "Astrology". With titles like "UFOs", "The Jesus Conspiracy" or "Bermuda-Triangle", it fostered conspiratorial thinking.

Luc Bürgin, who at Kopp-Verlag publishes on "forbidden archeology", edits the Swiss magazine "Mysteries". With 31,000 issues published in January 2010,[92] it is one of the bigger esoteric magazines. Its content, including advertisement, is much more occult than the articles in "Welt der Wunder", for example.[93] In the editorial of this issue, Luc Bürgin argues against Muslims, introduces "the number-magic of the Thora", and reveals the "secrets of bank-notes".

It is important to note that the texts concerned with these topics are not necessarily outspoken anti-Semitic or extreme-rightist in other aspects, but they promote these issues as topics of serious interest. Rhetorical questions such as "Free-Masons, do they really rule the world?" suggest a reality of secret societies and their assumed power, something which the extreme right also does.

Another example of the diffusion of esoteric material into a very popular magazine in Germany are the advertisements of the Kopp-Verlag, discussed above, in "ADAC Motorwelt", the magazine for members of Germany's most important association of motorists. In the advertisement of the issue of November 2009, Kopp promotes "Prophezeiungen über das Ende der Welt" ("Prophecies on the End of the World") by Fabio Ribeiro de Araudo; "Götterdämmerung: Die Rückkehr der Außerirdischen" ("Twilight of the Gods") by Erich von Däniken and "21. Dezember 2012: Das Ende unserer Welt?" ("21 December 2012: The End of our World?") by Adrian Gilbert.

Considering these examples, it is obvious that esoteric and especially conspiratorial thoughts penetrate the mass media and are not restricted to a small circle of readers.

VIII. Conclusion

The range of right-wing esotericism assembled in the present text reaches from overt neo-Nazism to comparatively harmless references in the mass media. The common thread in all examples presented is the connection to conspiratorial thinking.

Different types of esoteric right-wing material correspond with different kinds of hazard. The danger inherent in neo-Nazi esotericism does not lie in its quantity but in the easy access to heavily extremist thoughts like Holocaust denial through the Internet. Successful "esoteric entrepreneurs" generate a much greater danger through their popularity. With colorful Internet appearances and

92 See Mysteries, (2010) 1, p. 66 (Impressum).

93 See ibid., p. 34, advertisement for "ParaVideo – Ihr Videomagazin zu mysteriösen Themen" and of course a big advertisement for the Kopp-Verlag on the back page of this issue.

public lectures like those by David Icke, even strange ideas become available for a broader public. This is also true for the new "art" form of conspiratorial videos like "Loose change" or "Zeitgeist". These pictures attract even more people, especially youngsters, as illustrated by the frequent "views" on "YouTube". Above all, the impact and the importance of conspiratorial theories for right-wing esotericism deserve even further research. Now rumors about conspiracies easily enter texts and movies beyond the inner circle of occult extreme rightists, and often they come close to right-wing ideas.

Musical and Political Subculture - A Review of Attempts of Entrism

Stéphane François

In the West, some "young" musical subcultures[1] are closely connected with radical and extremist right-wing milieus. Right-wing radicals and extremists have attempted to infiltrate those "young" minority cultures in order to control them. In this text, I shall concentrate on the relationship between the so-called dark[2] musical scenes[3] and the neo-right wing and nationalist-revolutionary milieus.

These subcultures may be considered milieus bridging different subcultures and ideologies. They are a junction of a cultural web that is particularly hazy but - quite paradoxically - still easily identifiable. All of them wish to subvert the rules of the Western society, and to break taboos, particularly political ones. For this reason, it is difficult for external observers of this complex web to distinguish provocation from ideological commitment.

I. Targeted subcultures

The subcultures falling prey to this entrism are generally known as "dark music" or "dark cultures". The "dark" milieus are often politically acculturated. Due to this political acculturation, they are in fact quite open to these theories - all the more because some of them have developed points of view on certain topics that are quite close. We will return to this fact.

1 We will use in this study the term "subculture" rather than "counterculture" or "marginal culture". The term "counterculture" refers primarily to the collective memory to the students' counterculture of 1960s' California, while that of "marginal culture" has a negative connotation, harmful to the understanding of this phenomenon.

2 These "young" subcultures have roots in the literary and pictorial romanticism, particularly in the romantic "gothic", hence the name. Thus, persons operating in these environments often dress in black, and they play with romantic clichés: the tortured sexuality, decadence, the concept of sin, madness and torment of the soul, satanism, heathenism, esotericism, magic, etc. Generally, actors of these environments develop a pessimistic view of the world that can turn into nihilism. These styles of music are generally transgressive music and serve as safety valves.

3 We understand by "scene" the actors involved in the life of a musical register: groups, labels, distributors, press, radio, and the public.

Considering the sub-genres concerned, ideological entrism works more or less well. The truly gothic[4] milieus as well as the "dark wave" scene are more intellectual and aestheticized and flatly reject politics. They are less penetrated than the "industrial"[5] sub-genres, "dark folk"[6] or "black metal".[7] The latter are strongly characterized by a Eurocentric paganism, by esotericism in a wider sense, for example thelemism,[8] by subjects close to revolutionary-conservative thought (conservative vanguard, European nationalism, questioning of identity, etc.), and by topics frequently used as vehicles for what could be called "Mysterious History" in the 1970s.

In the 1960s and 70s, the interest in this history intending to bring up to date the occult bases of world history and especially of Nazism was kindled by Louis Pauwels via "The morning of the Magicians",[9] followed by his journal "Planète". In fact, a very strong interest in for what I called "Nazi occultism" in other texts prevails in these subcultures.

Since the mid-1980s, the subculture that had emerged from the "industrial music" has been fascinated by the most heterodox aspects of Nazism. This interest was sustained by the work of academics like Nicholas Goodrick-Clarke[10] as well as by the publication of the magazine "Aorta" by the Austrian musician Kadmon. "Aorta" was not only interested in various aspects of "Nazi occultism" and related topics. The fascination with the dark pages of European history, especially with the occultist aspect of the SS ideology, also played a major role for this interest that could be called "black romanticism". This is why the fanzines accorded ariosophy an important position. The French fanzine "Omega" was interested in the cross on the cover of the first album of Blood Axis ("The Gospel of Inhumanity"). The Austrian ariosopher Jörg Lanz von Liebenfels had used it before as the symbol of his Order of the New Templars - Ordo Novi Templi (ONT).

4 The gothic scene, musically multifaceted, includes literary and artistic components. Histrionic, tormented by religion and sexuality, profoundly sad and nostalgic (for a past that never existed), this scene has been born from the ashes of the punk movement (and partially of dandyism of glam rock) in the early 1980s.

5 This extreme music first appeared in the artistic avant-garde of the mid-1970s. It is characterized by an atonal and noisy music, hence the name. It is the successor of the most radical experiments of the psychedelic music, futurist, minimalist American music, Dadaism, and of the first punk bands.

6 The "dark folk" style is a sub-register of the industrial scene using mainly acoustic instruments, but has maintained the experimental side of industrial music. The themes of this style of music focus on the European paganism and heathenism, on the European folk traditions and on European history, with a marked preference for the dark chapters (Nazism, fascism, totalitarianism, etc.).

7 "Black metal" is a sub-register of the "metal" style, formerly known as "hard rock" or "heavy metal". It appeared in the mid-1980s. It is a trend of Black Sabbath, for desperate texts, of Kiss and Alice Cooper for makeup, and Led Zeppelin for occult texts.

8 "Thelemism" is the "religion" born of the magic's speculation of the British occultist Aleister Crowley.

9 Pauwels/Bergier, Le matin des magiciens.

10 Cf. Goodrick-Clarke, The Occult Roots of Nazism; id., Black Sun.

In this milieu, various initiatives develop rapidly around this topic. Thus, in 1994, in his album "Gotos Kalanda" Kadmon sets the poems of Karl Maria Wiligut to music. Later, Kadmon will dedicate an album, "Neuschwabenland", to a supposed Nazi base in the Antarctic - a place Hitler is claimed to have escaped to at the end of the Second World War. Basically, he only uses the theses of a literature on the fringe of occultism and of the extreme right wing, which popularized this idea with a certain success in occultist-conspiratorial circles in the 1970s.

In "black metal", on the other hand, the resort to "Nazi occultism" remains very superficial and is usually confined to titles of songs or albums, or to the names of groups like the Australian band Spear of Longinus. This milieu often refers to European pagan cults, too, with a general interest in Celtic and Germanic-Scandinavian forms of paganism. There are also references to "Heroic Fantasy" and to the pseudo-satanism expressed by Howard P. Lovecraft, especially in his cycle of novels "Cthulhu" and his "Necronomicon". In fact, these groups created a mythical world before the beginning of history where "super-warriors" in leather or metal armor fight dragons, evil beings, Gods, etc.

II. The context of entrism

Since the end of the 1970s, radical and extremist right-wing milieus in the West have been interested in "pop" music. The Italian radical and extremist right was the first to understand the relevancy of this culture at the time of the famous Hobbit camps, the name of the creatures in Tolkien's "Lord of the Rings". Between 1977 and 1979, young nationalist-revolutionary and neo-right wing young Italians gathered at those camps, which rapidly became fields of ideological exchange and experiments. This experience gave rise to a counterculture of the extreme right forming the counterpart of the leftist counter-culture. For a long time, though, the various radical and extremist right-wing currents considered the musical subcultures a form of decadence and not of subversion. This is why a music style committed to the extreme right became starkly visible for the first time a little later in a different milieu and independent of these reflections. It was "Oi! music",[11] the music of the skinheads coming from British workers' milieus. It developed in the punk period, i. e., in the late 1970s.[12] By the way, the leader of the band Skrewdriver comes from the punk milieu. The line taken by the band developed according to the political involvement of Ian Stuart, especially after his becoming a member of the *National Front*.

11 However, "Oi! music" is a generic term: Apolitical "Oi! music" and communist "Oi! music" played by Redskin groups also exist. It would be more correct to use the term "RAC" (for "Rock against Communism") or even the expression "Oi! RAC". But this terminology might be confusing to the reader unfamiliar with these musical styles.

12 Cf. Lescop, Mobilisation des corps, pénétration des esprits, pp. 244-271.

Still, this is a blatant case of musical hijacking with a strategy of entrism clearly reflected and elaborated by the *National Front,* namely the effort to seduce the British youth of the lower class. It may well be considered a textbook example with its attempt of capture, intimidation, recruitment of musicians, placement of magazines, networks, labels, and finally the organization of concerts and festivals. In the 1980s, "Oi!" affected all of Europe as well as the United States. Still today, in Eastern Europe, "Oi!" makes the headlines because of its extreme physical violence. In the 1980s, practically every right-wing extremist movement was more or less closely in contact with the skinhead movement. In those days, the "skinhead culture" dominated the extreme right, especially considering looks and music.[13] However, their extreme violence pinned the skins down in the limelight of the media. From this moment, the entrism of various little radical and extremist groups into the skinhead movement quickly becomes counterproductive.[14]

III. A favorable historical and cultural context

In fact, the atmosphere was favorable. There were important changes in the West after the surge of the oil prize in 1973/74. The intoxicating ideas of a political and social revolution had spread like wildfire among young leftists and hippies since 1967/68. In times of recession, they made way for a helplessness afflicting the whole Western world. This helplessness will explode in the musical cultures of post-punk, especially in the so-called "cold wave", due to its extensive use of synthesizers or at least the creation of "cold" aesthetics and atmosphere. The gothic scenes will emerge, "dark wave" and "dark folk". These musical scenes will radicalize the nihilism of the punk scene to the point where some former punk groups will abandon their militant anti-fascism and embrace an openly fascistic aesthetic. This does not necessarily indicate that all the members of those groups are fascists. But it will make the fans more susceptible to the important topics of the extreme right.

Still, some groups have passed the line. In the early 1980s, groups with a clear ideological frame of reference appear in different countries and in different musical subgenres: in "industrial music" especially Non, Death in June, Blood Axis, and Laibach; in "black metal" Burzum and Abruptum; in street rock with "Oi!" (Skrewdriver, emerged from the punk movement), etc. The latter are no cases of entrism. Instead, they are examples of the realization of a creative

13 Cf. Lescop, "Honnie soit la Oi!", pp. 109–128.

14 In the 1980s and 1990s, skinheads were in the spotlight of the media due to various acts of extreme violence (murder, assault, racist violence, ceremonies in honor of Hitler, etc.). While this phenomenon has more or less disappeared in Western Europe, it continues to be highly virulent in the countries of the former Soviet Block, for example in Russia (directed at Caucasians) or in Romania and Hungary (at Roms).

project, of a conviction rooted in a special musical project. By the way, both forms may exist side by side.

Some bands of this "industrial music" sub-genre agree with the milieus of the revolutionary/neo-pagan right on certain topics. This is made all the easier by these scenes' inheritance of the punk scene's partiality to provocation. For this reason, it is difficult to judge the situation and define a clear political position. The radical milieus profit from this situation which complicates scientific evaluation. Sometimes, there is no political discourse but it is still possible to determine the position of the group because of its special world view. In concrete terms, the views of these groups are clearly rooted in the currents of the conservative revolution and the various trends of the New Right: They develop similar topics like Nordic neo-paganism, European ethno-centrism, differentialism, and the defense of the native European cultures as well as an often virulent anti-Christianism. The fascination with European paganism and European history has thus simplified the reconciliation of these two universes.

In fact, groups of these dark cultures are quite often organically linked up to neo-pagan structures, especially to the Odinists, i. e., to the supporters of Germano-Scandinavian religions like the Icelandic Ásatrú, the Rune Gild of Edred Thorsson or the Odinic Rite of the Englishman John Yeowell. For example, Tony Wakeford was a member of Odinic Rite; Ian Read, the leader of the group Fire & Ice, formerly a member of Sol Invictus, is the head of the German edition of the magazine "Rûna", the official organ of Rune Gild. The same holds true for Michael Moynihan, by the way, who is one of the persons responsible of the neo-pagan magazine "Tyr". The musician Hilmar Örn Hilmarsson, a former member of the groups Psychic Tv and Current 93, succeeded Sveinbjorn Beiteinsson as dignitary of Ásatrú. We could multiply the number of examples.[15] But neo-paganism is so protean that it is impossible to position this neo-religion politically.[16] There are left-wing extremist and apolitical as well as right-wing extremist neo-pagans. This lack of clear political positioning is used by extreme right-wing activists to attract young and not quite so young people on their quest for identity offering them spiritual guidance. The extreme right-wing activists gamble on the ambiguities of neo-pagan history and on the fact that some neo-pagans, even though they belonged to the extreme right, were persecuted by the Nazi regime.[17]

15 Cf. for more examples François, Musique, ésotérisme et politique, pp. 238–259; The "Europagan" Music, pp. 35–54.
16 Cf. François, The Gods Looked Down, pp. 109–124; Le néo-paganisme et la politique, pp. 127–142; Les néo-paganismes et la Nouvelle Droite.
17 Cf. François, Le nazisme revisité.

IV. Facts about entrism

The radical and extremist milieus realized the strategic interest of entrism into the subcultural milieus. One of their most important goals was the "industrial music" that had come up in the late 1970s/early 1980s. It originated from the radicalization of experimental hippie music as well as of the punk wave. This music is openly nihilist and typically European.

For the extreme right activists, industrial music offers the undeniable merit of being totally "white". It is completely free from black influence - instead, its origins can be found in folk, classical, and contemporary European music. Furthermore, it is futuristic and often electronic. It takes advantage of fascist ceremonials, and indeed develops a markedly European-centrist and paganizing line. In fact, this scene with its conservative vanguardism was considered the chance to modernize the radical and extremist right in the West. These aesthetics are also well liked by some old neo-fascist fellow travelers. Thus, during an interview with the French neo-fascist leader Christian Bouchet, he confessed he loved this music he "would describe as European as opposed to Western. Politically, it is music whose apparent values, the underlying ideology, come the closest to what interests me. This is/was not the case with the rock identitaire français,[18] the Rac or Oi!".[19] More prosaically, "industrial music" or "black metal", even though they have a bad reputation, are much more acceptable to the media than "Oi!" - the latter having become repulsive because of the violence and the excesses of the skins.

These activists have realized that the interest in this music offers the possibility to spread their ideas. In the same interview, Christian Bouchet admitted his commitment to entrism "[i]n the 1980s, within the nationalist-revolutionary movement Third Way with Vivenza, Burgalat[20] and others. Like me, they belonged to the politburo of the splinter group. We were influenced by the German experience of nationalists protest songs and by the Italian one of counterculture (the Hobbit camps). We wanted our political current to have its own musical style as an alternative to Oi/Rac for the nationalist youth. At the same time we wanted to reach a population which we were not in contact with by creating a cultural proximity with it through this music. We set about this task with articles regularly published in our newspapers, with interviews (even Front 242 gave one!), with the creation of a label (Nouvelle Europe Musique, in English: New Europe Music), and of bands (Aion, LSVB, etc.). This strategy was continued by Nouvelle résistance.[21] Thus Lonsai Maikov was the musical chronicler

18 Rock identitaire français (RIF) is a nationalistic music genre associated with the French far right.
19 Interview with Christian Bouchet in 2005.
20 Bertrand Burgalat is a well-known musician. He was the organizer of parties for string instruments at Laibach. He dissociated himself from his former commitment.
21 Splinter group New Resistance.

of our bimonthly 'Lutte du peuple'.[22] We even expanded this strategy by creating fanzines and by an 'interest' in black metal considered a potential vehicle in terms of influence".[23]

Some fanzines of those days are attempts of remote control by extremist splinter groups. In France, some of them were published by Nouvelle Résistance or Troisième Voie.[24] The intention of those remotely controlled fanzines was "to show that the nationalist/pagan musical culture is also linked with black metal, death metal, industrial music, and hardcore".[25] This musical subculture has become an integral part of the revolutionary nationalist/neo-right wing culture. It is enough to visit the site of the online bookstore Librad owned by European nationalist-revolutionary activists (there are three "librad" sites, one in French, Italian, and German respectively). The subcultural publications and "European sounds", i. e., the musical styles listed in this presentation, occupy a significant part of the catalogue. This experience may be tested surfing the site of the youth forum of GRECE: a considerable part of the exchange of this forum concerns these musical styles, especially dark folk and industrial music.

According to Jean-Yves Camus, "consequently, and also because of the primacy of cultural activity which gives them both a strategic choice (the famous 'meta-political strategy' of the New Right) and a forced attitude (imposed by their numerical weakness and lack of perspective in the traditional political struggle), especially since the 1970s, many activists and groups, in France and elsewhere in Europe, have attempted to use the current forms of artistic expression as elements of their propaganda, as means of strengthening their groups' cohesion and as a vehicle for the subversion of society at the same time. In this strategic choice, nationalist-revolutionaries assign a special significance to music, more important than graphic arts, and doubtlessly equal to literature".[26]

Another purpose of entrism is the creation of political awareness or the influence of an already existing one. Since the 1960s, music has played an important role in the creation of political awareness of young adults. To reassure oneself, one only needs to recall the role and influence of protest singers in the rejection of the Vietnam War. Therefore, music may truly be considered a vehicle of identity. This is how it was presented by the omnibus volume "Musique et politique: Les répertoires de l'identité".

Music can also support the individual (the listener) and/or collective (the bandsmen) commitment to the resistance against cultural or political domination. In the 1980s, the left-wing "alternative rock" appeared on the scene as well as right-wing music like the Euro-pagan music and the "identity rock".[27]

22 Eng.: People's Fight.
23 Interview with Christian Bouchet in 2005.
24 Cf. Camus/Monzat, France.
25 Camus, Extrémismes en Europe, p. 487.
26 Camus, Préface, p. 10.
27 Cf. Darré, Prélude, p. 13.

V. Militant groups

Aside from the named facts about entrism, some important musicians of these scenes have a militant neo-fascist past. For a while, Michael Moynihan had no qualms admitting that for a certain period of his life, he had been a neo-fascist; Boyd Rice was a member of the American Front, a small right-wing extremist American group, and Tony Wakeford had been a leader of the Political Soldier faction of the *National Front*. We could also name Troy Southgate, leader of the group HERR and traditionalist revolutionary theoretician, i. e., more neo-fascist than perennialist, as well as the exponent of Norwegian black metal, Varg Vikerness, who is imprisoned for murder. Vikerness is a former skinhead and a notorious neo-Nazi activist who supported a small neo-Nazi group called Einsatzgruppe, which planned assassinations in Norway. In France, the French futurist musician Vivenza had been a member of the small group Troisième Voie before he became a monarchist and freemason. He edited a magazine called "Volonté Futurist". The organ of European revolutionary futurism (FER) promoted the glorification of the will and the technique of the fascist "total man" who creates himself.[28]

Michael Moynihan, mastermind of the group Blood Axis, also founded a publishing house, Dominion. Its best seller is a text about the Austrian ariosopher Karl Maria Wiligut, who was close to the head of the SS. Manfred Lenz, member of the East-German industrial music group Turbund Sturmwerk, contributed to the book "The Secret King: Karl Maria Wiligut Himmler's Lord of Runes".

Together with the American university professor Joscelyn Godwin, Michael Moynihan committed himself to the important task of publishing the works of Julius Evola in the United States. In addition, since 2002, Moynihan also publishes a luxurious journal "Tyr: Myth, Culture, Tradition". Besides musicians of the scene we are analyzing, theoreticians of odinism, a form of Nordic neopaganism, contribute to it as well as Alain de Benoist. In the first number of 2002, Moynihan published an interview with Georges Dumézil and Alain de Benoist that had originally appeared in 1978. Number 2 published another article of Alain de Benoist and a discussion between Alain de Benoist and Charles Champetier.

But Michael Moynihan's links with the neo-right wing French milieus do not end with the translation of contributions. In 2001, he contributed to the French revolutionary conservative magazine "Dualpha", which has turned into a publishing house run by the militant nationalist Philippe Randa. In fact, musicians of the most important Euro-pagan groups like Kadmon (Allerseelen), Robert Taylor (Changes), Michael Moynihan (Blood Axis), and Ain Soph, or perennialists like Alexander Rady (Scivias), Jean-Marc Vivenza and Thierry Jolif (Lonsai Maikov) contributed to this number dedicated to Evola.

28 Cf. François, La Musique europaïenne.

VI. Limitations

1. Limitations concerning the research of entrism

There are several limitations concerning the research of entrism as well as that of those groups. In the 1980s and 90s, the attempts of entrism could be observed by reading "fanzines", publications with a very limited edition, often A3 photocopies stapled together. They had developed during the punk phase and were published more or less by small groups (Napalm Rock, Omega, Hammer against Cross, Runen, etc.). Later, one of the difficulties in keeping up with these milieus is the disappearance of those fanzines. They are replaced by blogs and websites. Presently, militants of the extreme right, especially neo-Nazis and nationalist revolutionaries try forms of entrism at forums of certain Internet sites devoted to "black metal" if they have not been completely infiltrated yet. This entrism is facilitated by the naïve and apolitical attitude reasserted by the hosts of these sites. In fact, since the year 2000, it has become difficult to follow these attempts because the music is dematerializing: Sometimes, there are no longer CDs but only downloadable files. The only solution in this case is to check whether the group has a site on "myspace". This site permits the creation of an electronic page on which the groups can put their music online. The size of the complex web of "myspace" is impressive. The best way to move about "myspace" is to pass from one page to the next using shortcuts to "friendly" links - running the risk of losing one's way as well as one's time.

2. Limitations concerning the research of these scenes

For some years, we have witnessed two contradictory but complementary movements: the first is a mixture of lack of interest and distrust of groups that are ideologically tainted, and the second is the expansion of these groups within the subcultural dark milieus. This distrust originates from the wider political culture of the actors of these subcultures. My book "La musique europaïenne",[29] for example, sparked quite heated debates on their Internet forums defending or condemning my positions.

We have also noticed a decline of the number of new groups and of the renewal of the genre since the beginning of the new millenium. Furthermore, the weariness of political contents is becoming more and more overt. This is why some radical and extremist activists have a certain success in their attempt to penetrate the extremist milieus of the techno scene in Belgium, the Netherlands and France. This holds especially true for the sub-genre known as "gabber" or the "Lonsdale"-groups, named by the brand of clothes preferred by

29 Ibid.

the skins. The line taken there is reduced to its simplest expression and is overtly racist and nationalist.

Even though it is true that concerts of these groups have been cancelled due to the pressure of small anti-fascist groups, the Euro-pagan scene undeniably develops on the fringes of the Europhile extreme right. Right-wing extremist publications like "Réfléchir & Agir" in France are clearly interested in this scene. The Euro-pagan scene also interests the neo-Nazi milieu as is indicated by the favorable criticism of CDs of groups like Sol Invictus, Non or Death in June (whose name directly refers to the Night of the Long Knives) on the Internet site of the Svensk Front, a small Swedish neo-Nazi group, and on the site of the racist American national library by well-known negationists.

The right-wing commitment of a part of this scene causes its repression in some European countries, namely in the Germanic ones, i. e., Germany, Austria, and Switzerland. Albums have been forbidden, for example the Album "Brown Book" of Death in June in Germany, and in the beginning of this decade, concerts were cancelled: "Death in June" in Switzerland, "Ostara" in Germany and the Netherlands. These annulments resulted from the pressure of anti-fascist movements, but also from that of city fathers, especially in Switzerland. These groups do not propagate an ideology of the neo-Nazi or skinhead variety but still, they are under police surveillance. In interviews, some of them complain about being the objects of police curiosity. The police take these activities very seriously, sometimes with good reason. However, we have to keep in mind that the development of this scene (groups and fans) varies widely: while some remain on the level of provocation, others advance politically. Still another one will take root in the radical right wing milieus.

VII. Conclusion

Finally, we can conclude saying that the music genres studied here are used by small radical and extremist groups to build an identity with a double intention: 1) to reinforce the outlook on the world of the militant audience, and 2) to influence the audience that does not come from these ideological spheres. But we have to keep in mind the remark of Claude Lévi-Strauss who emphasized that "identity defines itself less through its postulation or affirmation than by its re-establishment and rebuilding".[30]

However, the main goal is a meta-political one: It is the attempt of activist groups as well as of publications from references that cannot be verified – for finding a good and reliable fanzine in these milieus is impossible – to bring about a certain degree of tolerance of the theses voiced by the extremist right wing.

30 Lévi-Strauss, L'Identité, p. 331.

Conclusion

Uwe Backes / Patrick Moreau

I. Right-wing extremism after the fall of the Iron Curtain

The fall of the Iron Curtain, the collapse of the Soviet Union, and the transformation of the communist regimes in Eastern Europe caused a deep break with tradition for the extreme left all over Europe. Did this also apply to the extreme right? Did its conditions for competition undergo a permanent change? Was it able to permanently profit from the fall of Moscow-oriented communism, and break out of the historical ghetto in which it had been trapped in many countries due to the end of the Second World War? The result is quite ambiguous. It calls for differentiation depending on the variant/expression, region, and time-frame considered. The contributions to this edition show that there can be no question of a general and lasting gain of political terrain in spite of some spectacular successes of extreme right groups.

On the one hand, the "crisis of the left" and the loss of importance of orthodox communist parties and groups opened up new opportunities for occupying the vacated terrain, for winning over the free protest potential and leading it into a new direction. On the other hand, anti-communism had lost considerable appeal as a factor for integration and a mobilizing topic. For the formations fixed on the "danger from Moscow", at least, a new structuring of the political agenda became necessary. Right-wing parties had not been able to establish themselves in all the Western countries where communist parties had been successfully enrooted as important elements of the party system. Spain and Portugal, for instance, are countries with a strong tradition of communist resistance against their authoritarian right dictatorships overcome only in the 1970s. Political newcomers from the far right remained unsuccessful. In contrast, in France and Italy, the right wing of the party system was solidly strengthened in the wake of the decline of the formerly strongest communist parties in Western Europe.

In many respects, Germany is a special case. Party communism had never been able to gain a foothold because of the deterrent reality in the eastern part of the country. But the extreme right was also unable to obtain any lasting success due to the after-effects of the trauma of the years 1933-1945. The epochal change of 1989/90 has not fundamentally changed this situation. But in spite of the continuing internal unification of the Eastern and Western German federal states, the situation in the East is similar to that of other countries in Eastern Europe. After decades of autocracy, the relative weakness of civil society (regardless of equalization efforts) corresponds with the relative vitality of the "uncivil society"[1] of xenophobic youth subcultures leaning toward violence and a strong NS-comradeship scene. These subcultures exist in a symbiosis with a regionally partly successful right-wing extremist party (NPD) which, in contrast to most formations in Western Europe, still stands largely under the spell of the NS-era. So, considering the extreme right, the country in the center of Europe consists of a strange mixture of "Western" and "Eastern" elements.

II. Parties and elections

The contributions of this edition cover a broad spectrum of right-wing parties which cannot all be considered right-wing extremist in the sense of a flat rejection of the fundamental values and procedures of democratic constitutional states. Some authors closely follow Cas Muddes' definition of the "populist radical right" family. This latter is characterized by the combination of nativism (defending the privileges of the native population against immigrants), authoritarianism (strong leadership, strong state), and populism (anti-establishment stand, the "man on the street" against "those up there").[2]

Thus, tensions (if not contradictions) arise concerning the ethos of human equality. The programmatic orientation and the political practice of right-wing parties show a wide range of variations from far-reaching system loyalty to fervent system disloyalty, and embrace "softer" and "harsher" forms of Euroskepticism. On important issues, they sometimes contain diametrically opposed positions (for example, Christian fundamentalist and neo-pagan, regionalist and ultra-nationalist convictions).

Has the potential electorate of the right-wing parties grown on the European level over the decades? After closely examining the six direct elections to the European Parliament from 1979 to 2009, the answer is no. Gilles Ivaldi shows that the sum of the total vote always remained below 8 %, even in the face of a broader definition of the realm of the phenomena. The right-wing parties were not able to found a uniform group in the European Parliament. Some (partially technical) groups deteriorated after a short time due to irreconcilable differences between the allies. The last one was the group Identity, Tradition, Sovereignty formed after the 2004 European Elections. Its end was brought about by anti-Romanian polemics of Alessandra Mussolini, the Italian MEP (Alternativa Sociale). The eastward expansion of the EU has not changed things. Even though, compared to 2004, the 2009 electoral result of the far right par-

1 Cf. Kopecký/Mudde (Eds.), Uncivil Society?
2 Cf. Mudde, Populist Radical Right Parties in Europe.

ties slightly improved (to 5.2 % according to Ivaldi's broader definition), they still remained far behind those of the years 1994 to 1996.

European elections are considered "second order elections". The electorate is much more inclined towards a protest vote than at national elections.[3] Nevertheless, Ivaldi's study reveals that this assumption does not always apply. The average electoral result of the preceding national elections is 0.4 % below the European result. Still, individual case studies indicate "winners" and "losers" at European elections among the far right. This is not always the result of the "second order" character of the elections. In Great Britain and France, for example, the respective parties profit from the proportional vote which is more favorable for smaller parties. In addition, David Marsh's diagnosis holds true: "European election results have an important domestic impact and provide a guide to the next general election results".[4]

Who are the voters of the far right parties? Kai Arzheimer's analysis is not limited to the European elections but includes a large number of national and comparative studies as well. The profile is relatively clear for Western Europe, even though there are deviations of individual cases. Concerning gender and the educational level, the picture is unambiguous: voters of far right parties are predominantly male and their formal education is below average. On the other hand, on the European level, general statements concerning age and social group affiliation are hardly possible. Strong trade union or church affiliation diminishes the tendency of a far right vote. In addition, contextual factors can be determined which favor the far right vote, for example, the framework of electoral law (proportional representation), and high unemployment unless its consequences are mitigated by the welfare state.

Concerning the connection between value system and vote, an "anti-immigrant sentiment" is the "most powerful predictor" according to Arzheimer. Guillaume Roux' contribution closely examines this connection. He demonstrates that there are different forms of "ethnic prejudice" which not all promote the tendency to elect the far right in the same way. The analysis is based on the European survey "Group Focus Enmity" initiated by Wilhelm Heitmeyer at Bielefeld University. A multiple regression analysis shows that "old-fashioned racism" in the sense of the assertion of a hierarchy of ethnic groups is not a good predictor of the vote of a party aiming at the marked reduction of immigration (supporters of the respective item have, for example, no special aversion toward ethnically "mixed marriages"). In contrast, in all the European countries where surveys were carried out, aversion toward cultural heterogeneity and a general opposition to Islam and Moslems are closely related with the far right vote.

For this reason, it hardly comes as a surprise that numerous far right parties have made Islamophobic programmatic elements the key issues of their election

3 Cf. Reif/Schmitt, Nine National Second-Order Elections.
4 Cf. Marsh, Testing the Second-Order Election Model, p. 606.

campaigns. Is this the new "winning formula" (following Herbert Kitschelt's terminology) that will guarantee success in the European countries? Patrick Moreau's study reveals that this assumption holds true only for some of the more successful far right parties. As a general rule, though, their success depends on their ability to articulate the key issues of their ideology and to introduce them into practical politics (immigration, defense of the welfare state, identity). In some special cases (the VB in Belgium and the LN in Italy), regionalist nationalism is added to these issues. The British example that is articulated around a white power racialist position remains a marginal case. In the East, the economic, social, and psychological context of post-communism, the instability of the political systems, and the lack of party loyalty of the voters are the reasons why the extreme right is represented on the political stage by strong electoral parties (Bulgaria, Romania, Hungary, Slovakia) but also by forms of extremist militancy (militia, guards, skinheads, etc.).

Do the contexts in the East and West differ? Prima facie, the communist heritage with its attendant corruption, its state captivity of the ex-communists, its collective disorientation, and the voters' fear of the future seems to be the dominant factor. However, one could also interpret the phenomenon of post-communism as a form of standardization of the political systems towards a common model for all of Europe: the change into a participatory democracy with free elections, the existence of a constitutional state, and the introduction of market economy have been leading to a continuing rapprochement of East and West. Due to the brevity of the post-communist period, two decades only, the phenomena of electoral and everyday protest (anti-Romani racism) are much more radical in the East than in the West.

The successful formations in Eastern as well as in Western Europe are different, and so are the unsuccessful ones. Uwe Backes shows in his examination, that they, too, must respond to the demands of the electorate with an attractive program. However, this condition is necessary but insufficient. Individual success/failure depends on numerous factors. The image is not coherent in this case. The profile of the parties with regard to their programmatic and strategic offer and opportunity cannot be summed up in one single term. At best, some factors may be pointed out that raise the probability of success. The political offer, for instance, ought to be presented with a certain populist agility and refrain from the ideologically dogmatic orientation on the role models of the interwar period. Further factors are a charismatic leadership, and the ability to campaign. Yet, even when such advantages meet high demand, success is not guaranteed. Besides structural conditions, situational factors (scandals, catastrophes, drastic historic events, etc.), coincidences, and fast-changing constellations of the personnel should not be neglected. The breakthrough of the REP in Berlin in January 1989 is a good example: Until then, the party had been virtually unknown and poorly organized. A provocative campaign TV spot attracted immense public attention. The REP entered regional parliament as a prelude to its European electoral success a few months later.

What are the consequences of the "radical right-wing populist parties" participating in government? Sarah L. de Lange investigates this question with cases of those formations entering into coalitions with moderate right-wing parties (like in Italy, Austria, and the Netherlands) as well as tolerating governments (like in Denmark, and Norway). De Lange is less interested in the conditions that "radical right wing populist parties" have to fulfill (research shows that the programmatic distance to the moderate right wing partner should not be too great and the share of seats in parliament not too small) than in the reasons of their attractiveness as coalition partners. Evidently, these parties "are more attractive coalition partners than other parties since they give mainstream right parties better opportunities for maximizing their control over office, policy, and votes". Normative evaluations concerning the democratic reliability of the coalition partners usually take second place behind the strategic considerations of the competition of the parties. These coalitions are made easier because, compared to other coalition partners, there are less programmatic differences on important issues. Furthermore, the right-wing populist parties are weak enough to be dominated in a government coalition. Comparing government coalitions in the Western with those of far right parties in Central and Eastern Europe (Estonia, Poland, Romania, and Slovakia), we discover a remarkable combination of left-wing social programs and authoritarianism not existing in this form in Western Europe. This explains unusual options and actual government coalitions.

Michael Meznik's and Tom Thieme's comparative study of the extreme right/right populist parties in Bulgaria and Rumania shows that programmatically and historico-politically, these parties draw on pre-communist nationalism as well as national communism of the real socialist era. Their charismatic leaders, Vadim Tudor and Volen Siderov, know how to combine this mixture of right and left-wing extremist elements with the rejection of national minorities (Romani people and Turks in Bulgaria; Jews, Romani people, and Hungarians in Romania) blamed for many evils. This is a distinct specificity of Central and Eastern European ultra-nationalism compared to its Western European forms: The controversy focuses on autochthonous minorities and, partly linked with it, on simmering territorial conflicts which have become virulent again after the end of the enforced Pax Sovietica. However, the authors accredit both charismatic leaders with a process of political moderation. But we cannot know the outcome or the effects of this process or its impact on the prospects of success of the right-wing parties presently moving towards the center.

This development does not seem to have greatly improved chances of an international cooperation of the far right parties. As Petra Vejvodová points out, historic conflicts over national borders usually prevent closer cooperation of Central and Eastern European ultra-nationalists. Apparently, it is closest between ideological hardliners inspired by the fascisms of the interwar period and/or by the concept of a "third position" (between capitalism and communism). In contrast, the "softer" formations have problems reaching a minimal agreement beyond a vague Euroskepticism and aversion towards Islam and immigration. Furthermore, the focusing on their leader brings forward personal vanities and rivalries. Thus, their relative weakness resulting from the small number of MEP seats is accompanied by the notorious incapability of effectively utilizing their full potential.

III. Militant scenes and subcultures

The more successful right-wing parties have broken away from the fascisms of the interwar period ideologically as well as strategically, reject violence as a means of politics, give priority to working within the institutions of representative democracy, and tend to avoid provocative action "in the streets". They have renounced classical racist arguments, and want to scatter any suspicion of anti-Semitism by forming alliances with Knesseth (far right) parties. The other parties try to use the militant scenes and subcultures as a reservoir for recruiting members. They draw on the fascination of the authoritarian/totalitarian past. Formations with an affinity with the NS have spread throughout Europe (even in countries that suffered the most terrible consequences of the national socialist occupation, like Poland). The far right parties sometimes provide their party political and parliamentary representation.

Jean-Yves Camus' contribution shows that in all European states, these are rather small marginalized minorities. Wherever they develop more strongly, form local strongholds, and penetrate sub-cultural youth milieus (skinheads, hooligans, "ultras") and paramilitary "defense leagues" (against the Romani people in Hungary, against Moslems in Great Britain, and against Turkish immigrants in Germany), they face strong civil societal counter-mobilization. To assess the situation realistically, we have to consider the fact that neo-national socialist groups have been a favorite object of manipulation for a long time. Initially, Eastern secret services used them in order to "to prove" the "fascist" character of Western capitalist states (of Germany first and foremost). Today, Muslim countries (Iran) often consider right-wing extremist groups strategic allies in their fight against Israel. Still, this should not be overestimated because the various scenes have their own roots, even if they sometimes consist of the sinister fascination with a bygone era. Many of these groups pose a serious threat to the minorities the extreme right concept of the enemy is focused on. This applies to the subcultural environment of neo-Nazi milieus (e.g. in Germany, Great Britain, Sweden, the Czech Republic) committing a large number of acts of violence (with numerous grievous bodily injuries). But it is also true for the rarer cases of strictly organized groupings of the type Combat 18. Their sophisticated planning is on the threshold to terrorism.

The NS-affine groups are also closely interwoven with the holocaust denying scene even though the latter constitutes a phenomenon sui generis. Intellectually, it nourishes from a strange mix of ideological influences and motivations.

This is evident due to the fact that (former) leftist intellectuals belong to its most prominent representatives. Furthermore, this phenomenon can sometimes be found in extreme left groups, too. As Jean-Yves Camus demonstrates, conspiracy theoretical constructions (the holocaust as a Jewish capitalist invention to justify the power of Israel) form the central link of a scene with sectarian traits in Europe and the USA. Its intellectual influence is frequently overestimated. But since the mid-1970s, its interpretations have been widely spread and accepted in the Arab Muslim world. They often serve to nazify Israel and the Jews while de-diabolizing historical national socialism. Islamist circles are responsible for the repercussions of this phenomenon in Europe. At times, they form strange alliances with right-wing extremists actually pursuing different goals but forged together by the common enemy.

Věra Stojarová's contribution investigates the paramilitary formations existing in some Central and Eastern Europe countries. Often attached to right-wing extremist parties, they claim to guarantee public security and order and fight members of social groups considered dangerous. "This is mainly the case with the post-Soviet formations that fight either for or against russification, or the CEE units set up to safeguard society from the Roma and what are seen as 'social enemies': criminals, gays, lesbians, drug-addicts, alcoholics, perverts etc.". Except for the Hungarian Guard, they do not wear uniforms, but they organize training sessions for their members. The more military and violent-prone they appear, the less they are capable of gaining social support beyond the narrow circle of their sympathizers.

Miroslav Mareš' paper deals with the vigilant activism against the Romani people in East Central Europe. He analyses this phenomenon in relation to the public discussion about the so-called "Roma question". Various forms of vigilantism are classified and described: "the monitoring of Roma crime" by public patrols and home guards, violent riots and how they are combated, lynching, and terrorist attacks. The reactions of the state and the Romani people are described, including the creation of Romani home guards. The author concludes that increasing vigilantism in East Central Europe could start an ethnic mass conflict, particularly if carried out by paramilitary or terrorist groups.

Stéphane de Tapia investigates a predominantly Western European and frequently neglected phenomenon among the Turkish immigrant communities. It is the small world of the "Grey Wolves", this name being a reference to one of their emblems. This subculture remains impenetrable, mysterious, and disquieting but does not seem all that dangerous for the European civil and political societies. The "Grey Wolves" exist in a Diaspora situation (e.g. in Germany, France, and the Netherlands) and set up their personnel network while isolating themselves from the majority societies. De Tapia shows this subculture to a certain extent reproducing "the Turkish-Ottoman model of cohabitation between *millet* (ethno-confessional communities recognized by the Ottoman Empire) but under different circumstances: here, it is the minority and, thus, cannot play a decisive role in politics".

IV. Cultural trends and political ideas

Taking stock of right-wing extremism in Europe would be incomplete without the cultural trends and political ideas that often cross borders and, despite all difficulties, offer the chance of transnational cooperation. In his contribution, Thomas Grumke presents two central ideological elements of an "international of ultra-nationalists": the "pan-Arian Weltanschauung" and anti-globalism. As the author shows, internationally active right-wing extremists do not fight just for the defense of one's nation from outside enemies any longer. They define nationality not by citizenship or geography, but by race. "Worth defending and protecting is not the nation as such, but rather the seriously endangered 'white race' [...] which is under massive attack in their ancestral nations by the 'international capital' that has no traditions, history nor scruples". "International capital" is considered dominated by Jews. "The result is a hard to digest brew of long-existing anti-Semitic or volkish theories and argumentations as well as alternative ingredients such as 'international (racial) solidarity', 'anti-imperialism', and 'foreigners out'". The pan-Aryan ideology is no longer slavophobic (like Hitler's Weltanschauung) but includes Eastern Europe and Russia in its defense of the "white world". Furthermore, it is closely related to the second ideological element: anti-globalization. According to this version, globalization is the attempt to destroy the national and ethnically racial cultures in order to create room for the unlimited action of Jewish-American dominated big business. "White patriots" need to join forces against this peril in order to defend their cultural and racial heritage.

In contrast, the ideology of the so-called "New Right" – though not homogenous – is intellectually far less simplistic. Since the end of the 1970s, the Frenchman Alain de Benoist has been considered its spokesman. He developed the concept of ethno-pluralism that has been adopted by many far right parties at least in theory. Instead of a hierarchy of valuable and inferior ethnic groups, it postulates the basic equality of all ethnicities. At the same time, the mixture of ethno-cultures is considered the road to their (unavoidable) degeneration. Tamir Bar-On demonstrates how – although having opened up for direct democratic and ecological influences and never a follower in the direct fascist tradition – de Benoist has stimulated right-wing fundamental critique of the representative democracy and, ethnicizing the political discourse, shaped a broad spectrum of far right formations. Among the "softer" parties, he considers the Italian LN rather than the French FN "a concrete model of a political outfit that mimics NR ideas".

Besides specific ideological influences, the readiness to accept ring-wing extremist political offers or – on the contrary – the enrooting of social defense mechanisms depend on cultural identity which has sometimes grown over a long time. One of its essential elements is the predominant way the European countries have dealt with the fascisms of the interwar period, with their own share in them, and with collaboration during the years of war. In his contribution,

David Art's central thesis is that far right parties' chances to develop depend on the dealing with the past, especially of the elites of the political mainstream. He demonstrates this using Germany, France, and Italy as examples. In Germany, a "culture of contrition" has contributed to the far right parties' not being able to succeed lastingly and remaining marginal. In contrast, in the early phase of establishing itself, the French FN was able to profit from the insufficient historical dispute about "Vichy". In the 1990's, a lively debate on collaboration rose and the "political class" used the past as a political weapon against the FN. This process helped contain the phenomenon. Thus, it seems to be a logical consequence that Le Pen's daughter, meanwhile the party's chairperson, has tried to break out of the political ghetto by moderating the discourse of the past and avoiding politico-historical danger zones. In Italy, the situation was entirely different: David Art observed a certain historic nostalgia for the fascist era spreading in politics and society, even in parts of the left wing since the 1980's. The MSI, besides the consequences of the Tangentopoli-scandal and the rise of Berlusconi, profited in its gradual transformation process into the reformed AN from initially positive statements about fascism (Fini 1994: "Mussolini was the greatest statesman of the 20th century"). They did not have disqualifying consequences similar statements had triggered in Germany and France. Regardless of these national differences, according to Art a "culture of contrition" has developed in Europe in which "an ongoing critical examination of historical complicity is becoming a pan-European value".

The last two contributions leave the level of mainstream culture and devote themselves to subcultures. Without their partly esoteric, partly eccentric creations, the presentation of the intellectual physiognomy of European right-wing extremism would remain incomplete. Their expansion, however, is not limited to extreme right milieus. Instead, through diverse communicative channels, it also seeps into social groups generally rather critical of extreme right ideas. This is true for right-wing extremist esotericism finding a broader audience in Internet media like YouTube. Its dangers are often underestimated since the ideas spread this way are always combined with absurd conspiracy theories considered too extravagant to be taken seriously. Yet, at times, the fantastic, irrational, and grotesque exerts extraordinary fascination. Nonetheless, it is necessary to differentiate between different types of esoteric right-wing extremist offers corresponding with different kinds of hazards since "the danger inherent in neo-Nazi esotericism does not lie in its size but in the easy access to heavily extremist thinking such as the denial of the holocaust via the Internet. Successful 'esoteric entrepreneurs' are able to generate a much greater danger through their popularity. With colorful Internet appearances and public lectures as, for example, those by David Icke, even strange ideas become available to a broader public". This holds true for the new "art form" of conspiracy theoretical videos of the type of "Loose Change" and "Zeitgeist". They can contribute to impart ideas hardly spread beyond the narrower circles otherwise.

Music is a medium transporting right-wing extremist ideas in a particularly effective way. It is well known that there are close connections between certain musical subcultures and right-wing extremist trends. Stéphane François explores a special field: the so-called dark musical scenes and the neo-right wing and nationalist-revolutionary milieus. However, it is not always easy to decide whether we are dealing with the sheer lust for provocation or the articulation of true political convictions. Doubtlessly, certain right-wing extremist groups use music to transport their ideas to youth milieus and to reach an audience far beyond the circle of their sympathizers. A sign of the spreading of these products is the commercial success of (not only) right-wing extremist profiteers who distribute them. A part of the revenue goes to extreme right organizations, and helps strengthen their competitiveness on the political market.

V. Final remarks

Despite these alarming developments, a sober taking stock of the development of the extreme right in Europe needs to emphasize its weaknesses rather than its strengths. The election results of the far right parties must be taken into consideration as much as the street activities of the militant scenes. Furthermore, one must differentiate between the consolidation of the European constitutional states and the problem of internal security even though both dimensions are connected.

The weakness of the far right parties clearly shows in their low representation in the European Parliament. In addition, they present an image of internal quarrels and conflicts and prove themselves unable to use their full potential. An individual national case study is able to identify a number of successful formations predominantly of the national populist type in Western as well as Eastern Europe. But even the strongest ones are incapable of exerting decisive influence on the political process of decision-making. Whenever they join governments as coalition partners, they appear acceptable because their more moderate partners are able to exploit their dominance. This situation has not changed in the states hit the hardest by the repercussions of the global financial and economic crisis. None of the European constitutional states consolidated for a long time has been de-consolidated by right-wing extremist formations. And even where the process of consolidation has not progressed too far yet, like in some of the new member states in Eastern Europe, this is due to more important reasons (like the deficits of the rule of law, mismanagement, corruption).

In some European countries (like France, Austria, and Switzerland), relatively successful far right parties seem to absorb the potential prone to violence. But there are also cases (like in Germany, Great Britain, and Sweden) where stimulating effects obviously predominate. There, electoral gains of far right parties (at least on the regional level) coincide with the vitality of militant scenes and the relations between both realms are sometimes symbiotic.[5]

It is evident that this situation causes serious problems considering internal security even if they do not seriously affect democratic consolidation. Negative economic effects are easily topped by the immaterial damage caused by the failure of an effective protection of minorities. Between the priorities of security and liberty, there is no patent recipe for dealing with generally disorganized and haphazard attacks as well as with terrorist threats. Furthermore, it is not only a question of state action but also of the civil society with prevention (civic education, intellectual altercations) being just as important as repression. No matter what the emphasis, we are dealing with a major challenge demanding permanent attention if the security issue is not to develop into a serious problem of consolidation on the long run.

5 Cf. Backes/Mletzko/Stoye (Eds.), NPD-Wahlmobilisierung; "Extrémisme et violence", Revue des Sciences Sociales, (2011) 46.

Appendix

Bibliography

Abdo, Nadeem: La vérité sur l'holocauste des juifs. Etude scientifique et historique sur la vérité des allégations sionistes sur "l'holocauste", Beirut 2007.

Adamson, Kevin/Florean, Sergiu/Thieme, Tom: Extremismus in Rumänien. In: Jesse, Eckhard/Thieme, Tom (Eds.): Extremismus in den EU-Staaten, Wiesbaden 2011, pp. 311-326.

Ágh, Attila: Hungarian Politics in the Early 21st Century: Reforms and Post-EU Accession Crisis. In: Südosteuropa Mitteilungen, 48 (2008) 2, pp. 68-81.

Ahlemeyer, Volker: The Coalition Potential of Extreme Right Parties in Western Europe, Cambridge 2006.

Albert, Gwendolyn: Hatred is the Cheapest Fuel: Political Power, not Economics, is behind Rising Czech Nationalism. In: Roma Rights Journal, 14 (1999) 1, pp. 23-33.

-/Redlová, Pavla: Racism in the Czech Republic: ENAR Shadow Report 2008, ed. by European Network Against Racism, Brussels 2009.

Albertazzi, Daniele/McDonnell, Duncan: The Lega Nord in the Second Berlusconi Government: In a League of its Own. In: West European Politics, 28 (2005) 5, pp. 952-972.

-/McDonnell, Duncan (Eds.): Twenty-First Century Populism: The Spectre of Western European Democracy, Basingstoke 2008.

Amaudruz, Gaston-Armand: Nous autres racists: Le manifest social-raciste, Montreal 1971.

-: Le procès Amaudruz: Une parodie de justice, Châtel-Saint-Denis 2000.

Andreescu, Gabriel: Extremismul de Dreapta în România: Centrul de Resurse pentru diversitate etnoculturală, Cluj 2003.

-: Romania. In: Mudde, Cas (Ed.): Racist Extremism in Central and Eastern Europe, London 2005, pp. 184-209.

Antakyali, François: La droite nationaliste dans les milieux turcs immigrés. In: Cemoti, 13 (1992), pp. 45-68.

Apfel, Holger (Ed.): Alles Große steht im Sturm: Tradition und Zukunft einer nationalen Partei, Stuttgart 1999.

Apostle, Richard/Glock, Charles/Piazza, Tom/Suelzle, Marijean: The Anatomy of Racial Attitudes, Berkeley 1983.

Art, David: The Wild, Wild East: Why the DVU Does Not Matter but the NPD Does. In: German Politics and Society, 22 (2004), pp. 122-133.

-: The Politics of the Nazi Past in Germany and Austria, Cambridge 2006.

-: Reacting to the Radical Right: Lessons from Germany and Austria, In: Party Politics, 13 (2007) 3, pp. 331-349.

-: The Organizational Origins of the Contemporary Radical Right: The Case of Belgium. In: Comparative Politics, 40 (2008) 4, pp. 421-440.

Arzheimer, Kai: Contextual Factors and the Extreme Right Vote in Western Europe, 1980-2002. In: American Journal of Political Science, 53 (2009), pp. 259-275.

-/Carter, Elisabeth: Political Opportunity Structures and Right-Wing Extremist Party Success. In: European Journal of Political Research, 45 (2006) 3, pp. 419-443.

Aslan, Fikret/Bozay, Kemal: Graue Wölfe heulen wieder: Türkische Faschisten und ihre Vernetzung in der BRD, Münster 2000.

Auer, Stefan: Das Erbe von 1989: Revolutionen für Europa. In: Osteuropa, 54 (2004) 5-6, pp. 31-46.
Austen-Smith, David/Banks, Jeffrey: Elections, Coalitions, and Legislative Outcomes. In: American Political Science Review, 82 (1988) 2, pp. 405-422.
Backes, Uwe: Das ideologisch-programmatische Profil der NPD im europäischen Vergleich. In: Backes, Uwe/Steglich, Henrik (Eds.): Die NPD, pp. 301-316.
-: Extremismus in Frankreich. In: Jesse, Eckhard/Thieme, Tom (Eds.): Extremismus in den EU-Staaten, pp. 131-148.
-: Political Extremes: A Conceptual History from Antiquity to the Present, London 2010.
-/ Mletzko, Matthias/Stoye, Jan (Eds.): NPD-Wahlmobilisierung und politisch motivierte Gewalt: Sachsen und Nordrhein-Westfalen im kontrastiven Vergleich, Polizei + Forschung, vol. 39, ed. by Bundeskriminalamt, Köln 2010.
-/ Steglich, Henrik (Eds.): Die NPD. Erfolgsbedingungen einer rechtsextremistischen Partei, Baden-Baden 2007.
Bailer-Galanda, Brigitte/Benz, Wolfgang/Neugebauer, Wolfgang (Eds.): Die Auschwitzleugner: "Revisionistische" Geschichtslüge und historische Wahrheit, Berlin 1997.
Baillet, Philippe: Pour la contre-révolution blanche: Portraits fidèles et lectures sans entraves, Saint-Genis-Laval 2010.
Bale, Tim: Cinderella and Her Ugly Sisters: The Mainstream and Extreme Right in Europe's Bipolarising Party Systems. In: West European Politics, 26 (2003) 3, pp. 67-90.
-/ Bergman, Tobjörn: A Taste of Honey is Better than None at All? Coping with the Generic Challenges of Support Party Status in Sweden and New Zealand. In: Party Politics, 12 (2006) 2, pp. 189-202.
Bardèche, Maurice: Nuremberg ou la terre promise, w. p., 1948.
-: Qu'est-ce que le fascisme?, Paris 1961.
Barkun, Michael: A Culture of Conspiracy: Apocalyptic Visions in Contemporary America, Berkeley 2003.
Barnes, Harry Elmar: Crucifying the Saviour of France: The Trial and Imprisonment of Marshall Pétain, London 2005.
Bar-On, Tamir: The Ambiguities of the Nouvelle Droite, 1968-1999. In: The European Legacy, 6 (2001) 3, pp. 333-351.
-: Where Have All The Fascists Gone?, Aldershot 2007.
-: Fascism to the Nouvelle Droite: The Dream of Pan-European Empire. In: Journal of Contemporary European Studies, 16 (2008) 3, pp. 327-345.
-: Understanding Political Conversion and Mimetic Rivalry. In: Totalitarian Movements and Political Religions, 10 (2009) 3-4, pp. 241-264.
Bastow, Steve/Benoist, Alain de: In: Blamires, Cyprian (Ed.): World Fascism: A Historical Encyclopedia, vol. 1, Santa Barbara 2006.
Beichelt, Timm/Minkenberg, Michael: Rechtsradikalismus in Transformationsgesellschaften: Entstehungsbedingungen und Erklärungsmodell. In: Osteuropa, 52 (2002) 3, pp. 247-262.
Beiträge zur Debatte, Rechtsradikalismus in Transformationsgesellschaften. In: Osteuropa, 52 (2002) 3/5/7/8, pp. 247-335, pp. 612-630, pp. 885-913, pp. 1056-1062.

Bell, John D.: The Radical Right in Bulgaria. In: Ramet, Sabrina P. (Ed.): The Radical Right in Central and Eastern Europe since 1989, Pennsylvania 1999, pp. 233-254.

Bennigsen, Alexandre/Lemercier-Quelquejay, Chantal: Les Musulmans oubliés: L'Islam en Union Soviétique, Paris 1981.

-/Lemercier-Quelquejay, Chantal: L'Islam dans les républiques musulmanes soviétiques. In: Carré, Olivier (Ed.): L'Islam et l'Etat dans le monde d'aujourd'hui, Paris 1982, pp. 143-168.

-/Lemercier-Quelquejay, Chantal: Le Soufi et le Commissaire. Les confréries musulmanes en URSS, Paris 1986.

-/Lemercier-Quelquejay, Chantal: Sultan Galiev: Le père de la révolution tiers-mondiste, Paris 1986.

Benoist, Alain de: Vu de droite. Anthologie critique des idées contemporaines, Paris 1977.

-: The End of the Left-Right Dichotomy: The French Case. In: Telos, 102 (1995), pp. 73-89.

-: Au-delà des droits de l'homme. Pour défendre les libertés, Paris 2004.

-: Bibliographie générale des droites françaises, 4 vol., Paris 2004/2005.

-: Demain, la décroissance! Penser l'écologie jusqu'au bout, Paris 2007.

-: The European New Right Forty Years Later: Tomislav Sunic's Against Democracy and Equality. In: The Occidental Quarterly, 9 (2009) 1, pp. 61-74.

- et al.: La cause des peuples, Paris 1982.

Benoit, Kenneth/Laver, Michael: Party Policy in Modern Democracies, London 2006.

Benz, Wolfgang: Realitätsverweigerung als antisemitisches Prinzip: Die Leugnung des Völkermords. In: Lipstad, Deborah (Ed.): Antisemitismus in Deutschland: Zur Aktualität eines Vorurteils, Munich 1995.

Bermeo, Nancy: Democracy and the Lessons of Dictatorship. In: Comparative Politics, 24 (1992) 1, pp. 273-291.

Bertelsmann Stiftung (Ed.): Strategies for Combating Right-Wing Extremism in Europe, Gütersloh 2009.

Betz, Hans-Georg: Radical Right-Wing Populism in Western Europe, New York 1994.

-/Immerfall, Stefan (Eds.): The New Politics of the Right, New York 1998.

Bezanis, Lowell: Volga-Ural Tatars in Emigration. In: Central Asian Survey, 11 (1992) 4, pp. 29-74.

-: Soviet Muslim Emigrés in the Republic of Turkey. In: Central Asian Survey, 13 (1994) 1, pp. 59-180.

Billiet, Jaak/Witte, Hans de: Attitudinal Dispositions to Vote for a New Extreme Right-Wing Party: The Case of Vlaams-Blok. In: European Journal of Political Research, 27 (1995) 2, pp. 181-202.

Biorcio, Roberto: La Padania Promessa: La storia, le idee e la logica d'azione della Lega Nord, Milano 1997.

Blamires, Cyprian P. (Ed.): World Fascism: A Historical Encyclopaedia, Santa Barbara 2006.

Bobbio, Norberto: Left and Right: The Significance of a Political Distinction, Chicago 1996.

Booth, James W.: Communities of Memory: On Identity, Memory and Debt. In: American Political Science Review, 92 (1999) 2, pp. 249-263.
Bora, Tanıl: Le nationalisme populaire et la "question kurde". In: La Vie des idées: Mensuel international sur le débat d'idées, 14 (2006), pp. 61-66.
-/ Can, Kemal: Devlet, Ocak, Dergâh: 12 Eylül'den 1990'lara Ülkücü Hareket, Istanbul 1999.
-/ Can, Kemal: Devlet ve Kuzgun: 1990'lardan 2000'lere MHP, third edition, Istanbul 2007.
Borre, Ole: Critical Issues and Political Alienation in Denmark. In: Scandinavian Political Studies, 4 (2000), pp. 285-309.
Bossi, Umberto/Vimercati, Daniele: Processo alla Lega, Milan 1998.
Botsch, Gideon/Kopke, Christoph/Rensmann, Lars/Schoeps, Julius H. (Eds.): Politik des Hasses: Antisemitismus und radikale Rechte in Europa, Hildesheim 2010.
Bouchet, Christian: Ainsi parle l'extrême droite américaine, Nantes 2005.
Bozarslan, Hamit: L'Islam turc en Allemagne Fédérale: identité et politique. In: L'Evènement européen, 8 (1989), pp. 87-98.
-: Une communauté et ses institutions: le cas des Turcs en RFA. In: Revue Européenne des Migrations Internationales, 6 (1990) 3, pp. 63-82.
-: Histoire de la Turquie contemporaine, Paris 2004.
Bozay, Kemal: "... Ich bin stolz, Türke zu sein!": Ethnisierung gesellschaftlicher Konflikte im Zeichen der Globalisierung, Schwalbach 2005.
Brigneau, François: Mais qui est donc le professeur Faurisson?, Paris 1992.
Brug, Wouter van der/Fennema, Meindert: Protest or Mainstream? How the European Anti-Immigrant Parties Developed into Two Separate Groups by 1999. In: European Journal of Political Science, 42 (2003), pp. 55-76.
Bruyne, Eddy de: Léon Degrelle et la Légion Wallonie: La fin d'une légende, Liège 2011.
Bugajski, Janusz: Political Parties of Eastern Europe: A Guide to Politics in the Post-Communist Era, New York 2002, pp. 662-664.
Bull, Martin/Newell, James: Italy Changes Course: The 1994 Elections and the Victory of the Right. In: Parliamentary Affairs, 48 (1995) 1, pp. 72-99.
Bulut, Ebru: Portrait d'une Anatolie assiégée. In: La Vie des idées: Mensuel international sur le débat d'idées, 14 (2006), pp. 35-44.
Bundesamt für Verfassungsschutz (Ed.): Argumentationsmuster im rechtsextremistischen Antisemitismus: Aktuelle Entwicklungen, Köln 2005.
Bundesministerium des Innern (Ed.): Verfassungsschutzbericht 2009, Berlin 2010.
Bustikova, Lenka: The Extreme Right in Eastern Europe: EU Accession and the Quality of Governance. In: Journal of Contemporary European Studies, 17 (2009) 2, pp. 223-239.
Butz, Arthur: Der Jahrhundertbetrug, Antwerp 1976.
BZÖ (Ed.): Bündnispositionen, Vienna 2009.
- (Ed.): Programm des Bündnis Zukunft Österreich, Vienna 2010.
Caldiron, Guido: La destra plurale: dalla preferenza nazionale alla tolleranza zero, Rome 2001, pp. 80-89.
Camus, Jean-Yves: Le Front national, histoire et analyse, Paris 1996.
- (Ed.): Extrémismes en Europe, La Tour d'Aigues 1997.
-: L'extrême droite aujourd'hui, Toulouse 1997.

-: Préface. In: François, Stéphane: La Musique europaïenne: Ethnographie politique d'une subculture de droite, Paris 2006, pp. 9-10.
-: Der Niedergang des Front National und die Zukunft der extremen Rechten in Frankreich. In: Spöhr, Holger/Kolls, Sarah (Eds.): Rechtsextremismus in Deutschland und Europa: Aktuelle Entwicklungstendenzen im Vergleich, Frankfurt a. M. 2010, pp. 165-175.
-: La notion d'identité divise les droites: pour combien de temps encore. In: La Règle du jeu, Paris 2011, p. 4.
-/Monzat, René: Les droites nationales et radicales en France, Lyon 1992.
-/Monzat, René: France. In: Camus, Jean-Yves (Ed.): Extrémismes en Europe, La Tour d'Aigues 1997, pp. 173-189.
Can, Kemal: Youth, Turquism and the Extreme Right: The "Idealist Hearths". In: Yerasimos, Stéphane/Seufert, Günter/Vorhoff, Karin: Civil Society in the Grip of Nationalism, Istanbul 2000, pp. 335-374.
Carey, Henry F.: Post-Communist Right Radicalism in Romania. In: Merkl, Peter H./Weinberg, Leonard (Eds.): The Revival of Right-Wing Extremism in the Nineties, London 1997, pp. 149-176.
Carter, Elisabeth: Proportional Representation and the Fortunes of Right-Wing Extremist Parties. In: West European Politics, 25 (2002) 3, pp. 125-146.
-: The Extreme Right in Western Europe: Success or Failure?, Manchester 2005.
Çeçen, Anıl: Atatürk ve Avrasya, Istanbul 1999.
-: Türkiye Cumhuriyeti Ulus Devleti, Ankara 2001.
Centre-Right Parties and Immigration and Integration Policy in Europe, special issue of the Journal of European Public Policy, 15 (2008) 3.
Ceresole, Norberto: España y los judíos: Expulsión, Inquisición, Holocausto, 1492-1997, Madrid 1997.
Champetier, Charles/Benoist, Alain de: La Nouvelle Droite de l'an 2000. In: Éléments, 94 (1999), pp. 10-23.
Christiansen, Ingolf/Fromm, Rainer/Zinser, Hartmut: Brennpunkt Esoterik: Okkultismus Satanismus Rechtsradikalismus, Hamburg 2006.
Císař, Ondřej: Transnacionální politické sítě, Brno 2004.
Coenders, Marcel: Nationalistic Attitudes and Ethnic Exclusionism in a Comparative Perspective: An Empirical Study of Attitudes toward the Country and Ethnic Immigrants in 22 countries, Nijmegen 2001.
-/Scheepers, Peer: The Effect of Education on Nationalism and Ethnic Exclusionism: an International Comparison. In: Political Psychology, special issue National Identity in Europe, 24 (2003) 2, pp. 313-343.
-/Scheepers, Peer/Sniderman, Paul/Verberk, Genevieve: Blatant and Subtle Prejudice: Distinct Dimensions, Different Determinants, Different Consequences? Some Comments on Meertens and Pettigrew. In: European Journal of Social Psychology, 31 (2001) 3, pp. 281-297.
Coffé, Hilde: Do Individual Factors Explain the Different Success of the Two Belgian Extreme Right Parties. In: Acta Politica, 40 (2005), pp. 74-93.
Collier, Paul/Nicholas Sambanis: Understanding Civil War, Washington 2005.
Conrad, Jo: Entwirrungen, Worpswede 2001.
Consolidated Texts of the EU Treaties as Amended by the Treaty of Lisbon, Norwich 2008.
Copeaux, Etienne: Le Rêve du Loup Gris. In: Hérodote, 64 (1992), pp. 183-194.

-: "Les Turcs de l'extérieur" dans Türkiye: un aspect du discours nationaliste turc. In: Cemoti, 14 (1992), pp. 31-52.
-: De la mer Noire à la mer Baltique: la circulation des idées dans le "triangle" Istanbul-Crimée-Pologne. In: Cemoti, 15 (1993), pp. 107-119.
-: Le mouvement prométhéen. In: Cemoti, 16 (1993), pp. 9-45.
-: Manuels scolaires et géographie historique: le cas turc. In: Hérodote, 74-75 (1994), pp. 196-240.
-: Les territoires de référence des discours identitaires turcs. In: Bonnemaison, Joël/Cambrezy, Luc/Quinty-Bourgeois, Laurence (Eds.): Le territoire, lien ou frontière? Identités, conflits ethniques, enjeux et recompositions territoriales, Bondy 1997.
-: Une vision turque du monde à travers les cartes de 1931 à nos jours, Paris 2000.
-: Claire Mauss-Copeaux, Taksim! Chypre divisée, 1964-2005, Lyon 2005.
Copsey, Nigel: Contemporary British Fascism: The British National Party and the Quest for Legitimacy, New York 2008.
Cuminal, Isabelle/Souchard, Maryse/Wahnich, Stéphane/Perrineau, Pascal: L'électorat de la protestation de Jean-Marie Le Pen. In: Perrineau, Pascal et al., Atlas électoral, qui vote quoi, où, comment?, Paris 2007, pp. 64-67.
Dachs, Herbert/Gottweis, Herbert/Gerlich, Peter: Politik in Österreich, Vienna 2006.
Dantschke, Claudia: Zwischen Feindbild und Partner: Die extreme Rechte und der Islamismus. In: Braun, Stephan/Geisler, Alexander/Gerster, Martin (Eds.): Strategien der extremen Rechten: Hintergründe - Analysen - Antworten, Wiesbaden 2009, pp. 440-460.
Darré, Alain: Prélude. Pratiques musicales et enjeux de pouvoir. In: Darré, Alain (Ed.): Musique et politique: Les répertoires de l'identité, Rennes 1996, pp. 13-14.
Debbaudt, Jean-Robert/Eburie, Robert: La vérité sur le complot nazi de Bruxelles (Huizingen), Brussels, undated.
Deschouwer, Kris/Delwit, Pascal/Hooghe, Marc/Walgrave, Stefaan (Eds.): Les élections régionales du 7 juin 2009, Bruxelles 2010.
Deutsche Stimme-Verlag (Ed.): Taschenkalender des Nationalen Widerstandes 2006, Riesa 2006.
Diamanti, Ilvo: Bianco, rosso, verde ... e azzurro: Mappe e colori dell'Italia politica, Bologna 2003.
Döring, Herbert (Ed.): Parliaments and Majority Rule in Western Europe, Frankfurt a.M. 1995.
-/Hallerberg, Mark (Eds.): Patterns of Parliamentary Behaviour: Passage of Legislation across Western Europe, Aldershot 2004.
Dorronsoro, Gilles: La nébuleuse Hizbullah, Istanbul 2004.
Downs, Anthony: An Economic Theory of Democracy, New York 1957.
Downs, William H.: Pariahs in Their Midst: How Belgian and Norwegian Parties React to Extremist Threats. In: West European Politics, 24 (2001) 3, pp. 23-42.
Drobnicki, John A.: Holocaust-Denial Literature: A Third Bibliography. In: The Bulletin of Bibliography, 55 (1998) 3, pp. 157-168.
Dubiel, Helmut: Niemand ist frei von der Geschichte, Munich 1999.
Dujardin, Vincent/Dumoulin, Michel/Gérard, Emmanuel/Wijngaert, Mark van den (Eds.): Nouvelle Histoire de Belgique, 3 vol., Belgium 2007.

Dumont, Patrick/Bäck, Hanna: Why so Few, and Why so Late? Green Parties and the Question of Government Participation. In: European Journal of Political Research, 45 (2006) pp. 35-67.

Duranton-Crabol, Anne-Marie: Visages de la Nouvelle Droite: Le GRECE et son histoire, Paris 1988.

Eatwell, Roger: The Rebirth of the "Extreme Right" in Western Europe? In: Parliamentary Affairs, 53 (2000), pp. 410-414.

-: The Extreme Right and British Exceptionalism: The Primacy of Politics. In: Hainsworth, Paul (Ed.): The Politics of the Extreme Right: From the Margins to the Mainstream, London 2008, pp. 172-192.

-/Goodwin, Matthew J. (Eds.): The New Extremism in 21st Century Britain, London 2010.

Establet, Roger: Comment peut-on être français?: 90 ouvriers turcs racontent, Paris 1997.

European Monitoring Center on Racism and Xenophobia, Thalhammer, Eva/Zucha, Vlasta/Enzenhofer, Edith/Salfinger, Brigitte/Ogris, Günther: Attitudes towards Minority Groups in the European Union: A Special Analysis of the Eurobarometer 2000 Survey, Vienna 2001.

European Parliament/Directorate General for International Policies (Ed.): The European Elections. EU-Legislation, National Provisions and Civic Participation. Study, Brussels 2009.

Europol (Ed.): EU Organized Crime Threat Assessment 2009, Brussels 2009.

Evola, Julius: Revolt Against the Modern World: Politics, Religion, and Social Order in the Kali Yuga Kali Yuga, Rochester 1995.

The Extreme Right in Contemporary Europe: History, Interpretation and Performance, special issue of the Journal of Contemporary European Studies, 17 (2009) 2.

Extrémisme et violence, Revue des Sciences Sociales, (2011) 46.

Ezergailis, Andrew: Anti-Semitism and killing of Latvia's Jews. In: Gilman, Sander/Katz, Stephen T.: Anti-Semitism in Times of Crisis, New York 1993, pp. 257-291.

Faye, Guillaume: Le système à tuer les peuples, Paris 1981.

-: La Nouvelle question juive, Chevaigné 2007.

Fenster, Mark: Conspiracy Theories: Secrecy and Power in American Culture, Revised and Updated Edition, Minneapolis 2008.

Fiala, Petr/Mareš, Miroslav/Sokol, Petr: Eurostrany: Politické strany na evropské úrovni, Brno 2007.

Fieschi, Catherine: European Institutions: The Far Right and Illiberal Politics in a Liberal Context. In: Parliamentary Affairs, 53 (2000), pp. 517-531.

Flemming, Lars: Das NPD-Verbotsverfahren: Vom "Aufstand der Anständigen" zum "Aufstand der Unfähigen", Baden-Baden 2005.

Ford, Robert: Who Might Vote for the BNP? Survey Evidence on the Electoral Potential of the Extreme Right in Britain. In: Eatwell, Roger/Goodwin, Matthew J.: The New Extremism in 21st Century Britain, London 2010, pp. 145-168.

Forza Nuova: Manifesto politico di opposizione, Rome, undated.

François, Stéphane: Musique, ésotérisme et politique: Naissance d'une contre-culture de droite. In: Politica Hermetica, 17 (2003), pp. 238-259.

-: The Gods Looked down: La musique "industrielle" et le paganisme. In: Sociétés, 88 (2005) 2, pp. 109-124.

–: La musique europaïenne: Ethnographie politique d'une subculture de droite, Paris 2006.
–: Le néo-paganisme et la politique: Une tentative de compréhension. In: Raisons politiques, 25 (2007), pp. 127–142.
–: The "Europagan" Music: Between Radical Right and Paganism. In: Journal for the Study of Radicalism, 1 (2007) 2, pp. 35–54.
–: Le nazisme revisité: L'occultisme contre l'histoire, Paris 2008.
–: Les néo-paganismes et la Nouvelle Droite (1980–2006), Milano 2008.
Frei, Norbert: Adenauer and the Nazi Past, New York 2003.
Freitag, Jan/Thieme, Tom: Extremismus in Schweden. In: Jesse, Eckhard/Thieme, Tom (Eds.): Extremismus in den EU-Staaten, pp. 329–343.
Friesl, Christian/Polak, Regina/Hamachers-Zuba, Ursula (Eds.): Die Österreicher innen, Wertewandel 1990–2008, Vienna 2009.
Fromm, Rainer: Rechtsradikalismus in der Esoterik. In: Christiansen, Ingolf/Fromm, Rainer/Zinser, Hartmut: Brennpunkt Esoterik: Okkultismus, Satanismus, Rechtsradikalismus, Hamburg 2006.
Gabanyi, Anneli Ute: Rumänien: Populismus als Instrument der Machtsicherung. In: Südosteuropa Mitteilungen, 48 (2008) 2, pp. 56–67.
–: Die Parlamentswahlen in Rumänien 2008. In: Südosteuropa Mitteilungen, 49 (2009) 1, pp. 64–75.
Gallagher, Tom: Exit from the Ghetto: The Italian Far Right in the 1990s. In: Hainsworth, Paul (Ed.): The Politics of the Extreme Right: From the Margins to the Mainstream, London 2000, pp. 64–86.
Garaudy, Roger: Die Gründungsmythen der israelischen Politik, w. p., 1996.
Gaudin, Jiří: Konečné řešení otázky cikánské v českých zemích, Prague 2009.
Gibson, Rachel: The Growth of Anti-Immigrant Parties in Western Europe, Lewiston 2002.
Giddens, Anthony: Beyond Left and Right: The Future of Radical Politics, Stanford 1994.
Gijsels, Hugo: Le Vlaams Blok, Brussels 1993.
Ginsborg, Paul: Silvio Berlusconi, New York 2004.
Givens, Terri E.: Voting Radical Right in Western Europe, Cambridge 2005.
Goldberg, Robert Alan: Enemies within: The Culture of Conspiracy in Modern America, New Haven 2001.
Golder, Matt: Explaining Variation in the Success of Extreme Right Parties in Western Europe. In: Comparative Political Studies, 36 (2003) 4, pp. 432–466.
Goodrick-Clarke, Nicholas: The Occult Roots of Nazism: The Ariosophists of Austria and Germany, 1890–1935, Wellingborough 1985.
–: Black Sun: Aryan Cults, Esoteric Nazism and the Politics of Identity, New York 2002.
–: Im Schatten der schwarzen Sonne: Arische Kulte, Esoterischer Nationalsozialismus und die Politik der Abgrenzung, Wiesbaden 2009.
Goodwin, Matthew J.: In Search of the Winning Formula: Nick Griffin and the "Modernization" of the British National Party. In: Eatwell, Roger/Goodwin, Matthew J. (Eds.): The New Extremism in 21st Century Britain, pp. 169–190.
–: The New British Fascism: Rise of the British National Party, Oxford 2010.
–/Ford, Robert/Duffy, Bobby/Robey, Rea: Who Votes Extreme Right in Twenty-First Century Britain?: The Social Bases of Support for the National Party and

the British National Party. In: Eatwell, Roger/Goodwin, Matthew J. (Eds.): The New Extremism in 21st Century Britain, pp. 191 - 210.
Govaert, Serge: Les griffes du lion: le nationalisme flamand à la veille de 2002, Brussels 2001.
Greven, Thomas/Grumke, Thomas (Eds.): Globalisierter Rechtsextremismus? Die extremistische Rechte in der Ära der Globalisierung, Wiesbaden 2006.
Griffin, Roger: The Nature of Fascism, London 1991.
- (Ed.): Fascism, Oxford 1995.
-: Foreword: Another Face? Another Mazeway? Reflections on the Newness and Rightness of the European New Right. In: Bar-On, Tamir: Where Have All The Fascists Gone? Aldershot 2007, pp. xii-xvi.
-: Modernism and Fascism: The Sense of a Beginning under Mussolini and Hitler, London 2007.
-: Modernity, Modernism, and Fascism. A Mazeway Resynthesis. In: Modernism/modernity, 15 (2008) 1, pp. 9-24.
Grumke, Thomas: The Transatlantic Dimension of Wight-wing Extremism. In: Human Rights Review, 4 (2003) 4, pp. 56-72.
-: Die transnationale Infrastruktur der extremistischen Rechten. In: Greven, Thomas/Grumke, Thomas (Eds.): Globalisierter Rechtsextremismus?, pp. 130-159.
-: Die rechtsextremistische Bewegung. In: Roth, Roland/Rucht, Dieter (Eds.): Die Sozialen Bewegungen in Deutschland seit 1945: Ein Handbuch, Frankfurt a. M. 2008, pp. 475-492.
-: Die transnationale Infrastruktur der rechtsextremistischen Rechten. In: Angelika Beer (Eds.): Europa im Visier der Rechtsextremen, Brussels 2009, pp. 9-25.
Grün, Michaela: Rechtsradikale Massenmobilisierung und "radikale Kontinuität" in Rumänien. In: Osteuropa, 52 (2002) 3, pp. 293-304.
-/Stankiewicz, Katharina: Spielarten des polnischen Rechtsradikalismus. In: Minkenberg, Michael/Sucker, Dagmar/Wenninger, Agnieszka (Eds.): Radikale Rechte und Fremdenfeindlichkeit in Deutschland und Polen: Nationale und europäische Perspektiven, Bonn 2006, pp. 170-199.
Gugenberger, Eduard/Petri, Franko/Schweidlenka, Roman: Weltverschwörungstheorien: Die neue Gefahr von Rechts, Vienna 1998.
Guillaume, Pierre: Die Verbrechernatur der Juden, Berlin 1944.
Günlük, Nergiz Canefe: MHP/MCP, the Turkish State and Alevi Turks: Dangerous Alliances, York 1994.
Güvenç, Bozkurt/Şaylan, Gencay/Tekeli, İlhan/Turan, Şerafettin: Türk-Islam Sentezi, Istanbul 1991.
Habermas, Jürgen (Ed.): The New Conservatism: Cultural Criticism and the Historian's Debate, edited and translated by Shierry Weber Nicholsen, Cambridge 1989.
Hainsworth, Paul: The Extreme Right in Western Europe, London 2008.
Hale, William: Turkish Politics and the Military, London 1994.
Harmel, Robert/Janda, Kenneth: An Integrated Theory of Party Goals and Party Change. In: Journal of Theoretical Politics, 6 (1994) 3, pp. 259-287.
Harwood, Richard: Starben wirklich sechs Millionen? Endlich die Wahrheit, London 1974.
Hate Crimes in the OSCE Region: Incidents and Responses. Annual Report for 2006, Warsaw 2007.

Hausleitner, Mariana: Wettlauf der Patrioten: Nationalismus in Rumänien. In: Jahn, Egbert (Ed.): Nationalismus im spät- und postkommunistischen Europa, vol. 2: Nationalismus in den Nationalstaaten, Baden-Baden 2009, pp. 599-626.

Hausser, Paul/Peiper, Jochen (Eds.): Wenn alle Brüder schweigen: Großer Bildband über die Waffen-SS, Osnabrück 1973.

Heinisch, Reinhard: Populism, Proporz, Pariah: Austria Turns Right. Austrian Political Change, Its Causes and Repercussions, Hauppauge 2002.

-: Success in Opposition - Failure in Government: Explaining the Performance of Right-Wing Populist Parties in Public Office. In: West European Politics, 26 (2003) 3, pp. 91-130.

-: Right-Wing Populism in Austria: A Case for Comparison. In: Problems of Post-Communism, 55 (2008), pp. 40-56.

Heller, Friedrich Paul/Maegerle, Anton: Die Sprache des Hasses: Rechtsextremismus und völkische Esoterik: Jan van Helsing, Horst Mahler, Stuttgart 2001.

Helsing, Jan van: Geheimgesellschaften und ihre Macht im 20. Jahrhundert oder: Wie man die Welt nicht regiert, Meppen 1993.

-: Die Kinder des neuen Jahrtausends: Mediale Kinder verändern die Welt, Fichtenau 2001.

-: Hände weg von diesem Buch, Fichtenau 2004.

-: Wer hat Angst vorm schwarzen Mann?, Fichtenau 2005.

-/Dr. Dinero: Das 1-Million-Euro-Buch, Fichtenau 2009.

-/Erdmann, Stefan: Die Jahrtausendlüge: Auf der Spur des Pyramidenrätsels, Fichtenau 2008.

Herf, Jeffrey: Reactionary Modernism: Technology, Culture and Politics in Weimar and the Third Reich, Cambridge 1984.

-: Divided Memory, Cambridge 1997.

Hlousek, Vít/Kopecek, Lubomír: The Far Right: Between Tradition and Change. In: Id. (Ed.): Origin, Ideology and Transformation of Political Parties: East-Central and Western Europe Compared, Farnham 2010, pp. 181-202.

Hofbauer, Hannes: Balkankrieg: Zehn Jahre Zerstörung Jugoslawiens, Vienna 2001.

Hofer, Thomas/Toth, Barbara (Eds.): Wahl 2008: Strategien. Sieger. Sensationen, Vienna 2008.

Hoffman, Stanley: Foreword. In: Rousso, Henri: The Vichy Syndrome, Cambridge 1994, p. viii.

Höhne, Roland: Der Sieg der Demokratie: Die Transformation der neofaschistischen italienischen Sozialbewegung MSI in die rechtsnationale Alleanza Nazionale. In: Backes, Uwe/Jesse, Eckhard (Eds.): Jahrbuch Extremismus & Demokratie, vol. 19, Baden-Baden 2008, pp. 89-114.

Holey, Johannes: Jetzt reichts!, Fichtenau 2009.

Horaczek, Nina/Reiterer, Claudia: HC Strache: Sein Aufstieg - Seine Hintermänner - Seine Feinde, Vienna 2009.

Huber, John D./Inglehart, Ronald: Expert Interpretations of Party Space and Party Locations in 42 Societies. In: Party Politics, 1 (1995) 1, pp. 73-111.

Human Rights First, 2008 Hate Crime Survey, New York 2009.

Human Rights Watch, Human Rights Watch World Report 1994 - Romania, New York 2004.

Icke, David: The Biggest Secret: The Book that Will Change the World, Wildwood 1999.

-: Le plus grand secret, tome 1 et 2, w. p., 2001.
-: Alice in Wonderland and the World Trade Center Disaster, Wildwood 2002.
-: Das größte Geheimnis: Dieses Buch verändert die Welt, 4th edition, Immenstadt 2009.
Ignazi, Piero: The Silent Counter-Revolution: Hypotheses on the Emergence of Extreme Right-Wing Parties in Europe. In: European Journal of Political Research, 22 (1992) 1, pp. 3-34.
-: Extreme Right Parties in Western Europe, Oxford 2003.
-: Legitimation and Evolution on the Italian Right Wing: Social and Ideological Repositioning of Alleanza Nazionale and the Lega Nord. In: South European Society & Politics, 10 (2005), pp. 333-349.
-: Partiti politici in Italia: Da Forza Italia al Partito Demoratico, Bologna 2008.
Imig, Doug/Tarrow, Sidney: The Europeanization of Movements? A New Approach to Transnational Contention. In: Della Porta, Donatella/Kriesi, Hanspeter/Rucht, Dieter (Eds.): Social Movements in a Globalizing World, Hampshire 1999, pp. 112-133.
-/Tarrow, Sidney (Eds.): Contentious Europeans, Lanham 2001.
Insel, Ahmet: Le nationalisme des "Turcs blancs". In: La Vie des idées: Mensuel international sur le débat d'idées, 14 (2006), pp. 55-60.
Ishiyama, John T.: Strange Bedfellows: Explaining Political Cooperation between Communist Successor Parties and Nationalists in Eastern Europe. In: Nations and Nationalism, 4 (1998) 1, pp. 61-85.
Ismayr, Wolfgang (Ed.): Die politischen Systeme Osteuropas, 3rd Edition, Wiesbaden 2010.
Ivaldi, Gilles/Swygedouw, Marc: Rechtsextremismus in populistischer Gestalt: Front National und Vlaams Blok. In: Decker, Frank (Ed.): Populismus in Europa, Bonn 2006, pp. 121-143.
Ivanov, Christo/Ilieva, Margarita: Bulgaria. In: Mudde, Cas (Ed.): Racist Extremism in East and Central Europe, London 2005, pp. 1-29.
Ivanova, Evgenija: Strah i žažda za văzmezdie, Sofia 2007.
Jackman, Robert/Volpert, Karin: Conditions Favouring Parties of the Extreme Right in Western Europe. In: British Journal of Political Science, 26 (1996) 4, pp. 501-521.
Jalali, Carlos/Pinheiro, Teresa: Extremismus in Portugal. In: Jesse, Eckhard/Thieme, Tom (Eds.): Extremismus in den EU-Staaten, pp. 299-312.
Jaschke, Hans-Gerd: Die Republikaner, Bonn 1993.
Jesse, Eckhard: Demokratieschutz. In: Jesse, Eckhard/Sturm, Roland (Eds.): Demokratien des 21. Jahrhunderts im Vergleich: Historische Zugänge, Gegenwartsprobleme, Reformperspektiven, Opladen 2003, pp. 449-474.
-: Wahlen 2009. In: Backes, Uwe/Jesse, Eckhard (Eds.): Jahrbuch Extremismus & Demokratie, vol. 22, Baden-Baden 2011, pp. 103-125.
-/Thieme, Tom: Politischer Extremismus in den EU-Staaten im Vergleich. In: Jesse, Eckhard/Thieme, Tom (Eds.): Extremismus in den EU-Staaten, Wiesbaden 2001, pp. 431-482.
Jesuit, David K./Paradowski, Piotr R./Mahler, Vincent A.: Electoral Support for Extreme Right-Wing Parties: A Sub-National Analysis of Western European Elections. In: Electoral Studies, 28 (2009) 2, pp. 279-290.

Johnston, Les: What is Vigilantism? In: British Journal of Criminology, 36 (1996) 2, pp. 220-236.
Judt, Tony: The Past is Another Country: Myth and Memory in Postwar Europe. In: Daedelus, (1992) 4, pp. 83-118.
Kailitz, Steffen: Die nationalsozialistische Ideologie der NPD. In: Backes, Uwe/ Steglich, Henrik (Eds.): Die NPD, pp. 337-353.
Kanzleiter, Boris: Jugoslawiens multiethnische Kriegsgewinnler: Paramilitarismus zwischen Krieg, Ethnisierung und kriminell-institutionellen Komplexen. In: Azellini, Dario/Kanzleiter, Boris (Eds.): Das Unternehmen Krieg: Paramilitärs, Warlords und Privatarmeen als Akteure der Neuen Kriegsordnung, Berlin 2003, pp. 99-117.
Kaplan, Jeffrey: Encyclopedia of White Power: A Sourcebook on the Radical Racist Right, Walnut Creek 2000.
Kappeler, Andreas: La Russie: Empire multiethnique, Paris 1994.
Karasimeonov, Georgi: The Party System in Bulgaria. In: Karasimeonov, Georgi (Ed.): Political Parties and the Consolidation of Democracy in South Eastern Europe, Sofia 2004, pp. 39-57.
Kieser, Hans-Lukas/Schaller, Dominik J. (Eds.): Der Völkermord an den Armeniern und die Shoah, Zürich 2002.
Kitschelt, Herbert: Diversification and Reconfiguration of Party Systems in Postindustrial Democracies, Bonn 2004.
-: Growth and Persistence of the Radical Right in Postindustrial Democracies: Advances and Challenges in Comparative Research. In: West European Politics, 30 (2007), pp. 1176-1206.
-, in collaboration with McGann, Anthony J.: Radical Right in Western Europe: A Comparative Analysis, Ann Arbor 1995.
-/Mansfeldova, Zdenka/Markowski, Radoslaw/Toká, Gábor: Post-Communist Party Systems: Competition, Representation, and Inter-Party Cooperation, Cambridge 1999.
Klassen, Ben: Nature's Eternal Religion, Lighthouse Point 1973.
Kleinpenning, Gerard/Hagendoorn, Louk: Forms of Racism and the Cumulative Dimensions of Ethnic Attitudes. In: Social Psychology Quarterly, 56 (1993) 1, pp. 21-36.
Knigge, Pia: The Ecological Correlates or Right-Wing Extremism in Western Europe. In: European Journal of Political Research, 34 (1998) 2, pp. 249-279.
Knight, Peter: Conspiracy Culture: From the Kennedy Assassination to The X-Files, London 2000.
Koogan, Kevin: Dreamer of the Day: Francis Parker Yockey and the Post-War Fascist International, New York 1999.
Kopeček, Lubomír: The Far Right in Europe: A Summary of Attempts to Define the Concept, Analyze Its Identity, and Compare the Western European and Central European Far Right. In: Central European Political Studies Review, 9 (2007) 4, pp. 280-293.
Kopecký, Petr/Mudde, Cas (Eds.): Uncivil Society? Contentious Politics in Post-Communist Europe, London 2003.
Köppl, Stefan: Extremismus in Italien. In: Jesse, Eckhard/Thieme, Tom (Eds.): Extremismus in den EU-Staaten, pp. 197-212.

Kovats, Martin: Možnosti a výzvy: Rozšiřování Evropské unie a romská/cikánská diaspora. In: Jakoubek, Marek/Budilová, Lenka (Eds.): Romové a cikáni: neznámí i známí. Interdisciplinární pohled, Voznice 2008, pp. 13-21.
Kriesi, Hans-Peter/Grande, Edgar/Lachat, Romain/Dolezal, Martin/Bornschier, Simon/Frey, Timotheos: Globalization and the Transformation of National Political Space: Six European Countries Compared. In: European Journal of Political Research, 45 (2006), pp. 921-956.
Krogstrup, Jesper: Immigration as a Political Issue in Denmark and Sweden, European Journal of Political Research, 43 (2008), pp. 610-634.
Kryštof, Roman: Romany Communities Ways of Living in Relation to Criminality (In the Known Territories of the Czech Republic and Slovakia). In: čověk v tísni - The Polis Project, 2007, pp. 11-14.
Kühnen, Michael: Lexikon der Neuen Front, w. p., 1987.
Kumar, Radha: Divide and Fall? Bosnia in the Annals of Partition, London 2007.
Küntzel, Matthias: Djihad und Judenhass: Über den neuen antisemitischen Krieg, Freiburg i. Brsg. 2002.
Landau, Jacob M.: Radical Politics in Modern Turkey, Leiden 1974.
-: Pan-Turkism in Turkey: A Study in Irredentism, London 1981.
-: The Politics of Pan-Islam: Ideology and Organization, Oxford 1990.
-: Ethnonationalism and Pan-Nationalism in Turkey and the Ex-Soviet Republics. In: Migration, 28 (1995), pp. 67-84.
-: Pan-Turkism: From Irredentism to Cooperation, Bloomington 1995.
Lange, Kai-Olaf: Populismus in den neuen Mitgliedsländern der EU: Potentiale, Akteure, Konsequenzen, SWP-Studie 16, Berlin 2009.
Lange, Sarah L. de: From Pariah to Power: Explanations for the Government Participation of Radical Right-Wing Populist Parties in West European Parliamentary Democracies, Antwerp 2008.
-/Guerra, Simona: The League of Polish Families between East and West, Past and Present. In: Minkenberg, Michael (Ed.): Historical Legacies and the Radical Right in Post-Cold War Central and Eastern Europe, pp. 123-155.
Laver, Michael: Party Competition and Party System Change: The Interaction of Electoral Bargaining and Party Competition. In: Journal of Theoretical Politics, 1 (1989) 3, pp. 301-325.
-/Budge, Ian (Eds.): Party and Coalition Policy in Western Europe, London 1992.
-/Hunt, W. Ben: Policy and Party Competition, London 1992.
-/Schofield, Norman (Eds.): Multiparty Government: The Politics of Coalition in Europe, Oxford 1990.
-/Shepsle, Kenneth: Coalitions and Cabinet Government. In: American Political Science Review, 84 (1990) 3, pp. 873-890.
Lebourg, Nicolas: Le monde vu de la plus extrême droite: Du fascisme au nationalisme-révolutionnaire, Perpignan 2010.
Lecœur, Erwan: Un néo-populisme à la française: Trente ans de Front national, Paris 2003.
Leonard, Mark: Europe without Frontiers: The Role of Political Parties in Europe's Future, London 1997.
Lescop, Gildas: "Honnie soit la Oi!": Naissance, émergence et déliquescence d'une forme musicale de protestation sociale. In: Copyright Volume! Autour des musiques actuelles, 2 (2003) 1, pp. 109-128.

–: Mobilisation des corps, pénétration des esprits: Des différentes tentatives d'investissement de la musique par l'extrême droite. In: Seca, Jean-Marie (Ed.): Musiques populaires underground et représentations du politique, Paris 2007, pp. 244–271.
Lévi-Strauss, Claude: L'Identité, Paris 1977.
Lévy, Bernard-Henri: L'Idéologie française, Paris 1983.
Linz, Juan J.: The Breakdown of Democratic Regimes: Crises, Breakdown and Reequilibrium, Baltimore 1978.
Lipsius, Stefan: Kommunistische Parteien in Albanien und Kosovo: Vorbild Enver Hoxha? In: Südosteuropa, 47 (1998), 10–11, pp. 534–546.
Lipstad, Deborah: Betrifft: Leugnen des Holocaust, Zürich 1998.
Literature Review of the SIREN project, Vienna 2002.
Lööw, Heléne: Nazismen i Sverige 1980–1997, Stockholm 1998.
–: Country Report Sweden. In: Bertelsmann Stiftung (Ed.): Strategies, pp. 425–462.
Lopušina, Marko: Tajne srpske policije, Beograd 2001.
Loubet del Bayle, Jean-Louis: Les non-conformistes des années 30: Une tentative de renouvellement de la pensée politique française, Paris 1969.
Lubbers Marcel/Gijsberts, Mérove/Scheepers, Peer: Extreme Right-Wing Voting in Western Europe. In: European Journal of Political Research, 41 (2002) 3, pp. 345–378.
–/Scheepers, Peer: Euroscepticism and Extreme Voting Patterns in Europe: Social cleavages and Socio-Political Attitudes Determining Voting for the Far Left, the Far Right and Non-Voting. In: Loosveldt, Geert/Swyngedouw, Marc/Cambré, Bart (Eds.): Measuring Meaningful Data in Social Research, Leuven 2007, pp. 71–92.
Lucardie, Paul: Das Parteiensystem der Niederlande. In: Niedermeyer, Oskar/Stöss, Richard/Haas, Melanie (Eds.): Die Parteiensysteme Westeuropas, Wiesbaden 2006, pp. 331–350.
Luebbert, Gregory: Comparative Democracy: Policy Making and Governing Coalitions in Europe and Israel, New York 1986.
Lupia, Arthur/Strøm, Kaare: Coalition Governance Theory: Bargaining, Electoral Connections and the Shadow of the Future. In: Strøm, Kaare/Müller, Wolfgang C./Bergman, Torbjörn (Eds.): Coalition Governance in Western Europe, Oxford 2008, pp. 51–83.
Lux, Georg/Sommersguter, Uwe: Das Jörg-Haider-Experiment: Partei der Lebensmenschen – Bündnis mit Zukunft? Vienna 2009.
Maddens, Bart/Billiet, Jaak/Beerten, Roeland: National Identity and the Attitude towards Foreigners in Multi-National States: The Case of Belgium. In: Journal of Ethnic and Migration Studies, 26 (2000) 1, pp. 45–60.
Mahieu, Jacques de: Précis de biopolitique, Montréal 1969.
Maier, Charles: The Unmasterable Past, Cambridge 1988.
Maigre, Marie-Elizabeth: Les deux visages du nationalisme islamo-turc. In: La Vie des idées: Mensuel international sur le débat d'idées, 14 (2006), pp. 45–54.
Mançо, Ural/Mançо, Altay (Eds.): Turcs de Belgique: Identités et trajectoires d'une minorité, Brussels 1992.
Marchi, Riccardo: Partido Nacional Renovador: Un'analisi della nuova estrema-destra portoghese. In: Trasgressioni, (2010) 50, pp. 57–80.

Marcus, Jonathan: The National Front in French Politics, New York 1995.
Mareš, Miroslav: Pravicový extremismus a radikalismus v ČR, Brno 2003.
-: Terorismus v ČR, Brno 2005.
-: National and Right-Wing Radicalism in the New Democracies: Czech Republic. Paper for the workshop "Right-Wing Extremism and its Impact on Young Democracies in CEE-Countries", Budapest, 27 November 2009, Friedrich Ebert Stiftung, Budapest 2009.
-: The Extreme Right in Eastern Europe and Territorial Issues. In: Central European Political Studies Review, 11 (2009) 2-3, pp. 82-106.
-: Extremismus in Slowenien. In: Jesse, Eckhard/Thieme, Tom (Eds.): Extremismus in den EU-Staaten, pp. 361-375.
-/ Stojar, Richard: Extreme Right Paramilitary Units in Eastern Europe. In: Mammone, Andrea/Godin, Emmanuel/Jenkins, Brian (Eds.): Mapping the Far Right in Contemporary Europe: Local, National, Comparative, Transnational, Oxford 2011.
Markovits, Andrei/Gorski, Philip S.: The German Left: Red, Green and Beyond, Cambridge 1993.
-/ Noveck, Beth: Germany. In: Wyman, David S. (Ed.): The World Reacts to the Holocaust, Baltimore 1996, pp. 428-432.
Marks, Gary/Hooghe, Liesbet/Nelson, Moira/Edwards, Erica: Party Competition and European Integration in the East and West: Different Structure, Same Causality. In: Comparative Political Studies, 39 (2006) 2, pp. 155-175.
Marsh, Michael: Testing the Second-Order Election Model after Four European Elections. In: British Journal of Political Science, 28 (1998), pp. 591-607.
Martin, Pierre: Le vote Le Pen, l'électorat du Front national. In: Notes de la fondation saint-simon, octobre-novembre 1996.
Mattila, Mikko/Raunio, Tapio: Does Winning Pay? Electoral Success and Government Formation in 15 West European Countries. In: European Journal of Political Research, 43 (2004), pp. 263-285.
Mauthe, Jan Christopher: Erfolgsbedingungen für Rechtspopulisten in Skandinavien: Schweden und Dänemark im Vergleich, Saarbrücken 2008.
Mayer, Gregor/Odehnal, Bernhard: Aufmarsch: Die rechte Gefahr aus Osteuropa, 2nd Edition, St. Pölten 2010.
Mayer, Nonna: The French National Front. In: Betz, Hans-Georg/Immerfall, Stefan (Eds.): The New Politics of the Right, New York 1998, pp. 11-25.
-: Ces Français qui votent FN, Paris 1999.
-/ Boy, Daniel (Eds.): The French Voter Decides, Ann Arbor 1993.
-/ Perrineau, Pascal: Les comportements politiques, Paris 1992.
-/ Perrineau, Pascal: Le Front national à découvert, 2nd Edition, Paris 1996.
McCulloch, Tim: The Nouvelle Droite in the 1980s and 1990s: Ideology and Entryism, the Relationship with the National Front. In: French Politics, 4 (2006) 2, pp. 158-78.
McGann, Anthony J./Kitschelt, Herbert: The Radical Right in the Alps: Evolution of Support for the Swiss SVP and Austrian FPÖ. In: Party Politics, 11 (2007) 2, pp. 147-171.
Meding, Holger: Der Weg: Eine deutsche Emigrantenzeitschrift in Buenos Aires, 1947-1957, Berlin 1997.

Meret, Susi: The Danish People's Party, the Italian Northern League and the Austrian Freedom Party in a Comparative Perspective: Party Ideology and Electoral Support, PhD thesis, University of Aalborg, Aalborg 2010.
Merkel, Wolfgang: Systemtransformation: Eine Einführung in die Theorie und Empirie der Transformationsforschung, 2nd Edition, Wiesbaden 2010.
Meznik, Michael: Extremismus in Bulgarien. In: Jesse, Eckhard/Thieme, Tom: Politischer Extremismus in den EU-Staaten, pp. 49-62.
-: Wer braucht die Vergangenheit? Eine Bilanz der Aufarbeitung des Sozialismus zwanzig Jahre nach der Wende. In: Österreichische Botschaft Sofia (Ed.): 1989/2009 - Reflexionen über die Wende in Bulgarien, Sofia 2009, pp. 79-89.
Mielants, Eric: The Long-term Historical Development of Racist Tendencies within the Political and Social Context of Belgium. In: International Journal of Comparative Sociology, 47 (2006), pp. 313-334.
Milo, Daniel: Slovakia. In: Mudde, Cas (Ed.): Racist Extremism in Central and Eastern Europe, London 2005, pp. 195-224.
Milza, Piere: Evropa v černých košilích, Praha 2006.
Ministero dell' Interno (Ed.): Rapporto sulla criminalità in Italia: Analisi, Prevenzione, Contrasto, Rome 2007.
Minkenberg, Michael: Die neue radikale Rechte im Vergleich: USA, Frankreich, Deutschland, Opladen 1998.
-: The Renewal of the Radical Right: Between Modernity and Anti-modernity. In: Government and Opposition, 35 (2000) 2, pp. 170-188.
-: Die radikale Rechte in den Transformationsgesellschaften Mittel- und Osteuropas: Konzepte, Konturen, Kontexte. In: Zeitschrift für Parlamentsfragen, 33 (2002) 2, pp. 305-322.
- (Ed.): Historical Legacies and the Radical Right in Post-Cold War Central and Eastern Europe, with an afterword by Sabrina P. Ramet, Stuttgart 2010.
Mohler, Armin: La Révolution conservatrice en Allemagne, 1918-1932, Paris 1993.
Monzat, René: Enquêtes sur la droite extrême, Paris 1992.
Moreau, Patrick: Die Rückkehr des Nationalpopulismus in Österreich. In: Totalitarismus und Demokratie, 7 (2010) 1, pp. 39-82.
Moroska, Aleksandra: Prawicowy populizm a eurosceptycyzm, Wrocław 2010.
-/ Sroka, Anna: Extremismus in Polen. In: Jesse, Eckhard/Thieme, Tom (Eds.): Politischer Extremismus in den EU-Staaten, pp. 283-298.
-/ Zuba, Krzystof: Two Faces of Polish Populism: The Causes of the Success and Fall of Self Defence and the League of Polish Families. In: Totalitarismus und Demokratie, 7 (2010) 1, pp. 123-147.
Mudde, Cas: Extremismus in den Niederlanden und in Flandern. In: Jahrbuch Extremismus und Demokratie, 8 (1996), pp. 242-256.
-: The War of Words Defining the Extreme Right Party Family. In: West European Politics, 19 (1996) 2, pp. 225-248.
-: The Single-Issue Party Thesis: Extreme Right Parties and the Immigration Issue. In: Western European Politics, 22 (1999) 3, pp. 182-197.
-: Globalisation: The Multi-Faced Enemy? In: CERC Working Papers Series, no. 3, University of Melbourne, Melbourne 2004.
-: Central and Eastern Europe. In: Mudde, Cas (Ed.): Racist Extremism in East and Central Europe, London 2005, pp. 267-285.
- (Ed.): Racist Extremism in Central and Eastern Europe, London 2005.

-: Racist Extremism in Central and Eastern Europe. In: East European Politics and Societies, 19 (2005) 2, pp. 161-184.
-: Politischer Extremismus und Radikalismus in Westeuropa - Typologie und Bestandsaufnahme. In: Backes, Uwe/Jesse, Eckhard (Eds): Gefährdungen der Freiheit: Extremistische Ideologien im Vergleich, Göttingen 2006, pp. 87-104.
-: Populist Radical Right Parties in Europe, Cambridge 2007.
Muižnieks, Nils: Latvia. In: Mudde, Cas (Ed.): Racist Extremism in Central and Eastern Europe, London 2005, pp. 101-128.
Müller, Wolfgang C./Strøm, Kaare (Eds.): Policy, Office, or Votes? How Political Parties in Western Europe Make Hard Decisions, Cambridge 1999.
-/Jenny, Marcelo: Abgeordnete, Parteien und Koalitionspolitik: Individuelle Präferenzen und politisches Handeln im Nationalrat. In: Österreichische Zeitschrift für Politikwissenschaft, 29 (2000) 2, pp. 137-156.
Mumcu, Uğur: Silah Kaçakçılığı ve Terör, Ankara 1998.
-: Tarikat, Siyaset, Ticaret, Ankara 1998.
Mussa, Giorgio (Ed.): Padania, identità e società multirazziale. In: Enti locali padani federali, (1998) 2, pp. XX.
Myrdal, Gunnar: An American Dilemma. The Negro Problem and Modern Democracy, New York 1944.
Nadeau, Jean-François: Adrien Arcand: führer canadien, Montreal 2010.
Nancy, Claude: Hacia un materialismo biologico: La caida del materialismo historico Claude Soas, Barcelona 2011.
Narud, Hanne Marthe: Voters, Parties and Governments: Electoral Competition, Policy Distances and Government Formation in Multi-Party Systems, Oslo 1996.
Nejčev, Simeon et al.: Volen Siderov: Meždu lăžata i istinata, Sofia 2007.
Nève, Dorothée de: Wahlen in Rumänien - eine ganz normale Katastrophe. In: Osteuropa, 51 (2001) 3, pp. 281-298.
Newell, James L.: Italy: The Extreme Right Comes in from the Cold. In: Parliamentary Affairs, 53 (2000), pp. 469-485.
Nohlen, Dieter/Stöver, Philip (Eds.): Elections in Europe: A Data Handbook, Baden-Baden 2010.
Nolte, Ernst: The Three Faces of Fascism: Action Française, Italian Fascism, National Socialism, London 1965.
Nordbruch, Claus: Völkermord an den Herero in Deutsch-Südwestafrika? Widerlegung einer Lüge, 2nd Edition, Tübingen 2006.
Norris, Pippa: Radical Right: Parties and Electoral Competition, New York 2005.
-: Radical Right: Voters and Parties in the Electoral Market, Cambridge 2005.
Novick, Peter: The Holocaust in American Life, New York 1999.
NPD: Argumente für Kandidaten & Funktionsträger: Eine Handreichung für die öffentliche Auseinandersetzung, Berlin 2006.
NRW-Ministerium für Arbeit, Gesundheit und Soziales des Landes Nordrhein-Westfalen, Zentrum für Türkeistudien (Ed.): Türkische Muslime in Nordrhein-Westfalen: Dialog mit einer neu etablierten religiösen Minderheit in NRW: Türkische Muslime und deutsche Christen im Gespräch, NRW-Ministerium für Arbeit, Gesundheit und Soziales des Landes Nordrhein-Westfalen, Düsseldorf 1994.

Ohlemacher, Thomas: Schmerzhafte Episoden: Wider die Rede von einer rechten Bewegung im wiedervereinigten Deutschland. In: Forschungsjournal Neue Soziale Bewegungen, 7 (1994) 4, pp. 16-25.
Oltenau, Tina: Rumänien: Vom Einparteiensystem zum Einheitsbrei? In: Segert, Dieter/Bos, Ellen (Eds.): Osteuropäische Demokratien als Trendsetter? Parteien und Parteiensysteme nach dem Ende des Übergangsjahrzehnts, Opladen 2008, pp. 147-166.
O'Meara, Michael: New Culture, New Right Anti-Liberalism. In: Postmodern Europe, Bloomington 2004.
OSCE/ODIHR (Ed.): Hate Crimes in the OSCE Region: Incidents and Responses - Annual Report for 2009, Warsaw 2010.
Padovani, Cinzia: The Extreme Right and Its Media in Italy. In: International Journal of Communication, 2 (2008), pp. 753-770.
Pallaver, Günther: "Die Lega Nord und die Konstruktion Padaniens". In: Fuchs, Gerhild/Tasser, Barbara (Eds.): Obiettivo sulla Pianura Padana: Visioni interdisciplinari di una regione geo-culturale italiana/Die Poebene im Blickpunkt: Interdisziplinäre Schlaglichter auf einen italienischen Kulturraum, Innsbruck 2009, pp. 111-125.
Pandurević, Vinko: Rat u BiH i paravojne formacije, Beograd 2004.
Pankowski, Rafał/Kornak, Marcin: Poland. In: Mudde, Cas (Ed.): Racist Extremism in Central and Eastern Europe, London 2005, pp. 156-183.
-: Die Liga der Polnischen Familien auf dem Weg zur Macht - eine Fallstudie zum Rechtsextremismus in Polen. In: Spöhr, Holger/Kolls, Sarah (Eds.): Rechtsextremismus, pp. 147-163.
-: The Populist Radical Right in Poland: The Patriots, London 2010.
Le Parti de la France, Les principes et les valeurs du Parti de la France, Paris 2009.
Pauwels, Louis/Bergier, Jacques: Le matin des magiciens, Paris 1960.
Paxton, Robert: Vichy France: Old Guard and New Order, 1940-1944 in 1972.
Payne, Stanley: A History of Fascism: 1914-1945, London 1995.
Pelinka, Anton: Country Report Austria. In: Bertelsmann Stiftung (Ed.), Strategies, pp. 29-58.
-: Vom Glanz und Elend der Parteien. Struktur- und Funktionswandel des österreichischen Parteiensystems, Innsbruck 2005.
Pérouse, Jean-François: La pomme rouge et le croissant de lune. Le monde (turc) vu par un "mafieux", Dossier: le nouveau "Grand Jeu" de la Turquie. In: Diplomatie, Affaires stratégiques et relations internationales, 36 (2009), p. 61.
Petreu, Marta: An Infamous Past: E. M. Cioran and the Rise of Fascism in Romania, Chicago 2005.
Petrova, Dimitrina: The Roma: Between the Myth and the Future, Budapest 2007.
Pettigrew, Thomas/Meertens, Roel: Subtle and Blatant Prejudice in Western Europe. In: European Journal of Social Psychology, 25 (1995) 1, pp. 57-75.
Peunova, Marina: An Eastern Incarnation of the European New Right: Aleksandr Panarin and New Eurasianist Discourse in Contemporary Russia. In: Journal of Contemporary European Studies, 16 (2008) 3, pp. 407-419.
Pfahl-Traughber, Armin: Renaissance der antisemitisch-antifreimaurerischen Verschwörungstheorie in esoterisch-rechtsextremistischen Veröffentlichungen. In: Reinalter, Helmut (Ed.): Verschwörungstheorien: Theorie - Geschichte - Wirkung, Innsbruck 2002, pp. 83-106.

-: Globalisierung als Agitationsthema des organisierten Rechtsextremismus in Deutschland. In: Greven, Thomas/Grumke, Thomas (Eds.): Globalisierter Rechtsextremismus?, pp. 30-51.
Philips, John: Macedonia. Warlords and Rebels in the Balkans, London 2004.
Piccone, Paul: Confronting the French New Right: Old Prejudices or a New Political Paradigm. In: Telos, 98-99 (1993-1994), pp. 3-23.
Pipes, Daniel: Conspiracy: How the Paranoid Style Flourishes and Where it Comes from, New York 1997.
Plasser, Fritz/Ulram, Peter A. (Eds.): Wechselwahlen: Analysen zur Nationalratswahl 2006, Vienna 2007.
-/Ulram, Peter A.: Analyse der Europawahl 2009: Wähler, Nichtwähler, Motive, Vienna 2009.
Porta, Donatella della/Tarrow, Sidney: Transnational Protest and Global Activism, New York 2005.
Quillian, Lincoln: Prejudice as a Response to Perceived Group Threat: Population Composition and Anti-Immigrant and Racial Prejudice in Europe. In: American Sociological Review, 60 (1995) 4, pp. 586-611.
Rassinier, Paul: Le Mensonge d'Ulysse, Bourg-en-Bresse 1950.
Reif, Karlheinz: National Electoral Cycles and European Elections 1979 and 1984. In: Electoral Studies, (1984) 3, pp. 244-255.
-/Schmitt, Hermann: Nine National Second-Order Elections: A Systematic Framework for the Analysis of European Election Results. In: European Journal of Political Research, 8 (1980), pp. 3-44.
Rémond, René: Les Droites en France, Paris 1982.
-: Les Droites aujourd'hui, Paris 2005.
Reuter, Gerd: Rechtspopulismus in Belgien und den Niederlanden: Unterschiede im niederländischsprachigen Raum, Wiesbaden 2009.
Reuter Jens: Die internationale Gemeinschaft und der Krieg in Kosovo. In: Südosteuropa, 47 (1998) 7-8, pp. 281-297.
Richter, Karl: Der Chaoskanzler. In: Opposition, 5 (2002) 1, p. 1.
Ridgeway, James: Blood in the Face, New York 1990.
Rigaud, Philippe: Continent Dark, Paris 2009.
Rigoni, Isabelle: Mobilisations et enjeux des migrations de Turquie en Europe de l'Ouest, Paris 2001.
Ringold, Dena/Orenstein, Mitchell A./Wilkens, Erika: Roma in an Expanding Europe: Breaking the Poverty Cycle, Washington 2006.
Robins, Robert S./Post, Jerrold M.: Political Paranoia: The Psychopolitics of Hatred, New Haven 1997.
Roček, František: Zeď (The Wall): Matiční - dokument o nejslavnější uliče světa, Ústí nad Labem 1999.
Rochtus, Dirk: Extremismus in Belgien. In: Jesse, Eckhard/Thieme, Tom (Eds.): Extremismus in den EU-Staaten, pp. 35-50.
Rodrigues, Peter R./Donselaar, Jaap van (Eds.): Monitor Racisme & Extremisme, Negende Rapportage, Amsterdam 2010.
Roger, Antoine: Les parties anti-système dans la Roumanie post-communiste. In: Revue d'Etudes Comparatives Est-Ouest, 31 (2000) 2, pp. 101-136.
Romsics, Ignác: Der Friedensvertrag von Trianon, Herne 2005.

Roques, Henry: Die Geständnisse des Kurt Gerstein: Zur Problematik eines Schlüssel-Dokuments, Deutsche Argumente, Leoni am Starnberger See 1986.
Rose, Richard/Mackie, Thomas T.: Incumbency in Government: Asset or Liability? In: Daalder, Hans/Mair, Peter (Eds.): Western European Party Systems: Continuity and Change, London 1983.
Roth, Heinz: Warum werden wir Deutschen belogen?, Witten 1973.
Rothkranz, Johannes: Die Sedisvakanzthese widerlegt? Antwort auf eine untaugliche Kritik von P. Gérard Mura, Durach 1999.
Rotter, Petra: Slovenia. In: Szajkowski, Bogdan (Ed.): Political Parties of the World, London 2005, pp. 532-537.
Rousso, Henri: Vichy Syndrome, Cambridge 1994.
Ruiter, Robin de: Die 13 satanischen Blutlinien, Durach 2000.
-: Der 11. September 2001: Osama bin Laden und die okkulten Kräfte hinter den terroristischen Anschlägen auf die USA, Durach 2002.
-: Im Namen der neuen Weltordnung. Der 11. September 2001 und andere Verbrechen gegen die Menschheit, Frankfurt a. M. 2004.
-: Worldwide Evil and Misery: The Legacy of the 13 Satanic Bloodlines, Enschede 2008.
Rydgren, Jens: Radical Right Populism in Sweden: Still a Failure but for How Long? In: Scandinavian Political Studies, 25 (2002) 1, pp. 27-54.
-: Explaining the Emergence of Extreme Right-Wing Populist Parties: The Case of Denmark. In: West European Politics 27 (2004), pp. 474-502.
-: Is Extreme Right-Wing Populism Contagious? Explaining the Emergence of a New Party Family. In: European Journal of Political Research, 44 (2005), pp. 413-437.
Sadovsky, Louis: Berlin 1942, Paris 2009.
Scharenberg, Albert: Plädoyer für eine Mehrebenenanalyse des Rechtsextremismus. In: Deutschland Archiv, 4 (2003), pp. 659-672.
-: Brücke zum Mainstream - Mainstream als Brücke. Europäische Rechtsparteien und ihre Politik gegen Einwanderung. In: Greven, Thomas/Grumke, Thomas (Eds.): Globalisierter Rechtsextremismus?, pp. 70-111.
Scheepers, Peer/Gijsberts, Merove/Coenders, Marcel: Ethnic Exclusionism in European Countries. Public Opposition to Civil Rights for Legal Migrants as a Response to Perceived Ethnic Threat. In: European Sociological Review, 8 (2002) 1, pp. 17-34.
Scheuch, Erwin K./Klingemann, Hans-Dieter: Theorie des Rechtsradikalismus in westlichen Industriegesellschaften. In: Hamburger Jahrbuch für Wirtschafts- und Gesellschaftspolitik, 12 (1967), pp. 11-29.
Schmitt, Hermann: The European Parliament Elections of June 2004: Still Second-Order? In: West European Politics, 28 (2005), pp. 650-679.
Schuman, Howard/Steeh, Charlotte/Bobo, Lawrence/Krysan, Maria: Racial Attitudes in America. Trends and Interpretations, 3rd Edition, Cambridge 1998.
Searchlight (Ed.): Lone Wolves: Myth or Reality?, Ilford 2011.
Sened, Itai: A Model of Coalition Formation. In: The Journal of Politics, 58 (1996) 2, pp. 350-372.
Seufert, Günter: The Impact of Nationalist Discourses on Civil Society. In: Yerasimos, Stephane/Seufert, Günter/Vorhoff, Karin (Eds.): Civil Society in the Grip of Nationalism, Istanbul 2000, pp. 25-48.

Shafir, Michael: The Mind of Romania's Radical Right. In: Ramet, Sabrina P. (Ed.): The Radical Right in Central and Eastern Europe since 1989, Pennsylvania 1999, pp. 213-232.
-: Marginalization or Mainstream? The Extreme Right in Post-Communist Romania. In: Hainsworth, Paul (Ed.): The Politics of the Extreme Right, London 2000, pp. 247-267.
-: Between Denial and "Comparative Trivialization": Holocaust-denial in Post-Communist East Central Europe, Acta n°19, The Vidal Sassoon International Center for the Study of Antisemitism, The Hebrew University of Jerusalem, Jerusalem 2002.
Shekhovtsov, Anton: The Palingenetic Thrust of Russian Neo-Eurasianism: Ideas of Rebirth in Aleksandr Dugin's Worldview. In: Totalitarian Movements and Political Religions, 9 (2008) 4, pp. 491-506.
-: Aleksandr Dugin's Neo-Eurasianism: The New Right à la Russe. In: Religion Compass, 3 (2009) 4, pp. 697-716.
Shields, James G.: The Extreme Right in France from Pétain to Le Pen, London 2007.
Shultz, Richard H./Dew, Andrea J.: Insurgents, Terrorists, and Militias: The Warriors of Contemporary Combat, New York 2006.
Simi, Pete/Futrell, Robert: American Swastika, Lanham 2010.
Sjöblom, Gunnar: Party Strategies in a Multiparty System, Lund 1968.
Skenderovic, Damir: Immigration and the Radical Right in Switzerland: Ideology, Discourse and Opportunities. In: Patterns of Prejudice, 41 (2007) 2, pp. 155-176.
Sniderman, Paul/Hagendoorn, Louk/Prior, Markus: Predisposing Factors and Situational Triggers: Exclusionary Reactions to Immigrant Minorities. In: American Political Science Review, 98 (2004) 1, pp. 35-49.
Spektorowski, Alberto: Ethnoregionalism: The Intellectual New Right and Lega Nord. In: The Global Review of Ethnopolitics, 2 (2003) 3, pp. 55-70.
Spöhr, Holger/Kolls, Sarah (Eds.): Rechtsextremismus in Deutschland und Europa: Aktuelle Entwicklungstendenzen im Vergleich, Frankfurt a. M. 2010.
Spruyt, Marc: Grove Borstels: Stel dat het Vlaams Blok zijn programma realiseert, hoe zou Vlanderen er dan uitzien?, Leuven 1995.
Stäglich, Wilhelm: Der Auschwitz-Mythos: Legende oder Wirklichkeit? Eine Bestandsaufnahme, Tübingen 1979.
Statham, Paul: Berlusconi, the Media, and the New Right in Italy. In: Harvard International Journal of Press and Politics, 1 (1996) 1, pp. 87-105.
Statistika Austria: Mikrozensus-Arbeitskräfteerhebung 2011, Vienna 2011.
Stefanova, Boyka: Ethnic Nationalism, Social Structure, and Political Agency: Explaining Electoral Support for the Radical Right in Bulgaria. In: Ethnic and Racial Studies, 32 (2009), pp. 1534-1556.
Steffen, Christian: Die Parteiensysteme Dänemarks, Norwegens und Schwedens. In: Niedermayer, Oskar/Stöss, Richard/Haas, Melanie (Eds.): Die Parteiensysteme Westeuropas, Wiesbaden 2006, pp. 67-108.
Steglich, Henrik: Erfolgsbedingungen der extremen Rechten in Deutschland: Die Bedeutung der Wahlkampf-Themen. In: Backes, Uwe/Steglich, Henrik (Eds.): Die NPD, pp. 55-74.

-: Rechtsaußenparteien in Deutschland: Bedingungen ihres Erfolgs und Scheiterns, Göttingen 2010.
Sternhell, Zeev: La droite révolutionnaire, Paris 1978.
-: Neither Right nor Left: Fascist Ideology in France (1983), Princeton 1995.
Stokes, Donald E.: Spatial Models of Party Competition. In: Campbell, Angus (Ed.): Elections and the Political Order, Wiley 1966.
Stöss, Richard: Die extreme Rechte in der Bundesrepublik: Entwicklung, Ursachen, Gegenmaßnahmen, Opladen 1989.
-: Zur Vernetzung der extremen Rechten in Europa. In: Arbeitshefte aus dem Otto-Stammer-Zentrum, No. 5, Berlin 2001.
-: Globalisierung und rechtsextreme Einstellungen. In: Bundesministerium des Innern (Ed.): Extremismus in Deutschland, Berlin 2004, pp. 82-97.
-: Rechtsextremismus im Wandel, Berlin 2010.
Strøm, Kaare: Party Goals and Government Performance. In: American Political Science Review, 79 (1985) 3, pp. 738-754.
-: A Behavioral Theory of Competitive Political Parties. In: American Journal of Political Science, 34 (1990) 2, pp. 565-598.
-/ Müller, Wolfgang C.: Political Parties and Hard Choices. In: Müller, Wolfgang C./ Strøm, Kaare (Eds.): Policy, Office, or Votes? How Political Parties in Western Europe Make Hard Decisions, Cambridge 1999, pp. 1-35.
Stýskalíková, Věra: Případ UÇK: Terorismus nebo guerilla? In: Souleimanov, Emil (Ed.): Terorismus: Válka proti státu, Prague 2006.
Sunic, Tomislav: The European New Right: Against Democracy and Equality, New York 1990.
Swaan, Abraham de: Coalition Theories and Cabinet Formations: A Study of Formal Theories of Coalition Formation Applied to Nine European Parliaments after 1918, Amsterdam 1973.
Swank, Duane/Betz, Hans-Georg: Globalization, the Welfare State and Right-Wing Populism in Western Europe. In: Socio-Economic Review, 1 (2003) 2, pp. 215-245.
Swyngedouw, Marc: National Elections in Belgium: The Breakthrough of the Extreme Right in Flanders. In: Regional Politics and Policy, 2 (1992) 3, pp. 62-75.
-: Country Report Belgium. In: Bertelsmann Stiftung (Ed.): Strategies, pp. 59-80.
-/ Ivaldi, Gilles: The Extreme Right Utopia in Belgium and France: The Ideology of the Flemish Vlaams Blok and the French Front National. In: West European Politics, 24 (2001) 3, pp. 1-22.
Sylvain, Bryan: European Son: An Interview with Alain de Benoist. In: The Occidental Quarterly, 5 (2005) 3, pp. 7-27.
Szabó, Maté: Movement and Counter-Movement Mobilization: The Gypsies and the Skinheads, Right-Wing Racists, and Anti-Racist Protest Movements in Hungary (1988-1995). In: Central European Political Science Review, 1 (2000) 2, pp. 143-173.
Szöllösi-Janze, Margit: Die Pfeilkreuzlerbewegung in Ungarn: Historischer Kontext, Entwicklung und Herrschaft, Munich 1989.
Taggart, Paul: New Populist Parties in Western Europe. In: West European Politics, 18 (1995) 1, pp. 34-51.
-: Populism, Buckingham 2000.

Taguieff, Pierre-André: Face au racisme, Paris 1991.
-: Sur la nouvelle droite: jalons d'une analyse critique, Paris 1994.
-: La nouvelle judéophobie, Paris 2002.
-: La foire aux illuminés, Paris 2005.
Tapia, Stéphane de: Rôle des flux migratoires et des réfugiés dans la construction d'un Etat: la Turquie. In: Cambrezy, Luc/Lassailly-Jacob, Véronique (Eds.): Populations réfugiées, de l'exil au retour, Paris 2001, pp. 119-148.
Tarchi, Marco: The Far Right Italian Style. In: Casals, Xavier (Ed.): Political Survival on the Extreme Right. European Movements between the Inherited Past and the Need to Adapt to the Future, Barcelona 2005, pp. 35-50.
Tarrow, Sidney: Power in Movement, 2nd Edition, Cambridge 1998.
-: The New Transnational Activism, Cambridge 2005.
Taylor, Charles: The Malaise of Modernity, Concord 1991.
Teitelbaum, Vivianne: Salomon, vous êtes juif? L'antisémitisme en Belgique, du Moyen Age à Internet, Brussels 2008.
Thieme, Tom: Hammer, Sichel, Hakenkreuz. Parteipolitischer Extremismus in Osteuropa: Entstehungsursachen und Erscheinungsformen, Baden-Baden 2007.
Thion, Serge: Vérité historique ou vérité politique?, Damascus 2005.
Todorova, Maria: The Courses and Discourses of Bulgarian Nationalism. In: Sugar, Peter F. (Ed.): Eastern European Nationalism in the Twentieth Century, Lanham 1995, pp. 55-102.
Tóth, András/Grajczjar, István: The Emergence of the Extreme Right in Post-Socialist Hungary and its Connections to Social Changes, report for the research project SIREN, Budapest 2001.
Trplan, Tomaz: Slovenia. In: Mudde, Cas (Ed.): Racist Extremism in Central and Eastern Europe, pp. 245-246.
Tsebelis, George: Nested Games: Rational Choice in Comparative Politics, Berkeley 1990.
Tufte, Edward R.: Determinants of the Outcomes of Midterm Congressional Elections. In: American Political Science Review, 67 (1975), pp. 540-54.
Türk, Fahri: Azerbaycan ve Orta Asya'da Değişim Sürecinde Ortaya Çıkan Turancı Siyasi Hareketler (1989-2007). In: Bilig, Türk Dünyası Sosyal Bilimler Dergisi, 51 (2009), pp. 205-230.
Vasilopoulou, Sofia: Varieties of Euroscepticism: The Case of the European Extreme Right. In: Journal of Contemporary European Research, 5 (2009) 1, pp. 3-23.
Vejvodová, Petra: Aplikace teorie extremismu na Dělnickou stranu, final thesis, Brno 2005.
Verberk, Genevieve: Attitudes towards Ethnic Minorities. Conceptualizations, Measurements, and Models, Amsterdam 1999.
Versluis, Arthur: What's Right? A Review Essay. In: Journal for the Study of Radicalism, 2 (2009) 2, pp. 153-58.
Waele, Jean-Michel de/Rea, Andrea/Delwitt, Pascal: L'extrême droite en France et en Belgique, Brussels 1998.
Wagner, Ulrich/Christ, Oliver/Pettigrew, Thomas/Stellmacher, Jost/Wolf, Carina: Prejudice and Minority Proportion: Contact Instead of Threat Effects. In: Social Psychology Quarterly, 69 (2006) 4, pp. 380-390.

Walker Fields, Ingrid: White Hope: Conspiracy, Nationalism, and Revolution in "The Turner Diaries" and "Hunter". In: Knight, Peter (Ed.): Conspiracy Nation: The Politics of Paranoia in Postwar America, New York 2002, pp. 157-176.
Waltson, James: History and Memory of the Italian Concentration Camps. In: The Historical Journal, 40 (1997) 1, pp. 169-183.
Warwick, Paul V.: Toward a Common Dimensionality in West European Policy Spaces. In: Party Politics, 8 (2002) 1, pp. 101-122.
Weber, Claudia: Geschichte und Macht: Die kommunistische Geschichtspolitik in Bulgarien 1944-1948. In: Richter, Angela/Bayer, Barbara (Eds.): Geschichte (ge-)brauchen: Literatur und Geschichtskultur im Staatssozialismus: Jugoslavien und Bulgarien, Berlin 2006, pp. 77-90.
Weckenbrock, Christoph: Die streitbare Demokratie auf dem Prüfstand: Die neue NPD als Herausforderung, Bonn 2009.
Welzk, Stefan: Globalisierung und Neofaschismus. In: Kursbuch, (1998) 134, pp. 37-47.
Widfeldt, Anders: Party Change as a Necessity: The Case of the Sweden Democrats. In: Representation, 44 (2008) 3, pp. 265-276.
Wilds, Karl: Identity Creation and the Culture of Contrition: Recasting "Normality" in the Berlin Republic. In: German Politics, 9 (2000) 1, pp. 83-102.
Williams, Phil: Violent Non-State Actors and National and International Security, International Relations and Security Network, Zürich 2008.
Winock, Michel (Ed.): Histoire de l'extrême droite en France, Paris 1994.
Witte, Hans de/Scheepers, Peer: En Flandre: origines, évolution et avenir du Vlaams Blok et de ses électeurs. In: Pouvoirs, (1998) 87, pp. 95-113.
Woods, Roger: Germany's New Right as Culture and Politics, New York 2007.
Yerasimos, Stéphane/Seufert, Günter/Vorhoff, Karin (Eds.): Civil Society in the Grip of Nationalism, Istanbul 2000.
Yerasimos, Stefanos/Seufert, Günter/Vorhoff, Karin (Eds.): Türkiye'de Sivil Toplum ve Milliyetçilik, Istanbul 2001.
Zaslove, Andrej: The Dark side of European Politics: Unmasking the Radical Right. In: Journal of European Integration, 26 (2004) 1, pp. 61-81.
-: Alpine Populism, Padania and Beyond: A Response to Duncan McDonnell. In: Politics, 27 (2007) 1, pp. 64-68.
-: The Populist Radical Right: Ideology, Party Families, and Core Principles. In: Political Studies Review, 7 (2009) 3, pp. 309-318.
Žečeva, Kristina: "ATAKA" - meždu nacionalizma i populizma, In: Polititičeski Izsledvanija, (2007) 3, pp. 49-65.
Zick, Andreas/Küpper, Beate/Hövermann, Andreas: Die Abwertung der Anderen: Eine europäische Zustandsbeschreibung zu Intoleranz, Vorurteilen und Diskriminierung: Eine Analyse im Auftrag der Friedrich-Ebert-Stiftung, Berlin 2011.
Zúquete, José Pedro: Portugal: A New Look at the Extreme Right. In: Representation, 43 (2007) 3, pp. 179-198.

Abbreviations

ABL	Agentura Bílý Lev
ADAC	Allgemeiner Deutscher Automobil-Club
ADR	Alternativ Demokratesch Reformpartei
ADŰTDF	Avrupa Demokratik Űlkücü Türk Dernekleri Federasyonu
AENM	Alliance of European National Movements
AGRA	Amis du Grand Reich Allemand
AIDS	Acquired Immune Deficiency Syndrome
AKP	Adalet ve Kalkınma Partisi
AN	Alleanza Nazionale
AN	Autonomous Nationalists
ANA	Albanian National Army
AS	Alternativa Sociale
ASALA	Armenian Secret Army for the Liberation of Armenia
AT	Austria
ATAKA	Partija Ataka
ATİB	Avrupa Türk İslam Birliği
BBP	Büyük Birlik Partisi
BDF	Bulgarian Democratic Forum
BE	Belgium
BfV	Bundesamt für Verfassungsschutz
BG	Bulgaria
BiH	Bosnia and Herzegovina
BNP	British National Party
BNS	Bulgarski natsionalen sujuz
BNYM	British Nationalist Youth Movement
BZÖ	Bündnis Zukunft Österreich
CCD-UDC	Centro Cristiano Democratico-Unione dei Democratici Cristiani e Democratici di Centro
CD	Compact Disc
CDA	Christen Democratisch Appèl
CDS-PP	Centro Democrático e Social – Partido Popular
CDU	Christlich Demokratische Union
CEDADE	Círculo Español de Amigos de Europa
CEE	Central and Eastern Europe
CEO	Chief Executive Officer
ČEZ	České Energetické Závody
CHP	Cumhuriyet Halk Partisi
CIA	Central Intelligence Agency
CKMP	Cumhuriyetçi Köylü Millet Partisi
CNRS	Centre National de la Recherche Scientifique
CO_2	Carbon dioxide
CODOH	Committee for Open Debate on the Holocaust
CR	Conservative Revolution

CSU	Christlich Soziale Union
CZ	Czech Republic
DA	Dekoloniseerimise Algatuskeskus
DC	Democrazia Cristiana
DE	Germany
DF	Dansk Folkeparti
DFP	Danish People's Party
DK	Denmark
DNA	Det Norske Arbeiderparti
DNSB	Danmarks Nationalsocialistiske Bevægelse
DP	Partido Democratico
DPP	Danish People's Party
DPS	Movement for Rights and Freedom
DS	Dělnická strana
DS	Democratici die Sinistra
DSSS	Dělnická Strana Sociální Spravedlnosti
DUP	Democratic Unionist Party
DVD	Digital Versatile Disc
DVU	Deutsche Volksunion
ECA	Europe and Central Asia
ECE	East Central Europe
EFD	Europe of Freedom and Democracy
EIP	Eesti Iseseisvuspartei
ELF	European Liberation Front
ENF	European National Front
ENR	European New Right
EP	European Parliament
ERSP	Eesti Rahvusliku Sõltumatuse Partei
ESM	European Social Movement
EU	European Union
EUL/NGL	European United Left/Nordic Green Left
EURONAT	Union of European Nationalists
EFA	European Free Alliance
EPEN	Ethniki Politiki Enosis
EVP	Europäische Volkspartei
EVS	European Values Study
FAP	Freiheitliche Deutsche Arbeiterpartei
FER	European Revolutionary Futurism
FI	Finland
FI	Forza Italia
FN	Forza Nuova
FN	Front National
FNb	Front National belge
FPÖ	Freiheitliche Partei Österreichs
FPTP	First-past-the-post

FR	France
FRP	Fremskrittspartiet (Norway)
FrP	Fremskridtspartiet (Danmark)
FSN	National Salvation Front
FT	Fiamma Tricolore
GERB	Graždani za Ewropejsko Razwitie na Bălgarija
GFE	Group-focused Enmity
GR	Greece
GRECE	Groupement de Recherche et d'Etudes pour la Civilisation Européenne
H	Høyre
HALDE	Haute Autorité de Lutte contre les Discriminations et pour l'Egalité
HNS	Hnutí Nnárodního Sjednocení
HOS	Hrvatske Obrambene Snage
HSP	Hrvatska Stranka Prava
HU	Hungary
HZDS	Hnutie Za Demokratické Slovensko
ICTY	International Criminal Tribunal for the former Yugoslavia
ID	Independence/Democracy
IDPS	Internally Displaced Persons
IHR	Institute for Historical Review
IKL	Isänmaallinen Kansallis-Liitto
IMF	International Monetary Fund
ISA	Institut für Strategieanalysen
IT	Italy
ITP	International Third Position
ITS	Identity, Tradition, Sovereignty
J İ TEM	Jandarma İstihbarat Terörle Mücadele
JN	Junge Nationaldemokraten
JSO	Jedinica za Specijalne Operacije
KD	Kristillisdemokraatit
KF	Det Konservative Folkeparti
KKE	Kommounistikó Kómma Elládas
KRF	Kristelig Folkeparti
KRR	Kommissarische Regierung des Deutschen Reiches
La.O.S./LAOS	Laikos Orthodoxos Sunagermos
LKÇK	Levizja Kombëtare per Çlirimin e Kosovës
LN	Lega Nord
LNF	Latvijas Nacionala Fronte
LPF	Lijst Pim Fortuyn
LPR	Liga Polskich Rodzin

ĽS-HZDS	Ľudová Strana - Hnutie za demokratické Slovensko
LV	Latvia
MAUP	Interregional Academy of Personnel Management
MÇP	Milliyetçi Çalışma Partis
MEP	Member of European Parliament
MG	Magyar Gárda
MHP	Milliyetçi Hareket Partisi
MIÉP	Magyar Igazság és Élet Pártja
M İ T	Millî İstihbarat Teşkilâtı
MNR	Mouvement National Républicain
MP	Member of Parliament
MP	Muhafazakar Parti
MpA	Movimento per le Autonomie-Alleati per il Sud
MPF	Mouvement pour la France
MS-FT	Movimiento Sociale Italiano - Fiamma Tricolore
MSI	Movimiento Sociale Italiano
MSZP	Magyar Szocialista Párt
MT	Malta
MTV	Music Television
MW	Młodzież Wszechpolska
NAFTA	North American Free Trade Agreement
NATO	North Atlantic Treaty Organization
NB	D'National-Bewegong
NCRV	Nederlandse Christelijke Radio Vereniging
ND	Nationaldemokraterna
ND	New Democracy
ND	Noua Dreaptă
ND	Nouvelle Droite
NDH	Nezavisna Država Hrvatska
NDP	Nouvelle Droite Populaire
NEO	New European Order
NG	Hungarian National Guard
NHB	Nationaldemokratischer Hochschulbund
NKVD	Narodnyy komissariat vnutrennikh del
NL	Netherlands
NL	New Left
NO	National Resistance
NOP	Narodowe Odrodzenie Polski
NPD	Nationaldemokratische Partei Deutschlands
NR	New Right
NRR	New Radical Right
NS	Národní Strana
NSDAP	Nationalsozialistische Deutsche Arbeiterpartei
NSDAP-AO	Nationalsozialistischen Deutschen Arbeiterpartei - Auslands-Organisation
NSi	Nova Slovenija

NSM	National Socialist Movement
NSS	Nové Slobodne Slovensko
NSV	Nationalistische Studentenvereniging
N-VA	Nieuw-Vlaamse Alliantie
NWO	New World Order
NYKP	Nyilaskeresztes Párt-Hungarista Mozgalom
OC	Organized Crime
OECD	Organization for Economic Co-operation and Development
OKW	Oberkommando der Wehrmacht
OMF-BRD	Organisationsform einer Modalität der Fremdherrschaft - Bundesrepublik Deutschland
ONT	Ordo Novi Templi
OSCE	Organization for Security and Co-operation in Europe
OS-DS	Ochranné sbory-Dělnické strany
ÖVP	Österreichische Volkspartei
PASOK	Panhellenic Socialist Movement
PC	Conservative Party of Romania / Partidul Conservator
PCF	Parti Communiste Français
PD	Partito Democratico
PDC	Partido da Democracia Cristã
PDF	Parti de la France
PdL	Popolo della Libertà
PDSR	Partidul Democrației Sociale in România
PiS	Prawo i Sprawiedliwość
PKK	Partiya Karkerên Kurdistan
PL	Poland
PLO	Palestine Liberation Organization
PNG-CD	Partidul Noua Generație-Creştin Democrat
PNR	Partido Nacional Renovador
PO	Platforma Obywatelska
PP	Progress Party
PRM	Partidul România Mare
PRO	Partei Rechtsstaatlicher Offensive
PRSH	Partia Revolucionare Shqiptare
PS	Perussuomalaiset
PSI	Partito Socialista Italiano
PSM	Partidul Socialist al Muncii
PT	Portugal
PUNR	Partidul Unității Naționale a Românilor
PUR	Partidul Conservator
PvdA	Partij van de Arbeid
PVV	Partij voor de Vrijheid
RAC	Rock against Communism
REP	Die Republikaner
RIF	Rock Identitaire Français

RNE	Russkoye Natsionalnoye Edinstvo
RNU	Russian National Unity
RO	Romania
RPC	Republican Party of Czechoslovakia
RPR	Rassemblement pour la Republique
RRWP	Radical Right-wing Populist Party
SD	Socialdemokraterna
SDS	Union of Democratic Forces
SE	Sweden
SFIO	Section Française de l'Internationale Ouvrière
SGP	Staatkundig Gereformeerde Partij
SI	Slovenia
SiD	Specialarbejderforbundet
SK	Slovakia
Smer	Smer - Sociálna Demokracia
SMP	Suomen Maaseudun Puolue
SNPU	Sotsial-Natsionalna Partiya Ukrainy
SNS	Slovenská Národná Strana
SO	Samoobrona Rzeczpospolitej Polskiej
SORA	Institute for Social Research and Consulting
SP	Slovenská Postpolitost
SPD	Sozialdemokratische Partei Deutschlands
SPÖ	Sozialdemokratische Partei Österreichs
SPO	Srpski Pokret Obnove
SPR-RSČ	Sdružení Pro Republiku - Republikánská Strana Československa
SRP	Samoobrona Rzeczpospolitej Polskiej
SS	Schutzstaffel
SSNP	Syrian Social Nationalist Party
SVP	Schweizerische Volkspartei
TİKDB	Avrupa Türk İslam Kültür Dernekleri Birliği
TT	Tvarka ir teisingumas
UACTI	Union des Associations Culturelles Turco-Islamiques
UÇK/KLA	Ushtria Çlirimtare e Kosovës
UÇK/NLA	Ushtria Çlirimtare Kombëtare
UÇPMB	Ushtria Çlirimtare e Preshevës, Medvegjës dhe Bujanocit
UDC	Unione dei Democratici Cristiani e Democratici di Centro
UDF	Union pour la Démocratie Française
UEN	Union for a Europe of Nations
UFO	Unidentified Flying Object
UK	United Kingdom
UKIP	United Kingdom Independence Party
ŰMİD-Der	University wing of Űlkü Ocakları
UNA-UNSO	Ukrainska Natsionalna Asamblea - Ukrainska Natsionalna Samooborona
UNMIK	Interim Administration Mission in Kosovo

UPK	Army for the Independence of Kosovo
US/USA	United States of America
USSR	Union of Soviet Socialist Republics
V	Venstre
VAM	Vitt Ariskt Motstand
VAPO	Volkstreue Außerparlamentarische Opposition
VAT	Value Added Tax
VB	Vlaams Belang
VHO	Vrij Historisch Onderzoek
VMO	Vlaamse Militanten Orde
VMRO-BND	Internal Macedonian Revolutionary Organization - Bulgarian National Movement
VNSA	Violent Non-State Affiliated Actors
VNV	Vlaams National Verbond
VU	Volksunie
VV	Věci veřejné
VVD	Volkspartij voor Vrijheid en Democratie
WAU	Women for Aryan Unity
WCOTC	World Church of the Creator
WUNS	World Union of National Socialists
WW II	World War Two
ZOG	Zionist Occupied Government
ZRS	Združenie robotníkov Slovenska

Index

Page references with star indicate a footnote.

List of Contributors

Prof. Dr. David Art, Tufts University, Department of Political Science, Medford, MA, USA

Prof. Dr. Kai Arzheimer, Institute of Political Science, University of Mainz, Germany

Prof. Dr. Uwe Backes, Hannah Arendt Institute for Research on Totalitarianism, Technical University of Dresden, Germany

Prof. Dr. Tamir Bar-On, Department of International Relations and Humanities, Tecnologico de Monterrey, Campus Queretaro, Mexico

Prof. Dr. Jean-Yves Camus, Institute for International and Strategic Relations (IRIS); Elie Wiesel University, Institute of Jewish Studies, Paris, France

Dr. Stéphane François, Laboratory Culture and Societies in Europe, CNRS/ University of Strasbourg, France

Dr. Thomas Grumke, Ministry of the Interior, North-Rine Westfalia, Düsseldorf, Germany

Ulrike Heß-Meining, Bundeswehr University, Munich, Germany

Dr. Gilles Ivaldi, CNRS, University of Nizza-Sophia Antipolis, France

Dr. Sarah L. de Lange, Political Science Department, University of Amsterdam, The Netherlands

Prof. Dr. Miroslav Mareš, Institute for Comparative Political Research, Faculty of Social Studies, Masaryk University, Brno, Czech Republic

Michael Meznik M. A., Institute of Political Science of the University of Vienna, Austria

Prof. Dr. Patrick Moreau, Laboratory Culture and Societies in Europe, CNRS/ University of Strasbourg, France

Dr. Guillaume Roux, The Security and Cohesion Department, Research Unit PACTE, CNRS, Grenoble, France

Dr. Vera Stojarová, Institute for Comparative Political Research, Faculty of Social Studies, Masaryk University, Brno, Czech Republic

Dr. Stéphane de Tapia, Laboratory Culture and Societies in Europe, CNRS/ University of Strasbourg, France

Dr. Tom Thieme, Institute of Political Science of the Technical University of Chemnitz, Germany

Dr. Petra Vejvodová, Institute for Comparative Political Research, Faculty of Social Studies, Masaryk University, Brno, Czech Republic

Wenn Sie weiterlesen möchten...

Marie-Janine Calic / Dietmar Neutatz / Julia Obertreis (Hg.)
The Crisis of Socialist Modernity
The Soviet Union and Yugoslavia in the 1970s

In den 1970er Jahren stieß die westliche Industriemoderne an ihre Grenzen. Ein ausgeprägtes allgemeines Krisenbewusstsein war die Folge. Wie aber stellte sich die Lage in Osteuropa dar? Gab es hier eine vergleichbare Entwicklung? Dieser Frage gehen die Beiträge am Beispiel der beiden sozialistischen Vielvölkerstaaten Jugoslawien und Sowjetunion nach. Untersucht werden Politik, Wirtschaft, Gesellschaft und Kultur, insbesondere die Nationalitätenfrage und die Außenpolitik. Dabei wird deutlich, dass sich beide Staaten in einer verborgenen Krise befanden, die sowohl aus der globalen Entwicklung als auch aus den inneren Widersprüchen des Systems resultierte. Die Krisensymptome waren in Expertenkreisen bekannt, wurden aber weder von der politischen Führungsspitze noch der breiteren Bevölkerung wahrgenommen.

Philipp Ther
Die dunkle Seite der Nationalstaaten
»Ethnische Säuberungen« im modernen Europa

»Ethnische Säuberungen« wurden nicht nur von Diktatoren, sondern auch von demokratisch gewählten Politikern veranlasst. Sie sind vor allem eine Folge des modernen Nationalismus und der Nationalstaatsbildung im 19. und 20. Jahrhundert. Dieses Buch bietet grundlegende Einsichten in eines der dunkelsten Kapitel des modernen Europa. Es befasst sich mit den Voraussetzungen »ethnischer Säuberungen« ebenso wie mit den Perioden und den verantwortlichen Akteuren von Flucht, Vertreibung, Zwangsaussiedlung und Deportation. Dabei beschränkt es sich nicht auf Osteuropa, sondern beleuchtet auch die Rolle der westlichen Großmächte. Der Autor spannt einen weiten thematischen Bogen von den Balkankriegen am Vorabend des Ersten Weltkriegs über die »ethnischen Säuberungen« während und infolge des Zweiten Weltkrieges bis zu den Bürgerkriegen im ehemaligen Jugoslawien und im Kaukasus der 1990er Jahre.